The School in American Society

Third Edition

The School in American Society

Third Edition

Ralph L. Pounds / James R. Bryner

The Macmillan Company, New York
Collier-Macmillan Publishers, London

Preface

The publication of the third edition of this book has given the authors an opportunity to review the purposes for writing it and for offering a college course in which it can be used. Courses for students in the field of education that will acquaint them with the trends and current characteristics of the American social order are widely taught throughout the United States. In contrast to the situation at the time of the first edition, materials for such classes now are widely available. In our own classes we have found the materials contained in this text to be effective. Many other schools throughout the country continue to find them satisfactory. Because of the contemporary nature of much of the material used for illustrations, it seemed advisable to prepare a new edition at this time. The period between the publication of the second edition and the present has been one of change, tension, and to some extent chaos and danger.

The basic topics and problems used in this text were selected from among those that contemporary scholars consider to be the major problems faced by our society. The aptness of these selections has been verified through examination of topics treated by writers and teachers in educational sociology and social foundations of education at major institutions. Many of the ways of setting forth, in clear but nontechnical language, certain of the problems drawn from economics and other of the social sciences were developed in connection with the classes at the University of Cincinnati. Both of the authors have presented their materials to class groups and have secured informal and formal criticism from the students. Rough drafts of all chapters have been reviewed by authorities.

This text in social foundations of education focuses on the general structure and problems of American society, with emphasis placed on the role of the school in guiding children and youth to analyze and select from alternative solutions. The authors (and, they hope, the readers) are, figuratively, standing in the doorway of the school, surveying the current cultural scene. A salient characteristic of the present culture is that we are in a state of rapid change. This book primarily is concerned with the important *trends* in that culture and their implications for the school.

Chapter 1 sets forth the importance of the rapidly growing field of social foundations of education and suggests problem areas in education to which this field of study may make significant contributions. Specific educational questions are listed. Complete, detailed answers to these questions may not be found in the book. Although some directions toward solutions are indicated in Part IV, it is felt that only continuous study of society by teachers and administrators can develop dynamic theories of curriculum and methodology for sound educational decision making. If static solutions had seemed feasible, the authors would have given the answers without need for indicating to the student the background in social trends and problems from which the solutions might be derived.

The authors encountered less difficulty in finding definitive answers to the questions "What is the nature of present social trends?" and "What is the nature of current educational problems?" than they encountered in suggesting alternative solutions to the problems. Some philosophic viewpoints not only interpret differently the sociological research on which curriculum construction is founded but also reject much of the psychological research that structures present methodology.

The authors have attempted to present without bias the conflicting philosophic viewpoints on the goals of the school. They have attempted to utilize both sociological and psychological research in formulating guidelines in curricular content and in pedagogical methodology. The reader probably will be able to determine, in general, the viewpoint of the authors with respect to the alternative points of view set forth in Chapter 15; the authors find themselves more in agreement with the experimentalist point of view as it is set forth in Chapter 15 than with any other. They find themselves in disagreement with some experimentalists, of course; like many other persons attempting to find answers to these problems, they are somewhat eclectic in their approach.

The primary responsibility for writing certain chapters was allocated between the two authors. Dr. Bryner had the responsibility for Chapters 6, 7, and 9. Chapters 14 and 16 were first drafted by Dr. Pounds, but both authors participated in the final organization and wording of these critical chapters. All other chapters were the original responsibility of Dr. Pounds. The very careful and critical reading and rewriting of many parts of the manuscript by both authors, however, means that the total book is the product of both.

The third edition of the book, although following the same format that has been successful in the earlier editions, does attempt to bring the information up to date, to condense as far as feasible all background material, to expand practical suggestions for the teacher, and to re-examine the entire text for clarity. In particular, much new material and a new approach are found in Chapters 9, 11, 12, 14, and 15.

Attention of the reader is called to the carefully correlated list of books and films found at the end of each chapter.

The authors wish to express their appreciation to the students who helped to establish the problems and to provide trial groups for trying out most of the materials of this book. They acknowledge indebtedness to the pioneer thinking and research of Harris, Ross, Snedden, Gillette, Dollar, Warner, Davis, Havighurst, Quillen, and others in the field of educational sociology for many of the ideas presented in this book as the thinking of the authors. The junior author is especially indebted to Dean I. James Quillen, Professor Paul R. Hanna, and Professor Oliver E. Byrd of Stanford University, and to Professor June Jentz of the University of Cincinnati. The senior author is indebted to some of his students and colleagues who have over the years offered suggestions and raised questions. He is especially indebted to Irene Thorman, his foster daughter, who edited his portion of the manuscript for clarity of language, typed the several drafts, and prepared the final copy. However, the responsibility for the final work is that of the authors, and they alone are to be held responsible for any errors or inaccuracies.

The authors also wish to acknowledge the materials that have been taken from numerous copyrighted sources. Recognition of permission granted by copyright holders is given at the appropriate places throughout the book.

R. L. P.
J. R. B.

Contents

Schools, Controversial Issues, and "Relevance" • The Freedom of the Teacher—Limits and Responsibility • The Process of Determining Educational Objectives • A Summary of Social Facts, Trends, and Problems • The Foreseeable Future • Education for the Foreseeable Future • Selected Bibliography • Selected Films

Illustrations

Tables

Part I

The Relation of School to Society

Part I focuses on the relationship of school to society. In the first chapter, which serves as an orientation to the entire book, the importance of society both to individual development and to the development of institutions is indicated. Stress is placed upon the reasons why teachers, administrators, and other persons interested in schools should know and understand social trends and their implications for the school.

Then in Chapter 2, materials are selected from the social sciences, primarily from anthropology and social history, concerning the way in which human society has evolved. The process of becoming "human" is discussed, as are the stages of human development and the significant characteristics that mark these stages. In Chapter 3 attention is focused directly upon the relationship of the school to the society in which it is found. Examples are given to illustrate how schools at different times in the past have been related to their societies.

1

Chapter 1
■□□□□□□□□□□□□□□□

Individual and Institutional Development in a Changing Culture

The period in which we are living has been variously described as an age of crisis, an age of anxiety, and an age of uncertainty. Although many earlier eras have been described In similar terms, and justly so, the problems of today are much graver than those of previous times, for several reasons:

1. They are more acute.
2. They are more complex.
3. They affect many more people.

The speed and efficiency of our transportation and communications facilities have brought us closer together. Rapidly increasing population has created problems of crowding, physical and psychological, and caused pollution of our physical environment—land, water, and air. The interdependence of each of us in the increasingly complex economic system has rendered all of us vulnerable to the threat of other economic disasters. Failure to meet the challenge of our problems thus may have far more disastrous consequences for the entire world than were possible in any previous period. The knowledge and the facilities needed for solving these problems are more adequate than ever before, but the question remains: "How can society—through education, in particular—use the available knowledge and facilities to solve these problems?"

THE PURPOSE OF THIS BOOK

It is the purpose of this book to set forth in some detail the nature of the present social order and, in an appropriate perspective, to show implications for the school.

Although attention is directed primarily toward society, the viewpoint is that of the professional educator, who is familiar with the nature and problems of education. The educator is standing on the "porch of the school," so to speak, looking out at the culture. The focus is on those aspects of the

3

culture that have particular significance for education. Because the scope of such a survey is vast, we must concentrate on large trends of broad significance, not on detail. We must use a telescope, not a microscope. It is obvious that we must sample—look at selected aspects typical of the whole. We must dip into the ocean and examine the sample drawn.

IMPORTANCE OF AN UNDERSTANDING OF SOCIETY FOR EDUCATIONAL DECISION MAKING

An understanding of the nature of society is essential for teachers and administrators who must make decisions concerning education in this rapidly changing world. Such understanding is important regardless of particular philosophical frameworks. (These philosophical choices are outlined in considerable detail in Chapted 15). Understanding of social changes and of changes in our knowledge concerning the nature of the world may affect the choice of a frame of reference. Even if we all believed that the main job of the school was to pass on certain fundamental, unchanging principles, an understanding of the society in which we live would affect the way in which each of us might apply those principles. Certain other values and principles that are subordinate to the "unchanging" ones may change as our cultures change. Because value choices, recommendations for curriculum, and other decisions depend upon the changing culture in which the school is found, it is crucial that the teachers and administrators understand the nature of the culture.

Following are examples of questions that demand of teachers and administrators more knowledge about their society:

1. What implications does the nature of present society have for the development of the content of curricular experiences?
2. To what extent does the changing nature of our society (an ever-accelerating change) affect the emphasis in curriculum upon subject-matter skills rather than the process of acquiring knowledge?
3. To what extent does the fact that the boys and girls now in school will live during their adult life in a world very different from that in which we now live affect the problem-solving techniques we teach them?
4. To what extent does the problem of changing values in a changing culture place a renewed emphasis upon the development and clarification of values as a part of the school's job?
5. To what extent does the urgency of some of the social problems arising out of social change place responsibility on the school to take leadership in helping our society change its institutions to meet these problems?
6. To what extent does some of the knowledge arising out of recent developments in the social sciences have implications for the quality of experiences in the school and for the teaching methods used?
7. What is the effect of changing life expectancy on the length of time to be spent in full-time schooling?
8. What is the effect of the increase in life expectancy on the amount of the energies of the school that should be devoted to adult education?

9. What effect should increasing specialization have on the diversity of educational programs?
10. What is the effect of increasing specialization upon the kind of general-education program we should have?
11. What is the effect of automation on the kinds of vocational and general-education programs our schools should have?
12. What is the effect of automation on the amount and kind of leisuretime activities, and what are its implications for the school?
13. What are the implications for the school of the necessity to teach "readiness to use unknown ways to solve unknown problems" (to use Margaret Mead's phrase)?[1]
14. What will be the effect upon school organization of the industrial trend toward a systems approach to management?
15. What will be the long-term effect upon school resources of currently increasing public resistance to property tax levies for school and municipal purposes?

THE GENERAL NATURE OF THE PRESENT SOCIAL ORDER

We shall now set forth some of the major general characteristics of the contemporary social order. One of the first things that strikes the observer is the tremendous diversity within cultures, even within one country like the United States. In our country, one language is spoken predominantly, there are many facilities for the circulation of ideas, and the population is highly mobile, yet there is great diversity. This heterogeneity may be attributed to many things. The seeking of freedom on American shores by many of our forefathers served to set, in many areas, patterns that have continued until today. The absence of an established church and the complete separation of church and state have served to encourage religious freedom and diversity. Hence there are nearly 250 religious bodies in the United States.[2] One of the most important factors contributing to variety in our culture is the fact that the encouragement of diversity is one of the fundamental principles of our democracy. "Unity in diversity" might well be a statement of one of our democratic goals.

The proliferation of occupations necessitated by a complex culture is the source of another set of factors differentiating our ways of life. *Dictionary of Occupational Titles* gave about 1,400 different kinds of occupations and thousands of job definitions as of 1966.[3] Each occupation carries with it a set of mores, including ways of thinking and a set of values. Each person lives in a subcultural occupational minority, even though he may be otherwise in a community majority group.

[1] Margaret Mead, *The School in American Culture* (Cambridge, Mass.: Harvard University Press, 1951), p. 40.

[2] The most available reference is the current issue of *The World Almanac and Book of Facts*. The 1971 edition lists 206 bodies. This does not count many minor movements and numerous unaffiliated congregational churches. A news item in the *Cincinnati Enquirer* (March 7, 1971, p. 6-F) quotes the *Yearbook of American Churches* that 247 religious denominations reported statistics voluntarily to it for 1970.

[3] W. Willard Wirtz, *A Supplement to the Dictionary of Occupational Titles,* Third Edition (Washington, D.C.: Government Printing Office, 1966).

There are also differences of national origin (the effects of which usually fade out in the third generation), regional differences, and differences in social status. (The cultural effects of social status will be discussed fully in Chapter 9.) In spite of the relative homogeneity of American civilization, there is great diversity according to geographical residence. The patterns range from those of the Maine fisherman to the many urban subgroups, as in New York City; from the Michigan "upper peninsula" to the resort culture of Florida; from the Southern culture of the state of Georgia to the many subcultures of the state of Washington; from the culture of Texas to that of California; from the cow country of Montana to the wheat fields of the Dakotas; from the culture of the upper class of the Eastern seaboard to the "hippie" culture of many of our cities.

To these complexities within our own country may be added those between countries; with the continual change in all modern cultures, there ensues a kaleidoscopic variety that defies complete description and makes difficult even a broad interpretation.

RAPIDITY OF SOCIAL CHANGE

Social change apparently is an inevitable accompaniment of human society. Even in those societies in which change is discouraged and that consequently remain almost static for hundreds of years, there is a slow cultural drift. In times of catastrophe, however, even previously static societies may change rapidly in order to adjust to changed conditions. A changing society is not a new thing; however, the rate of change does vary markedly from time to time throughout human history. The culture of primitive man continued for thousands of years with very little change, usually until change was forced from the outside. The Oriental type of civilization that eventually emerged out of an amalgamation of many cultures remained for long periods of time at a fairly constant level of development and with relatively unchanging mores.

In Western civilization, with its idea of progress, although founded on different bases at different periods and partially eclipsed during the Middle Ages, there has been a great deal of conscious change. Many times this change was deliberately brought about because of dissatisfaction with conditions evolving out of ferment from previous changes. With the advent of the scientific method and democratic forms of government, bonds were loosed, which gave rise to many events that fostered change. With every change that occurred, new potentialities for change emerged. It is said that the director of the Patent Office early in the nineteenth century resigned because he felt that his job was about done—1 million patents had been issued. However, each patent was a possible source of new patents. Each advance is the basis for several new ideas for other advances or changes. The wheel, the steam engine, and the vacuum tube were each the start of a whole series of branching avenues of discoveries. Thus the rate of change has been accelerating. It is exponential in rate of growth. The rate of change may be compared to that of a snowball, "the larger it grows, the faster it grows."

It has been said that George Washington would have been more at home in ancient Greece than in modern America. The age of the automobile, radio, television, jet planes, A- and H-bombs, and the astronauts may well cause us to say the same now of Woodrow Wilson. The following firsthand description, written around 1960, of the actual changes that have occurred within the lifetime of a middle-aged individual even in a rural community is illustrative of the pace of change:

I remember Mamma and the house where I was born. This house stood just off the village pike in the middle of a very large yard and was surrounded by many large trees and many outbuildings. Papa bought this house soon after my oldest sister was born, and my three other sisters, one brother, and I were born and grew up here. The house was of a long rambling style, much like the ranch style house of today, with the parlor (where we entertained special guests) in "front," and the very large kitchen at the "back." In between was the company dining room, a large hall, where we ate in the summer, and the "family" room, where we sat around the grate fire on winter evenings. On the right side of this grate was the stone churn—the cream must turn to make butter. In front of the fire my mother placed the quilt. By putting a table leaf across the quilting frames and setting the kerosene lamp on this leaf she could quilt late into the night. Mamma had little time to quilt in the daytime—there were too many other things to be done. My brother sat on the left side of the hearth in a rocker—the man was always given preference in our family—while I sat under the quilt on the floor.

I do not remember Papa very well because God took him away when I was only six years old. Papa was sick for a long time, but he did not go to the hospital. Few people in our village ever went to the hospital. Dr. Jacobs drove his horse and buggy seven miles from the city to see him. Mamma nursed him, and when he became very ill, the good neighbors came and sat up all night. They also cut wood for us to burn on the grate. They milked our cows, fed the pigs and cattle, and cared for the sheep. We didn't pay them. Neighbors always helped each other in their hour of need. We would help them when they became ill just as they had helped us. Papa was buried in our family burial lot on Grandma's farm. . . . Mamma said, "Jimmy was a good man—as men go." But she had a living to make and a family to raise and there was just one thing to do—go to work and do it. We never heard of "public welfare," and how could anyone make a living for five children in the city—especially when their only skill was sewing? My mother had worked as a seamstress before she married. She didn't go to college, not even to high school. She went to eighth grade, third part arithmetic. That was as far as you could go where she lived. When I worked buttonholes in a dress in a college sewing class, the teacher said they were excellent and gave me an A. Mamma said, "I wouldn't give you an F, they look like pig eyes instead of buttonholes." . . .

On Saturday we drove Miss Nancy, our buggy mare, into the city with the marketing. The marketing was butter, milk, and perhaps some chickens. We sold the eggs to the village store. With the egg money we bought flour, sugar, coffee, and kerosene. We didn't need many things from the grocery. We always had a good garden. This supplied us with fresh vegetables during the summer, and we canned enough vegetables for the winter months. We also canned peaches, pears, and grapes from the orchard, and blackberries from the woods. The potatoes and apples were stored in the cellar or "milk house" as we called it. The cabbages were buried deep in the ground so they wouldn't freeze. We grew most of our meat, too. We had fried chicken in the summer. When they became too large to fry, we stewed them and made dressing and dumplings to eat with them. Just about Thanksgiving time we butchered three or four hogs in the barn lot. We hired men to help butcher, but Mamma always cooked the lard in the black iron laundry kettles in the back yard. We cured the hams and sacked the sausage. This supplied us with pork and shortening for the entire year. We always ate the shoulders and middlings and saved some of the hams to sell. This was money in the bank, and everyone in our community who was "somebody" had money in the bank: The account grew ever larger, never smaller. This money that we saved had to take care of Mamma when she was old. When autumn came everyone wanted fresh meat to eat. So the farmers organized a beef club. This club met in our big barn lot every Friday, butchered a beef, and divided it among the members of the club.

On Sunday we wore our best clothes and went to the one-room country church. We had our Sunday school classes in the different corners of the church, and two Sundays in the month the pastor drove to our village and preached. Since we lived close to the church, it seemed to me that he always came home with us for dinner, especially in the winter when the roads got muddy and he couldn't get to the homes of many church members. We liked to have the pastor come. We put on the best white tablecloth and used the best silver and dishes. If he stayed all night, he slept in the parlor on the cleanest, fattest featherbed we had and under the best counterpane on the place —one that had been woven on the loom by Grandma.

When the pastor preached, he talked about man and his relation to God more than he talked about man's relation to man. He preached about the things we should not do rather than the things we should do. It seemed to me there were few things left to do. I was almost grown before I realized that "the old-time religion" was just something to preach about and wasn't really too different from the new religion. After singing "When the Roll Is Called up Yonder" or "Blest Be the Tie," we stood outside the church and talked for a long time. This was about the only time we had to be *social* with our friends and neighbors. This was where most of the young people in our community learned not to be afraid of the dark!

Miss Nancy and Miss Mary had both been married in the church. They had beautiful white gowns. My sister, Susan Ann, was the flower girl at each wedding. When Susan Ann was twenty-one, she married at home in our parlor. The house was decorated with roses from our own rosebushes, and our pastor performed the marriage ceremony. All the guests said Susan Ann was a beautiful bride. She wore a hat with two plumes on it, and she had made her own wedding dress. Secretly, too, she had embroidered all her underclothes. Thirty-eight years and fourteen children later her wedding band was removed for the first time since Robert put it there on their wedding day. It was removed after her death and given to her youngest daughter. Hazel and Lila were married in Tennessee during the "elopement era." Mamma thought "mighty little of it" —but, then, everyone was eloping. . . .

The forty to fifty families who make up this village lived very much the same way our family lived. Practically every farmer owned his farm of 150 to 250 acres. Most families were large enough to operate the farm in a gainful manner without hiring help; however, many families helped each other by "swapping" work. The social life centered around the church and school with a few "nice" parties sometimes. Nice parties did not include dancing and card playing. Most of the young people finished high school, found a mate in the village, married and "settled down" in the village to farm as their parents had done. A few young people, mostly girls, were ambitious and went to college in the nearby city. The idea of girls doing public work was slowly gaining consideration; and, since the teachers college was only seven miles away, many girls (twelve or fifteen) became teachers. The Lord "called" two of the young men to become ministers. Three girls went to the capital, twenty-five miles away, and took a business course. Practically all of the boys stayed home on the farm. In fact, many of them did not finish high school. Most people were interested in living the "good life" and carrying on their work on the farm. For many, many years the community boasted it had never had but one divorce. Some drinking was done, but this was just boys sowing their "wild oats"—they would settle down when they married.

Very slowly a few changes were being made in the community. Mr. Gibbs had had a telephone in the store for a long time. A telephone was needed in the store. When we needed to call Granny, we paid him a dime to let us use the phone. After a few years, eight of us formed a party line and each got a phone. Soon everyone who lived in the immediate village had a phone, but few families whose homes were on the mud roads had them. Mr. Gibbs bought the first car in our community. Mamma said he could afford it. He ran the post office and Uncle Sam paid him. Then the two churches, the school, and Mr. Gibbs got Delco light plants.

The farmers used to go to the city trading on "Court Day," but now they went every Thursday to the stock sales. They began to feel the need for cars to get there more quickly. With the purchase of cars, the mud roads had to be made into pikes. We got a car in our family when my brother was sixteen. Few women in the community were driving cars yet. Their place was in the home.

Sunday school rooms had been added to the churches and school buses now took the children to and from school.

In the summer of 1941, when I went home for a vacation, the old house I had lived in was torn down and Mamma was building a new and much smaller house—just large enough to care for the family that was left. The Rural Electrification Project had just been organized and everyone was discussing and organizing to have electricity put in their home. Mamma said we couldn't afford all these fancy new things, but it would be nice to have lights in the barn—she didn't care a thing about having them in the house. But other people were getting lights, so we got them too. A full-size basement was built under the new house, but Mamma wouldn't consider having a furnace put in. My brother insisted on having the bathroom built in the house, but Mamma could not see the necessity for installing the fixtures at that time.

By 1949 the farmers were buying tractors to farm with. Practically every farmer had a tractor by this time. Those who did not have them hired his neighbor to plow and help with his farm. There was only one hay-baler and one sheep-shearer in the community. The other farmers found it saved time and money to hire their hay baled and their sheep sheared. They were talking about hybrid corn, tobacco allotments, and more crop rotation. The farmers were going to the stock sales much more than formerly. Trading, buying, and selling was a much greater part of every farmer's life than it had been a few years before.

When electricity went into the homes, the women of the community immediately got electric irons, then electric churns. The next year's turkey crop was saved to buy an electric washing machine. Those who didn't have a washer in two years had suddenly found the old way of doing laundry just too backbreaking, so they bargained with a cousin and many families washed together until they could afford a washer. Refrigerators were the next "necessities." They reasoned with themselves how much food they could save with a refrigerator. When I was home in 1945, there were just a few electric stoves. Since that time practically every housewife in the community has an electric stove. Of course, some of the older people, like Mamma, have two stoves in the kitchen and often can be found cooking on both of them at the same time. Very few of the older people have invested in toasters and waffle irons. Their men folks still must have hot biscuits for breakfast and hot cornbread for dinner (noontime meal) so they have little need for these appliances. The younger families had just as soon eat toast for breakfast and they enjoy waffles in the evening sometimes, so they are investing in the smaller appliances as well as the larger ones.

Electric appliances and new ideas from the Homemakers Club have made the life of the farm wife much easier. The tractor and other farm equipment has left the farmer with "time on his hands." For this reason many of the older men in the community are buying more farm land to tend. In addition to these aids most of the people who can find a room in their old houses are having bathrooms put in. The newer homes are built with bathroom, furnace, and other conveniences just as homes in the city. As yet, there are very few food freezers, but each summer when I go home I find one or two more. They are no more expensive than keeping a frozen food locker in the city, they say. Many young people who finish high school are renting an apartment in the city and finding work at "Avon" or "The Factory." Those who continue to live in the village are building small homes on an acre or two of land and driving into the city to work. Most of the boys and girls are getting a job immediately after completing high school. College is too long and too expensive. Anyway, they can earn $40 or $50 a week with a high school education. Getting help on the farm or renting to a tenant is almost impossible. The older people, like Mamma, cannot adjust to this fast-changing life. Their children are too busy to care for them. When they are ill, they go to the hospital or to a nursing home. It is hard for them to understand young people who have land and don't raise a garden, who have barns and don't keep a cow, who buy all their clothes ready made, and who go to all the movies. Mamma says with all these conveniences they are always complaining about being tired and never have time for a thing.

Several years ago the people in each church said they needed a full-time pastor. So they built new parsonages with every modern convenience and hired a pastor to live on the field. Then the churches became too small and old-fashioned. Last year the Baptist Church spent $22,000 remodeling their church. The church now has its own baptistry, electric kitchen, and nursery. The nursery is equipped with a button system to summon the mother from the main auditorium when needed without disturbing the audience. Chimes that call the people to church each Sunday morning are quite an attraction in the community. The church music shows little improvement. Interest in church work is very keen. The young people have Daily Vacation Bible Schools and go to camp in the summer. Though little reading is done by the people themselves, they usually hire a graduate of a theological seminary for their pastor. Sermons are centering more around present-day living and world affairs. On the whole, it seems that the religious life of the community has kept pace with the changes in technology.

. . . I should say the educational life of the community has lagged far behind the religious and technological growth. This has perhaps been due to lack of interest on the part of the parents. In many respects, the teachers have done an amazing amount of work and good in the community. Their salaries have been much too meager for them to afford much additional training.

The one thing that has changed very little, if any, in this community is the "brand of politics." Feeling runs very high around election time, not only among the men, but also among the women. The big issue is not whether the candidate is a good man for the position, but how strong a Democrat or Republican is he. If politics were traced in most families, it would be found that at least 95 per cent of the people have the same politics their father, grandfather, and great-grandfather had. When "Ike" was nominated for President, all work was laid aside and many people in the village went to the homes where there were televisions (two in the village) to see and hear. The Democrats knew we would all starve to death when Ike became President, and the Republicans thought the Roosevelts would "bust the country" before they could get them out. . . .

Yes, the village is changing slowly, and with the change tension seems to be growing. As Mamma says, "With all of their conveniences and easy ways of doing things, they just race here and there—never time for a thing." Her grandchildren don't have time to eat a meal with her any more. In fact, the grandchildren all live in the city. They drive out to the village church on Sunday. The younger people prefer an easier job to having a large bank account. They buy things it would seem they can't afford. Their feeling of responsibility toward the older people is there, but their work prevents their getting around to help them often. And the older people won't leave their homes to live with the children. They still must take care of their farms. The younger people have a very great responsibility toward their immediate, small families. This is especially noticeable in the care and time that the fathers give the children. Their concept of moral values is still very high and many "recreations" are frowned on. They want their children to be educated, but they still feel that education means the three R's. Education is still for one thing, to help one make a better salary and live in an easier manner.

For the most part, I should say that the people in this community are a happy, contented group. They are interested in making money, having things, and doing things. But beyond this they have a set of values that are deeper and more enriching to them as individuals and as a group than money values.[4]

COMPARISONS OF PRESENT SOCIAL CHANGE WITH THE PAST

Aside from the rapidity and increasing acceleration of current social change, several characteristics distinguish the present changes from those of the past. In the first place, changes in the past tended to be either in the nature of a gradual cultural drift or in the form of a sudden "jump" resulting from catastrophic causes. In the past, life was lived on a precarious basis. Anything that upset the status quo necessitated major readjustments. Many catastrophes were caused by war and were followed by conquest and virtual or actual enslavement. Others were caused by failures of food supply or by epidemics and were widespread in effect. In modern times man has achieved greater physical security and has gained more ability to adjust to changes in physical environment.

Secondly, the changes in Western civilization that have produced the modern period are the result of man's increasing ability to understand, control, and change deliberately his physical environment. Each new invention or other form of change brings a host of further changes, widely spread through an increasingly complex and interrelated society. For example, the invention of gunpowder and the gun, although brought about for the purposes of advantage in fighting, was an important factor in the downfall of the feudal system, because the common footman with a gun was more than equal to the knight on horseback. The invention of the power loom and use of steam power destroyed the home craftsman because capital became neces-

---

[4]This statement was prepared by a graduate student of one of the authors from her own experience. Permission has been granted for it to be used with fictitious names.

sary to purchase the required machinery. Man became a wage earner rather than a craftsman. The threat of unemployment arose because of these changes in economic conditions.

In the third place, the increasing complexity and speed of communications make events in one part of the world affect the other parts. The specialization of the productive process makes one part of the country intricately dependent on the others. The economic system, instead of being self-adjusting, may tend to run away in booms or busts. Further, some parts of the culture tend to change more rapidly than others, thus throwing the parts out of relationship to each other. Each new change in society, instead of calling for a simple remedy which then serves until a new problem arises, calls for a remedy that itself is productive of further maladjustments.

Commenting on social change, psychologist Carl Rogers has said:

> I should like to point to the greatest problem which man faces in the years to come. It is not the hydrogen bomb, fearful as that may be. It is not the population explosion, though the consequences of that are awful to contemplate. . . . It is the question of how much change the human being can accept, absorb, and assimilate, and the rate at which he can take it. Can he keep up with the ever-increasing rate of technological change, or is there some point at which the human organism goes to pieces? Can he leave the static ways and static guidelines which have dominated all of his history and adopt the process ways, the continual changingness which must be his if he is to survive?[5]

A CONCEPT OF CULTURAL LAG

It is the differential in rates of change in the different parts of an interdependent society that gives rise to the phenomenon known as *cultural lag*. Usually changes in the material aspects of culture come first, followed by lags in institutional changes and in the ideas underlying those changes. Man seems to accept material changes more readily than institutional changes and seems to resist strenuously changes in fundamental ideological conceptions.

Some authorities have discarded at least partially the concept of cultural lag and speak of societal breakdown resulting from disarticulation—a lack of fitting together of parts. It would seem, however, that the concept of cultural lag still has great usefulness in describing these phenomena.

The amount of social lag or disjointedness of a culture varies, of course, with the amount of social change. If there is very little or no social change, obviously the lag, if it exists, is small. In times when social change was the result of a single force (which, when once applied, subsided as a force toward change), the lag quickly was reduced as the society readjusted to the relatively static new conditions following the initial impact. In Western civilization there has been a consistent change owing to new events occurring largely within the society. These continuously have brought about changes in certain parts of society and hence a lack of adjustment with parts that did not change. As Western society has entered the period of rapid social change, where each new change has set off a whole chain of other events, this lag has become acute.

[5] "Interpersonal Relations: U.S.A. 2000," reproduced by special permission from *Journal of Applied Behavioral Science*, Vol. 4, No.3 (1968), p. 266. Also Alvin Toffler, *Future Shock* (New York: Random House, Inc., 1970).

In the era of relatively slow but constant change in the late medieval and early modern periods, the lag between the material culture and the ideological and institutional culture, although not great in absolute amount, was greater in actual number of years. As people became more consciously aware of change and as ideas of progress developed, persons were able to adjust more quickly to many of these changes. However, the changes came with increasing rapidity and, even though the lag in time was much less, the absolute lag was still as great or greater in many cases. For example, a lag in time of two hundred years from the fifth to the tenth centuries might be a less "absolute" lag than fifty years in the nineteenth century.

Some of the important changes of the late modern period (from 1500 on) had implications that ran deeply into the most basic ideological concepts of people. These fundamental changes were resisted in certain areas because they challenged concepts to which man wished to cling at all cost. For example, the findings of modern science starting with the discoveries of Copernicus have challenged the basic assumptions of philosophy concerning the ultimate nature of the universe, and sometimes have caused men to cling to outworn institutional patterns because these patterns help protect cherished ideas against change. In some cases the institutions themselves, by their structure, tended to prevent adjustment to the social changes. Institutions, developed to meet certain needs under given conditions, tended to be rigid and to be obstructive when the need for change was obvious.

The individual is a product of the society in which he is born. If that society changes greatly during the lifetime of the individual, he may find it difficult to accept change even on superficial levels, not to speak of fundamental changes in his thinking.

The effect of cultural lag of various kinds may be seen in such phenomena as poverty and want amidst the plenty that modern technology is capable of bringing forth. Another example is the political lag in many overlapping governments surrounding large cities and the inability of suburban areas to merge their differences and join with the central area in an efficient governmental unit or in a well-planned set of coordinated subunits.

Rules of dress and personal appearance in many schools remain far behind current societal mores. Adoption by the students of the modern tactic of confrontation has forced some change; conflict has prevailed after reasonable arguments had been disregarded by the school. The current cultural conflicts, in schools and in society, are a sad commentary on man's ability to reason and upon his willingness to cooperate for the common good. The resolution of differences between countries by war is resort to a barbarian practice lacking rational justification for either the victor or the conquered.

THE CONTRIBUTIONS OF THE SOCIAL SCIENCES TO THE UNDERSTANDING OF MAN'S RELATION TO SOCIETY

The modern social sciences, such as history, sociology, psychology, anthropology, economics, and political science, have developed rapidly in the last few decades, using techniques adapted from the earlier-developed physical and life sciences. It is perhaps inherent in the nature of the various fields of study that mathematics should develop first, the physical sciences next, then the life sciences. and finally the social sciences. The sciences still lag, to some extent, in the same order as their development.

The scientific method of arriving at and applying facts is used in the social sciences just as in the other areas. However, there are many difficulties in its application:

The Problem of Maintaining Objectivity

Our own preferences and backgrounds cause us to see and interpret phenomena in ways that agree with our previous convictions. In the 1930's a scientist who knew in advance whether he was measuring a Negro or a white brain in a study of brain capacity thought he had honestly found that the Negro brain was less developed. However, when the work was checked by another, who was unaware of the racial type to which the brains belonged, no differences could be found.[6] We are not prejudiced about the properties of a metal; we are frequently prejudiced about matters relating to race, religion, and nationality.

The Problem of Formulating Useful Generalizations

The behavior of living creatures is so complex, the actions of humans so exceedingly complex, that it is difficult to make generalizations that will hold for most (or even many) situations. Persons acquainted with the "laws" and formulas of the natural sciences are disappointed with the necessarily guarded and qualified generalizations of the social sciences. Many persons do not realize that in modern Einsteinian science the generalizations from physics and chemistry are also considered to be only approximations. They are man-made generalizations of what usually happens in ordinary circumstances. Although it may be extremely probable that a phenomenon will happen as is predicted in the generalization, the whole quantum mechanics is on a probability basis; and furthermore, most laws are not even practically accurate except within certain limits. This places the physical sciences on exactly the same basis as the social sciences except that the probabilities are so much higher because the physical sciences deal with so many more of the basic elements concerned, usually atoms or electrons or their equivalent. One example from the physical science of meteorology, the prediction of the weather, where the factors are as complex as many in the social sciences, will serve to help the reader to visualize this point.

The Problem of Prediction

Many factors enter into the direction in which a society (or group) may move, one of which may be the influence of a prediction itself. It is extremely difficult to predict social conditions that will hold true over an extended period of time. Minor factors, difficult to measure, occur at opportune (or inopportune) times to make marked differences in outcomes. For example, if you are predicting something that will happen to the group, and the group is

[6]John Biesanz and Mavis Biesanz, Modern Society, Second Edition (Englewood Cliffs, N.J.: Prentice-Hall, 1959), p. 164.

sensitive to the prediction, the sensitivity may affect the outcome. If the National Safety Council should predict an alarmingly great number of accidents over a certain holiday weekend, the announcement might scare persons into driving more safely. The actual numbers killed would then not be as great as had been predicted on the basis of factors known at the time of prediction.

Difficulty in Experimentation

People are not guinea pigs. As social scientists and educators, we are not able to manipulate our subject matter as the natural scientists do. Because we cannot always manipulate our human subjects, we must manipulate our data by using statistical factorial analysis methods. This does not work as well, however, as if we could design the experiments and then manipulate our subjects in whatever way was best for checking the effect of the factors involved in the experiment.

Difficulty in Use of Terms

The social scientist must use the common language, but he must define his terms carefully. Consequently, he often employs the same words as those used by the layman, but In different senses. This causes a lack of clarity in communication when results, conclusions, or implications are announced.

The Role of Values in Conclusions

Many kinds of data are significant only in terms of values of the culture, and these may be in conflict or changing. Consequently, two persons using the same data frequently arrive at different conclusions or generalizations. In particular, in the area of social studies—let us take, specifically, economics —conclusions on the part of persons whose political philosophies are based on contrasting sets of values they hope to realize by means of a particular kind of social order may be quite different. For example, the viewpoint of the late Senator Robert A. Taft and that of the late labor leader Walter Reuther, in the period following World War II, were at opposite poles even though both were very well acquainted with economic "facts" and were well aware of the so-called laws of economics. Their different conceptions of the values to be achieved by the economic system led them to quite different conclusions.

In spite of these difficulties, the social sciences have made great strides, and there is a growing body of widely accepted knowledge in all of these sciences. The use of field studies, case studies, and statistical methods, coupled with the new techniques of "action research," have served to broaden the scope of study and to enable conclusions to be better applied. Bringing together conclusions from the various sciences to the solution of a problem has led to improved results.

Students of society have observed that a culture falls into three or more fairly distinct elements. Different parts of the culture affect its members differently. The first are the *universals*—those common customs, attitudes, and beliefs shared by almost all members of a cultural group, such as a common language or a common belief in democracy. The second can be termed the *specialties*—those elements of culture shared by persons of certain classes, localities, or occupations. The third may be called *alternatives*—characteristics shared by certain individuals but not common to all or even to the other members of the subgroup. Closely related to these alternatives are *individual peculiarities*. Examples of the two last mentioned include religion (in American culture), politics, and food habits.

Subcultures exist in a culture as relatively homogeneous as that of the United States, and they often tend to determine one's ways of behaving. Examples are minority groups, occupations, and so on. A given individual may have membership in several of these subgroups, each partially influencing his behavior.

Further understanding of the nature of culture may be given by the definition of certain terms. Societal cultures, or group habits, may be classified as *mores, folkways,* and *technicways.* The *mores* are those aspects of culture to which all individuals are expected to conform. The mores are supported by the strongest of sanctions, in contrast to the folkways, which are desired but not compulsory. Violations of the mores are immoral acts in the broadest sense of the term. In our society, monogamous marriages, right of private property, and prohibitions against murder, rape, or incest are part of our mores. *Folkways* are customs that persons are expected to follow, but violations do not involve serious consequences. Taking off your hat when addressing a lady is a folkway, but failure to follow it is not immoral. The term *technicways* is sometimes used to designate those new ways of behavior that have been developed and accepted as ways of adjusting to new technology. An illustration would be new dating behavior because of the use of automobiles.

Every culture has a hierarchy of values that provide its motivation and drive. Whatever the source of these values may be said by myth or tradition to be, they have arisen in almost all cases out of the past experiences and traditions of the group. The myths, quite often based originally upon facts but then greatly elaborated, tend to undergird the value symbols of the group. All of these together lead to a conception or picture of the universe and of nature and of the place of man in that universe.

Different groups of men probably developed independently and gradually a body of concepts about all men in relation to such areas as the nature of the universe, the place of man in the universe, the place of the individual within the group, and human nature and conduct. As each group expressed these concepts in more complicated form, they evolved into religion, philosophy, law, incorporating myths and folklore as well as the arts. Because of this independent development each group differs in its expression of its assumptions about the universe. However, the conceptions in the four different areas are always interrelated and are, relatively speaking, well integrated into one body of ideas.

THE APPROACH OF THIS BOOK

Our underlying assumption is that in order to understand questions such as those posed earlier in this chapter, it is necessary to understand the nature of society and at least part of the vast knowledge concerning man and the world that has been formulated by the social sciences in the last few years.

The book is organized into four parts. In Part I, "The Relation of School to Society," we have set forth in Chapter 1 an orientation to the importance of society to individual development and to the institutions man has created to help him in solving his problems. Then follows Chapter 2, in which we have brought together materials from anthropology and other sources indicating how human society has evolved and how man the animal has become human. In Chapter 3 we have indicated the historical relationship of schools to their societies, giving numerous examples from the history of education to cite how the school has tended to reflect the culture in which it is found.

In Part II, "Social and Economic Trends in America," we have set forth an overview of social and economic trends. Chapter 4 presents American social trends, first in chronological and topical order, then in a summary of contemporary social trends. Chapter 5 is given over to a discussion of the trends in the technological and economic realm. An attempt is made to acquaint the person who is not a student of economics with important facts about our industrial and economic system that anyone should know as a basis for understanding the many kinds of problems that face our society.

In Part III, "Problems Facing the Individual in Modern American Society," several chapters present a selection of the kinds of problems that modern American society faces: problems confronting members of a family; problems of mental hygiene in a period of rapid social change; problems of crime and delinquency; problems caused by intergroup relations, including the social class structure as found in America; problems of depressed areas, urban and rural; problems arising out of population pressures; problems related to the nature of representative government, including problems of communications media, propaganda, and public opinion; problems arising from the interdependent world of the present time. Although this list of problems is far from exhaustive, it should acquaint the student with the kinds of problems we face so that meaning will be given to the final clarification and summary in Part IV.

Part IV, "The Role of the School in Modern America," is a final summation of the role of the school in modern America. In the first of the three chapters in this section, Chapter 14, an attempt is made to clarify our central democratic values and the nature of the group process in our culture (group dynamics, the human sensitivity movement, and group therapy). The difficulties of the politics of dissent and protest, militancy, and the process of confrontation within a democratic framework are emphasized. In Chapter 15 is found a careful analysis of alternative viewpoints on the schools and social change. In the final chapter, Chapter 16, are summarized the main findings of the other chapters. The attempt is made to portray the role of the leader in a democratic situation and to indicate how his efforts can be directed toward helping the school to play an appropriate and effective role in this period of social change. The possibilities of the "foreseeable" future in our society are surveyed and implications for school practices are indicated.

Selected Bibliography

Banks, Olive. *The Sociology of Education.* London: B. T. Batsford Ltd., 1968. 224 pp.
Barber, Bernard, and Walter Hirsch (eds.). *The Sociology of Science.* New York: The Free Press, 1962. 662 pp.

Berrien, F. Kenneth. *General and Social Systems*. New Brunswick, N.J.: Rutgers University Press, 1968. 231 pp.

Bierstedt, Robert, and others. *Sociology and Contemporary Education*. New York: Random House, Inc., 1964. 138 pp.

Biesanz, John, and Mavis Biesanz. *Modern Society: An Introduction to Social Change*, Third Edition. Englewood Cliffs, N.J.: Prentice-Hall, Inc., 1964. 718 pp.

Blalock, Huber M., Jr. *Causal Inference in Nonexperimental Research*. Chapel Hill: University of North Carolina Press, 1964. 188 pp.

Blau, Peter M., and Richard A. Schoenherr. *The Structure of Organizations*. New York: Basic Books, Inc., Publishers, 1971. 445 pp.

Bonner, Thomas Neville, and others. *The Contemporary World: The Social Sciences in Historical Perspective*. Englewood Cliffs, N.J.: Prentice-Hall, Inc., 1960. 594 pp.

Borgatta, Edgar F. (ed.). *Social Psychology: Readings and Perspectives*. Chicago: Rand McNally & Co., 1969. 740 pp.

Brembeck, Cole S., and Marvin Grandstaff (eds.). *Social Foundations of Education: A Reader*. New York: John Wiley & Sons, Inc., 1969. 146 pp.

Brickman, William W., and Stanley Lehrer. *Automation, Education, and Human Values*. New York: Apollo, 1969. 419 pp. (Paperback.)

Butts, R. Freeman. *A Cultural History of Western Education*, Second Edition. New York: McGraw-Hill Book Company, 1955. 645 pp.

Calder, Ritchie. *Man and the Cosmos: The Nature of Science Today*. New York: Frederick A. Praeger, Inc., 1968. 219 pp.

Fabun, Don. *The Dynamics of Change*. Englewood Cliffs, N.J.: Prentice-Hall, Inc., 1967. 190 pp.

Greenstein, Fred I. *Personality and Politics: Problems of Evidence, Inference, and Conceptualization*. Chicago: Markham, 1969. 200 pp.

Gross, Carl H., Stanley P. Wronski, and John W. Hanson (eds.). *School and Society: Readings in the Social and Philosophical Foundations of Education*. Boston: D. C. Heath & Company, 1962. 666 pp.

Harrington, Michael. *The Accidental Century*. Baltimore: Penguin Books, Inc., 1964. 322 pp.

Havelock, Ronald G., and others. *Planning for Innovation*. Ann Arbor, Mich.: Publications Division Institute for Social Research, The University of Michigan, 1970. 538 pp.

Hodgkinson, Harold L. *Education, Interaction, and Social Change*. Englewood Cliffs, N.J.: Prentice-Hall, Inc., 1966. 256 pp.

Hofstadter, Richard, and Seymour Lipset (eds.). *Sociology and History: Methods*. New York: Basic Books, Inc., Publishers, 1968. 423 pp.

Holton, Gerald (ed.). *Science and Culture: A Study of Cohesive and Disjunctive Forces*. Boston: Houghton Mifflin Company, 1965. 348 pp.

Johnson, James A., et al. (eds.). *Introduction to the Foundations of American Education: Readings*. Boston: Allyn & Bacon, Inc., 1969. 441 pp.

Kallenback, W. Warren, and Harold M. Hodges, Jr. (eds.). *Education and Society*. Columbus, Ohio: Charles Merrill Books, Inc., 1963. 474 pp.

Kerber, August, and Wilfred Smith (eds.). *Educational Issues in a Changing Society*, Third Edition. Detroit: Wayne State University Press, 1968. 468 pp.

Kuhn, Alfred. *The Study of Society: A Unified Approach*. Homewood, Ill.: Richard D. Irwin, Inc., 1963. 810 pp. A detailed, theoretical analysis across disciplinary lines of the human society in its entirety.

Lear, John. "Predicting the Consequences of Technology," *Saturday Review* (March 28, 1970), 44–46.

Lipset, Seymour Martin. *Politics and the Social Sciences*. New York: Oxford University Press, 1969. 328 pp.

Lowry, Ritchie P., and R. P. Rankin. *Sociology: The Science of Society*. New York: Charles Scribner's Sons, 1969. 622 pp.

McIntosh, Donald. *The Foundations of Human Society*. Chicago: University of Chicago Press, 1969. 341 pp.

Mead, Margaret. *The School in American Culture*. Cambridge, Mass.: Harvard University Press, 1951. 48 pp.

Montagu, Ashley. *Man Observed*. New York: G. P. Putnam's Sons, 1968. 299 pp.

Myrdal, Gunnar. *Objectivity in Social Research*. New York: Pantheon Books, Inc., 1969. 111 pp.

National Science Foundation. *Knowledge into Action: Improving the Nation's Use of the Social Sciences*. Washington, D.C.: Government Printing Office, Special Commission on the Social Sciences of the National Science Board, 1969. 95 pp.

Nelson, Jack L., and Frank P. Besag. *Sociological Perspectives in Education*. New York: Pitman Publishing Corp., 1970. 230 pp.

Nisbet, Robert A. *The Social Bond: An Introduction to the Study of Society*. New York: Alfred A. Knopf, Inc., 1970. 448 pp.

———. *Social Change and History: Aspects of the Western Theory of Development*. New York: Oxford University Press, 1969. 335 pp.

Park, Robert E., and Ernest W. Burgess. *Introduction to the Science of Sociology*. Chicago: University of Chicago Press, 1969. 1,040 pp.

Platt, John R. (ed.). *New Views of the Nature of Man: The Monday Lectures*, 1965. 152 pp.

Riasanovsky, Alexander V., and Barnes Riznik. *Generalizations in Historical Writing*. Philadelphia: University of Pennsylvania Press, 1963. 239 pp.

Sanford, Nevitt. *Self and Society: Social Change and Individual Development*. New York: Atherton Press, 1966. 381 pp.

Sjoberg, Gideon, and Robert Nett. *A Methodology for Social Research*. New York: Harper & Row, Publishers, 1968. 355 pp.

Smelser, Neil J. *Essays in Sociological Explanation*. Englewood Cliffs, N.J.: Prentice-Hall, Inc., 1968. 280 pp.

Stocking, George W., Jr. *Race, Culture, and Evolution: Essays in the History of Anthropology*. New York: The Free Press, 1968. 380 pp.

Stretton, Hugh. *The Political Sciences: General Principles of Selection in Social Science and History*. New York: Basic Books, Inc., Publishers, 1969. 453 pp.

Wolff, Kurt H. "The Sociology of Knowledge and Sociological Theory," in Llewellyn Gross (ed.), *Symposium on Sociological Theory*. New York: Harper & Row, Publishers, 1959. 642 pp.

Selected Films

American Farmer (Ford Motor Co.), 24 min. An intimate and beautifully photographed story of a modern farmer and the changes wrought in his life by mechanization and scientific farming.

The American Road (Ford Motor Co.), 24 min. An excellent film on the change in American culture brought about by changing technology, particularly changes in transportation.

Anthropology and the Social Studies (Anthropology Curriculum Study Project), 20 min. Urban classroom discussion of a lesson from *Study of Early Man*.

The Individual (N.E.T.), 60 min. Problems facing the individual in a large society are discussed by exploring varied, dissimilar areas of American life and the common thread that binds individuals together—the need for self-identification.

Our Changing Family Life (McGraw-Hill), 22 min. The change from the farm family of 1880 to the urban family of today.

The Story of Prehistoric Man (Coronet), 11 min. This description of the life, appearance, habitat, and achievements of prehistoric man is reconstructed from authentic evidence, prehistoric tools and weapons, cave paintings and stone carvings, and skeletal remains. The periods of the Old and New Stone Ages are indicated and the geographical areas in which prehistoric man lived are mapped.

Chapter 2

■■□□□□□□□□□□□□□□□

The Evolution of
Human Society

We have seen the importance of society and its institutions in determining
the behavior of man and the relationship of social structure and social mores
to various human institutions. It now becomes important to focus our attention on the origins and development of human society. The development of
group mores and the ways in which changes in them came about are important elements in understanding modern-day man. The problems involved
in the conflicts of mores in changing and in interrelated and interdependent
societies have pertinence for our later discussion of the role of the school.
It is necessary to explore in detail the effects on and the implications for
social institutions of the social changes and the changed conception of the
nature of society and of man, as provided mainly by the science of social
(or cultural) anthropology. This will provide a basis for an understanding of
the various topics and problems to be taken up later.

SOCIAL MORES AND THE STAGES IN MAN'S DEVELOPMENT
Social Mores: The Result of Circumstance and Adaptation

Numerous attempts have been made in all ages to explain the differences in the customs or mores of groups. Among the attempts of groups
themselves to justify their unique customs or ways of doing, particularly
when they feared a breakdown by threatened change from within or without, is that of recourse to various supernatural sources. Peoples have attributed to direct or indirect contacts with deities or spirits, great or small,
mores ranging from legal codes such as that of Hammurabi or the Mosaic
law to food and marriage taboos and customs. Another approach attempts to
justify the "superior" way of life of one's own group by reference to its
superior racial inheritance, as did the Nazis.

Many of these explanations will not stand scrutiny. The modern study[1]
of "races," or even a casual reading of history, cannot support a "race"
theory. Modern students of race agree that inherited differences in abilities
or characteristics among races cannot account for "superior" modes of living.

[1]See George W. Stocking, *Race, Culture and Evolution: Essays in the History of Anthropology* (New York: Free Press, 1968).

21

The record of man's experiences indicates that the strong faith of a people in a supernatural source of their mode of life has often not withstood the ravages of time.

It seems evident to most students of the nature of man that the basic inherited structure of man and his potentialities has remained reasonably constant since the time of the first modern man, Cro-Magnon, 20,000 to 50,000 years ago, and that reasons for cultural changes must be looked for elsewhere. The viewpoint to be set forth in this chapter is at variance with many other theories of history that have been promulgated.

In the first place, the evidence of biology seems to indicate that the species *Homo sapiens* (that of modern man) secures by inheritance many fewer preformed behavior patterns than do other animals. In a later discussion of the social insects, such as the ant and the bee, we show that their social behavior is largely a function of inherited neural structure, mostly in the nature of reflexes. Man apparently inherits a much more plastic nervous system which enables him to absorb the culture in which he is born and to add to it. (This will be delineated more fully in the section "The Individual as a Product of His Society," later in this chapter.)

In the study of hundreds of primitive human groups that have survived to the present day, anthropologists have uncovered many patterns of social organization, some of which were more successful than others—at least as measured by modern standards of living. However, the success or lack of success of a pattern does not seem to indicate that the intrinsic nature of man is any more adaptable to one pattern than to others. Mead's study shows that in the various types of cultural organizations (individualistic, competitive, and cooperative) there are records of successes and failures and of problems and difficulties, fairly randomly distributed.[2]

It would seem that different mores are really accidents of history. In nonliterate societies each separate group (usually the tribe) needed to solve its basic problems of food and shelter. In time, it stumbled on methods that at least provided a minimal solution to each problem. Many other mores probably were added accidentally, even though they were not particularly functional, but through ingrained habit these soon gained the same status as those customs necessary to maintain existence.[3] This problem of the fixity of group mores, once they are established, is important enough to be looked at more fully later. Suffice it to say at this point that the type of mores established by a group, the changing of these mores, and the raising of the level of living seem to be a result of a concatenation (or coming together) of circumstances which provide favorable psychological, sociological, political, or technological factors appropriate to the time (including, of course, favorable geographic factors), not the result of inherited superiority or inferiority or the favor of the gods.[4]

[2]Margaret Mead (ed.)., *Cooperation and Competition Among Primitive Peoples* (New York: McGraw-Hill, 1937).

[3]See a humorous parody on the stubbornness of man's adherence to custom, using paleolithic man as an example in Harold Benjamin, *The Sabre-Tooth Curriculum* (New York: McGraw-Hill, 1939).

[4]See David McClelland, *The Achieving Society* (New York: Free Press, 1961), pp. 3–8. He explores many proposed one-factor explanations—and shows why they are implausible. S. Kuznets has also examined the causal relationship (recorded in many references).

The Stages in Man's Development

Students of human culture have used different methods of marking the various stages of man's development, for example, the hunting and fishing stage, the pastoral stage, etc.; or the Old Stone Age, the New Stone Age, and the Bronze Age. For the purposes of our discussion here it is more functional to describe the various stages in terms of the adaptability of the internal structures of the society to change or progress.

Under this approach the stages are (1) the primitive or nonliterate stage;[5] (2) a stage called Oriental because of its historical prevalence in the Oriental part of the world; and (3) a stage called Occidental or Western, again because it has been most evident in the Western area.[6] To these might be added (4) a modern stage, which may be in its early phases now.

In the nonliterate stage, man has made a minimal adaptation to his environment; particularly, he lacks a written language. Although the standards of food and shelter may be very meager (or may be fairly adequate in kindlier environments), each group has become accustomed to its ways and tends to resist change, especially sudden innovations from within or without. Often this fear of change is due to the fact that the initial effect of such innovations may well be quite unsettling. Sometimes a change may lead to disastrous results in terms of the stability of the group and its ability to meet its minimal needs. Thus, although some innovations might be of great value to the group, it hesitates to permit experimentation. Consequently, individualism as to new methods of behaving is discouraged except within prescribed patterns such as personal bravery in battle or skill in hunting and fishing.

At the Oriental level, man has raised considerably his standard of living and has a written language and a literature. Usually the civilization covers a considerable geographic territory. Quite often it is accompanied by a highly developed art and other expressional forms, such as a complicated ritualistic religion based on a rather complete mythology. Once having achieved this level—by processes to be described later in this chapter—these civilizations resist further change by various methods, such as ancestor worship or powerful religious taboos. Examples of this stage are the early Egyptian civilization and various other ancient civilizations of the Fertile Crescent, the sweep of productive land running east and south from Palestine through the Tigris–Euphrates Valley to the Persian Gulf. Such civilizations tended to remain constant for a great number of years (as did the Chinese) on a relatively high level unless changed by strong impact from an outside force.

In the Occidental-type (Western) civilization, a relatively high level of culture has been developed and definite mores have been established. The idea of progress or change has enough prevalence that individuals are somewhat free to experiment. At times an Occidental-type civilization may succeed in almost eliminating innovations; again, it may change rapidly. In most cases it is able to solve its crises by developing a mode of operation that enables it to adapt itself to the new change without complete disintegration

[5]The term *nonliterate* is apparently now preferred by scholars to either *primitive* or *preliterate*.

[6]It must be emphasized that the use of the convenient terms *Oriental* and *Occidental*, primarily because of accidental geographical reasons, does not imply differences in the biological potential of the peoples. The definitions of these terms, to follow in this section, are cultural and sociological rather than geographical, biological, or racial.

or conquest from without. However, there seems to be present in all Occidental civilizations a fear of change, a hangover of the thinking of the nonliterate and Oriental stages (transmitted by culture, not heredity, of course) that is constantly at war with progress.

It may be that there is emerging, or that there will emerge in the future, a type of civilization in which, because of man's increasing knowledge of himself and of his environment and the institutions he has created, he will deliberately set out to create the kind of society he desires. After he carefully clarifies his values and tests them in the light of their consequences, he will make full utilization of available knowledge and of procedures involving the scientific method in its broadest implication. He will further utilize the scientific method in bringing about changes in his institutions, or even in his values if necessary. in the light of any new conditions brought about by social changes. This stage might be classified as the modern stage.

Certainly the events of the late 1960's and early 1970's do not offer much hope of early arrival at the modern stage.[7] Although knowledge is increasing rapidly, the clarification of values and the integration of that knowledge in a deliberate attempt to realize these values on a broad scale throughout the world have been but perfunctory and relatively unsuccessful. As a matter of fact a case well could be made of retrogression in the five years preceding this writing; confrontation has been rampant between labor and management, between black and white, among social classes, between student and teacher (or principal, or president), between hard-hat and hippie.

Having reviewed briefly the stages in development, we shall now examine the three stages in more detail.

MAN IN THE NONLITERATE STAGE
General Characteristics of Nonliterate Man

In spite of some political theories holding that at some time in his existence man the individualist agreed with a group of his fellow men by a compact to work together for mutual ends (the "social compact" theory), it is now generally agreed that man probably has always been in association with his fellows. The evolution of human society starts, then, at least as far back as the first modern man, Cro-Magnon, who had approximately the same biological structure (including brain and nervous system) as contemporary man. All men from Cro-Magnon on, including the various modern races, belong to the same species, Homo sapiens. The date of Cro-Magnon man has usually been placed from 30,000 to 70,000 B.C.; however, earlier species of man are known to have been on earth nearly 5 million years ago. Cultural remains have been dated as far back as 2 million years by geological methods.[8] On geological and other evidence, the earth is generally believed

[7]In a recent article published in advance of his book The Identity Society (unavailable at this writing), William Glasser describes the Civilized Identity Society, which has been emerging the past twenty years. This might be the start of the "modern stage," which is found in the current youth movement in a society "in which human concern again centers on self-identity, self-expression, and cooperation." (William Glasser, "The Civilized Identity Society, Mankind Enters Phase Four," Saturday Review, February 19, 1972, p. 30.)

[8]Radioactive dating of stone semicircle at Olduvai site in southern Africa, on the oldest man-made structure so far found, as reported by John E. Pfeiffer, The Emergence of Man (New York: Harper & Row, 1969), p. 811.

to have been in existence for at least 4 billion years. Life has existed for over 1 billion years. The first mammals appeared over 150 million years ago. Man is thus a latecomer. The earliest known inscription appears to have been in Sumeria and is dated around 3300 B.C. This places the historic period as beginning at least 5,000 years ago.

Let us now look at the nonliterate period, which includes all men from approximately 50,000 B.C. to 3300 B.C. and many groups and tribes up to almost the present day. There is no evidence that early man of the *Homo sapiens* variety ever lived other than in groups. More details about the development of social institutions in primitive or nonliterate man will be given in the next section.

Certain characteristics are common to almost all groups of men in the nonliterate stage, even though there may be great variability in many aspects of cultural mores.

Early man had solved his problem of living on a very precarious basis. He understood neither his physical environment nor the causal relationships that lay behind his successful attempts to provide for his minimal needs. In general, he was fearful of change, perhaps as a result of experiences from time to time when individuals who attempted to innovate did upset the working relations and thus the meager adjustment of the tribe.

Nonliterate man, of course, operated in accord with ordinary causal relationships with respect to familiar things that, by trial and error, he learned could be controlled. In such activities as the felling of trees or the making of tools he acted in accord with causal relationships with much the same attitude as modern man. However, nonliterate man, understanding so little about the forces that operated in the world about, attributed much more to the "supernatural" than does contemporary man.

Whatever the reasons for the original mores may have been (including the necessity for a primitive technology), as time went on man forgot and tended to ascribe reasons that in most cases would not be verifiable by the use of scientific technique. Knowing himself as a creature that apparently could freely choose to do this and not do that, he tended to ascribe such freedom and personality to all other objects, animate or inanimate. This gave rise almost universally to a theory about the nature of his environment, the two different aspects of which are called respectively animism or animatism. Either or both of these might be present in a given group.

In the one form, *animism*, nonliterate man extended to inanimate objects the concepts formed as the result of his experience with animate objects: a stone, like a person, possessed feelings of love or resentment and the power to act on its feelings, just as his fellow men, himself, and other animals apparently did. Animism thus places a spirit in each inanimate object. The object can then be controlled by cajoling, pleading, worship, or other means of manipulation. The extension of the generalization of the spirit in a tree to the spirit of the trees (as in Druid worship) comes later. A complicated system such as the Greek and Roman pantheon, including gods of love, harvest, and so on, is a much later generalization. The extension of this concept to the abstract—but, in some cases, personal—God of the more modern monotheism is probably a later development, although vague concepts, such as the Manitou of some American Indian tribes, seem to have been of this general nature.

The other aspect of supernaturalism, *animatism*, seems to have been an extension of man's effort to control familiar objects by utilizing a supernatural science that can best be termed magic. Man tried to control the forces in a supernatural cause-and-effect relationship by means of certain rituals or formulas that probably had at some time appeared (by coincidence) to work and thus became a part of his thinking and action. Incantations, sorcery, and divination were a part of the magic, the use of which was quite prevalent in nonliterate man and persisted late into the Christian period of civilized man. Failure of the method usually was ascribed to errors in the procedure rather than the conception back of it. Skeptics existed, but they were usually merely skeptical of certain persons' power to use the ritual or of a particular formula used.

The use of taboo to control the behavior of individuals in the group is also an aspect of dealing with the supernatural. Because the supernatural is powerful, it is dangerous. Whatever the actual origin of the taboo, such as a food taboo originating from a coincidental or causally related sickness or death following eating, such origins in most cases have been forgotten. The reasons ascribed are almost entirely the appeasement of a spirit or the avoidance of danger from the supernatural power involved.

Nonliterate man, living as he did in a world of precarious existence, got his security through his fixed mores, his myths to explain religious rites, the superiority of his group to others, and taboos of various kinds to enforce conformity. In many cases, primitive tribes lived with little change for thousands of years. The breakdown of mores, sometimes through forces originating inside the tribe but more usually because of crises from outside the group, will be described in a later section. The fear of change has been held in such matters as public sanitation, vaccination, or fluoridation. The resistance, culturally inherited from the time that nonliterate man feared change as a threat to his security in a precarious world, may be a basis for some of the unreasoned conservatism found in modern culture.

Some cultural change existed at all times, even in those tribes that had the strongest antipathy toward change. This cultural drift in language, culture, social customs and institutions, and technology, although so slow as to be unnoticed in a generation, seems to have been universally present at all times in man's history and prehistory. "Nothing is constant but change."

Social Institutions in Man's Nonliterate Stage

Before looking at social institutions of nonliterate man, let us look at examples of social structure, cooperation, and even, by analogy, cultural institutions among the other animals.

The one-celled animal or plant does not show any social behavior or even sensitivity to similar plants or animals. All multicellular animals or plants do represent a type of social adaptation or cooperation, from the simplest coelenterate to the complex dinosaur, bird, or man. In the simpler forms such cooperation is carried out with practically no differentiation in function, as in the jellyfish, where any of the group of cells may act as both mouth and anal opening and thus have both food-taking and excretory functions.

At a slightly higher level, such animals as the sponge have adapted by living as separate entities but in a cooperative relationship. Higher still, animals such as wild cattle or wolves cooperate by grazing or preying in groups for mutual protection or for more successful hunting.

The group of animals below man that appears to have the most highly socialized structure is composed of the ants, bees, and similar species. Here we have a highly developed social structure with a differentiation of work among individuals. Examples among species of ants are specialized workers with a special anatomy for fighting; other ants for use as storage bins; and some with large jaws to crack hard-shelled seeds.

In these cases, all the social structure is by biological inheritance, which is preserved by successful survival and the consequent continuation of the species. There is no evidence of culture in the sense of the successful adaptations of one generation being passed on by language or imitation to the next. In some species, all possibility of such is prevented by the survival of the fertilized queen only, as in certain ants, or of the egg only in other insects. All such "social cooperation" is biologically produced and transmitted through inherited neural structures by the same well-known evolutionary procedures that have produced other physical structures.

A study of man has revealed the presence of the necessity for cultural adaptation. Although the helplessness of the infant is a characteristic that humans share with many of the other species, necessitating care in the early period, even the simplest adaptation of man to his environment seems to be culturally rather than biologicallly achieved. In other words, successful adaptation for humans is largely a result of a process of learning rather than merely a process of maturation, as it is in the other animals that are helpless at birth.

A comparison of man with the ape and other hominoid animals points up a great number of essential elements of difference. Animals of hominoid type can learn to solve problems of stacking boxes, can fit sticks together in the manner of a fishing pole, can play machines like slot machines in ways that seem much like those of humans. Animals, including the various hominoid species, are able to respond to language cues of various kinds and do have a sort of crude communication system using sounds.

In none of the animals that have been studied by anatomists is the speech center—that is, the portion of the brain that handles speech in man —developed so much as it is in man. Man is the only primate that has a brain sufficiently well developed to invent and to use language in the sense of developing abstract concepts. There is a difference between responding to cues or symbols in a concrete situation and being able to communicate in an abstract situation. Someone has said that when the mother bear is able to come back from a foraging trip and explain to the cub bears exactly how to travel in order to find the honey tree without any other demonstration than the sounds the mother bear emits, then we can assume that the bears have invented language and have learned to use it for communication.

Let us hear from a social psychologist:

> These results [with rats] differ sharply from those found with the human brain. While there is some evidence that human cries and exclamations—uttered in moments of excitement—are also controlled by the limbic system, *speech and language clearly depend upon neocortical areas*—areas for which there simply are no analogues in the brain of any other animal. These areas are, of

course, the well-known Broca and Wernicke areas in the left hemisphere of the human brain. It seems clear, as Robinson puts it, that "Human speech did not develop" out of "primate vocalization, but arose from *new tissue* (italics my own) which permitted the necessary detachment from immediate, emotional situations." Man's brain, *and man's brain alone*, is a language-supporting brain.

Corresponding to the neurological picture, is the psycholinguist's view of language. Almost every psycholinguist is impressed not only with the unique nature of language itself, but with its unique mode of achievement by the child. Whatever value so-called reinforcement or stimulus-response theories of learning may have for describing acquisition of motor skills by people, maze-learning by rats, and bar-pressing by pigeons, these theories are assessed as completely trivial and utterly irrelevant when it comes to understand that "stunning intellectual achievement," the acquisition of language by the child. Indeed in reading the psycholinguist's work, one is left with the impression that we will have to develop a species-specific learning theory for this species-specific behavior of language. I must confess that I agree with them. And if we ever achieve an understanding of language development, and if we learn how to push the *human* experience—then will we indeed be on our way.[9]

Man's ability to form a culture, therefore, depends on his higher ability to invent and use tools and his ability to invent and use a conceptual language in solving his problems. The development of language, particularly, allows him to communicate experiences toward the further solution of new problems. These powers enable him eventually not only to adapt himself better to his environment, but to adapt the environment to his needs.

Although little can be known of the early development of the two most ancient and primary institutions, the family and that other basically most face-to-face group, the tribe, the study of contemporary primitive peoples at differing stages in development does give us some clues. The human family unit, probably frequently polygamous in early primitive man, seems to be based on the sexual drive and the attractiveness of the female, coupled with her accessibility to sexual advances at times other than the oestrual period. It is also based on the necessity for the protection of the immature young, a necessity that man shares with many animals that also have a proto-family group with or without the presence of the male.

The tribe, consisting of persons usually related by blood, was probably developed for mutual protection and better success in getting food. The social relationships between individuals in these groups and individuals outside of these groups are carefully prescribed in most societies. Even the most individualistic societies, in which food-getting and other activities are neither competitive nor cooperative, still may define relations carefully between individuals on a basis of complicated social groupings.

Although social institutions are relatively simple in individualistic societies and in those societies whose technology is still at the gathering or hunting and fishing stage, they usually become progressively more complex in the harvesting (without planting) stage and among those who practice agriculture. In the case of the harvesters, access to the area of the food plant, grown without agriculture but still seasonal and needing storage as surplus, may be carefully controlled and allocated to various tribes or sub-

[9]David Krech, "Man's Participatory Evolution," *Current* (September, 1969). Used by permission.

tribal groups. In the agriculture stage, property is usually more precisely defined, although it is not always individually owned, nor are the products of the individual's work necessarily used by that individual and his family and kin alone.[10] Many variations and patterns, all of which determine the nature of the social institutions, are found. Some of these variations are discussed later in this chapter in the section on cooperation and competition.

Variations in Social Structure of Nonliterate Societies

Wide variations exist in the social structure and actions of the various primitive tribes. Many of these variations have existed down to the modern day and can be studied minutely. These studies of relatively simple nonliterate tribes may throw light on modern social problems. The examples used are drawn largely from relations in the institution of the family. The section that follows will discuss in detail variations in economic structuring and will take up cooperative, competitive, and individualistic societies.

The family as a face-to-face unit may vary from the married adults and their children to the patriarchal or matriarchal family with several generations of descendants. The family may be polygamous in either of two forms: *polygyny*, the marriage of one man to more than one woman; or *polyandry*, the marriage of one woman to more than one man. There is also one other form, very rare, the marriage of several women to several men. Polyandry is much more rare than polygyny.

Polygyny (frequently miscalled polygamy) is quite prevalent among nonliterate people and exists, or did exist, to some extent among relatively highly civilized groups such as the early Hebrews and the Mohammedans. Research among polygynous societies has failed to reveal the existence to any greater extent than in a monogamous society of widespread jealousy patterns or bickerings caused by unfaithfulness of husband or wife and attention toward others of the opposite sex.

Attitudes toward sex both within and without marriage vary widely. Only three groups reported in the literature, the New England Puritans, the Ashanti, and the Timne (the latter two from West Africa) seemed to taboo sex relations even within marriage except for procreation.

The nonliterate tribes in general seem not to taboo sexual relations before marriage and not to restrict them so completely to husbands and wives after marriage as in the Western world. (In this respect, the Western world has been far from absolute in practice, particularly in Europe, where a double standard with respect to prostitution persists.) It would be incorrect to say that nonliterate peoples are sexually promiscuous, because all such relations are subject to numerous controls and taboos. For example, the incest taboo is practically universal in all societies, even in those in which sex relations are fairly free before marriage.

The extension of permissive sex relations beyond husband and wife follows a careful pattern but one that varies from society to society. The most common practice is the extension to the sisters of the wife and to the

---

[10]See the discussion of the Tanala later in this chapter for a documented case of the changes in social structure that followed a change in the technology of food getting.

brothers of the husband. Extremely rare are such practices as the hospitality of wife lending to guests and the game of "putting out the light" in the multi-family home of the Ammassilik Eskimos.

Economic functions, status, and taboos are usually sharply differentiated between the sexes, and there is a wide range of variation in the status of women. The attitude toward women, the burden of work placed upon them, and their part in making important family, clan, or tribe decisions vary widely, although, in general, women have a lower status than that of the male. In cases where the women have real power, it is usually exercised "behind the throne"—that is, through the male.

This discussion of the variability of social institutions is not presented with the idea of emphasizing a complete relativity of choice, with one alternative as good as the other. Certainly the results from anthropological study indicate that institutions, though they vary greatly between societies, do have a relationship in a given society to the prevailing value systems and the other institutions of the society, even though they are apparently not in any sense preferable one to another on the basis of innate or inherent psychological or personality factors. Persons within Western civilization have tended overwhelmingly, as a result of attitudes developed out of their historical experience, to prefer complete monogamy after marriage as their ideal, even though this ideal is often violated. Indeed, a thoroughly rational study might well establish that this choice is fully justified in the present state of civilization and in relation to the other values desired in the culture.

Cooperation and Competition in Nonliterate Man

Margaret Mead has made a comparative study of the prevalent characteristics of a sample of thirteen nonliterate (primitive) societies in order to discover, if possible, any pattern of related factors favoring one society over another and some measure of the comparative success of these societies.[11] The thirteen groups, after careful analysis and study, were divided into three classifications: competitive, cooperative, and individualistic. The classification is based upon strong trends in the society rather than upon an exclusive trend. A competitive society, for example, does not refer to a society in which the individuals are in complete conflict, nor does cooperation mean complete solidarity. In many cooperative societies, competition as a motivation for increasing the contribution to the group may be present, although the results of the competition are widely shared.

A summary of important character and personality traits as related to these forms of culture as compiled from Mead shows no basic causal relationship or pattern behind the particular predominant characteristics of a culture. For example, cooperative societies may arise in geographic areas in which competitive societies are more prevalent, and vice versa. The traits are widely scattered among the different cooperative or competitive types.

Mead's study indicates that there is a plasticity about the adaptability by a group to a general cultural trait that parallels the plasticity of an individual. It has been established by psychologists that any normal newborn baby will take on almost completely the characteristics common to the

[11]Mead, op. cit., pp. 458–511.

society in which it is reared. This study tends to show that the range of possible successful societies is also quite variable in pattern. The argument that "human nature cannot change" or that "people are born that way" cannot be used to promote or to oppose any given social change that seems desirable on other grounds. This statement, of course, does not mean that a society, once having developed its mores or ways of doing, will of its own accord or by outside pressure change easily without some internal disturbance. Neither does it indicate that an economic system may be changed without a major or minor change in ideology or primary motivational characteristics of the society. It probably does indicate that a society might —in the light of a rational approach to problems of adjusting itself to a rapidly changing technology—develop a system compatible with that technology. It can do this without doing any violence to any basic drives or forces resulting from inherent personality characteristics of the individual or from any kind of inherent "natural social structure." For example, man apparently is not born acquisitive; he may acquire this characteristic from his surrounding culture.

Education of Nonliterate Man

Neither the school as an institution nor education as a function of society developed separately from other aspects and institutions of nonliterate man. Except for the fact that the family appears in all early human groups and that the separate offices of tribal government usually developed early, on the whole there was little separativeness about any of the institutions, customs, or ways of doing of nonliterate man. Life was fairly well integrated. Abstractions, specialization, and compartmentalization of life are results of more highly developed society.

The education of the child came about naturally in his participation in family and group life. The purpose of education, had it been formulated, would have been to induct the young child into the ways of doing, thinking, and believing—the folkways and mores—of the group. In other words, conformity was taught. The method was imitation: learning by doing. However, in the "activity program" of nonliterate man, creativity was not encouraged. The child was expected to learn well to do things in the ways they had been done. Although in many groups, both competitive and cooperative, he was encouraged toward individual excellence, there was little permissiveness in experimentation with new techniques. Such new techniques as did evolve seem to have come about by unconscious drift rather than by conscious effort toward improvement.

In almost all tribes there was no differentiation among persons responsible for teaching. Parents, other adults, and older children all participated in the effort to help the child grow into an adult. The ideology of the primitive group was instilled through conversation about spirits and taboos, through storytelling of tribal myths, and through religious ceremonies. Most primitives were fairly indulgent with their children; however, the mores of the group seem always to have been thoroughly ingrained by the time of adolescence.

The first vocation to become sharply differentiated among nonliterate people was that of medicine man or priest, who came to have exclusive knowledge concerning religious rites and exorcisings. These religious persons were the first who considered it a function of their office to play a special part in the education of the young. Many primitive groups had complicated rites at the onset of puberty, which tended to intellectualize the process and emotionally dispose the youth toward complete acceptance of the folkways and of his role as an adult. The school as an institution seems to have appeared only after the development of writing and reading skills. Because the priests were generally the most literate group in this dawning period of the civilized era, these schools were usually closely tied to religious institutions and religious leaders. Although the schools of Greece and Rome represented a more secular approach, education and religion usually have been very closely related in most cultures even to the present time.

The education of nonliterate peoples was tremendously successful in accomplishing its goal of conformity to folkways. Because the society was practically united in allegiance to its folkways and mores, and the child was imbued with them, he could do little else but be molded in conformity with the patterns of the tribe. A point worth mentioning here is that the method must always be considered together with the goal. In the primitive tribe, the complete activity approach—total participation in life situations—was used to develop a child who would be in complete conformity to the culture. There was little attention to creativity or to individual differences.

The Breakdown of Fixed Mores

It has been seen that once a group has developed a certain type of culture, it tends to resist change in that culture. This is probably due in part to fear of the unknown based on uncertainty of knowledge of the environment. It is also due to the fact that the adults of the group, who largely determine what mores are to be inculcated, have fairly fixed habits. However, if changes had not occurred, man would still be at a primitive level. Some groups improved technologically, achieved better standards of living, a written language, and a creative art, before others. Some of these changes came about very slowly by a kind of cultural drift and without the awareness of the group.

Numerous reasons have been given to account for these changes and for the variation in the times at which groups arrived at various levels of civilization. Among the reasons that have been advanced are divine help, superior racial inheritance, and geographical conditions. The first two can be ruled out, inasmuch as modern biology and anthropology do not disclose racial differences sufficient to account for the progress, and most of the gods and myths have long since been discarded. Certainly favorable geographical conditions were helpful. The early Oriental-type civilizations developed in relatively fertile regions in the southern part of the North Temperate Zone. However, not all groups in this zone developed at the same time, and most of them developed and then faded away.

Our discussion has made it apparent that the reasons for progress are multiple and involve fortuitous circumstances or coincidences. The speed and type of changes varied among the groups because of differences in acceptance of slow cultural change of the drift type, which permitted changes to occur in some groups and to proceed along different lines among different groups. However, the large breaks with past mores or folkways were brought about by events most of which might be considered disasters: drought, threatened famine, pestilence, fire, earthquake, war, and conquest. All served to *force* the group to move or change its ways. Contacts with other groups led to adaptions of superior practices from either group, sometimes peacefully. Sometimes the conquerors subdued the conquered but preserved the better part of their culture. Sometimes as a result of these cataclysms, but sometimes independently of them, new inventions occurred. When these inventions met a need or answered a problem for the group, they would be accepted. No one knows how many inventions that came "before their time" were rejected by the group.

When some groups had developed sufficient technology to permit considerable travel for trade or for conquest, they subjugated other groups over wide areas, thus facilitating diffusion of cultural practices. This stimulated further contact with other groups, not only permitting cultural diffusions and accretions but also probably further stimulating inventions and the acceptance of improved technologies and other folkways.

The experience of the Tanala tribe, faced with the necessity for changes in technology and the influence of those changes on other folkways, illustrates many of the points already made. The Tanala, a tribe in western Madagascar, until 200 years ago cleared land for rice by cutting and burning the trees growing on it. This method required that the land be left fallow after one crop of rice before it could be reused. Consequently the Tanala moved around and the land was owned by the tribe in general. They were cooperative and noncompetitive in their social relations, and government was informal.

Cultivation of wet rice, an idea introduced from the outside, changed all this. The land was reused, prolific profits were recognized, and very complicated arrangements were made for the use of land and the ownership of property. Government became complex. A king was installed and the attitudes of the people toward one another became suspicious and competitive.[12]

Through such breakdowns in fixed mores and through the process of invention, contact with others, and internal social change, the first civilization finally emerged around 5000 B.C. This stage in development can be measured by the appearance of a written language, by means of which there can be found a recorded culture usually diffused over a fairly wide area.

CHARACTERISTICS OF ORIENTAL CIVILIZATION

The ancient civilizations that achieved a written language and literature and developed cultures that extended over fairly wide areas include the Chinese, Hindu, Egyptian, Babylonian, Assyrian, Persian, and Hebrew. Some of these, notably the Chinese, maintained an almost unbroken and unchanged type and level of culture into modern times. Others continued with marked changes but still maintained their essentially "Oriental" character.

As set forth earlier in this chapter, the characteristics of the Oriental-type civilization are essentially those of a well-integrated culture of a re-

[12]Ralph Linton, *The Study of Man* (New York: Appleton, 1936), pp. 348–354.

latively high level, but with a tendency to resist change in the manner of primitive cultures. All the civilizations previously listed, in their ancient form, except possibly the Hebrew, meet the requirements of the definition.

The pattern of emerging civilizations of this type seems to have been that of conquest and unification by one tribe of a group of closely related tribes. In the case of Egypt this apparently came about by conquest, with the resultant unification forced from the outside by the Syrians. The period of cessation of intertribal hostility and the cross-fertilization of cultures after the conquest apparently often led to the consolidation of the cultures, resulting in esthetic, literary, and technological achievements. The development of a written language, and thus the more effective passing on of the cultural heritage, enabled many of these civilizations to exist with little change for long periods of time. Some of these, such as Egypt, had periods of ebb and flow marked by new conquests. Others rose and fell, to be eclipsed or absorbed into a new civilization by their conquerors. This occurred frequently in the Mesopotamian region. In spite of the fundamentally static conditions of these civilizations, a great number of their contributions, later absorbed by Western civilization, can be listed. Among them are astronomy, surveying, systems of time, the alphabet, legal codes, more advanced ethical and religious thinking, and advances in architecture.

CHARACTERISTICS OF EARLY AND MODERN WESTERN CIVILIZATION

It has been necessary to go into considerable detail to describe the non-literate peoples, even though it has not been as important to describe the Oriental stage so fully. We shall now describe in somewhat greater detail the characteristics of Western civilization, because this is the general climate under which American society has grown. Western, or Occidental, civilization has been characterized by the concept of the acceptance of change. It has been centered on the ideal of bringing about continual improvements within the culture, as though at different times the basis upon which improvements were made was different. In medieval days they were based upon the otherworldly religious concepts of the Church. In the age of enlightenment, the basis was reason or the rational process. In the modern age, it is the scientific method and the ideals of democracy. Even in periods when change was held down because of fixity of social structure, as in the feudal stage, there were always areas in which progress was taking place; so Western civilization never developed the static quality of Oriental-type civilization.

Early Western Civilization

The conquering of the tribes in the Attic (Greek) peninsula (some with a relatively high civilization) by various Aryan tribes calling themselves Hellenes appears at first to have followed much the same pattern as did that of the earlier Oriental civilizations. However, a group of independent city-states was founded, and the Greeks not only absorbed readily the earlier civilizations, but proceeded to improve upon them. The priestly caste did not play as predominant a role as in most Oriental civilizations. Although the majority of the Greeks believed in the familiar pantheon of gods, these gods were never taken very seriously, and a primarily secular state developed. As Greek civilization advanced to its great heights in the fifth century B.C., there was much questioning of religious ideas as well as a prevalent desire to change political and social forms. This was the product of a peculiar and probably accidental set of conditions that developed in the culture, rather than of a particularly superior Greek inherited ability. Neither the earlier nonliterate Greeks nor the Greeks of the modern period show a marked tendency toward mental or other abilities above those of other peoples.

The conquest of the Greeks by the related Macedonians and the later conquest of the then known world by Alexander the Great led to a diffusion of Greek culture and to an absorption by the Greeks and others of many cultural elements from the peoples conquered. The eventual conquest of the Greeks by the Romans, and the continuation of the *Pax Romana* that followed, ensured the spread of Greek culture and thought throughout the Mediterranean region. Although the weakening and eventual downfall of the Roman state gave rise to the Teutonic invasion from the north and to a temporary eclipse of learning and Greek culture, they were never totally lost. The incorrectly named period of the Dark Ages was not totally so. The questioning and scholarly pursuits in the early universities of the twelfth and thirteenth centuries led the way to the renaissance of Greek culture and traditions starting in the twelfth century and perhaps culminating in the fifteenth.

Modern Western Civilization

Finally, an upsurge of freedom and individualism led to a breakdown of the feudal type of society that had developed during the Middle Ages and to a weakening of the control of the universal church. There emerged, one after another, the three elements that may be said to distinguish modern civilization in the Euro-American or Western scene:

1. The discovery and widespread application of the scientific method. Although there were scientists before the gradual development of the scientific method in the fifteenth and sixteenth centuries (leading to Bacon's *Novum Organum,* 1620), there seems to have been little understanding or even recognition of the possibility of the use of the scientific method of experimentation resulting in tested knowledge. Aristotle, one of the most prolific scientists of all time, was primarily a classifier of observed facts. He did not use or understand the experimental method of science. He made many errors because of this. The commonly given example of these errors is his principle that all bodies fall at speeds proportional to their weights. This seemed rationally or logically true, and he never thought of testing it. Galileo put this to an experimental test with the dramatic experiment at the leaning tower of Pisa and disproved the principle in a striking vindication of scientific method.[13] Although this scientific experimental method, usually called Newtonian science, and its assumptions as to the nature

[13]Neglecting friction, all bodies fall at the same speed if dropped from the same height.

of the universe, have had to be reinterpreted and expanded by
Einsteinian science in recent years, it is this earlier version that has been
followed predominantly, and it is to this method that the great
achievements of modern scientists are almost entirely to be attributed.
2. The use of the scientific method to approach the solution of
technological problems involved in the production of the necessities for
life—the beginnings of the age of abundance.

The rapid growth in man's ability to feed, clothe, and shelter himself
by the application of the scientific method to his technological problems
is so much greater than that of previous periods in man's development
that this fact must be set forth as a differentiating characteristic of
modern times. As far as technology is concerned, in the industrialized
countries of the West this can be the age of abundance. This situation
is in contrast to that in most of the present nonindustrialized societies
of the earth and in practically all the previous ones. The lack of
abundance leads, on one hand, to privileges for a few within a class–caste
society (which includes in many cases slaves or peons) and, on the other
hand, to war for economic purposes—to take wealth from other groups.
A particular solution to the problem of supplying the necessities of life
in turn causes new problems. For example, we in America have an
economy of abundance with economic institutions largely geared to an
economy of scarcity. War is now uneconomic for us, because its waging
causes a greater economic loss than can ever be gained by victory.
3. The widespread acceptance of the democratic philosophy and the set
of values and the way of life it implies.

Although democracy as a form of government goes back well before the
modern era—Greece having developed it first—it has found complete and
widespread acceptance only in modern times. Even in some primitive tribes
there was participation of the members in the election of chiefs and in other
decisions. The ancient Greek democracy was a pure democracy in the sense
that all citizens participated in the making of laws as well as in the election
of officials to carry them out. However, the Greek citizenry was only a part
of the population, which included many slaves with few or no rights and
with no participation in government. The modern concept of and belief in
democracy are so widespread that, with the exception of the brief advent of
fascism, practically the entire world professes to be attaining it. Even Russia
and its satellites loudly vaunt the superior virtues of their economic democracy and their "people's republics" as opposed to our "bourgeois capitalistic
democracy." In spite of Russia's attacks on Western democracy, there is
probably more democracy in the world now than fifty years ago, measured
by any one of a number of objective criteria, such as number of voters,
diffusion of economic benefits, emancipation of women, and relations within such institutions as the family.

By and large, in the Western world democracy has come to mean much
more than just general suffrage and representative government. It has given
more rights to individuals and to minority groups in nongovernmental relations. It has affected philosophy in that it has challenged authorities who
refuse to allow their philosophic bases to be examined. To some persons
democracy has become a complete philosophy—a way of life. To many it

seems to mean a more equitable distribution of goods and services. It appears to have been the most dynamic force of the last century.

THE INDIVIDUAL AS A PRODUCT OF HIS SOCIETY

Against the brief survey of the development of modern society it is possible to examine with more understanding the relation of the individual to his society and the social institutions that affect his development.

The human infant is born with a much more plastic nervous system than are other animals. All animals except the human are born with preformed behavior patterns that cause animals of the same kind to develop very much the same behavior patterns regardless of environment. On the other hand, a man tends to take on the patterns of the culture into which he is born and reared.

Man seems to differ from the other animals in at least the following important characteristics:

1. He is born with very few preformed behavior patterns.
2. The human infant is born helpless and has a long period of infancy. He is absolutely dependent for physical survival on others. He is thus by nature socially dependent on others.
3. Humans are very sensitive to environmental stimuli. Some of their senses, such as smell, are not as well developed as those of other animals. However, they are sensitive to meanings as developed through experience with such stimuli.
4. Man has the ability to invent and to assimilate a language.
5. As a result of language capacity or the ability to use symbols in general, man is capable of problem solving, both through thought and through experience.

The conclusions of modern students of man can be summarized as follows: All modern men belong to the same biological species, *Homo sapiens.* Almost all development since about 25,000 years ago has been cultural rather than evolutionary or biological. If, by some time machine, a baby from a nonliterate tribe of 25,000 years ago could be whisked to modern time and placed in any home, he would, aside from his individual physical characteristics, grow up to become like a member of the modern family rather than the nonliterate people from which he came. By the same token, a baby taken from the interior of, say, South America to France would, if placed soon after birth with a French family, grow up to be in all respects a Frenchman (excepting certain physical characteristics, such as, possibly, skin color).[14]

Awareness of the dependence of the individual on society for his very " humanness," as well as for the distinguishing characteristics of those humans of his culture, has been developed out of recent psychological study. This point of view is in opposition to earlier ideas, such as those of Rousseau, that assumed the development of preformed patterns from within. It is also different from the ideas of the biological determinists, who, noting the

[14]Ralph L. Pounds, *The Development of Education in Western Culture* (New York: Appleton-Century-Crofts, 1968), pp. 8, 9.

inheritance of structurally based behavioral characteristics of other animals, posit the same in man.[15]

INSTITUTIONS, SOCIETY, AND SOCIAL CHANGE

The Nature of Institutions in a Changing Civilization

Returning now to the main story of the evolution of human society, we look at the role that institutions play. At the various stages in societal evolution, man has developed institutions to care for different aspects of his life as needs arise. In the broad sense, language, writing, property rights, and even fire may be considered institutions. Institutions may be defined broadly as agreed-upon ways of behaving in given life situations; or more narrowly, as an organizational framework used by a group when its members consciously join together to work for a certain purpose. For the moment, we refer to the more structural type of institution, such as the family, the tribal organization, religious groups, and the school.

These institutions are developed in a particular time in a particular culture and are structured in consistency with the folkways and mores of that culture. Change then comes about in that culture, gradually or rapidly. Individuals may change because they are born into the environment of the changed culture. Quite often, however, institutions are slow to change because they are not reborn in each generation. Sometimes their structure is such as to resist change or at least to assist conservative individuals who are opposed to the changes that have occurred (or that ought to occur to be consistent with the new needs of the culture). Institutions thus contribute to the cultural lag that so often is characteristic of changing societies, particularly those that are changing rapidly.

Institutional Arrangements in Society

The institutional arrangements of even the primitive (nonliterate) societies were complicated. Although the institutions in many cases were not clearly defined (except for the family), relationships in many areas where institutions did not exist were clearly defined.

The family is apparently the oldest of all institutions. The relationships among the members of the family, the kin included in the family concept, and the relationship with those outside are strictly prescribed in all cultures. These arrangements are so variable that the conclusion must be reached that they are probably the result of chance, rather than of any inherited tendency toward a particular kind of relationship. Regardless of the nature of these arrangements, they are usually very well defined and exert great force on the behavior pattern of the family members.

Another institution is that involved in the system for obtaining a living. The arrangements may vary from those of a simple society with little specialization to complex economic systems such as are found in modern industrialized countries, with an intricate system of exchange and an extremely

---

[15]An exceptionally good article summarizing knowledge of man's potential (as opposed to limitation) written by a psychologist at the National Center for the Exploration of Human Potential is Herbert A. Otto, "New Light on Human Potential," *Saturday Review* (December 20, 1969), pp. 14–17.

high degree of specialization. By the end of early childhood, the value systems and ways of behaving in whatever economic system is predominant in a given culture are usually absorbed along with other mores.

The institution of government includes the ways that people work together to promote the aims of their society, and its patterns are also extremely variable. The democratic form has emerged only recently. Government, among the institutions of society, has become more important as society has become more complex. It has absorbed many of the functions formerly performed by other institutions, including the family and even religious institutions.

The early beginnings of institutions of religion go back far in human history. The effort of man to understand the fundamental nature of the world and to come to terms with it has been ever present. Concepts and ways of behavior associated with religion are particularly resistant to change. For example, old pagan beliefs bitterly resisted the later monotheistic ideas. Ideas that became associated with monotheism, such as the Ptolemaic conception of the universe, were stubbornly held for a long time before they succumbed to the onslaught of man's knowledge gained by science.

Man's self-expression through activity (play) and creativity (art) has also been institutionalized. The total number of institutions in which modern man may participate is very great, and their structural arrangements are very complex. Moreover, the institutions are often in conflict with each other. This conflict is present even in periods of relatively slow change, even when not fully recognized by the individual, because of the complex nature of these institutions. He may conform in compartmentalized fashion to varying value systems set up by the many institutions in which at different times he plays a part, without recognizing the conflict.

Institutions as Affected by Social Change

Institutional arrangements are developed at a particular time to meet particular needs for a particular phase of man's life. Man's nervous system may permit him to adapt readily when the need for change is great, but institutional forces usually seem to resist strenuously demands for changes that threaten to affect the institution radically. Although institutions give stability to society and provide the individual with security (as early family relationships, for example), they also slow down adjustments made necessary by social change. Institutions grip the loyalty of man, narrow his vision, render him at times unable to see the reason for changes, and, even if he does see them, slow down his effort to bring them about.

One of the ideals held in common in all the major world religions and in political democracy is respect for the individual personality—belief in the importance of the well-being of the individual. All institutions should serve that end. They are the servants of mankind.

Institutions are valuable only if they contribute to the moral and spiritual values of human life. The family as an institution contributes to social stability and provides protection for the young. A family should be linked by affection rather than by authority to afford a training ground for wholesome human relations. Similarly, schools and other institutions justify their existence as they contribute to the growth, happiness, and well-being of individuals. The Declaration of Independence states that, "governments are instituted among men to promote their inalienable rights." Institutions should be subject to adjustments according to the needs and values of the individuals who function in them.

All social institutions tend to resist change. A function of education is to encourage continuing appraisal of existing institutions in relation to current and prospective needs. The schools should develop in all a strong sense of responsibility for community well-being and a willingness to devote themselves unselfishly to it.

INDIVIDUAL AND GROUP FRUSTRATIONS RESULTING FROM CONFLICTS IN CHANGING CULTURE

A large cultural area such as the United States does not really consist of one cultural group, although Americans may have some characteristics in common that distinguish them from members of other groups. There are wide differences in the mores of groups living in the hills of Kentucky, the open spaces of Arizona, the small towns of Ohio, and the great metropolitan areas such as New York. One of the factors affecting cultural change in America has been the transition from an agricultural to an industrial civilization, from rural to urban. Moreover, this has occurred so rapidly that many people now living in cities were raised in a rural community or small town with rural mores. The mobility of population, the lack of face-to-face relations with other members of his group, and the fragmented view of culture available to the typical present-day American have lessened his ability to adapt to the changed culture; but the major factor in the cultural confusions of the typical person has been the rapidity of cultural change. His idea structure has developed in one culture; he lives in another. He is usually unable (or unwilling) to operate according to his earlier idea system, and on the other hand he is unable to change in order to adapt completely to the new. Consequently, he is frustrated. Even at best, the tempo of the modern industrial society places a strain on those who sophisticatedly develop a modern urban point of view. Another conflict comes from the different generations. Where the parents make adjustment to the new society by becoming inured to the changing parts of it and maintaining their older ideas or standards successfully without inner conflict, the new generation changes and then finds itself in conflict with the old and with institutions that have not made the corresponding change. The institutional structure resists change, and it may be controlled largely by those who cling to old ideas.

The very real frustration resulting from the conflicts between an ideology of a childhood no long entirely adapted to the present and between various aspects or institutions of a culture that lag behind other aspects of the culture, in turn causes further individual and institutional conflicts and further maladjustment in our culture.

THE SCHOOL AND SOCIETY
The School as a Social Institution

In Chapter 3 there is set forth a detailed description of the evolving relationship of schools to their societies throughout the historic period. At this point, an over-all portrayal of the school as an institution is presented. The school as an institution evolved out of the educational function of the primitive tribe, the family, and the religious institutions. Although in Greece, and to some extent also in Rome, the school was secularized, by and large the school was closely related to religious institutions until the recent secularizing influences that produced separation of church and state also produced a school free of religious sectarianism. In England and Germany a cooperative relationship exists between the state and the church in educational enterprises, whereas in America the public school has become completely secular.

As the state took over from the family and the church the strictly non-religious functions of education, certain problems arose. How shall the schools be governed? What shall the school do about controversies in our society? Shall the school teach in accordance with the majority point of view, just as it is expected that the majority policies will be carried out elsewhere in government?

Out of the thinking gropingly done on these problems, certain principles have emerged that serve, by and large, officially and unofficially to determine school policy in the United States. The *de facto* operation of the school is in the hands of local lay boards elected for school purposes independent of other political controversy in a given community. The schools at first tended to limit education to literacy and to character traits that were agreed upon as desirable in our society. When the pressure of social events, such as the depression of 1930, forced upon the school consideration of controversial social issues, they were slowly admitted—with the proviso that the school, as such, would not take sides but would present the facts and arguments on the many sides of the issues to be explored.

The concept of the school as unique among governmental institutions has been slow to emerge. Some educational philosophers (as in Mexico) have come to think of the school as a fourth branch of government—the educational branch added to the executive, judicial, and legislative. Charles A. Beard explored this issue in a brochure written for the Educational Policies Commission of the N.E.A., *The Unique Function of Education in a Democracy.* He listed five major reasons for the school to be considered as unique and independent:

1. Scientific instruction is independent of politics.
2. The humanities have their independent imperatives.
3. The teaching of controversial questions calls for judicial prerogatives.
4. Preparation for citizenship transcends all partisan limits.
5. To education are entrusted enduring interests and values.[16]

The Lag Between the School and Society

In Chapter 3 we shall explore, among other generalizations in the history of the school, the following two, apparently conflicting: (1) schools tend to reflect the cultures in which they are found; (2) in changing cultures

[16]Charles A. Beard, *The Unique Function of Education in a Democracy* (Washington, D.C.: National Education Association, 1938).

they tend to lag behind rather than to lead the culture. At this point, it is sufficient to point out the nature and extent of the lag.

In Chapter 15 we shall note conflicting ideas among educational philosophers as to the importance of this lag. Indeed, some of the philosophers, humanists, who are most concerned about this lag, would agree entirely with Beard's assumption in the preceding section. Other philosophers, called social realists, who are concerned about narrowing the lag, are not so concerned about the independence of the schools from other political institutions.

The lag of the school behind society is no greater than that of many other institutions. Some of the reasons for the lag lie in the institutional character of the school. Other reasons will be explored later. Two of the most striking historical examples of lag are (1) the persistence of autocratic administrator–teacher relationships and teacher–pupil relationships long after the development of the democratic society, (2) the persistence of memoriter devices long after psychological research indicated that such learning was quickly forgotten and could not as readily be transferred to new situations.

In general, the social (or cultural) lag of the school may be discussed under three headings:

Administrative—Organization, Buildings, and Equipment. The slow change in administrative organization as better methods have been developed and the slow adaptation of buildings and equipment to newer design are very evident. Fifteen to thirty-five years may elapse before there is 95 per cent adoption of new school administrative and organizational methods.

Curriculum and Methods. Bringing textbooks up to date when new scientific facts are discovered is hindered by the amount of time it takes to get the items into a textbook and the text adopted by the schools. From ten to fifteen years may elapse. New curriculum organization based on modern educational research may be delayed still longer because of inertia or open opposition of teachers, administrators, and the public.

Methods and Teacher–Pupil Relations. The introduction of newer methods based on modern psychological research or on broadened purposes for education is delayed by the time lapse between the teacher's education and his years of service, by the lack of opportunity for teachers to keep abreast, and again by opposition of some teachers, administrators, and the public.

SUMMARY

This chapter has presented a survey of man's evolutionary development in relation to his culture. We have identified man's relationship to other animals and his development as a social creature largely influenced by his environment. We have traced his development through the three stages of civilization: the nonliterate, the Oriental, and the Western. We have indicated the importance of man's development to institutions and of institutions to man's development. We have related these developments to the school. We have also indicated some of the problems that arise out of the lack of adjustment between changes, in the culture in general and in man's institutions and ideologies.

In spite of the complexity of this analysis and the problems that it poses, there is perhaps room for optimism. In the early part of this chapter it was indicated that we might be in the early phases of what might be called a new level of civilization—called, for want of a better term, modern civilization. At this level it may be discovered that man has secured through science —physical, biological, and social—a sufficient understanding of the world, of himself, and of human relationships that he may be able to produce a type of educated individual and reconstructed social institution adaptable for the solution of the problems of each age and for the guidance and the direction of social change in directions most beneficial to himself. The role of the school in such a society is to maintain objective and unbiased presentation of truth, and development of scientific attitudes and democratic values in youth.

Selected Bibliography

Abel, Theodore. *The Foundation of Sociological Theory*. New York: Random House, Inc., 1970. 258 pp.

Allee, W. C. *The Social Life of Animals,* Revised Edition. Boston: Beacon Press, 1958. 233 pp. An interpretation, with human implications, of one of the most significant biological developments of recent years: the role of basic cooperative processes among living beings.

Baker, Paul T., and J. S. Weiner (eds.). *The Biology of Human Adaptability*. Oxford: Clarendon Press, 1966. 541 pp.

Berrien, F. Kenneth. *General and Social Systems*. New Brunswick, N.J.: Rutgers University Press, 1968. 231 pp.

Bloom, Benjamin S. *Stability and Change in Human Characteristics*. New York: John Wiley & Sons, Inc., 1964. 237 pp.

Blumenthal, Arthur L. (ed.). *Language and Psychology*. New York: John Wiley & Sons, Inc., 1970. 248 pp.

Bock, Philip K. (ed.). *Culture Shock: A Reader in Modern Cultural Anthropology*. New York: Alfred A. Knopf, Inc., 1970. 379 pp.

Borgatta, Edgar F. *Social Psychology: Readings and Perspective*. Chicago: Rand McNally & Co., 1969. 740 pp.

Buettner-Janusch, John. *Origins of Man: Physical Anthropology*. New York: John Wiley & Sons, Inc., 1966. 674 pp.

Calder, Ritchie. *Man and the Cosmos: The Nature of Science Today*. New York: Frederick A. Praeger, Inc., 1968. 219 pp.

Claiborne, Robert. *Climate, Man, and History*. New York: W. W. Norton & Company, Inc., 1970. 444 pp.

Cohen, Yehudia A. (ed.). *Man in Adaptation: The Cultural Present*. Chicago: Aldine Publishing Co., 1968. 433 pp.

Curti, Merle. *Human Nature in American Historical Thought*. Columbia, Mo.: University of Missouri Press, 1968. 114 pp.

Darlington, C. D. *The Evolution of Man and Society*. New York: Simon & Schuster, Inc., 1970. 753 pp.

DeFleur, Melvin L. *Sociology: Man in Society*. New York: McGraw-Hill Book Company, 1971. 640 pp.

Denzin, Norman K. (ed.). *Sociological Methods: A Sourcebook*. Chicago: Aldine Publishing Co., 1970. 590 pp.

Deutsch, Martin, Irwin Katz, and Arthur B. Jensen. *Social Class, Race, and Psychological Development*. New York: Holt, Rinehart & Winston, Inc., 1969. 423 pp.

Dobzhansky, Theodosius. *Mankind Evolving: The Evolution of the Human Species*. New Haven: Yale University Press, 1962. 381 pp.

Duberman, Martin. *The Uncompleted Past.* New York: Random House, Inc., 1969. 375 pp.

Dubos, René. *Reason Awake: Science for Man.* New York: Columbia University Press, 1970. 280 pp.

_____. *So Human an Animal.* New York: Charles Scribner's Sons, 1968. 267 pp.

Eiseley, Loren. *The Unexpected Universe.* New York: Harcourt Brace Jovanovich, Inc., 1969. 239 pp.

Emmet, Dorothy, and Alasdair MacIntyre (eds.). *Sociological Theory and Philosophical Analysis.* New York: The Macmillan Company, 1970. 232 pp.

Etzioni, Amitai. *The Active Society: A Theory of Societal and Political Processes.* New York: The Free Press, 1968. 698 pp.

Fabun, Don. *The Dynamics of Change.* Englewood Cliffs, N.J.: Prentice-Hall, Inc., 1967. 190 pp.

Fischer, Robert B. *Science, Man and Society.* Philadelphia: W. B. Saunders Co., 1971. 124 pp.

Foster, George M. *Traditional Cultures and the Impact of Technological Change.* New York: Harper & Row, Publishers, 1962. 292 pp.

Fraiberg, Selma. "Learning to Be Human," *Current,* No. 93 (March, 1968), 46–56.

Fried, Morton. *The Evolution of Political Society: An Essay in Political Anthropology.* New York: Random House, Inc., 1967. 270 pp.

Garn, Stanley M. (ed.). *Culture and the Direction of Human Evolution.* Detroit: Wayne State University Press, 1964. 98 pp.

Glass, H. Bentley. *The Timely and the Timeless: The Interrelationships of Science, Education, and Society.* New York: Basic Books, Inc., Publishers, 1970. 99 pp.

Goodman, Mary E. *The Culture of Childhood.* New York: Teachers College Press, Columbia University, 1970. 167 pp.

Gouldner, Alvin W. *The Coming Crisis of Western Sociology.* New York: Basic Books, Inc., Publishers, 1970. 528 pp.

Guskin, Alan E., and Samuel L. Guskin. *A Social Psychology of Education.* Reading, Mass.: Addison-Wesley Publishing Co., Inc., 1970. 211 pp.

Hall, Edward T. *The Hidden Dimension.* Garden City, N.Y.: Doubleday & Company, Inc., 1966. 201 pp.

Hallowell, A. I. *Culture and Experience.* New York: Schocken Books, Inc., 1967. 434 pp.

Hanna, Thomas L. *Bodies in Revolt: A Primer in Somatic Thinking.* New York: Holt, Rinehart & Winston, Inc., 1970. 308 pp.

Horowitz, Irving Louis, and Mary Symons Strong (eds.). *Sociological Realities: A Guide to the Science of Society.* New York: Harper & Row, Publishers, 1971. 545 pp.

Huxley, Julian S. (ed.). *The Humanist Frame.* New York: Harper & Row, Publishers, 1964. 432 pp.

Jonas, David, and Doris Klein. *A Study of the Infantilization of Man.* New York: McGraw-Hill Book Company, 1970. 362 pp.

Kormondy, Edward J. *Concepts of Ecology.* Englewood Cliffs, N.J.: Prentice-Hall, Inc., 1969. 209 pp.

Krech, David. "Man's Participatory Evolution," *Current,* No. 110 (September, 1969), 55–64.

_____. "Psychoneurobiochemeducation." Speech before the A.A.S.A. in *A.A.S.A. Official Report,* 91–105. Washington, D.C.: American Association of School Administrators, 1969. 215 pp. This is only one of many sources for reports of the research of Krech and others of the effect of drugs, hormones, environmental experiences, etc., on rats, with direct and important implications for man.

Lipset, Seymour Martin. *Politics and the Social Sciences.* New York: Oxford University Press, 1969. 328 pp.

———, and Leo Lowenthal. *Culture and Social Character: The Work of David Riesman Reviewed.* New York: The Free Press, 1961. 466 pp.

Lorenz, Konrad. *On Aggression.* New York: Bantam Books, Inc., 1969. 306 pp.

Markel, Norman N. (ed.). *Psycholinguistics: An Introduction to the Study of Speech and Personality.* Homewood, Ill.: Dorsey Press, 1969. 410 pp.

McIntosh, Donald. *The Foundations of Human Society.* Chicago: University of Chicago Press, 1969. 341 pp.

Mead, Margaret. *Cooperation and Competition Among Primitive People,* Enlarged Edition. Boston: Beacon Press, 1961. 544 pp.

———, and Rhoda Metraux. *A Way of Seeing.* New York: McCall Publishing, 1970. 335 pp.

Middleton, John (ed.). *From Child to Adult: Studies in the Anthropology of Education.* Garden City, N.Y.: Doubleday & Company, Inc., 1970. 355 pp.

Montagu, Ashley. "A Scientist Looks at Love," *Phi Delta Kappan,* Vol. LI, No. 9 (May, 1970), 463–68.

———. *Man in Process.* New York: The New American Library, Inc., 1961. 278 pp. A good presentation of man's social evolutionary development.

———. *Man Observed.* New York: G. P. Putnam's Sons, 1968. 299 pp.

Morris, Desmond. *The Human Zoo.* New York: McGraw-Hill Book Company, 1969. 256 pp.

———. *The Naked Ape: A Zoologist's Study of the Human Animal.* New York: McGraw-Hill Book Company, 1968. 252 pp.

Morton, John (ed.). *Biological and Social Factors in Psycholinguistics.* New York: American University Press, 1971. 215 pp.

Nisbet, Robert A. *The Social Bond: An Introduction to the Study of Society.* New York: Alfred A. Knopf, Inc., 1970. 448 pp.

Otto, Herbert A. "A New Light on the Human Potential," *Saturday Review,* December 20, 1969.

Park, Robert E., and Ernest W. Burgess. *Introduction to the Science of Sociology.* Chicago: University of Chicago Press, 1969. 1,040 pp.

Pfeiffer, John E. *The Emergence of Man.* New York: Harper & Row, Publishers, 1969. 477 pp.

Platt, John R. (ed.). *New Views of the Nature of Man.* Chicago: University of Chicago Press, 1965. 152 pp.

———. *The Step to Man.* New York: John Wiley & Sons, Inc., 1966. 216 pp.

Pounds, Ralph L. *The Development of Education in Western Culture.* New York: Appleton-Century-Crofts, 1968. 307 pp.

Pribram, Karl H. (ed.). *On the Biology of Learning.* New York: Harcourt Brace Jovanovich, Inc., 1969. 256 pp.

Richards, O. W. *The Social Insects.* New York: Harper & Row, Publishers, 1953. 219 pp.

Riesman, David. *Individualism Reconsidered and Other Essays.* New York: The Free Press, 1954. 529 pp.

———. *The Lonely Crowd.* Garden City, N.Y.: Doubleday & Company, Inc., 1956. 395 pp.

Rosenfeld, Albert. *The Second Genesis: The Coming Control of Life.* Englewood Cliffs, N.J.: Prentice-Hall, Inc., 1969. 327 pp.

Ruitenbeck, Hendrik M. *The Individual and the Crowd: A Study of Identity in America.* New York: The New American Library, Inc., 1964. 118 pp.

Sady, Rachel Reese. *Perspective from Anthropology.* New York: Teachers College Press, Columbia University, 1969. 98 pp.

Schur, Edwin M. *Law and Society: A Sociological View.* New York: Random House, Inc., 1968. 239 pp.

Shepard, Paul, and Daniel McKinley. *The Subversive Science: Essays Toward an Ecology of Man.* Boston: Houghton Mifflin Company, 1969. 453 pp.

Simpson, George Gaylord. *Biology and Man*. New York: Harcourt Brace Jovanovich, Inc., 1969. 175 pp.

_____. *The Meaning of Evolution: A Study of the History of Life and of Its Significance for Man*. New York: Bantam Books, Inc., 1967. 333 pp.

Smith, Mahlon B. *Social Psychology and Human Values*. Chicago: Aldine Publishing Co., 1969. 438 pp.

Snow, C. P. *Variety of Men*. New York: Charles Scribner's Sons, 1967. 270 pp.

Spindler, George D. (ed.). *Education and Culture: Anthropological Approaches*. New York: Holt, Rinehart & Winston, Inc., 1963. 542 pp.

Stocking, George W., Jr. *Race, Culture, and Evolution: Essays in the History of Anthropology*. New York: The Free Press, 1968. 380 pp.

Storr, Anthony. *Human Aggression*. New York: Atheneum Publishers, 1968. 127 pp.

Szent-Gyorgyi, Albert. *The Crazy Ape*. New York: Philosophical Library, Inc., 1970. 93 pp.

Teilhard de Chardin, Pierre. *The Phenomenon of Man*. New York: Harper & Row, Publishers, 1959. 318 pp.

Tyler, Stephen A. (ed.). *Cognitive Anthropology*. New York: Holt, Rinehart & Winston, Inc., 1969. 521 pp.

UNESCO. *Race and Science*. New York: Columbia University Press, 1969. 506 pp.

Walcott, Fred G. *The Origins of Culture and Anarchy*. Toronto: University of Toronto Press, 1970. 161 pp.

Warriner, Charles K. *The Emergence of Society*. Homewood, Ill.: Dorsey Press, 1970. 174 pp.

Warshofsky, Fred. *The Control of Life*. New York: The Viking Press, Inc., 1969. 181 pp.

Weinberg, Alvin M. *Reflections on Big Science*. Cambridge, Mass.: The M.I.T. Press, 1967. 182 pp.

Winch, Peter. *The Idea of a Social Science and Its Relation to Philosophy*. London: Routledge and Kegan Paul, 1958. 143 pp.

Wise, John E. "Science and Human Values," *School and Society*, Vol. 99, No. 2331 (February 1971).

Selected Films

The Color of Man (Columbia University), 20 min. Examines those conditions in the history of mankind which brought about differences in the color of man's skin. Shows the effect of modern science and transportation on these forces.

Earth and Its People Series (Louis de Rochement Associated), 20 min. each. Includes the following titles: Malaya—*Nomads of the Jungle*; Norway—*Farmer-Fisherman*; Java—*Tropical Mountain Land*; Guatemala—*Cross-section of Central America*; South Africa—*Riches of the Veldt*; and Argentina—*Horsemen of the Pampas*. Malaya film particularly is recommended.

Mirror of America (Norwood), 36 min. A reflection of the American way of life from 1914–1921, this movie portrays a cross section view of people and progress. It is a historical documentary taken from the Ford Film Collection recently presented to the National Archives.

Monkey into Man (Library), 20 min. Traces development through the baboon, gibbon, orangutan, chimpanzee, and gorilla, showing the family and social life of these animals and the variation in brain power among them. A comparison is made between the most intelligent of these apes and man.

Our Changing World (Ott and Methodist), 60 min. The story of the development of the earth since the beginning of time. The formation of the oceans and continents and the emergence of life are shown. Time-lapse photography is used to show the succession of higher forms of plant and animal life. Ends with the advent of man on earth.

Science and Superstition (Coronet), 10 min. Demonstrates technique for guiding elementary schoolchildren's thinking to scientific method. Shows means of helping children to conduct research and arrive at conclusions therefrom.

Small World (McGraw-Hill), 11 min. Children from some forty countries give their intepretation in drawings of the world from prehistory to the year A.D. 3000.

The Social Animal (Encyclopaedia Britannica), 29 min. Investigates some of the ways in which man is influenced and changed by society. Studies group pressures to conform and shows the consequences of publicly stating ideas contrary to one's private belief. From the Focus on Behavior series.

Social Change in a Democracy (United World), 29 min. Students in a social science class discuss the conditions that exist in a democracy and those that exist in a totalitarian state; they learn firsthand how a problem in their own community, arising from a social change, is solved by law and assembly rather than by violence.

Social Process (Encyclopaedia Britannica), 18 min. Patterns of behavior common to all cultures. Develops concept of social process from the statement, "Man seeks values through institutions using resources."

Social Revolution (Encyclopaedia Britannica), 18 min. Describes the process of social change, especially that instigated by technological developments. Illustrates the process with scenes of the industrial revolution in England, the French Revolution, emigration to the United States, and the rise of totalitarianism in Germany and Russia.

Southern Highlands (Ford Motor Co.), 22 min. Provides a picture of folk people and affords insight into their responses to the processes of change.

The Story of Prehistoric Man (Coronet), 11 min. This description of the life, appearance, habitat, and achievements of prehistoric man is reconstructed from authentic evidence, prehistoric tools and weapons, cave paintings and stone carvings, and skeletal remains. The periods of the Old and New Stone Ages are indicated and the geographical areas in which prehistoric man lived are mapped.

■□□□□□□□□□□□

The Historic Relationship
of Schools to
Their Societies

The fundamental thesis underlying this chapter is the following: Schools tend to reflect the societies in which they are found. There is a similar proposition, which may seem to be contradictory to the first but actually is not: Schools tend to lag behind their societies, particularly in periods of rapid social change.

THE NATURE OF THE SCHOOL AS A SOCIAL INSTITUTION

All human institutions are a product of culture and as such must be called social institutions. The word *institution* itself implies that the school is social. The school as an institution in most cases has been developed consciously by a people in order to carry out certain ideas deemed appropriate by them. Although the school as an institution sometimes has lost touch with its society and has tended to become a conservative force, it has always been established as an agency of society to carry out its purposes. Even where the schools have been institutions of a private nature, not controlled by any form of government, this still has been true.

In another sense the school itself is a social institution. Persons attending it learn the methods of their society—merely by living in a cultural milieu that reflects the society in which the school is found. Many times the lessons learned from the social structure of the school (reflecting that of the society) may be more important in the development of the individual than the course content—sometimes academic and little related to life—that the students learn. This appears to have been just as true in earlier schools as in those of the immediate past. However, it was not until the modern period that the importance of nonformal learning was recognized by the people directing the schools and consciously given some status, in the form of extracurricular activities, student organizations, and so on.

THE EARLY DEVELOPMENT OF THE SCHOOL AS A SEPARATE SOCIAL INSTITUTION

In Chapter 2 we went into some detail concerning the development of institutionalized education and some of the functions of the school among preliterate peoples. In the simple organization of preliterate peoples, there were no well-defined institutions in the sense of their having a separate structure from that of the total community. The family probably emerged first as a separate institution, together with the other trappings of tribal organization, probably just an extended family at first. The various forms of governmental organization, such as the office of chieftain or an advisory body of elders, may have emerged next as social institutions. Soon the religious activities of the tribe became institutionalized, with the development of a priestly caste with special training and activities.

In the more simply organized tribes, all the adults were responsible for the education of the children. Formal education was limited to mystic rites of initiation into the tribe; these rites usually were held for certain age groups or puberty groups. The children learned by doing, by imitation of what the adult did. Later on, certain persons, usually members of the priestly class, were given responsibility for the special training of children in the tradition and other formal instruction of the group.

Until a written language and literature appear, it is not necessary to develop a distinctly separate institution for the purpose of educating the young. When this happens it means that the group has reached the second level of development—the Oriental-type civilization. Those types of civilizations that first developed in the Fertile Crescent and in Egypt had a high level of culture; in most cases this culture was based upon amalgamation of existing cultures of various tribes. They also began to have a written language and literature. Similar changes were taking place in China. Only a few members of the culture at these early times could write or read. It became necessary, then, to train others to do this. Special schools were set up for those who were to be versed in reading and writing, who were to be the guardians of the culture. Usually these persons were closely connected with the religious institutions. In some cases there were also scribes (those who could read and write) whose functions were not necessarily religious. Special books were written for the instruction of the young, usually containing admonitions, words of wisdom, or important myths to be passed on to the next generation. Methods of instruction were devised for these schools. In many cases, however, the work of the schools became quite formal, with the main attention directed to the language *as such* rather than to the material to be taught.

Prior to the period of the Greeks, and for that matter practically until modern times, the school did not differ greatly from other institutions in its purposes or goals. Throughout most of the Fertile Crescent, in Egypt, and in China, the school was tied closely to either religious ceremonies or government or both. Its primary difference in function was in teaching persons to read and to write the literatures and to understand and to interpret the sacred literature of the society or culture. Education was usually limited to a relatively small portion of the total population. It was provided primarily for people who would have to use it in their governmental or religious tasks.

In that sense the school was vocational. In all the thinking about schooling that took place prior to the time of the Greeks, there seems to have been little conception of education as being a broadening experience or as being intellectually stimulating. Part of the reason, of course, was that early cultures were repressive or restrictive of innovation. It is not until we come to the Greek culture that we find any idea of progress or creativity. Because the school reflects the prevailing attitudes of the culture, it is not surprising that the schools of the pre-Greek period were as they were.

In the next four sections we shall discuss the school as an institution as it developed during each of four significant periods: the period of Greek influence, that of Roman influence, the medieval period, and the period of the revival of learning. In each case we will discuss briefly (1) the social and intellectual developments of the period; (2) the school as an institution; and (3) the goals of the school as they were established at that time.

THE GREEK SCHOOL AND ITS SOCIETY

The study of the Greeks and their civilization is an intriguing one because so many of the problems that they faced and the ideas with which they struggled were similar to our own.

It is difficult to understand why there developed on the Attic peninsula a different kind of civilization from that which developed in the Far East, the Middle East, or the Nile area. There had come into being on or near this peninsula, prior to the invasion by the various Greek tribes, two fairly highly developed civilizations, the Mycenaean and the Cretan. Their level of art and culture was quite high. These peoples were then invaded by certain Aryan tribes from the north, who called themselves the Hellenes but whom we call the Greeks. They were much less civilized. However, in conquering the old civilizations they absorbed them. Although there was an early period somewhat resembling our medieval period when the civilization tended to decline, it did eventually recover and reach new heights.

Instead of becoming one large group dominating the entire peninsula, the Greeks tended to develop politically into small city-states that were more or less independent. This left a great deal of local initiative for them to develop and experiment. Considerable differences existed among the various city-states, although a common language and a common alphabet and literature eventually developed. There was a contrast between the rigorous autocratic type of city-state, such as Sparta, and the much more democratic ones, such as Athens. However, in both cases the power to rule was dispersed fairly widely among an oligarchy. In Sparta the number of people who had freedom to make choices was probably, during most of the time, less than 5 per cent. The remainder of the populace were "free" men who were not citizens, plus a vast number of slaves. The same thing was true of Athens except that the number of free men was higher. Furthermore, the democratic rights held by the free men were much greater. Life was freer as a whole, and a great deal more individual initiative was allowed. Sparta was really a garrison state. It was at Athens that the liberal state, permitting a great deal of freedom of thinking, was developed. Publicly the state was religious; however, there was no priestly class that dominated it. There was no dogma that could cause a stifling of man's intellect. Authorities agree that the Greek level of culture was achieved largely as a result of accident of social structure rather than because of any superior inherited characteristics of the Greeks, for they were closely related by blood to many other Aryans who did not accomplish so much so early.

The Greeks never were able to solve the problem of getting along with each other, and the peninsula was beset by a succession of civil wars, which tended to weaken them greatly. They were finally conquered by Alexander the Great. The Greek culture, however, was dispersed throughout the Mediterranean region and eventually was absorbed by the Roman civilization. It had great influence upon Roman life and also on Christianity. It also had influence upon the Saracen, or Islamic, culture. During one period of history Greek influence was much greater upon the Saracen culture than it was upon Western civilization. A discussion of Greek developments would not be complete without considering at least three of the outstanding Greek teachers and intellectual leaders: Socrates, Plato, and Aristotle. These men constituted a kind of triumvirate, with the latter two each being a student of the older.

Socrates (469–399 B.C.) left no writings. Consequently it is difficult to determine exactly his ideas or his methods of teaching. Primarily he taught by a method that has become known as the Socratic method, a question-and-answer technique. When a pupil would come to him with a question to be answered, Socrates would retort with a question to the student. As the student began to answer that question and others to follow, he eventually discovered that he knew nothing. This is called the *ironic* or *destructive* stage. Then by a series of constructively worded questions, Socrates would build up the idea that he wished to place in the student's mind. This is called the *maieutic* ("giving birth to ideas," based on the Greek word for *midwife*) stage. Socrates thus apparently thought that one could get at truth by skillful handling of ideas. However, his questions were always related to life. Among the Greeks he comes closest to the pragmatic or modern experimentalist method. But he was not a thoroughgoing pragmatist in the modern James–Dewey sense.

Plato (427–346 B.C.), although a student of Socrates, represents a withdrawal from the practical period. Plato moved his classes away from the marketplace to the grove of Academius so that he would not be bothered by practical things. Hence comes our word *academic*—relating to things that are not necessarily practical. Plato developed a philosophical point of view that held that truth was decided ultimately by reason alone. Ideas existed apart from man's experience with things. To Plato the real world was a shadowy representation of the *ideal* world. The real end of education consequently must be to deal with those ideas. It must be abstract, intellectual. However, modern followers of Plato must, of course, remember that Plato's concepts about education were laid in the context of his time. Basic Greek education then allowed for the well-rounded development of the student, physically, mentally, and otherwise, through songs and literature and athletic activities. As shown by his suggestions for education contained in his *Republic*, he would continue this. Plato's emphasis upon the intellectual was, of course, the crowning part of the education he proposed for those people whom he believed capable of receiving it. However, for Plato this was not an exclusive form of education. Some of the modern followers of Plato attempt to define the education of the intellect as being the only kind of education worthy of the name. Plato's influence on the thinking of his time—and of the period to follow, when Greek culture was disseminated throughout the Mediterranean region—was immense. Through neo-Platonism, a mystical form of Platonic doctrine that spread throughout the area after Plato's time, he exercised a profound influence upon Christianity as it began to develop.

Aristotle (386–322 B.C.) was Plato's pupil. He agreed basically on most matters with Plato, but he had more interest in the things of this world— in material things. In the first place, Aristotle was a great scientist.[1] He wrote prolifically about practically all matters that are now embodied in the various fields of knowledge. Our organization of fields of knowledge still closely follows that of Aristotle. Artistotle was a collector and classifier of knowledge. Although he wrote many books on different phases of scientific knowledge, he did not understand the scientific method of experimentation as it has developed in recent years. Largely for this reason his work contained errors. Aristotle's philosophy as such did not influence Western civilization until about the twelfth and thirteenth centuries A.D., when his works, which had been lost, were recovered through Moslem schools. Aristotle's philosophy, with its acceptance by St. Thomas Aquinas and by the Roman Catholic Church, became dominant in the universities of Europe and in European thought for almost four hundred years. It was not until the coming of the scientific method that it began to be challenged seriously.

Platonic and Aristotelian ideas still exert a strong influence in Western civilization. They largely provide the basis for the perennialist point of view discussed in Chapter 15 of this book.

The Greek ideal of education, particularly in Athens and in other of the freer Greek states, was to develop the well-rounded, thinking individual. In Sparta the aim was more to develop a hardy, militaristic type of individual. In both cases, education was quite thorough and much broader than the purely intellectual. One of the significant differences between Athens and Sparta lay in the attitude toward freedom and toward freedom of thir. ͻ. It is well to note here, as in other cases, that the Greek schools put into action the Greek set of values and thus reflected their society.

THE ROMAN SCHOOL AND ITS SOCIETY

In the early Roman period, as in the early development of other peoples, the school was not clearly separated from the society. Primarily it was the job of the family to carry on education. When Rome began tu dominate the peninsula of Italy and the Roman state began to develop, schools as institutions began to separate from other institutions with respect to functions served. The early schools were private and seemed to be influenced little by either religious groups or the state. In the later Roman period, however, the state tended to exert much more influence. The Roman schools, just like schools in other countries, tended to reflect the nature of society whether or not they were run by the Church, by private nonreligious groups, or by the

---

[1]Aristotle was not, strictly speaking, a scientist in the modern sense, because he did not know or use scientific experimentation to validate his hypotheses. Nevertheless his observations and classification of scientific data were a contribution, in spite of the few (but major) errors in his work.

state. Roman schools in the early and middle period were divided into three levels: the *ludus*, or elementary school; the school of the *grammaticus*, or the intermediate school; and the school of the *rhetoric,* or the higher school. The Roman schools were primarily organized to develop citizens and to stress the duty of the citizens to their state. The schools of the rhetoric, for example, were never as broad in their approach as were the Greek schools even though they were modeled after them. There was emphasis primarily on speaking and oratorical ability. However, this was certainly considerably broader than similar education would be at present. There was little emphasis on the all-around development of the body, as there had been in Greek education. In the later Roman period the schools tended to degenerate, laying emphasis upon grammatical structure and form rather than upon thinking and the spirit. The study of philosophy itself never became a central feature of the school. The Romans were largely men of action rather than philosophers, and they tended to play down this aspect of education, which had been so prominent in Greece.

Only a small fraction of the Romans were educated completely (as was true of all countries until modern times). During the period of the decline of the Roman Empire, education tended to languish and to come more under the control of the emperor.

In the medieval period, which is discussed next, education was closely associated with religion. Neither in Greece nor in Rome (in contrast to most of the other countries that were contemporary with Greek and Roman civilization) were the schools closely tied to religious ideas. Education was primarily a secular function. This does not mean that the schools were antireligious or that they ignored religious materials. They simply were not controlled by the religious authorities, and their central purpose was not the teaching of religious ideas. Furthermore, the schools did not use members of the priesthood in teaching functions. Clerics were almost exclusively used during the medieval period—even into the period of the revival of learning.

THE SCHOOL AND THE SOCIAL CLIMATE IN THE MEDIEVAL PERIOD

The medieval period of history is generally considered to be roughly from the fifth century to the fifteenth. This period has been erroneously called the Dark Ages. Although there was a decline in learning and in the number of schools because of social conditions, they never disappeared. Furthermore during part of this time various forces produced an increase in the amount of learning and education. The decline of learning was due in part to the breakdown of the Roman Empire, the invasion of the Germanic tribes, and the early opposition of Christianity to pagan learning. Because pagan learning was the only kind of learning that existed, there was a tendency to look down upon schools and schooling of any kind other than religious. The first Christian schools, the catechumenal schools, were established before 500 A.D. and were connected with either a cathedral or a monastery. These schools and the later catechetical schools were established primarily for religious instruction. They often included instruction in reading along with that in theological doctrines. The best instruction in religion and theology was that developed for the clerics and took place mostly in the monasteries. Charlemagne (742–814 A.D) stimulated a considerable revival of learning by issuing several edicts to improve the education of the clergy and to establish other types of schools. However, this progress did not continue uninterrupted. The purpose of education was primarily that of instruction concerning Christian doctrines and preparing for the world to come —the "otherworldly" aim.

During this period of uncertain social conditions, many of the literary works of the Greeks and Romans were lost. Most of those preserved were from Plato. During the eleventh or twelfth centuries Aristotle's works were found and revived through contact with the Moslems. In the eleventh and twelfth centuries a group of scholars (called the scholastics) in the monasteries did a thorough reconciliation of Greek thinking (primarily that of Aristotle) with the Christian tradition. This philosophy, usually called scholasticism or Thomism (the latter term from St. Thomas Aquinas, 1225–1274), dominant in the Western world at least until the sixteenth century, was formally accepted by the Roman Catholic Church as its official philosophy in 1879 and has continued with some modifications to this day. Although no striking changes were brought about by the work of scholastics, intellects were stimulated in preparation for the revival of learning that took place from the fifteenth to the eighteenth centuries. There was practically no interest in science during the medieval period, and most of the errors that Aristotle had made were incorporated in the prevalent ideas. The revival of interest in things scientific foreshadowed the greater interest in the period of the Reformation and the scientific revolution, the seventeenth and eighteenth centuries—to be discussed later. Although kings and other nonreligious authorities took an interest in education from time to time, and sponsored schools and universities, primary control of the schools was in the hands of the clerics, and their primary purpose was religious—that is, to prepare people to be better Christians, to strengthen doctrines, and to get them ready for the world to come. Because both the political state and the Church were considered to be ordained by God and both were considered to be equally under His control, there was no such thing as separation of Church and state. Although there were disputes concerning the control of the Pope, by and large the political authorities were subservient to the religious authorities during the medieval period. Only a small percentage of persons were in school, were educated, or were literate. The interest in mass education was to await the period of the Reformation and the Counter Reformation.

One of the major contributions of this period was the founding of the university. Starting with the University of Salerno in the ninth century, many such institutions were founded throughout Europe in the medieval period. These became the repositories of learning and the centers for many new ideas. Though almost all scholars operated within the framework of the medieval outlook—the otherworldly, Christian outlook—they did maintain standards of learning as far as was possible during those times. The emphasis was upon the liberal arts and upon what was written in books rather than upon the development of new knowledge. The answer to a dispute was found by going to the authorities and attempting to reconcile the conflicting views. However, the freedom of the universities during this time laid an excellent background for the revival of learning and for the educational importance of the university in the early modern and contemporary scenes.

THE SCHOOL IN THE PERIOD OF THE REVIVAL OF LEARNING, FOURTEENTH AND FIFTEENTH CENTURIES

Starting with the work of Petrarch (1304–1374), the leaders of the period of the revival of learning were interested in changing the attention of the schools from otherworldly preoccupation to the joys of this world. This was primarily accomplished by a return to the use of the ancient Roman and Greek literary classics, all of which were much broader in outlook than the materials that had been used during the medieval period.

The political situation at this time helped to secularize education. There was a breakdown of feudalism, with the strengthening of the central monarchy in France and England and of the central power of the dukes and princes in Italy, Germany, and possibly Spain. In many cases the hold of the Church had weakened. The growth and development of town schools for the rising middle class helped to bring about a school based more upon the ideas of this world.

Many of the outstanding educational leaders of this period wrote books on their ideas. Da Feltre (1378–1446), at Mantua, Italy, who taught in a school maintained by a duke, had ideas concerning education that were surprisingly modern. Although the course of study was classical in content, there was mild discipline in the school and it was aimed at the harmonious development of mind and body. This seems more like the Greek ideal than the philosophy of other schools of its time. The work of such other leaders as Rabelais, who was very critical of the schools and other social institutions of his time, stands out during this period.

Although the revival represented a new orientation, it was not in complete opposition to the general orientation of this theologically centered period. The leaders were not in rebellion against prevailing theological ideas. They were merely placing more emphasis upon the affairs of men (humans). Hence they came to be called *humanists,* and the subjects they studied were called the *humanities.* During the sixteenth and seventeenth centuries, religious leaders accepted humanistic ideas and the two were encompassed together under the name of *religious humanism.*

In considering the pronouncements of earlier leaders on education, their ideas must always be examined in the light of the times. The suggestions for milder discipline or for consideration of individual differences of the student must always be considered in the light of the fact that the main aim was to produce the classically trained leader and upper-class gentleman. These schools were purely for the upper class and for the leaders. In almost all cases the emphasis was upon classical learning and the use of the classical languages. Only a few of these people believed that education should be conducted in the vernacular. There was still heavy emphasis upon grammatical form and upon a literary type of education. The revival of learning saw the beginnings of interest in scientific knowledge, but this interest still had little influence upon education.

THE SCHOOL IN THE PERIOD OF THE REFORMATION AND SCIENTIFIC REVOLUTION, SIXTEENTH TO EIGHTEENTH CENTURIES

During the sixteenth to the eighteenth centuries, the power of the Church was both weakened and strengthened. Through the Reformation movement, the northern part of Europe mostly broke away from the Church of Rome. On the other hand, the Church was strengthened immensely by the Counter Reformation as far as the southern part of Europe was concerned. It also was the period of the scientific revolution, which began to affect education. The Reformation itself reflected a strengthening of the power of the secular rulers against the Pope as well as a religious reformation. At the end of this period, the national states were pretty well established. This laid the basis for a national system of schools.

The Protestant reformers were much interested in the education of the masses. Although they did not have in mind the same kind of education for the masses as for the classes, at least they were interested in enabling them to read the Bible. This interest in the education of the masses did not, by and large, lead to any differences in school methods or curriculum. As a matter of fact, the Protestant schools under the influence of Luther and Calvin were probably more rigid and more repressive than earlier schools had been. They largely stressed memorization and learning of the rules of grammar. Luther's own concept of liberal education reflected the classics, in which he had been educated. The Protestant schools of this period were gloomy schools indeed. There was little emphasis on the child as an individual, on developing an educational program suited to his level, or on other such modern ideas.

A few developments during this period were the beginning of some things that were to come later. These were largely the results of the influence of modern science. It is generally felt that the work of Comenius (who is held by some to be the first modern educator) was influenced by the development of science. Comenius emphasized learning through sensory experience. He developed the idea of the textbook with pictures, so that the youngsters would understand the words that they were trying to learn. He was thus far in advance of his time, but he had very little influence because he was a Protestant bishop and in the minority in his section of Europe.

In Catholic Europe there was an improvement in education through the development of the Jesuit schools with quite high standards and through the work of the Jansenists and the Christian Brothers. Each of these groups set up special teacher-training programs in order to prepare better teachers. LaSalle of the Christian Brothers developed a special institute, which was one of the first examples of an institution largely for the training of teachers in the elementary school.

The developments of this time did not greatly affect the relationship of religion to education. The Protestant reformers were even more interested in continuing education in religion than were the humanist educators of the previous period. Even when the schools were taken more and more under the control of the civil authorities, it was still done for the central purpose of preparing people for the world to come. Not until the middle of the nineteenth century was there an emphasis upon a secular type of educational program. Moreover, the Calvinistic and Lutheran emphasis upon the state being subordinate to religious authority led eventually to education becoming a function of the state. They held that the state had the right to decide which religion should hold sway and to require all citizens to conform. The church became established in the sense that it was protected and supported by the state. Even when the state did not have the actual ownership and control of the school, there was increasing government interest in education. Edicts of princes and kings often determined the content of the school curriculum. This was especially true of some of the work of universities in France and England during this period, where through edicts the king controlled the emphasis in studies. One example is the move toward humanistic emphasis in the French schools as opposed to the earlier theological curriculum. In some cases, the king even took sides in theological controversies.

One other point might be made with respect to the attitude of religious authorities toward the developing sciences. Both the Protestants and the Catholics were strongly opposed to some of the findings of modern science. For example, both the Lutheran Protestants and the Catholics denounced the teachings of Copernicus that the sun was not the center of the universe. It was almost 100 years after the time of Copernicus that his ideas became widely accepted. This delay was largely due to the opposition of church leaders, who felt that the new ideas were opposed to their theology. On the other hand, men like Descartes tried to reconcile the new scientific view with the older theology; however, it was some time before Descartes was accepted by religious authorities.

THE DEVELOPMENT OF NATIONAL SCHOOL SYSTEMS, NINETEENTH CENTURY

Prior to the nineteenth century, education in Europe was predominantly either religious or private and was available to a very small segment of the population. Some national (state) systems of education developed in Germany during the Reformation period, as a part of the determination of the particular religion of the subjects of each of the German states. The purpose of such a national support of religion was primarily to give the young child a proper background to understand his religion, particularly in the Protestant faith.

With the French Revolution, the Napoleonic era in France, and the development of Germany under the Fredericks, a new purpose of education evolved: to use the school to raise the general level of the people for the welfare of the state. The Prussian kings were concerned about developing a minimum of education for their subjects in order to develop their state. In this period there was no thought of educating citizens to exercise the right of suffrage, because these were despotic states, albeit benevolent. During democratic periods there was emphasis in the French schools upon educating persons for freedom and for exercising the rights of citizenship; during periods of despotism this influence disappeared, only to be revived again under the next democratic government. Throughout Europe the prevailing emphasis in schools was on the indoctrination of the student with love for the emperor (or king) and with the religious viewpoint prevalent in the particular country. The German kings did espouse freedom of learning and teaching in the German universities for the purposes of fostering research; however, this was not carried into the *Gymnasien* and the elementary schools.

The general trend in the national school systems in France, Germany, and other European countries was toward two school types: the elementary school for the masses, compulsory for those who could not afford private tutors; and the secondary school for the classes, leading to the cultural development of the student divorced from work, and perhaps then to study at the university. Although there was much talk during the Reformation period concerning compulsory education for all, this ideal was not realized in Europe for some time. The first country in Europe to establish a compulsory system of education was the German state of Prussia. One of the next was the democratic United States of America. Although the reasons in both cases were nationalistic, certainly the climate of political thought in the United States was quite different from that of Prussia, and certainly the citizenship (voting) reason was more prevalent in the United States. There is evidence that some of the leaders in education in this country were considerably influenced by what was taking place in education in Europe.

The nineteenth century was the period when the work of the educational reformers became quite well known, although the work of the schools did not reflect to any great extent the teachings of such men as Herbart (1746–1827), Pestalozzi (1776–1841), and Froebel (1782–1852). The minimal influence of these men upon the typical school situation is an example of the lag of the school behind society in periods of rapid change. Very few of the teachers of Europe were well trained. Most saw learning as memorization, in spite of the emphasis of the theorists on concrete, realistic education. Only after people became concerned that there be changes in education, in line with the proposals of theorists, did there begin to be set up special schools for the preparation of teachers—professional teacher education. When people were fairly well satisfied with the education offered, there was little agitation for professional teacher education. In some cases there was opposition to it for fear that the school system would change and become more modern.

The development of the European national systems of schools did not change the relationship of church and state that had existed previously. Whereas the schools of the previous period had been primarily dominated by the church for religious reasons, the schools of this period were still largely influenced by the prevailing religion. This was true except at those times during the French Revolutionary period when anticlerical feeling caused the schools to become completely secular. Considerably later in the history of France, they were made secular again—around the turn of the twentieth century. Of course, in America they became secularized because America disestablished the church and adopted a policy of separation of church and state. This is one of the marked contrasts between the development of the American education system and the systems of European countries.

THE INFLUENCE OF DEMOCRACY ON EDUCATION IN AMERICA BEFORE 1865

The European colonists who moved to this country brought with them their European institutions. This was as true of the schools as it was of other institutions. The European schools of the seventeenth century (the period of early colonization) were aristocratic and classical. Such schools hardly suited life on the rugged coast of New England and in other parts of the colonial area. Many of the schools that were established were narrowly sectarian. The breakdown of the sectarian character of the colonies, together with the growing feeling that this education was not adapted to the life of the colonists, led to the languishing of educational standards in the early part of the eighteenth century. There was some revival of interest in education by the middle of the eighteenth century, as part of the renewed interest caused by the age of enlightenment in Europe, the growth of science, and the stirring ideas concerning the freedom of man. Outside of the New England colonies very little was done to make education universal because most people had not yet thought of education as being other than a private matter.

The schools in New England were public schools in the sense that they were established by the state even though they were narrowly sectarian. This was not true of schools in Europe. As the schools changed from being sectarian, in the early part of the nineteenth century, they remained public schools. Thus in America the principle of governmentally owned and operated schools was established. Also in New England during the colonial period the idea of having a committee of the town selectmen to run each local school was established. This arose partly because of the difficulty of communication between schools and partly because of the desire of the parents of each school to have control. Local school committees eventually became boards of education.

The attempts to establish a better secondary school, to take the place of the European grammar school, which had been transplanted to America, also represented an effort to develop an institution to meet the needs of life on this continent. The academy temporarily was successful, but it was to be replaced by the high school around 1890. The academy was often sectarian, and generally it was run privately. It developed later into a college-preparatory school even though it was not originally so designed.

The influence of the democratic spirit in America after the Revolution eventually caused the school system to take on the four characteristics of being (1) *free*, (2) *public*, (3) *nonsectarian*, and (4) *universal* (compulsory). The framework of the first three of these was developed in the period preceding the Civil War[2]—although all aspects were not fully realized. The fourth was not realized until well after the Civil War and in many states not until the twentieth century. One aspect of the development of universal education was the setting up of the American "ladder" system of education[3] as well as the compulsory aspects of the law.

We shall discuss the important trends during the period before the war under two headings: The Free Public School System and the Secular (Nonsectarian) School System.

The Free Public School System

The public control of our school system and its free aspect are so common now that we take them for granted. It is hard for us of the twentieth

---

[2]At one time persons in the South objected to the use of the term *Civil War*, preferring the *War Between the States*. Since the Civil War Centennial the term, used officially by the joint committees, is more acceptable.

[3]Under the so-called ladder system, a child may move without examination from one level of education to another and be transferred freely from one school system to another.

century to realize the tremendous struggle that occurred in order to bring about a free school system.

We have noted how the custom of having the school run under public auspices developed in New England. However, public control was not nearly so prevalent in some of the other states. In Pennsylvania, for example, many religious groups developed private schools. This differed from the situation of the theocratic states that set up the original *public* school system in New England—albeit a sectarian one. With the development of great heterogeneity of the population and with an increased demand for education, the question of payment of tuition began to be raised. This became increasingly important with the extension of suffrage to all people. At first this meant that persons of average wealth and wealthy people paid for their education by the use of the rate bill (being billed for their portion of the costs of education at the end of each term). In time, the question was forcefully raised as to whether a democracy could exist with universal suffrage unless all the people were literate. Thus it developed that public funds were made available for those who could not afford to pay for education. In this way universal education was established, with those who could afford to pay doing so directly, and with the fees of the rest being paid out of taxation. Of course, it was always difficult to know where to draw the line as far as the pauper was concerned. Some people of very modest means resented the idea of paupers getting free education. Furthermore, a great number of people who were not paupers and who should have been educating their children were not doing so. A vigorous battle for free public education was begun. This became a hot political issue in many of the state legislatures. The idea of free education for all, paid out of public taxation, was considered by many to be socialistic or communistic. Furthermore, it was held to be a denial of man's right to individual initiative toward education. In the state of Pennsylvania, for example, a permissive free school law was passed; but then the next assembly elected by the people contained a majority opposed to the free public school. However, a speech by Thaddeus Stevens swayed the legislature and allowed the bill to stay. His speech ranks as one of the great pleas for free public education.[4]

Gradually the advocates of free public education did win in the various states. In some states it was made obligatory on the school districts to furnish free education. In other states it was made permissive for the local boards of education. Moreover, the states and the local communities within the states were very uneven in providing free education even after it was legalized. It must also be remembered that free public education at first applied only to the elementary school. Free public education on a completely legal basis at the high school level came later.

The Secular (Nonsectarian) School System

We have seen that the early schools were largely sectarian. They were either public and sectarian as in the democratic states in New England or they were private and sectarian as in New York and Pennsylvania. Several fac-

---

[4] "Thaddeus Stevens' Speech Opposing Repeal of the Law of 1834," in Elwood P. Cubberley (ed.), *Readings in Public Education in the United States*, No. 121 (Boston: Houghton, 1934).

tors had led to the breakdown of the sectarian schools long before the legal matter was debated. One factor was the great religious heterogeneity of the colonies. In order to encourage people to settle in the various colonies, the concept of freedom of religion had to be extended to include the freedom from being taught a sectarian doctrine other than one's own in the schools. This tended to cause sectarian differences to be played down as far as school instruction was concerned.

Another factor was, of course, the disestablishment of the church. Several colonies had disestablished the church before the Revolution. In the federal Constitution the church was disestablished under the First Amendment. All the states eventually disestablished the church either by law or by constitutional amendment. When the new states set up constitutions, they all included sections preventing any kind of religious establishment, thus adopting officially the principle of the separation of church and state. Massachusetts was one of the late states to disestablish the church. However, Massachusetts had long had multiple establishment and in practice had fallen considerably away from "true establishment" before the passage of the law against establishment (1833). A third factor in eliminating sectarian instruction in the schools was the practical difficulty in deciding which sectarian doctrine was to be taught. Several board of education elections were fought in New England on the issue of whether trinitarian or unitarian doctrines should be taught, before the silliness of such a method of determination became apparent to most people. In many cases, by the time the states had decided on passing laws forbidding the teaching of sectarian doctrine in the schools, they no longer were teaching it in practice.

It must be remembered, in connection with the current discussions of teaching of sectarian religious ideas in the schools, that these people were God-fearing. It was out of their experience in attempting to teach sectarian doctrines that they decided it was impossible in a publicly controlled school system. This became even more apparent when compulsory education laws were considered. In this instance, pupils would be compelled to go to school and to receive sectarian doctrine if it were taught there. This, of course, would be contrary to the First Amendment of the Constitution as it has been interpreted by the United States Supreme Court.

THE EXPANSION OF THE AMERICAN SCHOOL, 1865 TO 1929

Whereas the period preceding the Civil War represents the beginning of the expansion of the school, with many solid bases being laid, it was in the period following this war that a tremendous expansion of both elementary and high schools occurred.

Starting with Massachusetts in 1852, the states in turn passed compulsory attendance laws until there was complete acceptance in principle of compulsory education with the Mississippi law of 1918. Although attendance laws were variously enforced by the different states and the range of years of required attendance varied considerably, the net effect was to establish the fourth of our principles of public education, namely, universal (compulsory) education. No longer did the parent have freedom to keep a child in or out of school as he wished. The child must attend school if he was physically and mentally capable of doing so. With the freeing of the slave and the coming of other non-Caucasians to the United States, the number of people of non-Caucasian races attending the public schools also increased.

After the turn of the century, some attention was paid to the raising of the standards of both training and certification of teachers. In about one hundred years we have gone from the early period of certification of teachers by lay examination (school boards) to certification by written professional examination and finally to state certification on the basis of credentials from accredited teacher-training institutions. There were also movements for the upgrading of elementary school standards, such as the demarcation of students into grades, the giving of objective examinations, and the setting up of standard courses of study.

The high school, which had its beginnings in the 1820's, expanded rapidly, and by 1870 it was seen to be the institution that would replace the old academy. Although ostensibly set up to take care of those who were not going to college, it soon developed a college-preparatory curriculum much like that of the academy it imitated and replaced.

The Kalamazoo decision in 1874 legalized the use of common-school money in public high schools. The high school thus became an important part of the public school ladder system, filling in the gap between the common or elementary school and the state university. The Committee of Ten (reporting in 1893), by setting up the principle that one subject is good as another, provided it is taught in the "right" way, reaffirmed the importance of the traditional subjects and in so doing tended to make the high school a preparatory institution, even though the committee recognized that the majority of students were not going on to college. It held, however, that the traditional college-preparatory subjects were good for training the mind, a mental-discipline argument. The Commission on Reorganization of Secondary Education, which published its report in 1918, developed a different concept as stated in the Seven Cardinal Principles. These are based on an analysis of the democratic culture. However, this did not influence the school curriculum very much.

Starting with 1890, the high school doubled its enrollment each decade through 1930. The high school thus became a "people's college" in which programs of all kinds were set up in order to meet the varying needs of the increased number and range of students. This rapid expansion of the public schools, in a period when there were not adequately trained personnel, led to many consequences. Standards of education, particularly at the higher levels, were not always well maintained. The salaries of the personnel were always low. Teaching in too many cases was something that one did while waiting for a job that would bring more income. This condition did not begin to be remedied until the 1920's, when increasing industrial expansion and the general prosperity of the country were such that teachers were paid somewhat better. In the depression period of the early 1930's and in the period following World War II, this situation of low salaries recurred.

THE UNCERTAINTY OF A PERIOD OF RAPID SOCIAL CHANGE IN AMERICA, 1930 TO PRESENT

The general characteristics of the period from 1930 to the present can be set forth roughly thus. First, the school was criticized during the 1929–

1934 depression for at least two reasons: (1) Its poor standards were held to be one of the factors that caused the Depression. (2) It was maintained that the school had not done a good job of teaching Americanism and therefore had caused people to become too radical. Second, during World War II, the school was looked upon as one of the bulwarks in helping the defense effort. In the third stage, following general social unrest, the school was again looked at critically and blamed for some of the unrest and lack of stability in our society.

The 1958 success of the U.S.S.R. in launching the first earth satellite, Sputnik I, launched a new criticism of American education. Our failure to be first in this field was blamed on the schools. Newspaper, magazine, radio, and television appeals were made for strong science and mathematical programs. Open condemnation was voiced of the current programs of fine arts and socialization.

At the very time the school was being criticized most for not fulfilling its function, it was being given the greatest tasks of its history. Throughout this period, however, there was a continued expansion of school enrollment, with the exception of a slight trough in the late 1930's and early 1940's because of the low birth rate of the Depression years. The great masses of people, wanting education and having great faith in its value, placed enormous burdens upon the school, both in numbers of children to be educated and in demands for increased services such as lunchrooms, health clinics, classes for the gifted and for the handicapped, and broadened curriculums. Furthermore, the school was unable to compete in salaries with other groups in the post-World War II period, as a result of inflation; therefore it had difficulty getting adequate personnel. It is ironic that educational leaders were criticized for having the school take on tasks that had been forced on it by social pressures, many times over the protests of educators who were, on the whole, very conservative.

One of the increasingly insistent criticisms of the school in the post-World War II period related to their inability and alleged lack of interest in teaching moral and spiritual values. The private religious schools of today are, and the schools of the sixteenth and seventeenth centuries had been, strongly oriented toward religious and theological ideas. Therefore, when the problems of the 1930's and the postwar period arose, it was argued that the public schools were not grounding people thoroughly in moral and spiritual values. In any period of social change, there has always been a period of reorientation of values and an increase in crime and other moral lapses. When this occurs, people seek some cause other than the difficulties of adjusting to a changing society. Noting that the schools did not specifically teach religious ideas, the critics hit upon this as being one possible reason. Actually the schools have not ceased teaching moral values just because they have ceased to teach religious doctrines. Early in the nineteenth century Horace Mann had advocated that they continue to stress moral teachings in his fight for the secularization of the school. But with greater emphasis on other things and the inability of the schools, under legal restrictions, to teach sectarian ideas (which in the minds of many persons, including many teachers, were inextricably tied in with moral and spiritual values), there was a decline in the formal teaching of moral precepts. In newspaper and magazine articles during World War II and after, the problem began to be stated more clearly: It is possible for the school to teach moral and spiritual values without using a sectarian theological base or without directly teaching religion? Many persons held that the school was already doing this and could continue to do it, although a greater stress could be placed upon the teaching of values. In 1952 the Educational Policies Commission published a book called *Moral and Spiritual Values in the Public Schools,*[5] in which they called on the schools to teach those moral and spiritual values that were common to our democratic society, regardless of differences in sectarian viewpoints. This point of view was accepted by many, and the schools have had a great revival of interest in attempting to teach moral and spiritual values as one of their aims. There have been three notable departures from this point of view:

1. Those who hold that the school cannot possibly teach moral and spiritual values without having a theological base. These people advocate a system of private religious schools, either financed by public funds or privately financed.
2. Others who advocate that denominational religious classes be established in the public schools and be given for credit.
3. Those who hold that the schools, while not teaching any one sectarian idea, can teach about religion. This is the point of view that has been sponsored by the Danforth Foundation and other influential groups.

The Supreme Court decisions forbidding the required use of prepared public prayers or the Lord's Prayer or any other religious exercises in the classrooms of the public schools seem to make it clear that such denominational classes cannot be established in the public schools under the Constitution as presently interpreted.

There recently has developed a new way of solving the problem of the conflict between the advocates of the teaching of religion in private schools and those of the continuation of the secular classes in publicly financed classes. This is the *shared-time* concept. It is thought by its proponents to be constitutional. All that would be required would be arrangements providing for the easy shift of students during the day from public schools to private religious schools. In secondary education credit for courses taken in part-time attendance at the public school would be transferred to the private school, or vice versa. Under this plan the child would take his religious classes and perhaps some other "theologically sensitive" courses such as social studies or literature in the church-related school and take his courses in mathematics, science, and others (e.g., vocational) in the public school. He would then get his diploma eventually from one of the two schools by the transfer of credit.[6] Title II of the 1965 Federal Aid to Education bill grants money to private religious schools (channeled through the public school in the area). This appears to be governmental (federal) approval of a limited shared-time concept.

Uncertainty over the role of the school did not come about entirely

[5]N.E.A., Educational Policies Commission, *Moral and Spiritual Values in the Public Schools* (Washington, D.C.: National Education Association, 1951). See further discussion in Chapter 14.

[6]N.E.A., *Religion in the Public Schools.*

because of a social struggle or the rapid rise of the masses wanting an education. It was also the result of increasingly conflicting philosophies that were developing as a result of the rapid social and intellectual change coming about in America and in the world.

The success of the protest movement with respect to civil rights for the black minority and later other minority groups led to the increasing use of protest, civil disobedience, and confrontation politics in the late 1960's and into the 1970's. Protests against U.S. involvement in Vietnam were the primary cause during the late 1960's. However, there was also agitation for changes in school and university policy. Black studies were introduced into both secondary schools and colleges as a result of such movements. There was also agitation for the increasing involvement of students in college governance. Some extreme militant groups wanted to politicalize the university, that is, force it to take positions on political and social issues and to reorient university programs in accordance with its political positions. (See Chapter 14 for more on student protest and university problems; see Chapter 15 for a look at related conflicting philosophies, including the "new left.")

EUROPEAN STIRRINGS IN RESPONSE TO DEMOCRATIC IDEAS AND SOCIAL CHANGE

Until recent times the European countries maintained more or less the type of school they had at the time of American colonization. Although common-school education had been made available to the masses, and most countries had compulsory education for four to six years, a great gulf existed between secondary and elementary education. Secondary education was held to be for the few. For example, in England a smaller percentage of persons went to secondary school than were going to colleges in this country during the immediate post-World War II period.

In the post-World War II period European schools experienced significant changes. Factors precipitating changes were the same forces that were affecting America, the attention the American educational system was receiving because of America's position of world leadership, and the contact with Americans in the armed services. Schools of various countries began to consider lengthening the required period of the common school. In England, France, and Germany great effort was made to increase the compulsory attendance period and to provide higher schools to meet the differentiated needs of youngsters. Under the impetus of the Education Act of 1944, education in England has undergone a great change. England is providing a broader education in the English modern secondary school and in the comprehensive school (the latter enrolling secondary-age students with many different backgrounds and a variety of goals in one school). There has recently been greater concern in England for the education of boys and girls beyond the age of fifteen to eighteen, an interest in providing more adult classes, and a very rapid increase in the amount of university-type education provided, somewhat the same as the increased interest in higher education that America started to have in the 1920's.

Only one other country claimed to provide as much advanced education for as great a number of persons as the United States. That country was the

U.S.S.R. By 1956 and 1957 information began reaching this country that Russia had developed an educational system, particularly of the technical type, that included ten years of school for the great majority of children. Also, the Russians were giving advanced training to a relatively high percentage of persons in the technical university or postsecondary schools. This education certainly was not as broad as that of other European countries, nor as broad as American education. It tended to be concentrated on the sciences, technical subjects, and the theory of communism. The economic and social status of the school teacher in Russia may be, relatively speaking, much higher than it is in the United States.

SUMMARY

The predominant theme underlying this chapter is that the school has developed as a separate institution in order to carry out the aims of its society—or at least the aims of the dominant portion of the society—for the education of the young. In the recent period of rapid social change, there has been confusion regarding the purposes of the school because there is confusion about predominating ideas of our culture. The problem of the separation of church and state and that of the relation between the sectarian and the secular also served to becloud the issue further. The recent advent of the space age, with the developing computer technology, has highlighted the urgency of these questions. In Chapters 15 and 16 we will attempt to clarify some of these conflicting concepts. In this chapter we have attempted to indicate how these things came to develop and to show the historic relationship of the school to its culture or its society. It has been shown that the school as a social institution is developed consciously by a people to carry out the ideals of a culture or segment of a culture. Once established, the schools, like other institutions, tend to lag behind their cultures. Much of what one learns has been learned outside of the school.

In this chapter brief descriptions of the school at different stages in man's development have been made to illustrate the theses: the tendency for schools to reflect their societies, and their lag behind its development. The recent changes in the school in Europe and in America in response to unprecedented social change and the resultant conflict with respect to the role of the school are set forth.

Selected Bibliography

Ablin, Fred (ed.). *Contemporary Soviet Education.* White Plains, N.Y.: International Arts and Sciences Press, 1969. 295 pp.

Bassett, G. W. *Innovation in Primary Education: A Study of Recent Developments in Primary Education in England and the U.S.A.* New York: John Wiley & Sons, Inc., Publishers, 1970. 209 pp.

Bayles, Ernest E., and Bruce L. Hood. *Growth of American Educational Thought and Practice.* New York: Harper & Row, Publishers, 1966. 305 pp.

Bettleheim, Bruno. *The Children of the Dream.* New York: The Macmillan Company, 1969. 363 pp.

Bowers, C. A. *The Progressive Educator and the Depression: The Radical Years.* New York: Random House, Inc., 1969. 254 pp.

Boyd, William. *The History of Western Education*, Seventh Edition. New York: McGraw-Hill Book Company, 1965. 489 pp.

Brembeck, Cole S. *Social Foundations of Education: A Cross-Cultural Approach*. New York: John Wiley & Sons, Inc., 1966. 544 pp.

Brubacher, John S. *A History of the Problems of Education*, Second Edition. New York: McGraw-Hill Book Company, 1965. 688 pp.

Burridge, T. D. *What Happened in Education: An Introduction to Western Educational History*. Boston: Allyn & Bacon, Inc., 1970. 146 pp.

Calhoun, Daniel (ed.). *The Education of Americans: A Documentary History*. Boston: Houghton Mifflin Company, 1969. 643 pp.

Cantor, Norman F., and Michael S. Werthman (eds.). *The History of Popular Culture*. New York: The Macmillan Company, 1968. 788 pp.

Carter, Harold J. *Intellectual Foundations of American Education*. New York: Pitman Publishing Corp., 1965. 653 pp.

Chambliss, J. J. (ed.). *Nobility, Tragedy, and Naturalism: Education in Ancient Greece*. Minneapolis, Minn.: Burgess Publishing Co., 1971. 213 pp.

Coben, Stanley, and Lorman Ratner (eds.). *The Development of an American Culture*. Englewood Cliffs, N.J.: Prentice-Hall, Inc., 1970. 235 pp.

Cohen, Alan, and Norman Garner (eds.). *Readings in the History of Educational Thought*. London: University of London Press, 1967. 272 pp.

Cramer, John F., and George S. Browne. *Contemporary Education: A Comparative Study of National Systems*, Second Edition. New York: Harcourt Brace Jovanovich, Inc., 1965. 598 pp. An excellent general source.

Cremin, Lawrence A. *American Education: The Colonial Experience 1607–1783*. New York: Harper & Row, Publishers, 1970. 688 pp.

_____. *The Transformation of the School: Progressivism in American Education, 1876–1957*. New York: Alfred A. Knopf, Inc., 1961. 387 pp.

Curti, Merle. *Human Nature in American Historical Thought*. Columbia, Mo.: University of Missouri Press, 1968. 114 pp.

Drake, William E. *Intellectual Foundations of Modern Education*. Columbus, Ohio: Charles E. Merrill Books, Inc., 1967. 369 pp.

Drucker, Peter F. *The Age of Discontinuity: Guidelines to Our Changing Society*. New York: Harper & Row, Publishers, 1969. 402 pp.

Fund for the Advancement of Education. *Education and American History*. New York: The Fund, 1965. 24 pp.

Gatewood, Willard B., Jr. (ed.). *Controversy in the Twenties: Fundamentalism, Modernism, and Evolution*. Nashville, Tenn.: Vanderbilt University Press, 1969. 459 pp.

Gillett, Margaret. *Readings in the History of Education*. New York: McGraw-Hill Book Company, 1969. 322 pp.

Good, Harry G., and James D. Teller. *A History of Western Education*, Third Edition. New York: The Macmillan Company, 1969. 630 pp.

Greaves, R. L. *The Puritan Revolution and Educational Thought*. New Brunswick, N.J.: Rutgers University Press, 1969. 188 pp.

Greer, Thomas H. *A Brief History of Western Man*. New York: Harcourt Brace Jovanovich, Inc., 1968. 594 pp.

Gutek, Gerald Lee. *An Historical Introduction to American Education*. New York: Thomas Y. Crowell Company, 1970. 256 pp.

_____. *Pestalozzi and Education*. New York: Random House, Inc., 1968. 178 pp.

Hartford, Ellis Ford. *Education in These United States*. New York: The Macmillan Company, 1964. 576 pp.

Hersch, Jeanne. *Birthright of Man: A Selection of Texts*, prepared under the direction of Jeanne Hersch. New York: UNESCO, UNIPUB, 1969. 491 pp.

Hook, Sidney. *Religion in a Free Society*. Lincoln: University of Nebraska Press, 1967. 120 pp.

Jaher, Frederick Cople (ed.). *The Age of Industrialism in America: Essays in Social Structure and Cultural Values*. New York: The Free Press, 1968. 400 pp.

Kidson, Peter. *The Medieval World*. New York: McGraw-Hill Book Company, 1967. 176 pp.

King, Edmund J. *Education and Social Change*. Oxford: Pergamon Press, 1966. 239 pp.

Martin, Malachi. *The Encounter: Why the Major Religions—Christianity, Judaism, and Islam—Are in Crisis, and How They Have Failed Modern Man*. New York: Farrar, Straus & Giroux, Inc., 1969. 488 pp.

Mayer, Frederick (ed.). *Bases of Ancient Education: Great Ideas of Education*, Volume One. New Haven, Conn.: College & University Press, 1966. 348 pp.

_____. *Foundations of Contemporary Education: Great Ideas of Education*, Volume Three. New Haven: College & University Press, 1966. 262 pp.

_____. *A History of Educational Thought*, Second Edition. Columbus, Ohio: Charles E. Merrill Books, Inc., 1966. 561 pp.

Mead, Margaret. *The School in American Culture*. Cambridge, Mass.: Harvard University Press, 1951. 48 pp.

Meyer, Adolphe E. *An Educational History of the Western World*. New York: McGraw-Hill Book Company, 1965. 516 pp.

Moos, Elizabeth. *Soviet Education in 1970*. New York: National Council of American-Soviet Friendship, 1970. 63 pp.

Muir, William K., Jr. *Prayer in the Public Schools: Law and Attitude Change*. Chicago: University of Chicago Press, 1967. 170 pp.

Nash, Paul. *History and Education*. New York: Random House, Inc., 1970. 338 pp.

Nisbet, Robert A. *Social Change and History: Aspects of the Western Theory of Development*. New York: Oxford University Press, 1969. 335 pp.

Perkinson, Henry J. *The Imperfect Panacea: American Faith in Education, 1865–1965*. New York: Random House, Inc., 1968. 239 pp.

Pounds, Ralph L. *The Development of Education in Western Culture*. New York: Appleton-Century-Crofts, 1968. 307 pp.

Power, Edward J. *Main Currents in the History of Education*, Second Edition. New York: McGraw-Hill Book Company, 1970. 640 pp.

Pulliam, John D. *History of Education in America*. Columbus, Ohio: Charles E. Merrill Books, Inc., 1968. 122 pp.

Riesman, David. *Constraint and Variety in American Education*. Lincoln: University of Nebraska Press, 1956. 160 pp.

Rippa, S. Alexander. *Educational Ideas in America*. New York: David McKay Co., Inc., 1967. 369 pp.

Shipman, M. D. *The Sociology of the School*. London: Longmans, Green, 1969. 196 pp.

Siceluff, Harry J. *Readings in the History of Education*. Berkeley: McCutcham, 1970. 168 pp.

Swift, David W. *Ideology and Change in the Public Schools: Latent Functions of Progressive Education*. Columbus, Ohio: Charles E. Merrill Books, Inc., 1971. 224 pp.

Tyack, David B. (ed.). *Turning Points in American Educational History*. Waltham, Mass.: Blaisdell Publishing Co., 1967. 488 pp.

Ulich, Robert. *A History of Religious Education*. New York: New York University Press, 1968. 302 pp.

Veysey, Laurence R. *The Emergence of the American University*. Chicago: University of Chicago Press, 1965. 505 pp.

Selected Films

Blue Like an Orange (McGraw-Hill), 25 min. A puppet film that shows the countless facets of an age-old art and reflects, from the Orient to the Occident, the world of both fantasy and hard reality in which humans live.

The Children's Republic (A.F.F.), 23 min. A new approach to education; operation of child-governed organization in France.

Clasping Hands (Grubbs), 20 min. How cooperation is taught In the French public schools.

Colonial Children (Ind.), 11 min. Re-enacts with authentic settings, costumes, and furnishings, the home life and self-sufficiency of a family in colonial New England during the late seventeenth century. Describes how colonial children received their education by studying at home and portrays the duties and chores of each member of the family. Reveals the spirit of helpfulness between families and emphasizes the vital role of religion in the home.

The Difference Between Us (N.E.T.), 60 min. A comparison of the secondary educational system in England and America.

Education in America: The Seventeenth and Eighteenth Centuries (Coronet), 16 min.

Education in America: The Nineteenth Century (Coronet), 18 min.

Education in America: Twentieth Century Developments (Coronet), 19 min.

Horace Mann (Emerson Film Corp), 19 min. Portrays important episodes in the life of Horace Mann, the "father of the common schools"; reviews his activities as teacher, lawyer, state senator, board of education member, and college president. Emphasizes his work in pointing up the need for well-built schools, good textbooks, democratic methods of learning, schools for teachers, and universal education in the United States.

Jean-Jacques Rousseau (Radim), 22 min. A biography of the French–Swiss philosopher, educationist, and writer Jean-Jacques Rousseau (1712–1778). Rousseau exerted a strong influence on eighteenth- and nineteenth-century writers and thinkers because of his theory of the tendency of society to distort the natural goodness of man, his advocacy of a return to the simple life, and his revolutionary views on man's fundamental rights and liberties. His passionate and eloquent writings influenced the course of the French Revolution and gave it the slogan, "Liberty, Equality, Fraternity."

Near Home (International Film Bureau), 25 min. A class and teacher study the English community in which they live. The use of resources at hand, problem-solving procedures, and the role of the teacher are vividly portrayed. The report in the community at the culmination of the project is especially well done. Developed as a teacher-training film.

Our Inheritance from the Past (Coronet), 11 min. This presentation of the contributions of the past to our modern life creates a better understanding and appreciation of historic advances. The fact that our modern world is actually a product of the past is made clear by studying past civilizations and their accomplishments.

Outposts of American Education (Near-East Col.), 20 min. Story of life at American colleges in Near East; also historic spots, peoples, cities of Greece, Turkey, Syria, Lebanon, Iraq.

Schools of Mexico (Ind), 10 min. Presents a comprehensive view of educational institutions from the ultramodern Ministry of Education in Mexico City to remote one-room adobe schools far in the interior. Includes normal schools, vocational and agricultural institutions, and kindergartens.

Small World (McGraw-Hill), 11 min. Children from some forty countries give their interpretation in drawings of the world from prehistory to the year A.D. 3000.

Soviet Education Today (University of Michigan), 72 min. A Soviet documentary with English sound and an American introductory statement.

Soviet Higher Education (Fifty Years) (NCASF), 30 min. It is claimed that in Czarist Russia 80 per cent of the people were illiterate. With the Revolution in 1917 Lenin opened a drive against illiteracy. We see footage from films made in the early period showing the backward state of education. With the first Five Year Plan in 1928, education began to make giant strides. In World War II, 334 colleges were reduced to rubble. Notwithstanding, 300,000 specialists were graduated in the war years. In 1967 there were 4.15 million students in 790 institutions of higher learning. The development of institutes, universities, and academies of all higher education is depicted with little flair but with substantial content, with the commentator providing many interesting facts. It is a good review.

Soviet Schools 1969 (NCASF), 30 min. In the year 1969 there were 49 million students in Soviet schools under the tutelage of 2.5 million teachers. Here is a leisurely up-to-date survey of Soviet schools in operation in a system that in 1970 is requiring of its boys and girls ten years of education. Early sequences center on younger children, then high school. By using electronic aids of all sorts, students are acquainted with all fields of Soviet endeavor, to open the way to choice of vocation. Attention to ill and handicapped; school for young workers in the factories; correspondence schools; history study focused on World War II; art training; children's exhibitions; summer camps. For classroom use might well be coupled with the film, "Soviet Higher Education."

Village School (BIS), 12 min. This documentary on education illustrates the philosophy underlying the British system of education.

Part II

Social and Economic Trends in America

In Part II is presented an over-all survey of the social and economic trends in the United States of America. Chapter 4 places in their historical setting the important social trends from the beginning of the American nation to the present time. Twelve current trends are summarized.

In Chapter 5 emphasis is placed on economic problems. A detailed analysis is made of the development of American technology and of the American industrial system. An appraisal of alternative economic choices facing the United States is also presented. Because economic and technological trends are basic to the over-all development of the society and to the other problems being considered, they are set forth in broad perspective early In the book.

Chapter 4

■■■■■□□□□□□□□□□□□□

An Overview of
American Social Trends

The job to be undertaken in this chapter may seem an almost impossible one in view of the fact that whole books have been written on one period of American history, even on one aspect of social change during one period. The attempt is made, however, to bring together in a clear picture the more significant American social trends and to show how they came to develop.

Many things confuse the picture. One is the disjointedness between the changes actually occurring and widespread verbal or ideological realization of the change. In some cases, the most vigorous denial of the fact of change was being made at the very time of occurrence of the change and its acceptance for all practical purposes. The confusion among the various spokesmen for the people in respect to the meaning of a particular change has also been evident throughout our history. As an example, the new Darwinian science was accepted, but in some cases the implications were seen in terms of reactionary ideas tending toward ruthless exploitation and antihumanitarianism. As a further example, new philosophic viewpoints underlying new social action were rejected, but the action was advocated on the basis of selected phases of the most ancient of traditional philosophic ideas. Certainly any clarification of trends in American society must recognize the two threads: (1) the actual changes themselves—many times wavering, partial, and hazy; and (2) men's ideas, particularly those of vocal spokesmen in literature and the arts, concerning the proposed or actual changes and the necessity for or opposition to them. The second thread, like the first, presents a chaotic picture, with almost all combinations of the traditional and the new, agitations for change and defense of the old being often mixed in the same individual.

PERIODS OF DEVELOPMENT OF AMERICAN SOCIAL TRENDS

We have divided the development into four periods similar to those used by Butts and Cremin in their book *A History of Education in American Culture.*[1]

[1] R. Freeman Butts and Lawrence A. Cremin, *A History of Education in American Culture* (New York: Holt, 1953).

The first period, "The Colonial Period, 1600 to 1779," covers the era from the beginning of colonization up to the time of independence from Great Britain. Many changes were brought about during this period by the colonists who had come to America to find religious and political freedom, or to gain wealth, or both. They experimented with various governmental forms that were to eventuate in a federal type of republic. By the end of this period the separation of church and state was coming about, and a bill of rights was being established to bulwark democratic processes.

The second period, "The Formation and Expansion of the Nation, 1779 to 1865," covers the actual formation of the nation and the coalescing of its institutional forms and precedents, and encompasses a rapid geographic expansion. The influence of the frontier on the further democratization of social and governmental institutions was very marked. The abolition of slavery and the enfranchisement of the Negro, which occurred at the end of this period, marked great progress in the strengthening and the extension of democratic institutions.

The third period, "Expanding America, 1865 to 1929," covers the time of the rapid industrial and further geographical expansion spurred by railroad development and by other forces of the industrial revolution. The effect of these forces was felt in ever-growing impact on social institutions. The development of more rapid communications, the increase in population, the change from rural to urban backgrounds, the effect of all these changes on the family and in turn on society, the cumulative effects of scientific changes on fundamental thinking (philosophy)—all are important aspects of social trends during this period.

The fourth period, "Contemporary Changes, 1929 to the Present," primarily is concerned with changes in the role of government with respect to the economic system, with a great shift from the earlier laissez-faire conception toward a "welfare state," and with other trends arising from America's position of world leadership. This period is especially difficult to evaluate and describe because it is too close for complete objectivity.

Each period will be discussed with the following types of changes as subheadings: Governmental and Political, Industrial and Commercial, Religious and Philosophical, Social Customs and Institutions.

THE COLONIAL PERIOD, 1600 TO 1779
Governmental and Political

The governmental and political institutions established in America during the early colonial period were largely transplanted from England. In the main, those groups who came to seek freedom from political or religious oppression did not grant such freedom to all those who arrived later in their colonies.

In the proprietary colonies such as New Amsterdam (later New York) and the Carolinas, a definite attempt was made to perpetuate a modified feudal system with a landed gentry. Many considerations, primarily economic but partially ideological, stemming from the ideas of French and British philosophers, prevented this feudalistic development.

New England at first was settled by people desirous of self-government and freedom. The Puritan majority initially established a theocracy and restricted the suffrage to orthodox property owners. This group also set up an established church in which it was difficult to distinguish church officers from civil magistrates. However, by 1700 a reaction had set in. Rising secular feeling, a large number of dissident sects (such as the Quakers and Baptists), and the interests of even the former strict Puritans in the growing commerce in rum and slavery led to a relaxation of strict Puritanism and to a widening of the gap between church and state.

The shortage of labor, the influence of the frontier, and the necessity for a common front against the Indians were all factors in the extension of self-government throughout the colonies. This came about through representative councils and through the widening of the suffrage, which, however, was still far from universal at the end of this period. The actual practices in the colonies were often more benevolent than the rules promulgated from abroad for the governing of the colonies. The colonies were in competition for settlers and tended to vie with each other in providing favorable conditions to attract newcomers.

By the time the homeland had begun to increase controls over foreign trade so as to threaten many of the colonists commercially, the people had had such a taste of freedom and had absorbed sufficient ideas concerning liberty that they were ready to stand up for what they considered their rights. The experience of the colonists in developing self-governing institutions under British rule and the experiences of the revolutionary Committees of Correspondence stood them in good stead when they were confronted with post-Revolutionary problems of creating governments.

Industrial and Commercial

The economy of colonial America was predominantly agricultural, with lesser interests in trade, lumbering, fishing, and trapping. Although the country remained essentially a land of farmers until the Civil War, even in the eighteenth century trade and commerce began to prosper. With this prosperity a wealthy merchant class appeared and the gulf between rich and poor widened. Economics invaded politics and religion when the merchant class gained power enough to resist the political control of the clergy and the landed gentry.

Climatic and geographic forces operated to fix a slave economy in the South, to stimulate attention on commerce in barren-soiled New England, and to make the rich land of the middle colonies the granary of the nation.

Economic considerations were perhaps decisive in the final action of the colonies leading to independence. Century-old English mercantilism, climaxed by irritating taxes and new measures of trade control, drove men of commerce into questioning the work of the Empire. Their protests were translated into action by the propertyless classes, who felt that abandonment of the old order would somehow bring them a new economic dispensation. The political and social ideas of Locke and others (discussed briefly in the next section) had permeated all classes, to provide ideological undergirding for movements toward greater freedom. In America, economic problems led men to feel that independence from England was the only method of achieving this freedom.

Religious and Philosophical

Although divided into many sects on refinements of theology, colonial Americans with virtual unanimity were believers in Christian theism. This conception held the universe to be governed by one God whose essence was infinite and spiritual. He was the all-good, all-wise, all-powerful being who created the world for man and operated it according to His laws. Man was created with a soul and a material body. The immortal soul linked man to God, and the body was a part of the world that tempted man to corruption. The escape from worldly corruption was provided by God in the form of Christ, whom all men should follow. The Bible was the word of God, and the highest type of knowledge emanated from God through the Scriptures. Man was to use the knowledge set forth in the Bible to reveal the Heavenly Father.

Based upon this common body of belief, sectarian differences were somewhat in the form of minor superstructures built upon a vast single foundation. The Calvinists (primarily the Puritans and later the Presbyterians) chose to emphasize predestination and election; the Anglicans, the sacraments and elaborate ritualism; the Roman Catholics, the sacraments, ritual, and a priestly intermediary; the Quakers, the inner life; the Lutherans, justification by faith and a priesthood of all believers. Of all religious groups in the colonies, the Calvinists and the Anglicans were the most numerous, and all "established" or "state" churches in the colonies were either Calvinist or Anglican. Of the two, the Calvinist church was, in the early period, the more authoritarian and its followers the more group conscious and aggressive.

The church in early New England was more than just that. New England was a theocratic state, with the magistrates of the town and the leaders of the church being the same person or persons who worked in close cooperation, and with the suffrage being denied to members of dissident sects. Although some dissidents were tolerated, Quakers and others (such as Roger Williams) who advocated religious tolerance and complete separation were persecuted and driven out.

By 1700 the extreme form of theocratic state as set up by the colonists in New England began to crumble. The preoccupation of the people with commercial developments, the coming of many new sects with diverse ideas, and a slackening of interest by the Puritans (now Congregationalists) in theological matters caused a separation of things civil from things religious; but the church still remained an established one. Later, other minor sects in New England were able to become established. This multiple church establishment continued in Massachusetts after the American Revolution and into the nineteenth century (until 1833), even after church and state had been completely separated in all other states.

The ideas of Newton, Locke, Berkeley, Hume, and others, which were influential in starting the rational movement in Europe called the Enlightenment, reached America during the early decades of the eighteenth century and exerted strong influence after the middle of that century. The Enlightenment was a reaction against the absolutism of government, classical mercantile economics, and rigid theology. It was based on a growing faith in the common man, in science, and in human reason. In politics it held that the rights of man were natural rights and were self-evident through the use of reason. In religion there was a growth in deistic ideas[2] which were held by many prominent leaders in the colonies, including Franklin, Jefferson, and Thomas Paine. The political ideas were more acceptable to the masses than the religious ones. Thus John Locke may well be considered as a source of much of the political philosophy underlying the Revolution and the new American government.

In the theological field, Calvinist views (but with less emphasis on predestination) were strengthened in the eighteenth century by a series of religious revivals, called the Great Awakening. These revivals were probably a reaction to the secularism and religious indifference that had become prominent in America. Spreading from Pietist sources in Europe, these revivals were spearheaded in New England by Jonathan Edwards and soon swept over the colonies. Religious forces throughout the colonies were given a new life under such leaders as George Whitefield. The educational influence was particularly significant. Denominational colleges were brought into being to propagate the creeds and doctrines of their founders. Religious leadership and power gained tremendously.

The Enlightenment did affect religious ideas among many individuals and among certain churches in several denominations. There was a questioning of church dogma, especially of the trinitarian conception of God, original sin, and eternal punishment. In 1785 King's Chapel in Boston, the first Episcopal church in New England, became the first Unitarian church in the Western Hemisphere.[8]

Social Customs and Institutions

Certainly not all immigrants to the United States during the colonial period had ideas favorable to social democracy. The views prevailing in Europe, which was witnessing the enormous upsurge of the middle classes, were transferred to America. The colonists were largely of this middle class, particularly of minorities whose political or religious rights had been oppressed. The upper class did not migrate. Neither did the peasants and the serfs of the lower class. The indentured servants and slaves of the colonies made up the lower class. The fact that the colonies were predominantly middle class did not mean that there were no class distinctions. There was a merchant and landed gentry who soon came to dress differently and to be addressed as "Mister" and "Mistress." There was also a lower middle class, members of which were addressed as "Goodman" and "Goodwoman." Members of an extremely lower class were often called only by their first, or Christian, names. These social distinctions persisted until well after the Revolution, although they never were as rigid as those in Europe; they broke down only where there were frontiers. Harvard continued to classify its students by precise rank, according to the father's status, until 1772.

[2]Deism—a belief in a personal god or creator who is unrevealed—opposes dogmatic orthodoxies based on revelation.

[3]Unitarianism is a religious doctrine that does not accept the trinitarian ideas of orthodox Christianity and has quite different ideas concerning the nature of the divinity of Jesus.

Class lines played an important part in separating loyalists from patriots at the time of the Revolution. The wealthy landowners of New England and New York were Tories and fled to Canada or England, and the merchants joined with the lower classes in the revolt. In the South the planter land-lords sided, by and large, with the patriot cause. The effect of the Revolution was to eliminate almost all the upper middle class of the North, the gentry.

THE FORMATION AND EXPANSION OF THE NATION, 1779 TO 1865

Governmental and Political

The United States was gradually becoming a secular society in which religious institutions played an important but increasingly subordinate role. Public attention was diverted to the growth of political democracy, the expanding role of the government, and the rise of nationalism. The achievement of independence inaugurated a struggle at home as to who was to rule. The earliest important conflict was that between the Jeffersonian ideas of democracy and the Federalist conception of rule by a wealthier class.

Jeffersonian doctrines, derived principally from the French humanitarian ideas of politics and economics, appealed to the frontier element, the small landowners, and the debtor class. The Federalists, adhering to the tradition of the English Whigs in opposing the wide extension of democracy, were supported by the wealthier merchants and the planter class. The struggle for rule was momentarily won by the wealthier class at the constitutional convention, but the Bill of Rights and the constitutions of the several states reflected the demand for democratic control and wider suffrage.

Voters who believed in a wider extension of democracy elected Jefferson to the presidency in 1800. This group conceived of political and economic freedom as meaning also political and economic democracy, and the Jeffersonian party controlled the national elections almost entirely during the earlier part of this historical period.

There was a trend toward increased federal control. A spirit of nationalism was also evidenced by the War Hawks, the pro-war party, in 1812. The first protective tariff was passed in 1816, and there were repeated increases in tariff rates until 1828. In this period political and economic ideas began to dominate the thoughts of men.

The majority of people in the western migration, particularly into Kentucky, Ohio, Indiana, and Illinois, tended to develop nationalist ideas, because they lost their identity with their original states as they intermingled in the new territory. They looked to the national government for the lands they purchased, and to the national government also for protection from the Indians.

The doctrine of states' rights developed by the South to defend itself and its agrarian economy against Northern capitalism, and the Northern assault on slavery, tempered the sense of nationalism. At the same time the Democratic party adopted the slogan of *manifest destiny*, which demanded expansion to the Pacific and to the Rio Grande. The Democratic party, appealing to the common man and the Southern voter, dominated the national scene almost entirely during the later part of this era.

Differences of many kinds, economic, political, and cultural, led to the Civil War, in which an agrarian minority in the South sought to preserve a distinctive way of life based on Negro slavery. The Southern move for independence was thwarted in the Civil War, and the indivisibility of the Union was established. Both nationalism and capitalism became increasingly important forces in the developing country.

Industrial and Commercial

The years following the Revolution, and particularly those after the War of 1812, produced a change in the economic system. The frontier retained an agricultural economy. Along the seaboard there was a shift from an agrarian to a commercial society, which led to the development of capitalistic enterprises. Cities grew, and a demand for improved communication and transportation resulted in construction of canals, better roads, and other means of travel. The Cumberland Road was begun. Fulton's steamboat began operations in 1809, and the *Savannah* crossed the Atlantic in 1819. The Erie Canal was opened in 1825, and the Baltimore & Ohio Railroad inaugurated service in 1828, although the steam locomotive did not appear until 1829.

The most significant development of these years was the triumph of the economic doctrine of laissez-faire capitalism. Throughout the United States there was approval of Adam Smith's ideas of laissez faire. This conception was based on a few fundamental principles, which were probably more nearly achieved in the early American economy than at any other time in the world's history. These principles were private property, the profit motive, free competition, flexible prices, and little or no governmental interference with business. The idea was that the owners of the numerous small business enterprises would compete freely with one another to produce an exchange of the goods and services required by people to meet their daily needs. The profit motive would provide the driving force, and the open market would serve as an automatic device for regulation of prices and quality of goods and services. It would not be necessary to have any kind of governmental regulation except to prevent dishonesty or misrepresentation. Even though America had already partially violated the ideas of laissez faire in passing a tariff law, the people still fully believed in them. The expanding American frontier helped to make laissez-faire principles successful at this time. The high tariff laws and the giving away of lands, however, were a direct violation of the pure principles of laissez faire.

The American economy entered an era of revolutionary industrial changes. The Industrial Revolution of eighteenth-century England had hit America in the early part of the nineteenth century.

The spirit of individualism stimulated new inventions and the growth of manufacturing. The application of technology to industry got underway: in 1790 Slater developed power cotton machinery; in 1793 Whitney invented the cotton gin; in 1797 the first cast-iron plow was made; and in 1803 the grain cradle was produced. In 1802 the Du Pont Powder Company was organized. In 1814 the first complete factory in America was established in Waltham, Massachusetts. Manning's mowing machine appeared in 1831, the reaper in 1834, the telegraph in 1835, the screw propeller in 1836, the vulcanization of rubber in 1839, photography in 1839, iron rails in 1840, and the sewing machine in 1846. These laid the bases for industrial society and simultaneously extended the benefits of the machine to man.

Business continued to expand and to lay the groundwork for the era of "big business" late in the century. Western Union, the first trust, came into being in 1851. Pork packing grew into a major industry in Cincinnati during the 1830's. The railroads became an important means of transportation. In 1850, when the federal government indirectly granted land to the Illinois Central Railroad, the government seemed committed to a policy of encouraging business activities. The National Bank Act of 1863 marked the long-deferred establishment of a sound national banking system. Sectional pressure and the ascendancy of the Democratic party kept the tariff generally low until the Republican triumph in 1860 ushered in a period when a high tariff became a permanent characteristic of the American economy.

Religious and Philosophical

The principal writers during the earlier part of this period were political philosophers, notably Jefferson, Franklin, and Paine. These men held a deistic conception of the world similar to that of the French humanitarians. Their championship of deistic ideas came about as a reaction to orthodox Calvinism; but, as Townsend has indicated, "deism is far too complicated a theory to be set down as a simple revolt against Calvinism." [4]

Muelder and Sears state that deism was dominant in the South.[5] Among intellectuals in New England, William Ellery Channing attacked the traditional Calvinistic views and proclaimed the Unitarian doctrine that "God is love, man is potentially noble, and religion is an excellent life." Channing defined religion as the "adoration of goodness," and his doctrine of "sweetness and light" was set over against the Calvinist dogmas of retribution and election.

In spite of these influences, the more orthodox forms of Christian theism were still the religious faiths of the majority of the people in the United States, but there were clear indications that the dominating influence of religion was on the wane. The traditional religious outlook was partially reinvigorated by a series of revivals called the Second Great Awakening, which spread among the pioneer settlements of the frontier and intermittently persisted past the Civil War. Calvinism was still the prevailing doctrine among those who were religious at the opening of the Jacksonian era, but the time was opportune for a new liberalism. As Parrington has stated, "It [Calvinism] was deeply entrenched in the inertia of custom, but intellectually it was in really desperate straits." [6]

Organized religious groups were feeling the effects of democracy and the liberation of the common man. A doctrine of self-expression was abroad in the land, and from it new cults were springing to life. Merle Curti has

[4]Harvey Gates Townsend, *Philosophic Ideas in the United States* (New York: American Book, 1934), p. 66.

[5]Walter G. Muelder and Lawrence Sears, *The Development of American Philosophy* (Boston: Houghton, 1940), p. 65.

[6]Vernon L. Parrington, *Main Currents in American Thought: The Romantic Revolution in America*, Vol. II (New York: Harcourt, 1930), p. 323.

termed this phenomenon *come-outism*, and he lists Shakerism, Perfectionism, Millerism, and Mormonism as products of the new liberalism.[7]

Transcendentalism, growing out of but going beyond Unitarianism, was in a sense a part of the romantic protest against the rationalism of the previous century. Transcendentalists such as Emerson, Thoreau, and Melville believed in a daily rebirth of God in each individual's soul, and they taught that the "divinity in man should rule the world." They held that each man, by "virtue of being identical with nature," must enjoy "equal rights and privileges." [8]

Organized religion, although sanctioning many social inequalities, was not entirely blind to the conditions resulting from industrialism. Reformers, often denouncing religious bodies, appealed to the spirit of the teachings of Jesus. Northern churches "declared war" on slavery. This declaration split all the major denominations, except the Roman Catholic, into sectional camps. The Seneca Falls Congress of 1849 proclaimed a beginning of a worldwide campaign for women's rights, and various other groups advocated reform movements.

Ralph Henry Gabriel has advanced an interpretation that during this period there emerged a new democratic faith. It rested, he says, on the earlier belief in a law-governed universe, but it also accepted the transcendental faith in the worth of the individual. The emerging of these ideas implied a faith in the superiority of American democratic institutions.[9]

Harvey G. Townsend has summarized the philosophic views of this period in these words:

> There was a dramatic issue . . . in America—heaven and earth had been sundered. The great question . . . was how they could be brought together again. The generation . . . had a firm grip on the earth. It was heaven which had escaped that generation. The geographical expansion, the exploitation of nature, and the discovery of vast riches in an uninhabited continent awakened acquisitive desires. Men became drunk with the idea of their own importance. They had lost the humility of the Puritans, and . . . they had lost a sense of the sacred and the holy. As a substitute for theology, they half-consciously accepted the notion that the world was made for man and perhaps by him.[10]

Social Customs and Institutions

The class structure, which had broken down considerably by the time of the Revolution, was further weakened by the removal of the props of feudal stability—primogeniture, entail, and quitrents.[11] These were almost

[7]Merle Curti, *The Growth of American Thought* (New York: Harper, 1943), pp. 309–313.

[8]Ibid., pp. 304–305.

[9]Ralph Henry Gabriel, *The Course of American Democratic Thought* (New York: Ronald, 1940), pp. 37–38.

[10]Harvey Gates Townsend, *Philosophic Ideas in the United States* (New York: American Book, 1934), pp. 85–86.

[11]*Primogeniture:* Limitation of land inheritance to the eldest son, to prevent breakup of large estates.

Entail: Restriction on the sale of large landholdings such as the William Penn estate in Pennsylvania.

Quitrent: A hangover from feudal days; original proprietor maintains title and the farmer-owner pays a perpetual but small rent.

universally abolished by the various states by the turn of the century. The reaction of the people against the establishment of the state church must be considered a part of this movement. Such establishments (that is, the official sponsorship of churches by government) came to be looked upon by Americans as a relic related to ancient feudalism. All establishment was gone by 1819, except in the state of Massachusetts (1833).

The property qualifications for voting almost universally were abolished during the first half of the nineteenth century. The Jacksonian attitude toward eligibility for public office (rotation in office) represents the extreme of this influence toward democratization of politics and toward equalitarianism. It resulted in the spoils system. Even the Jeffersonian Democratic Republicans had been doubtful in the early decades of the nineteenth century of the ability of the common man to carry on the business of government.

The democratization movement, although having a complicated set of multiple causes, was affected, more than by any other single factor, by the influence of the ever-advancing frontier, where the worth of a man was measured by what he could do, not who he was. Turner, writing in 1920, was among the first to study the relationships of the social conditions of the frontier to governmental and social institutions. His theory that life on the frontier continually influenced American political thinking and institutions is now widely accepted.[12]

The fact that there was a movement toward greater democratization does not mean that no social classes existed. The range in wealth and in possession of worldly goods still remained, especially in the East. The result of the development of industrial capitalism was an immediate rise of a very wealthy upper class and the appearance of a city proletariat. The latter were in some ways in a more pitiful condition than the peasant classes of the sixteenth and seventeenth centuries of Europe. The upper-class families, however, took care not to stand too aloof from the people. Distinctions in dress between the classes had practically disappeared by 1830. The labeling of persons of different classes by special names and courtesies tended also to fade out. The contempt that the upper classes in Europe had for work with the hands, which still persisted there, had almost disappeared during this period in America. All work was honorable. It was felt that everyone should work. Class lines were fluid, and it was relatively easy to move from one class to another.

AN EXPANDING AMERICA, 1865 TO 1929

Governmental and Political

Every period of American history seems to offer a repetition of the simplicity-to-complexity theme. That course of development was certainly present in the period between Appomattox and the Great Depression. In these years the American population quadrupled; statehood was bestowed on the last bit of land between the two oceans; seven amendments were added to the Constitution; a world war was fought in defense of security; the American people shared in the building of an organization of states to

[12]Frederick Jackson Turner, The Frontier in American History (New York: Holt, 1920).

preserve the peace of the world, although they themselves declined membership; and they sought to establish legislative control of colossal combinations of bankers, of industrialists, and of laborers. The government continued to aid bankers and industrialists, and it timidly ventured into a new field to extend a helping hand to farmers. Labor was little recognized until after 1932.

Even by 1929 the simple government at Washington had grown into a "wonderland of bureaucracy," with federal assistance of many kinds made available to businesses and to the public. Political habits, however, remained essentially unchanged. Although third parties came into existence as the result of special issues, they were soon absorbed by the two major parties. Suffrage was extended to women. New devices of secret voting and of direct government (such as initiative referendum and recall) were developed to aid in making a more honest and efficient government.

Chronologically, the United States passed successfully through the Reconstruction, the heyday of the cattlemen and the robber barons, and the war against Spain to liberate the Cubans and the Filipinos, which made the country a world power. It then survived the "trust-busting" and the "square deal" of Theodore Roosevelt, the "new freedom" of Woodrow Wilson, World War I and the League of Nations, the "normalcy" and scandals of Warren G. Harding, and the "jazz age" of Coolidge prosperity. By 1928 it had come into the administration of Herbert Hoover, the "Depression president."

Industrial and Commercial

Scientists and inventors again made a startling impact on the American economy. Transportation became more rapid: in 1869 the first transcontinental railroad was completed; in 1893 Clarence Duryea built one of the first automobiles; in 1903 the Wright brothers left the ground in a heavier-than-air machine; in 1911 the American continent was spanned by air in four days; and in 1919 the Atlantic was flown by a multipassengered plane. Communication, too, progressed: in 1866 the Atlantic cable was again laid, this time permanently; in 1876 Bell gave the world the telephone; in 1901 Marconi added the wireless telegraph; and twenty years later commercial radio broadcasting opened new vistas of entertainment, education, and sheer annoyance.

Strange new industries became both colossal and matter-of-course: meat packing, oil refining, rubber, automobiles, radio, road building, cosmetics, commercial nitrates, sporting goods, and many others. Technological advances took the farmer to the city and the city to the farm. Electric lights supplanted the "wonder light," the gas lamp, which in its turn had supplanted the "perfect light," the kerosene lamp.

Congress and the state legislatures repeatedly intervened to control the influence and operations of economic combinations and enterprises. Beginning with the Interstate Commerce Act of 1887, Congress passed a series of major laws to regulate the common carriers of the nation, taking up the job where the Supreme Court forced the states to relinquish it. Beginning with the Sherman Antitrust Act of 1890, Congress sought again and again to bring industrial combinations to a sense of public responsibility; a stream of laws was aimed at the improvement of the nation's banking system; various laws were enacted to adjust the rights and liabilities of organized labor; and pieces of legislation were directed at other public problems— pure food acts, corrupt practices acts, workmen's compensation laws, old-age pension acts, mothers' and widows' pension acts, educational aid acts, and many others.

The national economy of the years between 1865 and 1929 must be described as one of heightening capitalism, defended and abetted by the power of the government, and to an increasing extent restrained by well-organized and articulate labor. Despite the failure of certain classes, notably the farmers and the people in areas such as the rural South, to earn a proper income, the country was almost wholeheartedly in support of "rugged individualism." The doubts and compromises were to come out of the Great Depression of the next period.

Religious and Philosophical

Possibly the most significant development in thought during the early part of this era was the appearance of Charles Darwin's theory of evolution. *The Origin of Species* was first published in 1859, but the real impact of its ideas came several years later. As recently as 1925, the fundamentalists, adhering to a literal interpretation of the Bible, attacked the Darwinian concept in the famous Scopes trial in Tennessee.

The philosophical position of idealism was subjected to scrutiny when Peirce, James, and Dewey combined science and the temper of American life to formulate the philosophy of pragmatism. Basic to this development was a philosophical–psychological conception of how people learned. Faculty psychology, based on rationalism, was attacked by the empirical methods of the experimental psychology of Thorndike.

The extension of organized knowledge raised the material horizons of life. The contributions of modern science were great during this period. The new scientific ideas of Albert Einstein, although announced during this period, were to affect science greatly during the following period, and their effect on thought cannot be evaluated even yet. Einstein's theory of relativity, first announced in 1905, changed the conception of gravity, of light, and of the fundamental nature of space and the universe, and this gave physics and the other sciences an entirely new perspective.[13]

The revolutionary philosophy of the class struggle, enunciated earlier by Karl Marx and Friedrich Engels in the *Communist Manifesto*, had few converts in America, although it gained impressive acceptance in Europe in this period and eventually provided the battle cry of a large portion of the world. In Russia, Marxian philosophy—which has been described by Arnold Toynbee as a "reaction from and a criticism of the Western Capitalism"— was accepted by Lenin and his associates. In 1917 Lenin, Trotsky, and their followers successfully overthrew the Czar and attempted to establish a government based on Marxian principles. The importance of the 1917 Russian revolution must not be underestimated; for, as Toynbee has stated, Bol-

[13]Lincoln Barnett, *The Universe and Doctor Einstein,* Second Revised Edition (New York: Mentor, 1957).

shevism is the "only semblance of an effective external challenge to our society [Western civilization] since the Osmanlis' [Turkish faction] second failure to take Vienna." [14]

Social Customs and Institutions

As far as social customs and institutions are concerned, there actually were two separate periods from 1865 to 1929. The change in customs was very slight from 1865 to somewhat past the turn of the century. A variety of causes led to a rapid change in customs after 1900, with a great acceleration after World War I and through the 1920's.

In 1865, with the exception of some of the wealthy, the living conditions of most Americans were little improved over those of the European lower and middle classes. By 1900 there had been added, at least in the cities, many of the conveniences that now are called modern. Most middle-class homes had a bathtub and running water. There were electric lights in most city homes, although some still had gaslight. The rural areas were still in the kerosene-lamp stage, which had replaced the candle period some time after the Civil War. The rural areas were to continue in the period of the gasoline lantern (and their own private electric generators for a few of the wealthy farmers) into the 1930's before they received any extensive electrification.

At the beginning of this period the work week was quite long. Vacations were scarcely heard of, except for the very wealthy. The expense of travel (on trains or by the slower horse and buggy) and the amount of time involved practically precluded the ordinary individual from taking a vacation at a spot away from his own city. Even drives from the city out to the country were very rare. With the coming of the automobile, and particularly with the mass production of the Model T, this whole pattern was changed. Now the average person was able to go quickly out into the country or to visit relatives in some other town. Vacation spots for people of little means sprang up at the seashore and in the mountains. This was only one aspect of the changing social customs arising from ease of transportation. The whole set of customs with respect to dating and chaperones was changed by the automobile era. No longer was it possible to maintain the strict chaperoning that had accompanied the courting period. The effects of the automobile on the city and countryside were obvious: the movement of people to the suburbs, the improvement of highways, the filling stations, road markers, and billboards.

Let us now turn attention from such basic changes to some that on the surface may appear more superficial. In 1900, even in summertime, every woman wore a dress that swept the street. She had several layers of underclothes, including a chemise, drawers, corset, corset cover, and one or more petticoats. Men's clothing was very stiff and formal. The dressed-up man would have a high and stiff collar, and he wore a waistcoat (or what we now call a vest) under his coat even in hot weather. It was never proper for

[14]Arnold J. Toynbee, A Study of History, abridgment by R. C. Somervel (New York: Oxford University Press, 1947), pp. 203–204. It is important to note that Toynbee wrote this analysis well before World War II; and, as a matter of conjecture, the Japanese militarists might have been considered at a later time as an "external challenge."

a man to go hatless out of doors. In the early 1900's it was improper for a middle- or upper-class man to be in shirt sleeves. The change in styles came about very gradually, with the most rapid changes occurring after World War I, with the shortening of the dresses to the knees and the coming of sleeveless, low-necked dresses.

The so-called jazz age of the 1920's gave rise to many changes in conventions. Most of the Puritanical ideas of the early American period were done away with or minimized by the rapid changes that occurred during this period.

Class differentials in wealth were great, particularly during the period around 1900. Many millionaires had been created by the rapid industrial expansion of the country, and their fortunes were maintained partially through the lack of income tax. It was the fashion to display wealth by building elaborate homes and by having elaborate entertainments. Andrew Carnegie, one of the wealthiest men of the time, took in $23 million in the year 1900 with no income taxes to pay! Later on, when attacks were being made constantly against the "monopolists and the wealthy," ostentatious display lessened. With the coming of the income tax, and especially as it became increasingly progressive, the wealthy were much more heavily taxed.

Professional people around 1900 with a reasonably good income of $2,000 to $3,000 a year (which would be the equivalent of $12,000 to $18,000 now) lived much better than the corresponding class at present. One of the reasons for this, of course, was the fact that the average wage was quite low: $400 to $500 a year. It was easy for a man living on a professional income to hire other persons to work for him and to have at least one full-time servant. A professional income today will not support a full-time servant because domestic servants are getting incomes more nearly commensurate with those of professional people. On the other hand, the present mass production of goods, even though the cost of labor is much higher, enables many goods to be produced at relatively lower prices. The masses today can use articles that were not available except at a very high price to the wealthy few in the earlier period. Of course, many of the conveniences of today—electric vacuum cleaners, refrigerators, and so on—were not available at all then; they had not yet been developed.

In looking at the situation as a whole, we should remember that, even though at the present time we still have a wide differential between the upper and lower classes, the filth and poverty of the cities, particularly around 1900, were much worse than at present. The accident rate among workers was very high, and there was practically no workman's compensation. There was considerable child labor, with all its attendant bad effects on the health of the children. The average work week was about sixty hours, which left very little time for recreation. The average wage was quite low, $400 to $500 per year. Adjusting this wage to dollars of current purchasing power, that average wage would be the equivalent today of only about $2,100 per year. This is around one third of the average wage today, around $6,280 in 1970.[15]

---

[15]*Economic Report of the President,* January, 1971 (Washington, D.C.: Government Printing Office, 1971), pp. 216, 223. Labor force of over 86 million, counting armed forces but not unemployed; total wages and salaries around $540 billion.

Another interesting change came with respect to magazines. Magazines with mass circulation were almost unheard of before 1900. They were to come in the later part of this period, when persons had more time to read and magazines could be mass-produced more cheaply.

CONTEMPORARY CHANGES, 1929 TO THE PRESENT
Governmental and Political

The period from 1929 to the present can be said to be marked by two major themes in domestic politics and two in foreign relations, but it must be pointed out that in the twentieth-century world there can be no sharp distinction between the domestic and foreign problems of any nation.

Starting in 1929 with a serious breakdown in their economic and industrial system, Americans found that their first domestic problem was the organization of all their resources to end the Great Depression. Later it was necessary to bring about a *total* mobilization of the nation to fight the greatest war so far in history. The early period was dominated by the remarkable personality of Franklin D. Roosevelt, four times elected to the presidency. His program for domestic rehabilitation, termed the *New Deal*, called for a vast amount of legislation designed to lead to "relief, recovery, and reform." Much of this legislation was new in conception and liberal and progressive in nature, although roots can be found in controversies even prior to the days of the Populist agitation of the 1880's. The full impact of the New Deal on the eventual permanent trends in the philosophy of American government is as yet uncertain. The influence of the events of this earlier period on the Truman administration, and even on the following Republican administration, indicated that many New Deal changes seemed to be here to stay, including the concept of responsibility of government in stabilizing and bolstering the economy.

Foreign relations were dominated by two major themes. The first of these was the effort to reconcile American security with the growing belief that the people of the United States ought to share in solving the problems of the world. For a number of years the United States had adhered to a policy of economic nationalism, as exemplified by the passage of the Smoot–Hawley Tariff of 1930 and by the insistence on payment of war debts even when the debtor nations of the world had defaulted. Even Roosevelt, in the early days of his administration, bolted the London Economic Conference (1933), preferring to solve America's problems at home and alone. The attitude of the United States influenced the breakdown of the world economy. This hastened the rise of militarism in Japan and of nazism in Germany, helping to lay the groundwork for World War II. The apparent success of the isolationist foreign policies of the United States in increasing its own material prosperity was believed to be sufficient justification for refraining from closer economic collaboration with other nations. Effective neutrality legislation was sought at the same time that antiwar pacts were being framed and disarmament conferences were taking place. When isolationism eventually was abandoned, it was done in the name of national security.

Even before the end of World War II, the Roosevelt administration had turned to the second of the major foreign interests of the period, the preservation of the fruits of victory. The Atlantic Charter of 1941 was only the first of the persistent efforts of the Roosevelt administration to organize peace and understanding on the basis of morally defensible principles.

At the San Fransico conference of 1946, the United States was successful in its leadership in setting up the organization of the United Nations, which eventually settled in New York City. The United Nations is not a world government, but merely a body in which the opinions of the various nations can be sounded out and some action can be taken so long as it is supported by the nations concerned. During the early post-World War II period, many persons advocated that a world government be set up. In the 1950's actions taken by Communist China and other nations of the world led to a worsening of conditions and to a lack of faith in the cooperative method of the United Nations in solving problems. This led to a resurgence of nationalism in the United States and in some parts of Europe. This further led to a breaking apart of some of the cooperative efforts for the solution of international problems.

Although the United Nations was successful on many important but minor problems related to world peace, the major conflict between Russia and the United States deepened. This conflict, which developed into a cold war between the nations, became even graver when North Korean forces invaded South Korea. The United States had withdrawn its troops but had pledged support to the maintenance of the integrity of both the North and South Korean republics. When the South was invaded, the United Nations (Russia dissenting), with the heavy support of the United States, in both men and material, fought an indecisive war that eventually ended in an armistice.

The Eisenhower administration pursued a foreign policy very similar to that of the Roosevelt and Truman administrations. On the economic front it also had plans to use the powers of government, if necessary, in order to prevent economic depression should one threaten. The major differences claimed by the new Republican administration were a cleaner and more honest government and a greater emphasis upon private enterprise. The opponents of the Republican administration claimed that in this respect the aims and achievements of the two parties were not different. In spite of much political heat and smoke with reference to the tendency for the Democratic party to be favorable to a "drift toward socialism," both the Kennedy and Johnson administrations in the 1960's were middle-of-the-road movements. This is particularly evident when they are contrasted with the tendencies of the democratic parties in European countries, which were much more blatantly socialistic in their policies and trends.

During the latter half of the Johnson administration, attention centered on dissatisfaction with the Vietnam War. Johnson chose not to run, and Nixon won with a slight plurality over Humphrey. However, the Vietnam War and its extension into Cambodia continued into the 1970's and the Nixon administration had to deal with it amid problems of inflation, poverty, unemployment, protest movements, and riots in the United States.

Industrial and Commercial

Two considerations in the area of industrial and commercial developments invite attention: the course or fortunes of the national economy and the changing theory of that economy. The first can be quickly outlined. The Great Depression that began in 1929 reached its worst stage in 1932. Business casualties increased from 21,000 per year before the Depression to nearly 32,000 in 1932. In 1933 almost 20 per cent of the nation's banks closed. In March, 1933 (with the monthly average of 1924–1925 at 100), the index of industrial production stood at 60, construction at 14, factory employment at 61, factory payrolls at 38, and wholesale prices (1926 at 100) at 60.[16]

A slow upward trend began in 1933, was reversed temporarily in 1937, and then after 1939 reached prosperity on the basis of orders from belligerents and from the defense-minded government. American entrance into the war in 1941 brought full employment, high wages, and—inevitably—inflation. The national debt increased from $16 billion in 1930 to a peak of $270 billion in 1945. After dropping for a while in the late 1940's and in the 1950's it was to go to around $390 billion in 1970.[17]

The theory of the national economy underwent changes. Although Herbert Hoover, in a sense, was the precursor of the New Deal, it was President Roosevelt who threw tradition to the winds in a desperate effort to prevent complete economic collapse. The philosophy that emerged was both implicit and explicit: the government was no longer on the sidelines, it was an active partner of every legitimate business interest and the guardian of the welfare of every individual. This thinking meant food and shelter to millions of Americans, because at one time a third of the population was on federal relief.

The war itself emphasized the economic thinking that the government could rightfully use its power to set aside the operation of the "natural law" of supply and demand as the determinant of prices. This economic theory was not new, for rationing and priorities had been used in World War I. Price controls on consumer's goods, however, were a different feature; they were justified on the grounds that the national emergency was artificially curtailing supply and stimulating demand. Hence the "natural law" of the economist had no application.

Many fears were voiced that World War II would be followed quickly by a depression. There was quite a controversy concerning whether controls should be removed. Finally, because of political pressure, particularly from the members of the Republican party but also from other influential persons, price controls were abruptly taken off and there was a rapid inflationary period following World War II, which led to prices considerably higher than in the prewar period. Considerable time was spent by industry in replenishing the inventories that had become low during the war period, and the inflationary trend tended to cause the public to buy things rapidly, thus preventing stock on the shelves from piling up. At about the time when there might have been a mild recession as a result of piling up of inventory in industry's warehouses, the Korean War broke out and there was a rush to buy materials for the war. Consequently, a further inflationary trend

---

[16]Louis M. Hacker, *American Problems of Today* (New York: Appleton-Century-Crofts, 1938), p. 178.

[17]*Economic Report of the President* (Washington, D.C.: Government Printing Office, 1971), p. 270.

caused prices to continue to rise and therefore to accentuate further buying. During most of this postwar period, the national budget was unbalanced; and this, of course, added to the inflationary trend. Considerably more money was spent by the federal government than was taken in. The change of administration made little difference in this pattern. There was some decrease in the amount of money spent on domestic matters by the Eisenhower administration as compared with the Truman administration, but the worsening international situation, including a stepped-up military budget and aid to friendly governments, caused the federal budget to be considerably out of balance. It is difficult, therefore, to determine what would have been the policies of the Republican administration in normal times as opposed to those of the Democratic administration. The postwar period was not "normal times." Some wondered whether there would ever be "normal times" because there was envisoned a long period of cold or moderately hot war between the United States and the Soviet Union. Although the cold war between these two countries cooled off during the 1960's, the situation was complicated by the conflict between the Soviet Union and China within the Communist world, the American involvement in Southeast Asia, and the intensification of the Middle East crisis between Israel and the Arab countries.

Religious and Philosophical

By 1929 certain earlier religious views had been on the defensive for some time. Traditional social and ethical principles, including sex mores, were held by the conservatives to be allied to religion; and these were being violated. Religious interpretation of the Bible ranged from the literal and orthodox to more liberal positions. Complete atheism attracted only a small minority.

One trend appeared to be significant. Religious emphasis had been diverted from academic debates on divineness to the application of religious principles to problems of social welfare. Many ministers felt that theological problems were to be envisaged as they interacted with the industrialized world. One of these men, Reinhold Niebuhr, whose ministry brought him into personal contact with the industrial workers of Detroit, indicated that since he had "stopped worrying so much about intellectual problems" there was more of a thrill in preaching.[18] Niebuhr was largely concerned with the religious implications of economic, political, and social theory and practice. Although as a "neo-orthodox" he accepted an orthodox apostolic creed "as the whole genius of Christian faith" and advocated a Paulistic doctrine of original sin, Niebuhr attempted to synthesize traditional religious thought with modern sociological thought.[19]

Secular thinking, too, showed the impact of the Great Depression. Men turned increasingly to science to solve the dilemma, and there was a range of opinion concerning how we get and interpret knowledge. Some men

---

[18]Reinhold Niebuhr, *Leaves from the Notebook of a Tamed Cynic* (Chicago: Willet, 1929), p. 27.

[19]Reinhold Niebuhr, *Human Nature: The Nature and Destiny of Man*, Vol. I (New York: Scribner, 1941), pp. 260–265.

decried the emphasis on modern social and economic theories, reasserting the claims of the great tradition, which was based on the historical–philosophical outlooks of idealism, rationalism, and dualism. These reactions sometimes took the form of the new humanism as advanced by Stewart P. Sherman or Paul Shorey, of Catholicism as conceived by Jacques Maritain, or of intellectualism as proposed by Mark Van Doren or Abraham Flexner.

Other men, borrowing from Newtonian science and the positivism of Comte and Spencer, described the world as a machine that obeyed fixed natural laws in which supernatural and rationalistic interpretations had little place. These men believed in the scientific method, narrowly conceived. When the concepts of Newtonian mechanism were applied to explaining what caused man to function as he does, man was described as a complicated machine. The psychology of behaviorism stems from this view.

Reacting against intellectual rationalism and Newtonian mechanism was the point of view of experimentalism and experimental naturalism attributed to John Dewey and others. Drawing from all fields of knowledge, including the philosophic traditions of naturalism, empiricism, pragmatism, biology, anthropology, Gestalt psychology, and social psychology, this group attempted to devise a theory of life and education that they felt would assimilate many social and intellectual trends and would be appropriate for twentieth-century America. Experimentalism denied the traditional dualisms that separated man from nature, mind from body, individual from society, and knowledge from action. As Bode indicated, experimentalism held "that the world is all of one piece." [20] Human nature was not conceived as something fixed and eternal, but as a mode of reaction that had developed in a surrounding culture. Life was viewed as a continual interacting adjustment between an active individual and an active environment: in this adjusting process the environment influenced or changed the individual's behavior and, in turn, was changed by the individual's behavior.

In the 1960's two other philosophies tended to become emergent within the democratic culture: existentialism and logical positivism in the form of the analytical philosophy movement. Existentialism came to America out of the literary and logical movements among European philosophers that portrayed man as a tragic, grimly ludicrous figure in a world that lacked meaning. In this meaningless world, man has the awful task and the awful freedom to choose the nature of his being. He must face the problem of choice and the responsibility for the choice he makes. The philosophical analyst, on the other hand, tended to discount most of traditional philosophy as being meaningless and to reduce philosophy to the problem of clarification of the language philosophers use. This tended to rule out much of earlier philosophy, including pragmatism, and to interpret most value statements as meaningless.

The churches and religious thinking were influenced greatly by the changes in scientific and philosophical thinking. There was an increase of the liberal movement within the church and the further development of the "modernism" movement, which went much beyond the liberal thinking of the earlier period. The church as an institution prospered, however. The number of persons who were members of churches increased during the

[20]Boyd Henry Bode, How We Learn (Boston: Heath, 1950), p. 264.

1960's in all denominations—Jewish, Roman Catholic, and Protestant—to a level that probably included a higher percentage of the population than at any previous time in American history.[21] By 1970, however, all denominations were reporting either a decrease in membership or a per cent increase less than the population increase. Within the Protestant denominations there was a strong ecumenical movement. This was an attempt of the Protestant churches, which had separated again and again into many denominations to come back together because some of the reasons for which they had originally separated were now considered to be superficial. Several branches of the Methodist church joined together, and many other minor denominations were united into larger groups. Most of the Protestant groups also worked together through the Federal Council of Churches, which later merged into the National Council of Churches. Progress was made toward a more inclusive merger of Protestant churches in the United States in the C.O.C.U. movement (Churches of Christ Uniting). There was also a World Council of Churches, which took in most of the Christian churches of the world with the exception of the Roman Catholic Church. However, many denominations are still independent of each other administratively; and the big organizations like the National Council of Churches and the World Council of Churches are merely cooperative endeavors, rather than an actual union of the churches into one large group. With the administration of Pope John XXIII (1958–1963) came renewed interest in liberalizing the practices of the Roman Catholic Church. The calling of the Vatican II Ecumenical Council in 1962 and its continued sessions during the 1960's led to numerous changes in the policies and practices of the Church which made for much better relations between it and the other branches of the Christian church and the other world religions. In 1964 for the first time a Catholic diocese joined the State Council of Churches, hitherto Protestant (New Mexico).

Theologically the most spectacular controversy in Protestant theology arose over the "God is dead" assertion. For most it meant that the old conception of an authoritarian God was dead, and in Christian theology it meant a greater emphasis on Jesus. There were, however, wide ranges of views within each denomination and the clergy seemed much more liberal than laymen both in theology and in social views.

Social Customs and Institutions

The period from 1929 to the present represents an extension of the changes that had been taking place rapidly during the latter half of the previous period. In addition to the changes in the standard of living and the way in which goods were produced, there were changes in two other major areas. One was a change in the character of the family, and the other was the further change from the rural to the urban type of population.

We shall discuss the changes in the family briefly (they are treated more fully in Chapter 6). In the first place, caused by and paralleling other

[21]News item, Religious News Service, Cincinnati Times-Star, August 26, 1954. This item reported a church membership of 59.5 per cent, or 94 million persons in 1953. This is certainly a higher percentage than in 1800.

social changes, there was a considerable reduction in the size of the family. This took place first in the cities, but there was also a reduction in the size of the rural family. Even the population increases that were to come in the post-World War II period were not due so much to a greater number of large families as to the increased number of persons marrying and the increased number of families with one or two children that would have had none before.

The first noticeable characteristic about the family is, of course, the decrease in its stability—the increase in the number of divorces.[22] About one out of four marriages ended in divorce in the post-World War II period. The character of the families that did hold together had been changing. Because divorce had become easier and more socially accepted, the husband and wife tended to stay together on the basis of mutual affection.

Not nearly so much of the life of the family is now centered around the home. In earlier days the family earned a living in the home, and almost all recreation and even many important aspects of education were centered there. The home has now changed to a point that in some cases in which the mother works, it is little more than a place to get an occasional meal and to sleep. This last characteristic, of course, is an extreme example, because there were in the period of the 1930's and early 1940's numerous completely stable families. In spite of some predictions of a dire end to family life, most writers in the field have indicated that the family was in a transitional stage and that the kind of family that was to emerge also might be stable, although of a quite different character from the family of the 1850's.

The type of clothes worn, as well as other characteristics of living, have changed markedly during this period. The changes in the bathing suits worn at the beach are indicative of the changes occurring elsewhere. One-piece bathing suits for men and two-piece for women became quite prominent during the 1930's. The wearing of shorts in the home by women (at least in the suburbs) and, to some extent, by men was prevalent in the post-World War II period.

The wearing of very short miniskirts had reached its "high" by the end of the 1960's and the fashion makers decreed its demise, but many women defied the designers, refusing to surrender the freedom of the miniskirt and its companion "hot pants." See-through dresses worn by the sophisticated style-conscious and "topless" waitresses in many cities were features of the late 1960's. Frankness in literature about sex and downright pornography in both literature and the movies, with the liberal use of four-letter words, formerly considered obscene, became quite prevalent. It was difficult to prosecute for pornography in any of the arts because the definition of the line between realism and exploitation was almost impossible to make. The laws relative to any form of sexual relations between consenting adults were practically unenforced and unenforceable, and in many cases the laws were brought in line with practices (e.g., Connecticut in 1969).

By 1955 some aspects of recreation were reversing the trend that had occurred in the early part of this period. Recreation, for a time, had been

[22]Cf. discussion of recent divorce trends in Chapter 6.

taken out of the home. The development of radio in the 1920's and early 1930's, and of television in the 1950's, tended to keep people at home, although it could hardly be called family recreation. Some believe that television is killing the art of family conversation and limiting other forms of family group recreation. Commercialized recreational facilities, such as mass sports events, bowling alleys, and commercial movies, tended to dominate the period of the late 1930's and early 1940's and continued to be significant for adolescents who wished to get out of the home for their amusements during the 1950's.

A tendency toward an increased amount of travel was apparent in the 1920's. The amount of travel accelerated during the 1930's, was cut down during World War II because of gasoline rationing, and then increased rapidly. The increase in travel already in evidence before World War II was accentuated by the enormous number of young men and some young women traveling because of the war situation, either in uniform or in search of work at defense plants. They found out about other parts of the world and were interested in traveling all the more. Young men who except for the war would have grown up and stayed in their communities all their lives, were in Europe or the South Pacific, and they came back with a greatly broadened concept of the world in which they lived.

Americans continued to increase their mobility after World War II. In the 1950's over 30 million persons moved in a single year. Ten million families left their counties and 5 million of these moved out of their state.

During this period of time, almost everyone took some kind of vacation trip some time during every year. The tendency to travel in automobiles rather than by train was so great and the motel business so widespread that it was possible to go almost anywhere in the United States and find a clean and reasonably priced place in which to sleep at night. As motel and restaurant prices escalated in the 1960's, a new phenomenon kept vacationing America on wheels: trailers, mobile homes, and detachable camper bodies for trucks. Private and public camping facilities became common, many with central sanitary facilities which included shower rooms. As unemployment figures mushroomed in the late 1960's and early 1970's, great numbers of youth took to the highways with backpacks. Privately and publicly sponsored youth hostels appeared in large numbers in the United States for the first time, copied largely from the hostels in Europe. All these factors caused greater mobility of population. The net movement was to the west and north. There was also a tendency to move on a permanent basis from farm to city, and to states with pleasant climates, such as Florida.

The population movement from the country to the city is, of course, one of long standing in American culture. It was greatly accelerated with the rapid industrialization after 1900. The increasing productivity of American farmers enabled an increasingly smaller percentage of them to provide the food necessary for a more adequate diet for an increasingly large percentage of urban dwellers. Currently about 6 per cent of the total employed labor force are farmers. Seventy-five years ago the labor force was divided about equally between farm and nonfarm.[23]

[23]Economic Report of the President, January 1971, p. 293.

SUMMARY OF THE MAIN SOCIAL TRENDS

The purpose of this chapter has been to provide some understanding of the cultural setting in which the American educational system has arisen and in which it has striven to enhance those values in which its leaders have believed. The American history reviewed here is filled with twists and turns of many kinds. There have been problems always, each with its peculiar complexities and each doing something to induce a new perspective. Some awareness of these problems and of the conflicts they reflected and produced is necessary to an appraisal of the efforts of the school in its contributions to the society in which it exists and to suggestions for future trends in education and in society.

Perhaps, in the brief review of the nation's social trends, enough has been seen to indicate that at no time were Americans members of a static society. Events were always on the march; ever present was the fact of change.

To summarize the changes taking place in American society, we give in this section a list of trends, together with some of their implications for our society and specifically for education.

Trend I. Development of Atomic Energy and Automation

The potentialities of the development of atomic energy and the rapid movement toward complete automation of the production process not only make possible an abundant economy but also pose pressing problems for the American economic and industrial system. One of the most pressing problems of the last few decades is that imposed by the increasing technology of the American economic and industrial system. There have developed in recent years new trends in this area of improved technology, and the potentialities that have now been opened for atomic power have served to make this problem even more acute. The rapid trend toward complete automation has been almost completed in some of the newer oil-refining plants. The newer production processes apparently are going to require even less unskilled and semiskilled labor than did the earlier mass-production techniques based on the methods used in the production of the Model T by Henry Ford starting in the early 1900's.

A practically unlimited source of power will become available when the atomic power plant has been made successful and practical. This enormous increase of power arises from the fact that the fuel of the atomic power plant, the radioactive material, is not consumed in the same way as are coal, oil, or gas. In atomic furnaces new radioactive materials can be produced, which can be refined and used again in other atomic piles.[24] The use of atomic energy, therefore, gives almost unlimited production potential in terms of the quantity of products that can be produced automatically. This dawning age of plenty challenges the ability of our present distribution facilities to take care of the results of the increased productivity of our industrial system. The economic and industrial problems related to this and to other problems arising out of our industrial system will be discussed more fully in Chapter 5.

[24]The use of the fusion process (now used in the H-bomb), if it can be made technologically practicable, will further increase the amount of fuel because of the great quantity of heavy hydrogen in the oceans. (See Chapter 5.)

This trend has come about so recently that it is difficult to explore all the implications for education that are present in our contemporary culture. On the one hand, in a culture in which the production process has become largely automatic and in which there is tremendous power potential, there will be increased amounts of leisure time and an increased accentuation of the trends toward unskilled and semiskilled jobs, or toward jobs that require a minimum of skill in operating machines that are fairly automatic. On the other hand, it will mean, of course, an increasing number of persons with highly technical skills to design the automatic machines, to design the production systems under which they operate, and to prepare the blueprints for new machines in terms of new models and new products.

Trend II.   Increased Leisure Time Made Possible by Technological Efficiency

Because of rapid development in the efficiency of American technology, time previously required for the maintenance of a minimum standard of living has been released for use in leisure activities. This increased time for leisure pursuits has posed problems for the wise use of leisure in our society. In some cases, where leisure time has been used unwisely, it has been a contributing factor to increased delinquency and crime.

(1) There are some persons who would say that preparation for leisure-time activities is not basically the responsibility of the school, because it already has its own job to do and consequently should not be interested in expanding its program to include the development of resources within the pupils for the wise use of their leisure time. (2) Others, however, indicate that education should be concerned about all human possibilities and that the school therefore should teach the significance of our expanding technology. This point of view implies that the pupil could be helped to see the possibilities inherent in the increase in the extent of our material-centered living. It would also stress the need for the pupil to get ready to use his leisure time for the enrichment of life rather than to allow deterioration because of lack of wise use of such time. There is also a possibility that helping the person understand more fully his place in the quite often mechanical, routinized processes of the modern mass-production system will help him appreciate his work more, so that he will not look upon it as purely routinized and therefore will be able to enjoy it more and also do a better job.

Trend III.   Continued Social Lag of Institutions Behind Material Changes

Our modern society is characterized by a serious social lag caused by a failure of our institutions and our ideology to keep pace with the very rapid rate of material changes brought about by the expanding technology. This lag, of course, is the occasion for many of the conflicts of our society and for many of the problems that exist. The problem of the lag of the school has been fully discussed in the appropriate sections of Chapter 2 and throughout Chapter 3. The problem of lag in regard to economic problems is documented throughout Chapter 5.

(1) One point of view would say that this lag should be of little or no

direct concern to the school. The school is not concerned with current conflicts as such. The school's job is to pass on the basic values found in our cultural heritage and in this way help to avoid some of the difficulties that may arise because of conflict and change. (2) Other groups say that the school must help society change to the new ideas and ideals and work hard for changes in institutional arrangements adapted to whatever is implicit in the rapid social change and in psychological understandings found in our society. If the school will help to do this, the changes can be brought about by democratic means. If, however, the school and other institutions in our society ignore the necessity for subsequent change in our ideology, values, and institutions, it may be that the very foundations of our society will be threatened because of the fact that the basic institutions are too much out of gear with it.

Trend IV. Increased Demand and Necessity for Specialization and the Consequent Need for a Common General Understanding of the Universe as a Whole

The extremely complex nature of industrial and social relationships has resulted in the increased demand for expert knowledge and therefore in the need for specialists, particularly in the leadership roles in our society as well as in supporting roles (such as research). Such specialization raises problems of communication and mutual understanding and creates a need for all persons to have a common understanding of the currently available view of the nature of the universe and of knowledge as a whole. This leads to two implications for the school: (1) It must play an important part in developing the individuals who will become the specialists and helping those specialists maintain a well-rounded background. (2) It must develop some way of teaching to all an understanding of and respect for the contribution of the specialists but still maintain the ultimate control outside the oligarchy or minority of specialists. In the case of medical doctors, for example, to what extent must we leave the power to make certain decisions in their hands? To what extent should decisions relating to medicine that are social in nature be taken out of the hands of persons who may be somewhat biased in terms of their self-interest? The same question arises with respect to politicians or civil servants. To what extent must we leave technical decisions in their hands? To what extent must broad policy be brought back to and ratified by, for example, a board representing broader problems of school administration with a specialized school administrator, or to an analogous group in industry or in the various branches of government?

With an ever-increasing amount of knowledge to teach, doubling in some fields in ten years,[25] with a demand for greater specialization, the generalists were hard pressed to defend their case. Yet if people do not have a general grasp of the total world, how do they get perspective for their speciality, how do they communicate, and how do they fit their specialized work together? The increased necessity for general education to accompany specialization should be self-evident.

[25]This literally means that as much was learned in ten years as in all the previous years of man's history.

Trend V.   Increased Necessity for Cooperative Action and for a Sense of
Responsible Participation in All Cooperative Enterprises

The complexity of the modern industrial processes, the interdependence of different processes on each of many parts, and the necessity for various specialists and other persons concerned with a process to work closely together result in an increased necessity for cooperative action in almost all industrial as well as social enterprises and emphasize the need for an increased sense of responsibility for the results of any action. This tendency toward the necessity for cooperation brought about by the complexity of our society, and, particularly, the complex industrial process, has become evident in our modern society. The efficiency of the modern productive process depends on a very careful working together of all the various aspects of that productive process. This necessity for careful coordination apparently is present whether the matter concerned is an industrial production line, a complex engineering job, or some type of social process taking place in nonprofit-making enterprises. Research has shown that the failure of an individual to be successful on the job is due in more cases to his lack of ability to get along with other persons than it is to lack of skill. Increasingly the type of skill needed for industrial jobs can be learned very readily by the average individual on the job itself. There is an increase in semiskilled and unskilled jobs. Of course, a certain number of jobs, such as engineering and production design, require a high level of skill. Again, however, along with these skills is the necessity for knowing how to work cooperatively with others in the highly technical planning processes.

(1) Some persons would say that, in spite of this, the important thing to stress in our society is individualism. The individualist in our society will cooperate with others if it is profitable to him and if it is worthwhile for himself to do so. According to this point of view it would not be necessary to teach cooperation, because that would come about normally when the individual saw the necessity for it in terms of his own self-interest. Thus it would be the job of the school to teach each individual to be as highly skilled as possible in the contributions that he might make to a productive or a social process. (2) Others would stress that the school should, in addition, help the individual see the importance of his job in the total productive process, indeed the place of his work in society as a whole. Also, they would stress the importance of teaching in the school the necessity for cooperation, including experiences in working with others within the school, so that the child will learn the know-how of group endeavor and therefore be able to adjust better to the kinds of situations in which he will most certainly be placed when he leaves school. Except for a few very highly skilled jobs that require large numbers of specific skills to be learned in advance, the emphasis would be on the all-round development of the individual, including the ability to work with others, rather than on a very high level of specific skills. (3) Still another group feels that the necessity for cooperative action in modern society, plus the necessity for intelligent cooperative action of the entire group in the solution of the problems we face, means that the school must play a much more positive role. It must play that role in developing new techniques for our society to use in helping to reorganize itself on a more collective basis for the common solution of our problems, including production and distribution problems in our economic system. The necessity

for the school to take this particular role is brought about, they say, by the increasing complexity of the problems that we face, together with the increasing knowledge of the way in which our problems can be solved. The school is the institution best able to help society reorganize or reconstruct itself in such a way as to enable itself better to meet these problems.

Trend VI. Increased Necessity for Long-Range Planning

Modern technology, other aspects of the industrial process, and other complexities of modern life have necessitated an increase in the amount of careful long-range planning to ensure the maximum efficient use of our productive processes and, in consequence, the appropriate improvement in our modern living. There seems to be some opposition to this long-range planning when it is applied to governmental operations. It is difficult to see how, in a complex society such as we have now, there is any way in which we can avoid the necessity for making plans in advance so that complex devices and institutions can be geared to and developed in line with those long-range plans.

(1) Some persons object because they evidently feel that the long-range planning of any group, private or governmental, tends to restrict the freedom of the individual to make choices. If you have long-range planning, there must, of course, be some way to bring about the cooperation of individuals in such long-range planning. Certainly, they say, the school has no place in this, as its service should be devoted to helping the individual to develop, rather than to stressing procedures that may lead to the lessening of the importance of the individual and his decisions in our society. (2) On the other hand, some note that in spite of verbal opposition there is, in fact, increased planning by private enterprises as well as by nongovernmental and governmental social agencies. They hold that the school should teach persons about this necessity for planning so that they may be able to understand it and learn to make their own individual plans within the framework of the larger plans of our society. Furthermore, it should be the job of the school to *teach* people how to work with others on a cooperative planning basis, so that whatever plans are made are the result of the widest possible participation of individuals and groups in our society.

Trend VII. Increased Social Control and Its Increasing Remoteness

The present machine age has tended to reduce the direct personal relationship both between the producer and the consumer and between the worker and the manager, and thus to increase our dependence on new forms of social control (other than the former simple interpersonal relationships) in various aspects of our economy and our society, and has caused the source of the control to be increasingly remote from its individual beneficiaries. The use of machine processes in production brings about an apparent necessity for the productive system to be quite complex and to involve a large number of persons doing different tasks. The growing complexity of the productive and marketing systems has caused us to lose the person-to-person contact between the consumer and the craftsman that existed prior to the development of the industrial age. At the same time, the complexity of the industrial process has also caused the close interpersonal relationship between the worker and the entrepreneur or manager of the plant to be partially destroyed. The development of powerful labor unions, collective bargaining, and trade associations, and the ramification of governmental control in many aspects of life, all are indications of the growing amount of social control. This increased social control, of course, is resisted by certain elements of our population and accepted or promoted by other elements. At times, individuals have resisted social control when it was restrictive to them but have asked an extension of social control in areas favorable to their interests. This dichotomy of thought and action is quite common at present in the various groups of our society, and it includes, of course, persons in both labor and management groups. Sometimes persons may take one point of view in their consumer interests and another in their producer or other interests.

Time was when the most important matters that impinged upon local citizens were those under the control of the local government. Because of the complexity of society, many elements have moved more and more to higher levels of government. The schools, for example, have had their administration and financing transferred increasingly to the state level. Many other aspects of our society, involving as they do wide geographical areas, have become important on the federal level rather than on the local, county, or state level. This has been true not only in government but also in business organizations, with their many ramifying plants. It is true also of nongovernmental social groups such as organized charities, where one large Community Chest campaign has replaced many smaller campaigns. This tends to make relationships very impersonal, with a lack of direct contact, for example, between the individual giver and the agency, or worthy enterprises within that agency, to which the person is making his contribution. It is difficult for the individual to see clearly that the giving of his money enables him to help out someone who is sick or some poor child, because all the machinery of a complex social organization is between him and the actual recipient.

What role may the school play in the recognition of increasing social control? (1) On the one hand, we might strengthen the individual as a consumer by teaching him how to make wise decisions in the purchase of his clothing, for example, to avoid the necessity for extensive social control over such matters as the quality of materials and prices. (2) On the other hand, it certainly is true that we do have to have social control of some things because the matters of control are highly technical, such as the purity of our water supply, the competence of our doctors and teachers, and the soundness with which our buildings are constructed. This list of technical matters can be greatly extended. The complexities of checking on the satisfactoriness of matters of this type mean control and inspection of a very high level. One of the jobs of our schools would be to give an understanding of this, so that all would appreciate the necessity for social control.

The tendency of society to operate more and more on a highly abstract level requires, of course, the ability of the person to read and understand things on an abstract basis rather than on the concrete basis of an earlier period. This means that a higher level of education of our populace must be maintained. Communication must be established between the agencies and the people who must contribute to them or support them by their votes. This calls for a high level of literacy and interest. Both of these undertakings can be helped by the school as an institution developing an educated and functionally literate populace able to understand the complexities of the interrelationships of the remotely controlled social groups of which they are a part.

Trend VIII.   Increased Potential for Individual Differentiation

The growing recognition of the difference in individuals in our population, coupled with the abundance of an affluent society, is resulting in an increased differentiation in the provisions that can be made available to people in a democracy and, therefore, in increased potential for individual choice and creativity. Our rapidly improving industrial system is capable of providing goods and services of great variety, so that individuals can make a wide range of choices with respect to housing, clothing, and other consumer goods and rational needs. Despite this technical capacity for diversity, scholars in the 1950's and early 1960's saw a growing tendency in the United States toward conformity. In Riesman's study of the other-directed man, he spoke of the tendency in modern industrialized society toward conforming to the approval of the group as opposed to individualization of tastes, activities, and interests. However, there was conformity in the tradition-directed individuals who lived in the middle of the nineteenth century, although this conformity was to a much smaller group, both quantitatively and geographically. Consequently, people may have appeared to be more individualistic. Whatever conformity there is in the latter part of the twentieth century, it is conformity to a larger social group that has been tied together through mass circulation magazines, radio, television, and so on. This tends to make conformity even more uniform throughout a larger geographical area and gives the appearance of greater conformity. However much conformity may actually exist, it is increasingly possible for persons in our affluent society to make choices that are quite creative and individual.[26] The youth, "hippie" and otherwise, the blacks, and others have asserted their rights to their own life styles increasingly in the late 1960's and early 1970's.

This potential for greater differentiation in the possible services provided the individual, of course, also has implications for the kinds of education that need to be provided. (1) Differentiated programs are needed to meet the differentiated needs of the various individuals who go to the school. Equity of education does not necessarily mean the same education for all. (2) On the other hand, a general core of common knowledge should be provided in the school, so that people who are facing the same general problems in our society will have the required background. There are some differences of opinion on this particular problem. Some think that the school should be limited to serving the common needs of all. Others emphasize the different needs and to some extent may even de-emphasize the common needs in preference to a greater stress on specific individual needs, particularly vocational.

[26]See Alvin Toffler, *Future Shock* (New York: Random House, 1970), Chapters 12 to 14. He documents the present availability and the future potential for availability of a greater diversity of goods and life styles.

Trend IX.   Vigorous Assertion of the Rights of the Individual and Denial of
Traditional Authoritarian Controls over Human Conduct

The extreme diversity of our various cultural patterns, the very wide-
spread dissemination of the knowledge arising from the scientific method,
and the rise of the scientific attitude toward testing all hypotheses, together
with the generally changing and dynamic character of our industrial society
all have tended to weaken the authoritarian and conventional controls over
human conduct. This has been accompanied by the vigorous assertion of the
rights of each adult individual to determine his own private behavior, dress,
and general style of life. A breakdown of conventional controls over human
conduct has almost always been present in periods when society has been in
rapid change or has been rapidly deteriorating. At the present time, material
changes are occurring much more swiftly than at any other period in the
history of mankind, and they have been coupled with a profound change in
some of the basic ideological assumptions underlying our society. These
material and ideological changes, together with the general pattern of diverse
culture in America resulting from the many groups that make up our country
and our encouragement of diversity, have caused widespread denial of the
authoritarian controls that normally have helped to regulate human conduct.
This has been accompanied by a vigorous assertion of individual rights, which
has manifest itself in dress, literature, and the arts. By far the most spectacular have been changes in the attitude of the middle class (some freedom
had more frequently been accepted by the upper and lower classes), more
frequent divorce, increase of premarital and extramarital sex, the occasional
practice of wife swapping, and increased "communal living."

This breakdown in past controls over human conduct has caused some
to see weaknesses in our present educational system. (1) Some persons insist
that the primary reason for the breakdown of authoritarian control has been
the fact that the educational system has not stressed strongly enough the
traditional values of our culture. Others, of a more theological bent, have
held that the reason lies in the fact that our present public education, being
nonsectarian, has not been able to teach the theological foundations that help
to strengthen the many kinds of authoritarian moral controls. The net result
has been a considerable agitation for increased emphasis of the school on
traditional values, including, in some cases, emphasis on religious values to
an extent compatible with the traditional separation of church and state.
(2) There are other groups who hold that the breakdown in values is merely
a characteristic of all changing societies and that the remedy is not to be
found in the schools but within society itself, in terms of increased
family attention to such matters as the instruction of the young; better work
by the churches in attracting and maintaining the attendance of the young
at church services; and other religious education experiences. Some persons
of this same general point of view would hold that the lack of authoritarian
values is not in itself bad, and that our value systems will become more
stable as society stabilizes itself after passing through this period of rapid
change. To this group, the present period is not the forerunner of a time of
serious deterioration of our society. (3) Still another group would indicate
that we should place a great deal more stress on the common values *inherent*
in our culture, particularly those related to its democratic aspects. The main
job of the school from this point of view should be that of helping boys and

girls to clarify the values inherent in our democratic culture and to see what their implications are for human action in our society. (4) A group of extreme militants among the so-called new left, found mostly on college campuses, has called for a complete revolution to destroy the Establishment and "free humanity of the heavy hand of oppression."

Trend X.   Increased Strains and Tensions

The increased specialization of our society and the tendency for individuals to identify with occupational, class, or ethnic groups, have caused the society to become more compartmentalized into groups, both vertically and horizontally, thus deepening the strains and tensions in American life. There is an increased tendency for us to owe our main allegiance to the particular occupational or social group with which we are associated. Our political and economic ideologies tend to correspond more closely with those of the industrial group or social class in which we operate than with that of any other element of our population. There is a tendency, therefore, for action to be taken more often on the basis of this narrower class interest than on the basis of what may be good for society as a whole. It is, of course, true that there is greater mobility of persons from generation to generation (or even within one lifetime) between the various classes in America than there would be in most European or other countries at the present time. The person who is making his way from one class to another tends very quickly to assimilate the points of view of the new group. This mobility, therefore, tends to preserve the class structure. These fractionated points of view increase the problems that America is facing; but some inherent tendencies toward stability help to minimize these class differences. One characteristic of American society that helps to give stability is the identification of most persons with the middle class. Very few persons wish to classify themselves at the extremes. This is in marked contrast to many of the other countries of the world, where most people are at the extremes and think of themselves as being either wealthy or poor. (1) The school, because it is a nonsectarian, nonclass-interest institution in our society, probably has played a very important part in reducing class consciousness without consciously attempting to do so.[27] Most of our people attend public school, which helps them better to understand persons different from themselves. (2) Some persons feel that the school might play a more definite part in helping to reduce class tension by helping to explain the various points of view of the different classes (groups) in our society so that they will be better understood. The school might further help the pupil to see in broader perspective the problems of the entire society rather than that of the specific group to which his parents may happen to belong. (3) There are others, of course, who feel that the school should ignore these tension problems. They feel that focusing attention on problems will tend to accentuate them rather than to alleviate them. The school, according to this latter point of view, should emphasize the common culture of our society. This would help to mitigate the differential nature of our society, which tends to cause groups to come in conflict with each other.

[27]However, see the discussion of social class structure in Chapter 9.

Trend XI.   Developing Biological Technology, Population Pressure, and Pollution

Because of improved medical care and a better understanding of disease resulting in decreased infant mortality and in a sharp increase in longevity, the United States and the world are confronted with the possibility of enormous increases in population. This possibility raises problems as to the availability of food, living space, and the proper distribution of natural resources among and within the countries in face of uneven population distribution. It creates an immediate problem of air, water, and land pollution. Biological technology, currently in its infancy, adds to the potential of these problems. It ultimately will increase longevity, and it raises the possibility of producing new life in test tubes and by "cloning"; it also raises the possibility of "biological immortality" (by arresting the aging process).[28]
It is perhaps a strange anomaly that the two most serious problems the world is facing are so opposite in nature. The awful threat of the nuclear bomb, whether of the A or H variety, is the possibility of wiping out all life on this planet. On the other hand, if we do not have a serious atomic war or some type of disease that will decimate our population, we face the possibility, perhaps even as serious, of a world in which we will be so crowded that life will not be pleasant. The details in regard to our population will be discussed more fully in Chapter 11. However, at this point it should be noted that this increase in population is a matter not only of total numbers, and that it is uneven in the various parts of the world, but also of a change in the nature of the population, particularly in the numbers of people of an older age, above sixty-five, in each of the populations. This creates economic problems concerning the support of these people after their working period has ended. This involves their psychological as well as economic well-being. Further, it raises questions as to the distribution of the world resources, because in some cases, as in the underdeveloped countries, the population is rising much more rapidly than resources can be developed. In some cases, the resources are not there within the geographical area to support the population. Furthermore, eventually the question will be raised as to whether we can find room to house the people and provide any kind of worthwhile life. Housing already has encroached upon some of the agricultural land that could be used for the production of food. Although this is not an immediate problem in the next twenty-five years in the United States, it could become one soon. It is, however, an immediate problem in India and China.

The population of the United States is increasing at approximately the average rate of the increase in the world in general. The population in large countries such as China and India and in the South American countries is increasing very rapidly. The rapid increase, of course, raises the possibility that countries with less highly industrialized development and with values and a way of life not acceptable in Western civilization are increasing so much as to dominate eventually the rest of the world. Consequently, their population increase is not only a problem to India, to China, and to the South American countries, but a problem to all peoples of the world.

The problems of air, land, and water pollution are becoming over-

---

[28]Two of the best sources for this change are Gordon Rattray Taylor, *The Biological Time Bomb* (New York: New American Library, 1968) and Paul R. Ehrlich, *The Population Bomb* (New York: Ballantine, 1968). See also David Krech, *Psychoneurobiochemeducation* (Washington, D.C.: American Association of School Administrators, 1969).

whelming. In the highly industrialized countries the greater per capita use of all resources meant that the toleration level of pollution was reached and passed even before the more heavily populated but less developed countries (Chapter 2).[29]

The further development of biological technology, through increasing further man's longevity, developing "superior, test-tube" babies, "cloning" (i.e. nonsexual copies of individuals), and ultimately the possibility (after the year 2000) of arresting aging itself, and thus achieving biological immortality, raises problems beyond the limits of our imagination.[30]

Some of the implications for the school, of course, might include

1. Giving the boys and girls some understanding of the population problem and the unevenness of the population.
2. Helping them to understand the possibility of regulating family size so that they will have the family resources to meet its educational and other needs. The latter, of course, raises the question of birth control and birth control techniques. At the moment, because of the controversial nature of the methods of birth control to be used, not birth control itself, many schools are not in a position to provide information concerning the necessity for the use of birth control nor, of course, the methods to be used. The understanding of the economics and the problems entailed by the tremendous expansion of world population certainly ought to be presented to the students in our schools at some time during their educational programs.
3. Heavy emphasis on ecological problems and future alternatives made possible by biological technology.

Trend XII. America's Increased Involvement in a Position of World Power and Responsibility in the Space Age

Increased transportation, more rapid communication, and America's industrial and military power have thrust her, by necessity, into a position of world power demanding responsible leadership and action in the new age of space. The potential ability of any nation to destroy others (and possibly itself) in an atomic war, indicates the necessity for cooperative solutions to world problems and tensions. Even though change is the most evident feature of history, and even though history never repeats itself exactly, many unsolved problems persist from generation to generation. The aftermath of World War II revealed several persistent, unsolved problems. Although the power of Italian fascism, German National Socialism, and Japanese militarism was destroyed by the war, the problem of aggressive totalitarianism was not removed. With the peace there came to the forefront a totalitarian Soviet Union, which became one power of a two-powered world. Totalitarianism is certainly not a new development created in 1945. In its present form it has been threatening democracy since 1920, and its roots may be traced far back into history. Neither is it likely to be a unique characteristic of the few years after World War II, for it is probable that future generations will struggle with this same problem.

[29]Ehrlich, op. cit., especially pp. 110–130.
[30]Taylor, op. cit., p. 265, and Toffler, op. cit., Chapters IX, X, XI.

Many writers point out that World War II changed the attitudes of the American people in that more Americans started to think in worldwide terms; more Americans became conscious that an open society with a free flow of information and goods should be maintained; and more Americans felt that the United States should collaborate with the British Commonwealth, Western Europe, and Latin America. Yet it should be noted that these ideas are not basically new and that the underlying fundamentals of international relations have undergone no radical change.

Perhaps of all the trends listed, this is the one that might be questioned most in the light of the events occurring in the mid-1960's. Western Europe had emerged as stronger in its industrial and military power, and the Soviet Union had developed a great military force and had become a technical and industrial power. Numerous other nations as well had become stronger, and seemingly were challenging the leadership of America. Questions were therefore being raised concerning America's relative strength and also her ability as a world leader. It may well be that the concept of one nation taking upon itself the responsibility for the entire world will cease to be tenable. However, America continues to be a great military and economic power. This fact has not made America popular in the world, among either her friends or those who consider America their enemy. All this, of course, leads to some confusion in appraising the implications of America's position of world leadership. In the meantime, other nations are becoming industrially stronger (Germany and Japan, for example) and the climate of world opinion is opposed to domination by one or a few countries.

The long involvement of the United States in Southeast Asia, the drawn-out indecisiveness of this conflict, and the resultant draining of the energies of the United States led to much unrest in the United States (discussed in Chapter 15 and elsewhere). Cooperative solutions to these problems developed on a worldwide basis, rather than the use of force, seem the evident solution but one difficult to carry out in the light of Asian as well as Middle East threats and aggressions to neighboring countries and world peace and order. The United States has been divided internally as to its continued role in its position as the major world power. How can the nations of the world cooperate with each other in mutual interest? This will be discussed in the next paragraph and at more length in Chapter 13.

There are differences of opinion on what some of the preceding implications mean for the school. (1) There is a particularly vociferous minority opposed to all efforts of the United States that jeopardize even slightly its sovereignty, even by participating in such organizations as the United Nations. This group is especially fearful of such organizations as UNESCO (see Chapter 13). It opposes all efforts of the school to teach international-mindedness and to give information concerning UNESCO if this means, as they think it does, jeopardization of the patriotic love for America and a consequent weakening of the nationalism of American citizens. (2) Most educators apparently are in favor of teaching for better understanding of the other peoples of the world so that we can work together more cooperatively. (3) A small minority feels that the school ought to teach more positively ways in which we could strengthen international cooperation, including the possibilities of world government. The history of the world has been, of course, the progression of government from the level of the family to the tribe to the small nation, then to the present large nations that are predominant in the modern world. The next step, say these persons, is a government at the world level; and the schools ought to do their job of preparing people for this final and logical step, which would lead to world order and peace.

PERSISTENT VALUES IN AMERICAN CULTURE

In spite of the changes indicated by the twelve preceding trends, there are other ways in which the United States remains primarily the same, and these lie in the ideas that Americans hold dear. In many ways ideas are the heart of a nation's power; and most certainly Americans cherish the conception of liberty and man's place in society—a heritage derived from the Magna Carta and John Locke, among other sources. Although there are varying interpretations among our more than 200 million people, generally Americans still believe in such ideas as respect for truth, rule of law, sanctity of human life, open-minded critical inquiry, and freedom of the individual and of the mind. Many of these ideas are older than America itself; most have remained basically the same throughout all of American history, although means advocated or used to achieve them may have changed radically.[31]

Americans now appear to be in general agreement that our nation and the world have reached a turning point or crossroads. They seem to feel that the decisions and events of the next few years will fix the course of history for a long time to come. It may be that the atomic and hydrogen bombs, the prospect of space exploration, and the clash between the United States and Russia are the major conditioning factors of the period; but some writers have taken care to point out that there are problems of other kinds: economic rehabilitation and a more equitable distribution of income, overpopulation, the exhaustion of natural resources, general lawlessless, mass education, racial discrimination, and the utilization of the blessings of medical science. Unfortunately, technical advances have outstripped advances in the social sciences. America knows how to produce; but it has not solved the distribution problem *at home*. In spite of its obvious domestic failures, as evidenced by the masses of the poverty-stricken and swelling welfare rolls, America aspires to world leadership through helping the underdeveloped nations of the world to solve their problems both of production and of distribution. Social inventions are badly needed if Western culture as we know it is to survive.

The control of nuclear energy and other problems related to it must involve not only science, economics, and politics, but also philosophy, religion, and ethics. There are some grounds for hope that a solution may be reached, for the religious and philosophical problems of today are increasingly concerned with the place of the individual in society and the relation of society to the individual. To improve the material standards of living of the people of today is a mission commanding the same kind of moral fervor as formerly went into the task of winning their souls. There are some indica-

---

[31]Further discussion of the agreements and disagreements concerning the nature of American democracy appears in Chapter 14.

tions that mutual respect, cooperation, and understanding are increasing. A large number of organizations seeking racial and religious understanding have appeared in the last few years, and in 1946 the World Council of Churches had an auspicious beginning.

The question of freedom is at the center of the political and social problems. Some Americans are not sure that everyone should have the five freedoms advocated in America, and often Americans would deprive others of certain rights. This is a forceful reminder that freedom has to be fought for in every generation.

The late 1950's and the 1960's saw recurrent violence, assassinations, and riots. The arousing of the ghetto, the black power, and black nationalist movements and the general unrest among youth on the college campuses indicate the symptoms of serious problems.

The United States faces problems at home as well as abroad. Abroad neither isolationism nor withdrawal will be satisfactory actions. If America is to survive, Americans must face the issue squarely. She may try to achieve (through Marshall Plan, Peace Corps, and so on) a reality of all freedoms in an understanding, interrelated world. She may elect self-preservation through military dominance, as indicated in Korea and in Vietnam.

An interrelated world appeared to be a possibility at the close of World War II, but events since that time seem to indicate that instead there is a divided world. Two of the major powers, the United States and the Soviet Union, advance claims of being truly "democratic," although the Americans tend to measure democracy in political terms and the Russians to measure it in terms of economics. The United States, and for that matter all Western countries, according to Toynbee, has recently become aware of the challenge of the economic democracy implied in communism, because there is "an irresistible encroachment of planning in the once-unregimented economics of the democratic countries." [32] On the other hand, the Russians have put up a case for political democracy; they conceive the working class and peasants as the majority of the nation, and therefore they argue that the "proletarian democracy" expresses the "will" of the great masses of people more clearly than does the "bourgeois democracy" of the United States.

There is little doubt that Russian Communist ideas have had a tremendous influence in Eastern and Central Europe. The Soviet invasion of Czechoslovakia in 1968 indicates that they will maintain this at great cost. The extent of direct Communist influence within the United States, in spite of Toynbee's insight, is more problematical. The question, however, in which Americans are intensely interested is whether the great powers will engage in a struggle that might destroy Western civilization or whether they can coexist peacefully.

The challenge of the Sino-Soviet philosophy to the educational ideas of the United States is significant. If the educational system of this country is to meet the challenge successfully, it must inspire a continual struggle for freedom, for a living democracy, for a better distribution of worldly goods, and for the extension of democratic privileges to all people. These are the goals. The procedures and techniques are yet to be developed.

[32]Toynbee, op. cit., p. 400.

Selected Bibliography

Abt. Clark C. "Forecasting Future Social Needs," *The Futurist,* Vol. 5., No. 2 (February 1971).

Amalrik, Andrei. *Will the Soviet Union Survive Until 1984.* New York: Harper & Row, Publishers, 1970. 93 pp.

Arendt, Hannah. *On Revolution.* New York: The Viking Press, Inc., 1965. 343 pp. (Paperback.)

Armytage, W. H. G. *The Rise of the Technocrats: A Social History.* London: Routledge and Kegan Paul, 1965. 448 pp.

Bartels, Gilbert D. *Group Sex: A Scientist's Eye Witness Report on the American Way of Swinging.* New York: Peter H. Wyden, 1971. 298 pp.

Bell, Daniel (ed.). *The Radical Right: The American Right.* Garden City, N.Y.: Doubleday & Company, Inc., 1963. 394 pp.

Boorstin, Daniel J. *The Decline of Radicalism: Reflections on America Today.* New York: Random House, Inc., 1969. 142 pp.

Borgstrom, Georg. *Too Many: Study of Earth's Biological Limitations.* London: The Macmillan Company, 1969. 368 pp.

Braden, William. *The Age of Aquarius: Technology and the Cultural Revolution.* Chicago: Quadrangle Books, Inc., 1970. 306 pp.

Brickman, William W., and Stanley Lehrer (eds.). *Automation, Education and Human Values.* New York: Basic Books, Inc., Publishers, 1969. 419 pp. (Paperback.)

Bronowski, Jacob. "What We Can't Know," *Saturday Review,* July 5, 1969. A noted philosopher of science indicates some of the uncertainties of predictions of the possible future.

Browne, Ray B., Richard H. Crowder, and others (eds.). *Frontiers of American Culture.* Lafayette, Ind.: Purdue Research Foundation, 1968. 201 pp.

Burridge, T. D. *What Happened in Education: An Introduction to Western Educational History.* Boston: Allyn & Bacon, Inc., 1970. 146 pp.

Cantor, Norman F., and Michael S. Werthman (eds.). *The History of Popular Culture.* New York: The Macmillan Company, 1968. 788 pp.

Cetron, Marvin J. *Technological Forecasting: A Practical Approach.* New York: Gordon and Breach Science Publishers, Inc., 1969. 345 pp.

Chorafas, D. N. *The Knowledge Revolution.* New York: McGraw-Hill Book Company, 1968. 143 pp. (Paperback.)

Clark, Henry. "Physico-chemical Control of the Mind," *The Futurist,* Vol. 5, No. 4 (August 1971).

Coben, Stanley, and Lorman Ratner (eds.). *The Development of an American Culture.* Englewood Cliffs, N.J.: Prentice-Hall, Inc., 1970. 235 pp.

Cox, Claire. *The Fourth R: What Can Be Taught About Religion in the Public Schools.* New York: Hawthorn Books, Inc., 1969. 179 pp.

Darlington, C. D. *The Evolution of Man and Society.* London: George Allen and Unwin, 1959. 753 pp.

Davidson, R. Michael. "Man's Participatory Evolution," *Current,* No. 105 (March 1969).

Drucker, Peter F. *The Age of Discontinuity: Guidelines to Our Changing Society.* New York: Harper & Row, Publishers, 1969. 402 pp.

Duberman, Martin. *The Uncompleted Past.* New York: Random House, Inc., 1969. 375 pp.

Ehrlich, Paul R. *The Population Bomb.* New York: Ballantine Books, Inc., 1968. 223 pp. (Paperback.)

Ernst, Leonard. "Can Chemicals Stimulate Learning Capacity?" *The Education Digest,* Vol. 35, No. 9 (May 1970).

Ettinger, Robert C. *The Prospect of Immortality.* Garden City, N.Y.: Doubleday & Company, Inc., 1964. 190 pp.

Feldman, Saul, and Gerald Theilbar. *Life Styles: Diversity in American Society.* Boston: Little, Brown and Company, 1971. 480 pp.

Fellman, David. *The Supreme Court and Education.* New York: Teachers College Press, Columbia University, 1969. 229 pp.

Ferkiss, Victor C. *Technological Man: The Myth and the Reality.* New York: George Braziller, Inc., 1969. 336 pp.

Fischer, David Hackett. *The Revolution of American Conservatism: The Federalist Party in the Era of Jeffersonian Democracy.* New York: Harper & Row, Publishers, 1965. 455 pp.

Foster, George M. *Traditional Cultures and the Impact of Technological Change.* New York: Harper & Row, Publishers, 1962. 202 pp.

Freidel, Frank. *America in the Twentieth Century.* New York: Alfred A. Knopf, Inc., 1970. 692 pp.

Friedenberg, Edgar Z. *Coming of Age in America: Growth and Acquiescence.* New York: Random House, Inc., 1965. 300 pp.

Grane, Leif. *Peter Abelard: Philosophy and Christianity in the Middle Ages.* New York: Harcourt Brace Jovanovich, Inc., 1970. 190 pp.

Greaves, Richard L. *The Puritan Revolution and Educational Thought: Background for Reform.* New Brunswick, N.J.: Rutgers University Press, 1969. 188 pp.

Griffiths, William E. *Religion, the Courts, and the Public Schools: A Century of Litigation.* Cincinnati, Ohio: The W. H. Anderson Co., 1966. 244 pp.

Gross, Bertram M. (ed.). *A Great Society.* New York: Basic Books, Inc., Publishers, 1968. 362 pp.

Gutek, Gerald. *An Historical Introduction to American Education.* New York: Thomas Y. Crowell Company, 1970. 246 pp. (Paperback.)

Hacker, Andrew. *The End of the American Era.* New York: Atheneum Publishers, 1970. 239 pp.

Handler, Philip (ed.). *Biology and the Future of Man.* New York: Oxford University Press, 1970. 936 pp.

Harrington, Alan. *The Immortalist.* New York: Random House, Inc., 1970. 324 pp.

Harrington, Michael. *Toward a Democratic Left: A Radical Program for a New Majority.* New York: The Macmillan Company, 1968. 314 pp.

Hartman, William E., Marilyn Fithian, and Donald Johnson. *Nudist Society: An Authoritative, Complete Study of Nudism in America.* New York: Crown Publishers, Inc., 1970. 432 pp.

Hayes, Harold (ed.). *Smiling Through the Apocalypse: Esquire's History of the Sixties.* New York: McCall, 1969. 981 pp.

Heilbroner, Robert L. *The Future as History.* New York: Harper & Row, Publishers, 1968. 217 pp.

Henry, Jules. *Culture Against Man.* New York: Random House, Inc., 1963. 495 pp.

Jaher, Frederick Cople (ed.). *The Age of Industrialism in America: Essays in Social Structure and Cultural Values.* New York: The Free Press, 1968. 400 pp.

de Jouvenel, Bertrand. *The Art of Conjecture.* New York: Basic Books, Inc., Publishers, 1967. 307 pp.

Kormondy, Edward J. *Concepts of Ecology.* Englewood Cliffs, N.J.: Prentice-Hall, Inc., 1969. 209 pp.

Krech, David. "Psychoneurobiochemeducation," *American Association of School Administrators Official Report.* Washington, D.C.: American Association of School Administrators, 1969.

Lerner, Max. *America as a Civilization: Life and Thought in the United States.* New York: Simon & Schuster, Inc., 1967. (Paperback, Two Volumes.)

Lipton, Lawrence. *The Erotic Revolution: An Affirmative View of the New Morality.* Los Angeles: Sherbourne, 1965. 322 pp.

Lowenthal, Richard. *World Communism.* New York: Oxford University Press, 1966. 296 pp.

McGiffert, Michael (ed.). *The Character of Americans: A Book of Readings,* Revised Edition. Homewood, Ill.: Dorsey Press, 1970. 425 pp.

McHale, John. "Toward a Planetary Society," *Current,* No. 110 (September 1969).

"Man into Superman: The Promise and Peril of the New Genetics," *Time,* April 19, 1971. Special Section. An excellent up-to-date account of genetic, electrical, chemical possibilities for human improvement.

Marcson, Simon (ed.). *Automation, Alienation and Anomie.* New York: Harper & Row, Publishers, 1970. 479 pp.

Martin, Warren Bryan. *Conformity.* San Francisco: Jossey-Bass, 1969. 264 pp.

Mesthene, Emmanuel G. *Technological Change: Its Impact on Man and Society.* Cambridge, Mass.: Harvard University Press, 1970. 128 pp.

Michaelsen, Robert. *Piety in the Public School.* New York: The Macmillan Company, 1970. 274 pp.

Mitgang, Herbert (ed.). *America at Random: From the New York Times' Oldest Editorial Feature, "Topics of the Times," A Century of Comment on Americans.* New York: Coward-McCann, Inc., 1969. 286 pp.

Muller, Herbert J. *The Children of Frankenstein: A Primer on Modern Technology and Human Values.* Bloomington: Indiana University Press, 1970. 431 pp.

Nash, Roderick (ed.). *The American Environment: Readings in the History of Conservation.* Reading, Mass.: Addison-Wesley Publishing Co., Inc., 1968. 236 pp.

Nicholson, Max. *Environmental Revolution.* New York: McGraw-Hill Book Company, 1970. 366 pp.

Nobile, Philip (ed.). *The New Eroticism: Theories, Vogues, and Canons.* New York: Random House, Inc., 1970. 238 pp.

O'Neil, Robert M. *The Price of Dependency: Civil Liberties in the Welfare State.* New York: E. P. Dutton & Co., Inc., 1970. 351 pp.

O'Neill, William L. *Coming Apart: An Informal History of America.* Chicago: Quadrangle Books, Inc., 1971. 442 pp.

Platt, John Rader. *The Step to Man.* New York: John Wiley & Sons, Inc., 1966. 216 pp.

Power, Edward J. *Main Currents in the History of Education.* New York: McGraw-Hill Book Company, 1970. 628 pp.

Pribram, Karl H. (ed.). *On the Biology of Learning.* New York: Harcourt Brace Jovanovich, Inc., 1969. 256 pp.

Ramsey, Paul. *Fabricated Man: The Ethics of Genetic Control.* New Haven: Yale University Press, 1970. 174 pp.

Reich, Charles A. *The Greening of America.* New York: Random House, Inc., 1970. 399 pp. (Also paperback.) A book supporting the youth movement of the late 1960's and early 1970's.

Revelle, Roger, and Hans H. Landsberg. *America's Changing Environment.* Boston: Houghton Mifflin Company, 1970. 314 pp.

Rosenfeld, Albert. *The Second Genesis: The Coming Control of Life.* Englewood Cliffs, N.J.: Prentice-Hall, Inc., 1969. 327 pp.

Schaar, John H., and Sheldon S. Wolin. "Where Are We Now?" *Current,* No. 119 (June 1970).

Schon, Donald A. *Technology and Change.* New York: The Delacorte Press, 1967. 248 pp.

Shonfield, Andrew. "Futurology: A New Science?" *Current,* No. 105 (March 1969).

Sierra Club. *Ecostactics: The Sierra Club Handbook for Environmental Activities.* New York: Pocket Books, Inc., 1970. 288 pp.

Slater, Philip E. "Is American Culture at the Breaking Point?" *Current,* No. 119 (June 1970).

Smith, Page. *Women in American History*. Boston: Little, Brown and Company, 1970. 392 pp.

Spiller, Robert E., and Eric Darrabee (eds.). *American Perspectives: The National Self-image in the Twentieth Century*. Cambridge, Mass.: Harvard University Press, 1961. 216 pp.

Stambler, Sookie. *Women's Liberation: Blueprint for the Future*. New York: Ace Books, Inc., 1970. 283 pp.

Stover, Carl (ed.). *The Technological Order: Encyclopaedia Britannica Conference on the Technological Order*. Detroit, Mich.: Wayne State University Press, 1963. 280 pp.

Swomley, John M., Jr. *Religion, the State, and the Schools*. New York: Pegasus, 1968. 220 pp. (Paperback.)

Taylor, Gordon Rattray. *The Biological Time Bomb*. New York: The New American Library, Inc., 1968. 239 pp.

Tebbel, John. *The American Magazine: A Compact History*. New York: Hawthorn Books, Inc., 1969. 279 pp.

Theobald, Robert. *The Guaranteed Income: Next Step in Economic Evolution?* Garden City, N.Y.: Doubleday & Company, Inc., 1965. 233 pp.

De Tocqueville, Alexis (edited by O. P. Meyer). *Democracy in America*. New York: Doubleday & Company, Inc., 1969. 718 pp. (Paperback.)

Toffler, Alvin. *Future Shock*. New York: Random House, Inc., 1970. 505 pp.

Townsend, Harvey Gates. *Philosophic Ideas in the United States*. New York: Octagon Books, Inc., 1968. 293 pp.

Turner, Frederick Jackson. *The Frontier in American History*. New York: Holt, Rinehart & Winston, Inc., 1920. 375 pp.

Vandenberg, Steven G. (ed.). *Progress in Human Behavior Genetics*. Baltimore, Md.: The Johns Hopkins Press, 1968. 356 pp.

Warner, Aaron W., Dean Morse, and Thomas E. Cooney (eds.). *The Environment of Change*. New York: Columbia University Press, 1969. 186 pp.

Watson, James D. *The Double Helix*. New York: Atheneum Publishers, 1968. 226 pp.
_____. "Moving Toward the Clonal Man: Is This What We Want?" *Atlantic Monthly*, Vol. 227, No. 5 (May 1971).

Wogaman, Philip. *Guaranteed Annual Income: The Moral Issues*. Nashville: Abingdon Press, 1968. 158 pp.

Selected Films

The Age of Specialization (McGraw-Hill), 13 min. In a country store in 1900, a farmer, shoemaker, store owner and country doctor speculate about changes the new century will bring in their occupations. The contrast between the work done by the four men in 1900 and that done today is vividly drawn through technological changes in production, communication, and transportation.

American Farmer (Ford Motor Co.), 28 min. An intimate and beautifully photographed story of a modern farmer and the changes wrought in his life by mechanization and scientific farming.

The American Road (Ford Motor Co.), 25 min. An excellent film of the changes in American culture brought about by changing technology, particularly changes in transportation.

Atoms in Our Future (ICF), 15 min. Many important advances have taken place in the development of atomic power for use in medicine, in preservation of food, and in generation of electric power. This is a report of those advances, an assessment of what they mean to us, and an attempt to forecast possible future uses for atomic power.

Automation—Part I (McGraw-Hill), 34 min. The film points out the effect of automation on the work of various people. It compares the fabrication of a specific item by new methods and by methods standard five years earlier. It explores the many problems connected with the revolutionary development of automation.

Automation—Part II (McGraw-Hill), 25 min. The film illustrates automation in this country in the field of communication. In addition, the film depicts the problems created and their effect upon human relationships involving leisure time, unemployment, and retraining.

Automation—Part III (McGraw-Hill), 25 min. View of the payroll division of a large corporation shows how paper work is being taken over by machines, which leads to predictions of new industries resulting from the trend. The film shows that what is taking place is really an intellectual revolution, challenging teachers as well as workers.

Cities: Why They Grow (Coronet), 10 min. A study of our increasing urban population. By departing from the usual statistics and the sociological problems that are a result of the cities' growth, we learn that by observing what the workers of the city do we find out why the city grew.

Expanding World Relationships (U.S. State Dept.), 11 min. Contrasts the slow transportation and communication of Thomas Jefferson's day with the machine age, in which technological advances have lightened men's work and brought all the countries of the world into close contact and interdependence of raw materials and manufactured goods; emphasizes the necessity for world-wide cooperation.

Four Teachers (National Film Board of Canada), 60 min. Filmed in Japan, Poland, Puerto Rico, and Canada, *Four Teachers* presents many illuminating comparisons of the world of the classroom, of student–teacher relationships, of the status of the teacher in the community, of the importance placed on education in these four countries.

H-Bomb Over U.S. (Public Affairs Films), 10 min. A clear and direct scientific estimate of the impact of a 10-megaton H-bomb warhead on Los Angeles (as an example of a large U.S. city). The film presents no program of solutions; it does provide a clear, lively, and vital basis for discussion of civilian and military defense programs and the physical and moral aspects of nuclear war.

How Do American Schools Compare with Yours? (N.E.T.), 29 min. A forum with representatives comparing their school with American. Includes Australia, Guatemala, Norway, and Turkey.

Man in the Twentieth Century (CS-573), 18 min. Discusses the fact that man's material progress is now at a higher peak than ever before, but his daily routine is often one of dissatisfaction. Although he wants peace, his world is split into two conflicting philosophies—communism and democracy. Emphasizes that through public education and the United Nations, man is looking toward peace.

Man Who Changed the World (TFC), 11 min. Story of James Hargreaves, English spinner, whose invention of the spinning jenny in 1767 laid the foundation for the machine age. How the conflict between man and machine came about.

Of Time, Work, and Leisure (N.E.T.), 30 min. Dr. Sebastian de Grazia, on whose study film is based, believes we have lost the ability to enjoy leisure as time for thinking, rest, and so on.

Passion for Life (Brandon), 90 min. A dramatic French film with English subtitles describing how a schoolmaster vitalized learning in a village. His activities are atypical and represent a protest against the traditional French school. However, the film depicts some activities, such as the oral examination system, which are common in French schools.

Satellites, Schools and Survival (N.E.A.), 28 min. A pictorial history of education in the United States during the last half century. Points up the challenge of present problems. Shows close relationship of the American system of education to survival as a free nation. Interviews supplemented by dramatized section on our school since 1900 and a present-day class at work.

Schools of Mexico (Ind.), 10 min. Presents a comprehensive view of educational institutions, from the ultramodern Ministry of Education in Mexico City to remote one-room adobe schools far in the interior. Includes normal schools, vocational and agricultural institutions, and kindergartens.

The Second Hundred Years (Crane), 27 min. Traces an exciting hundred years of progress in America, with a glimpse of the future, in the colorful record of a pioneering company's growth to supply our modern comforts.

Section 16 (N.E.A.), 14 min. Traces the history of public education in America from the Dame Schools of early New England through the colonial schools of Pennsylvania, the one-room schools of the Middle West, the mission schools of the Far West, the accomplishments of Horace Mann and other leaders in education, up to the public schools of today. Narrated by Raymond Massey.

Social Revolution (EBF), 17 min. Traces the social changes during the past two hundred years.

Spare Parts for Human Bodies (ICF), 15 min. As replacement of damaged parts becomes commonplace in medicine, grave questions of morality, ethics, and legality arise. Does a man own his own body? When is a man legally dead? When physicians themselves disagree on this question, who has the right to define death?

Techniques for Tomorrow (Ford Motor Co.), 25 min. A description of one of the new automatic factories—an engine plant near Cleveland—and what it means for industry.

Village School (BIS), 12 min. This documentary on education illustrates the philosophy underlying the British system of education.

When Extremists Attack the Schools (O.E.A., N.E.A.), 30 min. Focuses on a growing problem for many American school systems today, as boards of education and local PTA's become primary targets for infiltration by extremist groups.

Chapter 5

■■■■■□□□□□□□□□□□□□

The Development of the
American Economy:
Problems and Alternatives

In the preceding chapter the over-all social trends in the United States were traced, with some mention of the developing American technology and of the American economy in general. In this chapter the development of the American economy will be described in greater detail.

In order to understand what is happening in the American economy, including the expansion of productivity and the increasing complexities of distribution in an urban, industrialized society, it is necessary that we trace the history of the economy from the time of the American Revolution. In general, this history starts with what has been called laissez-faire economics, the principles of which were more nearly realized in the early American frontier period than at any other time in American history, as was pointed out in the preceding chapter. Well before the Civil War, it had in practice broken down in a number of aspects. Governmental aid to home industries through tariffs and the expansion of American industry through the rise of various large companies and the consequent monopolies were all part of this picture, to be more fully discussed later. The industrial revolution, which began in Europe in the late 1700's and which came to America in the early 1800's, was one factor underlying the increase in productivity in the United States. However, as will be pointed out in more detail later in this chapter, America has experienced a series of industrial revolutions, each of a different nature.

OVER-ALL TRENDS IN THE AMERICAN ECONOMY

Several over-all trends can be identified and will be given more attention later.

1. The first of these trends is the development of the laissez-faire economy and its subsequent breakdown because of forces most of which originated within the economy itself. Other forces were changes in the nature of the emerging technology and in the structure of industrial enterprises.

2. The most outstanding of all these trends is perhaps the enormous expansion in productivity, in agriculture, in industry, in transportation, and in communication; most of this increase is a direct result of modern technological change. This is America's continual revolution.

3. Another outstanding change that took place during this period was the rise of the capitalistic system of control of the economy, as opposed to the small-shop and handicraft system of the earlier period. The development of "big" business, as opposed to the prevalence of small business, is seen by most students as a necessary characteristic of the development of American technology.

4. From 1870 to some time following the early 1920's, nearly the entire economy of America shifted from one of scarcity to one of plenty. The problem was to work out some system of distribution—some relationship between wages, availability of products, prices, and the maximum efficiency of the production system—that would enable the economy to keep operating without being flooded with unsold goods as it was during the period of the Depression.

5. Finally, then, the over-all trends in the American economy reveal a shift from the laissez-faire capitalism of the early period toward a mixture of both corporation and state capitalism, with some cooperatives, some state socialism, and some small private enterprise.

After a comparison of American productivity with that of other nations in the next section, the development and current extent of each of the preceding trends will be discussed. The way in which the productive processes are geared with the economy and the way in which the money economy operates in our system will also be described later in this chapter. In the latter part of this chapter we will take up in more detail the problems faced by the economy and will explore the possible alternatives to be used in attempting to solve them.

AMERICAN PRODUCTIVITY COMPARED TO THAT OF OTHER NATIONS

The full significance of trends in the American economy can be understood only as compared with economic development in the rest of the world. The people of the United States have lived better than those of other countries. This is true in the twentieth century even if we compare our periods of depression to the best times in other countries. The United States has approximately one fifteenth of the world's population and about the same proportion of the world's land area and natural resources, yet

American industry produces twice the goods and services of all European industry combined—including both Britain and the Common Market—and two and a half times more than the Soviet Union, which has a greater population than the U.S. It produces a third of the total production of all other countries in the world. The Americans have achieved this with only 7 per cent of the surface of the globe and 6 per cent of its population.

One third of all students in the world pursuing a higher education are American. The number of students, as compared to the total population, is double that of any other country. For every 1,000 inhabitants there are 29 Americans studying at a university, 18 Russians, 10 Europeans.

All by themselves the Americans consume a third of the total world production of energy, and have one third of all the world's highways. Half the passenger miles flown every year are by American airlines. Two trucks of every five on the road are American-made and American based. Americans own three out of every five automobiles in the world.[1]

The usual comparison of countries by annual gross national product (GNP) per person or by average annual income per capita can be misleading.[2] Figure 1 shows a comparison based on minutes of worktime required to earn enough money to purchase certain items in selected countries. Figure 2 shows similar comparisons between Moscow and New York City.

The increase in American productivity that has brought about its world leadership has been accompanied by an ever-decreasing work week. In the early part of the nineteenth century, the handworker usually had to work from twelve to sixteen hours a day to make a living. Now the four-day, forty-hour week is currently being favorably considered and adopted.

LAISSEZ-FAIRE ECONOMICS AND ITS BREAKDOWN

A set of principles and practices that can best be termed laissez-faire economics was accepted by the American people early in the development of the American economy. Adam Smith had published his book *Wealth of Nations* in 1776, just as the American colonists found it necessary to formulate for themselves an economic theory under which to operate. The American people had a fear of government regulation based on their colonial experience, and like John Locke they held a rather negative conception of the place of the state.

The Nature of Laissez-Faire Economics

The theory of Adam Smith, which came to be known as laissez faire, was based upon a few fundamental ideas or basic assumptions. The economic system would be characterized by very small businesses or productive enterprises, such as small firms, factories, and shops. These would compete with each other to produce and exchange the necessary goods and services. The competition of the numerous, independent, small producers on an open market would operate automatically to regulate prices. This market mechanism would serve, without the necessity for any positive governmental policy to coordinate it, to self-regulate all the activities that made up the economic life of the people in the best possible fashion. Not only was the government to interfere as little as possible except in cases of downright fraud, but any important interference by the government would theoretically serve to destroy or upset the balance automatically brought about by the free play of competition on the market.

As noted, in laissez-faire economics a great number of small, independent

[1]From *The American Challenge*, by J.-J. Servan-Schreiber. English translation copyright © by Atheneum House, Inc. Copyright © 1967 by Editions Denoel as *Le Défi Americain*. Reprinted by permission of Atheneum Publishers, New York.

[2]Great care must be taken in interpreting comparisons between the development of countries entirely on one measure such as GNP. For example, Kuwait has the highest per capita income in the world but is not economically developed. (Production of oil is the sole factor.) David McClelland, in *The Achieving Society*, discusses this fully (New York: Free Press, 1961), pp. 80–101.

Minutes of Worktime Required to Purchase:

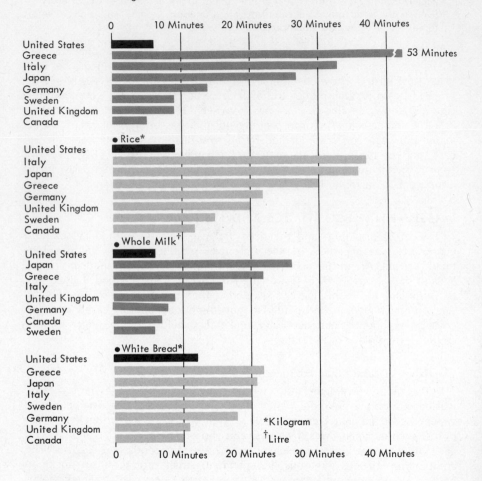

Figure 1. Factory workers' worktime cost of selected consumer goods (selected countries). National Industrial Conference Board, Inc.; 845 Third Ave.; New York, N.Y. Used by permission.

To compare living costs on an international basis, it is helpful to take certain staple goods (such as food) in each country, and determine how much worktime is actually required to earn identical or similar items. The ranking of countries according to worktime costs of particular goods indicates that time costs decrease as the degree of industrialization increases. The reasons for higher worktime costs in less developed countries appears to be because of the relatively low output per worker, which may be attributable to lack of education of the labor force

producers of various kinds and the absence of any kind of restraint of trade, governmental or otherwise, were presumed. It was assumed that if each of these small, independent producers operated in a way that was best for his own immediate self-interest, the entire system would operate for the best

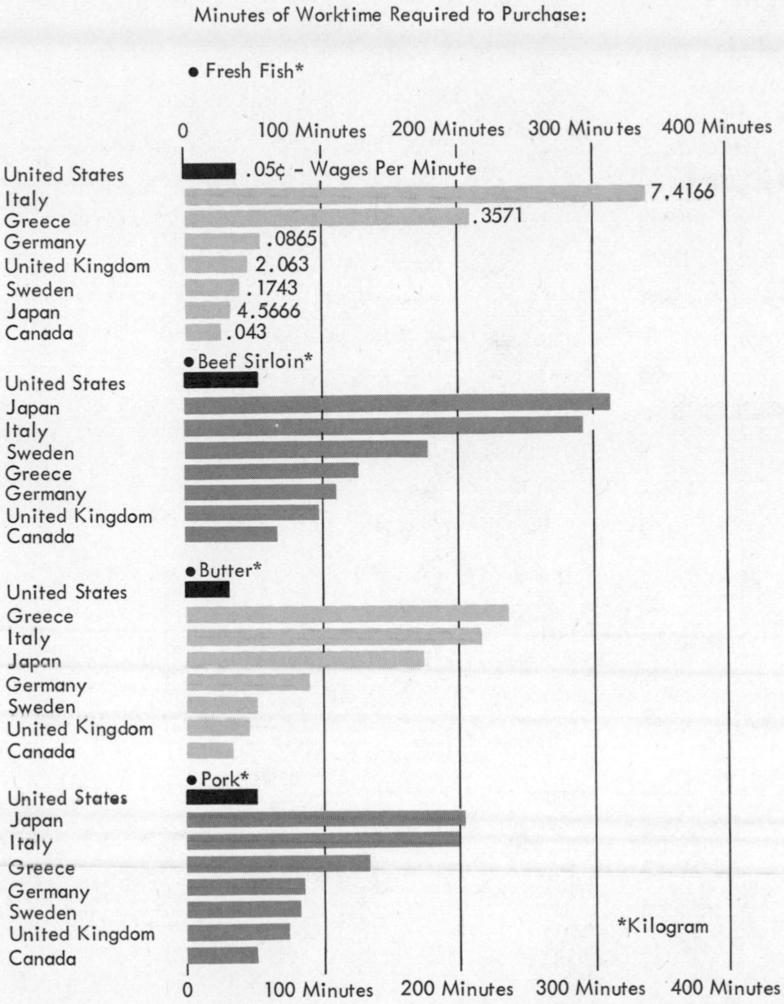

Minutes of Worktime Required to Purchase:

● Fresh Fish*

	0	100 Minutes	200 Minutes	300 Minutes	400 Minutes

United States .05¢ – Wages Per Minute
Italy 7.4166
Greece .3571
Germany .0865
United Kingdom 2.063
Sweden .1743
Japan 4.5666
Canada .043

●Beef Sirloin*

United States
Japan
Italy
Sweden
Greece
Germany
United Kingdom
Canada

●Butter*

United States
Greece
Italy
Japan
Germany
Sweden
United Kingdom
Canada

●Pork*

United States
Japan
Italy
Greece
Germany
Sweden
United Kingdom
Canada

*Kilogram

0	100 Minutes	200 Minutes	300 Minutes	400 Minutes

and a shortage of capital equipment. Consumer demand for certain foods depends a great deal on their costs in relation to costs of possible substitutes. For example, Swedish workers must spend approximately the same amount of worktime to purchase fish as British workers. However, since beef sirloin, one possible substitute, costs about four times more than fish in Sweden and only about two times more than fish in the United Kingdom, per capita consumption of fish is about twice as high in Sweden.

interest of the economy as a whole. If there was a producer who was charging exorbitant prices, he could not sell his product on the market. He would then be forced to bring his prices down. If there was a producer who was putting out inferior products, he also would not be able to sell on the market at the same price and would therefore be forced to reduce his price or not be able to sell his product. In any case, he would be driven out of the market unless there was a demand for a cheap, inferior product. To sum-

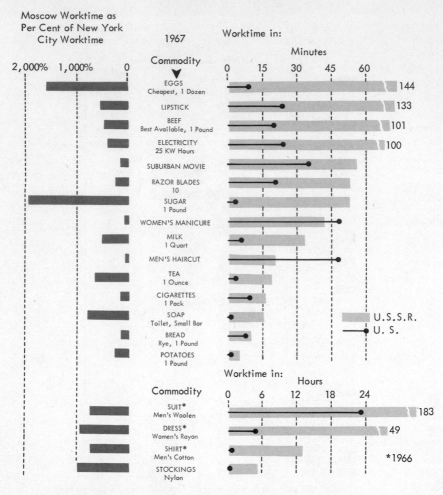

Note: Worktime figures were calculated on the basis of prices collected in Spring, 1967 and average earnings after income tax of male and female industrial workers in mid-1966.

Figure 2. Worktime required to buy selected commodities and services in Moscow and in New York City. National Industrial Conference Board, Inc.; 845 Third Ave., New York, N.Y. Used by permission.

marize, the characteristics of the economic system were private property, the profit motive, free competition, flexible prices, and little or no government interference with business.

Although the conditions on the American continent shortly after the Revolution fulfilled very nearly the assumptions of Adam Smith's theory, it is doubtful if his conditions ever were fulfilled perfectly anywhere at any time. It would be extremely difficult for a free market in the modern stage of transportation and communication to prevent one successful business from becoming large and monopolizing the market or dominating it in such a way as to be able to control prices. One of the interesting points about the history of American thought has been the persistence of the American people, and in many cases their intellectual spokesmen, in talking about the perpetuation of the laissez-faire economy long after it had been drastically modified. What we were *doing* in the gradual abandonment of laissez-faire practices and what we were still *saying* about the central ideas of our economy were quite often different.

Breakdown of Laissez Faire Before the Civil War

The government of the young American nation broke away from its neutral position in economic affairs early, as evidenced by the establishment of high tariffs for the protection of "infant" industries, bounties to the railroads, patent rights, and, later on, the giving away of the free land as homesteads in the West.

Conditions in early nineteenth-century America were very favorable for the expansion of an economic system. We had a virgin continent of excellent resources. We started our government at a time when the industrial revolution was getting under way, so that, in addition to the possibilities for the exploitation of our abundant natural resources, there was an opportunity to build our industries in accordance with the technological advances of the time. Our country was experiencing a rapid growth of population, including, of course, that which came about through the influx of immigrants throughout this period.

It is likely that Adam Smith had in mind the very small enterprises with which he was familiar in his day (1750–1780) rather than the large finance-controlled capitalistic enterprises that began to emerge after the Civil War and are quite typical of our industrial system in the latter half of the twentieth century. The development of the corporate system and the control of industry by corporations (rather than by single entrepreneurs or by partnerships) were only two of the factors that enabled large companies to develop. These large corporations could devote themselves completely to the dictates of profit and "good business," irrespective of any kind of moral purpose to maintain responsibility for the general welfare of their employees. This attitude was scarcely noticeable (even to a small extent) in the period immediately following the Civil War.

The laissez-faire system partially broke down, then, when government began to participate as more than an interested, neutral spectator. The participation usually was in favor of business enterprise. However, laissez faire also broke down partially in the agitation for laws controlling conditions of work. For example, the establishment of the textile mills in New England, which should have brought greater prosperity to the people, seemed to lead to the crowding of workers into cities, with relatively low wages, a long work week, and deplorably low living conditions. Conditions became so bad that many humanitarians of the 1830's and 1840's agitated for various kinds of reform laws, such as the reduction of the work week and prohibitions against child labor.

Corporate Monopoly Practices As a Threat to Laissez Faire

There was, therefore, some breakdown of laissez faire before the Civil War. But this breakdown was greatly increased in the period immediately following the war. The advent of the corporation as a prominent form of ownership of industrial enterprise, and the extension of legal and constitutional protection to the corporation as a person under Supreme Court decisions, led to a tremendous expansion in the size and power of the corporations in the postwar period.

It was estimated that in 1904 there were twenty-six trusts that controlled about 80 per cent of the production in their respective fields. Of these twenty-six trusts, eight controlled 90 per cent or more of the output of their respective products. Among these trusts were those that specialized in tin cans, cigarettes, agricultural machinery, oil, and shoe machinery. These corporations were the object of a vigorous "trust-busting" campaign during the administration of Theodore Roosevelt. This crusade actually did not break up very many trusts. As a matter of fact, no satisfactory answer to the problem of large business has as yet been worked out.

In 1946 an investigation made by a special governmental committee (included in the report *Economic Concentration and World War II*) showed that the 200 largest nonfinancial corporations, leaving out such firms as those in banking, owned 33.3 per cent of the total assets of all the nonfinancial corporations in 1909, 43 per cent of them in 1929, and 55 per cent in 1933.[3]

In addition to the concentration of assets into a relatively few corporations, there was an increasing tendency for only a minority of the stockowners to be in actual control, because the rest of them usually were apathetic or disorganized. A study made in 1933 showed that the Rockefeller family was controlling Standard Oil of New Jersey with holdings of 20 per cent of the outstanding stock. Similarly, the Du Pont interests controlled General Motors with holdings amounting to 32.6 per cent of the outstanding stock.[4]

A great number of people in the United States did own some stock, but stock ownership was concentrated in the hands of a few. For example, in an investigation made in 1937 it was found that 8 million persons in the United States received all the dividend payments reported by all corporations for that year. However, the Temporary National Economic Commission, which made this report, found that more than half of the total dividend payments received by individuals went to persons numbering fewer than 75,000, less than 1 per cent of the total number of stockholders in the nation.[5]

Ferdinand Lundberg, in *The Rich and the Super Rich*, has brought together recent statistics related to the unusual concentration of wealth in

[3]U.S. Special Committee Report, *Economic Concentration and World War II*, Senate Document No. 206, 79th Congress, Second Sess. (Washington, D.C.: Government Printing Office, 1946), pp. 6, 352.

[4]Adolph A. Berle and Gardiner C. Means, *The Modern Corporation and Private Property* (New York: Macmillan, 1933), pp. 102–103.

[5]U.S. Temporary National Economic Committee, Monograph No. 29, *The Distribution of Ownership in 200 Largest Non-financial Corporations* (Washington, D.C.: Government Printing Office, 1940), p. 13.

the United States. He cites Lampman and others (Smith and Calvert) to show that the "top wealth-holders"

owned 27.4 percent of gross and 28.3 percent of net prime wealth in 1953, but increased their share to 30.2 and 32.0 percent respectively by 1958. These data support Lampman's conclusion that the share of top wealth-holders has been increasing since 1949. Prime wealth, as they explain, is total wealth less the value of assets in trust funds and pension reserves.

But the top 11 percent of persons in the magic 1 percent (or 0.11 percent) held about 45 percent of the wealth of this particular group while the lower half or .50 percent held only 23 percent.

In a complex and comprehensive study prepared for the Board of Governors of The Federal Reserve System on the basis of Census Bureau data under the title *Survey of Financial Characteristics of Consumers*, the cold figures are officially presented on asset holdings as of December 31, 1962, removing the entire subject from the realm of pettifogging debates.

On that data the number of households in the country worth $500,000 or more was carefully computed at about 200,000. The number of millionaires at the year-end was more than 80,000 compared with Lampman's 27,000 as of 1953. Only 39 percent of these 200,000 had no inherited assets. These 200,000 at the time held 22 percent of all wealth, while 57 percent of the wealth was held by 3.9 million individual consumer units worth $50,000 or more.

The panorama of wealth-holding throughout the populace was as follows (in millions of units):

	MILLIONS		PERCENTAGE OF HOUSEHOLDS
All consumer units (Households)	57.9		100.0
Size of Wealth:			
Negative	1.0		1.8
Zero	4.7		8.0
$1–999	9.0		16.0
$1,000–4,999	10.8		18.0
$5,000–9,999	9.1		16.0
$10,000–24,999	13.3		23.0
$25,000–49,999	6.2		11.0
$50,000–99,999	2.5		5.0
$100,000–199,999	.7		1.25
$200,000–499,999	.5	Less than	1.0
$500,000–and up	.2	Less than	0.4

We see, then, that 1.4 million households owned 65 percent of investment assets, which are what give economic control. Automobiles and home ownership and bank deposits do not give such control. The economic power of the upper 200,000 is greater than indicated by their ownership of 22 percent of all assets; it amounts to 32 percent of investment assets.

Experts concede that a 5 percent ownership stake in a large corporation is sufficient in most cases to give corporate control. It is my contention that *general* corporate control lies in this group of 200,000 very probably and almost certainly lies in the combined group of 700,000 wealthiest households, slightly more than 1 percent, owning assets worth $200,000 and more.[6]

[6]Ferdinand Lundberg, *The Rich and the Super Rich* (New York: Lyle Stuart, 1967), pp. 10–11, 15, 16. Used by permission.

Some corporations, such as the Aluminum Corporation of America, lost part of their leadership in the field because of the effect of heavy demand on the output of some of the smaller companies. The income tax probably led to some reduction in the amount of total relative wealth held by individuals, and should have at least reduced the concentration of industry in the hands of a few corporations and the control of a particular industry by a few individuals. Apparently it did not stop it completely.

In the preceding discussion there is no attempt to point out that either size or concentration is bad or good. As a matter of fact, there is a difference of opinion among students of the problem, some indicating that the large corporation was an inevitable result of the trends taking place in American industry. Large corporations, by using mass methods, were able to produce goods much more cheaply than could many inefficient, small corporations. However, there was considerable evidence of price leadership and of agreements concerning price in some cases where there was still quality competition among firms, such as among the typewriter companies. A study of the changes in prices in the period from 1926 through 1938 indicated that there was a considerable difference in the amount of drop as a result of the Depression. In a government report prepared by Gardiner C. Means in 1939, it was found that in the "administered-price" group (that is, cases in which there was almost complete control of the prices of a given commodity[7]) prices fell by about 10 per cent from 1927 to 1935. In the case of the "market-price" group, where prices were set largely on the basis of what the product could bring in the market, there was a fall of more than 50 per cent during the period from 1927 to 1932. By 1935 prices had come back to within 25 per cent of what they had been in 1927.[8]

TECHNOLOGICAL CHANGE: AMERICA'S PERMANENT REVOLUTION

In an earlier section it was pointed out that American productivity had been made possible through tremendous changes in technology. *Technology* refers to the methods used in the productive process. It relates to the production of both goods and services. Technological change may increase both the quantity and quality of both goods and services. In the following sections it is planned to spell out a little more fully the extent of the technological change that has taken place in America.

The following point is clear in any discussion of technology. The output per man-hour has increased over a long period of years. This has been especially noticeable since 1929. The ability of this country to take care of civilian needs satisfactorily while maintaining supplies for an army of some 11 million men and giving aid to its allies during World War II indicates that this technological efficiency had improved. We do not have as accurate

---

[7]This discussion does not mean to imply that all cases of administered prices are due to corporation decisions or collusion. Policies of labor unions or even government regulations may be contributing factors.

[8]U.S. National Resources Planning Commission. *The Structure of the American Economy*, Part I: *Basic Characteristics*, pp. 145–147. A report prepared by the Industrial Section under the direction of Gardiner C. Means (Washington, D.C.: Government Printing Office, 1939).

figures on the amount of recent technological change. With the advent since World War II of automation (to be discussed more fully in the next section), there apparently has been another enormous increase in the technology. A rise of 35 per cent in production in American industry from 1947 to 1955 illustrates vividly the technological change that was taking place at that time.[9]

The increase in the pre-World War II period was striking. In 1936 Mordecai Ezekiel reported that the annual output per worker in agriculture had increased 140 per cent between 1870 and 1930.[10] This would mean that agriculture in 1930 was producing almost two and one-half times as much per worker as it had produced in 1870. These figures, of course, represent changes taking place before the more complete mechanization of agriculture. Comparable figures today would probably reveal an increase since 1930 equal to that from 1870 to 1930.

A study made by the Temporary National Economic Committee indicates that in four big segments of our economy the percentage increase in output per man-hour between 1909 and 1930 was as follows: manufacturing, 163.5; steam railroads, 81.7 (1914 to 1939); bituminous coal mining, 102.7; anthracite mining, 111.1.[11] These figures indicate, for example, that manufacturing had more than doubled—in fact, nearly tripled.[12] Some of the reasons for this amount of technological change will be discussed in the next section. However, there is evidence that technological change could have been even more rapid had it not been held back by monopoly and other interests that benefited by producing products that would not last as long as those products that could have been produced by inventions available at the time.

What are some of the factors underlying the rapid technological changes? Whatever the dynamics in back of the changes that did come about, they can be explained in terms of industrial "revolutions." Many history books speak of the industrial revolution as an event taking place at a specific time. In England the date given usually is the late eighteenth century, in America the early nineteenth. Actually what happened is of much longer duration and is much more complex.

The first part of the industrial revolution was the period of the development of new textile machinery in Europe (especially in England) from about 1750 on; of Eli Whitney's cotton gin, appearing in America in 1793; of the steam engine, which provided the power necessary to operate machinery to produce steel, to build better roads and canals, and later, to operate railroads and steamships.

The next period took place in America from about the time of the Civil War to perhaps the second decade of the twentieth century. The machinery used became larger. During this period there emerged the

---

[9]Adapted from U.S. Bureau of Labor Statistics.

[10]Mordecai Ezekiel, "Population and Unemployment," *Annals of the American Academy of Political and Social Science*, Vol. 189 (November, 1936), pp. 238–239.

[11]U.S. Temporary National Economic Committee, *Technology in Our Economy*. Investigations of Concentration of Economic Power, Monograph 22, 66th Congress, 3rd Session Senate Committee (Washington, D.C.: Government Printing Office, 1941), p. 90.

[12]Ibid., pp. 95–96.

vulcanization of rubber and the rubber industry; the petroleum industry and the application of its discoveries to the internal combustion engine; the development of better methods of communication such as the telegraph, telephone, and wireless telegraphy (early radio) of the late 1890's; and the production of high-speed printing presses that increased cheap production of books and magazines for mass reading.

A third step could be considered to be the "power age" or the "electric age." One of the characteristics of this age has been the development of the mass-production line brought about partially through the standardization (and therefore interchangeability) of parts. Most of the technological changes of the period from 1913 to 1940 can be ascribed to the improvement of production-line techniques, the improvement of the use of power—especially the use of electricity in running very complex machines, and the setting up of automatic machines that require only a minimum of control by the worker. Improvements in radio and the development of better high-speed newspaper processes also occurred during this time.

The fourth period of industrial revolution could be considered that occasioned by the use of automation and "atomic energy." It is just now beginning to show promise. Atomic power plants eventually will produce power in quantities unheard of in the days of the production of electricity from either steam or water power. This will enable some hitherto uneconomic processes to be undertaken, such as the converting of sea water to fresh water, the pumping of water from one area to another for irrigation, and the complete automatization of factories run by an abundant supply of power.

Automation itself, of course, is perhaps as important a revolution as any other. It means that the productive process will be made almost completely automatic. From the raw material to the finished product, automatic machines will feed the productive stream in a continuous process with little supervision. This has already occurred in some of the chemical industries where the flow process is possible. It is rapidly becoming widespread in the production of certain items, such as auto engines and TV chassis. When it can be applied to the productive process from raw material to finished product, it will mean another enormous increase in the output per man-hour. Far fewer but more highly skilled persons will be necessary to design, install, maintain, and operate the machines, as compared to the number manufacturing the same product previous to automation. Of course, the men released from one process could be absorbed in another, as cheaper products released purchasing power.[13]

Similar changes are taking place in agriculture. With the agricultural methods now available, it is likely that one fifth of our agricultural population with completely efficient methods could produce as much food and other agricultural products as are now being produced.

Other persons surveying the nature of the technological changes taking place in America have not felt it necessary to analyze the industrial revolution in separate phases, but have spoken of it as a "permanent revolution," industrial and otherwise. This means to these writers that America has always

[13]Excellent discussion of the long-range effects of automation and technology can be found in Toffler, op. cit., Chapters 2, 9.

been in a dynamic situation where something was continually happening to change the technology, and the changing technology was influencing other social changes. Consequently, we have never been in a completely static situation. "Revolutionary" changes have been occurring at all times. This has been so continuous that it is incorrect to speak of an "industrial revolution" or a "first industrial revolution." We are undergoing a permanent (or continuous) revolution in many aspects of American life at any given time.

Starting with the third quarter of fiscal year 1968, the productivity of the United States has not always kept up with unit labor costs. For example, in the first quarter of 1970, output per man-hour increased a little over 2 per cent and unit labor costs increased a little over 14 per cent.[14]

We have traced the development and the decline of laissez faire as a central set of principles underlying the American economy, and we have considered technological change and its accompanying industrial revolution. We shall now consider two other important trends in the American economy before making an analysis of the productive process. First we shall analyze the changing nature of the organization and control of enterprise itself. Then we shall indicate the changes in the relative amounts of different kinds of enterprises present in the structure of our industrial economy.

THE RISE OF BIG BUSINESS AND THE SHIFT TO MIXED CAPITALISM

In this section we shall trace the development of the way in which enterprises were owned and operated, as an indication of some of the changes that were occurring. The nature of the ownership and the size of the corporation in particular are central to the discussion. The shift from the economy of scarcity to one of plenty will be detailed. Then the tremendous shift of economic structure to a mixture of corporation and state capitalism, cooperatives, state socialism, and some small private enterprises will be traced.

The Rise of Capitalism, Corporations, Big Business

In the earlier period of the application of the laissez-faire philosophy of Adam Smith, most industrial enterprises were conducted as relatively small businesses, often owned by one entrepreneur. In many cases they were small shops or small factories employing only a few men. Sometimes the structure of ownership was complicated by a system of partnerships. As technology improved and the industrial process became more complicated, it was found that corporations provided for more efficient expansion and operation of industrial enterprises. The earlier ownerships or partnerships were not adequate for the size of organization made necessary by the type of economy emerging under the pressure of technological change. The Adam Smith theory could have applied as well to a system of goods exchange without any capital or money economy at all. Of course, the use of money does simplify the problem of exchange. The accumulation of large amounts

---

[14]*Time* (July 12, 1970), p. 67. President Nixon announced the appointment at this time of a National Commission on Production.

of money for the purpose of purchasing capital goods or means of production, however, constitutes a contribution that modern money methods have made to a better and more effective organization of our productive process. For this reason we speak of our system as a *capitalistic* system. It is the concentration of the ownership of capital goods, because of the concentration of wealth in the hands of a few persons or a group of people joined in a corporation, that makes the word *capital* significant as applied to our economy.

The corporation, with its board of directors and president operating under a charter granted in most cases by one of the states, was to pursue policies that were fairly flexible and was thus to expand readily to meet the demand for its product. The Supreme Court decisions of the late nineteenth and early twentieth centuries declaring the corporation to be a person in the sight of the law and therefore subject to the protection of the Fourteenth Amendment added to the effectiveness with which the corporation was able to operate.[15] The rise of capitalism and the discovery that corporations were the most effective way of handling modern mass-production methods led to the rise of big business. This phenomenon has been discussed earlier in relation to monopoly. However, even in industries where competition still existed, such as in automobiles, the size of the company seemed to be important in maintaining efficiency of operation. The mergers of many smaller automobile corporations in the 1950's serves to highlight this.

The reasons for the importance of the factor of size in success have been analyzed. In general, it is because large companies have greater operating efficiency than do small ones. The ability of some large corporations to control distribution outlets, again for efficiency and economy, illustrates another advantage.

The Temporary National Economic Committee, in *Technology in Our Economy,* found that in general the larger enterprises were able to employ a larger amount of electrical energy per man-hour. This same publication shows that these larger enterprises also could afford to employ larger research staffs.[16] This enabled the larger enterprises to refine old products, to create new ones, and to improve the productive process. It was also pointed out in this report that larger companies could more easily control patents, which made for greater economic concentration as well as efficiency. Larger enterprises were also able to provide more readily the huge advertising campaigns requisite to mass merchandising of present products and the introduction of new ones. In general, the larger the corporation, the higher is the rate of return.

The Shift from an Economy of Scarcity to One of Plenty

The history of mankind up until recent times (and of the major part of the world even at present) has been one of a continual striving for food and the other necessities of life in an environment in which there was not

---

[15]For example, see Hillman M. Bishop and Samuel Handel, *Basic Issues of American Democracy* (New York: Appleton-Century-Crofts, 1949), pp. 136–141. This contains excerpts of the Supreme Court decision in the case of *Lechner* v. *New York* (1905).

[16]U.S. Temporary National Economic Committee, op. cit.

enough to go around. The population and the desires and needs of the people have increased, by and large, more rapidly than has their ability to produce food and other necessities. A factor in this "scarcity," of course, has been the increasingly higher standard of living based upon an increasingly higher level of aspiration of mankind from the days of the cave man.

It has only been in the last few years, however, that at any point on the earth's surface a people was able to produce goods in such great quantities as to raise a serious problem of how to distribute those goods more equitably. The technological changes described are now coming about at such a rapid pace in America as to make this problem more acute.

Growth in the national product is rising at a more rapid rate than growth in the labor force, and the average income per family even when translated back into the constant dollar is such that the amount of equilavent dollars to be spent for household income for most years has been growing more rapidly than the price of the products bought. Although this generally rosy picture of the American economic system is blurred by the stubbornly high rate of unemployment and the threat of a higher rate through increased automation, it is likely that the rate of productivity will continue to rise and therefore the work week will continue to shorten. The effects of automation on the amount of technological unemployment, on the possibility of an accelerated shift from skills no longer usable, and on greater demands for highly trained persons to the detriment of those that are unskilled and to some extent untrainable are not known. One thing at least is certain—barring unforeseen economic or other type of disaster, the productivity of a highly industrialized nation can reach astronomical heights.

The Shift from Laissez-Faire Capitalism Toward a Mixed Capitalism

The third major trend is away from simple laissez-faire capitalism toward a mixture of many forms of structure for various enterprises.

We have noted that the predominant pattern of small enterprises of various kinds, operated largely by individual entrepreneurs, continued throughout the Revolutionary period, with respect to not only farms but also most small shops and industry. The exception in the case of farms was in the New Amsterdam–Hudson Valley, where there were some large tracts owned by the Dutch patroons, where other persons worked for the owner. There were also some large plantations in the South, the growth of which accelerated with the increase in slavery.

In the period from the American Revolution to the Civil War, there was an increase in the amount of enterprise controlled by those with money as opposed to that owned by the worker himself and run by him with a few assistants or apprentices. The period preceding the Revolutionary War could scarcely be called one of laissez-faire capitalism, because it was dominated by laissez-faire enterprises in which the worker had very little financial commitment other than his shop. In the succeeding period between the two wars, the change was in the direction of what can more nearly be called laissez-faire capitalism, because control through money was more predominant. In the period following the Civil War there was a rapid growth toward control by means of the corporation. The tendency for our production system to be dominated by one or a few corporations led to corporation capitalism and away from the strictly laissez-faire type.

In addition to this trend toward corporation capitalism, there was also a trend toward what Barnes has called a "state capitalism." This term is used here in the sense of the controls by state, national, or other branches of government over the policies and practices of private enterprise. Historically, this starts with the latter part of the nineteenth century when controls were established over the railroads as a result of the Populist revolt that occurred in the Midwest, largely over the inequity of railroad rates. These controls soon spread to cover many of the other so-called public utilities. These are businesses that are privately owned but are monopolistic by their very nature, because competition has no practical way of manifesting itself. Examples are electricity, gas facilities, and the telephone. In addition to the controls established over rates and other such matters in the public-utility field, there was, of course, the later establishment of workman's compensation laws and other laws dealing with minimum wages and conditions of work, applying to all industries. These amounted to control over the policies of all private enterprise. Then in the 1930's came a movement toward unemployment insurance and other laws dealing with minimum wages and conditions of work, again applying to all industries. These and other social security measures represent a further move toward state capitalism and added control over the policies and actions of private enterprises. These controls have been placed over institutions that are still "free" to set their own prices.

Cooperatives developed during this period. Producers banded together to form their own brokerage houses for the purchase of supplies and equipment and for the distribution of their products. The profits formerly absorbed by entrepreneur distributers or "middlemen" thus reverted to the producer-consumer cooperative owners. Examples of such corporations are the Farm Bureau enterprises and the cooperative elevators. The federal government has entered into the spirit of eliminating the middleman's profit through such activities as those of the Rural Electrification Administration.

There has also been a movement toward what might be called *state socialism*. This is the actual ownership and operation of various kinds of enterprises by the national, state, or local governments. It dates to the nineteenth century as far as many enterprises are concerned—for example, municipal ownership of the water system, the taking over of the fire-fighting enterprises, the collection of garbage by the city, and in some cases the operation of a municipal light plant or a transit system. It is also represented in some respects in the development of public power, particularly in the Northwest. In this case the power is usually distributed to anyone at its actual cost, including to local private power-distributing companies and to other businesses.

The public mail system and the public school system are still earlier examples of state socialism. A distinction can be made between state socialism and communistic enterprises at this point. As the terms are being used here, they are defined in a more technical sense than that in which the term *Russian communism* typically is used. In this stricter sense, a "socialistic" enterprise is one where the state or governmental subdivision operates the enterprise but sells the services at cost to the people. Examples of this would be water supply, a municipal light plant, or a public transit system. A communistic enterprise, technically defined, is one in which some branch of the government owns and operates the enterprise and supplies the services without cost to those who need it. Examples of this would be garbage collection, the public school system, and fire-fighting services.

It can be recognized readily that there has been a decided trend, and there still is a continuing trend, in the direction of socialistic or communistic operation of an increasing number of our enterprises. As a matter of fact, many of the services described in the preceding paragraphs are fully acceptable to most people. Terminology, of course, remains a very real problem. The strongest supporters of public postal and educational systems might present vigorous opposition if these systems were labeled as socialistic or communistic. It would seem that, in the light of the history, the question to be raised in the case of a proposed change is not whether the new direction is technically classified as socialistic, communistic, or capitalistic, but whether it is the most efficient and effective way of conducting the particular piece of business with due reference to its over-all effect upon the economy.

In spite of all these trends toward larger and larger corporations, and in spite of the fact that a very large percentage of our manufacturing is in the hands of a very few firms in each industry, there are still large segments of our economy in the hands of small private enterprises. This was largely true in the 1950's in the fields of farming and retail business. In the case of farming the amount of capital outlay necessary for efficient agricultural production had become so great as to lead to a sizable trend toward larger farms and absentee ownership. But there are still a large number of small individually owned farms. There are still a great number of small individually owned retail stores and establishments. This residue of smaller proprietors has been gradually reduced by the increasing trend toward larger farms and toward chain stores in almost all areas of retailing from groceries and auto accessories to big department stores. One of the outstanding aspects of this shift is the increasing domination of the whole industrial enterprise by the large corporation. Whether in newspapers; in radio, television, or movies; or in manufacturing, the advantages of the large corporation are becoming increasingly evident.

In the next section we shall analyze the nature of the productive and distributive processes in the present American economy before we consider, in the following chapter, some of the problems posed by all these changes in the American economy.

AN ANALYSIS OF THE PRODUCTIVE AND DISTRIBUTIVE PROCESSES

In this section an analysis is presented of the productive and distributive processes as they have developed and seem to operate at present in a modern industrial society such as that of the United States. The writers have attempted to do this by making the process as simplified as possible. It is their belief that even the most complex of processes can be understood by a layman. Although understanding a process sufficiently well to hold a general opinion is not the same as knowing it technically, in our democratic society such an understanding seems to be of paramount importance. As long as the person preparing the simplification does it honestly, with every attempt to convey the correct interpretation, it would seem to be a desirable service. There *is* danger, of course, of misunderstanding because of over-simplification. There are always many exceptions that cannot be put into a greatly simplified picture.

In order to explain the effects of technological change on a productive system, we have imagined a system in which there is at the start a balance between production and consumption. By means of a series of charts (Figures 3 through 7), we have attempted to show the situation existing in such an industry. This will be generalized to the whole productive process at times in this section in order to illustrate the effects upon the productive system if all industries were affected similarly or made the same decision with respect to technological changes.

Before the charts are discussed consecutively, some of the assumptions underlying them should be stated. In the first place, this is a static picture of the productive enterprise as seen at different times permitting only cer-tain kinds of changes and certain kinds of responses to those changes. It is assumed, of course, that no other changes occur during the period of dis-cussion. For example, there can be no change in the value of the dollar, no change in the amount of credit available, no change in the balance of trade, no change in the size of the federal budget surplus or deficit, no increase or decrease in the total public and private debt. These conditions are, of course, never realized because an economic system is a constantly changing, com-plex, interrelated system. The problems involved in the economic system per-haps can be understood if the system is considered simply. It is this pos-sibility of the simplification for nontechnical presentation of the very complex relationships existing within many aspects of the modern social and natural

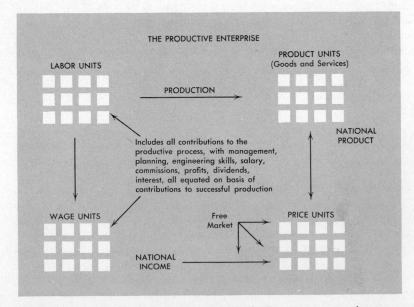

Figure 3. A balanced productive and distributive system—no changes.

world that makes it at all possible for every person to have some understanding of matters concerning which he must make decisions as a citizen. The authors do consider this feasible and present this illustration for the topic of economics.

It will be noted that in Figure 3 the productive process has been analyzed into four separate divisions. These are illustrated by means of formations of squares in the chart. One of these is called *labor units*. The utilization of these units (man-hours per week) in the productive process leads to the production of the product unit (goods and services), which on the national level can be called *national product*. The labor units, on the other hand, give rise to *wage units*. The total wage units are held to include all contributions to the productive process, including management, planning, and engineering skills, each being equated on the basis of its contributions to successful production. All wage units together can be termed *national income* when all the country's productive enterprises are included. This income from production or national income then goes into the free market to purchase the product units. The *price units* in a free market situation would be established by supply and demand conditions.

It should be pointed out that for purposes of simplification we have arbitrarily set up units so that we have in each case exactly twelve to start with. In the case of the labor units, they would represent such things as hours of labor per week, with management and other skills converted to the equivalent of other labor. The wage units would represent so many dollars per hour or per week. A size of unit has been chosen in each case such as to enable us to start out with exactly twelve units at the beginning of a balanced productive and distributive system. Similarly, we have chosen a unit for goods and services that enables the productive process to be listed as twelve such units during a given period, which could arbitrarily be a week, a month, or a year, depending on the size of the unit chosen. Similarly, for the price unit, a number of dollars has been chosen that would enable the price paid for the product to be on the basis of one price unit for each product unit at the beginning of the balanced productive and distributive system—twelve price units in all.

Now if there is no technological change and if the factory is putting out a number of product units sufficient to meet the normal demands of the society, as illustrated in Figure 3, we will have a balanced productive and distributive system, with the national income and national product (if considered on the national level) balanced, with no inflationary or deflationary trends, and with no piling up of goods in the warehouses.

Now let us look at Figure 4. One of the outstanding characteristics of our productive system has been the great increase in productivity. We have assumed in this chart that in a given period of time there has been a 33⅓ per cent increase in productivity. We have assumed that other things have remained constant in the charts that are to follow and have so indicated. The 33⅓ per cent increase in productivity is not out of line with the figures quoted in the section on technological change earlier in this chapter.

Let us note, therefore, what effects this increased productivity will have on the balance of production and distribution if there are no other changes. The first will be a 33⅓ per cent increase in the number of products (prod-

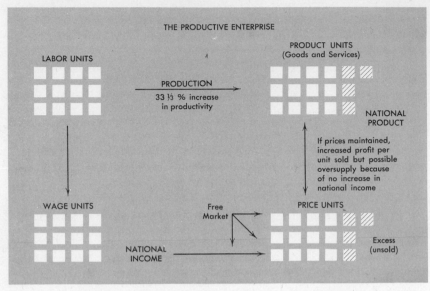

Figure 4. Increase in productivity—no other changes.

uct units). This has been indicated on the chart by means of adding four cross-hatched squares, indicating that one-third more product units are now available for the market. If the same prices are maintained and if the situation is generalized over the entire economy, there will be an oversupply if there is no other change in the total national income. Other factors that might affect the balance, such as increased credit from borrowing or the introduction of money from outside the nation, have been ruled out. The increased production would then mean that there would be an oversupply of goods and services. The services would go unpurchased and the goods would tend to pile up in the warehouse.[17]

Going back to Figure 4, the situation would then call for decisions by management and by others concerned (such as government). Let us suppose that the decision is made by management, as shown in Figure 5, to reduce the amount of labor units, because the same amount of labor can produce more goods and because the goods have not been purchased. Then we can reduce the number of labor units and produce as many goods; but of course, because there is no change in wages, we can produce goods much more

[17]It will be noticed that we have indicated that the profit per unit sold will be increased. Actually, because we have included profit in the wage units, this would not directly produce a decrease either in the wage units or in the national income. If the persons receiving the profits would expend the same balance in capital goods and consumer goods as would those receiving wages, theoretically this would make no difference in the productive economy. Consequently, the additional profits from the sale of sixteen product units as against twelve would then be spent in the market. This, generalized to the national level, would bring about a balance in the economic system. However, in a period of static or declining production, there is no incentive for a person to spend excess money gained by profits for capital goods or for new productive enterprises. Usually, therefore, the money gained through profits is withheld from the productive system, leading to a further slowing down of the process. This is more clearly shown in the flow chart in the next section.

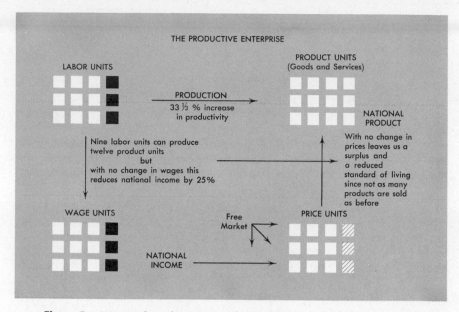

THE PRODUCTIVE ENTERPRISE

LABOR UNITS

PRODUCT UNITS
(Goods and Services)

PRODUCTION
33 ⅓ % increase
in productivity

NATIONAL
PRODUCT

Nine labor units can produce
twelve product units
but
with no change in wages this
reduces national income by 25%

With no change in
prices leaves us a
surplus and
a reduced
standard of living
since not as many
products are sold
as before

WAGE UNITS

Free
Market

PRICE UNITS

NATIONAL
INCOME

Figure 5. Increased productivity—reduction of labor to avoid oversupply.

cheaply and therefore make a better profit. If we reduce the number of labor units without increasing the wages, then the number of wage units will also be reduced. We indicate this on the chart by blacking out three of the twelve labor units and three of the twelve wage units, indicating that there are now just nine labor units and nine wage units. However, there still are twelve product units. But this, generalized on the entire national scene, means that there is less national income to take into the market to purchase the product units. With less national income and with no change in price, there will still be a surplus of products (indicated by cross-hatched squares), which cannot be purchased unless persons borrow money or go into debt, a condition that has been ruled out for the purpose of our present discussion. Consequently we again have an oversupply of goods and services that cannot be purchased. However, in this case, no more products are being produced, this will bring about a reduced standard of living, for not as many products can be sold as before. The result, then, of laying off men without reducing prices while still producing the same number of units as before would be to reduce the standard of living. One way of reducing the labor units, instead of laying off men, would be to reduce the length of the work week by an amount (one fourth) that would still produce as many units.[18]

Now let us suppose that we attempt to solve our problem by a reduction of the labor units without a reduction of the wage units. Because nine labor

[18]Some of our readers may perhaps be a little puzzled and disturbed by the fact that the reduction in labor and wage units amounts to one fourth, whereas productivity went up one third. Actually it is mathematically the same. The reduction in one fourth of labor units will enable the nine persons with a 33⅓ per cent increase in productivity to produce as much as twelve labor units did before.

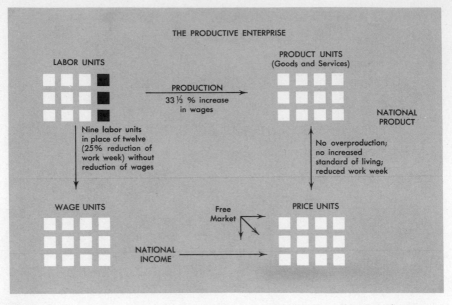

Figure 6. Increased productivity—reduction of work week with no reduction in wages.

units can produce as much as twelve, we could reduce the work week without a reduction in the amount of wages paid or the men employed. This can be done by raising the hourly or weekly wage by 33⅓ per cent. This plan is shown in Figure 6. Now it will be noted that we have reduced the number of labor units from twelve to nine but that the wage units stay the same; and so, generalized to the national level, the national income would stay the same. We are producing the same amount of units, so we have the same national product. The wage units (national income) then going out into the free market with the same price units enable the purchase of all the products produced. The net result of all this, generalized to the national level, means that we do not have overproduction, we are able to reduce the total amount of hours that we work, but we have no increase in our standard of living. We have merely reduced the amount of work that is necessary to maintain the same standard of living.

Now let us solve this problem in still another way. Suppose that we maintain the same amount of labor units, which would give us the same amount of wage units (with no change in the wages). We can thereby produce sixteen product units in place of the previous twelve (Figure 7). However, we can reduce the prices by 25 per cent, which means that, generalized to the national level, the same amount of income can absorb the 33⅓ per cent increase in product units. The twelve price units will purchase sixteen product units. The net result of this is that we have been able to absorb the increased production into our economic system in such a way that we have an increased standard of living without any change in amount of work week but with a reduction in prices. This tends to lead to a deflation and an increase in the value of money measured in products.

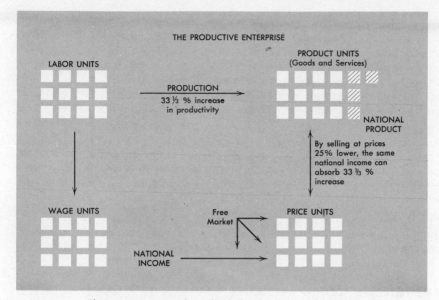

Figure 7 Increased productivity—reduction of prices.

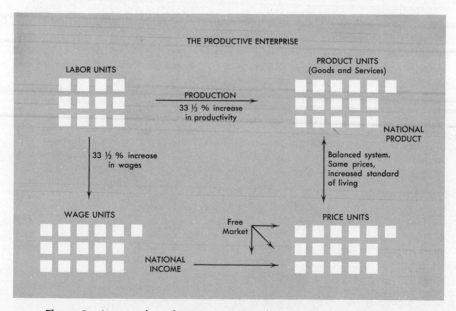

Figure 8. Increased productivity—increased wages: no change in prices.

Suppose, as is shown in Figure 8, we decide to pass along the increase in productivity to labor in the form of increased wages, so that they will be able to purchase the increased national product. We have therefore increased the number of wage units by four, a 33⅓ per cent increase. This would thereby increase national income by 33⅓ per cent. The product units of course have increased 33⅓ per cent (four on our chart). We thereby have again a balanced system. With the same prices we now have sixteen price units to correspond to the sixteen wage units that can produce the sixteen product units. We have a balanced system, with the same price per product but with an increased standard of living. This is a result of an increase in wages to correspond with the increase in productivity.

No attempt has been made in this explanation to indicate which of these methods should be used or whether it should be a combination of these.[19] The purpose was to clarify the effects of various decisions on industry itself, and, by inference, on our national economy if such decisions were universally made. It can be seen readily, and it will be shown more fully in the next chapter, that decisions of this kind have an important effect on depressions, inflationary trends, and other similar economic matters.

This presentation has been a static analysis of the productive process. In the next section, because our economic system is not really static, we are going to illustrate the dynamic process of the flow of money through our economy.

THE NATURE OF THE FLOW OF MONEY THROUGH THE ECONOMY

In this section we will portray the economic system as a circulatory system in which the flow of income to the economy is illustrated. The presentation, of course, again has been simplified greatly. The actually economic system is an extremely complex one, in which each of us with our income and purchasing power would be represented by little capillaries or pipes and in which other elements could be represented by many larger arteries, veins, and so forth.

Figure 9 represents a clarification of this simplified process by a relatively simple sketch.[20]

Before describing and defining the circulatory system in detail, the reader's attention is called to the fact that the gross national product, a representation of the nation's productive power, is a major driving force of the economy. At the other end the disposable personal income, which goes into the market for personal consumptive expenditures, represents also a major driving force of government expenditures and private capital investment.

One of the results of the recent study of economics has been the sharpening of the definition of certain terms used in that field and the development of reliable statistics on them. In Figure 9 we have used the latest statistics taken from the economic report of the president. We shall define

[19]Alternatives are presented in the latter part of this chapter.

[20]The statistical discrepancies in Figure 9 can be reconciled as follows: Some are due to rounding. Some are due to the statistical inadequacy of the data sources. For example, the national income amount necessitates the adding of government subsidies and subtracting business transfer payments. The personal income amount necessitates the adding of business transfer payments and inventory valuation adjustments. If the figure were three-dimensional, these extra flow pipes could be pictured. The discrepancy between gross savings and gross investment represents government surplus, a type of savings. The amount of net foreign investment must be added to incoming flow to give gross national product.

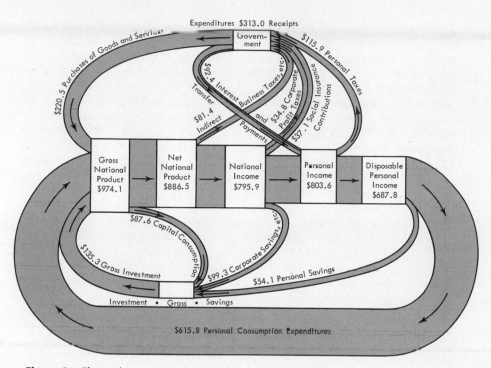

Figure 9. Flow of income and expenditures in 1970 (billions in 1970 prices). (Apparent discrepancies are the result of oversimplification of the chart. See footnote 20.)

some of the terms found in this figure as an illustration of the precise definition of certain indicators that can be carefully measured to indicate how our economy is progressing.

Gross national product (GNP) represents the total national output of goods and services at market prices. GNP measures the product attributable to the factors of production—labor and property—supplied by the residents of the continental United States. *National income* is the aggregate of earnings by labor and property from the current production of goods and services by the nation's economy. It is the sum represented by the compensation of employees, proprietors' income, rental income, net interest, and corporate profits; thus it measures a total factor cost of the goods and services produced by the economy. Earnings are inclusive of taxes on those earnings. *Personal income* is the current income received by individuals, by unincorporated business, and by nonprofit institutions (including pension trusts and welfare funds from all sources). *Disposable personal income* is equal to personal income less taxes on individuals.

Now let us look at the chart itself and follow through the analysis there given. The indication that is of greatest interest to economic statisticians is the gross national product. This was $976.8 billion for 1970). This figure less the capital consumption (that is, material spent by industry for building of new plants and purchasing of tools of production) becomes the *net national product*. The net national product less indirect business taxes becomes the national income. The national income less corporate savings and corporate profits and social insurance contributions plus interest payments and other government transferable payments becomes the personal income, the total amount received by individuals in our economy. The personal income less personal taxes gives us the disposable personal income—the amount that individuals have to spend in any given year. This was $684.7 billion in 1970. Some of this may go into personal savings and then back, of course, into various types of investment, as indicated in Figure 9. The various taxes collected by the different governmental units are also spent in the purchase of goods and services, which keeps the bloodstream of our economic system going and adds, of course, to the gross national product. The capital investment is a very important part of the economic system; it is investment of capital goods that facilitates machinery and processes for increased productivity. For example, if there were *no* money set aside in the productive process for the purchase of capital goods (those goods used to set up and develop the productive process itself), our productive system would become obsolete and eventually would disintegrate through normal wear and tear.

So long as this system maintains a fairly constant and balanced circulation, we have a relatively healthy circulation of money. If for some reason the consumers feel that they must purchase goods very rapidly, even borrowing money to do so (as, for example, in an inflationary period), then there tends to be an increase in the total amount of income, because the rate of acceleration affects the amount of income. The total national income is equal to the total of wages, salaries, rent, interest, and profit. If people spend their money rapidly so that it passes through many hands and therefore is counted several times in a given period, in effect we have more money in our economy, even though the actual amount of printed dollars may be the same. Other things that may affect the system are the pumping in of credit by governmental and private borrowing. The pumping out of credit by paying off debts also affects the system by reducing the amount in circulation. A "favorable" balance of foreign trade and the removal of products from the consumer market, as in the case of military products blown up or stored for future action, also affect the amount of income in circulation. In both cases the wages are available for the purchasers of consumer goods, but the goods are not available.

It is interesting to note that, as far as the flow of income is concerned, it makes no difference whether the wages and other income are secured through private enterprise or through governmental enterprise. For example, money paid to teachers for their services looks just the same to the economist as money paid to the doctor for his services on a private basis or as money used to buy products through private enterprise. Money paid for products bought from a publicly owned utility such as a water plant affects the economic system in exactly the same way as money paid for gas or electricity bought from a private electric company. Perhaps the amount of money set aside for capital improvement and the amount going into the division called profit may differ slightly in these respects, but as long as the money goes into the economic system, it affects the system in much the same way.

We will discuss later, at greater length, the problem of private versus public enterprise with respect to a working economy. Suffice it to say at this point that the incentive for production is held by the proponents of the private-enterprise system to be stronger in that system than it would be in the government-owned situation such as is found in extreme forms of socialism.

The nature and the development of the American economy have now been set forth. The remainder of this chapter will present some of the problems faced by the American economy and possible alternatives in the solution of these problems. In presenting facts indicating the problems of the American economy, the authors do not mean to condemn the nature of the economic system. It is an attempt to describe what has happened. Possible alternative actions designed to solve the problems presented are discussed fully in the latter part of this chapter.

PROBLEMS FACED BY THE AMERICAN ECONOMY
Concentration of Economic Power

Many big corporations have a large number of stockholders. In theory this might make it seem that the ownership of a particular corporation is actually quite widely dispersed. In fact, many of the holdings are very small ones. Most of the money value of the holdings in a given corporation is concentrated in the hands of relatively few persons. Because of the wide scattering of the various small shareholdings, quite often a minority of large stockholders with considerably less than half of the stock is able to control the company. Often a sizable portion of the stock may be owned by another company in a closely related business, such as the telephone and telegraph industries.

The control of proxies (signed delegations of voting rights) by the management, usually in conjunction with an already existing minority control, helps to prevent the overthrow of this minority control of stock. In many cases, the management itself controls the votes of the larger minority stockholders and thus can determine who the directors are to be.

Except in cases of stock manipulation (where the minority may manipulate a given company in order to cause a change in the value of the stock to its own betterment, even though it would not necessarily be an advantage to the company itself), such concentration is not always necessarily bad for the company or for the industry as a whole. It does, however, pose certain potential dangers if the interests of the minority in control are not consistent with the interests of the industry and with those of the country at large. The right to work in gainful employment is coming to be considered as one of man's basic rights. If the time should come when practically all the opportunities for employment were controlled by a few companies, which in turn were controlled by a minority, it would place in the hands of these persons more power than has ever existed in the hands of an oligarchy before in the history of mankind. However, we shall show in a later section that as far as the American scene is concerned, this is not as serious a threat to our freedom, at the moment at least, as it might appear to those who may wish to use the information for rabble-rousing.

Inequality of Wealth and Income

The second problem faced in American society is the inequality of wealth and income. When we talk about the low income of certain Americans, we must think of it within the American context. There is not as great a disparity betwen the income of the masses and that of the wealthy as that found within some of the undeveloped countries of the world. The income of the "underprivileged" class of America is well above the average income of the masses in some other countries, but this makes their deprivation nonetheless painful. They desire material comforts on the American standard.

There have been numerous studies made of the disparity of income. One of the most recent is that made by Michael Harrington, whose book *The Other America* was very influential in the development of the program of economic opportunity (the "antipoverty" program) in the mid-1960's. He indicated that there existed in America at that time approximately 50 million Americans, nearly a third of the population, living below the borderline of what could be considered a decent income with the American economy.[21] This at a time when American affluence was climbing and the middle class was able to have more than one automobile, better homes, even swimming pools and boats.

Ferdinand Lundberg in his study (published in 1968) has cited convincing evidence that in spite of middle-class affluence, there is a very small class of the "rich and super-rich" which is becoming relatively more wealthy in spite of income taxes and other devices for equalization of income.[22] The problem of depressed areas, both urban and rural, will be discussed in Chapter 10. At the moment, the problem of discrepancies in income between the upper and lower level is merely noted.

Monopoly and Administered Prices

It has already been seen, in the analysis earlier in this chapter, that the setting of prices has an important effect upon the economic process. Among the problems inherent in monopoly (or duopoly or oligopoly)[23] is the effect of such concentration of economic power in producing rigidity of price structure. This phenomenon is called by economists *administered prices*. It occurs in situations where prices are controlled, either by government (as in the case of utilities or during a war) or by a company (or group of companies) that sets prices at will.

It is possible that a monopoly, through the use of administered prices, can increase its income (based on profits) by maintaining prices at the expense of the amount of production. This may be especially bad during a period of depression in the business cycle because it further accentuates the trends already present.

It should be noted, however, that there are other factors that tend to mitigate the possible disadvantages in monopoly control. One of these is the fear of punitive measures by government, such as antitrust suits. Another is the fact that there really are no such things as absolute monopolies. Even

[21]Michael Harrington, *The Other America: Poverty in the United States* (Baltimore: Penguin, 1963), Chapter 1.

[22]Lundberg, op. cit., pp. 10–11 *et passim*. See quotations on p. 123.

[23]*Monopoly*: Control of a production of a product by one company; *duopoly*: control of production of a product by two companies; *oligopoly*: control of the production of a product by a few companies working in concert.

though a company may control the manufacture and sale of a given product, when the price becomes greater than the market can bear, the consumer tends to find substitutes or to delay purchases. This means that there will be some tendency toward self-regulation in any economy in which there is not an absolute control over the products that can be purchased by the consumer. The theory of this, known as *countervailing power*, will be discussed more fully later. It has been found that various powerful interests in our society tend partially to counteract one another, thus mitigating the possible force of monopoly or the concentration of economic power in the hands of a few.

Business Cycles

If the business activity in the United States over a period of years is measured on almost any scale, it tends to show peaks and valleys. This represents our business cycles.

This rapid variation in business activity leads to considerable waste in the production system. At times of low level, production capacity is not used efficiently and there is heavy unemployment, with resultant social disabilities and misery. The periods of boom may affect seriously other persons in the population because boom periods usually are accompanied by inflation, which means that persons on a fixed income may suffer from the lack of buying power. At this point we are not attempting to indicate the possible solution to the problem but merely to indicate that it is an important one. It is particularly interesting that the extremes of the business cycle seem to have been greater in the highly industrialized and advanced technology of America than they have been in some of the other countries of the world. It remains to be seen whether some of the remedies that have been worked out by government since the 1929 depression will be of any help in reducing the ups and downs of the business cycle or their effects.

Technological Unemployment

The paramount problem of the displacement of workers resulting from rapid technological development has been present for some time in our economy. Even though the total number of workers needed in the economy may remain the same or even be increased under an improved technology, there is the problem of the worker being displaced from one job and unable quickly to make the transfer to a new position.

With the advent of automation the situation may become quite acute, with very few men actually producing what a great number of men had produced before. This could lead to the production of an enormous quantity of goods per person, but it raises the question as to whether or not we shall be able to employ as many persons as before.

If automation were a simple matter of replacement of human labor by machines, there would be large-scale displacement of workers. In the automated factory of tomorrow, there may not be actual workers on the production floor. But large numbers of men will be required behind the scenes, as machine builders, machine installers, repairmen, controllers of machines, and "programmers" to prepare and feed information into the machines. In addition, highly educated specialists will be needed in newly created jobs as designers, draftsmen, systems engineers, and mathematicians. Finally, large numbers of managerial positions requiring the ability to analyze, make decisions, and assume risks will be created. This increase in the numbers of managers and the demands upon them may be the largest of all the social impacts of automation.

The workers needed per unit produced would certainly be less under automation. If the results of technology are reflected in lower prices, the workers per unit cost may be the same (in an economy with stable money). The productive capacity not used in one process must be routed into another to use the manpower and to absorb the purchasing power, both of which should be released by the new technology of automation if workers are released and prices lowered.

Because automation and technological unemployment do not affect the service industries in the same way that they do the production industries, we might expect that there would be a leveling off of persons employed in production even with increasing activity, productivity, and increase of those employed in services. This apparently is true. In 1920 there were about 14 million persons employed in the services-producing industries and 26 million in goods-producing industries. In 1952 there were approximately 27 million employed in each. By 1971 the number of persons employed in the services-producing industries had exceeded the number in the goods-producing industries, roughly 30 million and 49 million, respectively.[24]

The National Budget, Inflation, and Taxation

One of the outstanding phenomena among recent social trends has been the tremendous amount of money involved in governmental expenditures. The total money spent for all governmental purchases from 1929 to 1970 increased from $8.5 billion to $155.5 billion. Furthermore, in 1929 only $1.3 billion was spent by the federal government; whereas in 1970, $147.3 billion was spent by the federal government.[25] Of course a large part of the increase in the interim period was due, first, to an attempt to stop the Depression and, second, to the effort to achieve national security during World War II; the maintenance of military forces in Europe, Korea, and Southeast Asia; and preparation for other military eventualities. Regardless of the reasons, the size of the governmental budget has had an important effect upon the national economy. Much of the material required for war purposes was either stored in inventories or blown up in combat. Consequently, goods were not made available to be purchased on the market. Because the production of these goods required payment for raw materials and for labor, large amounts of money tended to be spent and thus set loose in the economic system. This excess of purchasing power over production made it necessary to establish controls on prices in order to slow the inflation of the value of money, and also to ration certain goods in short supply so

[24]United States Department of Labor, Bureau of Labor Statistics, *Occupational Outlook Handbook,* 1957, p. 25, chart 8. Updated with *Economic Report of the President,* 1972.

[25]*Economic Report of the President,* January 1971 (Washington, D.C.: Government Printing Office, 1971), p. 201.

that they would be distributed equitably among the people. This problem of controlling the value of money—or, putting it another way, the price of goods—then becomes an important one.

It is now thought that peacetime tendencies toward inflation and deflation can be controlled partially by the power of the Federal Reserve Board to control credit. A large part of the money available in the American economic system arises through the credit that can be given by a local commercial bank as loans. The bank needs to maintain only a certain proportion of its deposits in reserve. The rest can be loaned out again. Furthermore, the local commercial bank can, by going to a Federal Reserve bank with the loan paper (notes, mortgages, and so on), get additional credit, which permits it again to lend money on security loans. This pyramiding of credit can go on and on unless the cycle is topped by such regulations as those restricting the amount of the discount rate required by the Federal Reserve bank.

Problems Involved in the Growth of Unionism, the Expansion of Government, and the Pressure of Other Organized Power Groups

The early developments in the growth of larger power blocs go far back into the history of this country. Unionism is not a recent phenomenon; however, it has become a major industrial feature only in the last thirty or forty years. Section 7a of the National Recovery Act gave legal status to collective bargaining by labor and thus tended to give labor more power than it ever had before. This was in response to the increasing power held by industry, caused by the increasing concentration of power into the hands of fewer and larger corporations. The individual workingman was not able to bargain effectively with such massive antagonists as the large corporations. However, with the growth of unionism there has developed another establishment with policies often determined for the workers and imposed with possible threats to the total economy.

Because of the magnitude of problems of all kinds that we face, including the necessity for alleviation of suffering caused by depressions, there has been a rapid expansion of governmental services. This expansion is not entirely a recent phenomenon, for there has been a growth in the services demanded of the federal government over a long period of time. Many of these expanded services grew out of legitimate need for the aid that only the government could furnish, such as agricultural research, direct advice in helping farmers grow more crops, weather information, and other such services. It is difficult, when one starts to analyze any one of these services, to see how it can be eliminated, but the over-all result is that a sizable portion of the national income is given over to goods and services furnished by the federal government and by other governmental subdivisions.

In the growing concentration of industrial enterprises, labor, and government into larger and larger groups, agriculture was apparently losing out in the 1920's. In the 1930's the farmers combined politically with other proponents of the New Deal to secure various kinds of legislation to give it more power. By means of guaranteed parity payments, payments for land conservation, and other similar bounties, farmers were able to achieve what they considered to be their just share in the economy. Although they were still not well organized as a group, their voice was felt politically. By the late 1960's, however, this voice had lessened considerably, because of the rural–urban population shift.

The prospect of giant groups facing each other presents a quite different picture than that Adam Smith envisioned many years ago. It poses a problem of the place of the individual in the picture. Individuals are only small elements within large groups battling for power or for their "just" share of the national product. Then what place is there for individuality? The basic question is, "How can we maintain and protect the individual personality in a massive power conflict, such as has developed rapidly after the 1930's?"

The Place of Private Property in the Modern Democratic State

The concept of the right of private property seems to have developed quite early among some of the nonliterate peoples. We have seen, in the example in Chapter 2, how private property as an institution developed among the Tanala as a result of a change in technological process. Private property has always played an important part among the institutions the various civilizations have evolved as part of their total network of institutional arrangements. With the development of democratic theories, including those of the social and political philosophers preliminary to the development of democratic institutions, the idea of private property as being one of the basic rights became very prevalent. John Locke speaks of the rights of "life, liberty, and property." In the Declaration of Independence, this was changed (perhaps deliberately) to read "life, liberty, and the pursuit of happiness." At the time of the writing of the Declaration of Independence, men of property were only a small minority among the influential leaders. By the time the Constitution was written the propertied interests were much stronger. Numerous laws were passed quite early in the history of our country to limit the absolute right of property; for example, primogeniture (or the inheritance of all property by the eldest son) had been abrogated by laws passed early in the nineteenth century in almost all the states.

Basic growth of various forms of social legislation some time after the Civil War, such as the regulation of railroad rates, the regulation of other utility rates, the regulation of working conditions, has been considered to be an attack on the rights possessed by owners of industrial property. The battles over these laws were usually fought on the idea of the relative value of "property rights" versus "human rights." The development of extremely heavy inheritance taxes and of the steeply progressive income tax has served further to chip away at the "property rights" ideas in the American economy.

The right to property is not commonly considered to be an absolute right in America at present; for example, a person who owns a lot is restricted by zoning laws as to the kind of house or industry that he can build on it. The lot may be taken away from him under due process with compensation in order to build a schoolhouse, a road, or some other public construction. If he builds an industry on the property, he is restricted in many ways as to its working conditions, such as safety, hours of work, minimum wages, and so on. In general, then, the rights of private property of almost all kinds have been restricted by numerous laws supposedly in the public interest.

When property rights have conflicted with human rights, human rights have won out increasingly.

Despite the preceding, the right of private property in terms of the right to the ownership of instruments of production, to the distribution of product, or to the dispensing of services is held by the American people to be a fundamental one—within limits. In this respect the general tenor of opinion within America is different from that of the countries of the world that have tended to go toward socialistic (national) ownership of the instruments of production, or from the situation in Soviet Russia, where ownership of private property is mostly restricted to consumer goods.

Atomic Energy for Military and Industrial Use

One of the causes, and also a concomitant result, of our technological process has been the great increase in the amount of energy available for man's use. In the far past almost all the energy used was manpower. Later animal power was added, then wind and water power. In the recent past the tendency has been toward the fuel sources of power. These included first wood, then coal, then, of course, oil and gas. All such sources are potentially a form of energy derived from the sun. This is true even of water power, which is tied to the sun by the evaporation process and the subsequent falling of rain and the flow of the streams down to sea level. Gas and oil represent storage of potential energy through plant photosynthesis by action of the sun's rays. Power from such fuels is achieved entirely through the release of the energy latent in them by means of oxidation, and the consequent release of the stored energy (changed in form so that, after use, the energy is lost or dissipated). Atomic energy, however, embodies an entirely new principle. Here there is a destruction, in part, of the mass fuel material in return for release of enormous quantities of energy.

The development of atomic energy has been very rapid. The stimulus of competition, at first from the Nazis and later from the Russians, brought about the subsidization of research by all those governments that had the resources to put into the technological development of atomic power. The result was an extremely rapid growth of knowhow in this field.

Although some scientific work had been done before 1939, serious efforts toward the development of the atomic bomb were not made until about that time. On December 2, 1942, the first chain reaction based upon the fission process (breaking down of the molecules into simpler parts) was successful at the University of Chicago. On July 16, 1945, the first atomic bomb was exploded at Alamogordo, New Mexico.

The release of the bombs over Hiroshima and Nagasaki served in a destructive fashion to dramatize for the world the opening of the atomic age. From the very beginning it was felt that the fission process could be controlled for power purposes. On July 18, 1955, the General Electric Company announced the start of production of energy in an atomic energy plant that furnished electricity for power and light in West Milton, New York. This was just about ten years after the first bomb was exploded.

The hydrogen bomb employs a different process, namely, the fusion of lighter substances, such as deuterium (heavy hydrogen) or lithium. It was at first thought to be usable only in destructive explosives such as bombs or shells, and therefore to have no industrial application. Little success has as yet been achieved in efforts to develop the fusion process in such a way as to make it controllable and therefore available for atomic power purposes. The abundance of fuel for the fusion process opens completely new vistas of energy capabilities.[26]

Even in the use of "conventional" atomic energy, namely, the fission process, there are unusual possibilities for fuel because of the possibility of breeding. Let us now explain this process. U-235, the fissionable isotope, is a very scarce form of uranium. It makes up about 0.72 per cent of refined uranium. (The remainder is U-238.) The process of refinement is extremely complicated, and it takes a great amount of energy to get the relatively pure (99 per cent) U-235 used in an atomic pile. In a process known as *breeding*, quantities of U-238 placed in the atomic pile while the U-235 is undergoing reaction can be converted by the action of extra neutrons into plutonium, which can then be purified and used in other atomic piles just as U-235 is. The amount of fuel recovered from the first type of atomic pile is more than the amount of fuel used up in the reaction. Therefore there is no diminishing of the amount of fuel. Of course there is a potential limit in the amount of U-238 available in the world and the plutonium pile does not yield more fuel. However, the possible use of the fusion processes, coupled with the possible utilization of further information concerning the nature of the atom to lead to the use of other elements in fission or fusion, add enormously to the probable *potential* amount of energy available.

At the estimated rate of energy consumption for the year 2000, there will be sufficient atomic energy, based on uranium supplies *alone*, available for 1,700 years. The best estimate now is that the coal, oil, and gas supplies (if used alone) would last about eighty years at the rate at which we will probably be consuming energy in the year 2000.

The possibility of the utilization of this great amount of energy for increasing the productive capacity of the world challenges the imagination. Processes that have been economically impossible, such as the purification of sea water, the pumping of water over great distances to irrigate deserts, the synthesis of many products from raw materials, may all become possible. The amount of energy thus available to run automatic factories with very complex machinery almost completely without human guidance would be unlimited.

The dark cloud that hangs over all is the use of atomic power for destructive purposes. Indications are that two nations fighting an atomic war could very well destroy all human life on the globe, if not all animal and plant life. Whether this fact will lead to increased tension and war or whether the enormity of the power available in atomic energy will cause the groups to compromise on some "live and let live" basis remains to be seen.

---

[26]It has been asserted that sufficient amounts of heavy hydrogen (deuterium and tritium) exist in sea water to make it the net equivalent as a fuel to an equal amount of petroleum. Two methods have been pursued (without success at this writing): (1) the use of a very strong electromagnetic field, (2) the use of laser beams to heat the deuterium. The latter method is reported in the *New York Times*, November 22, 1970, p. 8E. On March 10, 1971, a news item in the *Cincinnati Enquirer* reported a successful attempt at Los Alamos Scientific Laboratory at producing hot ionized deuterium gas, or "plasma," a first step in the controlled-fusion process.

Man's Problems Ahead in the Economic Area

Before we examine the alternatives for the solution of problems that man faces, it may be well to summarize the main problems in the economic area. This list is not intended to be exhaustive.

1. How can we make adjustments in our production and distribution system to allow for extremely rapid changes in technology, including the effects of automation and atomic energy on production?
2. How can we prevent the extremes of the economic cycle, with its attendant boom periods and its inflationary trends, which are harmful to the person with a static income, and the bust periods (depressions), which are hard on the unemployed?
3. How can we avoid an undue concentration of economic power, which may endanger our individual liberties, without destroying the efficiency that grows from the advantages of large businesses?
4. How can we avoid the extremes of wealth and poverty, with the usual deterioration of character and personality at both of the extremes?
5. How can we avoid the rigidity of our economic system caused by the control of certain industries by monopolies or by a few companies that cooperate in maintaining a fixed price structure?
6. How can we operate the federal budget in periods of heavy military or social needs when large sums need to be expended, without causing undue hardship because of inflation or excessive taxes on certain groups?
7. How can we avoid the problems arising out of the large organized forces in our economy, such as monopolies, manufacturers' groups, labor groups, agriculture, and strong governmental pressure and regulation?
8. How can we provide for protection against the unexpected emergencies, such as unemployment, accidents, and sickness, and for retirement, without stifling the independence and initiative of the individuals involved?
9. How do we establish the just distribution of income and product to labor, management, owners, and government?

ALTERNATIVES FACED BY THE AMERICAN ECONOMY

In view of these problems, what are the possible alternatives faced by the American economy? Such possible alternatives might be discussed in several ways. They might be classified under the possibility of return to the traditional business system, the possibility of complete government ownership (socialism), the possibility of some combination of the two, or the possibility of movement toward more cooperatives. The writers have chosen to make the analysis a little more detailed to indicate a wide range of logical possibilities, though some of these alternatives are very unlikely to be chosen, and it is equally unlikely that any one of these will be selected exclusive of the others.

For the alternatives chosen by the writers for purposes of discussion, the reader is referred to Figure 10, "Alternatives Faced by the American Economy." These alternatives have been taken from many sources; they represent a logical array of choices. We shall start with the ones at the left of

Van Til	Traditional Business System	Restoring Competition	Leadership by Business	Two-Front Economy / Mixed Economies	Governmentally Planned	
Edwards and Richey	Negative Laissez-faire	Positive Laissez-faire	Administered Economy — by Business	Administered Economy — by Government		Socialistic Economy
Other terms; alternative proposals	Laissez-faire Individualism	Free market enforced by government action / "Trust-Busting"	Enlightened Self-Interest / Committee on Economic Development	Compensatory System / Keynesian Economics / Cooperatives	State Capitalism	Democratic Collectivism / State Socialism

Figure 10.   Alternatives faced by the American economy.

the chart, discussing and comparing the names given to each source of these possible alternatives.

Return to Negative Laissez Faire

The first alternative is frequently called the *traditional business system.* It is also sometimes called *negative laissez faire.* This is the traditional system as elaborated by Adam Smith,[27] in which the government would stay completely out of the affairs of business, leaving it to the operation of economic laws for any self-correcting influence. The government would conduct the punishment of persons who violate the law in such matters as honesty, but would exercise absolutely no positive action toward the working of the economic system. This is sometimes also referred to as the system of *laissez-faire individualism.* This system is based on the assumption that if each one works for his own immediate self-interest, the interest of society will be furthered through the automatic operation of the self-adjusting characteristics of the system.

Positive Laissez Faire

The next alternative, *positive laissez faire,* can also be considered as *restored competition.* In this case it is recognized that we have, in fact, moved a considerable way from the original laissez-faire idea. It would be the job of the government to exercise a positive influence to restore the original conditions. This was the purpose of what has been called the trust-busting program of the government. In this proposal there is set forth the anomalous idea of the government actually using its power in order to restore the laissez-faire system, which itself means "let alone." The idea is that

[27]Adam Smith, *The Wealth of Nations.* A classic published in many editions. See, for example, the Modern Library edition (1937).

if we can break down the power of large monopolies and restore competition, whatever is wrong with our economic system will be taken care of. The problem has been that trust-busting has not been able to accomplish much toward the restoration of laissez faire. Much faster than the government has been able to operate in the very complicated lawsuits that have been brought, industry has been combining and forming larger corporations, and more and more segments of our economy have come under either monopoly, duopoly, or oligopoly. It is difficult to say that there has been much positive action with respect to this particular alternative, even though it has been pursued as a government policy ever since the days of Theodore Roosevelt and by each of the administrations since—Republican and Democratic alike.

The first two alternative views were predominant before 1929 but are still widely held in the United States today. The remaining alternatives are those that came into prominence after the depression of 1929.

Administered Economy—Business Leadership

The next alternative has been called *leadership by business,* and sometimes the *administered economy,* of which two kinds may be listed: one being administered by business (discussed here) and the other being administered by government (to be discussed in a later section). The idea involved is that we have to recognize the fact that we live in an extremely complicated economic world that requires much coordinated planning and action. Someone (or some group) has to take the responsibility for this coordination and planning. The proponents of business leadership ask, "Who better could do this than the businessmen who are in positions where they can know what should be done?" Instead of each businessman working for himself, businessmen would work together to develop those policies that would be best for our economy. The enlightened self-interest of businessmen, in seeing more than just their noses and in looking ahead to the things that are happening and would happen in our economy in the future as a result of their plans, would enable them to make the kind of plans that would bring about a better economic system. There is self-interest operating here, but supposedly an enlightened self-interest rather than the extremely narrow form of self-interest that operated under the traditional laissez-faire system. A group of industrialists who call themselves the Committee for Economic Development was organized during World War II to pursue, more or less, proposals and actions based on this point of view. They have been at least partially in opposition to the National Association of Manufacturers and the United States Chamber of Commerce, which generally operate according to one of the two points of view already set forth, usually that of the traditional business system. The Committee for Economic Development, which includes some of our leading businessmen, has called upon business to take an interest in the welfare of the entire country and to pursue policies in regard to wages and other industrial practices that will lead to a better economic system.[28]

[28]The Committee for Economic Development, "Neither Right nor Left but Responsible" (pamphlet) (New York: Committee for Economic Development, n.p., n.d.).

An example of action (although somewhat ill fated) based on this point of view was the NRA, the National Recovery Act. This was sponsored by government, although it basically was leadership through business. Early in Franklin D. Roosevelt's administration the idea was developed that if the various industries could get together and agree upon fair codes of trade practices, then the government would enforce those codes. The representatives of an individual industry, such as, let us say, textiles, were first to agree on such things as the payment of minimum wages and the setting up of certain similar working conditions, and the government would then enforce the desires of the industry so that one business would not undercut another. The idea back of this was that if we could raise the amount of money being paid out to labor so that people had more mass purchasing power, then we would be able to get the economic machine going again. But if one business raised wages and another did not, then the one that did would be unable to compete. So the plan was that they would all get together and agree upon minimum wages, working conditions, hours, and other things, and perhaps even prices, and then the government would put the agreement into operation as an administrative law. Once this law was in force, all businesses, even the minority that had not gone along with the majority, would have to operate in accordance with it. Several hundred of these codes were put into operation. The Supreme Court of the United States declared the NRA unconstitutional in 1935, in the famous "sick chicken" case, as it was called *(United States* vs. *Schecter Brothers)*. Consequently this particular plan went out. But it appears that the Committee for Economic Development is not in favor of precisely this way of operating, because they tend to operate on the basis of voluntary cooperation among businessmen rather than to use enforcement by government as was done in the period of the NRA.

Dual Economy—Keynesian Economics

An alternative that became very prevalent throughout various parts of the world, including the United States in the late 1930's, has been called by Van Til the *two-front economy*. It is also sometimes called the *compensatory system*, and at times *Keynesian economics*, after Lord Keynes, a famous British economist who espoused the idea. Many of the policies brought about under the New Deal were based upon this theory, in spite of some of the criticisms that have been launched against Keynesian economics.

One of the characteristics of our capitalistic economic system, in spite of its many good points, is that it tends to lead into business cycles, or inflations and depressions. If the products of the factories are not bought, the deeper will be the depression, the more factories will be closed, and the fewer people will be getting money. We have not yet been able to eliminate depressions, but we can use the power of government to prevent depressions from being as acute as in the past. When the industrial system starts to go into a depression, dropping off in employment and production, then the government borrows money and pumps it into the credit stream. Such means as public works are used to provide work for people. Without such government aid, recessions become depressions.

Under the plan of older Keynesian economics, the government expands credit so that the cycle is prevented from going down as low as it might. On the other hand, as business begins to recover and starts up to new boom heights, the Keynesian theory then indicates that taxation must be heavy in order to prevent an inflationary boom. In other words, we take the purchasing power away from the people during the boom days and pay back the national debt so that we will be able, in the next depression period, to pour that money back into the economic system. What this system does at best is not to stop business cycles but to prevent them from going to extremes, a condition which has tended to become greater in recent years. The Keynesian economics was expressed in the early 1960's in the tax-cut method of placing more money in the hands of consumers. It was also used not only to prevent depressions but to maintain a steady rate of economic growth.

Administered Economy—Through Governmental Planning

The economy administered through governmental planning goes well beyond either economy administered by business or the two-front economy described in the immediately preceding section. In the two-front economy the government interferes very little with what is happening in private enterprise. Under a governmentally planned economy, the government does overall planning in terms of allocation of raw materials, minimum working conditions, and perhaps price controls, such as we have had in periods of inflation or periods of war (as, for example, World War II). Although there had been no well-defined program of administered economy by government consciously pursued in times other than war, the whole trend during the last fifty to seventy years had been toward more and more of what can be called state capitalism—or toward the policies of business being dictated by administrative law rather than being left to business itself. In general, except in wartime this has not included any attempt at restricting the amount of certain products produced, the controlling of prices, or consumer rationing, although quotas for certain farm crops have been set annually. During wartime such measures have been necessary in order to steer the economy into a productive program geared to meet military objectives. Most of the advocates of governmental planning think that we should bring together some kind of planning board (such as the National Resources Planning Board set up in the early 1940's) and determine just how the resources of the country should be used for the welfare of the people. Then various kinds of regulations, encouragement incentives, and other policies would be set forth by the government to see to it that the effort of our industrial system was employed in those areas where it would do the most good for our economy.

Socialistic Economy—Largely Governmentally Owned

A socialistic economy is an alternative not cherished by a large number of Americans. It is perhaps difficult for Americans to realize that, outside of America, ideas of this kind are widely held even in countries that are not communistic. Major political parties in France, Italy, and England hold modified ideas leaning toward a socialistic solution of some of the problems that their economies face. It is therefore worthwhile for those of us in

America to study this particular alternative, even though it is not likely to be accepted as a complete answer to our economic problems, at least in the near future.

The government geographically closest to the United States that approximates a socialistic approach is that headed by the Co-operative Commonwealth Federation of Canada, which has been in control in the province of Saskatchewan (but not of Canada as a whole) over a period of years. It is interesting to note that one of the things that this Canadian party has done within the province is to make available life insurance that can be bought at cost through provincial auspices. Another interesting item is that when you buy your automobile license you also must buy your liability insurance—at a slight additional cost. However, this particular party has made no major chances in the economy, although it does advocate some.

Distinction should be made here between democratic socialism and socialism of the type sponsored under dictatorships such as Russian communism. Most of the Socialist parties in noncommunistic countries are democratic; that is, they believe that the policies they want to bring about should be established through discussion and majority vote. This, of course, is in opposition to the attitudes of those Marxist Communists who think that it is necessary that there be a revolution in order to bring it about. Many of the socialists do base their philosophy on Marxist economics, as do the Russian Communists, but break with Marx with respect to the use of violence.

There is considerable difference among socialists, in both the United States and other parts of the world, as to the extent to which they would socialize the economy. Almost all of them agree that the noncompetitive types of enterprise, such as public utilities, should be publicly owned, either through the central government or through some local branch of government (state, county, or city). Most of them also agree that the major instruments of production, such as the manufacturing industries, should eventually be governmentally owned. When it comes to agriculture there is a marked disagreement among the different types of socialistic parties, with very few, among the democratic socialists at least, actually advocating nationalization or collectivization of farms on some kind of a public basis. Many of the democratic socialists (outside of communistic Russia) believe in the private ownership of personal property, such as clothing, cars, and, in most cases, housing. At least private housing is one of the alternatives of most of the democratic Socialist proposals. It is difficult to make an evaluation of this highly emotionalized, controversial issue within the present world scene without being, or appearing to be, somewhat biased. However, most Americans—and this includes most American economists—feel that the socialist "doctrinaire" theorists have oversimplified the problem. Although it might simplify the steps toward solution to have industry owned by government rather than by private enterprise, it does not necessarily solve the problems per se, as the British Labour Party discovered following World War II. Many of the basic economic problems of our society are still present even if we hand the ownership and management of an enterprise over to a representative of the government, or, theoretically, the people. We would still have a conflict of interest between management (which in the case of socialization is directly representative of the government) and the actual workers in industry. In other words, there can be strikes in government-owned enterprises, as Britain discovered. We would still have the problems of deciding how to distribute the proceeds of the productive process. Most American economists, although some of them may favor increased socialization, do not believe that socialization per se is an automatic solution to many of the problems that we are facing.

The social and political systems of the two parts of the world are more divergent than the economic systems. Both systems are characterized by industrialism, mass production, closer integration of industrial operations, and even an increasing measure of economic control and planning. The Russians have, thus far, been free of the scourge of the business cycle, but they have exposed themselves to the inflexibilities of planning, which may produce its own maladjustments. The Russian business manager serves as an agent of the state, just as the American corporate director serves as an agent of the stockholders. Even the financial structure and policies under which enterprise operates in the two systems are not as dissimilar as it might appear.[29]

Cooperatives—Private "Nonprofit" Enterprise

The history of the cooperatives actually goes back much farther than that of some of the other alternatives found here. As a matter of fact, the cooperative is not an independent alternative, but parallels, in a sense, several of the possible alternatives found on the chart. Cooperatives were organized only for a specific purpose, and their proponents did not make any claim that their particular method was one that would solve all problems. However, there are some outstanding enthusiasts who feel that if we could organize a large portion of our economy in the cooperative fashion— cooperatives of producers, perhaps cooperatives of distributors, cooperatives of consumers, retail stores organized without the profit motive but only from the motive of service ("production for use")—we would solve some of the problems that arise out of "exorbitant profits and concentration of too much wealth in the hands of a few people." Furthermore, they believe that this could be done on a basis that would avoid the alleged inefficiency of government-operated enterprises.

Other Possible Economic Analyses

In addition to the various alternatives listed, there are other possible economic analyses. Other possible solutions may come out of these analyses. In addition to the use of nonprofit cooperatives, there is also the idea of profit sharing. In this proposal, firms would be privately owned but would share the profits (or profits over a certain amount) with their workers, and in some cases also with the consumers. This is held to avoid the frequent conflict of interest between the workers and the management found under non-profit-sharing systems. We cannot go into the details of this and of other analyses, but brief résumés will be presented of a few alternatives that we feel are particularly pertinent or promising.

[29]Cf. George P. Adams, Jr., *Competitive Economic Systems* (New York: Crowell, 1955), p. 362.

Scandinavia—The Middle Way.   In the Scandinavian countries, Sweden, Norway, and Denmark, we find mixed economies that have gone farther away from laissez faire, perhaps, than any of the other countries of Western civilization. In Sweden, for example, the enterprise is divided as follows: private enterprise, one third; governmentally owned enterprises, one third; and cooperatives, one third. It is interesting and intriguing to note that during the period of the Depression, when such countries as the United States were suffering seriously, Sweden maintained a fairly even keel even though her exports were down because of the condition of world trade. Apparently by having a mixed economy (although perhaps there were other factors involved), she was able to avoid the excesses of the business cycle that affected the other countries of the world.

Drucker's "New Society."   Peter Drucker, in *The New Society*,[30] has made an analysis of the present American industrial system and points out that we are not headed either toward more socialism or communism or back toward laissez-faire capitalism. He makes an analysis of the industrial process particularly from the point of view of the production process itself in the individual enterprise, even when within the large corporation. This analysis is largely based upon the human relations existing within the enterprise. He points out that whether the eventual ownership of the enterprise is governmental, individual, or corporate, the same types of problems are faced in the relationship between management responsible for the over-all functioning of the productive process and the laborer carrying on some atomistic part of the process.

The laboring man, powerless as an individual in bargaining with management over his share of the proceeds of the productive process, has joined with others in organizing himself into a union. The union has been formed primarily for the purpose of trying to get for its members as large a share as possible of the returns from the productive process. In this narrow, limited view into which the union has been forced by the circumstances of its existence, the larger welfare of the productive enterprise, the worker, and the consumer sometimes is not considered. In some cases the union leadership has manipulated the members to serve its own selfish interests. In these cases it is imperative that the union itself be democratized in the opportunity for "feedback" from the rank and file to the union management.

Certain technical matters in regard to the productive process must be left with management. The narrow self-interest of the individual workers may be destructive of the productive process. Management must be in the position of making production decisions. Each enterprise must make a profit, whether operating as the only enterprise of a private company, as a government enterprise, or as one of the many atomistic enterprises of one large corporation.

Mr. Drucker thinks that his so-called *new society,* or *industrial society,* is "beyond" capitalism and socialism.[31] He apparently feels that his proposal would be less advantageous in an industrial system of the kind favored by democratic socialism than it would be in one in which the legal ownership

[30]Peter L. Drucker, *The New Society* (New York: Harper, 1950).
[31]Ibid., p. 351.

was still vested in private or corporate management hands. Management must be allowed to run the productive process on an efficient "business" basis, receiving whatever powers are necessary in order to make decisions consistent with the most efficient production.

Galbraith's Theory of "Countervailing Power." Another interesting analysis of the American capitalistic system is that of John K. Galbraith.[32] Galbraith has been concerned about analyzing the dynamics of the whole system, as opposed to Drucker's analysis of each enterprise within the system. Galbraith, however, agrees with Drucker that American capitalism has moved far away from laissez-faire capitalism as it was earlier conceived. He thinks that it has been gradually supplanted by a *differing* system; until now its success can be explained entirely in terms of a *differing theory*. This is the theory that he calls *countervailing power*. This explains the success of our economic system because of somewhat automatic regulation by the opposing giants, the many big corporations, big labor, and big government. This process replaces the automatic self-regulation of the old laissez-faire system.

As industry got larger and larger and control of the various productive processes became concentrated more and more in the hands of monopolies or oligopolies, an attempt was made to restore the competitive system by the means of "trust-busting." Galbraith indicates that this proves unsatisfactory because the large size of the industries is necessitated by the type of technology we have.

Monopolies, however, might well have tended to lead to inefficiency of the productive process and a static condition that would have been bad in terms of general industrial progress had it not been for the developing of countervailing power against monopolies. One of the bulwarks of this power is the force of the labor unions. With the help of the government, through the National Industrial Relations Act as well as through earlier laws passed to assist labor in its fight against management, the unions were able to obtain concessions in regard to their share of the returns of the productive process, as well as in other matters such as working conditions. Also, agriculture, a group that found it very difficult to organize itself to maintain its fair share of the productive process, was aided (after political pressure upon the government) through various forms of governmental action such as price-support methods.

According to Galbraith, these are not the only countervailing powers. Corporations are consumers of the products of other corporations. An example of this kind is supplied by General Motors and United States Steel. In other cases, corporations such as the Atlantic and Pacific Tea Company or Sears, Roebuck are marketing organizations and are able to match or even master the manufacturers in price and quality arguments. In between, and keeping an eagle eye over the procedure, is the force of the government, which has become over a period of years and still is becoming an ever stronger factor in the whole productive process through laws of various kinds to prevent any one element in the economy from overstepping itself. This

[32]John K. Galbraith, *American Capitalism: Concept of Countervailing Power* (Boston: Houghton Mifflin, 1952). See also John K. Galbraith, *The New Industrial State* (Boston: Houghton Mifflin, 1967).

whole process has led to a system of checks and balances, which Galbraith gives as the reason why the American capitalistic system has been able to go to great heights of productive efficiency and capacity.

People's Capitalism. Another possible interpretation of ways in which our economic system might move is toward what is called people's capitalism. Kelso and Adler, in their book *The Capitalist Manifesto,* indicate that the best direction in which the economic system could move would be toward more and more mass stock ownership.[33] This has happened to some extent, of course, for there is widespread ownership of the stocks in some of our large companies. There is, however, still high concentration of the deciding power of the companies in the hands of a relatively few persons. Kelso and Adler suggest that laws be set up to prevent overconcentration of stock ownership by a few people and to encourage the widespread purchase of stocks. Provisions could be made for people to buy stock in smaller quantities without the expense of purchase through a broker because this makes it somewhat prohibitive for small investors at present. Stock, for example, might be sold "over the counter" at banks or even stores. This proposal is based on making an economic system like profit-sharing companies in which the general public, workers and others, would feel an important vested interest in the capitalistic system, as do the present owners and managers.

According to an article in *Time* (June 24, 1970), Kelso has set up the Institute for the Study of Economic Systems in Washington, D.C.[34] His plan envisions loans to people without money; these loans would be paid back by the dividends from the stocks purchased. By abolishing corporate income taxes, the dividends might be as high as 20 per cent. The loss in corporate income tax would be made up by the greater take in personal income tax.

AMERICANS WILL PROBABLY SEEK A PRAGMATIC SOLUTION

In spite of the fact that all shades of opinion are present in the American social scene, the vast majority of Americans are probably very close to the middle of the road as far as range of opinion on the world scene is concerned. There are few Americans who are at the extremes of communism or other forms of dictatorial socialism, only a relatively few who are in favor of a thorough democratic socialism, and only a very few at the opposite extreme who would expound some form of neofascism or a closely related view. Some of our extreme reactionaries are very close to a fascistic point of view, even though not openly avowing such. This last group, in spite of the publicity sometimes given to them, makes up a relatively small portion of our population.

In spite of the vehemence with which Americans fight their political battles and in spite of the fact that they quite often seem to be irresistibly committed to one of a set of alternatives, the probability is that Americans in the future will continue to solve their problems in the same way as they have in the past. This is by the method of a pragmatic solution, one by one,

[33]Louis O. Kelso and Mortimer J. Adler, *The Capitalist Manifesto* (New York: Random House, 1958).

[34]See also Louis Orth Kelso and Patricia Hetter, *Two Factor Theory: The Economics of Reality* (New York: Vintage, 1968).

of the problems that they face. Americans apparently hesitate to theorize and thus solve a whole set of problems together. Once having achieved an immediate solution, they can rationalize it in terms of their present theory or as an exception to their theory, without developing a new theory to encompass the complete solution. It is quite likely that Americans will choose to improvise or to select solutions for a particular problem from the many alternatives listed above. This means that at times the solution will be delayed beyond the point at which it should be put into effect. However, there is apparently a growing feeling that economic problems can be solved by man because they *are* "man-made." Consequently, the public will not be very patient unless some sort of solution is attempted. The use of better measuring devices to determine the direction our economic system is going, on the one hand, and to determine the efficacy of economic remedies, on the other, will help to determine the direction of economic remedies and their success as they are tried.

RESPONSIBILITY OF SCHOOLS TO EDUCATE PUPILS TO UNDERSTAND CONSEQUENCES OF ECONOMIC TRENDS

Economic problems are basic to our lives. The growth of technical economic knowledge recently has been so rapid that very few of the American people understand such problems. It can be stated more strongly: the American people are economically illiterate. Conceptions about economics are held that are manifestly and demonstrably false. Many of the decisions that are made in economic matters must be formed through public opinion and public action. The people need to be better educated as to how the economic system works, what its problems are, and the possible alternatives for their solution.

Before we take up other implications in the study of economics, it is interesting to note that economists have recently become interested in studying education from an economic point of view. A good case in point is the study by Schultz.[35] This study of education has been interested in determining what the costs of education are if the loss of earning power while going to school is included. Typically, this has not been considered in the total when the amount of money spent on education is announced. Further, the economists are interested in knowing what is the return on investment in terms of "human capital." In searching for the sources of improved productivity in gross national product, one of the things which has to be considered is capital. The normal definition of this term refers, of course, to the plant, equipment, and methods of productivity used. However, the economists have discovered another factor called human capital, a part of the capital stock. Part of this human capital is related directly to education. Some of it is indirectly related to education to the extent to which the culture has been improved by education. The economists make an estimate concerning the rate of return on the investment in terms of improved national product as well as in terms of earnings that accrue to the individual concerned. Schultz reports that for four years of high school the

[35]Theodore W. Schultz, *The Economic Value of Education* (New York: Columbia University Press, 1963).

return on the investment was 14.3 per cent per year. College education had a return of approximately 11 per cent per year. Schultz reports a 35 per cent return per year on elementary education based on the return on the total cost over the life span of one's earnings.[36] The import of these data seems to indicate that education gives the highest return on the investment both from the standpoint of the investment by government and of the investment by the individual in loss of time and in money for his education.

Servan-Schreiber's comments are again appropriate here:

> Working from Denison's theory about the importance of education, two other scholars have made a comparative study of the United States and of other industrialized countries. The study of Dimitri Chorfas of the University of Washington covers 24 countries: that by the Frenchman, Raymond Poignant, together with the Dutchman, Kohnstamm, is the first complete comparative study of education in nine developed countries (of the U.S., the six Common Market nations, Britain, and the Soviet Union).
>
> They show that France, spurred by unprecedented population growth, has made great efforts. Between 1950 and 1960 the percentage of new teachers in France has been the highest in the world: a 126 per cent increase for secondary school teachers, and 102 per cent for teachers in lycees—against 75 per cent increase in the U.S. and 56 per cent in the U.S.S.R. For university professors the French growth rate is also the highest: an increase of 131 per cent, against 58 per cent in the U.S., 57 per cent in Britain, and 63 per cent in the U.S.S.R.
>
> This increase in the number of teachers has obviously been accompanied by an increase in the number of students, but not enough to bring France— which leads Western Europe—up to the level we need. In this respect, the chart by Professor Chorafas is instructive:

EDUCATION
(From the Chorafas Report)

COUNTRY	NUMBER OF STUDENTS IN 1966	AS PERCENTAGE OF THE POPULATION FROM 20 TO 24
United States	5,526,000	43 per cent
U.S.S.R.	4,000,000	24 ,, ,,
Japan	1,370,000	13.5 ,, ,,
France	500,000	16 ,, ,,
Italy	284,000	7 ,, ,,
Germany	280,000	7.5 ,, ,,
Canada	230,000	22.5 ,, ,,
Britain	165,000	7 ,, ,,
Sweden	62,000	11 ,, ,,
Belgium	54,000	10 ,, ,,

> Thus France and all of Europe lag far behind the United States, where 43 per cent of people between 20 and 24 are enrolled in colleges and universities. In the Soviet Union the figure is 24 per cent; while in Europe it varies between 16 and 7 per cent. Britain is in the worst position—which, according to Denison, explains a great deal about the current stagnation of Britain's economy despite a strong industrial base.

[36]Ibid., pp. 62–63.

During the most recent year for which figures are available, 101,000 people graduated from colleges in the Common Market countries (180 million population) as against 450,000 in the United States, with nearly the same population (190 million). Americans had four times as many graduates as the Common Market countries.

Looking at it by fields of study, the situation is even clearer, especially in science and technology. In the Common Market there were 25,000 graduates with degrees in science, or 1.1 per cent of those in their age group. In the U.S. there were 78,000 graduates in science, or 3.9 per cent of those in their age group. Thus the U.S. is producing scientists and engineers three times faster than the Common Market.

Finally, these reports show what chance children of manual laborers and less fortunate elements of the population have for higher education. In France, workers form 56 per cent of the population, but their children represent only 12.6 per cent of the students. The same is true in other Common Market countries: 11.5 per cent for Belgium, 10 per cent in Holland, and 7.5 per cent in Germany. In the U.S., on the other hand, *from three to five times as many children of workers and farmers have access to higher education as in the Common Market countries.*

Poignant concludes: "Looking at access to higher education from a social point of view, it is clear that the Common Market countries, individually and collectively, offer little opportunity for higher education to children in the lower income groups." By projecting Denison's theory of expansion, this partly explains American pre-eminence in the most advanced areas of science and industry. Here is where all the elements come together; growth and justice, education and mobility, industrial and intellectual progress. In the last part of this book we will try to zero in on these elements, for they can save us from fatalism and discouragement.

The growing "technological gap" between America and Europe is due primarily to a paucity of higher education, and thus to a relative weakness of science and research. But it is also due to an apparent inability—stemming from a refusal to make an investment, which is precisely the word, in man— to grasp and vigorously apply modern methods of management.[37]

Returning now to the discussion of the study of economics in the American schools: the authors hold that there should be a greater emphasis on economics in the school's curriculum. This does not necessarily mean emphasis on courses in economics. Economic ideas can be taught quite early in the elementary grades and in courses other than economics. Some of this is done now, but much more could and should be done. The fundamental concepts of economics can be made interesting and clear even to average persons in our population. Of course some of the more complex ideas of economics are for the specialist. What the average man needs to understand is the basic outline of economics. We have attempted to present such an outline of the fundamentals of our economic system in these two chapters.

Implications for education of the future growth of automation and of the possible ramifications of atomic energy, however, go much beyond the mere understanding of the economic system that now exists. The long-range question is, "Are we capable of developing a culture that does not depend upon work to give meaning to our lives?" Education must face this question. It calls for revisions in the curriculum, to train the new types of industrial

[37]Servan-Schreiber, op. cit., pp. 72–75. Used by permission.

workers needed—mathematicians, scientists, designers, skilled electronics operators, and those virtuosos who prepare the data-processing tapes. More importantly, everyone will need training to cope with more leisure time.

Man is not a loafer. He degenerates without something to engage his mind and muscles. Studies of workers who retired at sixty-five with no outside interest show many cases of nervous breakdown. In some companies the retired are allowed to go back to the shop and watch somebody else do their jobs.

After its introductory period automation may mean more leisure than man can tolerate. The job of the teaching profession will be to transform this leisure into meaningful activity, so that man may escape biological disaster.

Other implications for the school flow from an understanding of the nature of the free enterprise system through which America has been able to make great progress because of freedom, in the sense of the right to make suggestions and to carry them out. The authors would like to encourage some of the activities the schools have carried on in the past, while asking them to accentuate and extend them in the future.

The trend in the schools toward stimulation of self-expression and creativity and the more recent movement toward helping youth to work together in groups are elements which assist the school in teaching for values which are dominant in our free enterprise society.

The schools are doing a great many things in the area of creativity, group planning, and group work. From time to time it is necessary to clarify our thinking and to explore new possibilities of improvement in this area. Conflicts concerning the fine points of the meaning of *free enterprise* are not likely to have meaning in the early levels of school.

The school must help the child clarify those elements which are not in conflict. Moreover, criticism which teachers and other citizens make of interpretations of free enterprise should not be regarded as a criticism of free enterprise itself. Although teachers should have the freedom to express their own opinions in the classroom, the teacher should first fulfill his responsibility to discuss all sides of such questions. Such freedom is a part of our free enterprise system.

In summary, free enterprise in the United States is envisioned as one of the fundamental values of our democratic culture, a value which the school should emphasize. Although the school should not take sides when aspects of the concept are under dispute, the school should help actively and openly boys and girls to understand the concept and conflicting ideas concerning it at their level of maturity. Stimulating and developing creativity, independent and critical thinking, and the ability to work with others in group activity (without sacrificing individual creativity) are among the more important contributions that the school can make. The concept is to be thought of as applying as well to nonprofit-making enterprises, such a government, charity, and education. If America can maintain a kind of creative individuality in a world that requires a high degree of coordination, on one hand, and of skilled specialization, on the other, America's future is safe. She will be guaranteed the free flow of ideas and innovations necessary to the growth of society.

SUMMARY

In this chapter the development of one of the outstanding economic systems of the world has been described. The American industrial enterprise compared to that of other nations ranks quite high in total quantity, quality, and productivity per worker.

The first of the over-all trends in the development of the American economy was the rise of the laissez-faire economy and its subsequent breakdown caused by forces that originated within the economy itself and rose out of the emerging technology and the structure of the industrial enterprises. Outstanding also among the trends has been the expansion of productivity in all fields. The American capitalistic system has changed—from the small shop and handicraft system of the earlier period, to the finance-controlled capitalistic enterprises, and on to the large corporations characteristic of the "big business" of the modern period. Economy has shifted from one of scarcity to one of plenty, probably sometime in the 1920's. The over-all trend in the type of enterprises has been the basic shift from the laissez-faire capitalism toward a "mixed" capitalism consisting of both corporation and state capitalism, along with some cooperatives, some state socialism, and some small private enterprises.

The effect of the improved technology on a productive enterprise has been illustrated by charts, with the effect shown of the change in certain factors wages, workweek, prices (other factors being held constant) upon productivity. A description of the American economy in terms of the flow of goods and money has also been presented. The problems of the American economy have been listed: possible concentration of economic power; inequality of wealth and income; monopoly and administered prices; business cycles; technological unemployment; the unbalanced national budget, inflation, and taxation; the growth of big units, labor, government, business; and the changed notions concerning private property. Six alternatives for the American economic system have been set forth; negative laissez faire; positive laissez faire; administered economy by business; administered economy by government; two kinds of governmentally planned economy—i.e., "state capitalism"—"two-front" economy or "Keynesian economics"; and socialistic economy.

Other possible alternatives were discussed but it was pointed out that the Americans will probably seek a pragmatic solution to each of their economic problems as they face them rather than develop some type of clear-cut, doctrinaire base upon which to work out logically solutions for all problems faced.

Selected Bibliography

Abraham, William I. National Income and Economic Accounting. Englewood Cliffs, N.J.: Prentice-Hall, Inc., 1969. 232 pp.

Anderson, C. Arnold, and Mary Jean Bowman (eds.). Education and Economic Development. Chicago: Aldine Publishing Company, 1965. 436 pp.

Armytage, W. H. C. The Rise of the Technocrats: A Social History. London: Routledge and Kegan Paul, 1965. 448 pp.

"Atomic Power: Paradise Lost or Found," Cincinnati Enquirer (February 7, 1971), n.p. Excellent presentation of the possibilities and problems in the use of atomic energy.

Bach, George Leland. *Economics: An Introduction to Analysis and Policy*, Seventh Edition. Englewood Cliffs, N.J.: Prentice-Hall, Inc., 1971. 594 pp.

Bagdikian, Ben H. *The Information Machines*. New York: Harper & Row, Publishers, 1971. 359 pp.

Barnett, Homer G. *Innovation: The Basis of Cultural Change*. New York: McGraw-Hill Book Company, 1953. 462 pp. (Also paperback.)

Bazelon, David T. *The Paper Economy*. New York: Random House, Inc., 1963. 467 pp.

Becker, Gary S. *Human Capital: A Theoretical and Empirical Analysis, with Special Reference to Education*. New York: Columbia University Press, 1964. 187 pp.

Blaug, Mark (ed.). *Economics of Education: Selected Readings*. Baltimore: Penguin Books, Inc., 1968. 442 pp.

Boulding, Kenneth E. *Economics as a Science*. New York: McGraw-Hill Book Company, 1970. 157 pp.

Bowles, Samuel. *Planning Educational Systems for Economic Growth*. Cambridge, Mass.: Harvard University Press, 1969. 245 pp.

Bowman, M. J., et al. (eds.). *Readings in the Economics of Education*. Paris: UNESCO, 1968. 945 pp.

Brickman, William W., and Stanley Lehrer (eds.). *Automation, Education and Human Values*. New York: Apollo, 1969. 419 pp. (Paperback.)

Brzezinski, Zbigniew. *Between Two Ages: America's Role in the Technotronic Era*. New York: The Viking Press, 1970. 334 pp.

Calder, Nigel. *Technopolis: Social Control of the Uses of Science*. New York: Simon & Schuster, Inc., 1970. 376 pp.

Carter, Anne P. *Structural Change in the American Economy*. Cambridge, Mass.: Harvard University Press, 1970. 256 pp.

Center for the Study of Democratic Institutions. *A Conversation: Labor Looks at Labor*. Santa Barbara, Calif.: The Center, 1963. 32 pp.

Cetron, Marvin J. *Technological Forecasting: A Practical Approach*. New York: Technology Forecasting Institute, 1969. 345 pp.

Chase, Stuart. "Two Cheers for Technology," *Saturday Review* (February 20, 1971).

Cohen, Sanford. *Labor in the United States*. Columbus, Ohio: Charles E. Merrill Books, Inc., 1970. 704 pp.

Committee for Economic Development, Research and Policy Committee. *Economic Growth in the United States: Its Past and Future*. New York: The Committee, 1958. 63 pp.

_____. *Union Powers and Union Functions: Toward a Better Balance*. New York: The Committee, 1964. 42 pp. A statement of national policy by the Research Committee of the Committee for Economic Development.

Curtis, Richard, and Elizabeth Hogan. *Perils of the Peaceful Atom: The Myth of Safe Nuclear Power Plants*. Garden City, N.Y.: Doubleday & Company, Inc., 1969. 274 pp.

Darcy, Robert L. "Economic Education for Teachers: Preservice Program," *Bulletin of the National Association of Secondary School Pupils*, Vol. 49 (November, 1965).

Douglas, Jack D. (ed.). *Freedom and Tyranny: Social Problems in a Technological Society*. New York: Alfred A. Knopf, Inc., 1970. 384 pp.

Drucker, Peter F. *The New Society: The Anatomy of the Industrial Order*. New York: Harper & Row, Publishers, 1950. 356 pp. Believes that a "new society" is emerging in the American democratic culture that is neither capitalistic nor communistic. (In paperback also.)

Economic Report of the President: Transmitted to the Congress, February, 1971. With the Annual Report of the Council of Economic Advisers. Washington, D.C.: Government Printing Office, 1971. 306 pp.

Ellul, Jacques. *The Technological Society*. New York: Vintage Books, 1964. 449 pp.

Ferkiss, Victor G. *Technological Man: The Myth and the Reality*. New York: George Braziller, Inc., 1969. 336 pp.

Fischer, Robert B. *Science, Man and Society*. Philadelphia: W. B. Saunders Company, 1971. 124 pp.

Foster, George M. *Traditional Cultures and the Impact of Technological Change*. New York: Harper & Row, Publishers, 1962. 292 pp.

Fromm, Erich. *The Revolution of Hope: Toward A Humanized Technology*. New York: Bantam Books, 1968. 178 pp.

Galbraith, John Kenneth. *The Affluent Society*, Second Edition, Revised. Boston: Houghton Mifflin Company, 1969. 333 pp.

——. *American Capitalism: The Concept of Countervailing Power*. Boston: Houghton Mifflin Company, 1952. 216 pp.

——. *A Contemporary Guide to Economics, Peace and Laughter*. Boston: Houghton Mifflin Company, 1971. 382 pp.

——. *The New Industrial State*. Boston: Houghton Mifflin Company, 1969. 427 pp. (Paperback.)

Ginzberg, Eli (ed.). *Technology and Social Change: Columbia University Seminar on Technology and Social Change*. New York: Columbia University Press, 1964. 158 pp.

Goldman, Marshall I. *The Soviet Economy: Myth and Reality*. Englewood Cliffs, N.J.: Prentice-Hall, Inc., 1968. 176 pp.

Goldsmith, Maurice (ed.). *Technological Innovation and the Economy*. New York: Interscience Publishers, Inc., 1970. 292 pp.

Guillan, Robert. *The Japanese Challenge: The Race to the Year 2000*. Philadelphia: J. B. Lippincott Company, 1970. 352 pp.

Hacker, Andrew. *The End of the American Era*. New York: Atheneum Publishers, 1970. 239 pp.

Hansen, W. Lee (ed.). *Education, Income, and Human Capital*. New York: National Bureau of Economic Research, 1970. 320 pp.

Harrington, Michael. *The Accidental Century*. New York: The Macmillan Company, 1965. 322 pp.

——. *The Other America: Poverty in the United States*. New York: The Macmillan Company, 1962. 191 pp.

Heilbroner, Robert L. *Between Capitalism and Socialism: Essays in Political Economics*. New York: Random House, Inc., 1970. 294 pp.

Holstein, Ralph, Gerard Piel, and Robert Theobald. *Jobs, Machines, and People*. Santa Barbara, Calif.: Center for the Study of Democratic Institutions, 1964. 23 pp.

Howe, Irving (ed.). *The Radical Papers: Essays in Democratic Socialism*. Garden City, N.Y.: Doubleday & Company, Inc., 1966. 378 pp.

Jackson, Philip W. *The Teacher and the Machine*. Pittsburgh: University of Pittsburgh Press, 1968. 90 pp.

Kelso, Louis O., and Mortimer J. Adler. *The Capitalist Manifesto*. New York: Random House, Inc., 1958. 265 pp. Argues for a "capitalist revolution," which in essence would consist of the limitation of capitalist holdings to an individual family and the paying out of all earnings in dividends. All corporate income taxes would be abolished. The corporation would go to the market for additional capital needed for expansion.

Kelso, Louis O., and Patricia Hetter. *Two-Factor Theory: The Economics of Reality*. New York: Vintage Books, 1968. 202 pp.

Keyserling, Leon H. *Agriculture and the Public Interest Toward a New Farm Program*. Washington, D.C.: Conference on Economic Progress, 1965. 123 pp.

——. *Growth with Less Inflation or More Inflation Without Growth?* Washington, D.C.: Conference on Economic Progress, 1970. 79 pp. (Pamphlet.)

Kneller, George F. *Education and Economic Thought*. New York: John Wiley & Sons, Inc., 1968. 139 pp.

Kraft, Richard H. (ed.). *Education and Economic Growth*. Tallahassee: Educational Systems Development Center, Florida State University, 1968. 189 pp.

Kransberg, Melvin, Carroll W. Pursell, Jr. (eds.). *Technology in Western Civilization: The Emergence of Modern Industrial Society, Earliest Time to 1900.* Vol. 1. New York: Oxford University Press, 1956. 795 pp.

Kuhlman, John M. *Economic Problems and Policies.* Pacific Palisades, Calif.: Goodyear Publishing, 1969. 349 pp.

Kunkel, John H. *Society and Economic Growth: A Behavioral Perspective of Social Change.* New York: Oxford University Press, 1970. 368 pp.

Lapp, Ralph E. "Nuclear Power for Electricity," *Current,* No. 127 (March 1971).

Lear, John. "Predicting the Consequences of Technology," *Saturday Review* (March 28, 1970).

Lundberg, Ferdinand. *The Rich and the Super Rich.* New York: Lyle Stuart, 1967. 812 pp.

MacEwan, Arthur, and Thomas E. Weisskopf (eds.) *The Economic Problem: A Book of Readings in Political Economy.* Englewood Cliffs, N.J.: Prentice-Hall, Inc., 1970. 352 pp.

"The Man Who Would Make Everybody Richer," *Time* (June 29, 1970).

Marcson, Simon (ed.). *Automation, Alienation and Anomie.* New York: Harper & Row, Publishers, 1970. 479 pp.

Marriott, R. *Incentive Payment Systems.* London: Staples Press, 1961. 291 pp.

McClelland, David C. *The Achieving Society.* New York: The Free Press, 1961, 512 pp.

——, and David G. Winter. *Motivating Economic Achievement.* New York: The Free Press, 1969. 409 pp.

Mesthene, Emanuel C. *Technological Change: Its Impact on Man and Society.* Cambridge, Mass.: Harvard University Press, 1970. 128 pp.

Meynaud, Jean. *Technocracy.* London: Faber and Faber, 1968. 315 pp.

Michael, Donald N. "Cybernation: The Silent Conquest." Santa Barbara, Calif.: The Center for the Study of Democratic Institutions, 1962. 46 pp.

Morgan, James N., et al. *Income and Welfare in the United States.* New York: McGraw-Hill Book Company, 1964. 531 pp.

Morse, Dean, and Aaron W. Warner (eds.). *Technological Innovation and Society.* New York: Columbia University Press, 1966. 214 pp.

Muller, Herbert J. *The Children of Frankenstein: A Primer on Modern Technology and Human Values.* Bloomington: Indiana University Press, 1970. 431 pp.

Mumford, Lewis. *The Myth of the Machine: The Pentagon of Power,* Vol. II. New York: Harcourt Brace Jovanovich, Inc., 1970. 496 pp.

Myrdal, Gunnar. *Beyond the Welfare State.* New York: Bantam Books, 1969. 239 pp.

Nelkin, Dorothy. *Nuclear Power and Its Critics: The Cayuga Lake Controversy.* Ithaca, N.Y.: Cornell University Press, 1971. 160 pp.

Philipson, Morris (ed.). *Automation: Implications for the Future.* New York: Vintage Books, 1962. 456 pp.

Pincus, John A. (ed.). *Reshaping the World Economy: Rich Countries and Poor.* Englewood Cliffs, N.J.: Prentice-Hall, Inc., 1968. 176 pp.

Poor, Riva (ed.). *4 Days 40 Hours.* Cambridge, Mass.: Bursk and Poor, 1970. 175 pp.

Proxmire, William. *Report from Wasteland: America's Military-Industrial Complex.* New York: Frederick A. Praeger, Inc., 1970. 248 pp.

Ramsey, Paul. *Fabricated Man: The Ethics of Genetic Control.* New Haven: Yale University Press, 1970. 174 pp.

Reich, Charles A. *The Greening of America.* New York: Random House, Inc., 1970. 395 pp.

Revel, Jean François. *Without Marx or Jesus.* Garden City, N.Y.: Doubleday & Company, Inc., 1970. 269 pp.

Riesman, David. *Abundance for What? And Other Essays.* Garden City, N.Y.: Doubleday & Company, Inc., 1964. 610 pp.

Rogers, Virgil M. "What Teachers Should Know About Automation," *NEA Journal,* Vol. 52, No. 7 (October 1963).

Rohrlich, George F. (ed.). *Social Economics for the 1970's: Programs for Social Security, Health, and Manpower.* New York: Dunellen, 1970. 189 pp.

Rose, J. (ed.). *Technological Injury.* New York: Gordon and Breach, 1970. 224 pp.

Rosen, Bernard C., Harry J. Crockett, Jr., and Clyde Nunn (eds.). *Achievement in American Society.* New York: Schenkman, 1969. 653 pp.

Rostow, W. W. *The Stages of Economic Growth: A Non-Communistic Manifesto.* Cambridge, Mass.: Harvard University Press, 1960. 179 pp. A comparative study of national development based on a theory of economic growth.

Samuelson, Paul A. *Economics: An Introductory Analysis,* Eighth Edition. New York. McGraw-Hill Book Company, 1970. 810 pp.

Scheiber, Harry N. *United States Economic History: Selected Readings.* New York: Alfred A. Knopf, Inc., 1964. 583 pp.

Schultz, Theodore W. *The Economic Value of Education.* New York: Columbia University Press, 1963. 92 pp.

Servan-Schreiber, Jean-Jacques. *The American Challenge.* New York: Atheneum Publishers, 1967. 291 pp.

Sharpe, William F. *The Economics of Computers.* New York: Columbia University Press, 1969. 571 pp.

Sievers, Allen M. *Revolution, Evolution, and the Economic Order.* Englewood Cliffs, N.J.: Prentice-Hall, Inc., 1964. 173 pp.

Smith, Adam. *The Wealth of Nations.* New York: Modern Library, 1937. A classic. (Also in paperback, two volumes, 1963, Irwin.)

Staar, Richard E. (ed.). *Aspects of Modern Communism.* Columbia: University of South Carolina Press, 1968. 416 pp.

Staley, Charles E. *International Economics.* Englewood Cliffs, N.J.: Prentice-Hall, Inc., 1970. 400 pp.

Sykes, Gerald. *The Cool Millennium.* Englewood Cliffs, N.J.: Prentice-Hall, Inc., 1967. 280 pp.

Tesconi, Charles A., Jr. "Bureautechnocracy: An Emerging Organizational Pattern," *The Journal of Educational Thought,* Vol. 5, No. 1 (April 1971).

———. "Bureautechnocracy: A New Perspective on Schools and Society," *Proceedings of the Second Annual Meeting of the American Educational Studies Association,* Chicago (February 25–26, 1970).

Theobald, Robert (ed.). *The Guaranteed Income: Next Step in Socioeconomic Evolution?* Garden City, N.Y.: Doubleday & Company, Inc., 1967. 233 pp.

Toffler, Alvin. *Future Shock.* New York: Random House, Inc., 1970. 505 pp.

Touraine, Alain. *The Post-Industrial Society: Tomorrow's Social History—Classes, Conflicts and Culture in the Programmed Society.* New York: Random House, Inc., 1971. 244 pp.

UNESCO. *Readings in the Economics of Education.* Paris: United Nations Educational, Scientific and Cultural Organization, 1968. 945 pp.

U.S. Bureau of the Census. *Statistical Abstract of the United States: 1970.* 91st Edition. Washington, D.C.: U.S. Department of Commerce, Bureau of the Census, 1970. 1,018 pp.

Vaizey, John. *The Economics of Education.* London: Faber and Faber, 1962. 165 pp.

"Where Is the Dollar Going?" *Saturday Review* (March 6, 1971). Articles by Robert Leachman, J. A. Livingston, and Courtney C. Brown.

Wilson, Mitchell A., and the editors of *Life. Energy.* New York: Time, Inc., 1963. 200 pp.

Windham, Douglas. *Education, Equality and Income Redistribution.* Lexington, Mass.: D. C. Heath & Company, 1970. 120 pp.

Wirth, Arthur G. *Education in the Technological Society.* New York: Intext Educational Publishers, 1972. 237 pp.

Wogaman, Philip. *Guaranteed Annual Income: The Moral Issues.* Nashville: Abingdon Press, 1968. 158 pp.

Selected Films

A Is for Atom (GE), 15 min. An animated cartoon on basic atomic information.

The Age of Specialization (McGraw-Hill), 30 min. From the country store of 1900 to the complex specialization of today.

Allocating Our Resources (Carousel), 30 min. America has rejected the mechanism of total planning; however, because of our desire for fair distribution of goods or for reasons of efficiency, we have put some restrictions on a totally free market. The film illustrates some of the areas where the government has limited the free market as the sole criterion of economic allocation.

American Farmer (Ford Motor Co.), 28 min. An intimate and beautifully photographed story of a modern farmer and the changes wrought in his life by mechanization and scientific farming.

American Harvest (Jam Handy Organization), 29 min. Surveys American production, highlighting the latest developments in the mechanization of agriculture, the integration of agriculture with creative chemistry, and the newest, largest, and most efficient operations in agriculture, industry, transportation, and distribution.

America on the Edge of Abundance (Indiana).

Atomic Energy (Encyclopaedia Britannica), 10 min. Animated drawings on concepts fundamental to understanding the nature of atomic energy and its releases.

Atomic Power (McGraw-Hill), 28 min. A basic film on atomic power and on the bomb, produced by the March of Time.

Beginnings and Growth of Industrial America (Coronet), 11 min. Discussing economic and social change in the period between the Revolutionary and Civil wars, the film shows the development of American manufacturing from a system of home crafts to an industrialized factory system. Factors that contributed to industrial growth—inventions, investments, and labor—are explained. The film includes many reconstructed historical scenes, such as Hopewell Village and Slater's Mill.

Cage (McGraw-Hill), 29 min. Portrays Hugh Martin, a capable business executive, caught on the treadmill of a competitive society. Suggests that each man has to find his own way out of the cage that modern living imposes on everyone.

Capitalism (Coronet), 11 min. In this film students see some important aspects of the capitalistic system—private property, profit, competition, freedom of contract, and free enterprise. A high school radio forum provides an opportunity to listen to the conflicting opinions of several people, each of whom tries to tell what our system means to him.

The Case of Competition (Carousel), 30 min. The film points out that competition begets lower prices, provides a greater variety of products, and is generally favorable to all consumers. The film examines how government and business might view four subjects outside the area of competition—monopoly, labor, profits, and subsidies—and illustrates a "self-fulfilling prophecy."

Communism (UWF), 32 min. Documentary film on communism and its history, contrast between communism and the American system, and a warning to avoid labeling as Communists all who disagree with the majority.

Competition and Big Business (Encyclopaedia Britannica), 22 min. Assists in clarifying the meaning of competition by analyzing the role of big business in terms of its bearing on entry into the market, technological progress, and the problem of monopoly in a society where public interest and social responsibility is crucial.

The Cooperative and the Community (Social Science), 12 min. Shows high school students in a current problems class defining the difference between a private corporation and a cooperative. Defines and gives examples of three general types of cooperatives and then describes in some detail various marketing cooperatives.

Crossroads for America (Cincinnati Chamber of Commerce), 30 min. What America is, what it has to offer, and what it could become. The film exposes and explodes communism from a practical point of view.

The Edge of Abundance (N.E.T.), 60 min. British television explores consequences of computer-oriented society in the United States.

Enough for All (Massey-Harris), 40 min. A review of agricultural science and its application to modern farming. Basic scientific developments and techniques in the field of agriculture demonstrate the ever-increasing ability of agriculture to meet the food requirements of a growing population.

Farmers Working Together (United World), 19 min. Describes the operations, organization, and general activities of farmer cooperatives through the United States.

A Free Economy: Theory and Practice (Encyclopaedia Britannica), 30 min. The film outlines the essential ingredients of a classical, or laissez-faire, model of a free economy and shows how this has become a myth in the United States.

Goals and Growth (Carousel), 30 min. In the film it is explained how we must achieve continued or accelerated growth in the GNP. The importance of the question of choice, especially in the context of economic freedom, is revealed.

How We Live in America (The American Economic Foundation), 30 min. each. A series of nine films on economics. Factually well done. Strongly favorable to the American competitive system.

Introduction to Foreign Trade (Coronet), 10 min. First establishes the importance of foreign trade to our economy and then presents a general picture of the mechanics of international commerce. The role of monetary standards and control, national policies in reference to those controls, distribution of raw materials and markets are shown. Then, in an actual exchange of goods, the detailed domestic and foreign operations involved in the sale, shipment, and payment are portrayed.

Is Gold Obsolete? (ICF), 15 min. This film examines the traditional function of gold as a base for credit. Why has it lasted for so many centuries? Is it truly a satisfactory standard in modern times, or is the productivity of a nation a better gauge?

Knowledge and Skills (Association), 21 min. Alex Drier reports on today's growing need for workers with skilled and technological knowledge and shows how vocational training courses are preparing both young and old for future jobs.

A Look at Communism (NEP), 13 min. Basic philosophy, tactics, and strategy. A look at dialectical materialism, economic determinism, and atheism.

A Look at Socialism (NEP), 13 min. A thorough study of the philosophy and record of socialism in practice. Uses dramatization, actual scenes in England, and other material.

Man Who Changed the World (TFC), 11 min. Story of James Hargreaves, English spinner, whose invention of the spinning jenny in 1767 laid the foundation for the machine age. How the conflict between man and machines came about.

The Meaning of the Industrial Revolution (Coronet), 11 min. Tells of the beginning and the meaning of the industrial revolution.

Of Men and Machines (N.E.T.), 30 min. Investigation of man–machine relationships.

Productivity: Key to Plenty (EBF), 20 min. Emphasizes that greater use of machine power has given America top place in productivity, with resultant high standards of living. Research by the Twentieth Century Fund.

The Rise of Organized Labor (McGraw-Hill), 18 min. Explains the economic reasons that forced workers to join unions. Illustrates the past and present problems and responsibilities of unions in our economic system.

Seed for Tomorrow (Brandon), 20 min. Surveys the problems of the small farmer and discusses how the cooperative effort of the National Farmers Union can help the farmer to stay on the land.

The Story of Creative Capital (U.S. Chamber of Commerce), 16 min. A clever animated film of the evolution of business and capital investment in this country. It shows where capital comes from and what it does.

Sweden (McGraw-Hill), 22 min. Narrated by Walter Cronkite, this film explains the cradle-to-the-grave security experienced by the Swedish people. It answers such questions as, "Is it worth it?" "What are the drawbacks?" Swedish leaders in several fields are interviewed on the central issue of whether the nation's welfare state legislation is related to its chronically high rates of antisocial behavior.

Traveling the Middle Way in Sweden (Harmon), 90 min. Divided into three two-reel units, each of which may be obtained separately. A pictorial record of Sweden's progress through a coordination of public ownership and consumers and agricultural cooperatives. Unit I: Land of Sweden; Unit II: Consumer Cooperatives; Unit III: Agricultural Cooperatives.

Trip to Cooperative Europe (Co-op League), 20 min. A first-hand report on "co-ops" in seven of Europe's most cooperatively developed countries. Covers cooperative development from the original Toad Lane Store in Rochdale to the modern co-op factories in Sweden. Describes how the cooperatives of England, Scotland, France, Holland, Denmark, Finland, and Sweden are working to strengthen their nations' economies, which were badly shattered by the war.

Trouble in Paradise (Association), 12 min. An animated film that shows what inflation is, how to recognize it, and how to solve it. It shows further how it reduces purchasing power and threatens the foundations of free enterprise.

The '29 Boom and '30's Depression (Atlantis Productions), 45 min. Re-creating this period in American history, the film examines the prosperity and boom of the late 1920's with special attention to factors which later led to the Depression.

Two Views on Socialism (Coronet), 15 min. Arguments for and against the socialistic proposals.

U.S.A.: Trouble in Paradise (Audio-Visual Center), 50 min.

Valley of Tennessee (U.S. Government), 30 min. Change in agricultural methods made possible by TVA.

Valley Town (New York University), 27 min. The story of how machines made a boom town with factories running at top speed, stores crowded with shoppers, and money flowing freely and of how more machines broke it. Consider the problem of capable men thrown out of jobs because of high-speed machinery. Gives an idea of what this does to the spirit of the man and of the effect on the family. Finally offers as one solution the constant training of adults to keep them abreast of new developments for new and better jobs.

Waves of Green (Ford Motor Co.), 43 min. This is the dramatic pictorial story of the amazing development of American agriculture resulting from the combined efforts and skills of science and industry, the land-grant colleges, and, on the local level, the county agent.

What Is Automation? (Film Associates), 14 min. Automated factory where workers tend machines. (For junior and senior high school students.)

What We Have (American Economic Foundation), 15 min. An active, dynamic presentation of the meaning of the free-enterprise system—from the standpoint of production, consumption, and investment. Basic economic freedoms are pointed out.

Where People Count (Midland), 25 min. Story of two families and the importance of various kinds of cooperative to them; how co-ops begin and grow; democratic participation and ownership.

Why Play Leapfrog? (Harding College), 10 min. Shows how increases in wages result in increased prices. Points out that wage raises based on increased productivity increase purchasing power, but that wage raises without corresponding increases in productivity force prices higher, so that the two frequently leapfrog.

Years of Progress (Chrysler Corp.), 32 min. An informative picture whose primary objective is to acquaint students with the unique and outstanding facilities for research and engineering that exist for the purpose of creating new and improved products in the interest of broader services to public needs.

Part III

Problems Facing the Individual in Modern American Society

In Part III, the authors have selected typical problems in modern American society and have gone into some detail in an analysis of them. In many cases implications are drawn for the school, in the broad context of the point of view set up in the first two parts. The types of problems discussed in this part and the choice of individual problems for discussion within each type are not intended to be exhaustive; but it is hoped they will be typical and will give the student a well-balanced overview with respect to the important trends in the present American society, the nature of persistent current problems, and some of the implications for the school of these problems and trends.

Chapter 6

■■■■■■□□□□□□□□□

Problems of Family Life

It is fitting that our study of problems facing the individual in modern American society should commence with a consideration of the problems of the family. This most ancient and venerable institution has become one of the institutions most commonly identified as doomed to extinction in this era of rapid social change. Social critics have been predicting since before V-J Day that marriage and the family rapidly were becoming extinct. How accurate have these predictions been? In 1969 there were 2.146 million marriages in America, almost equaling the all-time high of 1946.[1] In a newsletter circulated privately to businessmen, predictions for the 1970's included growth in the number of families at 1.8 per cent per year.

It is not necessary to share a belief in the theory of the decline and fall of marriage and the family, of course, to recognize that "American families are in trouble—trouble so deep and pervasive as to threaten the future of our nation."[2] It is not only the United States that is experiencing this phenomenon. It is true of all modern industrial societies, but Patricia Coffin notes that marriage and the family are in more trouble in America than elsewhere. She states, "This disintegration of the home is a worldwide phenomenon, but the symptoms are most acute in our own materialistic-militarist society."[3]

It is undeniable that the functions of the family are changing. Parsons refers to this change as "differentiation," meaning the "increasing specialization that takes place so that certain functions formerly carried out by one unit are taken over by other specialized units, while the original unit concentrates on fewer functions."[4] Certainly the concept of "differentiation" differs dramatically from the concept of "disintegration" as pursued by many modern writers on marriage and the family. Many writers point to such evidence of "disintegration" as the rising divorce rate, the irresponsibility of youth, the Women's Liberation movement, isolation (and economic neglect)

[1] Joan Cook, "Marriage," *Ladies Home Journal*, September, 1971, p. 197.

[2] "The American Family: Future Uncertain," *Time*, December 28, 1970, p. 40.

[3] Patricia Coffin, "The American Family," *Look*, January 26, 1971, p. 21.

[4] Hyman Rodman, "Talcott Parsons' Views of the Changing American Family," in J. Ross Eshlemon (ed.), *Perspectives in Marriage and the Family* (Boston: Allyn and Bacon, 1969), p. 94.

of the aged, and the financial distress of near kin in extended illness. The differentiation theory accommodates these changes, not only conceiving of concentration on fewer functions but also conceiving of new functions created by the very nature of societal adaptation to industrial society. Of the eight traditional functions of the family—economic, status-giving, educational, religious, recreational, protective–procreational, and affectional—only the procreational and affectional remain.[5] The state (schools, police departments, welfare departments, and so on), the church, and the industrial society largely have assimilated the other traditional functions. A commonly accepted statement of the newer functions of the family is by Murdock, who postulates (1) that the nuclear family (man, woman, and minor children, if any) is universal in industrial society and (2) that it has four basic functions: (a) socialization, (b) economic cooperation, (c) reproduction, and (d) sexual relations.[6] Bell and Vogel further stress the differentiation of the nuclear family, as contrasted to the extended kinship family, in noting, "certain activities and functions performed by the nuclear family in industrial societies have increased in recent years. For example, the care of infants, household maintenance, and individual tension management, formerly performed in large part by the extended family or the community, are now almost exclusively the province of the nuclear family."[7] It is agreed that the family is changing but it seems to be here to stay.

The importance that students of the family attach to this institution as a determinant of the entire warp and woof of our present social fabric may be gleaned from the following statement:

> This broad overlap of generations is what makes the family, under our present type of social organization, the most basic of all social groupings. It is the institution recognized by society as being chiefly responsible for biological survival and social well-being, for it provides a socially approved method both of bearing and rearing children. The family provides almost the total social environment of the child for the first five years in its life and a very considerable portion of its environment for many years thereafter. It is the matrix of human personality. To this small primary group the state entrusts the initial care and training of its future citizens in the most formative period of their lives. This makes home and family the center of our total culture pattern.[8]

Despite the consensus among modern authorities with respect to the vital importance of the family, it is only in the past four decades that serious and systematic study of the family has been undertaken. In reviewing this research, Baber says, "All these efforts together have thus far been able to make only a slight impression on the work needing to be done."[9] Any serious consideration of family life courses for inclusion in the curriculum

---

[5]William F. Ogburn, "Social Change and the Family," in Robert F. Winch and Louis Wolf Goodman (eds.), *Selected Studies in Marriage and the Family*, Third Edition (New York: Holt, 1968), p. 60.

[6]Ira L. Reiss, "The Universality of the Family: A Conceptual Analysis," in Eshlemon, op. cit., p. 37

[7]Norman W. Bell and Ezra F. Vogel (eds.), *A Modern Introduction to the Family* (New York: The Free Press, 1968), p. 7.

[8]From *Marriage and the Family* (p. 1), by Ray E. Baber. Copyright 1953 by McGraw-Hill Book Company, Inc. Used with permission of McGraw-Hill Book Company.

[9]Ibid., p. 647.

has been of even more recent origin. The first impetus came from the youth on college campuses who wanted to know "how to meet desirable members of the opposite sex, how to attract them, how to choose a mate wisely, how best to practice sex relations and birth control, how to spend . . . money intelligently, and how to bring up children." [10] The noncredit, guest-lecture, loosely organized "courses" originally designed to meet this need gradually are giving way to systematic courses in family and marriage, which are given usually in the sociology department. Bowman takes an optimistic view of the quality of these courses, even though he recognizes their shortcomings in the lack of specialized preparation of the instructors, with attendant problems of inadequate materials and facilities designed for adapting the courses to the needs of prospective teachers. [11]

The high schools are beginning to see the need for family-life education, only to realize that adequate teachers are scarce. A report of one of the most comprehensive surveys of potential sources of teachers in this field in the high schools, with guidelines for their training, was published by the American Social Hygiene Association. [12]

Underlying this chapter, then, are three basic assumptions:

1. The family remains one of the most important institutions in modern culture.
2. Research on the family is limited, but enough materials of recent origin are available for a scholarly presentation.
3. Family-life education in the high school is in such an exploratory stage that any propositions presented by our authors must be considered as tentative suggestions only.

Proceeding upon these assumptions, this chapter will develop (1) the sociological significance of the family; (2) trends in the changing nature of the family; (3) reasons for the trends and present status in the changing nature, characteristics, and functions of the family; (4) problems facing the modern American family; and (5) tentative solutions to these problems, with stress upon family-life education from the cradle to the grave.

SOCIOLOGICAL SIGNIFICANCE OF THE FAMILY

The Family Remains One of the Major Institutions of Society

Several institutions have a pervasive influence upon most individuals from the cradle to the grave. The church, the state, and the family are prime among these. It is a commonly accepted tenet of the science of social psychology that those institutions that have primary contact with an individual make the most significant and lasting impressions upon both his personality and his behavior. The family, by definition, is a primary group. Burgess, Locke, and Thomas define the family in terms of the following four characteristics.

[10]Willard Waller and Reuben Hill, *The Family: A Dynamic Interpretation* (New York: Dryden, 1951), p. x.

[11]Henry A. Bowman, "Marriage Education in the Colleges," *Journal of Social Hygiene*, December 1949, 407–17

[12]American Social Hygiene Association, *Education for Personal and Family Living: A Working Guide for Colleges* (New York: American Social Hygiene Association, 1955).

1. The family is composed of persons united by the ties of marriage, blood, or adoption.

2. The members of a family typically live together under one roof and constitute a single household.

3. The family is a unity of interacting and intercommunicating persons enacting the social roles of husband and wife, mother and father, son and daughter, brother and sister.

4. The family maintains a common culture, derived mainly from the general culture, but in a complex society possessing some distinctive features for each family.[13]

A shorter and more workable definition is that used by MacIver: "The family is a group defined by a sex relationship sufficiently precise and enduring to provide for the procreation and upbringing of children."[14] Although MacIver wrote before the nuclear age, his definition certainly foreshadowed the current trend toward speaking of the *nuclear family* in the same sense that the previous generation of writers in marriage and the family spoke of the *conjugal family* (man, woman, and minor children, if any). Although the family usually is a primary group, bound by strong emotional ties, some families more nearly typify the impersonality of relations of the secondary group; in either case, the family influences personality development and behavior during the entire life span of most individuals. Brown states, "The extent to which the individual shows warmth and congeniality or is cold and reserved in relation with others is largely the product of the family pattern."[15] The family, then, builds the basic personality structure of our citizens. Certainly this is of major importance in any society.

The Family Is in Transition Because It Is Adapting to Conditions of Modern Life

The many changes that have occurred in the nature, characteristics, and functions of the family have led some writers to view its future pessimistically. Sorokin sees the family passing from a stage of instability to complete disintegration.[16] He sees divorce and separation becoming so common that marriage will become passé and children will be separated earlier and earlier from their parents. Anshen states, "The present collapse of marriage and the family is a perverted triumph of a profaned passion which in truth now largely consists in a reversion to abduction and rape."[17] Zimmerman is pessimistic about the survival of the family, seeing a parallel to the breakdown of Greek and Roman family life.[18] Russell hopes for the continuation of the family, because the affection of parents for their children makes the

[13]From *The Family*, 3rd ed., p. 2, by Ernest W. Burgess, Harvey J. Locke, and Mary M. Thomas. © 1963 by Litton Educational Publishing, Inc. Reprinted by permission of Van Nostrand Reinhold Company.

[14]Robert M. MacIver, *Society: A Textbook of Sociology* (New York: Holt, 1937), p. 196.

[15]Francis J. Brown, *Sociology of Childhood* (Englewood Cliffs, N.J.: Prentice-Hall, 1939), p. 111.

[16]Pitirim A. Sorokin, *Social and Cultural Dynamics*, Vol. IV (New York: American Book, 1944), p. 776.

[17]Ruth Anshen (ed.), *The Family: Its Functions and Destiny* (New York: Harper, 1959), p. 512.

[18]Carle C. Zimmerman, *Family and Civilization* (New York: Harper, 1947), p. 798.

family a far better place for the development of personality than are institutions for children.[19] His hope for the continuation of the family seems inconsistent with his continued championship of those factors in modern life to which the authors previously cited attribute the disintegration of the family: increased premarital sex, "trial" marriage without benefit of legal ceremony, and freedom to commit adultery after marriage. One of the better statements of modern pessimism, interestingly enough, is not by a serious scholar of the family but by a popular journalist, Patricia Coffin, who put together in a special issue of *Look* some articles of her own with articles by and interviews with such eminent writers as Dr. Benjamin Spock and Alvin Toffler, author of *Future Shock*.[20] The growing incidence of communal living, young unmarrieds starting families without benefit of wedlock, and the unconventional life style of some young married are portrayed in words and pictures.[21] The "wife-swapping" parties of California of the 1970's are not treated, apparently because they are considered as an aberration in life style of families that otherwise conform to the conventional family pattern, but such practices must have some significance for the future of the American family. The progressive social legislation and agitation for women's rights which have characterized Scandinavia in recent years may have had some influence on the growth of "group marriages" and other communes in the United States, but even in Denmark "the members have learned that for the sake of stability, sexual relationships must be kept monogamous" and that the children must have the security of a natural mother.[22] The prophets of doom point to these deviations from the norm as indicators of things to come, and they may be right, but the present evidence is fragmentary and inconclusive.

Many sociologists hold an optimistic view of the future of the family. Table 8, presented later in this chapter, statistically documents their position. Elmer reminds us that there is a considerable difference between reorganization and disintegration.[23] As Linton so aptly put it, "The ancient trinity of father, mother and child has survived more vicissitudes than any other human relationship."[24] The authors are inclined to agree with the statement of Burgess that the apparent disintegration of the modern family is only an expression of the symptoms of transition of a major social institution in changing its form from one adapted to a stable culture to one adapted to a rapidly changing culture.[25] This coincides with Parsons' theory of differentiation, as noted earlier. Patricia Coffin appears to be optimistic about the future of the family. Most of *Look's* special issue was devoted to

[19]Bertrand Russell, *Marriage and Morals* (New York: Liveright, 1929), p. 308.

[20]*Look*, January 26, 1971, pp. 21–86.

[21]See especially John Kronenberger, "Is the Family Obsolete?"; Betty Rollin, "What's Women's Lib Doing to the Family? Plenty!"; Patricia Coffin, "The Young Unmarrieds"; and John Poppy, "The Radical Family," all in ibid.

[22]Michael Durham and Enrico Sarsini, "From Denmark and Sweden: Experiments in Marriage," *Life*, August 15, 1969, p. 41.

[23]McC. Elmer, *The Sociology of the Family* (Boston: Ginn, 1945), p. 223.

[24]Ralph Linton, in Anshen, op. cit., Chapter 2.

[25]Ernest W. Burgess, "The Family in a Changing Society," *American Journal of Sociology*, Vol. 53 (May 1948), pp. 417–422.

positive discussions of the American family[26] and the lead article concluded with "the family is the basic pad from which our spaceship earth is being launched into the future." [27] Such interpretations are in harmony with the entire tempo of modern American life and education, where adaptability is becoming more essential to success in most fields than is stability. Adaptability as a major personality characteristic of the members of the family may well become the most important single factor in the success of marriage and family life.

It may be significant to note the marriage status of suburban males and other males as reported in the United States census of population, 1960. In suburban areas 73.9 per cent of all males were reported as married, whereas only 67.4 per cent of males in central cities and rural areas were reported as married. The metropolitan suburbs are characterized by a middle-class culture more typical of traditional American ideals than the more rapidly changing urban and rural areas. It may be that the status of the males living in the more fluid areas may be indicative of the shape of things to come. This would be true, of course, only if American culture were to move farther and farther away from the middle-class values cherished by the suburban dweller. Currently available evidence seems to point to the contrary. The statistical gradient is presented in Table 8; the percentage of married males in the population has remained constant at 68 per cent for the past two decades. The Great Society movement stresses involvement of the lower-class citizen in the development of solutions to his problems. The prized solution, at the time of this writing, seems to be to fit the lower-class inhabitant of the core cities and of impoverished rural areas with the job skills and the social attitudes that will enable him to move to the preferred suburban areas. These vast governmental programs reinforce the indoctrination of the schools toward prizing middle-class values, with the attendant higher marital status. Table 8 emphasizes the steadily increasing percentage of married males in the total population, 1890–1962, with a sharp upward gradient in the 1940's. Current statistics indicate that the family is, indeed, here to stay.

In the past 100 years we have shifted from a rural, handicraft society based on primary-group production with a variety of skills shared by the family group as an independent social entity to a highly specialized, interdependent, urban, industrial, secondary-group society.

We have experienced a complete cycle of the "three R's." In the past, the formal education of the family member was limited to basic instruction in reading, writing, and arithmetic. These skills were all that were needed to conduct the business and social affairs of the independent family group in a simple rural culture. Now the family and the school have to teach children to meet the basic problems of modern living in a highly complex, interdependent world. This necessitates delegating to the schools and to other agencies of an ever-increasing portion of the educative function of the family, which results in tremendous expansion in the curriculum of the school and in the scope of other governmental activities. Paradoxically, this

[26]Look, op. cit.; see especially Patricia Coffin, "The American Family" (lead article); Anne Gognebin, "Family Portraits, U.S.A."; Patricia Coffin, "A Happy Family"; Gary Snyder, "Prayer for the Great Family"; and Louis Botto, "The Executive Mother."

[27]Coffin, op cit, p. 22.

only emphasizes further the importance of the "three R's" as tools to unlock the content of the added curricular offerings. In modern America we are doing a better job of teaching the "three R's" to more people than at any time in any culture in the world.

Governmental programs are reinforcing the schools in placing stress upon literacy and computational skills through Operation Headstart, the Manpower Development Training Act of 1962, Job Corps and other programs of the Office of Economic Opportunity, the Elementary and Secondary Education Act of 1965, the Comprehensive Manpower Training Act of 1968, and similar programs. These programs tend to be operated with personnel recruited from the teaching profession. Along with the stress upon literacy and computational skills, effort is being made to impart middle-class values to the participants in these programs. (A group of professors employed as consultants to Federal Electric Corporation in the operation of the Job Corps Center at Kilmer, New Jersey, withdrew from their consultative role in protest against what they termed the "middle-class colonialism" of the policies of the Office of Economic Opportunity.) This new partnership of government with school and family in the education and training of lower-class children and youth portends an ever-increasing acceptance of middle-class values by the American populace. This assumes, of course, that the governmental programs will be more successful in dealing with these lower-class youth than were the traditional schools. It seems reasonable, however, to assume that the increased time and energy expended by the government will at least increase the effect of the schools in stressing such characteristics as honesty, punctuality, and chastity. In the face of the rising tide of juvenile delinquency and adult crime and of the high unemployment rate the significance of these contributions toward strengthening the moral and social fabric of America cannot be overestimated.

A fact of modern life in America is the shift from home to the school and to other governmental agencies of the responsibility for furnishing education in many areas that once were considered the exclusive prerogative of the family but that now have become areas in which the family has neither the technical competence nor the desire to educate the child. *Prime among these areas are experiences in social relationships and in direct participation in decision making.*

These shifts in the tasks of the schools have been accompanied by a shift in the nature of the school. Many authorities feel that the school no longer can be oriented to the past, focused upon simple transmission of the cultural heritage. The modern school must be oriented toward the present and the future, using history as a tool to solve present problems and to design a better future.[28] This may require a new kind of school, focusing on *people* in the social matrix. As Hamilton and Saylor note, "A curriculum design for a humanistic school should be focused directly upon the creation of conditions for fostering the development of human beings."[29] This not only alters the role of the school dramatically, but it also challenges the pre-eminence of the family in socializing the child, as was cited earlier. The

[28]Othanel B. Smith, William O. Stanley, and J. Harlan Shores, *Fundamentals of Curriculum Development* (Yonkers, N.Y.: World Book, 1950), p. 123.

[29]Norman K. Hamilton and J. Galen Saylor, *Humanizing the Secondary School* (Washington, D.C.: A.S.C.D., N.E.A., 1969), p. 48.

TABLE 1
Changing Characteristics of the Family

FORMERLY	NOW
Large	*Small*
Many children, with little personal attention given to each by the overworked mother. Average household size in 1790: 5.9.	Few children (1 or 2). They strive to be economically and socially independent of the family unit. 1940–1965: fluctuated around 3.7.
Consanguineal	*Conjugal*
Several generations under the same roof. Oldest man was the head of the family.	Husband, wife, and children. No parents or other relative. Accelerated in the 1940's—more new houses than new marriages.
Rural	*Urban*
Nine of ten families rooted to the soil. 1800: only five cities over 10,000. 1790: New York only city of 50,000.	More than half of the population living in urban areas over 50,000.
Agrarian (Producer)	*Industrial* (Consumer)
An economic unit. Self-sufficient.	Neither an economic unit nor self-sufficient. Income from outside home. No present or future security.
Authoritarian	*Democratic*
Mate selection by parents. Little or no courtship. Marriage for economic necessity; a partnership. Many children who received little attention, but had high economic value.	Weakened authority of parents over children. Mate selection by individual, based on romance. Husband and wife equal. Decisions reached in family council.
Patricentric	*Many Types*
Father head of household. Child followed father's vocation. Obedience to father first duty of child.	*Emancipated.* An urban phenomenon. Young parents. No plans for children until education is completed and/or business is established. Living in the present. Rebels against convention. *Patriarchial.* Father head of household by common consent, but family operates democratically. Typical of rural families (30 per cent of total U.S. population) and workingmen's residential areas. *Equalitarian.* Based on equality of husband and wife. Many working wives. Many decisions reached in family council. *Matricentric.* Mother head of household. Father commutes to work.
Institutional	*Companionship*
High degree of solidarity. Activities entered into jointly and cooperatively. Respect for secular and religious education. Permanence of marriage. Unplanned parenthood. Sense of duty. Economic necessity.	Low degree of solidarity. Individualism prevails, except in the rural areas. Little group participation in common activities. Education left to experts. Frequent divorce. Planned parenthood. Happiness the goal.

Note: Majority patterns are given, with the exception of "modern types" of families. The modern rural family tends to develop a majority pattern, but modern city families defy attempts at a single classification. All majority types in the charts on characteristics and functions, of course, exclude the many deviations from same in an attempt at clarity in presentation of trends.
Source: Adapted from Ernest W. Burgess, Harvey J. Locke, and Mary Margaret Thomas, *The Family: From Institution to Companionship* (New York: Van Nostrand Reinhold Company, 1963), pp. 63–72.

school seems to be assuming even greater roles, beyond those for which it is equipped. An example of what can happen in this situation is provided by "conservative" families who delegate the education of their children to "progressive" schools, thereby creating conflicts in the basic philosophies of the several family members.

The children and youth of the underprivileged segments of the American population increasingly are becoming involved in governmental programs of education and training. These programs foster even greater gaps between children and parents. Consider the situation, for example, of the Job Corps graduate who has been indoctrinated with middle-class values. He is uncomfortable in the home of his parents. He no longer thinks, acts, or believes as they do. He now has the job skills to enable him to purchase a home in the suburbs, and the social attitudes to enable him to live comfortably there. But he has discarded the social attitudes that formerly served him in the slums. If he returns to his "home," conflict is inevitable. He has no choice but to make a new life for himself apart from his family and his former friends.

The magnitude of these changes in the social matrix gives new perspective to the disorientation of the modern family. People are confused by the rapidity and complexity of change in modern life and are uncertain of procedures and values even in such traditional areas as the family. Much reorganization must occur in the form of the family, but one can state with certainty that the family will survive.

TRENDS IN THE CHANGING NATURE OF THE FAMILY

Changes in the characteristics of the family are presented in Table 1. A cross-sectional view of the trends in family life may be gained by looking next at the changing functions of the family. These are presented in Table 2. The underlying causes of these trends, and the problems they create, are presented in the next two sections.

RATIONALE OF CHANGE IN THE AMERICAN FAMILY

Industrialization, urbanization, the rising tide of individualism, and increasing governmental participation both in job training and in provisions for care of the aged are beyond the control of the family. These great national forces, however, have had immediate and profound effects upon the nature of the American family. Other forces in our culture have contributed to a lesser degree toward accelerating changes in the characteristics and functions of the family. Among these are national crises, such as wars and depressions, and cross-cultural marriages fostered by the increased mobility of our population. Most of these contributory forces, however, are natural outgrowths of the larger national forces earlier noted.

Industrialization

Chapter 5 traces the development of the American economy. Now let us see what these economic, industrial, and technological trends have meant for the American family.

TABLE 2
Changing Functions of the Family

FORMERLY	NOW
Reproductive	*Reproductive*
Fostered by: Taboos on extramarital sex experiences. Sense of duty of women. High economic value of offspring.	Hampered by: Breakdown of sex mores. Marital unhappiness. Birth control knowledges. Great economic liability of offspring. The birth rate rose rapidly from the early 1940's through 1955, with a sharp decline in 1955–1970 (25 births per thousand population in 1955; 17 births per thousand population in 1970).
Emotional	*Emotional*
Little attention to emotional adjustments. Marriage for economic necessity and partnership. Despite this, a high degree of emotional solidarity through functioning of the family as a unit, with the labor of all necessary for its maintenance.	Warmth and affection lavished on the young. Greater emotional attachment for the individual. Despite this, emotional stresses caused by: Extreme individualism of modern life. Care and training of young increasingly shifted outside the home. Consumerism. Commercial recreation.
Accultural	*Accultural*
Folkways and mores transmit the cultural heritage. Political beliefs, customs of dress, table manners, social manners, and the like shared by entire family.	Home atmosphere still a potent force in shaping the attitudes of the young. Despite modern individualism, high correlations exist between parents and offspring in cultural behavior.
Economic	*Economic*
Self-sufficient. Made own clothes, food, etc.	Needs depend on outside income. Most goods purchased. More women work outside home. Packaged foods or restaurant meals. Electric appliances do housework.
Educational	*Educational*
Secular and moral training mostly received in home.	School and church taking over both secular and religious training. Advanced education outside the home increasingly an economic necessity.
Protective	*Protective*
Head of house kept firearms. Legal business as unit.	Government taking over: police department, fire department, Social Security, etc. Life and health insurance policies.
Religious	*Religious*
Worship and church attendance an established part of family life.	Decrease in worship and prayers. Increased reliance on scientific explanation of natural phenomena. Decrease in supernatural beliefs and in church attendance.
Recreational	*Recreational*
Long hours of work. No place to go. Remained home. Play often frowned upon.	More leisure. Higher standards of living. More money and recreation. Growth of public facilities.

Source: Adapted from Ernest W. Burgess, Harvey J. Locke, and Mary Margaret Thomas, *The Family: From Institution to Companionship* (New York: Van Nostrand Reinhold Company, 1963), pp. 63–72.

First, the shift from family handicraft to factory production has forced the family to shift from a producer unit to a consumer unit. The emotional impact of this shift has been tremendous. Man needs to be needed. Children, and in some instances wives or husbands, have become economic liabilities. The producer in the family is the wage earner, who works outside the home for money with which he provides the material needs of all members of the family. The work of other members is less needed for the promotion of the material welfare of the family. The nonproducing members of the modern family lack the emotional security of the members of the older producer-unit family. The additional warmth and affection lavished on children and spouses by the modern wage earner can only partially compensate for the emotional security formerly provided through the simple fact of being needed.

Industrialization takes the father from the home for the major portion of the day, for at least five days per week. His commuting time plus work time plus meal time total almost the entire waking hours of the child. Some writers suggest that this factor alone is developing a majority pattern of matricentric families, for the mother has the primary contact with the children. Both boys and girls learn to turn to the adult woman in the household for guidance. What more natural development after marriage than for the boy-child grown-up to continue to turn to the adult woman in the house for guidance in family affairs?

Not all women in an industrial culture are content with the role of wife and mother. Tables 3 and 4 reveal significant trends in the number of women who are emulating the producer-male in the household. They are securing gainful employment outside the home, not just as a temporary measure but as a permanent way of life. Over one third of the married female population of the United States is employed through age sixty-four. This suggests that many women have chosen to continue working until they reach retirement age and can draw old-age insurance benefits under the Social Security Act, thus assuring themselves of a measure of independence in later years. It seems reasonable to predict that this trend will accelerate with the advent of the significant increases in taxes and benefits under the Social Security Act. The economic independence attained by these women, coupled with their equalitarian relations with fellow workers, has contributed heavily to the development of the equalitarian family. As the Women's Liberation movement (discussed in Chapter 9) gains, the economic independence of women may force even greater changes in the American family. The reverse, of course, is true; many families continue to cohabit not because of any continuing affection, but because of the economic interdependence occasioned by joint incomes. This too affects the traditional roles of husband and wife; she is no longer a dependent, but a full and equal partner. That not all females are willing to continue cohabitation in the face of unhappy marriages is shown in Figure 11, which indicates that nearly 9 per cent of white families and 27 per cent of nonwhite families are headed by females, with 45 per cent of the white females and 64 per cent of the nonwhite females apparently heading their family by choice (separated, divorced, or single).

The norm, however, remains the conjugal (nuclear) family. Table 4 revealed that in 1969 nearly two thirds of all women sixteen years of age and over were married and living with their husbands. Of these women 39.5

TABLE 3

Marital Status of Women in the Civilian Labor Force: 1940 to 1969

[Persons 14 years old and over through 1966; thereafter, 16 years old and over. As of March, except as indicated. Prior to 1960, excludes Alaska and Hawaii. Includes institutional population. Figures for 1940 based on complete census revised for comparability with intercensal series. Data for 1944–1969 based on Current Population Survey; see text, p. 1. Beginning 1955, figures not strictly comparable with previous years as a result of introduction into estimating procedure of 1950 census data through 1961, and of 1960 census data beginning March 1962. See table 35. See also *Historical Statistics, Colonial Times to 1957*, series D 33–35.]

YEAR	FEMALE LABOR FORCE (1,000)		Married			PER CENT DISTRIBUTION OF FEMALE LABOR FORCE			FEMALE LABOR FORCE AS PER CENT OF FEMALE POPULATION		Married		
	Total	Single	Total	Husband Present	Widowed or Divorced	Single	Married	Widowed or Divorced	Total	Single	Total	Husband Present	Widowed or Divorced
1940	13,840	6,710	5,040	4,200*	2,090	48.5	36.4	15.1	27.4	48.1	16.7	14.7	32.0
1944*	18,449	7,542	8,433	6,226	2,474	40.9	45.7	13.4	35.0	58.6	25.6	21.7	35.7
1947*	16,323	6,181	7,545	6,676	2,597	37.9	46.2	15.9	29.8	51.2	21.4	20.0	34.6
1950	17,795	5,621	9,273	8,550	2,901	31.6	52.1	16.3	31.4	50.5	24.8	23.8	36.0
1955*	20,154	5,087	11,839	10,423	3,227	25.2	58.7	16.0	33.5	46.4	29.4	27.7	36.0
1956	20,842	5,167	12,278	11,126	3,397	24.8	58.9	16.3	34.2	46.4	30.2	29.0	36.9
1957	21,524	5,378	12,696	11,529	3,450	25.0	59.0	16.0	34.8	46.8	30.8	29.6	37.6
1958	22,000	5,365	13,032	11,826	3,604	24.4	59.2	16.4	35.0	45.4	31.4	30.2	37.9
1959	22,376	5,162	13,586	12,205	3,628	23.1	60.7	16.2	35.2	43.4	32.3	30.9	38.0
1960	22,516	5,401	13,485	12,253	3,629	24.0	59.9	16.1	34.8	44.1	31.7	30.5	37.1
1961	24,199	5,663	14,612	13,266	3,924	23.4	60.4	16.2	36.8	44.4	34.0	32.7	39.0
1962	23,978	5,481	14,770	13,485	3,727	22.9	61.6	15.5	35.7	41.7	33.7	32.7	36.6
1963	24,675	5,614	15,362	14,061	3,699	22.8	62.3	15.0	36.1	41.0	34.6	33.7	35.8
1964	25,399	5,781	15,790	14,461	3,828	22.8	62.2	15.1	36.5	40.9	35.3	34.4	36.1
1965	25,952	5,912	16,154	14,708	3,886	22.8	62.2	15.0	36.7	40.5	35.7	34.7	35.7
1966	26,820	6,106	16,676	15,178	4,038	22.7	62.2	15.1	37.3	40.8	36.5	35.4	36.4
1967	27,545	5,915	17,486	15,908	4,144	21.5	63.5	15.0	39.7	50.7	37.8	36.8	35.9
1968	28,778	6,357	18,234	16,821	4,187	22.1	63.4	14.6	40.7	51.3	39.1	38.3	35.8
1969	29,898	6,501	19,100	17,595	4,297	21.7	63.9	14.4	41.6	51.2	40.4	39.6	35.8

* As of April.

Source: 1940–1958, Department of Commerce, Bureau of the Census; *Current Population Reports*, Series P–50. Beginning 1959, Department of Labor, Bureau of Labor Statistics; *Special Labor Force Reports*. Reprinted from *Statistical Abstract of the United States, 1970* (Washington, D.C.: Government

TABLE 4

Civilian Female Population—Total and Labor Force, by Age and Marital Status: 1969

[In thousands of persons 16 years old and over, except as indicated. As of March. Includes institutional population. See headnote, table 316.]

AGE AND MARITAL STATUS	Population	LABOR FORCE Number	Per Cent of Population	AGE AND MARITAL STATUS	Population	LABOR FORCE Number	Per Cent of Population
				Married, husband			
Total	71,919	29,898	41.6	present	44,440	17,595	39.6
16–19 years	7,159	2,665	37.2	16–19 years	817	289	35.4
20–24 years	8,040	4,554	56.6	20–24 years	4,600	2,204	47.9
25–34 years	12,285	5,334	43.4	25–34 years	9,982	3,686	36.9
35–44 years	11,927	5,884	49.3	35–44 years	9,851	4,470	45.4
45–64 years	21,414	10,356	48.4	45–64 years	15,475	6,665	43.1
65 years and over	11,094	1,105	10.0	65 years and over	3,715	281	7.6
Median age* years	42.2	39.5	(†)	Median age* years	42.0	41.2	(†)
				Other marital			
Single	12,689	6,501	51.2	status	14,790	5,802	39.2
16–19 years	6,172	2,288	37.1	16–19 years	170	88	51.8
20–24 years	2,850	1,979	69.4	20–24 years	590	371	62.9
25–34 years	1,071	866	80.9	25–34 years	1,232	782	63.5
35–44 years	599	433	72.3	35–44 years	1,477	981	66.4
45–64 years	1,147	779	67.9	45–64 years	4,792	2,912	60.8
65 years and over	850	156	18.4	65 years and over	6,529	668	10.2
Median age* years	20.3	22.4	(†)	Median age* years	62.0	50.1	(†)

*For definition of median, see preface.
†Not applicable.
Source: Dept. of Labor, Bureau of Labor Statistics; *Special Labor Force Report.* Reprinted from Statistical Abstract of the United States, 1970 (Washington, D.C.: Government Printing Office, 1970), p. 224.

per cent were in the labor force. They made up more than half (59 per cent) of the female labor force.

Several factors combine to set the stage for an unprecedented high in juvenile delinquency.[30] The growing child has no household tasks to occupy his time. Both mother and father may be working outside the home, so the child receives a minimum of family guidance in the utilization of his abundant leisure time. When immature minds are forced to rely on their own ingenuity for utilization of leisure time, unwise choices may be expected. The resultant experiences and associations set the stage for delinquent acts.

[30]See Chapter 8 for treatment of delinquency as a factor in modern life.

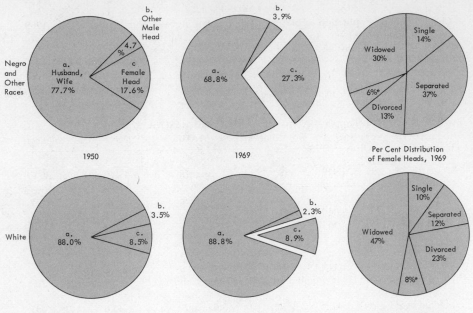

Figure 11. Family composition 1950–1969. [From *Road Maps of Industry* June 15, 1970 (New York: National Industrial Conference Board, 1970). Used by permission.]

Not all aspects of industrialization have been harmful to the family. Modern technology has increased productivity, which has shortened the work week. Modern appliances and packaged foods have cut the amount of time necessary for essential housekeeping chores.

Thirty years ago, the average housewife had to spend five to six hours of her day in the kitchen preparing meals. Today she spends less than half that time. That reduction is primarily due to her use of foods which are partially or fully prepared for her—foods that have built-in services. For example, bread, cake mixes, canned fruits and vegetables, canned soups, frozen foods of all kinds, baby foods, packaged dairy products, precut and prepared meats, prepared desserts including ice cream.[31]

An alternative point of view, shared by many housewives, is that "modern labor saving devices do not necessarily reduce the number of hours that housewives must work; they merely raise standards of cleanliness, meal preparation and child care."[32]

The shortening of the industrial work week and of the time required for housework theoretically makes possible more time for the family to spend as a unit. Manufacturers are remodeling the kitchen completely, to make it a spot for conversational family gatherings. The rising tide of individualism,

---

[31]William B. Murphy (President, Campbell Soup Company), "Revolution in the Kitchen: New Foods—Better Meals, Less Work," *U.S. News and World Report*, February 15, 1957, p. 56.

[32]Arlene Skolnick, "Stimulus-Response: Families Can Be Unhealthy for Children and Other Living Things," *Psychology Today*, August 1971, p. 18.

urbanization, modern transportation, and expanding commercial amuse-ments is retarding this return to family unity, except for television, which is at least bringing some families again into physical proximity, albeit without intercommunication. The trend seems to be the dispersion of the family to separate leisure-time activities.

Urbanization

Urbanization has further weakened the emotional security of the family. The rural family knew its neighbors and shared with them close ties of friendship, developing a community culture that further strengthened the security of the component families. The impersonal secondary-group society of the modern city isolates the family. This lack of family-to-family contact accentuates the dispersion of family members fostered by industrialization. The father tends to make his circle of friends among his business associates. The mother tends to associate with an entirely different group of families in her ladies' social clubs. The children may encompass still a third group of families by forming their friendships with their classmates at school. The minimal overlap of common acquaintances makes "family" gatherings for leisure-time activities a rarity. When they do occur, they are confined to the conjugal family rather than to two or more families sharing a common ex-perience.

A further weakening of family stability resulting from urbanization is the effect of the gathering of the forces of evil that occurs in any area in which population is concentrated. The drug problem mushroomed in the late 1960's and early 1970's, particularly among the youth, on an inter-national scale.[33] Many suggestions have been made for legalization of mari-juana and other "soft" drugs, with parallels made between their prohibition now and that of alcohol in the 1920's and early 1930's, but most people were rejecting such proposals in the early 1970's.[34] Social parasites have existed in all ages. The vendor of illicit entertainment must seek population centers to find a market. Not only youth but also parents may become in-volved in drunkenness, drug addiction, prostitution, theft, and other illegal and/or immoral activities, simply because the sources are readily available. Deviant social behavior by any family member causes family disorganization.

Urbanization and modern transportation have combined to foster a "transition from a sacred to a secular society."[35] The family no longer shares Bible reading. In many families the rush of modern living does not leave time for a simple prayer before meals. The church and the Sunday school have taken over the religious education of youth. The more than 250,000 ministers of the approximately 250 denominations in the United States do not say the same things about family life. Not only moral precepts but family con-cepts have suffered through lack of integration between home and church in the moral instruction of youth.

[33]"Federal Study Recommends Legal Use of Soft Drugs," *Star Phoenix*, August 26, 1971, p. 1.

[34]"Most Reject Utilization of Soft Drugs," *Star Phoenix*, August 27, 1971, p. 1.

[35]Clifford Kirkpatrick, *The Family: As Process and Institution* (New York: Ronald, 1963) p. 129.

Urbanization has had some salutary effects upon the family. The diversity of cultural activities in any metropolitan area offers great opportunity for the broadening of worthy interests and activities for all members of the family. Both industrialization and urbanization have contributed to improved family health; in the past century the life span of the average individual has increased from forty-five years to sixty-seven years. The cities have more than their proportional share of doctors and hospitals. Drugstores, life-squads, and the like are immediately available. Despite the *Time* analysis that in 1968 one fifth of the population was below the poverty line, with one seventh in substandard housing[36] (by modern standards), we are the healthiest, most prosperous, and longest-lived nation in history.

The term *urbanization* has been used to refer to the complex of technological and social aspects of life in the large city. Suburbs have characteristics different from those of central cities; these characteristics are developed in detail in Chapter 11. Often these characteristics, when stated statistically, fall between those for central cities and rural areas. For example, Table 5 shows that in 1960 this was true for the average size of the family, the sex ratio (the number of men per 100 women), and the per cent of the population eighteen years and younger.

TABLE 5

Family Size, Sex Ratio, and Per Cent Eighteen Years Old and Younger for
Central Cities, Suburbs, and Rural Areas, 1960

CHARACTERISTICS	CENTRAL CITIES	SUBURBS	RURAL AREAS
Size of private family	3.50	3.66	3.85
Sex ratio	90.9	92.2	104.3
Per cent 18 years of age and younger	32.3	37.2	39.0

Source: U.S. Bureau of the Census, *U.S. Census of the Population, 1960.* Volume 1, Characteristics of the Population. Part 1, U.S. Summary (Washington, D.C.: Government Printing Office, 1964), pp. 148–157.

Individualism

The philosophy of individualism in America began with the religious individualism of the early settlers, was accentuated by the familial individualism of the producer-family, and reached its economic height in Carnegie's "Gospel of Wealth." [37] Individualism remains an established part of the American way of life. Let us see how this emphasis upon individualism has affected the modern family.

Choosing a career and choosing a mate are two of the most important decisions in the life of a man. Historically, the family heavily influenced, if it did not actually dictate, both choices. The extreme emphasis upon individualism in modern America has developed a cultural expectation that the youth of the nation shall make these choices for themselves, with a minimum of parental guidance.

That the choice of youth should be on a basis that stresses individ-

36"Black and White Balance Sheet," *Time,* January 24, 1969, p. 35.
37Ralph Henry Gabriel, *The Course of American Democratic Thought* (New York: Ronald, 1940), p. 158.

ual happiness is to be expected. In discussing reasons for marriage, Baber
states:

> Why do people marry? The answers, if one went into detail, would be
> numerous, including sheer romance, desire for wealth or position, assurance of
> care in old age, a steady source of sex satisfaction, escape from unpleasant
> home conditions, love of children, perpetuation of family name, the expecta-
> tion of society, fear of ridicule if one does not marry, salary promotion or pref-
> erence, spite against another, and a host of other reasons. But all these are
> minor compared with the dominant urge for continuous and intimate com-
> panionship with a loved person.[38]

Individualism probably is the major underlying factor in changing attitudes toward divorce. Kirkpatrick states:

> There is also a pattern of individualism. The tendency is to think in terms of
> "what I want," of personal advantage, of good business. An individual who has
> just fired a secretary for inefficiency may take a dim view of his wife's in-
> adequacy as a household manager. While the home is the last refuge of collec-
> tivism in the sense that most property is communally owned, there is a growing
> tendency to think in terms of personal possessions and personal gains. If it is
> good business to break an economic relationship, why should it not seem desir-
> able to break up a family when personal satisfactions are not completely ful-
> filled? There is an impact then of individualism engendered by the economic
> system, which strikes powerfully at the traditional pattern of family life.[39]

National Crises

Depressions and wars are the major national crises affecting family life.
Economic depressions cause tremendous strain on the modern family. The
sole source of material necessities and pleasures is the wage earner's pay-
check. Even temporary unemployment severely dislocates the family budget.
Continued unemployment, such as occurs in periods of national economic
depressions, forces a complete reorganization of family finance. Burgess,
Locke, and Thomas report a study of the reactions to the depression of the
1930's.[40] They conclude that integrated, well-organized families meet and
solve depression problems with rational behavior and little emotional disturbance, emerging from the experience with greater family solidarity. Disorganized families tend to become further disorganized in the face of crisis,
and may even disintegrate through separation or divorce. Thus it appears
that national depressions are not one of the major determinants of family
structure, except as they intensify inherent family tendencies toward stability
or instability.

Although depressions do not seem to have a significant effect upon the
nature of the family, they have a definite effect upon marriage and divorce
rates, both of which decline sharply in times of depression.[41]

---

[38]From *Marriage and the Family* (p. 162), by Ray E. Baber. Copyright, 1953, by McGraw-Hill
Book Company, Inc. Used with permission of McGraw-Hill Book Company.

[39]Clifford Kirkpatrick, *The Family as Process and Institution*, Second Edition, p. 130. Copyright © 1963, The Ronald Press Co., New York.

[40]Burgess, Locke, and Thomas, op. cit., pp. 435–436.

[41] Philip M. Hauser, "Population and Vital Phenomena," *American Journal of Sociology*,
Vol. 18 (1942), p. 311.

Wars appear to have more varied effects upon the family. The entire supply of available marriage mates is disrupted by' such factors as men of military (and marriageable) age being concentrated in training camps or going overseas, defense industry towns becoming clogged with women workers, and seaports being flooded with transient hordes of pleasure-seeking males in uniform. Hasty marriages often are contracted between persons of badly matched backgrounds under the psychological tensions of a nation at war. A considerable portion of wartime marriages culminate in early divorce.[42] Of much more statistical importance is the drop in the marriage rate during war years, with a corresponding increase in the immediate postwar years. In the United States, for example, the marriage rate per 1,000 population fell from 12.2 in 1939 to 10.5 in 1944 and rose to 16.2 in 1946.[43] Parenthetically, one should not assume from these partial data that the long-term marriage rate is on the increase; quite the reverse is true.[44]

The large number of marriages in 1969 was mostly due to the war-babies that came of marriageable age.

After a careful analysis of the effects of World War I, World War II, and the Korean conflict upon American family life, Burgess, Locke, and Thomas conclude that wars, like depressions, are not major determinants of trends in family life.[45]

To the degree that war weakens institutions buttressing and supporting the family, it disturbs family relationships and is an indirect factor in family disorganization.

Family instability in American society is essentially a phenomenon of the transition from the institutional to the companionship type of family. The effect of a crisis like war is both to accelerate the transition and to introduce temporary disrupting conditions.

Certain factors favorable to family unity emerge in wartime. First, the actual danger to family members in war may draw them more closely together. When a member of a family enters the army, with the actual or potential dangers involved, petty difficulties may be forgotten and the family may become more united than before. Second, some men in the services, feeling that they are mere cogs in a huge machine, desire the intimate and personal appreciation of a sweetheart, a wife, or parents and may be drawn more closely to their families than formerly. Third, to most men a war is a disagreeable job, to be finished as soon as possible in order that they may return to civilian life, settle down, and enjoy home life, made all the more attractive by contrast with the army camp.

When one examines the divorce rates during World War II and the immediate postwar years, as presented in Table 6, it is well to guard one's thinking against the common-sense fallacy of assuming that a given reversal of a trend, resulting from temporary wartime conditions, is indicative of a permanent change. Divorce rates per 1,000 inhabitants jumped from 2.9 in 1944 to 3.5 in 1945 and 4.3 in 1946.[46] They declined almost as rapidly in the

[42]Burgess, Locke, and Thomas, op. cit., pp. 484–485.

[43]Metropolitan Life Insurance Company, "Recent International Marriage Trends," *Statistical Bulletin* (New York: Metropolitan Life Insurance Company, 1952), p. 2.

[44]See Table 7 for details.

[45]Burgess, Locke, and Thomas, op. cit., p. 486.

[46]For marriage and divorce rates see Table 7.

immediate postwar years, dropping to 3.4 in 1947 and 2.8 in 1948. From 1951 through 1962 they stabilized at about 2.2, then gradually rose through the 1960's to 3.3 in 1969, which is about what the long-term trend in rising divorce rate would have projected. Thus the dramatic fluctuation caused by the war apparently has not affected the long-term trend, a slowly rising divorce rate. This is in sharp contrast to the pessimistic predictions of some authors that by 1965 there would be one divorce for every two marriages. The apparent stabilization at about one divorce for every four marriages from 1947 through 1971 suggests that this ratio may not be exceeded significantly in the coming years; certainly it will not be more than one divorce for each three marriages. If this proves to be true, then the transitional period from the institutional to the companionship type of family may be nearing its completion.

Analysis of marriage rates does not present such a clear picture. The expected drop in the rate occurred during the Depression years, but it failed to materialize immediately in World War II, in fact, the first full year of American participation saw the highest marriage rate ever recorded in American history. One must remember, however, that marriage rates rise during periods of prosperity; one can only surmise that the forces of wartime prosperity following the Great Depression more than counterbalanced the effects of war. The typical pattern of depressed war rate followed by a dramatic postwar rise (as noted previously in the divorce rate) held true for 1943–1946. A disturbing facet of recent years is that marriage rates for the 1950's (rate per 1,000 females aged fifteen to forty-four) continued to be the lowest recorded since the Depression year of 1930, but Table 7 shows a steady upward trend in the 1960's. A marked upswing of the rate was expected, however, between 1965 and 1970, when large numbers of young people from the "baby boom" of the middle 1940's reached marriageable age. This prediction was fulfilled in 1969, when the marriage rate almost equaled that of 1949. A detailed listing of the data appears in Table 7.

There has been great debate among demographers about the significance of the birth rate. Suffice it to say here that the birth rate rose slowly from 1935 to 1955, and then suffered a sharp decline from 1955 to 1970.[47] It is too early to make a definitive prediction of long-term trends; but the rise in the marriage rate in the late 1960's, with an accompanying sharp increase in the number of women of child-bearing age, makes a sharp rise in the birth rate in the 1970's seem quite possible. For a full discussion of the birth rate, with detailed data in tabular form, see Chapter 11.

PROBLEMS FACING AMERICAN FAMILIES

Let us consider in roughly chronological order the family problems faced by the individual from birth to death.

Child Socialization

We have noted earlier the repeated reference by several writers to the importance of the first few years of life in shaping the basic personality of the child. We have also discussed the importance of the family in

[47]*Pocket Data Book, U.S.A., 1971.* Department of Commerce, Bureau of the Census, (Washington, D.C.: Government Printing Office, 1971), p. 59.

TABLE 6

Marriage and Marriage Rates, Divorces and Divorce Rates, United States

	MARRIAGES			DIVORCE		
	Total per Year (Thousands)	Rate per 1,000 Inhabitants	Rate per 1,000 Females 15–44	Total per Year (Thousands)	Rate per 1,000 Inhabitants	Rate per 100 Marriage
1887–1891	555	9.0	39.3†	31	0.5	6
1892–1896	609	8.9	38.7†	39	0.6	6
1897–1901	683	9.1	39.3†	52	0.7	8
1902–1906	829	10.1	42.8	67	0.8	8
1907–1911	919	10.2	42.9	81	0.9	9
1912–1916	1027	10.4	44.0	101	1.0	10
1920	1274	12.0	50.9	171	1.6	13
1925	1188	10.3	43.6	175	1.5	15
1930	1127	9.2	38.4	196	1.6	17
1935	1327	10.4	43.3	218	1.7	16
1940	1596	12.1	49.7	264	2.0	17
1941	1696	12.7	52.3	293	2.2	17
1942	1772	13.2	54.2	321	2.4	18
1943	1577	11.7	47.9	359	2.6	23
1944	1452	10.9	43.9	400	2.9	28
1945	1613	12.2	48.5	485	3.5	30
1946	2291	16.4	68.4	610	4.3	27
1947	1992	13.9	59.2	483	3.4	24

1948	1811	12.4	53.5	408	2.8	23
1949	1580	10.6	46.4	397	2.7	25
1950	1667	11.1	48.7	385	2.6	23
1951	1595	10.4	46.4	381	2.5	24
1952	1539	9.9	44.7	392	2.5	25
1953	1546	9.8	44.7	390	2.5	25
1954	1490	9.2	43.0	379	2.4	25
1955	1531	9.3	44.0	377	2.3	25
1956	1569	9.4	45.4	382	2.3	24
1957	1518	8.9	43.2	381	2.2	25
1958	1451	8.4	40.9	368	2.1	25
1959	1494	8.5	41.8	395	2.2	26
1960	1527	8.5	42.2	393	2.2	26
1961	1548	8.5	42.5	414	2.3	27
1962	1577	8.5	42.5	413	2.2	26
1963	1654	8.8	43.8	428	2.3	26
1964	1725	8.9	44.8	450	2.4	26
1965	1800	9.3	45.9	479	2.5	27
1966	1857	9.5		499	2.5	27
1967	1927	9.7		523	2.6	27
1968	2059	10.3		582	2.9	28
1969	2146	10.6		660	3.3	31

Compiled from (1) "Marriages and Divorces, United States, Selected Years, 1887–1966," in *The Economic Almanac, 1967–68* (New York: The National Industrial Conferences Board, Inc., 1967), pp. 14–15; and (2) Table 53, "Live Births, Deaths, Marriages, and Divorces: 1910–1969," and Table 75, "Marriages and Divorces: 1940–1969," in *Statistical Abstract of the United States, 1970* (Washington, D.C.: Government Printing Office, 1970), pp. 47, 60. Used by permission. Extrapolations (final column, 1965–1969) by Bryner.

TABLE 7

Marriages and Divorces: 1940 to 1969

(Prior to 1960, excludes Alaska and Hawaii. See also Historical Statistics, Colonial Times to 1957, series A 228, A 229, B 177, and B 179.)

MARRIAGE AND DIVORCE		1940	1950	1955	1960	1965	1966	1967	1968	1969
Marriages										
Total	1,000	1,596	1,667	1,531	1,523	1,800	1,857	1,913	2,059*	2,146*
Rate per 1,000 population		12.1	11.1	9.3	8.5	9.3	9.5	9.7	10.3*	10.6*
Rate per 1,000 unmarried women:										
15–44 years old		127.4	166.4	161.1	148.0	144.3	145.1	(NA)	(NA)	(NA)
15 years old and over		82.8	90.2	80.9	73.5	75.0	75.6	(NA)	(NA)	(NA)
Per cent married of population 18 years old and over:†										
Male		66.1	71.8	56.7	76.4	76.2	76.1	76.3	75.6	75.5
Female		65.4	70.9	71.9	71.6	70.5	70.3	69.7	69.2	68.9
Median age (years) at first marriage:† ‡										
Bride		21.5	20.3	20.2	20.3	20.6	20.5	20.6	20.8	20.8
Groom		24.3	22.8	22.6	22.8	22.8	22.8	23.1	23.1	23.2
Divorces (including annulments)										
Total	1,000	264	385	377	393	479	499	534	582*	660*
Rate per 1,000 population		2.0	2.6	2.3	2.2	2.5	2.5	2.7	2.9*	3.3*
Rate per 1,000 married women, 15 years old and over		8.8	10.3	9.3	9.2	10.6	10.9	(NA)	(NA)	(NA)
Per cent divorced of population 18 years old and over:†										
Male		1.4	1.8	1.9	2.0	2.5	2.5	2.4	2.6	2.6
Female		1.8	2.3	2.4	2.9	3.3	3.4	3.5	3.6	3.7
Median duration of marriage†	years	(NA)	5.3	6.2	7.1	7.2	7.1	(NA)	(NA)	(NA)
Children involved per divorce decree, average number		(NA)	(NA)	0.92	1.18	1.32	1.34	(NA)	(NA)	(NA)
Per cent of spouses separated, all families†		(NA)	1.3	1.5	1.5	2.0	1.9	2.0	2.1	2.2

NA Not available.

* Preliminary.

† Department of Commerce, Bureau of the Census; Current Population Reports, Series P-20.

‡ For definition of median, see preface. Beginning 1950, median age at first marriage based on sample.

Source: Department of Health, Education, and Welfare, Public Health Service; annual report, Vital Statistics of the United States, except as noted. Reprinted from the Statistical Abstract of the United States, 1970 (Washington, D.C.: Government Printing Office, 1970), p. 60.

194

TABLE 8

Marital Status of the Population Fourteen Years of Age and Over, 1890–1969

YEAR	MALE Total (Thousands)	Per Cent Distribution Single	Married	Widowed or Divorced	FEMALE Total (Thousands)	Per Cent Distribution Single	Married	Widowed or Divorced
1890	21,501	43.6	52.1	4.0	20,298	34.1	54.8	11.0
1900	26,414	42.0	52.8	4.8	25,024	33.3	55.2	11.3
1910	33,362	40.4	54.2	4.9	30,959	31.8	57.1	10.9
1920	37,954	36.9	57.6	5.3	36,190	29.4	58.9	11.6
1930	45,088	35.8	58.4	5.6	44,013	28.4	59.5	12.1
1940	50,554	34.8	59.7	5.5	50,549	27.6	59.5	12.9
1950	54,762	26.2	68.0	5.9	56,970	19.6	66.1	14.4
1960	60,582	25.3	69.0	5.6	64,875	19.0	65.6	15.4
1969	68,827	27.6	67.0	5.5	75,739	21.8	62.4	15.9

Compiled from the *Economic Almanac, 1967–1968* and the *Statistical Abstract of the United States, 1970.* Figures through 1950 are from the *Economic Almanac.* Figures for 1960 and 1969 are from the *Statistical Abstract.* Footnotes for each source follow: *Economic Almanac:* Note: Beginning 1960 data include Alaska and Hawaii. Totals for 1890–1940 include persons not reporting marital status (5 per cent of total at maximum).
Differences between the number of married men and the number of married women are due partly to the absence of husbands or wives from the country at the time of the enumeration. Examples are women whose husbands were in the Armed Forces overseas and immigrants whose husbands or wives were still abroad.
Data relate to total population for 1890–1940 and to civilian population thereafter. The latter includes members of the Armed Forces living off post or with their families on post, but excludes all other members of the Armed Forces.
Source: Bureau of the Census. Reprinted by permission from *The Economic Almanac, 1967–1968* (New York: The National Industrial Conference Board, Inc., 1967), p. 15.
Statistical Abstract: Statistical Abstract of the United States, 1970 (Washington, D.C.: Government Printing Office, 1970), p. 32.

transmitting the cultural heritage. The stress remains on child socialization as a major function of the nuclear family; as Bell and Vogel aptly put it: "No society, however simple, can persist in an orderly fashion without general orienting principles. . . . The significance of the nuclear family, with regard to the society's value system, stems from the fact that the nuclear family is the smallest social unit responsible for the preservation of the value system." [48] Now let us examine problems facing the child in these areas.

First, in this scientific age, parents are not quite sure they are equal to a task of this magnitude. For guidance in child rearing, parents eagerly read the publications of Gesell, Spock, Hymes, and other modern authorities. The philosophy of earlier treatises, such as Watson's *Psychological Care of Infants,*[49] was diametrically opposed to the central thesis of modern child-care techniques. The apparent confusion among the "experts" increases the insecurity of the parent. Insecurities and inconsistencies in parental guidance of children seriously hamper adequate personality development in these young citizens of our democracy.

Fortunately, modern authorities have available much research in the field of personality on which to base their advice. Modern techniques include an abundance of warmth and affection, especially for the very young child, to assure early emotional security and to free the infant for concentration on normal developmental tasks. They stress parental understanding of the strong egoism of the very young; the importance of the language of behavior; the need for being an attentive audience when the child feels that he has something important to express; the need for setting limits on the child's behavior, teaching him the bounds of behavior beyond which family and society say he cannot go; and the critical importance of assisting the child to evaluate himself, to decide which plans and goals are realistic for him.

The stress by the Women's Liberation movement for child-care centers to "free" mothers has not made much impression upon your authors. It is true that some mothers must work to provide family income; but this is at a price in the personality development of the child. As the eminent psychoanalyst Abram Kardiner has said, "You can't pay anyone to love your child. The monogamous nuclear family is the perfect environment for child development, for the incubation of feelings." [50]

Child developmentalists have little advice to offer the parent of the adolescent in today's affluent society. Today's adolescent is rebelling in far more basic ways than those of preceding generations. He seems almost like a five-year-old in his pleas to "Look at me!" He has no responsibilities during the long summer months. He rejects the materialism of adult culture while asking for his own room, his own TV, his own allowance, his own automobile, his own summer tour of Europe. The best advice, to date, seems to be to let him do his own thing—*on his own.* When he feels the need for family, he will return. This is little solace for concerned parents. How damaged will he be when he returns, *if* he returns? The massive love and

[48]Norman W. Bell and Ezra F. Vogel, *A Modern Introduction to the Family* (New York: Free Press, 1968), pp. 18–19.

[49]John B. Watson, *Psychological Care of Infants* (New York: Norton, 1928).

[50]Skolnick, op. cit., p. 22.

attention devoted to the child of today seems wasted, but the child developmentalists are convinced that their advice is sound. They question whether parents really have *loved* their children, or whether they have simply plied them with material comforts as a way to escape contact with them? The nuclear family has far too few contacts. If more real concern for each other were demonstrated, more real "listening" to one another occurred, more real affection were demonstrated, possibly the adolescent would not be so alienated from his culture.

"Many anthropologists and psychoanalysts have argued that the nuclear family is the fundamental building block of civilization, the basis of all societies, past, present, and future . . . the nuclear family arose as the family intensified the emotional bonds between its members and reduced those of outsiders." [51] What, then, has happened to "the emotional bonds" between parents and adolescents? This seems to be a phenomenon of the alienation of all youth from adult culture, to be discussed in Chapter 9, "Problems of Intergroup Relations." This is not meant to negate any of those sound principles of child-rearing enumerated previously.

All these modern techniques of child care are designed to build personalities who are creative and adaptable, who respect and show a genuine concern for others, who expect that same consideration from others, and who can make choices independently. These are personality traits that are essential to survival in a rapidly changing world. These techniques are understandably different from those designed to build personalities to live in the stable community of 100 years ago, where security was gained through extended-kinship families and where choices were made for youth by the family.

Modern parents are confused by the conflicting ideas on child-rearing of their own grandparents (who were reared in a stable culture), the ideas of Watson and others of the coldly "scientific" school of child-rearing that influenced their own parents, and the advice of the modern authorities. Development of a sound philosophy of child socialization is a very real problem for parents of today's child. If society is to progress, sound child-rearing practices must be followed. Personality defects acquired in infancy will handicap the child and his society for all of his life. If the parents remain confused, the child can find no sound foundation on which to build a healthy personality.

Secondly, complicating the confusion about proper child-rearing techniques may be the ambivalent attitudes of parents toward their children. "The child may be an economic burden to the parents, may conflict with parental ambitions or desire for freedom from responsibility; as a consequence, parents may develop the ambivalence of love and hate toward the child." [52] The reverse, of course, may be true; the imposition of necessary restraints upon the child may create temporary hatred toward the parent. But for so long as love remains the dominant emotion, this ambivalence is no real problem. No matter which way parents express their feelings, they assert strong hates and equally strong loves toward their children as a normal

[51]Ibid., pp. 18–19.
[52]Morris G. Caldwell and Laurence Foster, *Analysis of Social Problems* (Harrisburg, Pa.: Stackpole, 1954), p. 397.

part of parent–child relations. It is when the hate feelings lead to frequent rejection of the child that personality damage results.

A third problem in parent–child relations is the conflicting values between some homes and outside agencies such as church and school. The child is caught in a conflict of loyalties. He must disobey either the teaching of parents or the teachings of church or of school. If he disobeys the parent, family conflict probably will result; at the very least, family solidarity will be weakened. The conflict in values between lower-class homes and the school affects a significant portion of the population.

Fourthly, the individualism of the equalitarian, companionship marriage centers many of the family activities about adult interests. This is particularly true of suburban apartment dwellers. The child may have real difficulty in discerning himself as "an important person" when so few of the activities of the total family are centered about his interests. Failure to develop adequate concepts of self may result. This well may be the major problem facing the adolescent of the 1970's. He claims that adult society is "irrelevant." In terms of his definition, he is right; he cannot relate to adult society. Why? Maybe adults have been "too busy" or "too important" to relate to him. The European culture long has relegated the child to second-class citizenship, and the European university traditionally has been the scene of youthful rebellions.

Fifthly, the conflicts of adolescence are a major problem area for most families. The growing adolescent's need for independence from adult supervision, the conflict in values between the adolescent group and their parents, and the lessened control of parents over adolescent sex behavior are all bases for conflict.[53]

Finally, the high percentage of commuting husbands, working wives, and broken homes deprives the child of guidance by one or both of his parents for most of the time. Basic personality traits of these children are formed by persons other than the parents, who have intimate contacts with them in the formative years, nurses, babysitters, step parents, personnel of child-care institutions, and the like. Many of these children form very real feelings of inferiority and other negative personality traits because they feel that they are not important enough to be loved and cared for by their parents.

Careers and Family Roles

At first, careers and family roles seem to be a problem for women alone. Should the young woman get married, or should she embark upon a career? The modern woman, assisted by the equalitarian concept of husband helping the working wife with the housework and by the host of mechanical and other devices for reducing household drudgery, seems to be choosing both. Nearly two thirds of all women sixteen years of age and over are married and living with their husbands; 39.5 per cent of these women were in the labor force in 1969, approximately twice the number of working wives of the war years.

[53]The problems of adolescents are more fully treated in Chapter 7, under "Attaining Puberty."

This trend toward combined careers and families has created many problems for female youth. Should the young woman marry early and settle for a low-paying job? Should she defer marriage until after the college training necessary for a real career? "Even at the high school level there is the problem of emphasis on grade-getting in preparation for a job as compared with boy-getting in preparation for courtship, marriage, and mother-hood."[54] Should she have children? If so, how can she best manage simultaneously the roles of wife, mother, and careerwoman?

The young man must answer the same questions faced by the young woman as to the immediacy of marriage. Further, he must learn to compartmentalize his life into a career segment and a family segment. When work is brought home from the office night after night, no opportunities are provided for real family life.

Sex Behavior

Urbanization, the growth of scientific knowledge of birth control, and the lengthening period of formal education have accentuated the problems of modern youth in defining and conforming to changing sex mores. This does not necessarily mean that the problem of living within the sex mores is peculiar to recent generations. In sixty years the median age of first marriages for men declined from 26.1 to 20.4.[55] Thus we see that the period from the attainment of puberty to marriage has decreased in modern times for the average American; but this fact does not make the period any less traumatic. Paul Woodring, editor at large of *Saturday Review's* Education Supplement, points up the dilemma of the young:

> Human males reach their period of greatest sexual vigor and desire at a time prior to marriage, when the doors to socially approved sexual activity are closed to them, and the dilemma faced by girls, though different, is no less perplexing. Though some girls have strong sexual urges, more of them are motivated more by the desire to be popular with boys or by the desire to please one particular boy. The girl does not want to be thought old-fashioned, moralistic, or square.
>
> Although society has become more permissive [Woodring goes on], there is still no effective and accepted code of sexual conduct and each boy must decide for himself, and each girl for herself, where to draw the line. They need all the advice they can get from older people who presumably can take a longer view.[56]

Complicating the problem for modern youth is the supercharged atmosphere of sex stimulation that seems to pervade present-day culture. Sex is glorified in newspapers, magazines, and books; on billboards, radio, television; and in the cinema, where X ratings seem to be the mode of the 1970's. As a populace, we seem to be saturating ourselves with the physical aspects of sex. Becuse sex taboos largely have been based on the doctrines of ancient theologians, this verbal flaunting of the taboos may be expected in a society

---

[54]Clifford Kirkpatrick, *The Family as Process and Institution* (New York: Ronald, 1963), pp. 255–256.

[55]Ray E. Baber, *Marriage and the Family* (New York: McGraw-Hill, 1953), p. 585.

[56]Education U.A.A. *Special Report: Sex Education in Schools* (Washington, D.C.: N.S.P.R.A., N.E.A., 1969), p. 2.

that is in transition from a sacred to a secular base. That the flaunting is inconsistent, at least with parents, is revealed by parental insistence upon rigid adherence to their own interpretation of acceptable sex mores by their children, even though they themselves have violated them. In fact they may be violating their own verbalizations of the mores by "party behavior" at the very time they are insisting on chastity in their offspring! [57] The wife swapping of the 1970's is a case in point.

The "dating" complex that has grown up in the United States since World War I, combined with the automobile, has thrown young people upon their own moral resources in the area of sex behavior. They must decide for themselves the nature and the frequency of the physical intimacies permitted the opposite sex. Boys tend to be the aggressors in this area, both through earlier sex drive and through cultural expectation. The young lady must decide where to draw the line in the progression that leads from holding hands through kissing and fondling to coitus.

Despite the writings of Edward Carpenter, Ellen Key, Havelock Ellis, Bertrand Russell, Aldous Huxley, William Reich, and others, who preach varying degrees of sex freedom, the thoughtful writer has little difficulty in marshaling an array of arguments against premarital sex experience. Baber summarized these arguments as follows.

1. Premarital coitus will not prove whether the couple will be well mated and will make a successful sex adjustment in marriage. . . . Even if both reached full physical satisfaction, it would be no indication that they would be suitable marriage partners, for love is far more than a "sexual outlet."

2. Premarital sex experience, instead of being a helpful introduction to the sex life in marriage, may actually be one of the poorest possible introductions, especially for the girl. The act usually occurs after she has long resisted the idea and is finally persuaded against her better judgment. In such circumstance it is entered into not with anticipation and freedom, but with misgivings that magnify her normal inhibitions to such an extent that she gets no pleasure from the act.

3. Young folks of real character have great difficulty with their consciences when they indulge in sex behavior which they know runs squarely against all their home training, their moral and religious teaching, and the established tenets of society. Their sense of guilt makes them unhappy, especially when they think of the faith their parents have in them.

4. The possibility of pregnancy is a constant source of worry.

5. Frequently, when a young couple are in love and have engaged in sex relations before marriage, suspicions arise in the minds of each as to whether the other has had similar intimacies with others.

6. Furthermore, it frequently happens that a young couple who are engaged and begin sex relations do not marry after all. They feel differently, and conduct which they had justified in their own minds becomes just an illicit relationship.

7. The difficulty sometimes carries over into marriage, when either bride or groom has had previous sex relations and is afraid to tell the other . . . there is a tendency to try to wipe the slate clean by telling all, but it doesn't always work out as wished, for past indiscretions, even when consciously repudiated, still persist as lurking anxiety.

[57]Willard Waller and Reuben Hill, *The Family: A Dynamic Interpretation* (New York: Dryden, 1951), pp. 584–587.

8. Premarital sex relations sometimes lead to varying degrees of personality disorganization, especially in girls who have been reared with a high regard for moral and religious standards.[58]

To the psychological costs of irregular sex expression must be added the social costs. Exact statistics, of course, are unavailable, but it was estimated in 1953 that there were 150,000 illegitimate births and 350,000 abortions annually in the United States.[59] The 1968 figures for illegitimate births were more than double the above figures, as noted below in Table 9; 1973 estimates may double again.

The Children's Bureau estimates that one half of the illegitimate mothers are eighteen or younger.[60] This would mean that about one half of these

TABLE 9
Illegitimate Live Births, by Age and Race of Mother: 1940 to 1968

[In thousands, except as indicated. Prior to 1960, excludes Alaska and Hawaii. Includes estimates for states in which legitimacy data were not reported. No estimates included for misstatements on birth records or failures to register births.]

AGE AND RACE	1940	1945	1950	1955	1960	1965	1966	1967	1968
Total	89.5	117.4	141.6	183.3	224.3	291.2	302.4	318.1	339.2
Per cent of all births*	3.5	4.1	3.9	4.5	5.3	7.7	8.4	9.0	9.7
Rate†	7.1	10.1	14.1	19.3	21.8	23.4	23.6	24.0	24.1
	—	—	—	—	—	—	—	—	—
By age of mother:									
Under 15 years	2.1	2.5	3.2	3.9	4.6	6.1	6.2	6.9	7.7
15–19 years	40.5	49.2	56.0	68.9	87.1	123.1	135.8	144.4	158.0
20–24 years	27.2	39.3	43.1	55.7	68.0	90.7	92.5	101.6	107.9
25–29 years	10.5	14.1	20.9	28.0	32.1	36.8	35.5	34.5	35.2
30–34 years	5.2	7.1	10.8	16.1	18.9	19.6	18.4	17.3	17.2
35–39 years	3.0	4.0	6.0	8.3	10.6	11.4	10.5	10.1	9.7
40 years and over	1.0	1.2	1.7	2.4	3.0	3.7	3.4	3.3	3.3
By race of mother:									
White	40.3	56.4	53.5	64.2	82.5	123.7	132.9	142.2	155.2
Negro and other	49.2	60.9	88.1	119.2	141.8	167.5	169.5	175.8	183.9
Per cent of total	55.0	51.9	62.2	65.0	63.2	57.5	56.1	55.3	54.2

* Through 1955, based on data adjusted for underregistration; thereafter, registered births. For total birth figures used to derive these data, see table 53.
† Rate per 1,000 unmarried (never married, widowed, and divorced) women aged 15–44 years enumerated as of April 1 for 1940 and 1950 and estimated as of July 1 for all other years.
Source: Dept. of Health, Education, and Welfare, Public Health Service; annual report, *Vital Statistics of the United States*. Reprinted from the Statistical Abstract of the United States, 1970 (Washington, D.C.: Government Printing Office, 1970), p. 50.

[58]From *Marriage and the Family* (pp. 596–599), by Ray E. Baber. Copyright 1953 by McGraw-Hill Book Company, Inc. Used with permission of McGraw-Hill Book Company.
[59]Ibid., pp. 909, 916.
[60]Maud Morlock and Hilary Campbell, "Maternity Homes for Unmarried Mothers," Children's Bureau Publication 309, p. 13.

girls were enrolled in high school at the time of conception. This is a challenge for educators.[61] Many of these unwed mothers receive adequate care in reputable nursing homes and place their children, despite social disapproval amounting almost to ostracism in some parts of the United States, even if not in Scandinavia. Some fall victim to the adoption racket operation in "black market babies." In any case, most are forced to leave home and family for a "secret" lying-in and delivery period at the very time they most need sympathetic family guidance. The personality disorganization of these girls must be added to the social costs of bearing and rearing children in socially disapproved ways.

It has been estimated that perhaps 90 per cent of all abortions are performed on married women, especially wives in the twenty-five to thirty-five age group who already have several children.[62] Except when legally authorized to save the life of the mother, abortion commonly has been held to be the taking of life. Some states are changing their laws; but society pays the bill when human energies, and even human life, are wasted in these illegitimate and abortive results of irregular sex expression. Of these costs the economic one seems minor compared with the moral decay of society and the accompanying personality disorganization of its members. The women's liberation movement challenges this assumption, on the grounds that a woman should have the right to decide the utilization of her own body. The conservative elements of society agree—she should decide as to whether or not she should be involved in sexual intercourse—but they challenge her right to abortion as a solution to her own folly. Whether or not the right to sexual intercourse without regard to the consequences shall become a "right" of society is a decision reserved to posterity. Upon the moral standards of youth rests the solution of this problem.

Mate Selection and Courtship

For so long as the romantic ideal exists, mate selection cannot be a coldly scientific process in a culture in which people are free to choose their own mate, and probably it should not be. Much of the tenderness that makes of marriage a satisfying relationship in this era of individualism probably is based on physical attraction, and this sudden, mutual attraction is the basis of the romantic ideal.

One of the blocks to rational mate selection is that our cultural definition of "romance" encourages youth to idealize the loved one. In the first mad infatuation, love is blind to any and all faults of the object of affection. "If one is to use his head in mate selection, he must do it early. The only time in the process that the intellect is capable of functioning successfully is before, not after, one has fallen in love, for that rather rare pastime known as cerebration frequently varies inversely as the intensity of

[61]This is a challenge to families first. A family put a daughter into one of the strictest girls' schools so that they might feel she was safe. She had an abortion within the year. This is similar to the situation of families who cannot control their sons and hope that the military school or the army can teach them values that should have been learned at home.

[62]Baber, op. cit., p. 616.

emotion."[63] Parental or peer comments on the "ideal one" can lead only to conflict with the persons making the derogatory remarks.

A second block is the impetuousness of youth. Long engagements are not the fashion today. Often the infatuated couple rushes to the altar, only to discover after the honeymoon is over that their mate is not at all the person they thought they were marrying.

Fortunately, society has evolved several procedures that make mate selection a trifle less hazardous.[64] To begin with, children and youth make many contacts with members of the opposite sex in "dating" situations at an early age. Many of these relations appear to resemble sibling relations rather than approaches to mate selection. Secondly, the phenomenon of "going steady" (as puberty comes to pass and the "sibling" relations cease) provides firsthand experience with the complete cycle of infatuation–disillusionment–separation on a premarital basis. The caution provided by these experiences may make youth a bit more careful in the selection of the next recipient of their affections.[65] Finally, the courtship period itself normally allows for one to meet the parents and friends of the loved one. Obvious cultural dissimilarities may at least prolong the engagement. The additional time thus purchased not only allows for gradual dissipation of the intensity of emotion, with the return of a more rational viewpoint, but also provides much more material as a basis for rational consideration. Folsom indicates something of the variety of these materials.[66]

Prospective partners need especially to know each other's attitudes regarding the number and timing of children, their management and discipline, the role of the wife as homemaker or worker outside the home, and such other considerations as housing, accumulation of possessions, money, travel, extramarital friendships, the role of sex in life, and the duty of the family toward the community and its institutions. Each needs to know what the other is likely to do under emotional strain. Will he resort to drink, illness, quest of excitement, or will he retreat into a world of fancy? When hurt will she be cold for a long while toward the person who hurt her, or will she develop a rage which can be easily softened into love and reconciliation? She needs to know what he is apt to drop out of his life when he becomes busy and preoccupied; what pleasures he will most likely retain under these circumstances. She needs to know what is his pattern of work. Is it normal for him to become preoccupied for long periods with his work, punctuated by intense "sprees" which she may share with him by proper timing of her activities; or does he thrive best on a little work, a little play, a little love, each day with regularity? He needs to know whether she likes to save money cumulatively, or to save merely so as to keep always a little ahead of the game, or whether she is comfortable being always a little in debt. Each needs to know whether the other really wants to be told

[63]Ibid., p. 136.

[64]For excellent treatments of the courtship period, see part two of E. E. Le Masters, *Modern Courtship and Marriage* (New York: Macmillan, 1957). Also see Chapters 4–9 of Henry A. Bowman, *Marriage for Moderns* (New York: McGraw-Hill, 1965).

[65]There is no research evidence to document this conjecture.

[66]J. K. Folsom (ed.), *Plan for Marriage* (New York: Harper, 1937), pp. 96–97. Reprinted by permission of the publishers.

everything, or whether he would rather remain ignorant of possibly unpleasant facts which do not affect him.

Other factors also influence marital choices favorably. Families tend to live in neighborhoods composed of others of like cultural backgrounds. Bossard found that of the applicants for 5,000 consecutive marriage licenses issued in Philadelphia, nearly one quarter of the partners lived within two blocks of each other and more than one half lived within twenty blocks of each other.[67] Moreover, families who visit other families farther removed in residence tend to visit families of like backgrounds. This broadens the field of contact with possible life mates for children of both families, still within the framework of families of like acculturation. A further accentuation in this pattern of influencing the field of candidates from whom one might select a mate is parental attitudes of encouraging children to associate only with the "right" playmates. Normally, the "right" playmates means "our kind of people."

The importance of length of engagement and of similarity of cultural backgrounds, stressed previously, is further documented in Table 10, " Basic Background Factors in Marital Success," compiled by Waller and Hill after an examination of the research studies bearing on factors related to marital success. The other factors noted in the table may be beyond the control of the individual by the time that he has reached the age of mate selection. For the approximately one half of the population who do not marry within their residential area, knowledge of the importance of these factors is critical to propitious mate selection.

Certainly mate selection designed to produce happy marriages is one of the major problems facing youth today, not only for the sake of the individuals doing the selecting but for the future of the marriages of their children. Close examination of Table 10, in all five major areas, stresses the importance of happily married parents in the development of characteristics that are favorable for happy marriage of the children. Stability in marriage, in an individualistic age, depends on the continued happiness of both partners. The happiness of tomorrow's marriages will be largely determined by the wisdom employed in selecting today's mates. The future stability of the family will be determined by the happiness of the marriages of today.

Married-Pair Living

The newly married couple faces a host of new problems. The major task is that of submerging one's individuality in the building of a new unity between the married pair.[68] The personality of the newly formed family, with its offspring, will be a harmonious, integrating one or an inharmonious, disintegrating one largely to the degree to which the individual marriage partners willingly and cheerfully can subordinate individual desires to group welfare. In this age of individualism this is indeed a difficult task.

[67]James H. Bossard, "Residential Propinquity as a Factor in Marriage Selection," *American Journal of Sociology*, September 1932, pp. 219–224.
[68]J. L. Hirning and Alma L. Hirning, *Marriage Adjustment* (New York: American Book, 1956), pp. 257–278.

Another problem, inherent in modern culture, is sex. Never has any culture been bombarded with sex like the modern generation. The Madison Avenue blurbs in advertising and the X-rated films are obvious; the literature is less conspicuous, for fewer people read in this era of instantaneous communication. Examples of current titles are "The Dangers of the New Promiscuity,"[69] *Sex and the College Girl*,[70] and *The Return of Modesty*.[71] The modern housewife who responds to her husband's sexual advances with less than abandon may feel ashamed, and there is no reason for her to feel so. Sex is here to stay, but there is no reason for glorifying it as modern culture seems to do. A little common-sense talking out of sexual problems between man and wife could save many modern marriages.

The young couple is faced immediately with choices in furniture, life insurance programs, health, recreation, religious and social organizations, political affiliation, sex adjustment, and a host of lesser problems. Most of these, of course, are tied to that difficult problem, the family budget. Two people simply cannot maintain the same standard of living on a man's salary as he maintained when he was supporting only himself. The wife may choose to work; if so, this affects the couple's plans for children. If the choice is for an immediate family, soon three or four people may be living on the single salary. In such a case, the wife in the moderate-income bracket must assume the roles of mother, housekeeper, cook, seamstress, and keeper of the family budget if the couple is to make ends meet financially. The impact of these personal and financial problems on immature youth (approximately 70 per cent of all youth aged twenty to twenty-four already are married) is revealed in divorce statistics.[72] Many simply cannot cope with problems and quit early in the game. Most divorces occur in the first five years of marriage, and two thirds of all divorces are granted within the first ten years of married life.[73] A new solution may be imminent for these couples: part-time work for the wife. The *Saturday Review* states that these married women are

> Unwilling, or unable, to assume the responsibility of a conventional eight-hour day, five-days-a-week job . . . a national non-profit organization was founded in 1962 to seek ways in which mature women could combine family responsibilities with work in positions that are equal to their abilities. Called Catalyst (6 East 82nd Street, New York, N.Y., 10028) the organization is enjoying increasing success in placing women in positions in education, science and industry, and social work. . . . Catalyst contracted with the Massachusetts Department of Welfare to recruit, train and supervise fifty women to fill twenty-five full-time case worker jobs. More than 500 women applied.[74]

[69]Elizabeth Brodie, "The Dangers of the New Promiscuity," *Maclean's*, August 1971, pp. 14ff.

[70]Gail Greene, *Sex and the College Girl* (New York: Dell, 1964).

[71]Marjorie Harris, "The Return of Modesty," *Maclean's*, January 1970, pp. 31–35.

[72]Morris G. Caldwell and Laurence Foster, *Analysis of Social Problems* (Harrisburg, Pa.: Stackpole, 1948), p. 388.

[73]Howard Becker and Reuben Hill, *Family, Marriage, and Parenthood* (Boston: Heath, 1955), p. 685.

[74]Paul Woodring, "Education in America," *Saturday Review*, July 19, 1969, p. 45. Copyright 1969 Saturday Review, Inc.

TABLE 10

Basic Background Factors in Marital Success

	FAVORABLE	UNFAVORABLE	UNRELATED
Personality Characteristics	Permissive and considerate attitudes (both). Cooperative attitudes (both). Compatibility of temperament. Combinations where neither is neurotic. Combinations where both are intellectually superior.	Lacks self-confidence (husband). Man daydreams and woman does not. Man feels inferior and woman does not. Woman makes friends easily and man does not. Self-sufficiency in facing troubles alone (both). Proneness to argue points (wife). Unhappy temperament (both). Variability in moods (both). Feelings easily hurt (both).	Extroversion–introversion. Friendliness or offishness.
Cultural and Family Backgrounds	Similarity of cultural backgrounds. Similarity of educational level. Father of high occupational level (both). Firm but not harsh home training (both). Happiness of parents' marriage (both). Happiness of childhood (both). Conservative home backgrounds.	Dissimilarity in cultural and family backgrounds. Wife's cultural background higher than husband's. Residence in the city during childhood.	Number of siblings. Birth order in family. Differences in educational achievements of parents. Modernist or fundamentalist religious beliefs. Economic circumstances at marriage.

Sociability Factors	Frequency of attendance at church and Sunday school. Number of friends (both sexes). Residence in single-family dwellings. Social conservatism.	Unconventionality with respect to religion, sexual ethics, drinking. Religious inactivity.	Number of persons with whom one has "kept company."
Response Patterns	Love based on companionship. Length of acquaintance before marriage. Similarity between parent of opposite sex and affianced (both). Strong attachment to father (both).	Romantic infatuation as basis of love. Disapproval of marriage by parents (especially husband's). Conflict with father (both).	Amount of "petting" before marriage. Fear of pregnancy.
Sex Factors	Sex information received from parents first (both). Frank and encouraging attitudes of parents toward child's curiosity about sex (important for husband). Similarity in sex desires. Orgasm capacity in wife. Amount of pleasure wife experienced at first intercourse.	Premarital intercourse by either or both (low but negative relationship to subsequent marital adjustment). Fear of sex (wife). Prudishness and excessive modesty (wife). Husband–wife differences in strength of sex drive.	Sex techniques used. Frequency and duration of intercourse. Degree of pain exerienced by wife at first intercourse. Methods of contraception used.

Source: Reprinted from *The Family: A Dynamic Interpretation* (p. 352), by Willard Waller and revised by Reuben Hill. Copyright 1938 by Holt, Rinehart and Winston, Inc. Revised edition copyright 1951 by Holt, Rinehart and Winston, Inc.

Parenthood

The newly married couple may make a conscious choice of parenthood. Birth control information is as readily available as the family physician, except in Massachusetts where medical prescription of contraceptives is illegal. Even couples living within the moral framework of religions that ban the use of contraceptives are tending toward the modern mode of planned parenthood, through abstinence from sexual intercourse during the fertile period of the female.

Even this aspect of family and marriage is challenged by science. Parenthood may now be possible through artificial insemination from a male unknown to the natural mother, or by implanting in the womb of an infertile female eggs from a fertile female, thus making the natural mother unknown even when the wife actually "bears" the child. There is even the possibility of sperm banks and egg banks, with the baby conceived in laboratory glassware (*in vitro*), where both the natural father and the natural mother remain anonymous! Surely this has implications for such old words as *sex, love, family,* and *marriage.* As Rosenfeld says:

> There was no reason to doubt that the facts of life on which the whole moral structure rested would also remain essentially unchanged forever. But in the sciences forever has a way of turning out to be not so everlasting after all. We are now entering an era when, as a result of some new scientific discoveries, some mind-boggling things are likely to happen. Children may routinely be born of geographically separated or even long-dead parents, virgin births may become relatively common, women may give birth to other women's children, romance and genetics may finally be separated, and a few favored men may be called upon to father thousands of babies.[75]

Modern science produces visions exceeding the science fiction fantasies of only a few years ago, including the male retired to stud, pampered for only his sperm-producing capacity. This may be in the future, but this text will deal only with the *foreseeable* future.

There are two major facets of the birth-control aspects of planned parenthood. One involves the decision of whether to have children at all. The cost of bearing and rearing children obviously must result in other adjustments to most family budgets. If the wife worked previously to childbirth, the loss of her income coincides in time with an increase in family expenses. This may mean fewer party clothes (and fewer parties) and less frequent trips to the golf links, the hairdresser, the theater, the symphony, and the like. Couples who enjoyed travel during summer vacations may find that they no longer can afford it. The restaurant meal that used to be a regular routine now becomes a rare luxury.

Of course, this is all relative to the family income. It has been estimated that to rear a child to the age of eighteen it costs a family with an annual income of $2,500 nearly $8,000 in cash; the cost for a family with an income between $5,000 and $10,000 is over $16,000.[76] To the cash outlay

---

[75]From "Challenge to the Miracle of Life," by Albert Rosenfeld, *Life Magazine,* June 13, 1969, p. 40. © 1969 Time, Inc.

[76]Louis I. Dublin, "The Cost of Raising a Child in Higher Income Families," *Statistical Bulletin,* Metropolitan Life Insurance Company (January 1944).

must be added the personal services required to rear a child; parents invest many hours in bathing, feeding, clothing, training (educating, socializing), and entertaining the child. This total cost is more than some families are willing to bear.

The second aspect of birth control, once the decision to bear children has been reached, involves regulating the number and spacing of the children. The economic and personal-service costs of rearing children definitely affect the total number of children in the family. (As noted in an earlier section, when birth-control techniques are faulty, abortions may be induced in the effort to control family size, particularly in the group of married women aged twenty-five to thirty-five who already have several children.) The health of the baby is a major factor affecting spacing of children. The National Committee for Planned Parenthood claims that when births are one year apart, the loss of babies is nearly 50 per cent higher than when the births are two years apart.[77] The adverse effects of too closely spaced babies upon the health of some mothers is another reason for the widespread practice of birth control for the spacing of children.

Once the baby has been born, the process of child socialization proceeds. These parent–child relations have been discussed in pp. 196–198. However, we should review a major point, discipline, on which so many parents and teachers are confused; it is the crux of the socialization process, on which depends the success of the child in developing self-direction and self-control. As Brown puts it:

> A complicating factor in the American home is the lack of standardization regarding maturity. Among primitive people, the initiation ceremony marked the transition from child to adult. In our times, a person must be 21 years of age to vote In all but one state; he is allowed to work at ages varying from 14 to 18, depending on the state laws; the age at which young people can marry is a matter of state lines, varying from age 12 for girls and 14 for boys, with parental consent, to age 21 for both, without parental consent. The variation in the attitude of parents toward the maturity of their children shows similar contrasts, from those who believe that home discipline should be retained until marriage —and sometimes afterward as well—to those who assume that young children should be given much the same sense of responsibility as adults.[78]

The Empty Nest

Married pairs are often startled to discover that their "babies" have grown up. The departure of the last child from the home for college or for marriage signals the start of a period of major readjustments for both parents. "The period after children marry is typically a long one—some 25 to 30 years for the average couple . . . a post-parental period, lasting from approximately age 45 to age 65, when retirement typically calls for a change of roles; and a retirement period."[79] The father faces a less serious problem

---

[77]Baber, op. cit., p. 546.

[78]Francis J. Brown, *Educational Sociology*, 2nd ed. (Englewood Cliffs, N.J.: Prentice-Hall, 1954), p. 240.

[79]Ruth Shonle Cavan, *The American Family*, Fourth Edition (New York: Crowell, 1969), p. 486.

than his wife, for he has devoted a relatively larger portion of his interests and energies to his occupation, with correspondingly less involvement in the process of child rearing. Moreover, his occupation offers him not only an outlet for the energies that formerly were expended in the family situation, but also the opportunity to escape the place so full of memories of the recently departed children. The mother is in a less favorable position. Her child-bearing and child-rearing span is comparatively short.[80] She reaches the stage of the empty nest in physical and mental condition appropriate for many more years of useful service, only to realize that her life's function apparently is complete. The empty house symbolizes the emptiness of the years ahead. Her emotional adjustment may be difficult.

Parents who have kept alive interests other than parental duties can cope more successfully with this crisis. This is particularly true if the companionship roles of husband and wife have been satisfactorily fulfilled through the years of parenthood. The married pair who can "do what they always wanted to but hadn't the time because of the children" receive assistance in adjustment not only from the revived interests but also from the mutual reinforcement of the sympathetic mate. This type of married-pair adjustment builds a much more stable foundation for the childless years ahead than the individual adjustments through mutually exclusive interests such as father's vocation and mother's social clubs.

These can be the happiest years of life. Those who are forty-five to sixty-five have been called the command generation, for they control so much of the economic, political, and social life of the nation; they are the generation referred to by youth as the "Establishment." They represent only one fourth of the population, but they earn more than half of the nation's income.[81] They seem to have "better physical health, greater resistance to disease and superior emotional stamina." [82] But they have problems. Work may have lost its appeal because of too many years of sameness; this can be true for both gainful employment and housework. The independence of the young, or even gratuitous advice from the children, may be hard to accept. The normal aging process may be perceived with such exaggeration that hypochondria develops. Plateaus of achievement may terminate the promotional process and one may awaken to realize one is in a "dead-end job." This is the time of life to assay one's assets, explore avenues that promise emotional fulfillment, and make basic plans for the decades ahead. Some couples find, to their delight, that the initial period of the "empty nest" is the first time that they have had time and resources to "be married."

The Aged

The extended-kinship family of rural America considered the care of the aged a family matter. The shifts from rural to urban residence, from agriculture to industry, and from extended-kinship family to conjugal family

[80]Paul C. Glick, "The Family Cycle," *American Sociological Review*, Vol. 12 (April 1947), pp. 167–168.

[81]Ted J. Rakstis, "Generation in the Middle," in *Blue Print for Health: Generation in the Middle*, Vol. 23, No. 1 (Indianapolis: Blue Cross Association, 1970), p. 11.

[82]Ralph Bugg, "Caution! Men at Work," in ibid., p. 82.

have combined with increased longevity to create an increasing number of old people who are unemployed, impoverished, and unable to depend upon their family for support. (For a discussion of this problem, see Chapter 11.)

The economic support of the aged is still a legal responsibility of the family in many states. Further, the folkways of the extended-kinship family linger in the memories of the people. A major factor is that children who love their parents cannot see them suffer economic deprivation without making some effort to relieve their suffering. In discussing the problem of economic dependency of the aged, Kirkpatrick says:

> The familial group in the past has taken heavy responsibility for support of the aged. Now the OAA program creates confusion in regard to the roles of the familial group and the state. The laws of some 35 states still bear witness to the social expectation that consanguineal and affinal relationships imply responsibility for aged family members who are in need.
>
> In some 14 of these states OAA benefits are withheld on the assumption that relatives should bear their share. Contributions from relatives determined by complicated schedules must be deducted from the old age assistance benefits. The aged may even be encouraged to sue their own relatives to obtain these contributions, thus jeopardizing familial good will and discouraging voluntary contributions. Since the relatives of the aged are often poor, they may take aged relatives into their own homes unwillingly, with a possibility of familial disharmony. Confusion as to the responsibility of family and state is further indicated by the laws in about half the states which seek to recover OAA payments from the estate of a deceased beneficiary. The total effect of efforts by the state to coerce support of the aged by family members is probably a weakening of voluntary cooperation.[83]

The burden of economic support of aged family members often is unfairly distributed among the children. Married children readily shift the burden to the single sibling, especially if this sibling still resides with the aged parent. Even when the burden is shared, the yoke may be heavy. The life insurance programs, pensions, social security programs, and the like mentioned in Chapter 11 may relieve this burden in many cases. The sharp rises in social security taxes and benefits, together with the concurrent legislation on Medicare, may portend a future in which the aged will retain economic independence, even to the extent of provision of home care for the physically feeble and/or incapacitated. Governmental programs, financed from payroll deductions in the productive years of the worker, seem to be moving rapidly in this direction. Realization of these programs is not yet here; however, it may be closer than is commonly realized. The size of the over-sixty-five group is increasing, as is its political awareness. National organizations of the aged are springing up. There soon may be an "aged vote" bloc influencing state and federal legislation; if so, financial support of the aged by government is certain to increase.

Aside from the loss of economic independence, two major problems face the aged parent. One is loss of status. This varies by class level.

[83]Clifford Kirkpatrick, *The Family as Process and Institution*, Second Edition, p. 549. Copyright © 1963, The Ronald Press Co., New York.

In the lower class the context is one of a relatively unified mutual-aid economy in which old folks manage their statuses in a larger kinfolk entity. In the upper class, old people normally retain status and honorific positions, including power, to the end. In the middle classes old people retain status only if they are economically competent and worthy. A middle-class person loses social respectability when he no longer can hold his own economically.[84]

The aged who have lost status face a major adjustment problem. To have advice to their own children rejected as being old-fashioned or impractical is bitter medicine for the person who has guided these children through the years of their mental immaturity. An even greater gap exists between the aged and the grandchildren, who sometimes have difficulty even in communicating.

The second major problem is one of social isolation. The conjugal family has no place for grandparents or for aged aunts and uncles. Even when physical residence is enforced, social communication is at a minimum. Ways of thinking, behaving, and even of speaking have changed so rapidly in American culture that there is little real basis for social interaction among three generations. Old age is becoming increasingly a lonely time for most persons. One explanation of this phenomenon is the disengagement theory of aging. The older person is simply less involved in the social system than when he was in his productive years. Old social roles have been abandoned. There are no significant new roles assigned by the system to the aged, so the aged person withdraws both physically and emotionally from a world which has no use for him.[85] The only social contacts which have meaning for him become those with age mates, and they, too, have no societal roles. Creative use of leisure time with persons of like ages seems to offer the best hope for mental health for the aged. In the "retirement colonies" of Florida, California, and the Southwest, such activities are readily accessible, but less than 1 per cent of the aged leave their states,[86] so many aged persons have difficulty in establishing the needed contacts. They truly are "The Old in the Country of the Young"; they are 20 million aged in a country with nearly 100 million persons below the age of twenty-five. (Just under half the population is under the age of twenty-five!) [87] (Anticipated life span is shown in Figure 12.) The problem, of course, lies in the *causes* for disengagement. Retirement is the obvious cause for the male or for the employed female. This is *not* true of the "housewife," who really sees no change except that her husband is "underfoot" and needs coddling much more. The real problem is the culture, which "tends to place youth on a pedestal, high above any other age, to be honored, admired, emulated and even worshipped . . . older women forget to remember that beauty has its gradations. There is beauty in childhood, in adolescence, in adulthood, in middle age, and in the

[84]Willard Waller and Reuben Hill, *The Family: A Dynamic Interpretation* (New York: Dryden, 1951).

[85]Frank Itzin, "Social Relations," in Adelin M. Hoffman and William D. Bechill (eds.), *The Daily Needs and Interests of Older People* (Springfield, Ill.: Thomas, 1970), pp. 137–162.

[86] "The Old in the Country of the Young," *Time*, Vol. 96, No. 5, p. 42.

[87] "America's New Look, as the Census Sees It," *Changing Times*, August 1971, p. 13.

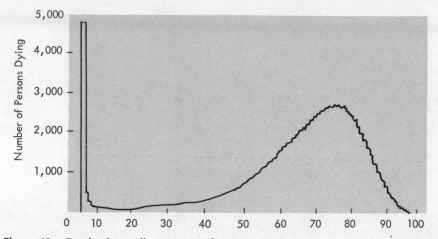

Figure 12. Deaths from all causes (peak at 77 years). [Source: Dr. Alex Comfort, *Conquest of Aging* (Saskatoon: University of Saskatchewan, 1968), p. 11. Used by permission.]

older years." [88] The culture seems in no mood to change, so the aged must adjust to it, preferably with age mates.

Family Disorganization

Not all families enact a continuous drama, with a resident cast, from the cradle to the grave. The actors change in far too many casts. Family disorganization occurs when there is serious and prolonged conflict or when the family unit is broken. Either of these situations suggests an unhappy family. The members of the family carry their unhappiness with them to work and to play, infecting society with their tensions. Society pays for the unhappy family.

Divorce, legal separation, or desertion normally come only after serious and prolonged family conflict. The obvious remedy for these causes of broken homes is to discover and to eliminate the causes of unhappy marriages. The legal causes of divorce, listed in the order of the number of states recognizing their validity, are as follows: adultery, cruelty, desertion, insanity, pregnancy at marriage, bigamy, separation, indignities, drug addiction, violence, and fraudulent contract.[89] The real causes of the family discord preceding desertion, separation, or divorce are more elusive. Basically, all conflict results from blocking of goal-seeking behavior.[90] Whenever the gratification of the wishes of one marriage partner means frustrating the desires of the other, there is conflict. These bases of marital unhappiness are as broad as life itself. The "obvious" remedy must elude the social scientist, at least for the time being.

[88]Maxwell S. Cagan, *There's Gold in Your Golden Age* (Minneapolis: T. S. Denison and Co., 1963), p. 61.
[89]*Information Please Almanac* (New York: Macmillan, 1965), p. 304.
[90]See Chapter 7.

If a positive approach were taken—that is, concentrating on the building of happy marriages—then more rapid progress might be made toward reducing the number of unhappy times. We have indicated earlier that the building of healthy personalities in children, with stress upon adaptability and upon consideration for others, is the best possible preparation for happy marriage. The importance of this second trait (consideration for others) is noted by Cohn in the negative sense by referring to disruptive marriage behavior as "an orgy of the ego . . . an indulgence of the gratification of the immediate desires of man or wife without regard to family, children, or state . . . individualism gone made." [91]

The common causes for broken homes are death, separation, and divorce. One marriage in four was terminating in divorce in the 1960's, as shown earlier in Table 7, and nearly two thirds of all divorces involved one or more children, as shown in Table 11, but divorce accounts for only a small portion of families headed by only one parent. Hunt indicates that about 10 per cent of all broken homes are headed by divorced persons, approximately twice as many by those legally separated, and nearly three fourths by individuals who have been widowed. [92]

TABLE 11

Per Cent Distribution of Divorces and Annulments, by Number of Children
Reported According to Duration of Marriage: Divorce-Registration Area, 1963
(Based on Sample Data)

DURATION OF MARRIAGE	ALL DIVORCES AND ANNULMENTS	NUMBER OF CHILDREN REPORTED			
		NONE	1	2	3+
		Percentage Distribution			
Under 1 year	100.0	84.8	11.2	1.7	2.3
1–2 years	100.0	57.5	34.6	6.3	1.5
3–4 years	100.0	38.5	35.5	20.5	5.5
5–9 years	100.0	28.7	22.0	25.9	23.5
10–14 years	100.0	24.4	15.9	23.2	36.5
15 years and over	100.0	34.5	19.2	19.5	26.8
Total	100.0	38.4	23.9	18.7	19.0

Source: *Divorce Statistics Analysis, United States—1963*, Public Health Service Publication No. 1000, Series 21, No. 13 (Washington, D.C.: Government Printing Office, 1967), pp. 34–35.

When children are involved, the problems of broken homes are magnified. Truxal and Merrill emphasize that it is the unhappy marriage that poisons the world of the child. Whether the marriage is broken psychologically by bitter and continuous conflict, or legally by divorce, or by separation or death, the child loses an emotional security that he may never recover. [93]

[91]David L. Cohn, "Are Americans Polygamous?" *Atlantic*, August 1957, pp. 30–33.

[92]Elgin F. Hunt, *Social Science* (New York: Macmillan, 1955), p. 186.

[93]Andrew G. Truxal and Francis E. Merrill, *Marriage and the Family in American Culture* (Englewood Cliffs, N.J.: Prentice-Hall, 1953), pp. 545–546.

Remarriage of the surviving spouse (or of the separated or divorced spouse retaining custody of the children) may provide economic security for the children and eventual emotional security, but not until many difficult adjustments have been made. New roles need to be defined not only between the newly married couple but also between at least one spouse and one or more children. When both partners bring children to the marriage, many new relationships and roles need to defined. Unfortunately, there is no script to follow; each member must "ad lib" his way, defining his own role in the group.

Some emotional support is given to the family broken by death through the bereavement rituals designed by society. Friends and neighbors gather, saying only complimentary things about the deceased and offering material assistance during the adjustment period. The divorced person has no such ritual to support him. The tendency is to condemn the defects of one or both spouses and possibly to ostracize those involved.[94] The family separated by desertion often has no public notice taken of their plight until the initial shock of the separation has been dissipated; by that time the "deserter" frequently has returned home. The person separated by a legal step short of divorce suffers much the same discrimination as the divorced person. Statistics reveal little of the human suffering involved in broken homes. Death may mean the passing of the one human being with whom genuine affection and respect was shared, or it may mean release from a drunken, sadistic monster. Divorce normally is the result, not the cause, of family suffering; but, especially with children, it may cause much new or further suffering.

As far as desertion is concerned, "It would appear that a figure of 100,000 deserters per year is conservative. This would be roughly one desertion to every four divorces—1950." [95]

If one adds the divorce and desertion totals and compares them with the marriage totals, one can well understand the concern of many for the future stability of the family. In recent years this ratio has been approximately one desertion and four divorces for every sixteen marriages; in short, nearly one third as many homes annually are being broken by desertion and divorce as are being created by marriage. Fortunately, not all broken homes involve children. Childless couples are twice as prone to divorce as couples with children; further, as the size of the family increases, the likelihood of divorce decreases.[96] In addition, in homes broken by death, the great majority of these involve marriage partners over sixty-five; obviously, fewer young children are present in homes with parents over sixty-five.

In summary, family disorganization occurs when there is serious or prolonged family conflict or when the family unit is broken. The bases of marital unhappiness are as broad as life itself, but extreme individualism is the greatest contributor. The greatest hope for reducing the number of unhappy marriages destined for dissolution by desertion or divorce seems to be in premarital and marital counseling designed to create happier marriages, thus

[94]Ernest W. Burgess, Harvey J. Locke, and Margaret Thomas, *The Family: From Institution to Companionship* (New York: American Book, 1963), p. 460.

[95]Baber, op. cit., p. 494.

[96]Ibid., pp. 502–503.

providing a better environment for the development of healthy personalities in the offspring. The basic personality traits needed are adaptability and consideration for others. Divorce and desertion affect over 300,000 minor children each year.[97]

PROPOSALS TO IMPROVE FAMILY STABILITY

In a culture exhibiting as much free choice by the individual as is apparent in modern America, education of the individual is the surest approach to the solution of social problems. However, in any urbanized, industrialized culture, the government increasingly restricts the freedom of the individual in order to protect the welfare of the group. Social legislation is necessary, therefore, to assist the individual in the solution of problems that are partially or completely under governmental regulation. In Chapters 9 and 10 considerable space is devoted to necessary social legislation designed to improve the physical and social welfare of the individual in terms of health, housing, vocational opportunity, and economic welfare. All of that legislation is applicable to the individual as a family member.

Legislation

Special social legislation is needed in the field of family stability. Our present medley of divorce laws is a national disgrace. "The confusion produced by the difference among state laws is well known; a man may be a respectable married man in New Jersey and a bigamist in New York State." [98] Even the Supreme Court has reversed its position on migratory divorce on three separate occasions within a seven-year period.[99] The moral of the story seems clear: persons had better stay married, or else marry, divorce, remarry, and live the rest of their lives within the same state.

The alternatives may be charges of bigamy and illegitimacy, and confusions regarding inheritance of property.

Another aspect of divorce law that needs clarification is alimony. State differences are considerable; the range in percentage of divorce cases involving alimony, from state to state, is approximately from 10 per cent to 50 per cent.[100] The range in size of award may be as great as from $1 per month to a New York award of $90,000 a year.[101] Certainly there is social justification for alimony. The middle-aged wife who has neither training nor experience in earning a living cannot be expected to culminate twenty years of keeping house and rearing children with a penniless start on a new life. Neither can the sick or aged be cast upon the charity of society. On the other hand, alimony "careerists" have abused the alimony provisions of the law. Many women stoutly refuse alimony, maintaining that they are well qualified to support themselves; others insist upon support in a style far better than the

[97]Waller and Hill, op. cit., p. 542.
[98]Ibid., p. 502.
[99]Baber, op. cit., pp. 477–478.
[100]Ibid., p. 480.
[101]Ibid., pp. 481–482.

former husband's income can maintain. Despite the provision of the federal Constitution that individuals cannot be imprisoned for debt, nonpayment of alimony is an offense punishable by imprisonment. The thesis is that the defaulter is not being jailed for debt but for contempt of court in refusing to pay. The penalty obtains in some states even though the wife is using the alimony to support both herself and a new husband. Alimony may be claimed by the wife even though she is the "guilty party" in the divorce. Certainly the changed political, social, and economic status of women in the modern world entitles men to a re-examination of the alimony statutes.

The greatest single change that needs to be made, however, is in the concept of the "guilt" of one party to the marriage as a condition to divorce. The legal theory is that a divorce is granted to the injured party because of some violation by the other of the marriage mores or customs which govern the married state. A couple cannot agree to get a divorce. If any evidence of such collusion comes out in a trial for divorce, the judge is in duty bound to throw the case out of court. Such a state of affairs makes criminals out of every couple who jointly decide that their interests and those of society would be served best by a dissolution of their marriage. Much more important, from the viewpoint of the stability of marriage, their legal lines of communication are severely restricted from the time of their decision to separate. For prosecution of the case, the law insists that they must be antagonists rather than two adults cooperatively trying to solve a problem. Basic to this assumption is the theory that if the guilt of one is proved, then divorce is the just punishment for the offender. Divorce is not so impartial; both parties suffer from it. Further, society pays a large part of the cost in terms of the unhappiness of both parties, loss of time and energy in court procedures, the turning back into the marriage market of poor matrimonial risks, and the emotional and economic problems of the dependent children who may be involved in the divorce action.[102] The emphasis needs to be shifted legally to a consideration by the court of whether the divorce action is in the best interests of the parties involved and of society. The American Bar Association has advanced a proposal based on a counseling relationship between the court and the marriage partners. Claims of success in reintegrating marriages on the verge of divorce have gone as high as 90 per cent.[103] Evidence of the willingness of couples to try again if someone will encourage them to do so is gleaned even from the cold statistics of the divorce courts: Marion County, Indiana, reports that about 45 per cent of the divorce suits filed there never even come to trial.[104] Certainly we need to change the function of our divorce courts from one of "trying guilt" to one of "trying to help."

Social agencies have been working recently on agreements concerning qualifications for the marriage counselor. If such specially trained persons were available, they might well prevent most divorce cases from ever coming to trial. Waller and Hill comment on the promise of this field as follows:

[102]It is estimated that a total of three children under eighteen are involved in every five divorce actions.

[103]David G. Wittels, "Perjury Unlimited," *The Saturday Evening Post*, February 18, 1950, p. 138.

[104]*Indianapolis News*, December 2, 1953, p. 34.

No activity is at present more chaotic and none is riper with promise than the salvaging of families through skilled counseling. A husband and wife are worried about their heated tiffs; a parent feels that friction at home is producing anxiety in a child; a doctor has a patient whose home difficulties are delaying his recovery; a lawyer finds that his client needs his marriage strengthened, not dissolved; an employer has a good workman who is falling down on the job because of personal problems; a minister desires advice regarding care for a member of a family in his church; an engaged pair wonder whether they are ready to marry, they have so many doubts and mixed feelings—these are problems for the marriage-and-family-counseling agency which yesterday would have been solved over the backyard fence or with the help of an older relative. Or worse, they are problems that might have been postponed indefinitely, never to be solved.[105]

It is hoped that the day will come when every divorce court judge will insist upon counseling by a member of his staff before agreeing to hear a divorce case.

Education

The period in which family life education is most desperately needed is young adulthood. Readiness for learning is at an optimum, and the need for learning is evidenced by the high divorce rate in the early years of marriage. The student body of these adult education classes, however, should not be limited to young adults. The need is for enrollment by engaged couples, other single young adults, the newly married, married people with unresolved problems, ministers, doctors, and teachers. As we noted earlier, the minister, doctor, and teacher often are called upon in the role of marriage counselor. All too often they possess neither the knowledge of family life nor the techniques of counseling requisite to adequate fulfillment of the role.

The content of such adult education classes in family living should include at least the following: study of and practice in democratic principles of family living; development of a set of moral and ethical principles on which to base family decisions; human dynamics, with special stress upon the courtship and marital roles of the adult couple; sex relations in marriage —personal hygiene, birth control, and planned parenthood; the human development of the child through adolescence; home management, including family finance; consumer education; the wise utilization of leisure time; planning for the periods of the empty nest and of old age; and techniques of counseling.

Increasingly, the battle centers around sex education. Some of the critics of sex education (biological facts *plus* ethical values) really want sex *information* only disseminated.[106] Proponents of sex *education* propound diametrically opposed views: "Current programs in the schools, say Esther Schulz, associate director of the Sex Information and Education Council of

---

[105]From *The Family: A Dynamic Interpretation*, by Willard Waller and revised by Reuben Hill. Copyright 1938 by Holt, Rinehart and Winston, Inc. Revised edition copyright 1951 by Holt, Rinehart and Winston, Inc.

[106]Louis J. Karmel, "Sex Education, No! Sex Information, Yes!" *Phi Delta Kappan*, Vol. 52, No. 2 (October 1970), pp. 95–96.

the United States, are weighted with biological or reproductive information. Little is offered to assist students to face real life situations." [107] Some victories, of course, have been won by ultraright-wing forces. "In August, 1969, the Louisiana State Legislature by a vote of 94 to 4 banned sex education for Louisiana pupils." [108] This is part of a "concerted campaign being launched around the United States to arouse public fear and suspicion of sex education in public schools." [109] Fortunately, not all legislatures are responding to this fear campaign. The Illinois legislature in 1965 passed a Sex Education Act.[110] Among the guiding principles developed by the Illinois Sex Education Advisory Board and issued by the State Superintendent of Public Instruction are, "Family life and sex education is concerned with both facts and values. Sex education should be broadly conceived and planned as an integral part of education for personality and character development. . . . Illinois youth should be sex-educated, not merely sex-informed or indoctrinated." [111]

Not all sex education, of course, is concentrated upon young adults. Sound programs start in the earliest years. As the *Education U.S.A. Special Report* stresses.[112]

> The teacher of the young child takes him with all his good, bad, or indifferent sex information, tries to satisfy his curiosity and to relieve any anxieties by giving clear, simple, honest answers to his questions.
>
> Teachable moments can center around the arrival of a new baby in someone's family. Young children are fascinated by babies, and the teacher can capitalize on this interest by emphasizing the miracle of a new life, the wonder of reproduction.

From primary education to higher education, the moral aspect of sex education continues to preoccupy educators. Basic moral and psychodevelopmental issues are involved; for example, consider the issues posed by a recent article ostensibly related to sex mores:

> To the extent that they are present, morality becomes an integral part of the human being, not role behavior or something plastered on:
> 1. *What the individual is asked or expected to do must be in harmony with his essential nature.*
> 2. *A sense of being an acceptable, belonging, worthy individual is essential to a stable, mature morality.*
> 3. *The example of important "others" is of much significance.*
> 4. *An atmosphere of openness and honesty in which all issues and various possibilities can be given full consideration is needed.*[113]

[107]*Education U.S.A. Special Report: Sex Education in Schools* (Washington, D.C.: N.S.P.R.A., N.E.A., 1969), p. 5.

[108]Douglas R. Mackintosh, Kathy L. Glassman, Nancy Richard, and Shelley C. Herman, "Sex Education in New Orleans: The Birchers Win a Victory," *New South*, Vol. 25, No. 3 (Summer 1970), p. 46.

[109]Ibid., p. 46.

[110]*Sex Education in Schools*, op. cit., p. 6.

[111]Ibid., pp. 7–8.

[112]Ibid., p. 17.

[113]Lester A. Kirkendall and Deryck Calderwood, "Changing Sex Mores and Moral Instruction," *Phi Delta Kappan*, Vol. 46, No. 2 (October 1964), pp. 65–66.

The content increasingly includes an honest confrontation with the basic facts of (physiological) life.[114] The content is basically the same as that noted for adult education, with high school and college counselors rendering personal, vocational, and marital counseling. The teacher competencies and methodologies are basically the same as those to be outlined in Chapter 9. Areas that currently are weak are the assimilation of high ideals and the development of skills in critical thinking.[115] The historic separation of church and state, with proscription against doctrinal instruction, has led many good teachers to evade their responsibility to help youth develop a set of moral and ethical principles that will guide life decisions. This is part of the cultural tradition the school is charged to transmit.[116] In the two decades since the publishing of *Moral and Spiritual Values in the Public Schools*, the courts have held repeatedly that nonsectarian moral training is legal. Modern authorities in curriculum continue to stress the need; as Saylor and Alexander state, "definition of ethical behavior in various types of response situations, and the development of attitudes that give concrete expression to cultural values are within the potentialities of social education." [117] The neglect of moral and ethical curriculum by many good teachers may well be a heavily contributing factor in the secularization of our society. This weakening of the moral fabric of our people adds considerably to the emotional insecurity of our times, which further distorts the judgment of all. Man needs the security of something greater than himself to which he can cling in times of trouble. Too many families are trying to find the answers to their problems in the physical world alone. Religious expression has been a basic need of man from time immemorial. Teachers probably exceed constitutional limitations in their emphasis upon Christian holidays, yet they fail to guide children in the development of those daily moral and ethical principles that all of us so badly need for guidance in coping with life's problems. The family cannot survive so long as man and woman find their only strength in each other.[118]

SUMMARY

The family always has constituted a significant social group, but sociological research on family life is of recent origin. Some sociologists interpret this research to indicate that the family is disintegrating. The authors concur with the contrasting interpretation that disorganization is only a symptom of the adaptation of the family to a rapidly changing culture. Urbanization, industrialization, and increasing governmental participation are changing the size, functions, characteristics, and stability of the family. There is evidence of a shift in family structure from an institution to a companionship, based

[114]Nancy Gay Faber, "Sex for Credit," *Look*, April 1, 1969, pp. 39–45.

[115]See Chapter 12 for brief *schema*.

[116]Educational Policies Commission, *Moral and Spiritual Values in the Public Schools* (Washington, D.C.: N.A., 1951), pp. 6–7.

[117]J. Gaylen Saylor and William M. Alexander, *Curriculum Planning for Modern Schools* (New York: Holt, 1966), pp. 90–91.

[118]The legal separation of church and state in America need not mean the abandonment of moral and ethical principles in the schools. The American moral code has as strong roots in our secular history as it has in doctrinal teachings.

upon equalitarian roles of family members and with stability dependent upon continued happiness of its members.

The major problems facing the American family are child socialization, dating, choosing a career, development of physically and morally satisfactory sex behavior, selection of a mate, courting, definition of family roles, parenthood, and adjustment to the stages of the empty nest and of old age. Family disorganization may occur at any of these stages. Basic personality traits of adaptability and consideration for others are the greatest integrating forces in building harmonious, effective families.

Social legislation is sorely needed to improve present divorce procedures. Education, however, offers the greatest hope for successful transition of the family to a new form adapted to present society; it is increased stability of the family, not improved methods of dissolution, that is needed. Basic to this education must be concern for wholesome personality development of children, for it is upon the personalities of today's children that the future of the family depends. Educators need to recognize that modern youth is faced with a bewildering variety of decisions; sound moral and ethical principles on which to base those decisions must be integrated into total personality development. Upon the moral and ethical integrity of modern youth rests the future of America.

Selected Bibliography

Look, The American Family. January 26, 1971. Special issue; sixty-five pages. Positive and negative views on the universality and permanence of the family. Illustrative examples of homosexuality, unwed couples, communal marriage, career women, and the happy family. Suggestions for constructive child-rearing practices and stable marriages.

Look, The American Woman. January 11, 1966. Special fifty-page feature. Interesting cross-sectional overview of problems facing the modern American woman.

Barash, Meyer, and Alice Scourby (eds.). *Marriage and the Family: A Comparative Analysis of Contemporary Problems.* New York: Random House, Inc., 1970. 418 pp.

Baruch, Dorothy. *How to Live with Your Teen-agers.* New York: McGraw-Hill Book Company, 1963. 261 pp. A guide for parents.

———, and Hyman Miller. *Sex in Marriage: New Understandings.* New York: Harper & Row, Publishers, 1962. 277 pp.

Bartell, Gilbert D. *Group Sex: A Scientist's Eyewitness Report on the American Way of Swinging.* New York: Peter H. Wyden, 1971. 298 pp.

Bell, Robert R. *Marriage and Family Interaction,* Third Edition. Homewood, Ill.: Dorsey Press, 1971. 600 pp.

Bowman, Henry. *Marriage for Moderns,* Fifth Edition. New York: McGraw-Hill Book Company, 1965. 709 pp. This college text emphasizes the importance of attitudes in marriage. Comprehensive presentation of most aspects of premarriage and marriage relations and conduct. Films are available that are correlated with the text.

Burgess, Ernest W., Harvey J. Locke, and Mary Margaret Thomas. *The Family: From Institution to Companionship.* New York: American Book Company, 1963. 582 pp. Analysis of historic forces that are changing the family from institution to companionship. Stresses role of family in shaping personality. Claims family is successfully adapting to social change.

Carter, Hugh, and Paul C. Glick. *Marriage and Divorce: A Social and Economic Study.* (Vital and Health Statistics Monographs, American Public Health Association.) Cambridge, Mass.: Harvard University Press, 1970. 451 pp. This book provides comprehensive, up-to-date coverage of the demographic aspects of marriage, divorce, and widowhood and includes statistics on marital status and health, the influence of race, and a chapter on single people.

Cavan, Ruth Shonle. *The American Family*, Fourth Edition. New York: Thomas Y. Crowell Company, 1969. 556 pp. Popular textbook for college-level courses in marriage and family relations.

Duvall, Evelyn Millis. *Family Development*, Fourth Edition. Philadelphia: J. B. Lippincott Company, 1971. 525 pp. Popular textbook for college-level courses in marriage and family relations.

_____, and the Class in Methods and Materials in Teaching Family Relations, Syracuse University, Summer 1949. *Family Life Materials.* Syracuse: Syracuse University Press, 1949. 52 pp. Text and reference books; annotated lists of pamphlets; annotated lists of professional periodicals; annotated lists of films and filmstrips; glossary of frequently used terms.

Education U.S.A. Special Report: Sex Education in Schools. Washington, D.C.: National School Public Relations Association, N.E.A., 1969. 48 pp. Brief presentation of legislative trends. Extensive guidelines for institution of school programs of instruction for all age levels.

Ellis, Albert, and Robert A. Harper. *Creative Marriage.* New York: Lyle Stuart, Inc., 1961. 288 pp. Popularly written. Psychiatrically oriented.

Farber, Bernard. *Family: Organization and Interaction.* San Francisco: Chandler Publishing Co., 1964. 536 pp. Organized in three sections: General aspects of family life, contemporary family structure and membership, and interaction between family members.

Feldman, F. L., *Family Social Welfare: Helping Troubled Families.* New York: Atherton Press, 1967. 386 pp.

Ginzberg, Eli. *The Life Styles of Educated Women.* New York: Columbia University Press, 1966. 224 pp. Based on detailed reports of women in graduate study from 1945 to 1951, this study concludes that educated women are not constricted or discontented, but have and exercise a multiplicity of options to realize the goals they set for themselves.

Grey, Alan L. (ed.). *Man, Woman, and Marriage: Small Group Process in the Family.* New York: Atherton Press, 1970. 225 pp.

Harbeson, Gladys. *Choice and Challenge for the American Woman.* Cambridge, Mass.: Schenkman Publishing Co., Inc., 1969. 185 pp. A study of the career patterns open to the American woman of today and tomorrow, with statistics and research studies to support the thesis that American women must be prepared for roles and life patterns differing from the traditional role.

Hoffman, Adelin M., and William D. Bechill (eds.). *The Daily Needs and Interests of Older People.* Springfield, Ill.: Charles C Thomas, Publisher, 1970. 493 pp.

King, Edith W., and August Kerber. *The Sociology of Early Childhood Education.* New York: American Book Company, 1968. 234 pp.

Kirkpatrick, Clifford. *The Family as Process and Institution.* New York: The Ronald Press Company, 1955. 651 pp. This book elaborates the dilemmas of families in our inconsistent culture and portrays the family process as successive dramas over the life cycle of familial experience. Reflects a lifetime of research and teaching courses on the family.

LeMasters, E. E. *Modern Courtship and Marriage.* New York: The Macmillan Company, 1957. 619 pp. Emphasizes "subcultures" of the adolescent, the male, the rural dweller, class levels, and other groups. Excellent section on the American courtship system. Crisp, effective, readable.

"Man into Superman: The Promise and Peril of the New Genetics," *Time*, April 19, 1971. Special Section. An excellent up-to-date account of genetic, electrical, chemical possibilities for human improvement.

Milne, Lorus J., and Margery Milne. *The Ages of Life.* New York: Harcourt Brace Jovanovich, Inc., 1968. 296 pp.

Neubeck, Gerhard (ed.). *Extramarital Relations.* Englewood Cliffs, N.J.: Prentice-Hall, Inc., 1969. 205 pp.

O'Neill, William. *Divorce in the Progressive Era.* New Haven: Yale University Press, 1967. 295 pp.

Reik, Theodor. *Of Love and Lust: On the Psychoanalysis of Romantic and Sexual*

Schulz, Esther D., and Sally R. Williams. *Family Life and Sex Education: Curriculum and Emotions.* New York: Bantam Books, Inc., 1971. 623 pp.

Instruction. New York: Harcourt Brace Jovanovich, Inc., 1971. 281 pp.

Seward, Georgene H., and Robert C. Williamson (eds.). *Sex Roles in Changing Society.* New York: Random House, Inc., 1970. 419 pp.

Sex Information and Education Council of the United States (eds.). *Sexuality and Man.* New York: Charles Scribner's Sons, 1970. 239 pp.

Sexual Behavior. Interpersonal Publications. A serious magazine devoted to authoritative information about sex.

Taylor, Donald L. (ed.). *Human Sexual Development.* Philadelphia: American Medical Book Publishers, 1970. 420 pp.

Zimmerman, Carle, and Lucius F. Cervantes. *Successful American Families.* New York: Pageant Press, 1960. 226 pp.

Selected Films

Age of Turmoil (McGraw-Hill), 20 min. The picture goes from one adolescent type to another, focusing on behavior that mirrors the emotional turmoil of the persons involved.

Before They Say "I Do" (National Council of Churches), 28 min. As a young couple walks down the aisle to be married, a series of flashbacks traces the role of the clergyman and the physician in premarital counseling. Includes birth control information and the part family planning plays in marriage.

Being in Love (N.E.T.), 30 min. Maturity in attitudes toward love and varying needs of individuals.

Boy to Man; Girl to Woman (Churchill Films), 16 min., each title. Film deals with the physical and emotional changes that occur during adolescence. Junior and senior high school students should see both *Boy to Man* and *Girl to Woman* to understand the processes and problems of both sexes.

Children's Emotions (McGraw-Hill), 20 min. Shows sources of common emotions. Discusses normal fear, anger, and jealousy, and points out dangers of emotions.

Choosing for Happiness (McGraw-Hill), 14 min. Portrays through dramatized situations the reactions of a girl to various boyfriends and her rejection of all of them—and they of her; and suggests that the girl should re-evaluate herself and her demands on others. Follow-up filmstrip: thirty-eight frames.

Early Social Behaviour (ERPE Classroom Films), 10 min. Illustrates the social significance of the home through scenes reflecting parent–child relationships. Analyzes the social behavior of ten children, eight weeks to seven years old. Stresses individual differences and sibling relations.

The European Experience (N.E.T.), 30 min. Small-family concept, compulsory education, and emancipation of women in European countries.

Families First (New York State Department of Commerce), 17 min. By a series of everyday episodes in the lives of two contrasting families, this film demonstrates the causes of tensions, frustrations, and antisocial attitudes as well as the results of affection, achievement, and harmonious personality adjustment.

Family Circles (McGraw-Hill), 31 min. Shows how the role of the family has changed in our society, placing emphasis on the relation of home and school. The importance of recognizing the child's emotional needs is shown in four parents' attitudes in their homes.

From Generation to Generation (Contemporary/McGraw-Hill), 27 min. The story of human reproduction is told as an integral part of the universal pattern of nature. Childbearing is seen as an emotional and spiritual experience. Animation is used to describe the physiology of conception and reproduction.

Happy Family Planning (PPWP), 6 min. This charming, witty animated cartoon explains in pictures and musical accompaniment the benefits of family planning and methods. Wordless except for the names of the contraceptives, shown in seven languages. "Happy" is the word for this film designed especially for hospital family planning clinics and useful in many different national settings.

How Much Affection? (McGraw-Hill), 20 min. Dramatized presentation of situations and questions concerning the extent of physical affection between a couple who is going steady.

Human Growth (E. C. Brown Trust), 20 min. Demonstrates for parents how sex education can be handled smoothly. Provides the classroom teacher with a suitable instructional aid for presenting the biological facts of sex.

In Time of Trouble (McGraw-Hill), 14 min. Portrays the family minister counseling a young married couple and helping them understand the reasons for their disagreements and ways in which satisfactory adjustments can be made. Follow-up filmstrip: thirty-six frames.

Introduction to Birth Control (PPWP), 15 min. A simple, straightforward presentation of birth control methods and an introduction to reproduction physiology. Designed for clinic use. Revised in 1968.

Is This Love? (McGraw-Hill), 14 min. Contrasts the romances of two college girls, one impulsive and eager to get married, the other wishing to go more slowly through the stages of dating, courtship, going steady, and engagement. Concludes with open-end questions directed to the audience.

It Takes All Kinds (McGraw-Hill), 20 min. Portrays a series of young couples reacting to tense situations; relates their reactions to their possibilities for marriage success or failure, and emphasizes the point that marriage partners should be carefully chosen.

Jealousy (McGraw-Hill), 16 min. Portrayal of a young wife, jealous of her husband, and her gradual realization that her behavior is an expression of her dissatisfaction with her role as a homemaker. Follow-up filmstrip: thirty-eight frames.

Life with Grandpa (March of Time), 17 min. Portrays problems confronting older people in our society: disease, economic insecurity, emotional difficulties. Suggests several solutions.

Marriage Is a Partnership (Coronet), 16 min. Shows some of the realities of early marriage adjustment; considers specific problems of in-laws, finances, housing, job adjustment; exemplifies arguments, responsibilities, decision-making, loyalties.

Marriage Problems (N.E.T.), 30 min. Young couples are often victims of their own unrealistic expectations in marriage.

Marriage Today (McGraw-Hill), 22 min. Dynamic treatment of goals and ideals of married love. Three couples are depicted: one idealizing marriage, one working toward building a secure future, and one in the process of adjusting interests and day-to-day living.

Meeting Emotional Needs in Childhood (New York University), 33 min. Shows children's need for security for emotional development.

Meeting the Needs of Adolescents (McGraw-Hill), 19 min. Attempts to indicate some of the things parents can do to prepare their children for the future.

The Merry Go Round (Contemporary/McGraw-Hill), 23 min. Psychotherapist Albert Ellis, columnist Ann Landers, and educator Mary Winspear present their views on teenage sexual behavior. This film dramatizes a dating situation in which a boy and girl are considering premarital sexual experience. Encourages teenage discussion.

The Parents (N.E.T.), 60 min. A documentary report on the changing problems of today's American parents and their attempts to find identity, meaning, and purpose in their lives.

Preface to a Life (United World Films), 29 min. Parental influence on a child's developing personality, illustrated by episodes showing the effects of an overly solicitous mother and an overly demanding father contrasting with the healthy childhood resulting when both parents accept their child as an individual.

Questions and Answers About Birth Control (PPWP), 30 min. A group of young adults ask Dr. Alan F. Guttmacher the questions they have about birth control. The answers are frank, direct, and factual and are supplemented by line drawings and actual contraceptive devices. Cleared for television.

Social Development (McGraw-Hill), 15 min. Factual description of the developmental changes in children's social behavior. Most of film centers on the preschool years.

The Steps of Age (International Film Bureau), 25 min. Portrays the confusion, fears, and far-from-easy struggle to understand herself that Mrs. Potter, age sixty-two, faces as she embarks on the last quarter of her life. The picture suggests that people need to begin early in life to handle well the situations that come with increasing age.

This Charming Couple (McGraw-Hill), 19 min. Shows how the marriage of a couple who refused to evaluate realistically each other's good and bad points ended in divorce.

Trouble in the Family (N.E.T.), 90 min. Family therapy, in which family is treated as a unit, is discussed.

When Should I Marry? (McGraw-Hill), 19 min. A minister advises a young couple, eager to marry, by describing the experiences of two other couples who married at an early age.

Who's Boss? (McGraw-Hill), 16 min. Portrays a young married couple, both of whom are individualists, their differences, and their decision to adjust their differences through cooperation. Follow-up filmstrip: thirty-six frames.

Who's Right? (McGraw-Hill), 18 min. Dramatization of a quarrel between husband and wife, caused by her seeing his forcefulness as "bossism" and by his labeling her good taste as extravagance. Follow-up filmstrip: thirty-six frames.

Chapter 7

■■■■■■■□□□□□□□□□

Problems of Mental Health in an Era of Rapid Social Change

We are living in an anxious age. A multitude of personal and social pressures are impinging on individuals and on groups, creating personal tensions and cultural stresses that threaten to destroy us. The 1970 *Yearbook of the Association for Supervision and Curriculum Development* enumerates some of these stresses, and their cultural genesis, as it states, "The social changes brought about by the technological, social, and knowledge revolutions . . . have resulted in social upheaval and disorientation; in rebellions and riots; in frustrations, alienation, fear, and hatred; and in a nation divided between affluence and poverty, between blacks and whites, between the establishment and the dissenters, and between those over and those under 30 years of age."[1] Alvin Toffler underscores the societal reasons for personality disorganization in the modern world when he defines future shock as, "shattering stress and disorientation that overwhelms people who experience too much change in too short a time."[2]

Not all nervous and mental diseases are caused by the pressures of modern social living. Serious personality disturbances usually have multiple and deep-seated origins. There is no single cause of mental illness. Nevertheless, isolation of single causes and single catalytic events is an essential step in the diagnosis and treatment of the illness. Such diagnosis and treatment, of course, is the prerogative of the trained person, such as the clinical psychologist, physician, or psychiatrist. The purpose of this chapter is to introduce laymen and professional educators to the general area of mental hygiene as a vantage point from which to assay the role of the teacher in promoting sound mental health in the children under his charge.

Teachers may sigh, "But we cannot cope with *all* the problems of society. Our task is to pass on that for which we are uniquely fitted and with

[1]Mary Margaret Scobey and Grace Graham (eds.), *To Nurture Humaneness: Commitment for the 1970's* (Washington, D.C.: A.S.C.D., N.E.A., 1970), p. 204.
[2]Alvin Toffler, "How to Take the Sting out of Future Shock," *The Cincinnati Enquirer Magazine*, Sunday, January 10, 1971, p. 10.

which society has charged us: the basic skills, the cultural heritage, and moral values. We are not psychiatrists; we are unequipped to deal with problems of mental health." Nevertheless, a growing body of literature (oriented to both school and community health) reflects the sentiment of the Division of Special Education of the Ohio Department of Education: "It is impossible to escape the conclusion that the schools are in the mental health business . . . . they are the only agency outside the home that has an intensive and complete impact on that segment of the population most vulnerable to mental health problems and most amenable to change." [3]

The dimensions of the problem are staggering. "In its third annual report to the United States Senate and House of Representatives, the Joint Commission on Mental Illness and Health estimated that seventeen and a half million people in our country had nervous or mental illness needing treatment." [4] The total cost of mental illness in the United States has been estimated to be in excess of $3 billion a year.[5] Table 12, to be presented later in this chapter, indicates 1,361 million cases of emotional disturbances were treated in 1968. These are only the cases of record; it is assumed that many of the emotionally disturbed were not treated. This documents earlier predictions that "one out of every ten persons in the United States is emotionally or mentally maladjusted and needs treatment for some personality disorder." [6]

THE RELATIONSHIP BETWEEN PHYSICAL AND MENTAL HEALTH

Mental hygiene is the study of the causes of poor mental health and of the techniques for improving and maintaining sound mental health. The study of causes is complicated by the fact that mental illness is not distinct from bodily disease.

Probably every case of physical disease has some effect on mental health, and vice versa. An outstanding example of this may be the asthmatic attack due to allergy, with fear superimposed and often becoming dominant. Hence the treatment often becomes psychiatric in nature, even though a physical cause initiated the attack. Some psychiatrists look upon asthma as purely psychological in origin; others accept an allergic explanation, plus psychological overlay.[7]

Further examples of the relationship between physical and mental health are found daily in doctors' offices, where patients exhibit very real symptoms of physical pain, although there is no apparent organic basis for pain. Common examples are psychosomatic back ache and nausea.

Prolonged emotional conflicts may even produce real changes in bodily tissue, changes that we call physical disease. Ulcers of the stomach, certain

[3]S. J. Bonham and T. M. Stephens (eds.), *Mental Health Planning in Education* (Columbus: State of Ohio, 1964), p. 17.

[4]Edgar Loar, *Social Aspects of Mental Hygiene*, unpublished paper, University of Cincinnati, 1964, p. 1.

[5]Rashi Fein, *Economics of Mental Illness* (New York: Basic Books, 1958), p. 38.

[6]George Thorman, *Toward Mental Health* (New York: Public Affairs Committee, 1950), pp. 22–23.

[7]Oliver E. Byrd, *Causes of Mental Illness*, unpublished paper, Stanford University, 1950.

types of heart disease, and other comparable physical ailments may be so induced. Such physical illnesses, when caused by emotional disturbances, are called psychogenic, meaning that they are psychological in origin. Fink records successful psychotherapy in a case involving "alternating diarrhea and constipation, abdominal colic, mucus and sometimes blood in the stools."[8] One of the symptoms of anxiety is fatigue. "Anxiety effect, like the fear arising from perceptible danger, involves an arousal of the entire organism . . . anxiety effect is not merely heightened emotion. It is itself unpleasant; when intense, it is painful and fatiguing."[9] The incidence of anxiety-induced fatigue is presented by a physician, Dr. William M. Goldberg, as he says, "Fatigue has become one of the major reasons people visit physicians today—and only 15 per cent of the cases can be traced to organic illness. The other whopping 85 per cent of the people involved have psychological hangups."[10] Because these cases have a psychological origin, successful treatment of physical illness depends upon removal or amelioration of the psychological causes of the physical condition.

Just as emotional disturbances may cause physical disease, so also may physical deviations cause mental illness. Any or all of the physiological "causes" of mental illness in the paragraphs to follow may form only a small portion of the total picture, but the picture certainly would be incomplete without them. This isolation of physiological phenomena is not to be interpreted as an indication of dualistic thinking on the part of the authors. We believe in the organismic nature of man, that any physiological or psychological phenomenon manifested by an individual affects both the mind and the body of that individual. Nevertheless, some phenomena are related most closely to injuries, disease, or malfunctions of the bodily structure, and these may be classified for clarity of discussion as primarily physiological in nature. Other phenomena are related primarily to emotional reactions to symbolic stimuli or to other persons, or to external situations in general, and these may be classified as primarily psychological. This section comprises an attempt to list some of the major physiological phenomena affecting mental health, in an endeavor further to emphasize that forces affecting the physical aspects of man also affect the mental aspects.

Infections

Infections are a more widespread source of mental illness than was previously thought. Worry over chronic illness, even excessive susceptibility to the common cold, may so upset a person that petty irritations become magnified, tensions mount, and emotional unbalance results. A less obvious result of infections is the damage to the neural system caused by impurities deposited by the infections in the bloodstream.[11]

[8]David Harold Fink, *Release from Nervous Tension* (New York: Simon & Schuster, 1963), pp. 33–34.

[9]Frederick F. Lighthall, *What Research Says to the Teacher: Anxiety as Related to Thinking and Forgetting* (Washington, D.C.: N.E.A., 1964), p. 9.

[10]Bill Trent, "If 10 Percent of Your Life Is Exciting, You Are a Lucky Person," *Weekend Magazine*, August 21, 1971, p. 16.

[11]J. Victor Greenebaum and Louis A. Lurie, "Encephalitis as a Causative Factor in Behavior Disorders of Children," in Oliver E. Byrd (ed.), *Health Instruction Yearbook, 1948* (Stanford, Calif.: Stanford University Press, 1948), p. 66.

Nutritional Deficiencies

Nutritional deficiences have much the same twofold effect. In addition, they may result in physical impairment of one's ability to meet the demands of his everyday world; frustrations may result from the inability to perform tasks that the nutritionally adequate person could accomplish with ease.

Accidents

Accidents, especially traffic injuries, involve all the preceding hazards. Accidents are traumatic, and may cause persistent worries. These emotional problems are accentuated by the incidence of sharp blows to the head, resulting in direct and immediate injury to the brain. Brain injury may cause disabilities such as lack of muscular control, loss of speech, or loss of ability to think coherently.

Anemia

Anemia, if severe, may result in insufficient supply of oxygen to the brain. The resultant damage to the brain may be more serious than that occasioned by a sharp blow to the head.

Deterioration of Brain Tissue

Thorpe lists deterioration of brain tissue, such as that accompanying senility or hardening of the arteries, and growth of foreign tissues in the brain (whether benign or cancerous), as among the most frequently recognized causes of organic psychosis.[12]

Food Allergies

Food allergies may cause severe disturbance to otherwise well-adjusted persons if the allergy is such that it results in inflammation of the brain, with resultant damage to its tissue.[13] The social effects of food and other allergies are similar to those discussed in the next two items.

Glandular Deficiencies and Imbalances

Glandular malfunction may be a direct cause of mental illness, such as glandular imbalance related to depression, or it may result in social maladjustment. A glandular imbalance leading to obesity, for example, could cause serious damage to the personality. This may be true even though the particular personality being damaged never has been rejected or ridiculed. The simple knowledge that one is very different from one's fellows may prevent development of adequate concepts of self. This knowledge may lead one to imagine that one is being rejected and ridiculed.

[12]Louis P. Thorpe, *The Psychology of Mental Health* (New York: Ronald, 1960), p. 203.

[13]T. Wood Clarke, "The Relation of Allergy to Character Problems in Children," in Oliver E. Byrd (ed.), *Health Instruction Yearbook, 1950* Stanford, Calif.: Stanford University Press, 1950), pp. 70–71.

Physical Defects

Physical defects, such as facial disfigurement, may have social effects similar to those resulting from glandular deficiencies. A second major result of limitations of one's ability imposed by physical defects is the frustrations that accompany inability to participate effectively in the activities enjoyed by one's age mates. A heart condition or an allergy to dust may prevent a boy from playing baseball. This enforced separation from his age mates not only may cause immediate frustration but also may lead to isolation of the boy from the group in other activities. Man is a gregarious creature; he does not thrive on isolation.

Alcoholism

Alcoholism is one of the leading causes for commitment to mental institutions. The cause of alcoholism is not entirely clear. It is generally agreed, however, that alcoholism is the result of personality disturbance rather than the cause. Bloch synthesizes the research in an interesting refutation of the well-intentioned but misguided propaganda of prohibition zealots.[14] That alcohol in itself may be a contributing factor to personality disorganization, however, on a solely physical basis, may reasonably be assumed from the disclosures of the Yale University Laboratory of Applied Psychology. Nutritional deficiency was shown to be one aspect of excessive consumption of alcohol; it results not so much from the specific action of alcohol upon the body as from the disturbance of the ordinary vitamin balance.[15]

Drugs

Drugs are another source of possible mental disorder. Many drug addicts lead useful and productive lives, relatively unaffected by their habit.[16] It is the withdrawal of drugs that causes the addict intense physical and mental anguish. "The resulting physical shock to the organism may be severe in many cases, even after the cure has been attained." [17] It must be admitted that the physical damage of the withdrawal shock probably is of less importance in personal demoralization than the association with the criminal procurers of drugs or the effects of methods necessary to obtain money to buy expensive drugs. In any discussion of physical causes of mental illness, however, drug addiction deserves at least passing mention.

THE RELATIONSHIPS OF EMOTIONAL NEEDS TO MENTAL HEALTH

Now that we have established the relationship between physical and mental health, let us cite an authority who negates the importance of that relationship:

[14]Herbert A. Bloch, *Disorganization, Personal and Social* (New York: Knopf, 1952), pp. 443–449.

[15]Ibid., p. 446.

[16]Ibid., p. 459.

[17]Ibid., p. 461.

The fact that human beings are not self-sufficient but must live in an inter-dependent society where other human beings are also engaged in the pursuit of their goals and desires leads inevitably to a succession of interpersonal conflicts. For the most part, the rules of social life establish a framework in which indi-viduals are able to interact with one another and to help each other toward the mutual satisfaction of their goals. But, inevitably, situations occur in which the course of life does not go smoothly and problems arise. The ability to cope with these difficult situations without undue pain to oneself or others is one of the common criteria used for distinguishing "mental health."

Such a conception assumes that the causes of these psychological disorders lie in the interaction between long-term personality dispositions of individuals and the realities of their life situations. It rejects the notion that there is a fun-damental medical cause in the sense that there is some organic malfunction-ing.[18]

Despite the recent dialogue on the topic, most textbooks still classify mental illness as organic or functional. In 1970 Martin commented, "mental illness is a disorder, disease, or disturbance that keeps a person from living as happily and healthily as he—and perhaps others—would like. Considered more technically, it is a complex of brain disorders."[19] Deviant behaviors resulting from physical causes may be considered as organic disorders. Emotionally induced deviant behavior, however, is functional illness. It is these functional mental illnesses with which we shall be concerned in the remainder of this chapter.

The major causes of mental illness are psychological in nature. Although many single causes enter into any serious case of mental illness, the damaging effect of most of them may be traced to the denial of man's basic emotional needs. Many listings of these needs have been published by many eminent authorities: psychiatrists, psychologists, sociologists, anthropologists, educa-tors, and others. For purposes of discussion here, the organization sug-gested by the sociologist Thomas is used.[20] He reduces basic emotional needs to four major areas: response, recognition, new experience, and security. Following this presentation will be a brief discussion of "self-actualization."

Response

Thomas uses the term *response* to refer to that warm, intimate relation-ship found between individuals in primary groups. The cuddling, the fondling, and the terms of endearment employed by a loving parent are evidence of a responsive feeling. The billing and cooing of young lovers is another good example of responsive behavior. The degree of responsive feeling is not measured by the innate worth of its recipient; it is determined by the depth of emotional attachment felt by the bestower of affection. Margaret Ribble refers to the evidence of this feeling as "mothering" and stresses the importance of adequate mothering in the development of per-sonality.[21] Although there is not unanimous agreement among authorities in

[18]Norman M. Bradburn, *The Structure of Psychological Well-being* (Chicago: National Opinion Research Center, 1969), p. 2. Used by permission.

[19]Lealon E. Martin, *Mental Health, Mental Illness: Revolution in Progress* (New York: McGraw-Hill, 1970), p. 18.

[20]W. I. Thomas, *The Unadjusted Girl* (Boston: Little, Brown, 1923), p. 4.

[21]Margaret A. Ribble, *The Rights of Infants, Early Psychological Needs, and Their Satisfac-tion* (New York: Columbia University Press, 1943), p. 9.

child development, Ribble's position is indicative of the trend in the literature away from the austerity of the child-rearing practices recommended by some pediatricians in the 1920's. "Mother provides his first social contact with another person. He begins to trust mother, who becomes the object of his feelings of affection. The capacity to feel affection develops out of the positive effects of this first relationship." [22] The wire-surrogate studies at the University of Wisconsin, where monkey infants who received inadequate "mothering" withered and died despite adequate nutrition, further document Ribble's position. Experts in child development now are emphasizing the importance of giving an abundance of love to very young children in order to foster the development of an inner sense of adequacy and security. Although the innate worth of any individual may not determine the number or intensity of responsive behaviors received by that individual, it becomes readily apparent that the number and intensity of responsive feelings received by the individual will determine his own feelings about his innate worth. Mental health is primarily a matter of emotional balance, only secondarily a matter of intellectual perception.[23] The stabilizing effect of a strong sense of personal adequacy can hardly be overestimated. This sense of personal adequacy is best developed through an abundance of responsive behaviors showered upon the infant. It is best maintained by the continuing evidence of responsive feelings throughout the life of the individual.

The effectiveness of responsive behavior in the development and maintenance of wholesome personalities is directly related to the degree of response that the recipient feels toward the giver. Persons who hold the following roles in the successive primary groups clustered about any individual bear a responsibility for showing responsive feeling toward that individual: parents, siblings, teachers, "best friends," lovers, mates, and children. Those persons in our culture who seem to need the most encouragement to display affectionate behavior are fathers and teachers. Some fathers seem to feel that it is unmanly to display affection toward their children, especially toward their sons. Some teachers seem to feel that it will ruin their discipline if they display affection toward their students.

Response is a basic emotional need of man. Failure to meet this basal need often results in disturbed personalities, already off-balance and susceptible to severe mental illness.

Recognition

A second emotional need is for recognition. By this Thomas refers to the more impersonal acclaim accorded by members of secondary groups. The teacher will fill a role either in one of the primary groups surrounding the child or in one of the secondary groups, dependent partly upon the age of the child and partly upon the personality of the teacher. The teacher is in a key position to accord acclaim, as he not only evaluates all the child's school

---

[22]Ronald G. Poland and Nancy D. Sanford, *Adjustment Psychology: A Human Value Approach* (St. Louis: Mosby, 1971), p. 6.

[23]Even our perceptions are colored by our feelings. Emotional blocks may make it impossible for any given individual to perceive the "truth" about colorful political personalities, much less about himself.

work but also structures the classroom situation so as to accord or deny the individual child the acclaim of his peers. The teacher does not always recognize his own importance in controlling to a significant degree the amounts of both response and recognition received by the school-age child. The three R's are paramount, "to fit the child to get along in the world." Teachers need to realize that jobs are lost not so often because of ineffectiveness in the three R's or in technical skills as because of ineffectiveness in human relations. Basic to good human relations is sound mental health. Basic to sound mental health is meeting one's basic emotional needs. Specifically, awarding recognition bolsters one's sense of personal adequacy through the feeling of one's worth that comes with the acknowledgment by others of a job well done.

Unlike response, recognition is directly related to the "worth" of the individual. This is particuarly so in our competitive American culture. The more outstanding one's accomplishments are, the greater is the amount of recognition accorded. But recognition need not be limited in our classrooms to only the "best" products. Primary-grade teachers seem to be particularly skillful in eliciting group recognition of even the "poorest" products. A primary child will glow with pride over group acclaim of the first completed project, even though the rest of the group had mastered that phase of their work months earlier. For older children, differentiated tasks need to be devised. Each child can do something well; teachers of older children need to discover these limited abilities and to assign these particular tasks only to the child who can do nothing else well. They need to follow up with warm personal recognition and with guidance of group recognition of the completed task, even though it is such a menial task as carrying in the realia for a class-culminating activity.

New Experience

The term *new experience* we should like to define as both different and independent experiences. To state that one needs only "new" experiences is trite. Personality is learned. All learning is based upon experience. With no new experiences one not only ceases to develop as a person, one also reaches a plateau in other areas of learning.

This drive for different and independent experiences is evidenced at a very early age. One who knows a two-year-old child intimately knows why some psychologists refer to this as the "wastebasket age." His eager, inquisitive fingers are everywhere. He delights in emptying the wastebasket just to see what is in it. The three-year-old may cross that forbidden traffic artery just to see what is in the next block. The ten-year-old may plan with his gang for Huckleberry Finn adventures—a trip on a raft down the Mississippi—not only to enjoy the rigors of camp life and to explore the unknown, but also to demonstrate that he can exist for considerable periods of time in unusual circumstances independent of the protection of his family. Teachers must meet this need if they are to safeguard the mental health of their children. Classroom situations need to be varied, to provide children not only with different group approaches but also with independent experiences.

This need for different and independent experiences persists through-out life. Adults may enjoy much of their adventure vicariously, through books and films and television programs, but they do satisfy their need, or suffer emotionally from the deprivation.

Security

The final basic emotional need listed by Thomas, security, may be de-fined as the preservation of inviolability of self and the freedom from anxieties and fears. Certainly experiencing adequate amounts of response and recognition will contribute greatly to emotional security. One can never receive too much love.

One can, however, receive only love and protection, without a corre-sponding balance of new experience, and become emotionally insecure despite massive doses of affection and acclaim. Child developmentalists refer to this phenomenon as overprotection. Mother loves her child so much that she cannot bear to see him climb on a chair. She cannot bear to see him play with other children, for fear that he might catch a contagious disease. She is anxious about his walking alone to school, for fear that he might get hit by an automobile. She is fearful that he might be hurt by working with tools with his father or by engaging in team sports with his classmates. So she protects him from all these possibilities by preventing him from having the experiences that might produce them. She loves him unwisely. It may be that she loves him not enough, that she loves herself so much that she cannot bear the pain of seeing him endure the ordinary ills of boyhood. The personality damage to the growing child is many sided: development is retarded because of limited new experience; fears of specific situations are effectively taught through mother's obvious fear of them; and a general feel-ing of anxiety is learned through constant association with a fearful mother. Tense teachers, too, create tense children; but teacher relationships are neither so constant nor so intense. The fact remains, however, that anxiety is contagious.

Related to this need for independence of experience as a means for attaining emotional security is the concept of inviolability of self. The child who always had to be tucked into bed and kissed good night may suddenly slam the bedroom door in our faces as she approaches adolescence. She needs to establish herself as an independent person. She wants no encroach-ment on her private domain. An example from earlier life is the inquisitive toddler who wanders the length of the train aisle, peering solemnly at each new passenger as he approaches his chair, but as soon as one of the passengers attempts to pick her up, or even to talk to her, she retreats hastily to the security of her mother's skirts. To reach into adulthood for examples, how many executives will allow their secretaries access to every drawer in their desk? Or allow their sons free access to all their clothing? Each of us needs some things orplaces to call his very own. Similarly, some dreams are shared with no one, not even wives, mothers, or sweethearts. Some inner-most recesses of our hearts must remain inviolate, or we have nothing left to call our very own. This inviolability of self is essential to emotional security.

The attainment of security, however, involves more than just the psychological experiences of inviolability of self and adequate amounts of response, recognition, and new experience. It involves also protection of the physical welfare of the young. When baby is cold and wet and hungry, he is insecure. When mother changes and feeds him, holding him gently in the warmth of her arms, he is learning that the world is a good place in which to live; he is building emotional security. Provision of the physical things that make this a good world in which to live is essential to the emotional security of the human organism. These are such things as food, shelter, clothing, and recreation. Not all of us have as much as others; but all must have at least minimal amounts if we are to create and maintain an emotionally secure populace. Basic to the attainment of physical security in our society are skills in problem solving, both for personal attainment of this world's goods and for the solution of social problems that threaten the security of all mankind.

SELF-ACTUALIZATION

Modern psychologists have postulated more sophisticated hierarchies of needs than Thomas. Maslow, for example, has structured basic needs of humans; he places physiological needs (food, clothing, shelter, safety) at the bottom, love and belonging needs (similar to the Thomas statement) next, and self-actualization and intellectual needs at the top of the pyramid.[24] It has been said that Carl Rogers believes that man has only one basic need: self-actualization. Maslow has been the individual most identified with the term. Lazarus speaks of "Abraham Maslow and Carl Rogers, who view successful adjustment as the achievement of self-actualization—that is, the successful expression of the highest potentialities of which a person is capable." [25]

The need for self-actualization seems to be the mode of modern society. In the affluent society, physiological needs are passé; the hippie claims that his needs are few—food, clothing, and shelter—and that his welfare check will provide them while he "self-actualizes" or finds "the real me." The white-collar worker dabbles in sensitivity training [26] or visits his psychoanalyst. The alienation of youth from the Establishment is another case in point; many youths are rejecting the work ethic as a Puritan anachronism in modern society. Self-actualization is the "in thing." Some members of the middle class are challenging not the theory but the implementation. If welfare checks are supporting youth in their search for "the real me," then who is paying the bill? Why should over-thirty Joe support under-thirty Moe in his search for self-actualization? This creates intergroup conflict, apparently in denial of what some modern psychologists are postulating as a basic need of man. That educators agree on the importance of self-actualization as a major

[24]B. Claude Mathis, John W. Cotton, and Lee Sechrest, Psychological Foundations of Education (New York: Academic Press, 1970), pp. 416–417.
[25]Richard S. Lazarus, Personality and Adjustment (Englewood Cliffs, N.J.: Prentice-Hall, 1963), p. 18.
[26]Donald Thomas, "T-Grouping: The White Collar Hippie Movement," Phi Delta Kappan, Vol. 49, No. 8 (April 1968), pp. 458–459.

goal of education is noted in the 1966 *Yearbook of the Association for Supervision and Curriculum Development.* It says in part, "A world that seems to be in a continual state of crisis . . . calls for each human being to reach a kind of maturity and a depth of understanding not commonly achieved today. We will refer to this positive growth as self-actualization and take the stand . . . that fostering this in all young people will be a vital and rewarding enterprise and well worth the effort entailed." [27]

To return to the quote from Bradburn at the beginning of this section, the current controversy over the right to self-actualization "leads inevitably to a succession of inter-personal conflicts." The implications for mental health are obvious. Society has too few jobs for its members (over 6 per cent unemployment in 1971, with the bulk of the unemployment among the culturally disadvantaged and the young). Man abhors inactivity, he will find goals to pursue. (In the absence of work opportunity, why not reject the work ethic in favor of attainable goals? Western man has been taught that he has the "inalienable right to life and property." Why should he contribute taxes for the support of the rebel?)

These are only a few of the emotional stresses prevalent in modern society. To summarize this brief presentation, prolonged denial of any of the basic emotional needs will tend to cause mental illness. The method of denial, however, is not always obvious. These needs are psychological and their description is elusive. They are even more difficult to recognize in the everyday world. The authors, therefore, will attempt in the next three sections to survey some of the broad social areas in which man's basic emotional needs are being met or denied. Social relations with groups and individuals in this interdependent world will be surveyed, with attention to limitations of physical, economic, and social environments. Personal adjustment to new ways of living—being born, starting school, making sex adjustments, choosing an occupation, selecting a mate, entering military service, and attaining retirement—will be considered. Finally, some attempt will be made to indicate some of the cultural limitations placed on the process of realistic goal setting by the individual; special attention will be paid to unrealistic levels of aspiration, incompatible goals, restriction of alternatives (especially in the field of recreation), and religion, both as a source of strength and as a source of weakness.

SOME SOCIAL CAUSES OF POOR MENTAL HEALTH

Fear Occasioned by an Interdependent World

Anxiety is contagious. Research has shown that anxiety should be considered a communicable disease and that the chief method of spreading it is through sound (voice, loud noises, and so on).[28] Toffler speaks of "de-stimulating tactics" to combat anxiety-producing sound. He says, "We employ a de-stimulating tactic, for example, when we storm into the teenagers' bedroom and turn off a stereo unit that has been battering our ear-

[27]Walter B. Waetzen and Robert R. Leeper (eds.), *Learning and Mental Health in the School* (Washington, D.C.: A.S.C.D., N.E.A., 1966), pp. 99–100.

[28]Jurgen Ruesch and A. Rodney Prestwood, "Anxiety," in Oliver E. Byrd (ed.), *Health Instruction Yearbook, 1950* (Stanford, Calif.: Stanford University Press, 1950), p. 72.

drums with unwanted and interruptive sounds." [29] Children especially are apt to absorb the tensions of parents or other adults. Is it any wonder that we are living in an anxious age? Modern methods of communication have brought the furious sounds of global conflict into the living room of nearly every American child. Television screens report the battles of World Wars I and II, the sobbing of Vietnamese orphans as they wander aimlessly through the rubble of their cities, and the battle tactics of the armed forces as they maintain a state of readiness for our protection in the event of a third world war. Films of race riots in our own cities come into our homes through televised news reports. Television, radio, and newspapers are an essential link in the chain that is slowly binding the entire globe into one world. The prospect of one-world unity seems to frighten many people even more than the specter of the continuous armed conflict that seems to the concomitant of a divided world. These fears are being communicated as specific fears from one adult to another, and as a generalized feeling of anxiety from adults to their children.

Limitations of Physical Environment

In our complex, interdependent modern world the sources of fears and anxieties are found in all of man's relations with man and with the physical world in which he finds himself. For example, the relationship between the rice fields of China and the mental health of the children of Middletown, U.S.A., is not obvious; but it is very real. The unrest in the Far East today is in part a reflection of the inability of the land to support such a large population in an agricultural economy. When man's physical existence is threatened by starvation, tensions mount and drive him to action. Evidence of such behavior was the surge of the Chinese army over the Yalu River. Televised scenes of weeping Korean orphans directly disturbed American children, for the orphans depicted were similar to them in age. More sweeping in effect, though less obvious, is the transmission of anxiety from adults to children when adults become disturbed by this evidence of the inadequacy of the rice fields of China. The confusion over the causes and goals of the Vietnam conflict, coupled with the heavy casualty rates in the escalated stages of the war, accelerated and extended the anxieties of both adults and children. These anxieties may be blamed on a Communist plan for world conquest, or they may be attributed directly to the physical deprivations suffered by the Vietnamese as a result of their environment.

Limitations of the Economic System

Let us come closer to home for another example of the contagiousness of anxiety, leaving limitations of the physical environment in the Far East for a brief sketch of one limitation of the American economic system. We turn to opportunities for vertical mobility in American society. True, the term *limitation* is used here in a relative sense. One of the great strengths of American democracy has been its tradition that "any boy can become

[29]Toffler, op. cit., p. 10.

president." Recent evidence of the operation of that tradition is the rise of a relatively unsuccessful haberdasher to the presidency of the United States. Despite that recent dramatic evidence, the trend has been toward a diminishing of opportunity. As business corporations have become larger and more complex, the junior executive posts have come more and more to be filled by sons of the senior executives. Harvard, for example, draws its student body largely from the homes of the well-to-do. It places its graduates in positions of eminence, at least partly because of the social connections made by students during their years at Harvard.

College enrollments are growing because of an increasing population of youth of college age but only slightly over half of the young electorate of the country have completed even a high school education. Median years of school completed, by states, range from 8.7 in South Carolina and Kentucky to 12.2 in Utah.[30] Education is one of the major ladders of vertical mobility in modern America. For as long as nearly half of the nation's children are being denied a high school education, the opportunities for that half to become president are being materially decreased.

The denial of the education ladder for vertical mobility to a large segment of the population has destructive effects far beyond the anxieties it creates in the minds of young people facing the problem of vocational placement with inadequate preparation. It limits further contact with middle-class culture in a society that is based on middle-class values, thus making individual problems of life adjustment more difficult in all areas. Stated negatively, it fosters juvenile delinquency and adult crime. Basically, it is a denial of vocational and intellectual security to those who come from homes already faced with physical insecurity.

Limitations of the Class–Caste System

A third major source of tensions in American society is the limitation imposed by our class–caste system. The authors hold no brief for a classless society. In all cultures, at all times, man has rewarded his leaders with power, prestige, and money. Admitting the necessity for such unequal (but equitable) division of this world's goods and services, the fact remains that those on the lowest rung of the economic ladder must have enough goods and services for adequate existence if they are to remain physically and mentally healthy. Our caste system, however, discriminates on a basis other than leadership (or other productive) ability. Color of skin has denied first-class citizenship to some 20 million Americans. The clash between the ideals of equality and brotherhood embodied in the Judaeo-Christian tradition and the reality of class privilege causes many anxieties and insecurities.

Our class–caste system, then, has limited opportunities for the achievement of security. Restrictions are placed on the individual on the basis of his economic class, color, or religion. These limitations will be developed in Chapter 9. All of us are aware of the tensions created by these denials of man's needs. Social legislation may increase these tensions for brief periods in restricted areas, but the proud record of America is a gradual lessening of

[30]*Statistical Abstract of the United States*, 1970 (Washington, D.C.: Government Printing Office, 1970), p. 112.

these tensions through reductions in discriminatory practices. We note these tensions here only as another source of the many anxieties of our times. Any anxiety is contagious; it affects not only one's own class, race, creed, but all of America.

Making Adjustments to New Ways of Living

Being born is probably one of the greatest shocks suffered by any human being. The baby is faced with the task of doing many things for himself that the mother had been doing for him, such as breathing, eating, eliminating, and adjusting to changes in the temperature and humidity of the air about him. He had not even supported his own weight; mother had suspended him in a bag of liquid. The postnatal period, or first ten days of life, is one of great adjustment to a new way of living.

Other periods in one's life that necessitate great readjustment to new modes of living are starting to school, attaining puberty, leaving school to earn one's living, beginning married life, entering the armed forces, and retiring. To these may be added the major readjustments faced by selected portions of the populace as they move from rural to urban areas, from one state or region to another with sharply different ways of living, or from one country to another.

Any period necessitating major readjustments to life's problems endangers mental health. It is in these periods of stress that personality damage may be done to the mentally healthy person and that severe mental illness may develop in the previously mildly unbalanced individual. Evidence from the battle zones of World War II indicates the significance of these periods of stress for the mental health of our most physically and mentally fit young men:

> Ordinarily neuropsychiatric disorders are thought to occur only in weaklings or in individuals with personality defects. This is not true. Information at hand indicates that a significant proportion of the neuropsychiatric casualties are occurring in individuals who give no history suggesting predisposition. Under the extremes of stress and fatigue of modern combat the most stable individual may reach his breaking point. Thus the presence of neuropsychiatric disorder must be looked for in normal as well as predisposed individuals.[31]

Even those well-adjusted individuals with emotional security and a high level of problem-solving ability, who cope successfully with the less traumatic problems of life, may find adjustment to new modes of living extremely difficult.

The Preschool Period. The preschool period of rapid growth in all aspects of development—motor, intellectual, school, and emotional—encompasses the most critical years of personality formation.

> The basic personality traits and reaction patterns are acquired in this period (early childhood) and are, for the most part, merely strengthened in the succeeding years. . . . In the home the young child encounters the initial experiences

[31]Robert J. Carpenter, "Early Recognition and Treatment of Neuropsychiatric Conditions in the Combat Zone," in Oliver E. Byrd (ed.), *Health Instruction Yearbook, 1944* (Stanford, Calif.: Stanford University Press, 1944), pp. 88–89.

which determine whether he will develop a sense of personal security and of being loved and accepted; in the home the child meets the situations which determine the extent of his sense of adequacy and of personal worth.[32]

But this does not mean, as some of the earlier psychologists had contended, that personality patterns are rigidly set by the age of six. Sherman lists "critical periods in the growth of personality" through the "crystallization period—variously estimated as occurring between the ages of 35 and 45." [33] More recent psychologists extend this period. Kurt Haas, for example, says, "We describe the give and take of living by saying that the person has *adjusted*, and continues to adjust for so long as he participates in the world." [34]

It seems obvious that there is greater danger of basal personality damage at the very youngest ages. It seems somewhat less obvious that the cumulative effect of a life of emotional instability would make the older person more susceptible to severe mental illness. This is not to imply that mental illness is a prerogative of old age. At least 150,000 children are seen in psychiatric clinics each year.[35] Schizophrenia, the leading cause of first admissions to mental hospitals in 1950, was most commonly found in youth.[36] As we discuss briefly each of the periods creating stress, two factors should be kept in mind. First, although emotional security and problem-solving ability will enable most individuals to experience transitional periods successfully, they are a potential source of danger to the mental health of every individual. Secondly, "personality maladjustments" and "functional mental illness" are probably varying intensities of the same psychological phenomenon and are found at all ages.

Starting to School.   Certainly the young child is expected to make major readjustments as he enters school life. "Children growing up . . . are literally captured by aspects of their milieu, which mold them." [37] The small size of the modern American family provides the average child with relatively few individuals with whom he must share the affection of his parents. In this strange new world called the school, he must share with thirty or forty other equally self-centered children the attentions of the teacher. By and large, his needs had taken priority at home. As a very young child, he consumed his meal under the complete and undivided supervision of his mother before his parents sat down to dinner. Just before the age of entering school he had moved to the family dinner table at their regular dinner hour, but his needs still were the center of attention. Smaller portions were arranged for him. Special provisions were made to prevent his spilling food. Little games were played to make certain foods more attractive. If his father commuted to work, the family dinner hour may have been the major period of the

[32]Barney Katz and George F. J. Lehner, *Mental Hygiene in Modern Living* (New York: Ronald, 1953), p. 75. Used by permission.

[33]Mandel Sherman, *Mental Hygiene and Education* (New York: McKay, 1945), pp. 58–60.

[34]Kurt Haas, *Understanding Adjustment and Behavior* (Englewood Cliffs, N.J.: Prentice-Hall, 1970), pp. 229–230.

[35]Katherine Glover, *Mental Health—Everybody's Business* (New York: Public Affairs Committee, Inc., 1953), p. 23.

[36]Ibid.

[37]Haas, op. cit., p. 206.

day in which he and his father had time to visit (in his terms, to play) with each other. Now he must learn to participate in kindergarten lunch periods where he is only one of a large group, receiving only one thirtieth of the attention of the sole adult present. Food is very important to the young child. The relative impersonality of the school lunch program may present a very real problem to him.

His freedom of movement is curtailed, and even the ways in which he receives his directions are changed. In the home he had free access to the cookie jar and to the toilet facilities. For the most part he played when, where, and with what he pleased. Now he must adjust to routines, to taking turns, and to sharing. He must learn to take directions from written symbols on a chalkboard or chart, as a member of a group, rather than receiving the individual oral instructions, to which he had been accustomed. He must learn that for the authority of only two parents there has been substituted the authority of many individuals—bus driver, teacher, principal, nurse, dentist, custodian, traffic policeman, and safety patrol boy—some of whom have only infrequent contact with him. Little children need much affection and close physical contact with adults at this period if they are to make a satisfactory adjustment. True, basal personality patterns are taking shape, but they have not formed completely. They are subject to great modification now and to lesser modification in later life. A normal, healthy, outgoing child may be transformed by a harsh first-grade teacher into a shy, withdrawn child or into a hostile, aggressive one.

Attaining Puberty. The attainment of puberty is another great milestone in personality development. Freud makes more of the sex drive than most modern psychologists, but most of us are forced to agree with him that the prolonged period of (legal) infancy in modern man has created a host of problems that adolescents in earlier cultures did not face. Biologically, most children are mature before they enter senior high school. If they have aspirations for professional life, they must remain dependent upon their parents for at least seven more years of schooling—three of high school and four of college. If they have vocational aspirations higher than semiskilled labor or the lower echelons of the distributive trades, they must postpone marriage for at least the three years requisite to the completion of high school. Further complicating the picture are compulsory education and child-labor laws that limit the amounts and kinds of employment available to them until the normal age of completion of high school.

Youth is biologically ready for procreation, then, several years before our society will sanction marriage, and premarital intercourse violates both the social and the religious mores of our culture. The biological organism is driving youth to the satisfaction of its needs. Society says that sexual desires cannot be satisfied. Many youths, of course, defy conventions and satisfy the biological urge, but they only intensify their emotional conflicts through guilt feelings and lowered moral standards as youths, and through excessive worry about the sexual behavior of their own children when they become parents of teen-agers.

The adolescent faces the problem of identity, or "Who am I?" The White House Conference on Children and Youth is widely quoted on this topic:

With the onset of adolescence another period of personality development begins. As is well known, adolescence is a period of storm and stress for many young people, a period in which previous certainties are questioned and previous continuities no longer relied upon. Physiological changes and rapid physical growth provide the somatic base for the turmoil and indecision. It may be that cultural factors also play a part, for it has been observed that adolescence is less upsetting in some societies than in others.

The central problem of the period is the establishment of a sense of identity. The identity the adolescent seeks to clarify is who he is, what his role in society is to be. Is he a child or is he an adult? Does he have it in him to be someday a husband and father? What is he to be as a worker and an earner of money? Can he feel self-confident in spite of the fact that his race or religion or national background makes him a person some people look down upon? Over all, will he be a success or a failure? By reason of these questions adolescents are sometimes morbidly preoccupied with how they appear in the eyes of others as compared with their own conception of themselves, and with how they can make the roles and skills learned earlier jibe with what is currently in style.[38]

Leaving School to Earn One's Living.   Whether the youth leaves school at the end of the sixth grade or at the completion of the doctorate, many of his problems will be the same: establishing a life independent of his family,[39] becoming established in a vocation or a profession, assuming full legal and moral responsibilities for his actions, selecting a mate, establishing and supporting a family, making choices of social and political allegiances, and assuming responsibility for adult citizenship. It seems as though at both the beginning and the end of one's school life a whole host of critical decisions are forced upon one as a result of entering a new way of life. Many youths drift along the path of least resistance with apparent serenity but later regret bitterly those casual decisions as they assess their accomplishments and survey the future from the reality of middle age. The time of leaving school is a critical age in terms of personal mental health, even though the emotional conflict may be delayed for many years.

One of the choices of youth most dramatically affected by an era of rapid social and technological change is the choice of a vocation. The choice of a semiskilled vocation, with its high job obsolescence, gives little real security to the employee. Technological unemployment—the elimination of jobs through the invention of labor-saving machines—may wipe out the family source of income just as the new baby is arriving. Complicating this picture is the fact that the percentage of semiskilled jobs is increasing. These semiskilled jobs are the ones most susceptible to technological unemployment. The recent trend of entire factories toward automation eventually may wipe out all but a handful of these jobs in production work.

A second change in the composition of the labor force that will affect youth's choice of vocation is the decline of the extractive occupations: farming, mining, and forestry. This is coupled with a sharp increase in the distributive and service trades: retail sales, repair, and maintenance. It is

---

[38]Debora Brink, *Readings in Mental Hygiene: Principles and Practices* (New York: Selected Academic Readings, 1969), pp. ERS–8A. Used by permission.

[39]Youths who attended colleges outside their home community have made many of these adjustments, but even for them graduation symbolizes final severance of many major family ties, especially financial ones.

becoming increasingly difficult for a youth to drift into the occupation of his father. Many youths are having to select from a host of new jobs created by the rapid changes in our technology and our whole social order.

Beginning Married Life. No matter how cooperative and understanding one may be, learning to share one's life with another person is accomplished only through conflict. To begin with, one may learn that the person one married is not at all the person one thought he was marrying. The fastidiously perfect beauty queen may be a sloppy housekeeper. The handsome "prom trotter" may refuse to leave his fireside. Further, few individuals realize just how carefully they have preserved their inviolability of self until they discover that their mate expects to share all their most intimate secrets, their feelings, and their thoughts. Petty incidents become magnified out of all proportion to their significance, and serve as focal points for venting pent-up hostilities. Sharpening the pencils with a razor blade may provoke a scene when the real source of irritation was the wife's curiosity about an office deal that had not gone well.

Sharing also means giving up. Bowling may have to be discontinued. Favorite television programs may have to be forgotten. One is no longer free even to choose one's own friends, for they must be acceptable also to the mate. The weekly trip to the hairdresser may not be within the family budget, even though it was a pleasant necessity when the girl was working. If the wife continues working, business and professional women's club meetings may have to be skipped in order to do the ironing or to clean the house. In the 1970's the courts of the United States were granting one divorce for every four marriages. In 1945 an all-time high was reached of one divorce for every 3.3 marriages.[40] Need more be said about the emotional impact of marriage, if one fourth of our modern marriages are ending in complete failure and dissolution? And what of the emotional conflict in those unhappy marriages that never reach the divorce courts?

What can we predict for the future of the mental health of our nation, as measured by the stability of marriage as an institution? Children are involved in nearly half of all divorce cases. It is true that often a child can be happier and feel more secure when living with one parent with a minimum of confusion and conflict than when living with both parents amid a storm of criticisms and accusations, but the "child's basic difficulty in the disappearance of one or more parents arises from the fact that his parent could care so little for him as to desert him." [41] His basic security is threatened by the disruption of the marriage of his parents. If we are concerned that the marriages of the future become more stable, society must assume responsibility for more and better marriage counseling in an attempt to improve the happiness of current marriages. "Education for successful marriage begins in infancy. Upon the success of today's families depends the success of those established a generation hence." [42]

Fulfilling Military Service. Many young men will state bitterly that

---

[40]*The Economic Almanac, 1958* (New York: The National Industrial Conference Board, Inc., 1958), p. 16.

[41]J. S. Plant, *The Envelope: A Study of the Impact of the World upon the Child* (New York: Commonwealth Fund, 1950), p. 22.

[42]John Biesanz and Mavis Biesanz, *Modern Society* (Englewood Cliffs, N.J.: Prentice-Hall, 1964), p. 247.

military service was the most difficult period in their entire lives. Statistics at least partially will support their statements. "For every soldier hospitalized in World War II for wounds due to bombs and shellfire, there was one (or more) hospitalized for an emotional difficulty. The great majority of emotional crack-ups occurred during the first three months of training." [43] When one considers the sources of man's emotional security—family, friends, job, locality—this high incidence of personality disturbance in the early months of training is readily understandable. The civilian-soldier is suddenly torn away from all his emotional anchors. He usually has little choice in his new life as to his associates, the type of job to which he will be assigned, or even his freedom of movement. Regimentation and restraint are thrust upon individuals trained from birth to exist in a free society. To attempt to escape from this disagreeable situation is to be stigmatized as a traitor. The civilian-soldier has no choice but adjustment or discharge as an emotional deviate. Despite the draft card burnings of the middle 1960's, and Vietnam protest demonstrations persisting into the 1970's, the stigma attached to the draft dodger persists. The "bleed-in" staged by students at Indiana University, where thousands of students gave blood for shipment to military hospitals in Vietnam, still symbolizes the spirit of patriotism characteristic of the great majority of American youth.

If the civilian makes a satisfactory adjustment and becomes a "good soldier," then new emotional stresses are placed upon him. The fatigue, sleeplessness, irregular diet, physical danger, noise, and confusion of battle may break even the best-integrated individual. It is no wonder that reports from all theaters of operation indicated that neuropsychiatric disorders caused more hospital admissions than did all battle casualties.[44] In the current conflict, drug addiction is becoming a major problem in Vietnam. The question remains: Is the problem the ready availability of drugs in Asia, or is it another evidence of the psychiatric casualties of war?

Entering Retirement. We realize what a great source of emotional security we find in our jobs when we see the aimless wandering and early demise of men and women forced into retirement by compulsory age limitations on service. Many of these unfortunates only complicate their own problems by voluntarily severing ties with many other sources of security; they leave children, friends, and places with which they have been associated all their lives to move to the "retirement colonies" of Florida and California. They are "starting a new life" almost in the sense of the army draftee: new climate, new house, new associates, new occupation, and usually a restricted income. About all they retain of their old life is their mate, their personal and household possessions, and their freedom of movement. Of those who remain in their old homes, the former wage earners face major readjustments to an entirely new way of life.

Moving from Rural to Urban Areas or from One Region to Another Region with Sharply Differing Folkways. The impersonality, loneliness, bustle, and confusion of a large city have a seriously disintegrating effect upon the personalities of many persons born and reared in rural com-

---

[43]Katz and Lehner, op. cit., p. 426.
[44]Ibid.

munities. Old sources of security have been left behind. Ways of doing things are strange and different. Apartment dwellers are not the neighbors that the folks back home were. Clothing is worn differently. Speech patterns are strange. All of these differences and many more make the newcomer visible as an "outsider" and tend to keep him that way. New friends are few and far between, and loneliness can overwhelm one.

Toffler suggests that the *number* of changes involved in moving to a new locale may be more destructive of sound mental health than just loneliness.

> One who is moving to a new residence is a classification into which more than 100,000 Americans fit on any given day, yet they are seldom thought of as a group. . . . Dr. Herbert Gerjuoy, a psychologist on the staff of the Human Resources Research Organization, terms it "situational grouping." . . . By temporarily bringing together people who are sharing, or are about to share, a common adaptive experience, he argues, we help equip them to cope with it. A man required to adapt to a new life situation loses some of his basis for self-esteem. He begins to doubt his abilities![45]

Toffler suggests "half-way houses" to assist rural migrants in their adjustment to urban living. He stresses the need for retention of some of the old ways of living in the new situation, to minimize future shock.

Moving from One Country to Another. The immigrant faces all the preceding problems, but they are intensified because of the greater degree of difference in ways of doing, thinking, and believing. To these barriers to social integration may be added the extra visibility of a foreign accent or of a foreign tongue being spoken in the home, a difference in skin color, and even a "foreign" name. The difficulty of finding emotional security in a strange culture is probably the greatest single reason for the formation of "foreign colonies" in large cities. This segregation may afford immediate relief from tension; but it only intensifies the long-range problem, because It slows the process of the cultural integration that is essential to the eventual acceptance in the culture that in turn is prerequisite to finding emotional security in the new culture.

Cultural Limitations on Realistic Goal Setting

Goals must be set in the major areas of living in order to give direction and meaning to life. Frustrations result from the inability to set goals, to achieve unrealistic goals, or to achieve incompatible goals simultaneously. These frustrations are caused by the absence of realistic goals. Conversely stated, *the achievement of realistic major life goals fosters sound mental health*. By realistic goals we mean attainable goals that contribute to the integration of the individual and to the maintenance and improvement of the culture. The major limitations upon the setting of realistic goals by the average individual is the tendency of parents to encourage youngsters to set life goals without due consideration of the children's innate abilities. Upper-class parents tend to encourage aspirations beyond the child's ability;

[45]Toffler, op. cit., p. 14.

lower-class parents sometimes discourage capable children from pursuing professional goals.

The four broad areas of life in which one should concentrate his mental health efforts are work, love, recreation, and a personal philosophy.[46] Rogers comments on the difficulties in the last area, in what he refers to as "The Fundamental Discrepancy." By this he means that most persons assimilate their values from the culture—from parents, teachers, ministers, best friends, and so on—without questioning the validity of these values for one's unique self. Operating within a value configuration at variance with one's real desires maintains constant tensions, often to the point of serious disturbance. As Rogers puts it:

> I believe that this picture of the individual, with values mostly introjected, held as fixed concepts, rarely examined or tested, is the picture of most of us. By taking over the conceptions of others as our own, we lose contact with the potential wisdom of our own functioning and lose confidence in ourselves. Since these value constructs are often sharply at variance with what is going on in our own experiencing, we have in a very basic way divorced ourselves from ourselves, and this accounts for much of modern strain and insecurity. This fundamental discrepancy between the individual's concepts and what he is actually experiencing, between the intellectual structure of his values and the valuing process going on unrecognized within him—this is a part of the fundamental estrangement of modern man from himself. This is a major problem for the therapist.[47]

We shall speak, in a later section, of scientific problem solving as a strategy for setting realistic goals in these major areas of life: work, love, recreation, and a personal philosophy. We have noted these critical areas in Chapter 6. As a family member or as an individual, however, most individuals set their major life goals not on the basis of rational problem solving but on the basis of emotional attitudes. These attitudes have been conditioned by the child-rearing practices of parents and by other forces in the cultural matrix. The extent of such emotional goal setting is not amenable to scientific measurement, but informed opinion is reflected in the statement attributed to the dean of the school of education in a major American university: "We feel our way through life on the basis of our emotions. We think only as a last resort, for thinking is painful."

Unrealistic Expectations of Parents

A significant source of culturally imposed frustrations is the tendency of upper-class parents to encourage their children to set a level of aspiration that is unrealistically high. This level is related to the child's concept of himself, and it will determine the types of goals that he sets for himself. The mean intelligence of children of professional parents will correlate about 0.50 with the mean intelligence of their parents, regressing toward the mean

[46]Oliver E. Byrd, "Mental Health for the Normal Person," unpublished paper, Stanford University, 1950.
[47]Carl R. Rogers, *Freedom to Learn* (Columbus, Ohio: Merrill, 1969), p. 247. Used by permission.

intelligence of the total population.[48] Many professional parents, however, want their children to be as competent as themselves, or more competent. They anxiously watch for the first baby step, the first word, and other indicators of development and eagerly compare developmental status with that of the children of their friends and relatives. The child constantly is reminded of superior progress. He is encouraged to think of himself as a very superior fellow indeed. Ambitions in sport, vocational choices, and other goals will be based on the expectation of superior accomplishment. What does this do to the personality of the individual of near average ability when he constantly fails to achieve superior accomplishment? He may make a choice early in life, for example, to become a physician. His orientation for years has been toward that goal, but he makes such a poor record in premedical training that he is denied admission to medical school. A major readjustment to a new choice of a life work must be made. Both the making of the new choice and the period of adjustment to it will be very trying. Setting a more realistic original goal was prevented by the unrealistic expectations of the parents.

On the other hand, the discouragement by lower-class parents of the professional ambitions of their children, whose ability may be far above average, may contribute to self-recrimination by such a child who drifts into a dead-end job, with the attendant anxieties and frustrations. However, the major tragedy here seems to be the waste of human resources.

Ambivalent Cultural Values of Individuals

Another major source of externally imposed frustrations lies in the ambivalent patterns of our culture. We offer the child inconsistent guidance in making important choices. How will the child feel about people of another color if brotherly love is taught in the home and racial segregation is practiced in the schools, or vice versa? Or how will he feel if the most important agencies for education in his life—home, school, and church—all preach brotherly love but practice discrimination? How will the child feel about honesty if he is scolded for stealing an apple and made to return it, only to hear dad brag about a "sharp deal" in which he made a big profit at the expense of a gullible customer or business associate?

Ambivalent Cultural Values of Groups

A major source of internally imposed frustrations is the effort of the individual to work simultaneously toward incompatible goals (or apparently incompatible goals). Such dilemmas may be personal, as in the case of the girl who cannot decide between two prospective mates or between a mate and a career. On the other hand, it may be largely a social dilemma, even though the selection of the alternative may be almost wholly up to the individual. We have mentioned earlier the moral conflict of the child who experiences inconsistent racial attitudes at home and at school. The child has little choice about maintaining membership in the home and the school.

[48]Anne Anastasi, *Differential Psychology* (New York: Macmillan, 1964), pp. 275–279.

He does have autonomy, however, in pledging allegiance to various sub-groups within the school and the community. For example, a student may accept or reject membership in a school sorority, a Y.W.C.A. youth group, or a Sunday school class. Simultaneous membership in all three of these groups may involve behavior that violates the customs of one or more groups; friendship may be expected in the Y.W.C.A. group toward a girl who was excluded by the sorority. Such friendship may baffle the sorority sisters, who cannot understand such behavior from "one with such a good background—associating with trash just isn't done!" "In these cases, the individual is not reacting contrary to his past experience, as might at first appear. This would be psychologically impossible. His (her) behavior is the result of psychological membership in various conflicting groups."[49] Simultaneous membership in many conflicting groups may be maintained to the ultimate improvement of the individual. Awareness of their differences may provide for more realistic evaluation of all the groups and for more sound moral choices. In some cases, however, as in the case of open conflict between a labor union and a political party, the individual may be forced to choose affiliation with one group at the expense of surrendering friendships in and cherished ideas of the other group. Such a forced choice, of course, gives very real pain and may cause serious personality damage. An illustration of such damage is the adoption of dogmatic attitudes in defense of the organization chosen. The gradual growth in the rigidity of personality that may result from such painful choices not only may impair one's problem-solving skills but also may leave one less prepared to bend rather than to break under other emotional impacts.

Impoverished Cultural Environment

Some goals may be recognized as poor ones but may be structured by limitations of the physical environment. The young adult may "choose" movies, bars, and "lovers' lanes" as preferred entertainment solely because they offer the only recreational facilities available in the community. The frustrations that come from such forced choices are keeping many good young teachers out of some rural communities. They are draining the potential leadership in many other areas of life from some areas of the hinterland, as young people gravitate to metropolitan areas that offer sports, the fine arts, and intellectual stimulation. The effects on mental health of the "bar–lovers'-lane" routine were discussed earlier under the headings of Alcoholism in this chapter and of Sex Behavior in Chapter 6.

Religion

Religion may be a source of strength or of weakness. Man can comprehend the finite; he can only contemplate the infinite. When scientific explanations of life's problems and mysteries have proved inadequate, when tensions seem unbearable, peace may be attained through faith in the ultimate wisdom of a Supreme Being in so arranging events. Religious faith can be a great source of emotional security.

[49]Ibid., p. 628.

Religion as a source of weakness has both social and personal implications. On the social side, there have been religious wars and discrimination against religious sects throughout recorded history. On the personal side, religious teaching is often the source of the greatest emotional disturbance—the dichotomy between the perfection taught and the imperfection practiced on all sides.

Another personal aspect of religion as a source of emotional disturbance concerns the basic reorientation of the thinking patterns of modern Western man. For the Western world the day of "one faith, one king, one country" has gone forever. For the unreasoned acceptance of the authority of church and state we have substituted the application of Newtonian science to most areas of life. Religious freedom is one expression of this reorientation in thinking. A man no longer must belong to the Universal Church or be damned to eternal fire (and secular persecution); he has the right to make his individual peace with God, either alone or within the religoius sect of his choice. But as man probes the eternal mysteries of life in search of religious faith, he cannot escape his problem-solving frame of reference. He wants to understand, to explain, the meaning of life and the nature of God.

> To call things supernatural is no explanation of them according to the modern scientists, for to explain is simply to point out the natural connection between phenomena. The new general attitude has become so instinctive and so much a part of our world-view that most of us never think of interpreting extraordinary any more than ordinary occurrences in other than a naturalistic way. Fairies, witches, ghosts, angels and demons, once freely assumed to account for all sorts of phenomena, have simply dropped out of the mind of the average modern man and no longer play a part in his experience. Not that their existence has been disproved, but that they have become superfluous.[50]

Man needs the security that has been supplied by religious faith. The Communists have used this need and have avoided the conflict between modern naturalistic thinking and the unreasoned acceptance of a religious dogma by making of communism a secular religion, one that demands a fanatical adherence to its dictates.

> He alone has the true faith. The party line alone is truth. To it he owes blind obedience. It is his God on Sinai delivering the law. Any deviation from the dictates of the party line must be confessed as a sin. To a Communist, the state is the all-powerful, all-embracing Numen (Universal God). The party leaders are high priests and exercise the enormous social control of a priesthood.[51]

Probably more important than the "faith" noted above (since it applies to the party members) is the fact that the Soviets have put everybody to work and have attached high praise to its performance. Some, probably many, though not party folk, enjoy better mental health because they feel that they are engaged in a common enterprise. Further strengthening their mental health is the climate of political opinion in Russia. The average man has few

---

[50]Arthur C. McGiffert, *The Rise of Modern Religious Ideas* (New York: Macmillan, 1951), p. 36. Used by permission.

[51]Biesanz and Biesanz, op. cit., p. 27.

choices to make; hence, he has few anxieties concerning the "right" de-cisions. One can only speculate as to the effect of purges and reversals of the party line on the mental health of the average man in modern Russia.

Western man has reached no easy solution. He is committed to the freedoms implied in the individual, scientific search for truth. He is bound by the thinking patterns of that search as he tries to establish an individual faith. He cannot accept on a supernatural basis the spiritual values enshrined in the Judaeo-Christian tradition.[52] There seems to be an unconscious realiza-tion that the moral and spiritual values that he needs to give direction and meaning to his life must arise from the experiences of modern culture, but the church teaches that the source of these values is divine revelation, as recorded in the Bible. The intensity and significance of the conflict caused by the attempt to apply naturalistic thinking to mystical phenomena cannot readily be measured. Some writers take a more pessimistic view of the dualism of reason and faith in the modern world than do your authors, but the presence of the problem cannot be denied. The position of one writer is that "we shall continue to develop intellectually and emotionally mal-adjusted people so long as the total educational influences of our culture perpetuate this split between the head and the heart—between modern man's tested methods of achieving knowledge and control and his ideal objects of aspiration, allegiance, and devotion."[53]

As the church moves into the modern world, the age-old dichotomy between faith and reason seems to be diminishing. The Ecumenical Councils have striven valiantly to relate religion to modern man. Texts by a prominent clergyman (*The Power of Positive Thinking,* 1956; *Stay Alive All Your Life,* 1957; *The Amazing Results of Positive Thinking,* 1959; *The Tough-Minded Optimist,* 1961; *Sin, Sex and Self Control,* 1965) read more like psychiatry for the layman than like religious treatises. Frankly psychiatric texts (for example, Cecil Osborne, *The Art of Understanding You* [New York: Pyramid, 1967]) quote freely from the Scriptures, and they deliver basically the same messages as popular texts in mental hygiene authored by psychologists and physicians (such as Murray Banks, *How to Live with Yourself* [New York: The Institute Press, 1953] or John A. Schindler, *How to Live 365 Days a Year* [New York: Fawcett, 1969]). Modern man is being assisted by religion in rec-onciling faith and reason.

ADJUSTMENT MECHANISMS INDICATIVE OF POOR MENTAL HEALTH

The problem situations in the preceding sections have implied a need for action by the individual. The well-integrated individual will react both emotionally and rationally to problem situations. It is only when emotional reactions become habituated as the major "solutions" to problems that poor mental health is indicated. In this section we shall list some of the better-known emotional reactions that are typical of most people. Individuals with

[52]Many individuals, of course, do accept spiritual values on a supernatural basis. The ad-herence of devout Catholics to church dogma is a case in point.
[53]John L. Childs, *Education and Morals* (New York: Appleton-Century-Crofts, 1950), pp. 124–125.

good mental health use them sparingly and accompany or follow them with rational attacks upon their problems. Persons with poor mental health use them excessively and often employ them as their only response to problem situations.

As the following sections are read, whether from the point of view of one's own personal mental health or from the point of view of the teacher searching for help in her classroom, it is well to remember the caution by Fritz Redl in the foreword to *Conflict in the Classroom*:

> Whatever we say in the excitement and rush of the moment about emotional disturbances," it makes a great difference whether we talk about *the emotionally disturbed child* or about behavior which obviously indicates a *state of emotional disturbance.* Such behavior may be the clear indication that we have to deal with a youngster whose emotional health or characterological development is in some jeopardy. However, it may also be an indication that we have a youngster before us who is certainly in conflict, but in a conflict that does not come entirely from within and is attributable to a world which does something to him that shouldn't happen—a world wherein the life of the child is set awry and to which he responds by trying to fend off the pathogenic impact.[54]

Anger

We refer here to emotional outbursts of *anger*. When this anger is directed against people, it is referred to as *aggression*. When anger is vented against things, it is referred to as *destruction*. When anger is repressed, or when it is a constant, deep-seated feeling indicative of many unresolved frustrations, we refer to it as *hostility*. By whatever name, this emotional reaction and its accompanying behavior are ineffective techniques for solving problems and they accelerate mental illnesses. Levy emphasizes the fact that aggression is not a constructive form of tension release by noting that it is invariably followed by compulsive self-punishment, restoration (restitution), rationalization, or all three.[55] These compulsive behaviors are indicative of the heightened level of tension that follows aggressive behavior. The aggressive behavior to which we are referring is not rational aggression in socially approved ways, but unadulterated anger which results in antisocial behavior.

Withdrawal

Withdrawal from the conflict situation is a common response at the unconscious level. Tensions may be relieved through withdrawal techniques, but such withdrawal indicates either abandonment of the goal or postponement of goal-seeking activity. In either case the relief is only symptomatic; the immediate tensions are relieved, but the source of anxiety is unchanged. At best, withdrawal maintains a status quo of unresolved frustrations and a potential source of intense and prolonged anxiety.

[54]Nichlas J. Long, William C. Morse, and Ruth G. Newman (eds.), *Conflict in the Classroom* (Belmont, Calif.: Wadsworth, 1965), p. v. Used by permission.
[55]Levy, op. cit., pp. 397–410.

Some of the common withdrawal techniques will be sketched very briefly. Physical withdrawal from the conflict area may be a perfectly rational action, if there is real physical danger and/or if there is no goal to be attained by remaining. It is the habituation of this response to frustrations that builds anxieties; unresolved frustrations mount in number, tensions multiply, and more severe withdrawal techniques are demanded. In psychological withdrawal the person lives in an inner world into which no conflict can intrude. Emotional equilibrium is maintained through emotional apathy. This is incipient schizophrenia, a psychosis perennially causing the greatest number of admissions to mental hospitals. Regression to less mature levels of behavior is another withdrawal defense against tension. The sick or younger person is not expected to be able to cope with adult problems. Occasional use of the regression technique does little harm. A good cry may relieve tensions and leave one more relaxed, which may aid in problem solving if one soon retackles the problem. Continued infantile behavior, however, neither solves perplexing problems nor builds confidence for meeting new ones. Psychosomatic illness is one form of withdrawal behavior. The inefficient bank clerk or bookkeeper may develop an upset stomach, backache, sleepiness, or other physical symptoms of distress as the time for the examination of the books approaches; if he is ill enough, he can stay away from work while his books are being examined. Postponement of decision and compulsive use of alcohol or narcotics are withdrawal techniques that have been discussed earlier. The use of fantasy is another withdrawal technique that has consequences all the way from beneficial effects on mental health to development of psychosis. Daydreams are common in childhood. The vicarious achievement of daring deeds through fairy tales, comic books, movies, radio, television, and adult fiction may serve a very real emotional need for recognition for most of us. It is when the individual resorts to fantasy in the compulsive fashion of the alcoholic, to escape reality, that we recognize the symptoms of serious mental illness.

Rationalization

Rationalization is an easy way out of difficult situations, because it involves merely inventing plausible statements as to the desirability of the status quo. This may mean attributing altruistic motives to selfish behavior, claiming insightful behavior upon the fortuitous resolution of an unwise decision, feigning indifference or dislike of a group by which one has been rejected, and the like. If the original goal was unrealistic, rationalization probably promotes better mental health. The danger is that rationalization involves fantasy. Such distortions of fact may make future goals even more unrealistic.

Repression

Repression of our real reasons for behavior, while verbalizing rationalizations until we actually are unaware of our real motives, may lead to marked mental illness. The real motives usually are so socially unacceptable as to cause shame and humiliation if we admit them, even to ourselves. An example is that of the young man who has homosexual tendencies. He is so ashamed of them that he disavows all interest in sex, on the basis of moral precepts, until he himself actually has forgotten why he became so sexually moral. Such behavior involves tremendous tension, to the point of severe physical fatigue.[56]

Projection

Projection of our original motives on another is a mechanism that has its amusing as well as its tragic aspects. For example, a respectable businessman was standing at a bus stop, innocently reading his newspaper. A frustrated spinster was standing beside him. As the bus arrived and he moved to board it, he accidentally brushed against her. She had him arrested for indecent advances. The woman had so wanted to be touched, though not admitting it to herself, that she actually thought that he had run his hand caressingly over her body.

Sublimation

Sublimation refers to the channeling of the energy generated by a primitive urge into culturally or ethically high patterns of behavior. According to some psychoanalytical theories of genius, some of the finest art and music is attributed to sublimation of the sexual drive into esthetic experiences. For some persons, in some situations, sublimation is the only possible positive adjustment.

Identification

Identification is one of the more important of the adjustment mechanisms. The importance of the adult model in shaping behavior patterns of children and youth can hardly be overemphasized. If a child likes an adult and is liked in return, the behavior and personality patterns of the child may show a striking similarity to those of the adult model. This can be one of the major forces contributing to sound mental health when the child selects wholesome models. It can be a most disrupting influence when the models are socially or emotionally deviant, or when two or more models adopted by the same child hold conflicting values or exhibit conflicting behaviors.[57]

SEVERE MENTAL DISTURBANCES REQUIRING SPECIAL CARE

The diagnosis and cure of advanced cases of mental illness require long and complex treatment by highly specialized personnel. The inexpert meddling of the lay person can only make the eventual rehabilitation of the mentally ill more difficult. It is probable that the meddling of well-intentioned but poorly prepared classroom teachers and inexpert psychiatrists has

[56]Katz and Lehner, op. cit., p. 50.
[57]Lee J. Cronbach, Educational Psychology, Revised Edition (New York: Harcourt, 1964), pp. 424–434.

accentuated the problems of some individuals who were suffering from curable mental illness. Many of the functional psychoses probably are only accelerated neuroses. "The conviction is becoming widespread among psychiatrists, psychologists, and sociologists that the same kind of personal, social, and environmental factors are operative in preparing the ground for and in precipitating the functional psychoses as in the case of the neuroses."[58]

This section is designed to emphasize the fact that emotional deviates differ in behavior from normal individuals only in the intensity of the frustrations experienced and the frequency and appropriateness of the techniques employed to reduce their tensions. As Katz and Lehner put it:

> Maladjusted people differ from those who are well adjusted principally in degree. They use the same defense mechanisms as adjusted individuals, but they use them more rigidly and in ways which are less desirable socially. The difference can be stated as follows: Whereas the adjusted individual uses mechanisms sparingly and appropriately, the moderately maladjusted person uses them frequently and inappropriately, and the psychoneurotic or psychotic individual depends on these mechanisms constantly and frequently uses them in ways which antagonize, repel, and in general, alienate him from other people.[59]

The very terms *adjusted* and *integrated* indicate the relativity of mental illness, if we remember that we are referring to emotional balance. One is never really "adjusted" or "integrated," except for brief moments. We are constantly "adjusting" to new influences, and we are constantly "integrating" new experiences into our total personality. To be technically correct, one would speak of "well-adjusted" people when referring to those of sound mental health. The emotional deviate simply has more difficulty in adjusting. He exhibits the same behaviors and uses the same techniques for adjustment as anyone else; he simply does not use them as effectively. Consequently, he remains further off balance than the normal individual. All of us will recognize some of our own behaviors in descriptions of deviant behavior; that does not mean that we are neurotic or psychotic (although, in fact, we may be); it means simply that we are recognizing "human behavior."

For a presentation of the major neurotic and psychotic syndromes in language understandable to the lay person, the reader is referred to Carroll.[60] The hysterias, psychasthenias, neurasthenias, schizophrenias, paranoia, and manic depression are outlined in accordance with classification developed by the American Psychiatric Association. These states require the attention of highly trained specialists and are beyond the scope of this text. The incidence of clinically treated cases is noted in Table 12. The rapid growth of community health services is emphasized by the decrease in the rate per thousand of the population treated in out-patient psychiatric clinics. The authors view as a most constructive move this shift in treatment of the severely emotionally disturbed from remote institutions to community clinics, where the patient continues to receive the emotional support of loved ones. Furthermore, it is quite probable that community services reach

[58]N. Cameron, "The Functional Neuroses," in J. McVicker Hunt (ed.), *Personality and the Behavior Disorders* (New York: Ronald, 1944), Vol. 11, p. 869.

[59]Katz and Lehner, op. cit., p. 55.

[60]Herbert A. Carroll, *Mental Hygiene: The Dynamics of Adjustment* (Englewood Cliffs, N.J.: Prentice-Hall, 1964), pp. 239–291.

TABLE 12

Patients in Mental Hospitals, Outpatient Psychiatric Clinics, and Institutions for the Mentally Retarded: 1935–1968

(In thousands, except rate. As of end of year. Prior to 1960, excludes Alaska, and 1961, Hawaii. Completeness of reporting varies from year to year.)

YEAR	TOTAL PATIENTS	HOSPITALS FOR MENTAL DISEASES			OUTPATIENT PSYCHIATRIC CLINICS			INSTITUTIONS FOR THE MENTALLY RETARDED		
		Total* Number	Rate†	Fed-eral‡	State and Coun-try§	Total	Non-VA clinics	VA clinics	Total* Number	Rate†	Pub-lic‖
1935	(NA)	422	331	23	389	(NA)	(NA)	(NA)	97	77	93
1940	(NA)	479	364	34	434	(NA)	(NA)	(NA)	105	80	101
1945	(NA)	522	409	45	463	(NA)	(NA)	(NA)	119	94	113
1950	(NA)	580	386	54	513	(NA)	(NA)	(NA)	135	90	128
1955	(NA)	634	390	60	559	(NA)	(NA)	(NA)	151	93	144
1958	(NA)	621	363	62	545	(NA)	(NA)	(NA)	162	94	154
1959	965	618	354	63	542	181	140	41	166	95	158
1960	994	611	343	62	536	211	166	45	172	96	164
1961	1,040	603	333	63	527	263	212	51	174	96	167
1962	1,069	591	322	62	516	296	242	54	182	99	167
1963	1,102	579	311	62	505	339	281	58	184	99	177
1964	1,153	566	299	62	490	400	337	63	187	99	180
1965	1,179	550	287	62	475	436	369	67	193	101	187
1966	1,244	523	270	57	452	524	450	74	197	102	192
1967	1,295#	493	252	53	426	609	530	79	193#	99#	193
1968	1,361#	457	231	48	399	711	627	84	193#	98#	193

NA Not available.
* Includes patients in private hospitals or institutions, not shown separately.
† Patients per 100,000 population estimated as of July 1. Total population used for 1935; civilian thereafter.
‡ Includes veterans with mental disorders resident in VA hospitals and, through 1965, all patients in public health service hospitals at Fort Worth, Tex., and Lexington, Ky.
§ Includes patients in State-operated psychopathic hospitals and, through 1950, in city hospitals.
‖ Includes city institutions through 1945.
#Excludes patients in private institutions for the mentally retarded.

Source: Department of Health, Education, and Welfare, Public Health Service; Patients in Mental Institutions; Mental Health Statistics-Current Facility Reports; Annual Statistical Report of Outpatient Psychiatric Clinics; Data on Patients of Outpatient Psychiatric Clinics in the United States; Mental Health Statistics, Series A; Veterans with Mental Disorders Resident in Veterans Administration Hospitals; and unpublished data.
Reprinted from Statistical Abstract of the United States, 1970 (Washington: Government Printing Office, 1970), p. 73.

many more of the patients in early stages of disturbance, when the prognosis for cure is much more favorable.

PROBLEM SOLVING AS A STRATEGY FOR MAINTAINING SOUND MENTAL HEALTH

Certainly the problem-solving process is not a technique to be suggested to psychotic individuals as a method for regaining mental health.

Individuals in advanced stages of psychoneurosis may no longer be able to attack life's problems rationally. But the normal and mildly maladjusted person who learns to apply the problem-solving technique to life situations may expect to enjoy sound mental health. This is not necessarily true in every case (battle fatigue can occur in the best-integrated individual), but a scientific approach to life's problems offers the greatest hope for sound mental health.

This is neither the time nor the place for a detailed discussion of the problem-solving technique. Dewey,[61] Thorndike,[62] and others[63] have presented in great detail both the technique and ways of learning it. If the reader is unfamiliar with the application of scientific method to life situations, the authors recommend intensive readings in the field.

The basic problem of mental hygiene lies in the blocking of the individual in his attempts to satisfy his needs. Success in the fulfillment of needs results in feelings of satisfaction and the release of tension. Failure to satisfy needs sets the stage either for the adjustment mechanisms discussed in a previous section or for a constructive learning situation, the successful conclusion of which will contribute to sound mental health.

In the face of failure, the well-adjusted individual will marshal his knowledge and skill to cope with his frustrations in a rational fashion. Mary Elizabeth Keister has this to say:

> Mental hygienists have employed the concept of failure in two ways. They have used it in connection with a situation which is ultimately impossible for the individual to overcome because of his own incapacity; under such circumstances it is important for him to realize this fact and adjust himself to the idea of impossibility. In a second sense, they have thought of failure as a step in the process of solving a problem, as involved in the individual's working his way out of a difficulty.[64]

Adjusting by realizing the impossibility of a situation is obviously more difficult than thinking of failure as a step in the problem-solving process, because it involves emotional as well as intellectual acceptance of failure. The second procedure treats failure as a temporary state in the application of provisional tries for the solution of the problem and eventual success. We shall consider first the rational adjustment of the individual to limitations of self; secondly, we shall discuss some of the common rational attacks on surmountable sources of failure.

Understanding and Acceptance of Self

We have indicated in an earlier section some of the child-rearing practices that contribute to unrealistic conceptions of self. In a prior section we took a brief look at physical disabilities. It may seem relatively simple to

[61]John Dewey, How We Think (Boston: Heath, 1933), pp. 106–115.

[62]Robert L. Thorndike, "How Children Learn the Principles and Techniques of Problem-Solving," Learning and Instruction: Forty-ninth Yearbook of the N.S.S.E., Part 1 (Chicago: University of Chicago Press, 1950), pp. 192–216.

[63]See Chapter 12 for a brief schema.

[64]Mary Elizabeth Keister, "The Behavior of Young Children in Failure," in Barker, Kounen, and Wright (eds.), Child Behavior and Development (New York: McGraw-Hill, 1943), p. 429.

the objective observer to assess the physical and mental capabilities of an individual in terms of the goals that he may set realistically for himself. It is, in actuality, an extremely difficult task for any individual when the individual is inferior in any aspect, because objective appraisal violates his sense of personal adequacy. The rational person, however, is forced to conclusions of limitations of self when faced with insurmountable difficulties. Then comes the most difficult task of all, a realistic acceptance of these limitations as à basis for setting new and attainable goals.

Aggression

The problem-solving approach involves an aggressive attack upon the cause of failure. This may be either at the physical or at the verbal level. The boy who was too poor to afford a college education but whose football prowess and high grades in high school earned him a football scholarship exemplifies the virtue of both types of aggression. Physical aggressiveness on the football field and verbal aggressiveness in the classroom demonstrate, respectively, his ability to score touchdowns and his understanding of the concepts presented in texts and lectures. Both aggressive behaviors are essential if he is to achieve his goal of a college education. Despite the negative connotations of the word *aggression* in our modern world, our football hero's behavior is a positive expression of a virtue highly prized in that same world, a drive to assert oneself, to excel. The successful assault on barriers to goals, in socially approved ways, is the reaction to frustration most conducive to sound mental health. Such aggression is a rational attack upon the very source of the anxiety.

Circumvention

The goal may be achieved by following a circuitous path to the original goal. A stenographer may have her heart set upon the prestige and the salary that accompany the position of private secretary to the boss. The barrier, in this case, may be a very efficient secretary to a junior executive. The seniority practices of the firm may make it quite clear that the secretary to the junior executive has first claim to the position as secretary to the boss when that position becomes vacant. A circuitous route to the original goal may be followed through moving to a firm where seniority practices are not followed.

Substitution

If prestige and money are the crucial goals of the stenographer cited previously, the position of wife of the boss may make a quite satisfactory substitution for the position of secretary to the boss.

We assumed earlier that the only barrier to attainment of the stenographer's goal was the seniority practices of the business firm. Now let us assume that the roles are reversed, that our subject is the secretary to the junior executive and holds seniority and that the stenographer is promoted over her head because of our subject's demonstrated inability to handle the high-level routine demanded of the secretary to the boss. The problem now becomes one of understanding and accepting one's limitations. This task will be considerably eased if the original goal is not simply abandoned but if substitution is made. An example of such a substitution might be to become the best possible secretary to a junior executive. Such a goal is attainable, because the secretary already has demonstrated an ability to be a "good" secretary to a junior executive. She needs only that bit of extra effort and extra training to achieve the assurance that she is the "best possible secretary." Attainment of this goal will bring the feelings of success, adequacy, and achievement that contribute to personal mental health.

Not all substitution, of course, is appropriate. Particularly poor substitutions, from the viewpoint of mental hygiene, seem to be those of academic goals for social ones. The withdrawal from attempts to improve social skills will result in a progressively crippled social life. Cronbach notes, "Not only artists like Van Gogh and Beethoven, but also scientists like Cavendish are celebrated for their moodiness, eccentricity, and temperamental outbursts as well as for their work. These men achieved, but they appear to have been far from happy." [65]

Choice Between Goals

A choice between conflicting goals has to be made, and it must be made by taking reality into account. A girl has to choose between mates if she is to marry one of them. A man has to choose at an early age between professions if either profession involves a prolonged period of specialized training.

If such a choice is made with a "now let's wait and see if this is the right decision" attitude, the period of anxiety that accompanies decision making is either prolonged until the final psychological choice (emotional commitment to the intellectual choice), when the decision is proved correct, or intensified, when the choice is proved poor. A sound approach to such decisions involves making one deliberate and final choice, a choice as scientifically sound as is possible at the time of decision, and a willingness to accept the consequences of a wrong decision. This procedure terminates, at the time of the choice making, the period of anxiety that always accompanies choice. Freedom from this anxiety assists the individual in making this a good choice and in maintaining the emotional equilibrium necessary for coping successfully with all the new choices that occur in everyone's lifetime.

Choice Between Values

We have noted earlier what Rogers refers to as the "fundamental discrepancy," the discrepancy between the values one professes and the values motivating one's behavior. The problem is both social and ethical. It is social in that one assimilates his values from society, both his verbalized ones and his functional ones. It is ethical in the sense that behavior which violates a person's own moral beliefs causes pain. The problem-solving approach to

[65]Lee J. Cronbach, *Educational Psychology* (New York: Harcourt, 1954), p. 532.

these discrepancies—a logical, introspective, conscious analysis of one's own value system—may lead to a healthy questioning of one's own values. The solution to the problem may be a restructuring of a person's entire value system. Once a person reconciles his behavior with his conscience, many tensions will disappear. Many of one's socially assimilated values really are not relevant to the world in which one may operate. The problem-solving approach may assist one in determining which values are "right" for oneself, even though they are not considered "right" by society because they deviate from the norm. Bradburn presents Szasz's conception of the ethical dimension of mental health as follows:

> Ethical considerations are brought into play because behavior is continually judged in terms of the social-psychological norms of society. Behavior that is considered a "mental health problem" usually involves thoughts, feelings or actions arising from life problems that either the person himself or others around him judge to be a serious violation of "normal" behavior. Such judgment assumes that there is a correct standard with which to compare the behavior and that this standard has some validity above and beyond the individual's own feelings, beliefs, or actions.[66]

The older concept of the healthy personality stressed adjustment to societal norms. This eliminated stress, for the individual simply conformed and was "happy," what Lazarus refers to as the contented-cow approach.[67] Many modern psychologists are considering stress as a normal part of life and are defining the healthy personality as one which can cope effectively with stress; in short, the healthy personality uses stress as a motivator to achievement. Maslow and Rogers are not so concerned about achievement; they stress self-actualization, not social (economic, political, professional) achievement, despite Maslow's concept of the self-actualizing individual as one who is altruistic, dedicated, self-transcending, and social. The self-actualizing person must have highly developed skills in problem solving; he must be making choices constantly as to what is right for him versus what society expects of him. Certainly the 1966 *Yearbook of the Association for Supervision and Curriculum Development* gives highest priority to problem-solving skills when it states:

> Specifically, these new directions in education must occur for pupils to become self-actualizing persons.
>
> 1. Pupils must select areas of learning or problems which are significant to them.
> 2. Pupils must learn how to think creatively and flexibly.
> 3. Pupils must learn to generalize from data and to group ideas in meaningful clusters, if they are to solve problems.
> 4. Pupils must be taught to generate models and theories to explain phenomena.
> 5. Pupils must learn ways to test hypotheses and make critical judgments.
> 6. Pupils, at some point, must arrive at a decision and take a stand.[68]

[66]Norman M. Bradburn, *The Structure of Psychological Well-being* (Chicago: National Opinion Research Center, 1969), p. 3.

[67]Richard S. Lazarus, *Personality and Adjustment* (Englewood Cliffs, N.J.: Prentice-Hall, 1963), p. 18.

[68]Elizabeth Monroe Drews, "Self-actualization: A New Focus for Education," in *Learning and Mental Health in the School* (Washington, D.C.: A.S.C.D., N.E.A., 1966), pp. 97–98.

IMPLICATIONS OF MENTAL HYGIENE FOR THE SCHOOL

The recurring emphasis in this chapter has been upon the importance of emotional security and of problem-solving skills in the attainment of sound personal mental health. The prevalence of mental disturbances has been indicated, the relationships between physical and mental health and between emotional needs and mental health have been explored, various causes of poor mental health have been sampled, and defense mechanisms indicative of poor mental health have been summarized briefly. In all these discussions the stress has been upon the significance of emotional security and of rational problem solving.

These strategies are not designed primarily to rehabilitate damaged personalities or even to prevent mental illness. Emotional security and skills in problem solving are designed to promote and to maintain sound mental health. An issue of the *Review of Educational Research* devoted to mental and physical health states that "education's task in relation to mental health is to find ways to get all children through the educational process as effectively as possible." [69] It defines this educational process by citing goals of education presented by Biber in 1967: "(a) sensitivity to the world around one, (b) the development of techniques and attitudes for learning by discovery, (c) the development of cognitive power and intellectual mastery, and (d) the support of the synthesis of learning through opportunity for symbolic expression." [70]

How can a teacher fulfill these responsibilities? We offer five specific suggestions.

1. The teacher must be able to be both permissive and firm. She must love children and be willing to make allowances for their behavior when they are tired or hungry or sick. Most important, she must be patient when children are frustrated and are striking out at her in an attempt to relieve their tensions. But she must also be firm and clear in setting the boundaries for behavior. Children need to know what is expected of them if they are to build behavior patterns that will conform to at least a nucleus of societal expectations. Further, the mental-health-oriented teachers must assist in breaking what Kubie refers to as the "conspiracy of silence." Children and youth must be free to analyze their experiences and feelings. Only through full and free exploration may children and youth receive moral education based on personal decision making. The authors agree that it is "more important that a child be taught to be moral—that he becomes capable of moral choice, and, hence, fully human—than that he be right in the sense of conforming to the established dictates of society." [71] The nature of the permissiveness of the teacher and the involvement of the student in the decision-making process perhaps is best stated by Kubie:

> This does not, however, force us to the impossible conclusion that every teacher must be an analytically trained psychotherapist or that every school

[69] Eli M. Bower, "Mental Health in Education" in *Review of Educational Research: Mental and Physical Health*, Vol. 38, No. 5 (December 1968), p. 449.

[70] Ibid., p. 450.

[71] William F. O'Neill, "Existentialism and Education for Moral Choice," *Phi Delta Kappan*, October 1964, Vol. 46, No. 2, p. 49.

child must be psychoanalyzed. It brings us rather to conclude that all education should be conducted in an atmosphere in which the universal and recurrent emotional disturbances and repressive tendencies of childhood can be resolved as soon as they arise, and before they become chronic. The child's fifth freedom is the right to know what he feels; but this does not carry with it any right to act out his feelings blindly. This will require a new mores for our schools, one which will enable young people from early years to understand and feel and put into words all the hidden things which go on inside of them, thus ending the conspiracy of silence with which the development of the child is now distorted both at home and at school. If the conspiracy of silence is to be replaced by the fifth freedom, children must be encouraged and helped to attend to their forbidden thoughts, and to put them into words, i.e., to talk out loud about love and hate and jealousy and fear, about curiosity over the body, its products and its apertures; about what goes in and what comes out; about what happens inside and what happens outside; about their dim and confused feelings about sex itself; about the strained and stressful relationships within families, which are transplanted into schools. All of these are things about which school must help children to become articulate in the schoolroom.[72]

2. The teacher must learn how to listen! Children will be articulate only if they have a sympathetic audience. Teachers too often sound like directive counselors. It is not suggested that they substitute the one-way street (client to counselor) of the nondirective counselor for the one-way street (counselor to client, or teacher to pupil) of the directive counselor. What is requested is participatory listening—dialogue—entering into another's experiences. For specific help in learning the skills of listening and for insights into the therapeutic values accruing to students, the teacher is directed to John Drakeford, *The Awesome Power of the Listening Ear.*[73]

3. The teacher must possess the professional skills that are necessary for understanding the needs of children. Permissiveness and firmness are sound foundations on which to build a classroom environment that will provide emotional security for children, but each child has both normative and unique needs. The teacher must discover the unique needs of each child if she is to assist him in building realistic plans for the satisfaction of those needs. Only if his needs are satisfied can he be emotionally secure.

4. The teacher must possess a high level of problem-solving ability and must develop a host of techniques for assisting children in learning the attitudes and skills necessary for effective problem-solving. The students *must* be intimately involved in the decision-making process. The process seems to be learned through application. The teacher, then, will need to assist students in discovering, clarifying, and attacking major problems of significance to them. He will need to guide students in evaluating the success of their endeavors, in formulating new plans of attack when faced with failure, and in maintaining an attitude of continuing appraisal of successful endeavors.

5. The teacher must identify those mental health specialists in the community to whom she may turn for assistance. Bower reports a definition by

---

[72]Lawrence S. Kubie in Richard Jones, *An Application of Psychoanalysis to Education* (Springfield, Ill.: Thomas, 1960), pp. vii–viii. Reprinted by permission.

[73]John W. Drakeford, *The Awesome Power of the Listening Ear* (Waco, Texas: Word Books, 1967).

Hobbs of the scope of competencies of such personnel: "the mental health specialist must be a person of broad scientific and humanistic education who knows something about schools, courts, churches, welfare programs, recreation, cultural deprivation, family life, and human ecology. He must also know how to increase his effectiveness by working through and with the people in such programs." [74] Smith and Hobbs report significant growth in the "comprehensive community mental health center" in the wake of the *Mental Health Study Act of 1955*, the Congressional funding of state needs and resources studies in 1962, the partial funding for construction of community mental health centers in subsequent years, and the commitment to pay part of the cost of staffing for 1965–1970.[75] Dorken points out that not all the fully qualified personnel described in the *Review of Educational Research* currently are available for staffing community health centers.[76] Psychiatrists find private practice more lucrative. There is a severe shortage in trained personnel in all categories needed by the centers. But teachers need to search for competent help where they can find it: health clinics, psychological services of central school offices, guidance counselors, and so on. The teacher's task is to "get all children through the educational process." Mental health specialists can help her perform that task.

SUMMARY

We live in an anxious age. The tensions of the cold war, the insecurity of an industrial economy, the insecurities of the class–caste system, and the unique problems of urban living have fostered a national disease of anxiety, one which is highly contagious. Diagnosis and treatment of the mental illnesses stemming from this generalized anxiety and from other sources are not as far advanced as the diagnosis and treatment of physical illnesses.

This chapter only touches upon the varied causes of mental illness and the relationships among them. A broad overview of the complexity of the problem is attempted, in an effort to sensitize the beginning teacher to the magnitude of problems other than those of academic content that affect both the academic and social learning of her pupils. Stress is placed upon structuring classroom situations in which children are free to learn, situations providing an abundance of response, recognition, security, and new experience for the pupils.

Milestones of personality development are sketched and suggestions are made to teachers for ways in which school experiences can foster, or hamper, development of the wholesome personalities essential to effective citizenship in a democracy. Conscious effort has been made to write in lay language, in the hope that this chapter will serve as the springboard for many parent–teacher conferences and as a stimulus for parents to digest the entire text as a means of strengthening the parent–teacher relationship.

[74]Bower, op. cit., p. 448.

[75]M. Brewster Smith and Nicholas Hobbs, "The Community and the Community Health Center," in Bernard G. Guerney (ed.), *Psycho-therapeutic Agents: New Roles for Non-professionals, Parents, and Teachers* (New York: Holt, 1969), pp. 28–29.

[76]Herbert Dorken, "Behind the Scenes in Community Mental Health," in Arthur J. Bindman and Allen D. Spiegel (eds.), *Perspectives in Community Mental Health* (Chicago: Aldine, 1969), p. 127.

Stress is placed upon problem-solving techniques as a means toward sound mental health. The psychology of the decision-making process still is imperfectly understood, but a wealth of literature is available concerning the formal processes of attacking a problem. Implications for mental health of the various reactions to problem situations are developed.

The final section of the chapter, "Implications of Mental Hygiene for the School," summarizes the pedagogical principles developed in the context of the presentations of the problems of mental health.

Selected Bibliography

Allport, Gordon W. *Becoming: Basic Considerations for a Psychology of Personality.* New Haven: Yale University Press, 1955. 106 pp. A quite readable presentation for the beginner of the concepts presented in the more technical psychiatric treatises.

Baruch, Dorothy Walter. *New Ways in Discipline.* New York: McGraw-Hill Book Company, 1949. 200 pp. A penetrating analysis of the principles of child discipline which includes alternative patterns for parental leadership in dealing with pre-school- and school-age children.

Bettelheim, Bruno. *Truants from Life: The Rehabilitation of Emotionally Disturbed Children.* New York: The Macmillan Company, 1964. Pp. xii + 511. Through four detailed case studies the author illustrates the nature and scope of the work carried on at the Sonia Shankman Orthogenic School of the University of Chicago.

Bradburn, Norman M. *The Structure of Psychological Well-being.* Chicago: National Opinion Research Center, 1969. 318 pp.

Branden, Nathaniel. *The Psychology of Self-esteem: A New Concept of Man's Psychological Nature.* New York: Bantam Books, 1971. 242 pp.

Brenecke, John H., and Robert G. Amick. *The Struggle for Significance.* Beverly Hills, Calif.: Glencoe Press, 1971. 347 pp.

Carroll, Herbert A. *Mental Hygiene: The Dynamics of Adjustment,* Fourth Edition. Englewood Cliffs, N.J.: Prentice-Hall, Inc., 1964. 408 pp. Technical explanations in terms understandable by the layman.

Crow, Lester D., and Alice V. Crow (eds.). *Mental Hygiene for Teachers.* New York: The Macmillan Company, 1963. 580 pp. A guide for teachers to the needs and problems of learners, with the emphasis on human relations in the classroom.

Downie, R. S., and Elizabeth Telfer. *Respect for Persons.* New York: Schocken Books Inc., 1970. 165 pp.

Drakeford, John W. *The Awesome Power of the Listening Ear.* Waco, Texas: Word Books, 1967. 126 pp. "Must" reading for teachers.

Haas, Kurt. *Understanding Adjustment and Behavior.* Englewood Cliffs, N.J.: Prentice-Hall, Inc., 1970. 519 pp.

Heaton, Margaret M. *Feelings Are Facts.* New York: National Conference of Christians and Jews, 1962. 60 pp. Suggestions for helping children to analyze their feelings and to make wholesome adjustments to them.

Hoopes, Ned E. *Who Am I?* New York: Dell Publishing Co., Inc., 1969. 286 pp.

Janis, Irving L., and others. *Personality Dynamics, Development, and Assessment.* New York: Harcourt Brace Jovanovich, Inc., 1969. 859 pp.

Jonas, David, and Doris Klein. *Man-Child: A Study of the Infantilization of Man.* New York: McGraw-Hill Book Company, 1970. 363 pp.

Katz, Barney, and George F. J. Lehner. *Mental Hygiene in Modern Living.* New York: The Ronald Press Company, 1953. 546 pp. Simple, clear, comprehensive coverage of the mental hygiene aspects of all areas of modern living.

Kurzweil, Z. E. *Anxiety and Education.* New York: Thomas Yoseloff, 1968.

LaBenne, Wallace D., and Bert I. Greene. *Educational Implications of Self-concept Theory.* Pacific Palisades, Calif.: Goodyear Publishing Co., Inc., 1969. 144 pp.

Lazarus, Richard S. *Personality and Adjustment.* Englewood Cliffs, N.J.: Prentice-Hall, Inc., 1963. 118 pp.

Long, Nicholas J., William C. Morse, and Ruth G. Newman (eds.). *Conflict in the Classroom.* Belmont, Calif.: Wadsworth Publishing Co., Inc., 1965. 515 pp.

Menninger, Karl, and others. *The Vital Balance: The Life Process in Mental Health and Illness.* New York: The Viking Press, 1963. 530 pp. Synthesis by a recognized scholar in the field of the changes that have taken place in scholarly thought regarding mental health in the past fifty years.

Poland, Ronald G., and Nancy D. Sanford. *Adjustment Psychology: A Human Value Approach.* St. Louis: The C. V. Mosby Company, 1971. 233 pp.

Purkey, William W. *Self Concept and School Achievement.* Englewood Cliffs, N.J.: Prentice-Hall, Inc., 1970. 86 pp.

Redl, F. *Children Who Hate.* New York: The Free Press, 1965. 286 pp. Utilizes case studies to tell what these aggressive children are like, how it feels to live with them, and how people can survive with such children.

———, and William W. Wattenberg. *Mental Hygiene in Teaching.* New York: Harcourt, Brace & World, 1959. 562 pp.

———, and David Wineman. *Controls from Within: Techniques for the Treatment of the Aggressive Child.* New York: The Macmillan Company, 1965. 332 pp.

Rogers, Carl R. *Freedom to Learn.* Columbus, Ohio: Charles E. Merrill Books, Inc., 1969. 358 pp.

———, and others. *Person to Person: The Problem of Being Human.* Lafayette, Calif.: Real People Press, 1967. 276 pp.

Sahakian, William S. (ed.). *Psychology of Personality: Readings in Theory.* Chicago: Rand McNally & Company, 1963. 504 pp. Brings together generous selections from the writings of twenty-one prominent psychologists. Use of primary sources exclusively brings the students into direct contact with the significant theories of personality.

Scobey, Mary Margaret, and Grace Graham (eds.). *To Nurture Humaneness: Commitment for the 1970's.* Washington, D.C.: A.S.C.D., N.E.A., 1970. 255 pp.

Shirley, Hale F. *Pediatric Psychiatry.* Cambridge, Mass.: Harvard University Press, 1963. 796 pp. Highly recommended for reading by parents and by teachers of young children. Language of the text is readily comprehensible to professional teachers and to most parents.

Sykes, Gerald (ed.). *Alienation: The Cultural Climate of Our Time,* Vols. I, II. New York: George Braziller, Inc., 1964. 1,237 pp.

Tanner, Laurel N., and Henry C. Lindgren. *Classroom Teaching and Learning: A Mental Health Approach.* New York: Holt, Rinehart & Winston, Inc., 1971. 448 pp.

Toffler, Alvin. *Future Shock.* New York: Random House, Inc., 1970. 505 pp.

Torrance, Ellis Paul. *Constructive Behavior: Stress, Personality, and Mental Health.* Belmont, Calif.: Wadsworth Publishing Co., Inc., 1965. 432 pp.

Waetjen, Walter B., and Robert R. Leeper (eds.). *Learning and Mental Health in the School.* Washington, D.C.: A.S.C.D., N.E.A., 1966. 174 pp. Synthesizes current theories of learning and mental health. Designed for the sophisticated scholar of curriculum. Too technical to be useful to the average teacher.

Selected Films

Children Without (N.E.A.), 30 min. Too many children in American cities are without parental love and care, without the basic requisites of daily living, without the many experiences that help them develop their potential. This film takes the viewer into a Detroit public school where teachers and counselors establish the warm relationships such children need and provide positive learning experiences for them. Focus is on white poverty.

The Emotional Dilemma (N.E.T.), 60 min. New methods and treatment for mental and emotional problems are discussed.

Emotional Health (McGraw-Hill), 21 min. Shows interviews of a college student with a physician and then with a psychiatrist, who uncovers his fears and helps him to become emotionally adjusted; uses occasional flashbacks to the boy's childhood.

Feeling Left Out (Coronet), 13 min. Attempts to stimulate understanding for the socially isolated and offers suggestions to meet the problems involved in dealing with them.

Feeling of Depression (McGraw-Hill), 30 min. Presents the case history of a businessman who suddenly suffers feelings of great despondency. An examination of his earlier life reveals the reasons for his plight and suggests help.

Feeling of Hostility (National Film Board of Canada), 27 min. Case history of Clare, showing how feelings of insecurity in childhood produce a lonely person underneath the outward appearances of success. Calls attention to various compensatory devices expressive of feelings of hostility.

Feeling of Rejection (National Film Board of Canada), 21 min. Presents the case of Margaret, who as a young adult had not yet learned to make decisions independently. When she goes to a psychiatrist to learn the reasons for her headaches and tired feeling, she reveals that when a child she was afraid of losing the love of her parents and friends and, as a result, learned to acquiesce to all their demands. When she realizes the cause of her trouble, she begins to assert herself and becomes well adjusted.

The Game (National Film Board of Canada), 28 min. (Available through McGraw-Hill Book Company.) A casual relationship that ceases to be casual and confronts a teen-age boy with an agonizing moral dilemma.

The Great Rights (Brandon), 14 min. A humorous animated film which dramatizes the way life in this country might be without the Bill of Rights. Without flag waving, the film subtly conveys our privileges as individuals as well as our need to protect them by protest and responsibility.

The Individual (N.E.T.), 60 min. Problems facing the individual in a large society are discussed by exploring varied, dissimilar areas of American life and the common thread that binds individuals together, the need for self-identification.

Meeting the Emotional Needs in Childhood: The Groundwork of Democracy (Department of Child Study, Vassar College), 32 min. Opens with a scene of students graduating from college, then shows and analyzes behavior in various childhood situations related to needs and experiences that shape adult behavior. Causes are shown, along with suggestions as to how problems might be met by those working with children.

Nation's Mental Health (McGraw-Hill), 18 min. A survey of the mental health problem for community and other adult groups and for beginning students in psychology and education.

Neighbors (International Film Bureau), 9 min. A startling presentation of the way in which violent disputes may arise from the most trivial incidents. A modern parable of the latent hostility in local issues, as we see two men fighting over a flower. This film has been particularly good with emotionally disturbed youngsters and potential dropouts.

Overdependency (National Film Board of Canada), 32 min. Deals with understanding the causes of overdependence, with the discussion presented through flashbacks to childhood experiences.

Phoebe (Contemporary/McGraw-Hill), 29 min. The moving story of a teen-age girl who finds herself pregnant and reviews what led to her plight and what it will mean in relation to her parents, the boy, her teachers, her education and herself. A professional production, well photographed and acted.

A Place in the Sun (Encyclopaedia Britannica), 6 min. A very short cartoon-type film which uses analogy to show that each person must have his place in the sun for any to survive.

Preface to Life (United World Films), 30 min. Portrays the influence which parents exert on the developing personality of the child. The oversolicitous mother and the overly demanding father are contrasted with parents who accept their child as an individual.

Problem of Pupil Adjustment (McGraw-Hill), 2 reels, 39 min. *First reel*, "The Drop-out": In an employment office Steve Martin, on the day he should be graduating from high school, sits reminiscing about things gone awry at school and his succession of mediocre jobs held after dropping out of school. Shows Steve's eagerness as a freshman, then the withering effect of repetitious drills over textbook material that seemed pointless. Truancy comes easily and, finally, becomes his escape. *Second reel*, "The Stay-in": Explains how one high school has reduced its drop-outs to less than 5 per cent of its total student population. Stresses learning in terms of student interests and shows how even "required" subjects are made vital by enlightened teaching methods.

Self-conscious Guy (Coronet), 10 min. Feelings of self-consciousness keep a high school boy from doing classwork well or making friends easily. He discovers that many of his classmates suffer from similar feelings. Works to become better adjusted by thinking about others, developing skills, taking part in activities, and finally developing a perspective on his own relationship to his social situations.

Shyness (McGraw-Hill), 23 min. Shyness in children, its causes, and how, through a greater understanding by parents and teachers, this problem may be dealt with. From the lonely existence of a typically shy adult, the film turns to a study of three children: Anna, shy but wistfully wanting association with others; Jimmy, whose excessive timidity is really a symptom of profound emotional disturbance; Robert, aloof but happily independent. Studying their conditions, a psychiatrist from the child guidance clinic reveals the confidence-destroying demands of parents that predisposed the children to shyness. Together teacher, psychiatrist, and parents bring about a change in the children's attitudes.

Understand Your Emotions (Coronet), 13 min. A general understanding of emotions, what they are, what they do, where they come from, and how they are changed. Shows that emotions have main effects on the body, on both voluntary and involuntary behavior, and that people have different emotional responses to the same stimulus pattern.

What's on Your Mind? (National Film Board of Canada), 11 min. This documentary film explains modern psychiatry and clinical psychology. The film opens with a definition of psychiatry and shows in close-up a case of schizophrenia.

You Are Not Alone (Association), 32 min. An emotional health documentary that dramatically tells the story of a businessman who suffers a disappointment that creates great emotional anxiety. Emphasizes self-understanding and emotional adjustment.

Chapter 8

■■■■■■■■□□□□□□□□□

Problems of Crime
and Delinquency

In the early stages of man's development almost all the problems he faced as a community member were those that resulted from disasters in his physical world or from his contacts with neighboring tribes. Today many of our important social problems come from stresses and strains within the society. As community members we still face some disasters that are due to forces beyond our control. Floods, fires, earthquakes, hurricanes, volcanic eruptions, tidal waves, and the possibility of bombings may challenge the resources of a community. Problems of traffic conditions, problems of eliminating slums, and similar municipal problems must be faced squarely by individuals in their own communities, if we are to have, from the grass roots, a strong nation and a good world. Overshadowing these physical and external problems, however, are major problems of human relations developing *within* the society. One such major set of problems relates to the area of adult crime and juvenile delinquency. This chapter will concentrate on the implications of crime and delinquency for the local community.

EXTENT OF CRIME IN THE UNITED STATES

The cost of crime in the United States, ranging from minor felonies to actions of highly organized gangs and syndicated gambling, has been estimated from $30 billion to as high as $50 billion. These estimates include the cost of damages done by criminals as well as the expenses of apprehending, convicting, and confining them. By far the largest number of crimes are those against property. Next in frequency are those against persons.

Although murders as the result of gang warfare are prominent in the United States, many more are caused by temporary anger between persons who are known to each other. In addition, murders are sometimes committed by psychopaths. The criminal homicide rate for the United States between the years 1955 and 1969 rose over 30 per cent, to 7 crimes per 100,000, the highest number and the greatest percentage increase of any country that keeps crime statistics.[1] Moreover, homicide represents only

[1] National Commission on the Cause and Prevention of Violence quoted in U.P.I. dispatch, March 21, 1969.

part of the violence in the United States. For example, the suicide rate is almost twice as great for any given year. Furthermore, accidental deaths run about 100,000 annually.

A part of the picture of trends in crime is the increase in the amount of white-collar crime. Such matters as embezzlement, confidence games, and stock market manipulation, as well as other marginal practices (such as dishonesty on the part of watch repairmen and garage mechanics), have increased considerably in American society in recent years. Such trends, together with the prevalence of crimes against property (robbery, theft, and gangster racketeering), indicate the extreme emphasis upon the economic motive lying behind most crimes.

In a careful and pioneering study, Sutherland[2] revealed the extent and nature of white-collar crime. He found that in business, white-collar criminality takes the form of misrepresentation of financial statements of corporations, manipulation on the stock exchanges, direct and indirect bribery of public officials, misrepresentation in advertising and sales, embezzlement and misapplication of funds, short weights and measurements and misgrading of commodities, tax frauds, and misapplication of funds in receiverships and bankruptcies.

Illegal sale of narcotics, abortions, illegal services to criminals, fraudulent reports in accident cases, unnecessary treatment, fake specialists, restriction of competition, and fee splitting are forms of criminality found in the medical profession. Fee splitting is illegal in many states and a violation of the conditions for admission to the profession in all states. The physician who takes part in fee splitting sends his patient to the surgeon who charges the highest fee rather than to the one who is most skilled. Reportedly, two thirds of the New York City surgeons split fees, and more than one half of the physicians in a Midwestern city who answered a questionnaire on this point, favored fee splitting.

These varied types of white-collar criminality can be reduced to two categories: misrepresentation of asset values and duplicity in the manipulation of power. The first is the equivalent of fraud or swindling; the second is similar to the double cross. The latter can be illustrated by the corporation director who purchases land which he knows the corporation will need and sells it at a high profit to his corporation. Here the offender holds two antagonistic positions, one of which is a position of trust, which is violated in the interest of the other position.

The damage to social relations resulting from white-collar crimes is more important than the financial loss. These crimes create distrust, which lowers social morale and produces large-scale social disorganization. Other crimes produce relatively little effect on social institutions or social organizations.

ORGANIZED CRIME

One of the characteristics of modern crime trends is the increasing tendency for crime to become highly organized. The beginning of this trend

[2]Paraphrased from Edwin H. Sutherland, "White-Collar Criminality," *American Sociological Review*, Vol. 5, No. 1 (February 1940), pp. 1–5 *et passim*.
   See also fuller statement in Edwin H. Sutherland, *White-Collar Crime* (New York: Dryden, 1949). See also Gilbert Geis (ed.), *White Collar Criminal: The Offender in Business and the Professions* (New York: Atherton, 1968).

can be found in the prohibition era of the 1920's, when gangs organized for the distribution of bootleg liquor. The trend has continued to the present. Organized crime can be seen in gambling activities, the drug traffic, prostitution, labor racketeering (protection), "Murder Incorporated," and so on.

The effects of crime (organized or not) upon the public are many. Stock manipulation and other marginal business practices eventually increase the cost of a product to the public. Racketeering control of such industries as trucking and construction also increases the cost to the public. Some legitimate industries are owned by organized criminals. Emphasis upon gambling activities diverts a lot of money to nonproductive enterprises. The total energies persons devote to these activities could very well be devoted to constructive enterprises that would add to the total amount of goods and services in our country. The demoralizing influence of the close tie-in of gang leaders to local municipal governments and sometimes the "respectability" of the very wealthy gangsters have a bad effect upon the youth and others of our society.[3]

The Drug Problem

One of the problems that has become especially acute, particularly among adolescents, is that of the increased use of habit-forming or otherwise harmful drugs. The drug about which there is the greatest concern is that obtained from the poppy, opium and its various derivatives. It is usually used in the form of heroin. The use of marijuana, a drug that does not have an effect on the user as powerful as that of the opium-derived drugs but that is very difficult to stamp out, is also now very prevalent in the United States. It is probably not habit forming, except psychologically, but it may lead to the use of habit-forming drugs whose effect is more serious.

There is some sentiment among experts that the possession of marijuana not be illegal or at least that it be made a misdemeanor rather than a felony.

Another type of drug that is prohibited except under special experimental or medical conditions is that comprising the hallucinogens (LSD, mescaline and so on). Drugs that are permitted but that are dangerous if not taken under a doctor's care include amphetamines (pep pills) and barbiturates (sedatives).

The use of narcotics, except for medicinal purposes, is illegal. Any traffic in these drugs is a felony. There is great variation in the extent to which the narcotics laws are enforced in various parts of the country. Furthermore, there is great variation in the penalties provided by the laws of the various states and cities. The use of narcotics results in a serious habit, which requires that the addict be given very special treatment. Aside from the harmful effects produced directly by the drug, there is the demoralization of the person in terms of his efforts to obtain it. Because drugs are very expensive (as well as illegal) and because the habit usually requires

---

[3]See Ralph Salerno and John S. Thompkins, *The Crime Confederation* (New York: Doubleday, 1969) for excellent documentation of organized crime. But see also Norval Morris and Gordon Hawkins, *The Honest Politician's Guide to Crime Control* (Chicago: The University of Chicago Press, 1969), Chapter 8, who argue that the existence of the Mafia (or Cosa Nostra) never has been proved.

increasing amounts, the addict is willing to go to any length to obtain money to buy the drug. He will engage in criminal acts, sometimes induced by the seller of the drug, in order to obtain it. By legal definition, of course, all addicts are criminals. Therefore it is easy to be driven into other types of criminal acts once one has become a drug addict.

Gambling

Gambling has existed from time immemorial and exists in various forms to the present day, from the "harmless" private bet and the private poker party to carefully organized syndicated gambling. In some states a certain amount of control has been obtained by legalizing gambling, as in parimutuel betting at races.

In spite of the fact that the gambling addict is always in hopes that he will be able to make a strike, mathematical study of gambling devices indicates that in the long run there is no chance for the gambler. Even if gambling machines were honest, the odds are so set as to favor entirely the gambling operators. Many of the gambling devices are not honest. Just enough winnings are allowed the customers to keep up their interest. The same is true with cards, numbers, and so on.

Because gambling involves many persons and much money, it has become closely allied with corrupt politics. Many persons, thinking there is no harm in some gambling, wink at the violation of the laws in those states prohibiting it. This plays into the hands of the gambling racketeer. Many persons who need money badly for the necessities of life spend it on the various types of gambling, including the numbers racket. The numbers, or policy, racket is based on the sale of chances on the payoff of some number, which may be obtained from the total number of stock or bond sales or some other figure that has at least a semblance of being unfixed. However, in many cases such numbers can be fixed. Even though the numbers racket involves relatively small sums of money from each individual each day, the annual take is very large, and it comes mainly from people who can least afford to lose it.

CRIME AND POLITICS

By far the worst problem related to organized crime is that of the possible corruption of the local municipal government. It is unlikely that organized crime can operate successfully on any large scale without the connivance of the local force. By conniving with the ward politicians and other local political bosses, some of whom may even be racketeers themselves, persons engaged in organized crime are able to get protection from arrest. Whenever arrests and convictions do occur, they usually involve a person who is not important in the total picture. Through access to great amounts of money, the organized criminals are able to hire brilliant lawyers who use legal devices in such a way as to make them almost immune from successful prosecution. It is all too well known that such famous gangsters as Al Capone were finally convicted only for income tax evasions, not for the more serious crimes of which they were guilty.

This possibility of a fundamental breakdown of law enforcement at the local level places the crime problem squarely in the hands of the people of the various communities. By electing the right people to office and by taking an interest in their government, particularly by supporting noncorruptible officials, the citizens of a community can minimize the crime in their community. However, many citizens either are indifferent or are interested in being able themselves at times to have access to one or more of the illegitimate enterprises. Every person who seeks to have his traffic ticket "fixed" is technically in the same position as those who buy protection from the police to carry on illegal enterprises. Those participating in illegal gambling, even for a spasmodic special occasion, are also contributing to the corruption of their city government.

Legal Prohibition Versus Legalized Control

One of the big controversies arising out of the relationship between crime and politics relates to difference of opinion over the respective merits of prohibition versus legalized control. As a first case in point, let us look at the prohibition of the manufacture and sale of alcoholic beverages. This legal step, opposed by a large minority of United States citizens, led to the racketeering gangs of the 1920's who managed to finance themselves through the sale of alcoholic beverages to many otherwise law-abiding citizens. The repeal of prohibition managed to eliminate this source of revenue. However, the gangs have continued, largely ensconced now in the fields of gambling, narcotics, and other illegal activities.

The proponents of legality think that if such marginal pursuits as gambling could be controlled so as to reduce the gambling take and a campaign of education concerning the harm of gambling could be conducted, we could eliminate the gamblers' influence and their payoff protection, on the one hand, and reduce the amount of gambling in the community on the other. There is very little sentiment for the legalization of the use of narcotics. In this case most persons think that this traffic, which actually involves few people, can be eliminated through more careful and uniform law enforcement. This would have to be accompanied by increased access to institutions for the treatment of addicts. There are even some who argue for legalized prostitution, which is still prevalent in Europe and was almost universal during the Middle Ages and later.

The difficult problem of the better enforcement of prohibition laws as against a careful system of legalized control in these areas of gangster activities is one that requires careful study. On that level, it is a social problem. On the level of helping the individual to solve his problems related to it, it becomes an educational problem.

Morris and Hawkins make one of the strongest cases for eliminating all matters where individuals are not victims of another's violence from criminal action, thus leaving the police free to spend their efforts on "real" crimes and not to enforce "private" morality.[4] They propose eliminating the following from the criminal code:

[4]Norval Morris and Gordon Hawkins. *The Honest Politician's Guide to Crime Control* (Chicago: University of Chicago Press, 1969).

1. Drunkenness (except when driving).
2. Narcotics and drug abuse (sale to be controlled).
3. Gambling.
4. Disorderly conduct and vagrancy.
5. Abortion (under qualified auspices).
6. Sexual behavior (between consenting adults in private).
7. Juvenile delinquency (except in cases where the offense would also apply to adults).

Development of Corruption-Free Municipal Government

One of the most important problems related to the crime situation is corruption in the local government. This has come about for a wide variety of reasons. One is the indifference of the average urban dweller to his city government. Another is the attempt to fight city election battles on the basis of some national political affiliation. If a city is predominantly of one party the municipal government tends to stay in power regardless of the efficiency or honesty of the administration. Over a period of years this tends to lead to corrupt government. From time to time, in the large cities, various reform groups have attempted to bring about good government by electing good officials. In most cases such efforts are sporadic and the cities soon resume their traditional practices. Efforts have been made in some of the cities (mostly medium-sized and small ones so far) to set up a politics-free government based on the city manager or commission plan. There have been other efforts to make the city elections nonpartisan so that they would not be related to national or state politics.

Other Problems of Enforcement

There are other problems of law enforcement related to the crudity of police methods, quality of police work, and the restrictions of the courts to protect the innocent from injustice.

In the first place, many proponents of "law and order" are more concerned about "order" than justice. Challenges to the status quo are against order. Consequently, police methods aimed at "putting down" anyone who protests are condoned. This leads to a lack of respect for law enforcement officers and to "law" itself. The quality of police officers needs to be raised and their freedom from harassment by defenders of the status quo as well as from the crime syndicate must be protected.

The many decisions of the Supreme Court in the last few years to protect the rights of the accused are well taken. However, because of a lack of knowledge of proper procedures by police, the individual's rights sometimes were violated and the cases thrown out, sometimes the guilty along with the innocent. Effective policemen can work within the court's restrictions, but this requires a highly educated, competent police force, well paid, well organized, well trained, and protected in their job from reprisals, political or physical. On the other hand, the attempts on the part of radical defendants to make a travesty of court trials also is detrimental to law enforcement. The recent decision (1970) of the Supreme Court in the *Allen* case gives the judge the right to maintain proper conduct and decorum in the courtroom. (More discussion of these topics will be found in Chapter 14.)

JUVENILE DELINQUENCY

Although in the legal sense the primary distinction between delinquency and crime relates to the age of the persons involved, the concept of delinquency also implies a completely different attitude on the part of society. This difference in attitude between acts committed by younger persons and those of older persons goes back far in the history of mankind. Among the Romans and Greeks younger persons were not held to be responsible for crimes that they had committed. This same point of view prevailed in the Napoleonic Code. In the English jurisprudence, however, there was little differentiation among children, youths, and adults until relatively modern times. The Chancery Courts of England were sometimes used for special legal processes, including cases involving children. Not until 1899 was there one special court in the United States for juveniles. In that year the first juvenile court was set up in Illinois.

The Nature of Juvenile Delinquency

A delinquent is someone below a given age, as defined in the law of the specific state, who commits an illegal act for which society must take some kind of action. This age is usually set at sixteen, seventeen, or eighteen. In practice, delinquency is generally held to involve something more than a one-time minor infraction of the law. In the first place, the concept includes repeated violations; in the second place, it denotes violations by someone who deviates consistently from expected normal behavior. It does not include, therefore, the common misbehavior of persons who are normally co-operative toward society. The use of the term *delinquent* ranges from its application to someone who has persistently violated the law but has not been detected, to someone who has been taken into the juvenile court and actually adjudged to be a delinquent.

It is likely that, for most purposes, a sociological and psychological definition is more helpful than a strictly legal one. Furthermore, it is probably better not to define the term too strictly but to leave it somewhat amorphous. In general, then, the writers are using the term *delinquency* in the following sense in this chapter and other parts of this book: *Chronic and persistent failure (of young persons) to conform to the expectations of the society as a whole.* This would mean that some persons are delinquent even though they are not before a juvenile court. It would also mean that in some cases persons might be delinquents legally but not be delinquent in terms of this definition. An example of the latter case would be that of a child who ran afoul of his family where the family itself was somewhat antisocial. In this case the child's behavior would conform to that of society as a whole but not conform to that of the family, and the child, consequently, might be falsely remanded by the family to the court.

The writers are of the opinion that just as normal personality is the product of culture, so is deviant personality. Both crime and delinquency are caused. It is so important that pliable, plastic youth be handled on a psychological and sociological basis, rather than on a legalistic one, that it is essential for the society to set up special procedures. The use of the juvenile court to handle these cases—a procedure that is now almost universal in the United States and is spreading to other parts of the world—is one illustration of this point of view. Before going into the details of these procedures, let us see exactly what the nature of the problem is.

Trends in Delinquency

Most of the statistics quoted in the field of delinquency are not completely accurate. This is true for a number of reasons. There are differences in the definition of delinquency in the several states, both in terms of the general types of behavior called delinquent and in respect to age range. Delinquency figures include only court cases and not those handled by other agencies. Good agency handling of delinquency cases may preclude the need for court. The discrepancy in figures varies from state to state and from time to time.

Most authorities are agreed that in the post-World War II period there has been a sizeable increase in the delinquency rate in the United States. The figures may vary in different parts of the country. They may vary in a given year from two to three youths per hundred up to about six or seven youths per hundred who are actually picked up by police, some of whom are before the juvenile court (or its equivalent) in any one of the several states or jurisdictions. The F.B.I. reports 1,500,215 arrests under the age of eighteen (not counting minor traffic cases) in 1969.[5] A much greater number were dealt with directly by the police but did not go to juvenile or other courts. This represents an increase of approximately 240,000 in the number appearing before the courts in 1968.[6] According to this figure, the number of juvenile delinquents is rising faster than the population as a whole is increasing.

Studies of trends over a period of years have indicated that delinquency rates, as well as crime rates, periodically rise and fall. Delinquency rates, unlike crime rates, tend to rise during periods of prosperity and full employment. They also tend to rise during war periods. Both of these conditions were present during World War II. They were also present during the period of heavily increasing delinquency from 1950 to 1955, a period during which there was a draft for the Korean "affair" and general unrest with respect to national security but a high level of prosperity. In addition, it may well be that periods when the public is very much interested in delinquency may cause the rate to appear to rise even farther, merely because the enforcement agencies are more zealous in the apprehension and prosecution of delinquents.

Differentiated Rates by Socioeconomic Backgrounds and by Other Factors

Almost all available studies indicate that the delinquency rate is much higher in industrial areas (where the families are of a lower socioeconomic

[5]*Uniform Crime Reports for the U.S., 1969* (Washington, D.C.: Federal Bureau of Investigation), p. 124.
[6]See 1968 report, p. 126.

status and are poorly housed) than in the better residential areas. Among the important factors behind this difference are the lack of recreational facilities in the former areas and the poor facilities in the home, as well as the standards of conduct that are more likely to be learned by the young person and to bring him into conflict with the law.

Part of the difference in delinquency rates in the two types of areas must be attributed to the fact that a child who is apprehended in a lower socioeconomic area is more likely to be brought before the juvenile court and thus to become a "statistic." In the better areas the case is likely to be settled without being taken into court, and thus it does not go on the record. In some cases, in the more wealthy residential areas, the influence of prominent persons who are acquainted with the parents of the delinquent prevents anything at all from being done. However, most sociologists agree that there is a "real" differential of rates, which is not totally accounted for by this difficulty with the statistics.

In the recent postwar period there has been a greater increase in delinquency in the low-delinquency areas (that is, the areas with the higher socioeconomic status) than there has been in the formerly high-delinquency areas. There has been a significant increase in both types of areas.

Youth Gangs

An important aspect of the problem of juvenile delinquency is the youth gang. The youth gang meets a very definite need that the youth apparently has for adventure, a feeling of belongingness, and a desire to lose oneself in some type of "cause." Although not all gangs are necessarily delinquent or criminal, a large portion of those in urban areas do tend to be so. They tend to become schools for delinquency and crime. In some cases the law is broken through episodes arising from competition with some other gang. In other cases the group has joined together in order to have a thrill, "borrow" automobiles, or actually commit thefts or sex crimes.

This problem is especially difficult to solve because the work of the juvenile court and other agencies tends to be nullified by the strong forces of the gang, which do fulfill a real social and psychological need of the youth. The problem is one of redirecting the activities of the gang toward constructive social efforts. This can be done through increased recreational facilities, competitive athletics, and other worthwhile youth projects. However, the problem of getting the gangs interested in these things is not an easy one.

Delinquency and Social Factors

Persons working with the problems of delinquency, and other concerned citizens, are always attempting to find a cause for it. Authorities are fairly generally agreed that there is no one cause nor one "pat" solution. This problem, like so many social problems, has various causes. Sometimes factors that might normally appear relatively insignificant and that in other circumstances would not lead to delinquency may cause a particular child to become delinquent. Reasons such as comic books, poor housing, oppressive teachers, and broken homes, which have been given as causes for juvenile delinquency, probably are not the basic causes. However, they may be factors that trigger delinquent behavior if other conditions are also unfavorable.

An analysis of the reasons for the increase of delinquency at the present time probably would reveal some of the following general social condition. First, we should list the general insecurity of the world at the present time, which results from war and the threat of war and from economic insecurity. Second, closely related to this economic insecurity, we should list the fact that our society measures success by material criteria. This places enormous pressure upon the individual, the youth as well as the adult, to display those material things that have become the symbols of success. He is sometimes thoroughly tempted to use shortcuts to get them, such as stealing an automobile or other objects that are evidence of material prosperity. This results in increases in crimes against property. Another factor is the very great mobility of the people, with the problems of adjustment that result from that mobility. Persons who live in relatively settled neighborhoods tend to develop sets of values and ideals that are not threatened as long as they stay in the slower-changing community. Moving into a new group tends to challenge these values and may cause the individuals to do things that they would not otherwise do. The sedate businessman who "goes on a toot" when he is in a strange town is an example of this at the adult level. This sort of behavior can be duplicated many times, especially by children, in the relatively anonymous environment of the large city. Still another factor, of course, is the changing mores of our times. These changes lead to confusion of choices. The conflict between the mores of youth and the mores of adults leads to confusion, and this, in turn, can cause persons to assert that there are no moral standards. Consequently, many youth and young adults are not motivated by a clear set of values or moral standards. Still another factor is the difficulty of finding adequate facilities for the wholesome use of leisure time, particularly playgrounds and recreational centers in the urban areas. In spite of the fact that many cities have done excellent work in trying to develop leisure-time activities, there probably still are not completely adequate facilities in any of the cities of the United States. Another factor that probably affects delinquency is the attitude in our society toward lack of emphasis upon the individual as such and on his responsibility for his own actions. This attitude has become increasingly prevalent. It results from the increasing complexity of society, the increasing emphasis upon group activity, and the increasing lack of recognition of individual achievement. Institutions such as the home, the school, and the church can do much to combat all these trends and to counteract to some extent the harm that these attitudes may do to youths and adults of all ages.

THE JUVENILE COURT

The *juvenile court* is the name applied to the specialized institution now used by all fifty states, the federal government, and the various territories for handling the delinquency cases of special groups of persons who are below a given age. The definition of the type of cases to be handled by this court apparently varies with the political jurisdiction. In many states it is defined to include all cases "below a certain age." In other states it may be the cases of persons between certain ages, such as between twelve and seven-toon incluoivo, ac in Ohio. In Ohio there is a *children's registry* for children twelve years of age and under.

The philosophy of the juvenile courts is that the cases of immature, plastic children should be handled differently from those of hardened criminals. In a sense, the juvenile case is not a criminal one at all. The child is neither "charged" nor "tried." He is carefully studied and some recommendation is made. This may sometimes entail sentencing for a period of time in a reform school. A very careful study is made of the problem by psychologists, sociologists, and others before any recommendation is made to the judge. There are no lawyers. The action of the juvenile court, or the referee, is taken on the basis of the sociological and psychological factors rather than on the basis of the crime per se.

One of the important methods used by the juvenile court, as well as by other criminal courts for minor offenses by younger adults, is to pass sentence but to withhold it pending a probation period. The delinquent is assigned to a trained probation officer to whom he must report periodically. This probation officer works with him on any problems he may have; when the probational period ends, he is free from any sentence that the delinquency might have entailed. The work of the probation officer has been relatively successful. Its success depends upon a great many factors. The child or young criminal going back into the same environment sometimes has considerable difficulty. If he has served a certain amount of time in a reform school prior to the probational period, this hangs over his head. Sometimes the probation officers are not as well trained and as skilled in handling their cases as they should be. A major block to effective probation work is the extremely large case load of the probation officer.

The opinion of most criminologists and experts on juvenile delinquency is that the philosophy of the juvenile court, by and large, is the one under which we must solve our delinquency problems. Those improvements that are needed are in the quantity and quality of the facilities available for the study of the child and of the places to send him for rehabilitation when necessary. In many cases juvenile courts are handicapped by inadequate funds for staff and facilities. At present the facilities for detention and rehabilitation are very poor. Many of the so-called reform schools are really schools for crime. They are poorly staffed and poorly equipped, with very few facilities for the actual study of juveniles or for remedial work. Some of the farms that have been set up with relatively small groups on large areas of land under fairly wholesome conditions have done a reasonably good job with respect to rehabilitation.

Judge Walter G. Whitlatch has reported on a decision of the U.S. Supreme Court (In the Matter of Gault, 387, U.S. I [1967]) which has brought about great changes in juvenile-court procedures.[7] The *Gault* case was concerned primarily with due process of law in juvenile courts. The decision did not say that the juvenile court must now follow criminal-court adversary proceedings. The juvenile court can proceed informally as a judicial inquiry. Nor did it say that a child is entitled to a jury trial. The decision did not hold that records must be kept in juvenile-court proceedings, but a strong recommendation was made that this be done.

[7]Walter G. Whitlatch, "The Gault Decision—Its Effect on the Office of the Prosecuting Attorney," *The Ohio Bar*, January 8, 1968, pp. 41–52.

The Supreme Court made three specific rulings in the *Gault* case:

1. *Notice of hearings and charges.* Advance notice of scheduled court proceedings must be given so that preparations can be made. This notice must enumerate, with particulars, the alleged misconduct.
2. *Right to counsel.* The parent and child have the right to retain counsel and to be specifically advised of the consequences of waiving this right.
3. *Self-incrimination.* The alleged delinquent may no longer be required by the court to answer questions which might incriminate him.

Children are entiled to due process of law and fair treatment. Questions of the relevance of due-process requirements in juvenile courts should be resolved in favor of the child, if this can be done without undermining the court's rehabilitative objectives.

The U.S. Supreme Court in subsequent cases will define *due process* more definitively. The problem seems to be to determine what forms of procedural protection are necessary to determine fundamental fairness, without imposing unnecessarily rigid restrictions on the juvenile court.

Let us now return to an examination of the court itself. In spite of the fact that the philosophy under which the juvenile courts operate and the general methods that are used are appropriate in the light of what is known about the nature of juvenile delinquency, there is much to be said about the way in which the philosophy is carried out. Some of the criticisms of "mollycoddling" launched against juvenile courts are, in reality, results of poor methods of administration, lack of enough personnel, or lack of trained personnel. Criticisms have been made (which seem, in some cases, to be substantiated) that youthful delinquents brought in by the police sometimes are released and returned home before the police can return to the precinct. Although the extent to which this occurs may be exaggerated, in many cases the investigation is probably quite perfunctory. It is difficult to see how a juvenile investigation can be carried out without bringing in the parents and without putting some responsibility on them for whatever rehabilitation program may be worked out. In some cases the parents are not of the type to participate in such cooperative planning. However, this does not negate the need for a thorough investigation to include conferences with parents and others, such as ministers, or youth-group leaders, who have some knowledge of the juvenile and could help in his rehabilitation. School people should be of great assistance in this area. Unfortunately, some juvenile courts tend to ignore school personnel or even to reject assistance proffered by the school. Much of the criticism of the juvenile court probably can be laid to a lack of effective administration or a defect in carrying out its ideals rather than to the philosophy of the court itself. Possibly one of the new areas to be explored is that of increased involvement of the parent in responsibility for the delinquent act and in the rehabilitation and educational program.

EDUCATIONAL IMPLICATIONS

The facts concerning crime and the problems originating from crime do, of course, have implications for the school. Our citizens should be aware of the extent and importance of crime as a problem in our society. They should also be aware of the danger of such problems as narcotics and gambling. Positive emphasis in the curriculum should be on values that would tend to counteract any tendencies toward criminal action on the part of the person. Most of the implications for rehabilitation of the persons who tend toward criminality are the same as the implications for treating delinquency. The educational implications for the treatment of the delinquent are of two sorts. One is to take care of those who have become so delinquent that they require a special treatment, either in the form of clinics or in the form of some kind of school for rehabilitation. The other implication is to secure the help of the various agencies trying to work with children in serious need in the predelinquent stage.

Child Guidance Clinics

It is necessary that each school system or community have full facilities for the study of individual children who have become serious problems either in school or in other institutions and who are either potential delinquents or already delinquents. These child guidance clinics should be quite extensive. Each child must be dealt with individually. Opportunities must be given at times for the child to reside at the clinic so that he can be studied. In many cases an investigation of the family and other environmental conditions must be made. Such clinics are an essential part of the total handling of many problems of behavior or delinquency.

Schools for the Socially Maladjusted

There are schools for those who are not so bad as to need complete separation from society, to be sent to the so-called reform school, but who may need to be taken out of their home environments for a period of time. These schools are usually resident schools, often in a rural area outside of town, where there can be a farm program and usually also some special type of educational program directed toward the rehabilitation of the children.

Classes must be small, teachers must be specially trained, and facilities for individualized work must be made available. Facilities for further psychological and psychiatric study of the children must be available. The length of time the child stays at the school should be determined by careful study and restudy of the individual and his home. Some of these schools have been very successful in rehabilitating some cases involving badly maladjusted delinquents.

General Implications for Schools and School Programs

School programs have an important part to play, particularly in the prevention of delinquency. One important item is the attitude of the teacher toward his pupils and particularly toward those who are serious behavior problems in school and, therefore, potential delinquents. Whatever the treatment given to behavior problems in a school, there must be a real warmth of understanding and every effort must be made to give genuine meaning to the school program. A teacher who works in a neighborhood where the backgrounds of the children are quite different from the background of the teacher himself must learn to understand these unfamiliar cultures if he is to work effectively with them. Even when cultural differences do not exist, to some extent the teachers, the adults of one generation, tend not to understand the boys and girls of another generation, because of the present rapidity of change. This disparity in points of view is bad enough in a community where the teacher comes from the same general socioeconomic status. The problems are complicated when the socioeconomic statuses, attitudes, and mores are markedly different. Probably the single most important thing the school can do is to take a *genuine personal interest* in each child.

In addition to the teachers' attitudes and understanding, there needs to be a heavy emphasis in the curriculum upon those matters that will help the coming generation to work toward the solution of social problems so that fewer situations conducive to the development of behavior and delinquency problems will exist. This means, among other things, an emphasis on developing skills in helping people to get along with each other. (See Chapter 9.) It also means heavy emphasis upon the ideals and practices of good family living, so that the graduates of our schools who are normal boys and girls will go out equipped with the attitudes and desires to develop good family living. (See Chapter 6.)

Mental Health Program of the School

Efforts should be made to develop a good mental health atmosphere in all schools. Antagonism between groups of teachers or between teacher and principal does not result in a situation where wholesome personalities can be developed readily. Some of the suggestions that have been covered in Chapter 7 are applicable here in a program for developing a good mental health atmosphere.

SUMMARY

Crime in the United States has become a very important social and political problem, in terms of both the amount of money involved and the effect the criminal and his crimes has on the rest of society. Prominent in the increase in crime is the increase in the amount of white-collar crime. Much crime is related to the problem of control or prohibition of certain things, such as the use of alcohol, the use of narcotics, gambling, and prostitution.

In the United States the juvenile delinquent generally is treated differently from the adult criminal. The special court, the juvenile court, at present has an adequate point of view but an inadequate staff to do the job assigned to it. Juvenile delinquency has increased markedly, particularly in its spread into the previously low-delinquency areas, those of the middle and upper classes. The implications for education point toward providing services for the help of children who are socially maladjusted and hence potential delinquents; help can be given through special schools and classes as well as by specialized personnel. Important implications for school programs based upon good mental health principles can also be formulated.

Selected Bibliography

Abelstrom, Winston M., and Robert J. Havighurst. *400 Losers*. San Francisco: Jossey-Bass, 1971. 246 pp.

Abruzzi, William. "Why Penalties for Pot?" *Saturday Review*, May 22, 1971.

Barkun, Michael (ed.). *Law and the Social System*. Chicago: Aldine-Atherton, 1972. 128 pp.

Blachly, Paul H. (ed.). *Drug Abuse: Data and Debate*. Springfield, Ill.: Charles C Thomas, Publisher, 1970. 322 pp.

Blavat, Herbert, and William Flocco. "A Survey of a Workable Drug Abuse Program?" *Phi Delta Kappan*, Vol. LII, No. 9 (May 1971).

Blum, Richard H., et al. *Society and Drugs*. San Francisco: Jossey-Bass, 1969. 400 pp.

———. *Students and Drugs*. San Francisco: Jossey-Bass, 1969. 399 pp.

Blumberg, Abraham S. *Criminal Justice*. Chicago: Quadrangle Books, Inc., 1970. 212 pp.

Byrd, Oliver E. *Medical Readings on Drug Abuse*. Reading, Mass.: Addison-Wesley Publishing Co., Inc., 1970. 274 pp.

Carroll, Charles. *Alcohol: Use, Non-use and Abuse*. Dubugue, Ia.: Wm. C. Brown & Co., 1970.

Center for Law and Education, Harvard University. "Special Reports: Drugs, Discipline, and Disruption," *Inequality in Education*, No. 8. Entire issue.

Chambliss, William J. *Crime and the Legal Process*. New York: McGraw-Hill Book Company, 1969. 447 pp.

"A Children's Ombudsman? Planning a Children's Advocacy System," *Current*, No. 125 (January 1971).

Clark, Ramsey. *Crime in America: Observations on Its Nature, Causes, Prevention and Control*. New York: Simon & Schuster, Inc., 1970. 346 pp.

Cohen, Bruce J. (ed.). *Crime in America: Perspectives on Criminal and Delinquent Behavior*. Itasca, Ill.: Peacock, 1970. 506 pp.

———. *Turbulent Times*. New York: Sidney Hillman Foundation, 1970. 9 pp. (Pamphlet.)

Donahue, George T., and Sol Nichtern. *Teaching the Troubled Child*. New York: The Free Press, 1969.

Douglas, Jack D. (ed.). *Crime and Justice in American Society*. Indianapolis: The Bobbs-Merrill Co., Inc., 1971. 297 pp.

Downie, Leonard, Jr. *Justice Denied: The Case for Reform of the Courts*. New York: Frederick A. Praeger, Inc., 1971. 224 pp.

Evans, Wayne O. "Mind Altering Drugs and the Future," *The Futurist*, Vol. V, No. 3 (June 1971), 101–104.

Farber, Seymour M., and Roger H. L. Wilson (eds.). *Control of the Mind: Man and Civilization*. New York: McGraw-Hill Book Company, 1961. 340 pp.

Fitts, William H., and William T. Hamner. *The Self Concept and Delinquency*. Nashville: Mental Health Institute, 1969. 96 pp.

Fleisher, Belton M. *The Economics of Delinquency*. Chicago: Quadrangle Books, Inc., 1966. 127 pp.

Fortune. *Youth in Turmoil*. New York: Time-Life Books, 1969. 159 pp.

Gagnon, John H., and William Simon (eds.). *Sexual Deviance*. New York: Harper & Row, Publishers, 1967. 310 pp.

Garabedian, Peter G., and Don C. Gibbons (eds.). *Becoming Delinquent: Young Offenders and the Correctional Process.* Chicago: Aldine Publishing Company, 1970. 304 pp.

Gardner, Erle Stanley. *Cops on Campus and Crime in the Streets.* New York: Pocket Books, 1970. 156 pp.

Geis, Gilbert (ed.). *White-Collar Criminal: The Offender in Business and the Professions.* New York: Atherton Press, 1968. 448 pp.

Gibbens, T. C., and R. H. Ahrenfeldt. *Cultural Factors in Delinquency.* Philadelphia: J. B. Lippincott Company, 1966. 201 pp.

Gillers, Stephen. *Getting Justice: The Rights of People.* New York: Basic Books, Inc., 1971. 228 pp.

Glaser, Daniel (ed.). *Crime in the City.* New York: Harper & Row, Publishers, 1970. 308 pp.

Glueck, Sheldon, and Eleanor Glueck. *Delinquent and Non-delinquent in Perspective.* Cambridge, Mass.: Harvard Press, 1968. 268 pp.

Gnagey, William J. *Controlling Classroom Misbehavior.* Washington, D.C.: N.E.A., 1965. 31 pp.

Goode, Erich (ed.). *Marijuana.* New York: Atherton Press, 1969. 197 pp.

Graham, Hugh Davis, and Ted Robert Gurr. *The History of Violence in America.* New York: Bantam Books, 1969. 822 pp.

Grinspoon, Lester. *Marihuana Reconsidered.* Cambridge, Mass.: Harvard University Press, 1971. 443 pp.

Hart, Harold H. (ed.). *Drugs: For and Against.* New York: Hart, 1970. 239 pp.

Health-PAC Workshop. "Methadone or Therapeutic Communities," *Current,* No. 120 (August 1970).

Hirschi, Travis. *Causes of Delinquency.* Berkeley: University of California Press, 1969. 309 pp.

Hoopes, Ned E. (ed.). *Who Am I? Essays on the Alienated.* New York: Dell Publishing Co., 1969. 286 pp.

Hoover, John Edgar. *Crime in the United States, 1969.* Washington, D.C.: Government Printing Office, 1970. 185 pp. Published annually.

James, Howard. *Children in Trouble: A National Scandal.* New York: David McKay Company, Inc., 1970. 340 pp.

Johnson, Elmer Hubert. *Crime, Correction and Society,* Revised Edition. Homewood, Ill.: Dorsey Press, 1969. 745 pp.

Kaplan, John. "Dealing with Drugs—What Legal Status for Marijuana?" *Current* (November 1970), 44–47.

_____. *Marijuana: The New Prohibition.* New York: Pocket Books, 1970. 402 pp.

Knudten, Richard D. (ed.). *Crime, Criminology and Contemporary Society.* Homewood, Ill.: Dorsey Press, 1970. 448 pp.

_____. *Crime in a Complex Society: An Introduction to Criminology.* Homewood, Ill.: Dorsey Press, 1970. 775 pp.

Kvaraceus, William C. *Anxious Youth: Dynamics of Delinquency.* Columbus, Ohio: Charles E. Merrill Books, Inc., 1966. 291 pp.

Ladd, Edward T. "Pills for Classroom Peace?" *Saturday Review,* November 21, 1970.

Land, Herman W. *What You Can Do About Drugs and Your Child.* New York: Pocket Books, 1969. 169 pp.

Lerman, Paul (ed.). *Delinquency and Social Policy.* New York: Frederick A. Praeger, Inc., 1970. 488 pp.

Levine, Murray, and Adeline Levine. *A Social History of Helping Services: Clinic, Court, School and Community.* New York: Appleton-Century-Crofts, Inc., 1970. 315 pp.

Lewis, Barbara. *Sexual Power of Marijuana.* New York: Wyden, 1970. 177 pp.

Louria, Donald B. *The Drug Scene.* New York: McGraw-Hill Book Company, 1968. 215 pp.

MacIver, Robert M. *The Prevention and Control of Delinquency.* New York: Atherton Press, 1967. 215 pp.

Marin, Peter, and Allan Y. Cohen. *Understanding Drug Use: An Adult's Guide to Drugs and the Young*. New York: Harper & Row, Publishers, 1971. 163 pp.

Maslow, Abraham, *Religions, Values and Peak Experiences*. Columbus: Ohio State University Press, 1964. 123 pp.

May, Rollo. *Man's Search for Himself*. New York: W. W. Norton & Company, Inc., 1953. 281 pp.

McLuhan, Marshall, and Quentin Fiore. *War and Peace in the Global Village*. New York: McGraw-Hill Book Company, 1968. 190 pp.

Minton, Robert J., Jr. (ed.). *Inside: Prison American Style*. New York: Random House, Inc., 1971. 325 pp.

Montagu, Ashley. *On Being Human*. New York: Schuman, 1950. 125 pp.

Morris, Norval, and Gordon Hawkins. *The Honest Politician's Guide to Crime Control*. Chicago: University of Chicago Press, 1969. 271 pp.

Moskowitz, Ronald. "Leaving the Drug World Behind," *The Education Digest*, Vol. XXXV, No. 9 (May 1970).

Moynihan, Daniel P. *Violent Crime: The Challenge to Our Cities*. New York: George Braziller, Inc., 1969. 85 pp.

Nordin, Virginia Davis. *Gault: What Now for the Juvenile Court?* Ann Arbor, Mich.: Institute for Continuing Education, 1968. 218 pp.

Parker, Harold K. "On Making Incorrigible Youths Corrigible," *The Education Digest*, Vol. XXXV, No. 9 (May 1970).

Passow, A. Harry (ed.). *Education in Depressed Areas*. New York: Teachers College, Columbia University, 1963. 369 pp.

Platt, Anthony M. *The Child Savers: The Invention of Delinquency*. Chicago: University of Chicago Press, 1969. 230 pp.

Report of the National Advisory Commission on Civil Disorders. New York: Bantam Books, 1968. 700 pp.

Rosenberg, Bernard, and Harry Silverstein. *The Varieties of Delinquent Experience*. Waltham, Mass.: Blaisdell Publishing Co., 1969. 165 pp.

Salerno, Ralph, and John S. Tompkins. *The Crime Confederation*. Garden City, N.Y.: Doubleday & Company, Inc., 1969. 424 pp.

Saltman, Jules. *Marijuana and Your Child*. New York: Grosset & Dunlap, Inc., 1970. 123 pp.

Schreiber, Daniel (ed.). *Guidance and the School Dropout*. Washington, D.C.: N.E.A., 1964. 214 pp.

Schurr, Edwin M. *Law and Society: A Sociological View*. New York: Random House, Inc., 1968. 239 pp.

———. *Our Criminal Society*. Englewood Cliffs, N.J.: Prentice-Hall, Inc., 1970. 244 pp.

Sheviakov, George V., and Fritz Redl. *Discipline for Today's Children and Youth*. Washington, D.C.: N.E.A., A.S.C.D., 1956. 64 pp.

Silberman, Charles E. "Give Slum Children a Chance," *Harper's Magazine*, Vol. 228, No. 1368 (May 1964).

Smith, Roger W. (ed.). *Guilt: Man and Society*. Garden City, N.Y.: Doubleday & Company, Inc., 1971. 314 pp.

Stearn, Jess. *The Seekers: Drugs and the New Generation*. Garden City, N.Y.: Doubleday & Company, Inc., 1969. 383 pp.

Stratton, John R., and Robert M. Terry (eds.). *Prevention of Delinquency*. New York: The Free Press, 1969. 334 pp.

Sutherland, Edwin H. *White Collar Crime*. New York: Holt, Rinehart & Winston, Inc., 1949. 272 pp.

———, and Donald R. Cressey. *Criminology*, Eighth Edition. Philadelphia: J. B. Lippincott Company, 1970. 659 pp.

Toffler, Alvin. *Future Shock*. New York: Random House, Inc., 1970. 505 pp.

Tyler, Gus (ed.). *Organized Crime in America: A Book of Readings*. Ann Arbor: University of Michigan Press, 1962. 421 pp.

U.S. Riot Commission Report. *Report of the National Advisory Commission on Civil Disorders*. New York: Bantam Books, 1968. 609 pp.

Vaz, Edmund W. (ed.). *Middle-Class Juvenile Delinquency*. New York: Harper & Row, Publishers, 1967. 289 pp.

Wasserstein, Bruce, and Mark J. Green (eds.). *With Justice for Some: An Indictment of the Law by Young Advocates*. Boston: Beacon Press, Inc., 1971. 400 pp.

Westley, William A. *Violence and the Police: A Sociological Study of Law, Custom and Morality*. Cambridge, Mass.: M.I.T. Press, 1971. 222 pp.

Winslow, Robert W. *Society in Transition: A Social Approach to Deviancy*. New York: The Free Press, 1970. 408 pp.

Worsnop, Richard L. "Juvenile Offenders," *Editorial Research Reports*, Vol. 1, No. 6 (February 11, 1970).

Yablonsky, Lewis. *The Tunnel Back: Synanon*. New York: The Macmillan Company, 1965. 403 pp.

Selected Films

Children of the City (BIS), 31 min. Frank discussion of juvenile delinquency problems illustrating practice of Scottish courts under recent act of Parliament. Story of three boys accused of petty thievery—how overcrowding and shortage of recreation facilities breed delinquency—how education, social, and civic authorities unite in treating delinquents.

Children's Village (McGraw-Hill), 19 min. Produced at the Children's Village, Dobbs Ferry, N.Y. This film shows the work of this well-known institution in the rehabilitation of delinquent boys. Founded in 1951, the village is today a community of more than fifty buildings and 400 boys. It is both a school and a preadult society in which each boy learns and works. It has its own businesses, shops, and banks; selects its own mayor, judge, and town clerk; and pays its own taxes to run its own community projects. We are shown a new boy, Richard, who is accepted by the community, and how he reacts to his new environment.

Children Without (Anti-Defamation League), 30 min. Shows a Detroit public school where teachers and counselors establish the warm relationships such children need, and provide positive learning experiences for them.

Crime in the Streets (N.E.T.), 60 min. Film examines two aspects of juvenile crime: the quality of police protection and programs for rehabilitation of offenders.

Dropout (Atlantis Productions), 27 min. Studies the case of a school dropout. Explores the reasons for his action and the results.

Marked for Failure (N.E.T.), 59 min. Educational problems of deprived children in Harlem.

Police Power (N.E.T.), 60 min. Debate on role of police power, including conflicts between civil liberties and police methods, attitudes of police and the public toward one another, and the effect of Supreme Court decisions on police authority.

Portrait of a Disadvantaged Child (N.E.T.), 59 min.

Portrait of the Inner City (N.E.T.), 58 min.

Portrait of the Inner City School: A Place to Learn (N.E.T.), 59 min.

Semester of Discontent (N.E.T.), 60 min. Issues behind the mounting wave of unrest in the nation's universities are investigated.

Superfluous People (Atlantis Productions), 54 min. This film argues that welfare aid is a material and moral problem. It looks at people in trouble. It presents the thoughts of social workers, clergymen, authors, educators, and city planners.

Chapter 9

Problems of
Intergroup Relations

Successful societies probably always will be stratified. Without leadership and without power vested in the hands of the leaders, there is anarchy. A central thesis of this book is that democracy is the best method yet devised for the selection of those leaders and for the prevention of the abuse of power by the leaders. Recognizing this, we realize further that American democracy has not yet developed fully; we have many problems. A parallel thesis is that American educators bear a responsibility for recognizing current American problems and for providing leadership in the search for solutions. It is the responsibility of American educators to recognize the diverse groups in American culture, to become aware of the problems created by conflicts of interest among these groups, to ameliorate the suffering caused by conflicts (especially as it affects the personality development of school children), and to develop adult citizens who can meet these conflicts with mutual respect, reason, cooperation, and high morale.

Adequate treatment of intergroup problems would require a series of volumes. This chapter briefly will sample in sequence: (1) the basic problems of intergroup relations in America; (2) reasons for the origin and persistence of these problems; (3) proposed action toward their resolution; (4) the role of the school in treating them; and (5) the continuing school integration crises

BROAD AREAS OF INTERGROUP PROBLEMS

Most of the intergroup problems in America today fall into the areas of social class, race, religion, national origin, and regional differences. Each of these broad areas will be discussed. In the contemporary scene, two additional groups merit discussion: women's liberation and youth. The continuing crisis in school integration will be treated in a concluding section, as the authors feel that the traumatic nature of resistance to school integration is not only a question of racial prejudice, but a matter of social class differences among those being integrated. Treatment of school integration will be limited to content and to alternative solutions. The *strategies* of protest

—confrontation, riot, strike, and so on—will be discussed under "Protest and Confrontation Politics" in Chapter 14.

Class Differences

In spite of the fact that America generally is considered to be a class-less society, social stratification is a major source of intergroup problems in this country today. One reason for the popular impression that America is relatively free of class differences probably lies in the high degree of vertical mobility in American culture; that is, one can move readily from one class to another. The popular phrase "Any boy can become President" epitomizes America's pride in her relative freedom from the rigid class barriers that inhibit vertical mobility in many cultures. The extremity of the phrase also emphasizes the popular belief that vertical mobility is more easily accomplished than is actually the case. Despite relative mobility, great masses of the American populace suffer from discrimination based on social stratification. This is particularly true of the lower-class Negro.

Class barriers in many societies are so rigid as to approach a caste system, wherein one is born into a certain caste and can never escape it, no matter how great his individual abilities. The Negro has been relegated to such a caste status in America. Within the Negro caste, one finds class differences quite similar to those described in succeeding sections of this chapter as an integral part of the total American culture.

Caste status has become increasingly infuriating to the young black in contemporary society. Recent advances by the black and by the culturally disadvantaged have greatly benefited the expanding middle class, leaving the urban lower class even further behind. In 1940 approximately 5 per cent of all blacks were middle class. By 1970 approximately 25 per cent of all blacks had attained middle-class status, but the majority of blacks remained poor and increasingly frustrated.[1] The gains achieved by their black brethren only emphasized the injustice of their own plight. They reacted violently in the 1960's.

Social research has indicated that class differences in America make important differences in the behavior of individuals in at least four areas: sexual behavior, values and motivation, such cultural practices as child rearing, and political and economic ideologies. The differences often serve as bases for the rationalization and reinforcement of prejudices.

Because of the importance of class differences affecting the entire populace of the nation, we shall develop in some detail (1) the Communist theory of class structure and struggle; (2) the development of class structure in America; (3) the method of analysis of contemporary social structure in America; and (4) the nature of contemporary American social structure.

The Communist Theory of Class Structure and Struggle. Although the Afro-Asian bloc is moving toward a "third world" (as an addition to the current popular terminology of the "Western world" and the "communist countries") the contemporary conflict is between two main ideologies: democracy and Marxism. Struggle between the social classes is basic to

[1]Thomas F. Pettigrew, "Racially Separate or Together?" *Journal of Social Issues*, Vol. XXV, No. 1 (1969).

Marxist theory. It is, therefore, pertinent at this point to examine the Marxist theory of class struggle and structure in relation to what has happened in America. According to Marxist theorists, the class struggle in modern times was to result in all existing classes being reduced to two major social classes, the proletariat (or working class) and the bourgeoisie.[2] Marx postulated that the rich would become richer and the poor would become poorer. He based his generalization on certain trends that were present during the period in which he wrote, nineteenth-century industrialized Europe. Events of recent years, particularly in the United States, have tended to demonstrate that in this respect the Marxist analysis is faulty. It is true that the wealthy have accumulated more wealth; but so have the poor. Amelioration of the living conditions of the lower-middle and lower classes since 1900 has been tremendous. Even though there is a wide economic difference between the upper and lower classes, the gulf between them has not become wider. Furthermore, many persons in the lower classes have risen in class level through occupational or professional advancement. This means that there has been a very considerable increase in the size of the middle class. Although there is a large group of wealthy persons in America, neither the number of those persons nor the amount of wealth above the middle-class level has increased proportionately until very recent years. Lundberg has brought together recent statistics related to the concentration of wealth in the United States.[3] As the middle class has expanded, so has the number of millionaires, a natural concomitant of inflation. He points out, however, that the wealthy group now has greater power, because of its control of corporations, and that probably 1 per cent of the families in America control the corporate wealth. Despite this growth in corporate control, the number of the super-rich is growing at a not much greater rate than the growth of the general population. It is likely that the programs of economic legislation starting with the antitrust laws and continuing with the regulation of utilities, the income tax, the social legislation and executive orders and agencies of the Franklin D. Roosevelt administration, and probably the increased strength of labor unions, all have served to prevent Marx's predictions from coming true. Rather than all classes being reduced to two sharply defined groups, at least six groups, whose lines of demarcation are very hazy, have been identified in the contemporary American class structure.

The Development of Class Structure in America. The colonists brought to this country many of the class distinctions that had existed in Europe. Because for the most part the upper class did not migrate, the colonists were mostly middle- and lower-class persons. Certain class distinctions existed well into the period of the development of the American republic itself.[4] Some class lines tended to become obliterated by the time of the Revolution. The Revolution accelerated this trend by eliminating a portion of the wealthy landowning class and thus reducing the extent of class differences. In addition, the whole climate of political opinion affected by the Age of

[2]Louis Untermeyer, *Makers of the Modern World* (New York: Simon & Schuster, 1955), pp. 26–33.

[3]Ferdinand Lundberg, *The Rich and the Super-Rich* (New York: Lyle Stuart, 1967).

[4]These class distinctions are discussed in some detail under "Social Customs and Institutions" in Chapter 4.

Enlightenment in Europe was toward greater emphasis upon equality and brotherhood, which tended to blur class lines.

On the American frontier a man was worthwhile for what he could do, not for his class status. The frontier tendency toward blurring of class lines had great influence on what was occurring in the more settled East. This does not mean that there were no classes. There was considerable range in wealth and in the possession of worldly goods. There were no sharp lines between the classes, however, except perhaps those between the wealthy mill owners and the laboring groups.

Especially in the larger cities, social class distinctions tended to become somewhat more fixed in the period following the Civil War. In most of the large cities a society consisting of the "best families" developed; frequently there was a special book to list them. Of lesser status was a group of wealthy persons who tended to associate together, and who had both wealth and tradition. Then there was the great mass of people, who quite often tended to associate on the basis of their commercial or professional ties. Next in status came the unskilled laborers and the lower classes.

The expansion of the economy during the latter half of the nineteenth century promoted the accumulation of wealth, with accompanying vertical mobility, but cultural practices among the classes necessitated major reorientation of habits of speech, dress, and social courtesies on the part of those aspiring to raise their class standing. The climate of opinion that followed the administration of Theodore Roosevelt was such that there was a reaction against the extremely wealthy, and the open display of wealth typical of the early 1900's tended to decline. After 1913, the income tax tended to remove the great surplus of wealth even from the very rich. The present social structure maintains wealth as one of the indexes of social position, but family tradition still is an essential ingredient of entry into the upper-upper class.

Methods of Analysis of Contemporary Social Structure in America. Research in class structure has tended to be based upon empirical findings, although sometimes hypotheses are set up, to be verified later by experimentation or by field study. The Lynds felt that in Middletown there was a twofold social class system: one of the business class and one of the working class. In a later study, *Middletown in Transition*, they divided the working class into two groups.[5] Another study by Centers divided the United States into a fourfold class system, including upper, middle, working, and lower classes.[6]

By far the most thorough and far-reaching study of American class structure has been done in a series by W. Lloyd Warner and his associates. Basing their work entirely upon an empirical analysis of thoroughly detailed data in specific towns in which they worked, these investigators have postulated a class system as follows: upper upper, lower upper, upper middle, lower middle, upper lower, lower lower. The major techniques employed in arriving at this classification system and assigning persons to it involved

[5]Robert S. Lynd and Helen M. Lynd, *Middletown in Transition* (New York: Harcourt, 1937).
[6]Richard Centers, *The Psychology of Social Classes* (Princeton, N.J.: Princeton University Press, 1949).

the development and application of two indexes: (1) an index of status characteristics consisting of such criteria as occupation and place of residence and (2) an index of participation in social activities revealing the social class rating of persons in the community by other members of the community.[7]

Although the Warner studies have been subjected to some criticism, they are by far the most far-reaching and penetrating of all available studies. They seem to indicate definitely that there are social classes and that people are aware of them. Class consciousness is illustrated in such areas as selectivity of social invitations and differential codes of conduct toward selected groups.

The Nature of Contemporary Social Structure.   A careful study of the research done by Warner and by other researchers indicates that social class structure is a fact in America and must be taken into account in any analysis of the American scene. We have indicated earlier that even within the Negro caste a class structure can be identified, which is similar to that found in the Warner studies.

As a result of the empirical study of Yankee City, a heterogeneous industrial city in New England, Warner and his associates found it to be divided into classes as postulated. The class structure of Yankee City is shown in Figure 13.

Race, social reputation, religion, national origin, and wealth all entered into the composite picture that comprised the class structure of Yankee City. Old American stock, Swedes, Russians, and Negroes had class preference in that order. The basis for prestige was social reputation. The upper-upper, old-family native-born formulated standards and ideals which served as models of social conduct for the lower-lower, who lacked job security and were unskilled and poorly housed. The norm was a middle-class society. In the Warner study, the upper class was predominantly Episcopalian in religious faith; the lower class was predominantly Catholic, Jewish, or religiously unaffiliated.

To be born into one of the classes does make it difficult to move into another. In spite of the difficulty, there is a great deal of vertical mobility in the American scene. It probably is becoming increasingly difficult for one to move from the lower-middle class or the lower class to the position of executive in the industrial world. But by means of higher education, albeit with a struggle because of economic handicaps, a person can move from the lower class into such a profession as teaching, law, or medicine, and thus break out of class bonds.

The breaking of lower-class bonds through higher education is popularly thought to be becoming more difficult; the ever-increasing costs of college education are cited. Statistics on college enrollments do not support this position; an ever-increasing proportion of college-age youth are enrolled in college. True, many modern youth are enrolled in terminal courses in two-year colleges or in similar courses at major universities, but the fact remains

[7]There is a series of books in the study, but see especially W. Lloyd Warner and Paul Lunt, *The Social Life of a Modern Community*, Yankee City Series, Volume 1 (New Haven: Yale University Press, 1941). Newest paperback edition of this data appears as W. Lloyd Warner et al., *Yankee City* (New Haven: Yale University Press, 1963).

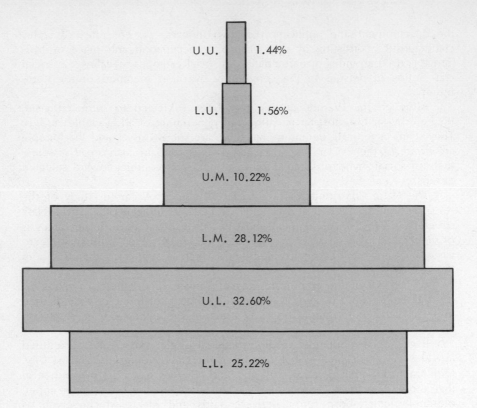

Figure 13.   The class hierarchy of Yankee City. [From W. Lloyd Warner et al., *Yankee City* (New Haven: Yale University Press, 1963), p. 43. Used by permission.]

that more and more of today's young are receiving at least some college education. The campus associations not only prepare them for technical vocations with relatively higher salary and status, but also significantly modify their value patterns and cultural behavior.

If one has assimilated the middle-class mores emphasized in our public schools, breaking lower-class bonds relieves misery. If an individual becomes an urban professional person, however, while maintaining lower-class standards of dress, language, and personal habits, he may become an unhappy isolate. He belongs professionally with one group and socially with another; he receives only an uneasy tolerance from each group and no real acceptance from either, with an attendant reduction in his personal emotional security. Fortunately many such professional men marry middle-class wives who re-educate them, but such marriages may have turbulent beginnings, or even may culminate in divorce, because of these class-value conflicts. If both members of a marriage of urban professional people maintain lower-class mores, unhappiness almost certainly will result. In the small rural community, however, the professional members may achieve greater social and emotional security by conforming to the lower-class mores of the community.

There can be an overemphasis on the class structure of America because it is less restrictive here than in many other countries. However, to ignore the existence of the lines, even though they may be somewhat blurred, is to ignore one of the important facts about American culture. Especially in the larger cities, class distinctions are important in modern America.

So far as the schools are concerned, there probably is an *under-emphasis* upon social class and its implications for education. Silberman notes that "variations in school inputs seem to have little effect on students' academic achievement, while variations in their family background have substantial impact." [8] This topic will be discussed in detail under "Continuing School Integration Crisis" at the end of this chapter, with special reference to the Coleman Report.

Racial Differences

The anthropologists maintain that two facts alone are important for any definition of race. They state that a race is a large group of people (1) possessing in common certain distinctive physical characteristics that are (2) determined by heredity. Such a "pure" race has not been located in the modern world. The most commonly accepted scientific classification of the modern races of mankind is the Negroid, or "black"; the Mongoloid, or "yellow-brown"; and the Caucasian, or "white." [9] Laymen often confuse "race" with natural characteristics, confusing genetic and political concepts. Hitler utilized these confusions, identifying "Aryans" as the master race. Further confusions relate to linguistic, religious, or cultural differences. For example, Judaism is a religion and Hebrew is a language; there is no Jewish "race."

Racial differences pose some of the most traumatic problems in intergroup relations facing the American populace today. The Negro suffers most from racial discrimination. The American Negro has been relegated to second-class citizenship solely because of skin color. This historic fact has made very real differences in the behavior of both whites and blacks. The resentment over deprivation of their birthright has made large numbers of the American Negroes militant in their fight for first-class citizenship. Highly articulate Negroes with great organizational abilities have capitalized on this militancy. The clarion call of the freedom sermon is effectively expressed in Martin Luther King's Letter from a Birmingham Jail.

> . . . I am in Birmingham because injustice is here. Just as the prophets of the eighth century B.C. left their villages and carried their "thus saith the Lord" far beyond the boundaries of their home towns, and just as the Apostle Paul left his village of Tarsus and carried the gospel of Jesus Christ to the far corners of the Greco-Roman world, so am I compelled to carry the gospel of freedom beyond my own home town. Like Paul, I must constantly respond to the Macedonian call for aid. [10]

[8] Charles E. Silberman, *Crisis in the Classroom* (New York: Random House, 1970), p. 73.
[9] Stewart Henderson Britt, *Social Psychology of Modern Life* (New York: Holt, 1941), p. 427.
[10] Martin Luther King, Jr., *Why We Can't Wait* (New York: New American Library, 1964), p. 77.

Unfortunately, even the most capable of the Negro leaders cannot control the lunatic fringe of their followers, witness the bloody and apparently senseless riots in Washington, Detroit, and so on, in the 1960's.

Moderate Negro leaders such as King were being pushed aside by late 1964, and many responsible Negro leaders had considered King to be radical in early 1963. Negro militancy mushroomed in 1963 and 1964. The year 1965 saw the responsible leaders further losing control, while spontaneous street riots broke out with no apparent leadership or organization. The extended riots in Watts, California, in the summer of 1965, finally communicated to the leaders of the power structure of America that the Negro was committed to a genuine grass-roots rebellion. Clear need had been demonstrated for prompt and positive programs to strike at the roots of the conditions of poverty which generated a Watts. Congress saw the need and embraced in toto the legislative programs proposed by President Johnson for the War on Poverty. A realistic appraisal of the situation appeared in the August, 1965, issue of *Change,* publication of the Center for the Study of Democratic Institutions.

> Members of the Center, like most Americans, have been discussing the meaning of the Los Angeles riots and speculating about what should now be done. There is general agreement that repressive or punitive measures make no sense. "It depends on what you're aiming at," one staff member commented. "Some people want to strike back because of the discomfort and guilty feelings that the riots have caused in them. So they ask for more police, and want the entire community penalized. This course will merely insure bigger and more costly commotion in the future. The right thing to aim at is a program that will do away with the conditions—personal, economic and social—that brought on the uprising in the first place. The effort should be to show that an intelligent city can learn from its mistakes by turning the devastated area into a model community."[11]

The preceding comments made in *Change*—antedating the Coleman Report by a full year—still make sense, but progress in attaining these goals seems painfully slow even though the summers have been less "hot" as America has moved into the 1970's. Extremist groups, both black and white, further contribute to the turmoil of the times. Such groups as the Klu Klux Klan, the White Citizens Council, National Association for the Advancement of White People, the Black Muslims, and the Black Panthers deliberately inflame both the white man and the black man. Unscrupulous leaders, both black and white, use these extremist groups for personal ends. Among the many and varied causes of the Watts and other riots of the 1960's must be counted the hate-fostering activities of these extremist groups. The death of Martin Luther King has made the proliferation of leadership in Negro groups, and their instances upon continued autonomy, as visible as the conflicts among the various white groups. A *Time* special issue, "Black America 1970," comments:

> Today most blacks and thoughtful whites have accepted the fact that leadership on the magnitude of a Martin Luther King is uncommon in any race or time. . . . The black movement today is factionalized. . . . there is sharp disagree-

[11] "Can We Learn from the Riots?" *Change,* Vol. 1, No. 6 (August 1965), p. 1. Used by permission.

ment among the traditional integrationists, best symbolized by King and the N.A.A.C.P's Roy Wilkins: the black nationalists, of whom CORE's Roy Innis and U.S's Ron Karengo are leading spokesmen; and the Marxist-oriented revolutionaries represented by the Black Panthers.[12]

Graphic illustrations of discrimination against the black segment of the population follow. The graphs refer to "blacks and other minorities," or to "blacks and other races" or to "nonwhite"; but it has been reliably estimated that 92 per cent of all nonwhite minority group members in America are black, so the graphs do closely approximate the black picture.

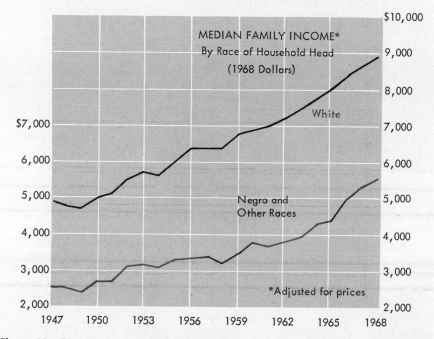

Figure 14. Economic status of the Negro in the United States. [From *Road Maps of Industry* (New York: National Industrial Conference Board, 1970). Used by permission.]

Figure 14 reflects the growth of the American economy from 1947 through 1968, with a growth in family income for both black and white. The significant item for blacks is that the late 1960's showed a narrowing of the gap between black and white family incomes, both in real wages and in the percentage spread. No graph, of course, presents a complete story. The complete gap is not apparent, for black families on the average are larger than white families and consequently have a greater drain on their income.

Figure 15 throws further light on this problem, as it shows that the dramatic gain by college-trained blacks has distorted the average for all black families. Most blacks are still poor! Whether one computes family income from Figure 14 or individual income from Figure 15, blacks will have an income of only two thirds that of whites.

[12] "Black America, 1970," *Time*, April 6, 1970, p. 18.

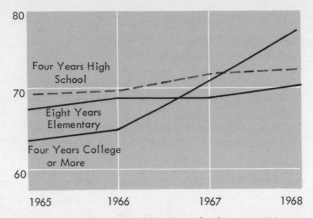

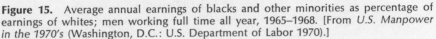

Figure 15. Average annual earnings of blacks and other minorities as percentage of earnings of whites; men working full time all year, 1965–1968. [From *U.S. Manpower in the 1970's* (Washington, D.C.: U.S. Department of Labor 1970).]

Figure 16 tells the story of improvement in the 1960's in some major areas of family concern. Again, both blacks and whites have made gains, with a slightly higher relative gain by blacks, but with the blacks still in a poorer relative position.

Another area in which civil rights legislation has made a difference is detailed in Figure 17. This is an especially important area, as the post-industrial society provides fewer and fewer jobs for unskilled labor.

Graphs and statistics tell of relative gains for the black, but they come too slowly. In one decade the blacks have made probably the greatest social and economic gains of any ethnic group at any period in American history, but they also had the furthest to go. In the early 1970's, the Nixon administration seemed to be saying, "Let us pause to catch our breath. Let us cool off a bit. Let us consolidate our gains before moving on." This will not satisfy even the moderate Negro, let alone the militant black. Silberman has reminded us that revolutions feed on hope, not despair; without doubt the decade of the 1960's, particularly the latter half of the decade, has given the black man ample reason to hope that he is at long last on the road to first-class citizenship. He is in no mood to wait for a traffic signal; he is pushing down hard on the accelerator. This maintains him, of course, on a collision course with the same white groups who fought him every step of the way in the 1960's. The 1970's may see not a cooling off, but a resumption of the long, hot summers of the middle 1960's. The whites will fight to retain jobs and to maintain de facto segregation.

Segments of the Negro population have become outwardly subservient to the white man. The confusions in the American culture as to the value to be placed upon aggressiveness make it easy for the white man to rationalize his prejudices; no matter whether the Negro fights for his birthrights or accepts the status quo, the white man rejects the Negro's behavior as containing either too little or too much aggressiveness. The Negro who maintains a judicious balance in his behavior is not credited with wisdom, for selected portions of his behavior are misrepresented by the white as

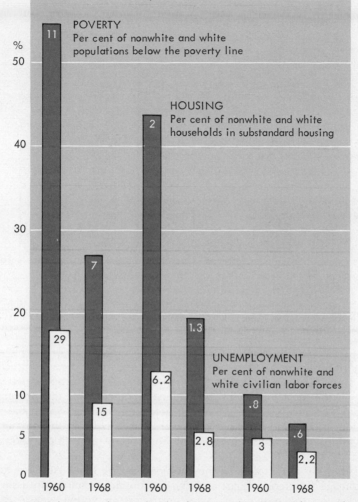

Figure 16. Nonwhite vs. white in levels of poverty, housing, and unemployment in 1960 and 1968. (Figures in bars are millions of people or households. Shaded bars represent nonwhites; white bars represent whites.) [From "Black and White Balance Sheet," *Time*, January 24, 1969. Used by permission.]

examples of both extremes. The deep prejudice felt by many whites, com- bined with the high visibility and large numbers of the Negro (approximately one of every ten Americans), have made the American Negro the center of the greatest intergroup conflict in America today. The contemporary Negro rebellion intensifies this conflict on all levels. Some authorities on human relations, as well as some scholars in the field of social psychology, are con- jecturing as to whether the greatest potential source of conflict lies in this very segment of the Negro populace. The subservient Negro is labeled an "Uncle Tom" and rejected by his own people. To the resentment engendered by his subservience is added the pain of social isolation. Normal outlets for relief of tension are denied, for the role of subservience demands a calm

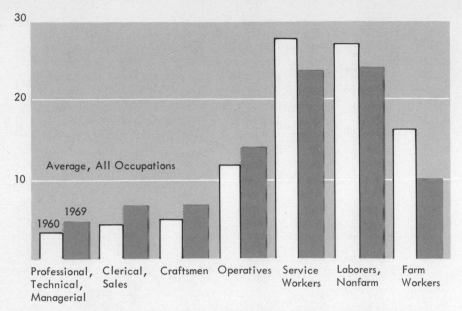

Figure 17. Occupational shifts of blacks and other minorities in terms of per cent of total employment, 1960 and 1969. [From *U.S. Manpower in the 1970's* (Washington, D.C.: U.S. Department of Labor, 1970).]

demeanor. In the face of a genuine Negro rebellion, how long can the "Uncle Toms" contain their wrath? When and how will it be vented? These are among the most intelligent, best-adjusting Negroes. If the power structure does not take intelligent action before this group joins the Negro Revolution, it may find itself out of power. This may be in the best interests of the future of America, but it will come only after long and violent struggle.

Possibly the most tragic of the problems facing black America today is the self-image fostered in black children by American culture. In a survey of the studies on the growth of racial awareness in young Negro children, Guy summarized as follows:

> Ausubel [(D. C. Ausubel, "Ego Development Among Segregated Negro Children," *Mental Hygiene*, 1958, Vol. 42, pp. 362–369)] stated that the Negro child inherits an inferior caste status and almost inevitably acquires the negative self-esteem that is the realistic ego reflection of such status. Through unpleasant contacts with white persons and with institutionalized symbols of caste inferiority (e.g. segregated schools, neighborhoods, amusement places)—and, more indirectly, through mass-media and the reactions of his own family—he gradually becomes aware of the social significance of racial membership. He soon learns that skin color is important, that white is to be desired, dark to be regretted. He perceives himself as an object of derision and disparagement, as socially rejected by the prestigeful elements of society and as unworthy of succorance and affection. Having no compelling reasons for not accepting this officially sanctioned negative evaluation of himself, he develops deeply ingrained feelings of inferiority.

Finally, according to Bronfenbrenner [U. Bronfenbrenner, "The Psychological Costs of Quality and Equality in Education," *Child Development*, 1967, Vol. 38, pp. 909–925] not only does the Negro child feel powerless; he feels worthless as well. At the core of his sense of inferiority is the awareness of being black. From the age of three onward, Negro children begin to prefer white skin to black and to think of Negroes in general and themselves in particular as ugly, unwanted, and "bad." [13]

American culture seems to give the black child only two choices: Uncle Tom or Black Panther.

Evidence of discrimination against the Negro exists in nearly every area of American life: housing, recreation, church membership, economic opportunity, and education. Negroes have a larger incidence of disease and a shorter life span than whites, largely because of deficiencies in health facilities, education, housing, and economic opportunity. Negroes have suffered a greater ratio of delinquency and crime than have the whites, largely because the discriminatory practices of the whites have forced Negroes to live in conditions that breed vice; for example, the big-city slums are largely owned by absentee landlords who perpetuate slum conditions for personal profit. Furthermore, if the Negro tries to escape slum conditions by moving out of them, he finds that houses in desirable locations are not readily available to him. If he does succeed in locating in a desirable area, for sale signs are likely to sprout on his neighbors' lawns.

Finally, the whole complex of lower-class Negro culture violates the middle-class mores of the white, Anglo-Saxon, Protestant majority group in America. Honesty, cleanliness, and thrift are noticeably deficient in large segments of lower-class American Negro culture. The white man accepts none of the blame for this, any more than he accepts the blame for similar deficiencies in lower-class white culture. Rather than examine his own discriminatory practices, which have forced a large proportion of the Negro population into a lower-class way of life, he shrugs his shoulders in superior fashion and says, "Negroes are born that way." These are the attitudes which must be overcome if the War on Poverty is to be accepted and successful. Mr. Van Henderson, Associate Director for Program Services of Atterbury Job Corps Center, commented on this attitude in 1966; the same comments probably are still valid today:

> In a social situation such as the Watts riots, we cannot assume that there is any one given cause, but many causes. The unorganized and leaderless lower classes of the Negro society can be considered dangerous. They must have education and leadership. President Johnson's War on Poverty programs are not a luxury but a necessity. The whole of American society depends upon all Americans operating as a unified force to combat the racial, economic, social, and morale problems of the Negro. Our whole system is threatened. We must unite as Americans, not as Negroes and Whites, to preserve the greatest way of life yet extant.

Watts is not the only area of Los Angeles, of course, which has erupted into racial violence. East Los Angeles is the home of some 400,000 Mexican Americans. Like the 500,000 blacks of Watts, they are disadvantaged. *Business*

[13]David C. Guy, *The Growth of Racial Awareness in Young Negro Children and Some of Its Effects*, unpublished paper, Montclair State College, 1971, p. 14. Used by permission.

Week writes of the Mexican *barrio* that "Unemployment runs at least to Watts 15 per cent, the high school drop-out rate hovers around 50 per cent, and housing is dilapidated."[14] Despite the similarity in the cultural milieu, the congruity of the riots, and the proximity in space, hundreds of millions of dollars (federal, state, and private) and thousands of social researchers flooded Watts in the late 1960's and ignored the *barrio* of East Los Angeles. The 92 per cent of the nonwhite population who are black continue to preoccupy the nation. The 8 per cent who are not black but who still are socially isolated by skin color and both culturally and economically disadvantaged receive little attention. The growing populations of Mexicans in Los Angeles, Puerto Ricans in New York, and Cubans in Florida may force some consideration of the Spanish Americans in the 1970's. In the Southwest, some progress has been made; Spanish-language textbooks and Spanish-speaking teachers are fairly common. Most of the population, however, is not in the areas where progress has been made; the Spanish-speaking sections of metropolitan areas are the potential areas of conflict. Why should conflict be needed for progress? Despite Silberman's cynicism (see quotation, page 322), the authors have faith in the basic humaneness of the American people. Why cannot Spanish-speaking Americans be treated as Americans, not as "minority problems"? The answer, as the authors see it, is that the problem is not simply one of race. The *ghetto* and *barrio* dwellers are suffering from the same economic and social problems faced by all the waves of white immigrants from Europe, the lower-class milieu of cheap labor in the big city. The white immigrants did not escape completely; there still is a large white lower class in the United States. But skin color relegates nonwhites to a caste status, from which escape remains extremely difficult even under the recent civil rights legislation.

Orientals are held in minority status in most places where they are found in America, but usually they are not subject to the type of discrimination suffered by Negroes. The Oriental problem is a minor one in the total American culture because of the small number of Orientals presently in this country and because of our restrictive immigration policy. But the human misery suffered by any individual Oriental is nonetheless severe: the Nisei (Japanese-American) camps of World War II offered a dramatic example of the cruelty of the majority group in America to a minority group.

The American Indian is the one ethnic group that can escape caste status if it so desires. Because of their low visibility, many Indians can leave the reservation and start a new life if they so choose. This is more true for some tribes, of course, than it is for others. Substandard education, housing, health facilities, and economic opportunity characterize the several Indian cultures in America today. All these factors make especially difficult the breaking of lower-class bonds, even though caste status is escaped.

Although severe cultural conflicts currently exist in some sections of the country between Indian groups and the white majority group, the relatively small numbers of the American Indian and his low visibility make the Indian problem a relatively minor one on a national scale. This does not lessen for the individual Indian the human misery caused by deprivation and dis-

[14] "The Barrio Wants a Better Deal, Too," *Business Week*, August 14, 1971, p. 72.

crimination suffered by those who choose to remain with their relatives and friends in the Indian areas, or who live in white areas and are discriminated against.

Unlike the situation in the United States, the Indian problem is very much in the consciousness of Canadians. They currently have no solutions, but they are working hard at the problem as a matter of national conscience. The confusion engendered by growing Indian ghettos in the cities, disproportionate numbers of Indians in jails, inappropriateness of provincial curricula for "bush" Indians, severe grade-level retardation, and excessive drop-out rate possibly are best expressed in the subtitle of a publication by a leading university center for research on Indian problems, "Here We Are— Where Do We Go?"[15]

Cultural pluralism seems to be the logical answer for the Indian, but who honors his culture? In American textbooks when the U.S. Cavalry wins an Indian battle, it is a glorious victory in the march of progress, but when the Indian wins, it is a massacre. The source material is clear. The U.S. Cavalry and other frontiersmen were involved in their share of massacres, including the wiping out of entire Indian villages of women and children, but the textbooks avoid such facts. Some school districts are rewriting history, including the contributions of minority groups, but the Indian still is by-passed in most instances. The California statute of 1968 included them in the School Code reference of minority groups to be studied, along with Negroes and Mexicans; but the Illinois statute of 1967 is more typical— Negroes and twelve enumerated European groups, with the Indian included, if at all, in the etc.[16]

Religious Differences

Religious discrimination is on a long-term decline in America. Anti-Semitism is our largest religious problem. Entire sections of our large cities have become largely Jewish, at least partly because the Jewish family that moves into a Christian neighborhood does not receive full social acceptance by the neighbors. This social distance is emphasized in our public schools, where Christian holidays are joyously celebrated but where the Jewish child who remains at home to celebrate a Jewish holiday often is counted as an unexcused absence and given make-up assignments. This works a special hardship on the Jewish child because his whole culture prizes education and places a premium on good relations with the teacher.

Discrimination against Jews in the better hotels is declining, but discrimination persists in some establishments. Some housing areas still have restrictive covenants in the deeds against sale to Jews and Negroes. These restrictive deeds have been declared illegal, but "gentlemen's agreements" are an effective technique in continuing discriminatory practices.

The economic recession of the late 1960's fostered legislative actions against the Jew—not advertised, not widespread, but nonetheless painful for

[15]Thecla Bradshaw and André Renaud, *The Indian Child and Education: Here We Are— Where Do We Go?* (Saskatoon: University of Saskatchewan, 1971).

[16]*Education USA Special Report: Black Studies* (Washington, D.C.: National School Public Relations Association, N.E.A., 1970), pp. 5–9.

the Jewish child who was discriminated against. Public monies were becoming increasingly scarce. Out-of-state quotas for college admissions were established by many legislatures, and specific group quotas were established by many private colleges, enumerating the ten states which included great centers of Jewish population. One Wisconsin legislator, in arguing against the 1967 regulation of the Board of Regents limiting out-of-state students to 15 per cent, and a later more restrictive bill in the legislature, is quoted as saying, "It was to get rid of the Kike from New York and the dirty niggers."[17]

Dorothy Rabinowitz comments, "He [the Jewish student] is visible and overrepresented both among radicals and just plain social changers; he always has been. . . . As goes the current proposals of enlightenment, he goes; and, indeed he goes first, farthest, and fastest. That is the tradition which does not change."[18] The general public, however, has not seemed to identify campus radicalism with Jewry. The Jewish child in the public elementary or secondary school continues to outperform his classmates in academic achievement and in social leadership. The tightly knit families and religious community continue to give emotional security to the young. Anti-Semitism does not seem to be a major problem at this time.

Anti-Catholicism has increased in recent years. The constitutional separation of church and state in the schools may be at least partly responsible. Separately maintained schools may lead to lack of understanding between groups with different backgrounds (Roman Catholic versus Protestant, Jew, and those with no religious affiliation), although two recent studies, separated by half a continent, found no empirical evidence to support this assumption.[19,20] The point on which federal aid to the schools foundered in several sessions of Congress has been the method of distribution within the states as related to children in private and parochial schools versus children in public schools. Many Congressmen could not accept federal aid to private or to parochial schools, even under a "child benefit" theory of state distribution of funds. In the aftermath of the Supreme Court decision of May 17, 1954, holding racial segregation unconstitutional, the racial problem has overshadowed the religious one, but the religious issue alone effectively blocked federal aid to schools. The crux of the problem is that some states furnish free transportation, textbooks, health services, and the like to all children of the state; some states furnish money for the support of education only to public school children. N.E.A.-sponsored bills have proposed that any new federal aid funds be distributed in the same fashion as other state funds. Some Protestants as well as some Catholics have attacked this provision. A high point of the controversy was reached in the widely publicized debate between Eleanor Roosevelt and Francis Cardinal Spellman in 1954; then debate subsided until the early days of the Kennedy administration. The emphasis on federal aid to education shifted from "general" aid

[17]Dorothy Rabinowitz, "Are Jewish Students Different?" Change, Vol. No. III, 4 (Summer 1971), p. 49.

[18]Ibid., pp. 48–50.

[19]Joseph H. Fichter, S.J., Parochial School (Notre Dame, Ind.: University of Notre Dame Press, 1958).

[20]Peter H. and Alice S. Rossi, "Some Effects of Parochial School Education in America," Daedalus, Vol. 90, No. 2 (Spring, 1961), pp. 300–328.

to highly specific programs for provision of science equipment, language laboratories, government loans and grants to college students, and so on. The Catholic universities profited from these federal funds. Much furor has been created in educational and in religious circles over this use of federal funds to further Catholic higher education, thereby further contributing to the consolidation of anti-Catholic prejudices.

The Elementary and Secondary Schools Act of 1965 carried the principle of the "child benefit theory" into categorical federal aid to all schools —public, parochial, and private—in such areas as textbooks, transportation, compensatory education, and so on. Other federal acts which provide significant aid to pupils in parochial and private schools are the National School Lunch Act of 1946, Agricultural Act of 1949, Federal Property and Administrative Services Act of 1949, Science Foundation Act of 1950, Economic Opportunity Act of 1964, Higher Education Act of 1965, Child Nutrition Act of 1956, National Highway Safety Act of 1966, and the Vocational Educational Amendments of 1968. Many states have statutes providing for public support for parochial and private schools in such areas as bus transportation, textbook loans, school lunch, health services, and so on. Several states are considering issuing vouchers to pay for the education of *all* children in their jurisdictions.[21]

Such expanding aid to parochial and private schools, of course, has met with organized opposition. A surprising source of opposition is the National Association of (Catholic) Laymen, who contend that, "the parochial system has outlived its usefulness and ought to be phased out." [22] The prestigious Education Commission of the States, however, seems to feel that "state aid to nonpublic schools may no longer be a question of 'whether' to help, but 'how.' . . . We can no longer avoid the realization . . . that the future of private schools will have an effect on our public school system." [23] Opposition groups agree that the "effect" is relevant, but they disagree as to the nature of the effect. They contend that the Constitution forbids it and that the economic realities of the times do not allow the taxpayer adequately to support one system, let alone two or more systems. Further complicating the picture is the number of private academies mushrooming in the South as a means to maintain segregation, although the language of most of the acts specifically excludes from federal support any school clearly practicing segregation, and the courts have denied funds in cases where state funds had been so allocated.

There has been much discussion on the effect of separate parochial school systems in maintaining religious discrimination against Catholics. At the very least, separate school systems limit contact between Catholic children and children of other faiths. This deliberate segregation of children could mean limiting the growth of understanding between the groups, limiting friendship ties, and even building antagonism by fostering differences. In the light of recent studies that find no evidence to support these assumptions, it seems more likely that anti-Catholic sentiments have continuing

---

[21]*Education U.S.A. Special Report: Religion and the Schools* (Washington, D.C.: National School Public Relations Association, 1970), p. 13.
[22]Ibid., p. 18.
[23]Ibid., p. 3.

reinforcement from the feeling among many non-Catholics that the vigorous growth in the parochial school system of the Roman Catholic Church has been accompanied by growing Catholic resistance to public school taxes. Now that state and federal monies are going to parochial schools, possibly for *full* support in the foreseeable future, the economic factor seems destined to accentuate anti-Catholicism further.

Religious discrimination against Catholics has been most pronounced in the area of job opportunities. In the 1920's to write the word *Catholic* in the space provided for religious preference on some job application forms was equivalent to ensuring rejection of the application; on others, religious preference was the deciding factor in choosing between equivalent candidates. Civil rights legislation designed to assist the Negro has proved of significant value to the Catholic job hunter. Many states now have civil rights laws, enforced by separate civil rights commissions, making it illegal to identify a job candidate by race, color, or creed. These laws were codified at the national level by the Civil Rights Act of 1964. Both labor and management are experiencing major difficulty with this act. If one cannot discriminate on the basis of sex, then does a man also lose his job after the birth of his first child? Or a second illegitimate child? These are common management policies affecting women. Test cases are in the courts at the time of this writing. The language of the act appears clear. Management policies affecting only women appear doomed. It appears equally clear that personnel practices discriminating against Catholics in employment are illegal. The Civil Rights Commission will police the action.

As in the case of anti-Semitism, parental fears of intermarriage probably play a significant part in building anti-Catholic and anti-Protestant prejudice in children. Research evidence indicates the instability of mixed-faith marriages, thereby reinforcing the fears of parents. Whatever the reasons, there seems to be some increase in anti-Catholicism in recent years. Of course, this is not to suggest that individual Catholics cannot overcome the generalized feeling of anti-Catholicism. John Fitzgerald Kennedy broke the religious barrier; others can do so.

National Differences

National differences, fortunately, are mainly of historic interest in America; the treatment of Spanish Americans is the primary exception. During the past generation there has been little immigration. Our high population mobility has helped to disperse the second generation from the "foreign colonies" in our large cities. With differences minimized through removal of the foreign accent and through dispersion of residence throughout the total population, second-generation immigrants have only minor problems of acculturation. Some discrimination based on national origins still persists, but severe problems are limited to a few recently immigrating groups.

This has not always been true in America. The waves of Irish in the 1850's, the Germans in the 1880's, and the southeastern Europeans in the twentieth century have suffered, each in their turn, from discriminatory practices of the established residents. In times of prosperity the immigrant was welcomed as a source of cheap labor but was held at a social distance as an inferior being. He did not talk, dress, think, or even eat like Americans. He had different ideas on how to rear his children. His diet seemed peculiar. In short, he was different. Because he was different, he must be inferior. Because he was inferior, he was not acceptable to "100 per cent" Americans. He could secure housing only in slum areas; because the areas where he lived had a high incidence of crime and violence, he was blamed for "crime waves." In times of economic depression, discriminatory practices grew much more severe. He was blamed for the depression. He was vilified by movements such as the Know Nothing Party of the mid-nineteenth century, the Ku Klux Klan of the 1920's, and the National Council for American Education of the post-World War II period. He was subject to all the physical misery of the lowest class in times of depression, plus the psychological torture of the social outcast.

Spanish Americans currently are subject to many of these discriminatory practices. Puerto Rican immigrants, particularly in the New York City area, suffer considerable discrimination. The unskilled laborer with limited or no command of the English language receives only the lowest-paying positions and lives in the least desirable quarters. Acculturation is to the norm of his neighbors, the lower-class American Negro. Itinerant Mexican laboring groups have similarly severe problems in the Southwest and Far West, as do Cuban refugees in Florida.

Mixed marriages of Spanish Americans and Negroes produce offspring subject to the minority-status problems of both groups.

Sex Differences: Women's Liberation

The Equal Pay Act of 1963 (passed as an amendment to the Fair Labor Standards Act), Title VII of the Civil Rights Act of 1964, and Executive Orders 11246 (September 1965) and 11375 (October 1967) apparently codified the demand by the Women's Liberation movement for the end of economic discrimination on the basis of sex before the leaders of Women's Liberation even sounded the battle cry. MAPI Memorandum IR-28 refers to this complex of laws as "a formidable legal mandate calling for equal employment of women in the workplace." [24]

It may be true that "Partly as a joke, Congressman Howard W. Smith of Virginia, then 81, added 'sex' to the section of the 1964 Civil Rights Act that prohibited discrimination on the basis of 'race, color, religion, or national origin", [25] however, feminists rapidly capitalized on the "joke," with approximately 20 per cent of the charges of discrimination in employment filed in the late 1960's with the Equal Employment Opportunity Commission. The complaints got results. Hosts of new jobs opened to women, who were now employed as jockeys and telephone switchmen, for example. Working conditions changed dramatically for others; for example, airline stewardesses won the right to work after the age of thirty-two. Soon we may anticipate female firemen, disc jockeys, and garbage collectors and an expanded role

---

[24] "Equal Pay for Equal Work," *Industrial Relations Memorandum*, August 28, 1970 (Washington, D.C.: Machinery and Allied Products Institute, 1970), p. 2.

[25] "The New Feminists: Revolt Against 'Sexism'," *Time*, November 21, 1969, p. 54.

for the women's auxillaries of the military forces, possibly even with equal status in all areas, including combat duty.

Women's Liberation as a formal movement seems to have begun with the formation in 1966 of NOW (National Organization for Women). A strong, unified, national organization did not develop from NOW, but in the late 1960's and early 1970's a number of splinter groups formed simultaneously, espousing similar and dissimilar goals, all under the generic umbrella of Women's Liberation. The common denominators seemed to be (1) membership from the upper middle class, particularly college students and faculty, with a strong urge to relate to the working-class woman but with relatively little success, as evidenced by the small size of most units; (2) militant espousal of women's rights in those areas where women traditionally have felt oppressed but have not expressed their grievances publicly: (a) abortion laws, (b) unequal pay for equal work, (c) management opportunities (not covered under the Equal Pay Act of 1963, but included in Title VII of the Civil Rights Act of 1964 and the Executive Orders of 1965 and 1967), and (d) need for free child-care centers and other special conditions of employment related to child bearing. Some autonomous units and some vocal minorities within units are much concerned with rights for lesbians, cohabitation, and so on, but preoccupation with sexual activities does not seem to be the mode of the new feminist. Brassiere burning may be dramatic, but it misses the point of the movement. The Womens' Liberators generally seem to be intent upon equal status with men in all areas of life. As Marilyn Bender put it, "Women's Liberation is a catch-all label for the second phase of the movement for total equality for slightly more than half of the United States population. In the first phase, women won the vote. Now they're going for broke." [26]

In the early 1970's management seemed the hardest nut for the Women's Liberators to crack. Orth and Jacobs comment, "women certainly have begun to push, but changes in male attitudes do not appear to reflect the extent of that pushing." [27] They note that surveys of male and female executives report that approximately 40 per cent express mildly or strongly unfavorable attitudes toward women in management, with approximately another 25 per cent indifferent. The title and tenor of their article, however, give hope to women; they classify as outmoded the behavioral norms and role expectations reflected in such traditional (and current) male comments as, "Women can't work while they have young children," "Women executives make everyone uncomfortable at staff meetings," "Women are emotionally incapable of coping with crises," and "Women have to stay near to where their husband works." They report that, "For every woman with a title there are many men with lesser titles and higher pay," but they also comment that, "The signals of change are obvious; younger men and women have become more and more alike . . . traditional roles are breaking down." [28] It may well be that changing family roles may coordinate with civil rights legislation

[26]Marilyn Bender, "The Women Who'd Trade in Their Pedestal for Total Equality," *New York Times*, February 4, 1970, Section C, p. 30.
[27]Charles D. Orth, III, and Frederich Jacobs, "Women in Management: Pattern for Change," *Harvard Business Review*, July–August 1971, p. 140.
[28]Ibid., pp. 141, 142.

to give the American woman greater access to management positions; but in 1970 nearly half the personnel of major corporations were women, but less than 10 per cent of the supervisors and managers were women. The same pertains to many other professional fields in America. Women represent 1 per cent of the engineers, 3 per cent of the lawyers, and 7 per cent of the doctors; further, women's pay is often less than half that of men.[29]

The Women's Liberation movement, of course, is not limited to America. Japan's widespread labor shortage of the early 1970's (six jobs waiting for every high school graduate) has given Japanese women access to jobs as taxi drivers, ship builders, teachers, secretaries, and even managers.[30] Canadian women have been successful in focusing national attention on the abortion laws, with great hope of success in actually forcing legislation for free and legal abortions.[31] The expressed concern in Canada is sexual; in Japan it is economic; but in both cases the overriding theme is equality with men. And who can grant this equality? The Establishment, controlled in America by the WASPs who are the husbands and fathers of the leaders of Women's Liberation. Despite these ties, one sociologist comments, "How many of us are on the outside and alienated from the Establishment? Surely students, the black and the poor. And women." [32]

What does this mean for the school? Many analyses of the child and adolescent literature commonly found in school textbooks reveal clear definition of male and female roles. The male is intelligent, adventurous, successful. The female is charming, supportive, and a home body. Are these portrayals realistic? If not, do we need a whole new set of literature, or merely teachers intelligent enough to assist children and youth in critical comparisons of the romanticism of their texts with the realities of life? More importantly, how should the new realities of an era of Women's Liberation affect teacher's attitudes and behavior toward children and youth? Must, or even should, we insist upon girls behaving like "little ladies," should teachers continue to tolerate boys dominating the positions as class officers and on student councils? What about the traditional social amenities? Who should open the door or hold the chairs for whom? The authors are not suggesting that teachers should proceed as though the Women's Liberation movement already had achieved perfect equality between male and female; after all, the militant Liberationists were a tiny minority of the total population in the early 1970's, even though they claimed to speak for all women. The authors are suggesting that teachers study their own communities for local reaction to the goals of Women's Liberation. We are not proposing that teachers immediately "teach as the community expects." We do maintain that it is the professional responsibility of the teacher to know *what* the community expects, whether it be equality for all persons in all areas of life or a strong demand that women return to the homes and free jobs for the "breadwinners," particularly in times of economic recession.

[29] "The New Feminist," op. cit., p. 54.

[30] Japanese Women Join the Lib Movement," *Business Week*, April 10, 1971, pp. 70–72.

[31] Marlene Dixon, "On Women's Liberation," *The Sheaf*, January 19, 1971, pp. 4–5.

[32] Kate Millett, "Libbies, Smithies, Vassarites," *Change*, Vol. 2, No. 5 (September–October 1970), p. 43.

Age Differences: Youth

Seldom does any single age group, cutting across lines of class, race, religion, and ethnic origin, speak with a single voice, in tones loud enough to command national attention, but such is now the case with youth. The age range of youth is approximately between eighteen and twenty-nine. Voices come from different quarters, with superficially different messages— lower-class youth have no jobs, black youth suffer both social and ecomonic discrimination, urban youth have no hostels for their summer nomadism, high school youth are embattled over dress and grooming, college youth have no control of the curriculum, hippy youth are restricted in the use of drugs and in sexual freedom—but the common message is clear: *Alienation from the Establishment.* One might say that the common factor is resistance to the draft for the hateful war in Vietnam, for both boys and girls of all ages are protesting; but this seems to be a symptom, rather than a cause, of the psychic unrest of the youth of our times.

How serious is the problem? This age group consisted of nearly one of every five Americans in 1970.[33] Of this number the range of "expert" opinion is all the way from "an overwhelming majority of the young—as many as 80 per cent—tend to be traditionalist in values".[34] to "the institutional and parental power base has been shaken by the sudden and volcanic force of the young."[35] The preponderance of the literature seems to favor the latter view. Both sides cite research studies, sometimes the same studies with different interpretations. What does seem clear is that the youth movement *is* of major concern to the nation. It does not matter whether 20 per cent or 80 per cent of youth are affected, whether campus youth are truly speaking for all youth, whether this is the traditional generation gap or a unique phenomenon of our times; what matters is that the nation perceives it as a unique problem. If it is so perceived, then it is a problem, and the problem is compounded by defensive reactions to it by authority figures: parents, police, and civic and school officials.

Not all adult reactions, of course, are defensive. The *Report of the CASSA Curriculum Subcommittee on Current Status of Student Involvement in Curriculum Development in California High Schools, 1969–70* indicated that nearly 20 per cent of all California schools allow student involvement in curriculum development, and that the great majority of the student-involving schools had begun the practice within the preceding two years.[36]

The youth movement may be led by a minority of youth but if so, certainly that minority is getting results. An *Education USA Special Report*, dated

[33]Extrapolated from *Advance Report, 1970 Census of Population (PC–V2–1)* (Washington, D.C.: Bureau of the Census, February 1971). Data compiled, in part, by halving the Census data for the twenty-five to thirty-four age group for inclusion with other data on the eighteen to twenty-nine age groups; this probably underestimates the twenty-five to twenty-nine age group, but is sufficiently close for the "one in every five Americans" cited.

[34]Joseph Adelson, "What Generation Gap?" *The New York Times Magazine*, January 18, 1970, p. 11.

[35]Mario D. Fantini, "The Student Movement and School Reform," in Hart and Saylor (eds.), *Student Unrest, Threat or Promise?* (Washington, D.C.: A.S.C.D., 1970), p. 47.

[36]"Students are Changing the Secondary School Curriculum," *NASSP Spotlight*, No. 97 (March–April 1971) (Washington, D.C.: N.A.S.S.P., N.E.A., 1971), p. 2.

1969, commences, "Bubbling like supercharged soda, student unrest exploded in 1968 and sprayed the high school landscape with boycotts, demonstrations, sit-ins, picketing, vandalism, and violence."[37] It proceeds to identify the major causes of high school student unrest as (1) race, (2) dress and grooming, (3) curriculum, (4) personnel (inept teachers), and (5) regulations for personal behavior and organizational structure (rigid administrators). Principals have reported each of the preceding five areas as major factors in over one third of their school protests.

Although the preceding five areas may be the verbalized issues, the editors of *Education USA Special Report on High School Student Unrest* felt that the basic messages of students were the following: "(a) Listen to us— for all you know, we might have something. (b) Treat us like adults and maybe we'll act that way. (c) Cut us in on the action—it's our school as well as yours. (d) Teach us what we need to know *now*, so that we can use it in our lives."[38]

It should not take sophisticated professionals to give us these messages; all that we need is to *listen* to our own students. Direct quotes from a young black participant on a panel sponsored by the editors of *Today's Education* follow:

> Basically, my school has the same problems that exist in all of our schools. There has to be a change in the traditional ways of education, and it has to come soon. . . . The courses today do prepare you for college, but we need courses to teach people how to get along. Let's face it. The conditions in this country are coming to a point where pretty soon things are going to blow. So, teaching people how to work with each other is important.[39]

And it does not require adults to point students in constructive directions for peaceful change within the system. *The Shape of Education for 1970–71* reports a number of activities initiated and conducted by youth, ranging from tutoring ghetto children in Minneapolis to ecological research in Schenectady.[40] Elsila reports on students actually organizing and operating their own shared-time high school, with a black studies curriculum in the Freedom Annex of Eastern High School in Washington, D.C.[41]

The college research follows the pattern of research on high school unrest understandably, for the college disturbances preceded the high school disruptions, and probably for the same reasons, although it is not necessarily true that the college unrest "filtered down to the high school," as claimed by many disturbed high school principals. In discussing the problems of youth in the modern world, Maxine Greene looks through the other end of the telescope in saying, "we older people are the immigrants, the aliens in the new technological world. . . . We think too seldom about what it

[37]*Education USA Special Report: High School Student Unrest* (Washington, D.C.: N.S.P.R.A., N.E.A., 1969), p. 1.

[38]Ibid., p. 7.

[39]"What's Troubling High School Students?" *Today's Education*, September 1970, pp. 32–33.

[40]"New Brand of Activist: The Student Volunteer," *The Shape of Education for 1970–71* (Washington, D.C.: N.S.P.R.A., N.E.A., 1971), pp. 62–64.

[41]David Elsila, "A Student-Run Accredited School; D.C. Strivers Create Their Own Thing," *American Teacher*, Vol. 53, No. 3 (November 1968), p. 12.

is like to be young in a country apparently dominated by a military-industrial complex impervious to individual desire and demand." [42] Fantini posits an interesting theory, that we who went through the Depression and World War II are the lucky ones; we escaped the monotony facing modern youth. He says of youth, "Their parents have provided them with comfort, yet they crave the sensations of struggle. . . . Many are exhilarated by the revolutionary game, for it provides them with the risks and rewards which suburban monotony has taken away." [43] Peter Marin seems to be speaking for most of the writers on the subject when he says, "the psyche of this culture is post-industrial, relatively unrepressed, less literate and vocal, a new combination of elements, almost a new strain." [44] Mario D. Fantini, co-author of *Toward a Contact Curriculum*, probably best summarizes when he says:

> All students are responding to their visions of themselves as victims— victims of an institution and a society-at-large which have repeatedly and undeniably refused to recognize them. Even the most disparate splinter groups are expressing common, and essentially emotional, grievances. All students, regardless of specific affiliations, want to be *seen*; they want to be acknowledged as thinking, feeling human beings. Second, they want to participate in the process of their education. How very obvious it seems—look, if this school is supposed to be for *me*, then let me tell you how I feel about it. Finally, students want their curriculum to be applicable to their individual lives—culturally, politically, socially, and personally. The cry for "relevance" is also painfully self-evident; who wants to study something he can't "relate" to? All three of these demands, though they have political translations like "democracy" and "freedom," stem from the most fundamental human needs, needs which the school has persisted in ignoring.[45]

What does this mean for the school? One approach might be to step back a bit from the problem, and see what "outsiders" think of it. A staff writer for *MacLean's*—admittedly not impartial, for American social and economic structures dominate Canadian life, but at least a most interested and involved non-American observer, states: "On the Left, there's Jerry Rubin and Abbie Hoffman urging a violent revolution. On the Right, there's Richard Nixon and Spiro Agnew calling anti-war demonstrators 'effete snobs' and 'bums.' And that's the problem. Americans no longer reason together. They choose up sides. . . ." [46]

In a summary of this series of short articles, James Eayrs notes: "The derangement of democracy in America may persist past 1972, but it can't go on forever. We can't do much about it, but then we don't need to do much about it. Americans are now their own severest critics. Along with avenging destroyers intent on burning the place down are men of good will intent upon rescue, and we should wish them well." [47]

[42]Maxine Greene, "The Spectrum of Disenchantment," in Hart and Saylor (eds.), op. cit., pp. 4–15.

[43]Fantini, op. cit., p. 55.

[44]Peter Marin, "The Open Truth and Fiery Vehemence of Youth: A Sort of Soliloquy," *The Center Magazine*, Vol. 2, No. 1 (January 1969), pp. 61–64.

[45]Fantini, op. cit., pp. 51–52.

[46]"How to Live Next Door to America Without Getting Burned," *MacLean's*, Vol. 83, No. 8 (August 1970), p. 1.

[47]Ibid., p. 8.

Can we reason together? If so, we need first to heed the advice of our students, to listen to one another; and Nichols points out that we listen at only a 25 per cent level of efficiency, but he also points out ways we can improve our efficiency.[48] We need, as a part of listening to one another, to treat our students as *persons*, not as inferior beings. The teacher has been the monarch of the classroom for too long. Now comes the revolution! Either the king listens, or he will be deposed. This will be especially hard for teachers; they recently have won their battles to be included in policy decisions within the school and they will not readily share this hard-won right with others, especially students. *The Education USA Special Report on High School Student Unrest* offers many suggestions to teachers. Let us close with an extensive quote from that report, directed to administrators but equally applicable to teachers:

> Where there exists a closed system—where rigid control and repression are emphasized . . . where "law and order" are paramount . . . where the administration and the teachers "know what is good for the student" . . . where students' concerns come AFTER the course content . . . where the curriculum is revised and the dress and behavior code has been laid down by the administration . . . where the student is only a number or a faceless unit in the class— there we will find the psychosocioeducational mix for student unrest, for disorder, violence, and riots. . . . When the confrontation comes—and it will in the "closed system" described above—the administrator would do well to review the following insights on coping with the tensions and disruptions of militant youth:
>
> > Feelings of distrust, animosity, rage, and frustration will almost always be directed toward what the dissident group perceives as a focus or seat of authority (power). This will probably be the superintendent and/or principal. These feelings will not be clearly articulated but will likely be expressed in radical, irrational accusations—frequently in the form of general or gross indictments based on a single or, at best, a few specific examples. For instance: "The teachers are prejudiced—we want that stopped—Now!"
> > Because of a natural tendency for most youth to suspect the adult, the unconcerned or noninvolved student can be quickly enlisted in the dissident group by either an effective emotional appeal by his peers or an overreactive repressive response from the authorities.
> > Repressive force—excessive to the need—will result in more intense dissidence. Overreaction is self-defeating because it strengthens the position of the radical leadership—among the uncommitted as well as the committed.
> > Although violent disorder must be met with adequate controlling force, a climate receptive to negotiation and discussion must be assured the responsible, rational spokesmen among the dissidents. Channels for communication must always be kept open, by direct or indirect means.
> > In most instances, the administration will have to give up some things. This sharing power or conceding changes need not mean appeasement or concession. Student grievances are not always unreasonable, invalid or wrong. Indeed, it matters less whether the grievance is valid than that the grievance is genuinely felt by the students. If problems didn't exist in the minds of students, there would be no dissidence to begin with. Real or imagined, these problems must be dealt with.

[48]Ralph G. Nichols, "Do We Know How to Listen? Practical Helps in a Modern Age," in J. Jeffey Auer (ed.), *The Rhetoric of Our Times* (New York: Meredith, 1969), pp. 227–236.

Trust—the most vital element of all—may have to be achieved through risk-taking. This may involve sharing power, permitting students to make a poor decision, admitting you're wrong, abandoning traditional rules and regulations, placing reasonable student concerns above all else!

Students do not want to take over schools—they want to be heard, and heeded.

In negotiating on grievances, students want results, not promises. Deferral and postponement only heighten suspicion and ill will. Even a negative decision, given with reasons promptly and concisely, will minimize any credibility gap. It might prevent, and will defuse much of the dissidents' ammunition.[49]

Regional Differences

As we have indicated in Chapter 11, there are great currents of population movement in America. Some of these relocations of large segments of the population cause severe problems of intergroup relations. The Southern white mountaineer who moves to the industrial cities of the North enters an entirely new culture, where he may experience discrimination from the established residents. The Southern Negro who moves from the cotton fields to the Northern cities must adjust to new ways of living; his problems of adjustment may be accentuated by discrimination based on both color and regional differences. The pensioner who retires to the West Coast may be resented by families with school-age children as a potential threat to the passage of school tax levies, and by the general populace as a potential drain on the entire taxable wealth of the state through eligibility for state pensions. The problems of each group are different and are specific to the characteristics and needs of the groups involved, but the general pattern of discrimination through fear of the newcomer is employed against most of them.

So it goes for the victims of discrimination, whether the prejudice is based on differences in social class, race, religion, national origin, or region. Each minority group is different from another, but all suffer discrimination, for as Hirsh so aptly put it, "the victims of prejudice have little to do with the cause of it. They are likely to be people whom a tragic combination of circumstances has rendered both accessible and vulnerable and therefore eminently suited for victimization by those casting around for someone on whom to unleash the full force of their fears."[50]

RATIONALE OF INTERGROUP PROBLEMS

There must be some reason or reasons for Americans who profess to believe in democracy to violate those beliefs by maltreating fellow Americans. This dilemma is compounded when one reflects that most Americans profess to adhere to the values of the Judaeo-Christian tradition, and that discrimination and persecution violate all the precepts embedded in these

[49]Reprinted by special permission from *High School Student Unrest*, pp. 4–5. Copyright 1969, National School Public Relations Association.

[50]Selma G. Hirsh, *The Fears Men Live By* (New York: Harper, 1955), p. 104.

faiths. Teachers need to summarize the salient facts of the psychology of groups in an attempt to clarify these reasons.

We have tended to treat the diverse groups in America on a majority–minority basis. The majority have power on their side, so we have not concerned ourselves with their problems. This does not mean that they have no problems, for the deterioration of the moral fiber of the majority group through discriminatory practices that violate their values is a major reason for the psychic unrest of our times. Allport estimates that "group prejudice is an active force in the lives of perhaps four-fifths of our fellow-citizens." [51] In the following brief presentation of the social psychology of discrimination, perhaps the implications for deterioration of the moral fiber of the majority group will become more clear. The major purpose of this section, however, is to enable educators better to understand the psychology of prejudice as a first step in formulating plans to combat it.

Minority Status

Minority status is not a quantitative affair, but a qualitative one. The basis for minority status is lack of power and prestige. The evidence of minority status is discrimination. The attitudinal configuration that leads to discrimination is prejudice, namely, an attitude of prejudging individuals on the basis of their race, social class, religion, national origin, region, or some other characteristic.

Origins of Prejudice

How does prejudice come about? Basically it stems from a feeling that one culture, class, race, religion, or other group is superior to another. Then how do we get that way? Why do we feel superior? Much new knowledge has become available on the dynamics of prejudice. A monumental series has been completed under the sponsorship of the American Jewish Committee.[52] In a popular interpretation of this series, founded in great part on *The Authoritarian Personality*, Hirsh states that "the central thesis of this book is that people are prejudiced because they are afraid. They use their prejudices to conceal their fears." [53]

Men suffer from fears largely because they fail to develop as children the basic emotional security necessary for the integrating personality. Disturbed personalities may reach for emotional security through feelings of superiority. If an individual feels that his group is superior to another group, he enjoys the personal security of his own worth as compared to that of individuals of the "out-group"; he also enjoys the group security gained by power of group action. Hitler capitalized on this phenomenon of group psychology by propagating the myth of Aryan superiority.

---

[51]Gordon W. Allport, *The Bigot in Our Midst* (New York: American Jewish Committee, 1957), p. 2.

[52]Max Horkheimer and Samuel H. Flowerman (ed.), Studies in Prejudice Series: *The Authoritarian Personality; Dynamics of Prejudice; Anti-Semitism and Emotional Disorder; Rehearsal for Destruction;* and *Prophets of Deceit* (New York: Harper, 1949–1950).

[53]Hirsh, op. cit., p. xi.

Another major origin of prejudice is the sociological fact that majority influence establishes the patterns of behavior for any society, and that minorities are "judged" by their degree of conformity to the established cultural norms. The white Anglo-Saxon Protestant is dominant in contemporary America. Middle-class values are the cultural norm. Any other color, national origin, religion, or class value will be prejudged by the majority group in terms of its degree of conformity to the majority pattern. Your authors maintain in a later section on the integration crisis that this was a major source of the resistance to school integration. Your authors feel that white parents did not picket the public schools of New York City because their children were attending school with Negroes and Puerto Ricans, but because their children were in classes with children whose cultural background did not allow them to progress academically at the same speed as children with middle-class backgrounds. In short, they felt that their children were being sacrificed on the altar of integration. This is a common source of tension in our culture. Those persons now accepted as middle class strive to maintain their place, while others exert great effort to become middle class themselves.[54]

The civil rights legislation of the late 1960's seemed to herald the decline and fall of the WASP, with his domination of the cultural norms of America: honesty, neatness, punctuality, devotion to duty, hard work, sense of public service, rational approach to problems even in the midst of swirling passions, and, admittedly, repression of dissenters, rigidity in maintaining the Establishment. The January 17, 1969, issue of *Time*, however, points out that the WASP still represents 55 per cent of the population; holds almost 90 per cent of the directorships of the fifty largest corporations; holds about 80 per cent of the directorships of the ten largest banks and of the richest universities; and is still overwhelmingly in control of law firms and brokerage houses, Congress, the officer cadre of the Armed Forces, and the policies of both major political parties.[55] The events of the late 1960's have shaken the WASP hold on the value systems of America, but they have not broken it. California is shearing the hairy jobless of unemployment insurance benefits, on the grounds that their appearance makes them unavailable for employment.[56] Deviants still are being "prejudged" by the majority group.

Another good example of judging by degree of conformity to the established cultural norms is provided by discrimination based on national origin. The newly arrived immigrant was the subject of much discrimination. He had left his old culture but had not yet assimilated the new. He clung to old ways of doing things because he knew no other ways. He might not even have had a working knowledge of English. Second-generation immigrants were reared in the new culture and assimilated as many of its patterns as were not in violent conflict with parental patterns. The third generation virtually escaped discrimination based on national origin, for the new ways of living were firmly entrenched, but social class discrimination

[54]Margaret Rasmussen (ed.), *Implications of Basic Human Values for Education* (Washington, D.C.: Association for Childhood Education International, 1964), p. 38.

[55]"Are the WASPs Coming Back? Have They Ever Been Away?" *Time*, January 17, 1971, pp. 24–25.

[56]"The Hairy Jobless Are Shorn of Benefits" *Business Week*, July 24, 1971, p. 34.

might persist because of the relegation of his grandfathers to the lower class. Individuals may escape class bonds. The middle-class values taught in the public schools are their greatest aid in escape.

Finally, the psychological climate of the times may intensify mild prejudice into overt discrimination by the majority group. This may be only verbal, as exemplified by name calling. More often it develops into denial of job opportunities, with the attendant deprivations in health, nutrition, housing, and clothing. Some of the crises in men's affairs that accentuate prejudice are wars, depressions, floods, drought, and other national calamities. In such times the psychological insecurity of the majority group leads them to seek a scapegoat. Minority groups are convenient victims on which to vent their frustrations. It has been reported, for example, that there was a high correlation between the incidence of Negro lynchings in the South and the price of cotton.

The psychological climate of the times also may intensify existing prejudices through actions of the minority group. The mass sit-ins, freedom marches, forced school integration, and so on, of the 1960's undoubtedly forced many whites to re-examine their prejudices. Undoubtedly many persons who considered themselves only mildly prejudiced became much more prejudiced when their children were bused from the white, suburban school to the predominantly Negro school in a slum neighborhood.

Economic and social insecurity accentuates prejudice. As any group is forced to share its material wealth with another group, the "have" group rejects the "have-not" group. This seemed dramatically true of lower-middle-class America in the early 1970's. Schneider speaks of the "alienation of a large segment of the population, the white working class . . . . up to sixty or seventy million (persons) . . . . from $5,000, or $6,000 to somewhere around $15,000 a year . . . . the buffer between the ghetto and the affluent society." [57] He negotiates through his union for a good raise, only to see it decimated by inflation. He sees the opening of crafts to uncontrolled apprenticeship programs. Unless new jobs are created, this means unemployment for him. He sees the college-bound sons of outer suburbia deferred from the draft, while his sons go to Vietnam. He sees cut-backs in aerospace and related industries as the Vietnam War de-escalates, with no governmental provisions for rapid conversion to a peace-time economy. San Francisco, for example, with a construction boom in the downtown area, still had a 1970 unemployment rate of 15 per cent in the building trades. Not only are jobs in mass production and many crafts mind-deadeningly repetitive, they also are held in contempt by society, so one is bored on the job and ashamed off the job. These are precisely the jobs threatened by automation, and the lower-middle-class American has no training for any other kind. The political parties give him no platforms or candidates which clearly sharpen party differences on issues, so the ballot box offers little hope of relief. Even the streets are no longer safe; violence no longer is confined to the ghettos. Welfare, child care, and so on, are not available to him, but the tax support comes from his salary, for the benefit of those making almost

[57]Michael M. Schneider, "Middle America: A Study in Frustration." *National Elementary Principal*, Vol. L, No. 5 (April 1971), p. 32.

as much as he. He is desperate. So how does he react? As Schneider puts it, the "white working class guy is more likely to transfer his economic and social frustrations into racial and ethnic prejudices, and now we are seeing more and more overt hostility."[58] Is the backlash against gains provided the lower classes through civil rights legislation? Of course; this is a typical case of fear translated into prejudice. Schneider fears that this will lead to further violence from a new group. He says, "If he yields to demands for super-seniority for black workers, his family will suffer—really suffer. He will fight for his job before he gives in."[59]

Perpetuation of Prejudice

An oversimplification of the basic reasons for the persistence of prejudice and discrimination in a democratic Judaeo-Christian nation would be the statement that prejudice persists because of (1) ignorance and (2) insecurity. Both are broad terms. Some space will be devoted to delineating the ways in which ignorance and insecurity perpetuate prejudice.

By *ignorance* we mean lack of understanding, both of one's own self and of other people. A man does not always possess full knowledge even of the values by which he guides his own life. He may pledge $1,000 to his church for the support of African missions and secure the $1,000 by charging exorbitant rentals to Negro inhabitants of his slum tenements. He may be convinced that he gave to the mission fund because of Christian compassion for fellow human beings. Could it be that he really pledged because his church group expected it of one in his financial position, and that he fulfilled that expectation in order to maintain his social status? If so, then ignorance of one's own motivations, with the attendant failure to live by a consistent set of values, is one major reason for the perpetuation of prejudice. Certainly the first step toward success in intergroup relations is to "know thyself."

Ignorance of the conditions in which one's fellow man lives certainly is a contributing factor toward the perpetuation of minority status. Full knowledge of minority cultures and full understandings of *why* different groups behave differently would provide a sound basis for rational solutions to intergroup problems. This knowledge must be implemented by emotional conditioning designed for acceptance and appreciation of others.[60] Absence of accurate data about minority groups fosters stereotyping, tabloid thinking, racism, and chauvinism. This is not meant to imply that the supply of knowledge alone will yield significant returns in improved intergroup relations; experience with informational programs has indicated their limitations, as will be shown later. Effective use of informational techniques involves utilizing knowledge as a first step in emotional acceptance of likenesses. Understanding without identification is of limited effectiveness; what is needed is empathy, not sympathy.

Insecurity is a second major block to the brotherhood of man. Basically, all insecurity is psychological, but for purposes of discussion, two broad

[58]Ibid., p. 38.
[59]Ibid.
[60]Hilda Taba (ed.), *Elementary Curriculum in Intergroup Relations* (Washington, D.C.: American Council on Education, 1950), p. 25.

areas contributing to insecurity will be discussed separately: denial of man's emotional needs and denial of man's physical needs.

One means of finding emotional security is through association with people like oneself in order to convince oneself of one's own worth. This leads to the formation of "in-groups." The in-group then comprises a pressure group to foster its own welfare. Discrimination against other groups thus enhances not only the political, social, and economic welfare of the group but also bolsters the psychological security of its members through a feeling of superiority to other groups. When things go wrong the minority group becomes a scapegoat, thus allowing the majority group to escape guilt feelings (feelings of inferiority) for allowing its affairs to deteriorate. The challenge to the white Anglo-Saxon Protestant "in-group" during the integration crisis of the early 1960's led to frustrations among Caucasians so evident that a national candidate for office attempted to capitalize on the white backlash. It is a tribute to the white man's conscience that, despite his obvious feelings of insecurity in the face of the apparent power of the Negro minority group, no significant block of votes seems to have been delivered to the candidate, with the possible exception of the eleven states of the old Confederacy.

Tabloid thinking plays a significant part in perpetuating prejudice. Man thinks only as a last resort, for thinking is painful. What is more natural than the acceptance of stereotyped concepts as a basis for justifying the venting of his anger and frustration on a minority group? Why complicate matters by thinking of individuals when we can rationalize our discrimination against an individual by claiming that his entire group is characterized by negative traits? Verbalizing these stereotyped concepts leads still others of our own group into tabloid thinking; thus is started a new cycle of bigotry, spreading from the newly affected individual.

Allport notes, "Besides venting our fury upon scapegoats for their alleged vices, we go still further and blame them specifically for our *own* sins and shortcomings. The term psychologists give to this mental twist is projection." [61] Projecting our faults upon others allows us to escape our feelings of personal guilt, thus bolstering our emotional security.

Economic insecurity results in spending less for food, clothing, shelter, and recreation, if not in actual deprivation. Economic insecurity tightens the bonds of the majority group and intensifies its discriminatory practices to protect its own welfare; at the same time it intensifies scape goating to relieve guilt feelings and to reassert its own status. Previously mild prejudices may grow into bigotry under the pressures of physcial insecurity. There seems to have been some recognition of the importance of this aspect of the situation in the federal War on Poverty commencing with the Economic Opportunity Act of 1964 and continuing through a series of legislative and executive actions designed to relieve economic insecurity.

Nonrational Nature of Prejudice

The preceding discussion of the social psychology of discrimination presupposes a basic knowledge of the psychology of learning on the part of

[61]Allport, op. cit., p. 4.

the reader. Let us briefly summarize at this point the psychology of the learning of attitudes as it affects the preceding discussion.

Discrimination is overt action. Prejudice is the attitudinal configuration that motivates the act of discrimination. Like most attitudes, *prejudice is learned nonrationally*. Davis[62] says that attitudes are learned (1) by integration of numerous specific responses of a similar type; thus, a series of unpleasant emotional experiences with a certain group of people will lead one to generalize, "All such people are unpleasant," without any rational investigation of the total group; (2) through a single traumatic experience; (3) through general approach or withdrawal tendencies; and (4) through imitation of the attitudes of others in order to secure their affection.

The nonrational nature of prejudice has implications for educators, both in the original learning of these attitudes and in the relearning process that supplants negative attitudes with positive ones. Nonrational, emotional experiences are the ones that implant prejudice. The educator needs to utilize this knowledge. The approach to intergroup problems must not be a coldly scientific one or it is doomed to failure. Attitudes are not formed in rational fashion. Rational approaches need to be strongly reinforced through presentation in highly emotional situations. The teacher needs to be an "actor," with a sound working knowledge of all the dramatic techniques available to the intergroup educator. This is true both for the original implantation of attitudes and for the supplanting of negative attitudes. Psychiatrists utilize psychodrama for securing maximum emotional involvement of the individual in psychiatric treatment of negative attitudes. The educator does not have the technical competence necessary to use psychodrama, but sociodrama and other techniques that secure a relatively high degree of emotional involvement are available to him. The preceding observation by Davis about the adoption of the attitudes of others in order to gain their favor certainly operates daily in classroom and playground situations; children often adopt the attitudes that the teacher displays toward members of minority groups. Teachers need to demonstrate clearly their friendly feelings toward minority-group members; they must utilize emotional techniques with individuals and groups if they are to be successful in supplanting negative attitudes and implanting positive ones.

The preceding is not meant to imply that educators are not currently using emotional techniques. The daily pledge to the flag, class discussion of emotionally charged problems, the satisfaction of successful committee work with members of other groups, the warm smile and hug of the primary teacher for the newcomer in her room, and the use of dramatic films are but a few examples of the many ways in which educators are recognizing the interdependence of intellectual and emotional learnings.

TOWARD THE RESOLUTION OF INTERGROUP PROBLEMS

The short-term solution to intergroup problems in America seems to be legal action to protect the rights of minorities and to improve the economic and social status of underprivileged groups. The long-term solution seems to

[62]Jerome Davis, "Study of 163 Outstanding Communist Leaders," *Proceedings American Sociological Society*, Vol. 24 (1930), pp. 42–45.

be education. Both legal action and educative forces must be brought to bear on those areas where the effects of discrimination are most severely felt: employment, housing, recreation, and education. Industry must bear a major share of the responsibility for ending discriminatory practices in employment. Labor must open the doors to apprenticeships in the skilled trades. The public schools bear a major responsibility, but full discussion of the role of the school will be deferred until the final sections of this chapter. Federal legal action—including federal legislation, presidential investigations, executive orders and enforcement agencies, and Supreme Court decisions—and agencies of education other than the schools will be discussed.

Legal Action

Social legislation needs both to protect the legal rights of the populace and to improve the economic and social welfare of all citizens. We shall discuss briefly American social legislation and other steps of a legal nature currently affecting minority groups, with some consideration of the speed with which such steps should proceed.

Legal Steps to Protect the Rights of Minorities. Laws do not, of course, eliminate prejudice. However, a state may be neutral with respect to the acts of the citizen affecting the rights of minorities, or it may be positive in taking measures to prevent acts of discrimination against those minorities. Some states, such as Nazi Germany or the Union of South Africa, have taken active steps to deny or restrict rights and privileges to certain minorities. The trend in recent years in the United States has been toward positive efforts on the part of the government to protect the rights of minorities. Earlier governmental action was less vigorous.

Most of these legal measures have been taken since 1941, under the pressures of World War II and of post-World War II events. President Franklin D. Roosevelt in 1941 and 1943 issued executive orders prohibiting discrimination on government contracts and requiring a clause in such contracts that would prevent discrimination against any employee or applicant because of race, creed, color, or national origin. He set up the Federal Fair Employment Practice Committee to police these executive orders. After World War II President Truman attempted to make the FEPC a permanent agency, but the proposal was turned down by Congress. President Truman soon afterward issued an executive order declaring nondiscrimination to be government policy and requiring the same policy of all government contractors. In 1953 President Eisenhower confirmed the policy of nondiscrimination; in 1955 he set up a President's Committee on Government Employment Policy to supervise the nondiscrimination program in federal employment. The President's Committee on Government Contracts set up by President Eisenhower in 1953 continued the work of President Truman's early committee in this area. By 1956 at least fifteen states had FEPC laws. However, some of these laws were in the nature of general education, persuasion, and consultation. Many of the latter were not very effective even in this area. In addition, thirty-six towns and cities (many of these in states not having FEPC laws) had set up their own fair-employment groups by 1956. Presidents Kennedy and Johnson capitalized on the climate of the early 1960's to secure formalization of nondiscriminatory (and, in many instances, compensatory) employment practices among the large corporations through the President's Committee on Equal Employment Opportunity's "Plans for Progress" programs.

In 1945 President Truman set up a committee on civil rights[63] which investigated the condition of civil rights for minorities and made a report in 1947. A considerable change has been made in the segregation rules of the armed forces. Starting in 1946 changes were begun and by 1954 almost all the segregation practices of the armed forces had been eliminated. In 1946 the Navy opened all its jobs to Negroes and slowly began to mix the races. In 1948 the Air Force did the same. Although the Army made some earlier attempts to integrate, it was not until the period of the Korean War that in-integration actually was achieved and given a first test in battle. By June, 1954, all Negroes were serving in nonsegregated units.[64] By contrast, Civil Service regulations prohibiting discriminatory practices continued to be ignored through the 1950's.[65] It was not until the late President Kennedy made it clear to the heads of all government agencies that he expected them to increase the number of Negroes in government jobs, especially in jobs at the middle and upper levels of responsibility, that integration became truly effective in the Civil Service structure.[66] The most sweeping civil rights law since Reconstruction days was signed into law by President Johnson on July 2, 1964. The thirteen titles of the Civil Rights Act of 1964 encompass voting rights, places of public accommodation, public facilities, public education, commission on civil rights, federally assisted programs, equal employment opportunity, registration and voting statistics, intervention and procedure, community relations service, and miscellaneous provisions.

Title I of the Elementary and Secondary Education Act of 1965, together with the ensuing regulations and program guides of the U.S. Office of Education, provided the financial base for compensatory education. Although ESEA was not limited to black children, the spirit and the language of the HEW administrators focused attention on those educationally deprived children who were black. Program Guide 44 says in part, "Applicants for Title I funds should design effective compensatory education programs which include, where appropriate, measures for fostering integration in the community."[67] All children within target area schools, of course, benefited from the compensatory programs, and the intent was to *fund them adequately.* The guideline was that compensatory programs designed to supplement the

[63]*To Secure These Rights: The Report of the President's Committee on Civil Rights* (Washington, D.C.: Government Printing Office, 1947).

[64]Cf. George Eaton Simpson and J. Milton Yinger, *Racial and Cultural Minorities: An Analysis of Prejudice and Discrimination* (New York: Harper, 1953), pp. 451–455. Also Elgin F. Hunt, *Social Science: An Introduction to the Study of Society* (New York: Macmillan, 1955), p. 259.

[65]Mahlon T. Puryear, Associate Director of the National Urban League, in an unpublished speech at the 1963 National Conference of the Urban League.

[66]Charles E. Silberman, *Crisis in Black and White* (New York: Random House, 1964), p. 241.

[67]ESEA Program Guide #44 (excerpted in *Is It Helping Poor Children?* Washington, D.C.: Washington Research Project and NAACP Legal Defense and Education Fund, Dec. 1969, p. 69), Section 5.5.

regular program of the school should add 50 per cent to the per-pupil cost of the total program (regular plus compensatory).[68] There has been some feeling, supported by HEW audits, that much of Title I money in fact has supported many children *beyond* the target school areas; the more common examples are (1) learning resources centers designed to serve an entire school district rather than just the target schools and (2) language and science laboratories utilized by large schools enrolling only small numbers of children from target areas with high concentrations of low-income families.[69] The point, however, is that Congress continued enacting legislation and the president's office continued issuing executive orders through the late 1960's strongly encouraging integration.

In the early 1970's, support of integration by the executive branch of government was at least halted, if not reversed. In March 1970 President Nixon delivered an 8,000-word statement which *Time* has reported as "his message: desegregation, yes; integration, no." [70] Major points in the message were stress on the preservation of the neighborhood school and opposition to busing for purposes of achieving racial balance in the schools. Sixteen months later, in the face of court-ordered busing for integration and of carefully formulated HEW regulations for the same, President Nixon stated, "I have consistently opposed the busing of our nation's school children to achieve a racial balance . . . I have instructed the Attorney General and the secretary of HEW that they are to work with individual school districts to hold busing to the minimum required by law." [71] At the time of this writing, the President and many Congressmen seemed to be in the mood to legislate against busing for integration either by constitutional amendment or by appropriations acts which deny federal funds to school districts integrating by busing.[72] In a book review of *The Southern Strategy* the reviewer presents the carefully documented report of changes in the HEW staff during the early years of the Nixon administration and the author's conclusion that the "administration's tactics in removing unwanted liberal administrators borders closely on the fine art of the spoils system." [73] The evidence was neither clear nor complete in the early 1970's. Neither militant integrationists nor white racists were happy with President Nixon's middle-of-the-road stance. But the spirit of the proposed School Emergency Assistance Act of 1971 and of the Executive directions to HEW for implementation seemed to be a considerable retreat from the Civil Rights Act of 1964 and the executive support given to it.

Prior to the enactment of the Civil Rights Act of 1964, Supreme Court decisions with respect to the enforcement of civil rights provisions and with respect to declaring unconstitutional certain laws and practices had been more important than new laws. Starting with the *Gaines* decision concerning the right of Negroes to higher education and continuing to the school

[68]Ibid., p. 69, Section 4.7.
[69]*Is It Helping Poor Children?* (Washington, D.C.: Research Project and NAACP Legal Defense and Education Fund, December 1969), p. 5.
[70]"Desegregation Yes; Integration No," *Time*, April 6, 1970, p. 15.
[71]"Bus Stop," *Time*, August 16, 1971, pp. 14–15.
[72]Ibid.
[73]"Republicans Keep Whistling Dixie," *Business Week*, August 7, 1971, p. 7.

segregation decision of 1954, the Court has strongly affirmed a nonsegregation policy in the schools. This is consistent with the many decisions dealing with segregation on railroads, in public parks, and so on. The 1954 school segregation decision is a complete reversal of the *Plessy* vs. *Ferguson* decision in 1896, which confirmed a law requiring racial segregation and which has been called the separate-but-equal decision. Implementation of the Supreme Court decision of May 17, 1954, has been another matter. Ten years after the decision, only one Negro child in 100 was attending school with white pupils in the eleven states of the old Confederacy.[74] A dramatic illustration of the effect of the Civil Rights Act of 1964 and of the executive enforcement of it under the Johnson administration, is the increase to 18 per cent of Southern Negroes in schools with whites by 1969.[75] *De jure* segregation had been pursued with "all deliberate speed" from 1954 through 1964, then the courts really got tough. By 1970 courts were ordering school districts to bus all students in order to bring *each school* within the district to the same black–white student ratio as prevailed within the entire district. In Los Angeles, for example, this meant busing to achieve racial balance in some 560 schools—a staggering financial, administrative, and public relation's headache for the school system.

De jure segregation remains a major problem in the South, where integrated housing patterns have been the tradition. The rural South has no alternative but to integrate, and rapidly. The Southern cities, however, in the late 1960's rapidly were developing patterns of *de facto* segregation similar to that of the North; the white residents are fleeing to the suburbs. In the early 1970's the courts were attempting to force integration through busing, paired schools, shared time, and/or any reasonable plan presented by the school district. The Stennis amendment, providing "that it shall be the policy of the United States for the school desegregation law and guidelines established by the 1964 Civil Rights Act and by the 1966 Elementary and Secondary Education Act amendments to 'be applied uniformly to all regions of the United States in dealing with conditions of segregation by race' . . . ,"[76] initiated Congressional retrenchment from the previously strong integration tone of the civil right's legislation of the 1960's. The South appeared intent upon building a defense against integration of *de facto* districts in its cities, based on the new Stennis principle of "equality of treatment," replacing the discredited "all deliberate speed." In the late 1960's, advocates of the "equality of treatment" principle could point to the fact of judicial and executive recognition of de facto segregation in the North as legally acceptable. By the early 1970's, Northern courts were eliminating de facto segregation by orders for metropolitan consolidation, with integration to be achieved by busing. School segregation seemed to be doomed, both North and South.

Among other developments has been the increase in the setting up of public and private intergroup agencies to assist in the protection of the legal rights of minorities and to work for the improvement of their status. Where-

[74]"A Decade of Desegregation," *Education U.S.A.*, May 14, 1964.

[75]Alexander M. Bickel, "Desegregation. Where Do We Go from Here?" *New Republic*, February 7, 1970.

[76]"School Desegregation and the Southern Strategy," *The New South*, Vol. 25, No. 2 (Spring 1970), p. 39.

as most public agencies are less than twenty years old, the leading private agencies have contributed more than fifty years of service to date. It has been estimated that there are nearly 100 private agencies with national scope, a somewhat lesser number of state private agencies, nearly 300 local private agencies, and about 50 municipal (public, tax-supported) intergroup relations agencies—all with paid staffs. The National Association of Intergroup Relations Officials publishes an annual directory of agencies with paid staffs. Activities consist of legal aid, publications, public meetings, behind-the-scenes intervention, and other strategies designed to improve intergroup relations.

Legal Measures Designed to Improve Economic and Social Status of Underprivileged Groups. Many of the social changes that have been inaugurated by the federal and state governments from the Depression years to the present have been of special value to underprivileged minorities. Although these measures were designed to relieve distress from a number of causes, they have been especially helpful to the minorities that have been economically underprivileged. Federal laws dealing with minimum wages, unemployment benefits, housing, school lunches, aid to dependent children, relief, old-age insurance, medical aid, and other kinds of social security have been of great help to the underprivileged segments of our society. Although there are many problems here that have not as yet been alleviated completely (Dewhurst estimates that in 1950 one fifth of the population was ill fed, one fourth ill clothed, and one third ill housed;[77] *Time* estimated that in 1968 one fifth of the population was below the poverty line, with one seventh in substandard housing[78]), certainly the net result of these laws has been to reduce the amount of serious suffering in the lower, underprivileged classes and thus to reduce the extremes of poverty in the United States. The March on Washington on August 28, 1963, the high point of good feelings between activists in the civil rights movement and white people sympathetic to the cause,[79] seems to have triggered a series of legislative acts designed to alleviate poverty: the Anti-poverty Act, Appalachian Relief, and so on. Possibly the most spectacular achievement in legal steps to guarantee the rights of all persons throughout the United States to equal opportunity in the purchase and rental of housing was the Civil Rights Act of 1968. Equally as important, if somewhat less known to the general public, was the Supreme Court decision in the case of *Jones* vs. *Mayer* on June 17, 1968, promptly after the passage of the Civil Rights Act. The Court linked the most recent Civil Rights Act to the very first, the Civil Rights Act of 1866. The Court found that the "1866 Act was designed to do just what its terms suggest: to prohibit all racial discrimination with respect to the rights enumerated therein—including the right to purchase or lease property."[80] It seems ironic that a loophole in the 1968 Act was plugged by enforcement of an 1866 Act, which could lead one to wonder if the 1968 Act were necessary, if only

[77]J. Frederick Dewhurst et al., *America's Needs and Resources: A New Summary* (New York: Twentieth Century Fund, 1955), pp. 158, 194, 224.

[78]"Black and White Balance Sheet," *Time*, January 24, 1969, p. 35.

[79]William Lee Miller, "Civil Rights in the North," *Current*, No. 52 (October 1964).

[80]"Civil Rights Legislation," *Law*, Vol. 3, No. 1, September 1968, p. 2.

the 1866 Act had been properly enforced. However, the Court maintained that the two laws supplemented one another: that the 1866 Act applies only to discrimination based on race, whereas the 1968 Act bars discrimination on grounds of religion and national origin.

The Timing of Democratic Legal Action. Legislation that does more than to codify the mores precipitates conflict. A good example of this is the Southern reaction to racial integration in the public schools. Many Southern cities and states had laws that codified the mores of the Southern whites on this issue. The Supreme Court has held these local laws unconstitutional. Where even the supreme law of the land, the Constitution, conflicts with local mores, violence erupts.

Legislators need to be aware of this basic sociological fact when drafting laws. Legislation that departs too radically from the established mores may cause more human misery than it alleviates. In the case of racial integration in the schools, Gunnar Myrdal points out that the white man's conscience is probably the greatest force operating toward eventual acceptance by the South of the Supreme Court's reinterpretation of the Constitution.[81] In one sense, this is codification of national mores before they had been assimilated fully by one section of the country. This was bound to lead to sectional conflict. One wonders, as one observes the caste status of the Negro in the North, if these mores had solidified fully in any section of the country.

Writing twenty years later, Silberman agrees with Myrdal that codification in advance of the mores causes conflict, but he questions Myrdal's interpretation of the white man's motivation:

> Gunnar Mydal concluded that "the American Negro problem is a problem in the heart of the American," and titled his monumental study of the Negro *An American Dilemma.* Myrdal was wrong. The tragedy of race relations in the United States is that there is no "American Dilemma." White Americans are not torn and tortured by conflict between their devotion to the American creed and their actual behavior. They are upset by the current state of race relations, to be sure. But what troubles them is not that justice is being denied but that their peace is being shattered and their business interrupted.[82]

Social legislation, of course, must go beyond the mores; otherwise there would be no need for such legislation. There is a fine line of demarcation, however, between social legislation that will be reluctantly accepted and social legislation that will precipitate bitter and prolonged conflict designed to divide the nation further. This psychological evaluation in terms of predicted acceptance or rejection should be a critical factor in the consideration of even the most needed social legislation. Democracy has demonstrated its ability to achieve *peaceful* change, at a moderate pace, through cooperative action. This seemed to be the administration line in the early 1970's. The white backlash of 1967 had cooled until the economic recession occurred, then it was revitalized as unemployment rose, clearly showing public sentiment to be out of sympathy with enforced integration. (We

[81]Gunnar Myrdal, *An American Dilemma* (New York: Harper, 1944).

[82]Charles E. Silberman, *Crisis in Black and White* (New York: Random House, 1964), p. 10. Used by permission of Random House, Inc., and Jonathan Cape Ltd.

have previously quoted the "Nixon message" as "Desegregation, Yes; Integration, No.") Coupled with the changing public sentiment were the Coleman Report (showing little value in compensatory education and little gain in integration, in terms of pupil achievement) and the perverse effects of the elimination of *de jure* segregation in Southern cities. Bickel notes:

> Integration soon reaches a tipping point. If whites are sent to constitute a minority in a school that is largely black, or if blacks are sent to constitute something near half the population of a school that was formerly white or nearly all-white, the whites flee and the school becomes all, or nearly all black; resegregation sets in, blacks simply changing places with whites. . . . The questions to ask are whether there is any way to prevent the whites fleeing, or whether there are gains sufficient to offset the flight of the whites in continuing to press the process of integration.[83]

Bickel clearly feels that we were going too far, or too fast, or in the wrong direction. Nixon apparently agreed with him. The general public seemed to feel the same way. It may well be that two wrongs did not make a right, that the South was wrong in its stubborn resistance to the elimination of *de jure* segregation as found unconstitutional by the courts and declared illegal by the Congress, and that the nation was wrong in too vigorous pursuit of forced integration in the late 1960's. One thing is certain: conflict resulted. It is to be hoped that the 1970's will see economic prosperity; that is the best hope for the civil rights movement to achieve peaceful change, at a moderate pace, through cooperative action.

Industrial Recruitment and Employment Practices

Concurrent with legal action by the government and partly as a result of it, industrial recruitment and employment practices have altered the complexion of racial discrimination significantly in employment in recent years. This has been a key area of progress. Of what use are integrated restaurants if the average Negro cannot afford the price of a meal? Acquisition and retention of something more than menial jobs is the only solid base on which the Negro can build.

Management Practices.   Writing in the immediate wake of the "long, hot summer" of 1963, Reverend Martin Luther King, Jr., was caustic in his comments concerning management practices.

> The summer of 1963 was a revolution because it changed the face of America. Freedom was contagious. Its fever boiled in nearly one thousand cities, and by the time it had passed its peak, many thousands of lunch counters, hotels, parks and other places of public accommodation had become integrated.
> Slowly and unevenly, job opportunities opened up for Negroes, though these were still more impressive in their promise than in their immediate numbers. In the larger northern cities, a more significant change in employment patterns took shape. Many firms found themselves under fire, not because they employed Negroes, but because they did not. Accustomed to ignoring the question, they were forced by its sudden overwhelming presence into a hasty search

[83]From "Desegregation: Where Do We Go from Here?" by Alexander M. Bickel, *The New Republic*, February 7, 1970, p. 519. Reprinted by permission of *The New Republic*, © 1970, Harrison-Blaine of New Jersey, Inc.

for absolving tokens. A well-trained Negro found himself sought out by industry for the first time. Many Negroes were understandably cynical as the door to opportunity was flung open to them as if they were but recent arrivals on the planet. Nevertheless, though the motives were mixed, the Negro could celebrate the slow retreat of discrimination on yet another front.[84]

No less caustic were the critics of the new hiring policies. The public image of the large corporations undoubtedly suffered from the bitter satire of such writers as Art Buchwald.

> Ever since the Negroes have been protesting job discrimination and threatening to boycott any company that doesn't hire Negroes, the major corporations have been searching desperately to have at least one Negro on the payroll in something more than a menial position. For the first time the college-educated Negro is being wooed by large companies who need him desperately to avoid a national boycott. . . .
>
> The search is going on very quietly and no one is willing to talk about it, but the competition is getting so fierce that we wouldn't be surprised if it went something like this. . . .
>
> Two vice presidents of the Mackerel Soda Co. are sent to interview Thomas Jefferson Jones, who holds a B.S. and an M.A. and a Doctor of Philosophy degree from MIT. Before Birmingham, Mr. Jones was working as stock-room clerk in a large New York department store. But now everything has changed.
>
> "Mr. Jones," the first vice president says, "we'd like you to join our company in an executive position."
>
> "If I understand you correctly," Mr. Jones says, "you'd like me to be your executive Negro."
>
> "No, no—that's not it at all," the second vice president says. "We've been searching for some time for somebody with your qualifications to head up our Interdepartmental Bottling and Sales Liaison."
>
> "What is that exactly?"
>
> "It's a new job which would require you to consult and report and make suggestions on managerial procedures that could improve consumer interest on a company level."
>
> "I see," Mr. Jones says. "But you'd want me to sit near the door."
>
> "As a matter of fact, we would, but that has nothing to do with the job. . . ."[85]

It would appear, to an impartial observer, that writings such as those quoted from King and Buchwald underrate the intelligence of top management officials in the larger corporations. The "spontaneous" search for the well-qualified Negro graduate by the larger corporations commenced no later than 1960. Management was preparing for the holocaust which seemed bound to come, and which the Southern Baptist Leadership Conference and allied organizations delivered in the summer of 1963. By the time the President's Committee on Equal Opportunity presented industry with a code, hiring policies already had been revised. Industry signed the code, claiming that it only codified their existing practices. It does seem significant, however, that industrial recruitment of Negroes on college campuses experienced a

[84]From *Why We Can't Wait* by Martin Luther King, Jr. (Harper & Row, 1964), p. 127. Used by permission.

[85]Art Buchwald, "How It Goes with New Hiring Policy," *Cincinnati Enquirer*, September 13, 1963. Reprinted with permission from the *New York Herald Tribune*.

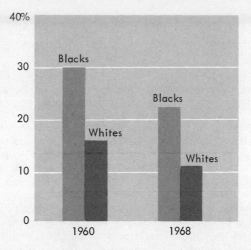

Figure 18. Unemployment rates by race for persons dropping out or graduating from high school. [From *U.S. Manpower in the 1970's* (Washington, D.C.: U.S. Department of Labor, 1970).]

sharp increase in the 1963–64 school year.[86] Further evidence of the acceleration of pace in employment of Negroes appeared in a report on the President's Committee on Equal Employment Opportunity on the "Plans for Progress" program, "Employment of non-whites in management categories rose by 43.4 per cent and by 37.4 per cent in professional and administrative jobs . . . in technical jobs, 31.6 per cent."[87] Despite these gains by skilled and college-trained blacks, the unemployment gap between whites and blacks newly entering the labor market remained almost constant through the 1960's, as shown in Figure 18.

In the face of the rapidly increasing size of the labor force in the 1960's (the bumper crop of war babies were entering the labor market), it is surprising that the gap did not increase. Probably the major reason that Negroes were even able to "hold their own" proportionally was the economic militancy of the blacks. Early leadership was taken by the National Urban League, supported by informal groups of Negro ministers, in demanding "compensatory" employment practices. Management of most of the larger companies appeared to be honestly endeavoring to practice *equal* employment opportunity for all Americans, regardless of race, color, or creed. They were "compensating" for the difficulties experienced in locating well-qualified Negro applicants by intensifying recruitment activities designed to locate and attract Negro applicants.

This was not the type of "compensatory activity" acceptable to Negro leaders. Mr. Whitney Young, Jr., Executive Director of the National Urban League, was the most vocal spokesman for the position that the Negro is "owed" compensation in all areas of life—employment, housing, recreation, education, and so on—for three centuries of maltreatment in exactly the

[86] "Industry Rushes for Negro Grads," *Business Week*, April 25, 1964, pp. 78–82.
[87] "Negroes Push for Employment Opportunities," *Dun's Review and Modern Industry*, Vol. 83, No. 6 (June 1964), pp. 59–60.

same sense that the G.I. was compensated for *four years* of "lost" time during World War II.[88] Silberman discussed the Urban League in 1964 as follows:

> The Urban League is proposing that when a Negro and a white have equal qualifications for a job, the former should be given the preference. Militant Negro organizations are demanding considerably more; they are insisting, in effect, that business firms hire Negroes not because they are qualified but because they are Negroes. And they are developing a good deal of muscle to back up their demands for preferential hiring. The most widely used technique is the boycott, or "selective patronage campaign," as Negroes prefer to call it. "Don't buy where you can't work" campaigns were frequent during the 1930's, but they were sporadic and only occasionally effective. The contemporary use of the weapon began in the early sixties in Philadelphia. The campaign was organized and directed by a group of Negro Ministers (some 400 ministers co-operated) with no formal organization. The ministers' technique is to approach one company at a time, usually a manufacturer or distributor of consumer products for which a number of competing brands are available—a baker, a dairy, an oil company, a supermarket chain. If the company refuses to negotiate with the ministers, it is given an ultimatum to hire a specified number of Negroes in specified job classifications before a given date; if the demands are ignored, a boycott ensues. With four hundred ministers using their pulpits to announce the boycott, a substantial portion of the Negro population takes part. Some firms—Pepsi-Cola and Esso, for example—have come to terms without a boycott. Others held out—but generally not for long; Gulf Oil capitulated in twelve days, Sun Oil in three months. All told, the ministers have won concessions from twenty-four firms so far. The technique has spread to Boston, New York, Atlanta, Detroit, and other cities, and is bound to be widely imitated. As Rev. Ralph Abernathy, Rev. Martin Luther King's chief lieutenant, says, "Not every Negro is able to go to jail, but every Negro can stop buying a particular brand of bread or milk or gasoline." [89]

Other black groups adopted the successful strategy of the local boycott, and organized for action. In 1966, for example, Reverend King appointed Reverend Jesse Jackson to establish a Breadbasket office in Chicago; since then Reverend Jackson has set up other bread basket operations in such major cities as Los Angeles, Milwaukee, Indianapolis, Brooklyn, Houston, and Cleveland. Possibly his most spectacular success was the sixteen-week boycott of the more than forty supermarkets operated by A. & P. in Chicago's black neighborhoods. The chain finally signed a contract to hire 268 more blacks, stock some twenty-five black products, and to use black-owned companies for janitor services, garbage removal, and rodent extermination.[90] The Jackson success story could be told many times, only the names, the organizations, and the locales change. The significant points seem to be (1) the organization and control of the operations were at the local level, and (2) they got results.

Labor Practices. Labor is not as vulnerable as management. Of what use is a boycott of a particular union as a technique for gaining admission

---

[88]Whitney M. Young, Jr., "Domestic Marshall Plan," *New York Times Magazine*, October 6, 1963.

[89]Charles Silberman, *Crisis in Black and White* (New York: Random House, 1964), pp. 238–239. Used by permission of Random House, Inc., and Jonathan Cape Ltd.

[90]"Jesse Jackson: One Leader Among Many," *Time*, April 6, 1970, p. 20.

into the union? To the discerning Negro, the situation is critical. Of the 18.5 million union members, the 1.5 million Negro card holders are concentrated in the poorest-paying jobs.[91] For the most part the craft unions historically have excluded Negroes.

The only feasible solution to the problem of admission of Negroes to trade unions providing apprenticeships for skilled labor seems to be government intervention. The government may be moving in this direction. Adequate laws presently are on the books, if the government chooses to enforce them. In the mid-1960's such enforcement activities were not readily apparent. The President's Committee on Equal Employment Opportunity seemed to be busily engaged in pressuring management to employ Negroes at all corporate levels. They did not seem to be quite so busy in pressuring labor unions to admit Negroes to apprenticeship programs that would qualify them for the very jobs for which management was supposed to employ them.

Public reaction to riots in major cities[92] expedited government action, largely in the form of "behind-the-scenes" persuasion of labor leaders to open the union memberships to blacks voluntarily. The first "foot in the door" appeared to be the acceptance of trainees from Job Corps and other Manpower programs into all AFL–CIO unions at the apprentice level. There was a veritable explosion of these federally sponsored retraining programs in the late 1960's—MDTA, NYC, JOBS, New Careers, Mainstream, Upward Bound, and so on—culminating in the Comprehensive Manpower Training Act of 1969.[93] These and other activities have led to sufficient labor reform to create a real "white backlash" among union members. Again, the psychological questions arise: (1) how much pressure should the government maintain in the effort to narrow the unemployment gap between black and white and (2) how much easing of pressure will the Negroes tolerate? *Business Week* interprets the pieces of legislation ensuing from the Comprehensive Manpower Training Act of 1969 (such as the Emergency Employment Act of 1971) and the regulations issued to implement the Act as of high priority in helping the disadvantaged within the framework of a much broader and more important program:

> Now, for the first time, a comprehensive, coherent manpower program is emerging that would dovetail with broad economic policy. Through a coordinated system of training and placement programs it would seek to ensure that the entire U.S. labor force is utilized to best advantage in prosperous times. In downswings of the business cycle, it would create jobs with government money to take up the slack. When all the pieces are in place, this new manpower policy could join monetary and fiscal policy as a third major tool for managing the U.S. economy.[94]

Such a powerful and comprehensive program surely must enlist the cooperation of the labor unions. The black appears well on his way to full union membership.

[91]Whitney M. Young, Jr., "Discrimination in Labor Unions," *Vital Speeches of the Day* (New York: City News Publishing Company), p. 535.

[92]"Why Race Riots Strike 'Nice' Northern City," *Business Week*, No. 1822, August 1, 1964, p. 24.

[93]*Washington Monitor*, December 1, 1969 (Washington, D.C.: N.S.P.R.A., N.E.A., 1969), p. 83.

[94]"At Last, A National Manpower Policy" *Business Week*, August 7, 1971, p. 48.

National Urban League.   The Urban League is often mentioned by company executives as being the most professional of the Negro groups. It specializes in working on Negroes' employment and housing problems, whereas agencies such as NAACP, CORE, and SNCC concentrate on education and voting. Urban League activities not only are nonviolent in nature, they lead to positive "action" programs. Active cooperation among the Urban League, industry, and philanthropic foundations has resulted in large cash grants to institute and/or further retraining programs for Negroes.[95] There seems to be no question of the need for such retraining programs.[96] The Manpower administration refers to it as a "growth industry" in the tabulation presented in Table 13.

TABLE 13
Manpower Training: A Growth Industry

FISCAL YEAR	FEDERAL SPENDING* (MILLIONS OF DOLLARS)	TRAINING SLOTS
1963	$56	59,200
1964	142	125,800
1965	433	510,200
1966	615	808,800
1967	796	808,400
1968	802	823,800
1969	1,030	910,700
1970	1,429	966,400
1971	1,637	1,187,200

Reprinted from the August 7, 1971 issue of *Business Week* by special permission. Copyright © 1971 by McGraw-Hill, Inc.
* Funds obligated under MDTA, EOA, & Social Security Act.

The Negro suffers from cultural deprivation that handicaps him in the beginning reading programs of the elementary grades of school, in acceptance of vocational guidance in secondary school, and in development of positive attitudes in college courses and in job seeking. There is a critical shortage of well-qualified Negro labor in all but the unskilled categories. The Urban League had taken beginning steps in the retraining program by 1964 and had completed a highly successful year in placing already trained Negroes in appropriate positions through the National Skills Bank.

The basic proposals of the National Urban League[97] in 1963 were the following:

---

[95] "Negro Push for Employment Opportunities," *Dun's Review and Modern Industry*, Vol. 83, No. 6 (June 1964), pp. 59–60.

[96] Stephin Habbe, "Hiring Negro Workers," *The Conference Board Record*, Vol. 1, No. 6 (June 1964), pp. 16–19. Stephin Habbe, "Recruiting Negro College Graduates," *The Conference Board Record*, Vol. 1, No. 8 (August 1964), pp. 7–9.

[97] Mahlon T. Puryear, "Problems and Trends in Job Development and Employment" (unpublished speech before the 1963 National Conference of the Urban League at the Statler-Hilton Hotel in Los Angeles, July 29, 1963).

1. A basic skills program for the "hard-core" unemployed Negro. The League was dissatisfied with existing federal retraining programs, claiming that most Negroes enrolled in government-financed retraining programs were being trained for menial occupations—practical nursing, shirt pressing, cooking, and service station operation. Negroes were conspicuously absent in most of the programs in electronics, machine trades, welding, drafting, and other skilled areas.
2. Demonstration projects to increase opportunities in apprenticeships. Suggested activities were improving the preparation of Negro youth through general and vocational education (the Deutsch research and demonstration project in ten New York public schools and five day-care centers is an excellent example of a successful demonstration project in general education); changing the attitudes of Negro youth *and of their parents* concerning Negro aptitude and opportunity in the skilled trades; changing the attitudes of the unions; and changing the attitudes of management.
3. An experimental recruiting and placement program for Negro college students. The main thesis was that the Negro colleges were providing inadequate guidance and inadequate placement service. It was the responsibility of government and industry to provide these services for the students enrolled in Negro colleges. Industry recruitment programs were proposed for Negro students in Negro and integrated colleges.
4. A National Skills Bank. This proposal was to establish in one central place the names, qualifications, and availability of any persons who wished to be considered for employment in a variety of work situations. The National Skills Bank was to be financed by the federal government but was to be managed exclusively by the National Urban League.

Securing commitments from governmental leaders for legislative programs designed to achieve most of their objectives but failing to secure governmental support for the National Skills Bank, the Urban League turned to the great foundations for financial support. Supported by funds from the Rockefeller Foundation, the National Skills Bank was established and widely publicized. A survey is done by each of the local Urban Leagues across the country to determine availability of jobs for Negroes, and companies' interest in cooperation in such a program. By late 1964 chapters of the National Skills Bank had been established in sixty-five cities. The National Urban League trains the personnel of its local chapters in how to contact Negroes in their communities, to understand their job skills, and to stimulate their desire for improvement. Once job candidates are identified, they are called in for personal interviews. The interviewers are often personnel specialists who themselves work for local companies. Through this process, a pool of available Negro talent is built up job level by job level. If applicants are not available in an area to match an employer's particular request, the National Urban League headquarters, where a master file is maintained, is contacted. The employer's request is matched with an applicant closest to the company and a meeting is arranged. The Skills Bank differs from private employment agencies in several respects: it operates nationally, and no fee is involved; its primary aim is to help more Negroes to gain entry to job levels where few or none are now employed.

The black businessman also learned how to help himself. His activities coordinate with and extend the services of the Urban League. The Urban League matches individuals with jobs. The National Association of Black Manufacturers matches contractors with contracts. As the civil rights movement entered the 1970's, the federal government appeared to compensate for its opposition to busing for school integration by strengthening its weapons against industry in the fight for civil rights. The word was out: it was no longer enough to promise to look for black subcontractors; one must take affirmative action, and document the search. A real boon to big contractors, and to black subcontractors in search for jobs, was the ability to match subcontractors and black subcontractors quickly through a telephone call to Colonel Ted Adams; National Association of Black Manufacturers; Room 608, 1101 Seventh Street, N.W.; Washington, D.C. 20036.

Education

Education is a continuous process from the cradle to the grave. The following discussion will be oriented to this broader definition of education, with the role of the formal school deferred to a later section.

Application of Consistent Values to the Solutions of Life's Problems. Democracy, Judaism, and Christianity should be more than a political philosophy and religious faiths. Many persons hold that the application of the Judaeo-Christian tradition in the American social scene should clearly indicate a way of life based on the values common to both democracy and the Judaeo-Christian tradition. There should be little conflict between Christians and Jews in arriving at a common set of values.[98] Briefly stated, the American value system includes mutual respect, cooperation, rational thinking, and faith in the future.

Man needs constantly to be re-educated in the consistent application of these values. Conceptual grasp of a set of values is meaningless unless the values are *applied* to all areas of life. Parents, teachers, and peers all bear a civic responsibility to assist in this educational process through precept and example.

Mutual respect involves both understanding one's fellow man and treating him as a brother. Confucianism goes beyond even the Sermon on the Mount in this respect; it expects one to do unto others as *they would have one do unto them.* This demands full understanding of one's fellow man. No one can know fully all the diverse groups in America, but consistent operation on a principle of mutual respect would eliminate the fears of the unknown and the pseudofeelings of superiority that are at the roots of all prejudice. Further, it would lead one to search for *causes* when a group behaved in an apparently unexplainable way, rather than to treat them as stereotypes and scapegoats.

Cooperation involves the full efforts of *all* groups in the solution of common problems; it cannot consist of the majority group reaching a decision and handing it down to the minority group. Again, the very handing

[98]Those values common to all Americans are more fully developed in Chapter 14, with clear implications of their effects on the moral and ethical principles of both theists and nontheists.

down of cultural decisions, such as proper dress, diet, and common courtesies, implies that the majority group is superior in that it knows the only "right" ways. Cooperative action on such problems often discloses the fact that there are many "right" ways. Sometimes the minority way of behaving proves to be the preferred way, as witness the gradual adoption by the socially elite of the loose, comfortable summer wear of the men of the lower classes. Formerly, a gentleman never appeared in public without his coat; such vulgarity was reserved for the masses at such popular resorts as Coney Island. Now short-sleeved sport shirts are acceptable to all classes for casual wear.

Rational thinking strikes at one of the roots of prejudice: ignorance. Rational thinking demands factual data on which to base hypotheses. If the overwhelming weight of scientific data on the equality of races were accepted by all men, then racism would diminish. As indicated earlier, the difficulty lies in securing emotional acceptance; surrender of one's prejudices threatens personal security through closing the escape valve for venting frustrations. Other problems of intergroup relations are not so readily susceptible to solution by rational thinking, even if men could be induced to think rationally in prejudicial areas; for example, no system of government to eliminate class differences has yet been devised. Rational thinking can minimize the adverse effects of social stratification, however, by providing a four-point program designed (1) to develop each person to his maximum potential; (2) to provide equitable opportunities to all—political, economic, social, and educational; (3) to help individuals to establish realistic life goals; and (4) to help individuals to be happy in the position in life that they must fill.

The behavioral scientists are bringing both the programmed learning strategies of Skinner and the counseling strategies of Rogers to bear upon training laboratories designed to improve skills in problem solving. This gives new hope for rational approaches to the emotional problems of intergroup education. Some materials are available commercially, such as the *Problem-Solving Program* booklet published by the NTL Institute for Applied Behavioral Science.[99] Others are in the process of development by leaders of training laboratories. Research evidence of their effectiveness is not yet available, but they do represent a promising new approach to rational thinking.

Faith in the future is the very antithesis of psychological insecurity. It is emotional in nature and correspondingly difficult to define in operational terms. Basically, if one has faith in his fellow man and in the use of cooperation and reason for the solution of common problems, then faith in himself and in the future should result. Maintaining faith in the future becomes increasingly difficult in an age of atomic missiles and sputniks. First steps, for educators, lie in building the confidence of students in their classmates and in their teachers through cooperative classroom mastery of demonstrably important and difficult learnings.

Effective and Noneffective Techniques in the Changing of Attitudes. We have stated earlier that prejudice is perpetuated through ignorance and insecurity. Prejudices based on insecurity are extremely resistant to modifica-

---

[99]*A Problem-Solving Program for Defining a Problem and Planning Action* (Washington, D.C.: N.T.L. Institute, 1969).

tion, and there is some evidence that all prejudices are so based. These prejudices may belong to the group or they may be personal. Examples of the two types are (1) the scapegoating of one group by another to relieve group frustrations and (2) the expression of psychoneurotic symptoms of authoritarian personalities. Prejudice based on group insecurity may be made more susceptible to change by removing the source of group frustration. Prejudice based on rigidity of personality requires a reorientation of basic personality structure before pressures for attitudinal change can be effective.

Programs of information, per se, have not been effective in the reduction of prejudice. Americans pride themselves on their rational approach to life; they fail to recognize their own prejudices, believing them to be reasoned conclusions. Programs of factual information may modify attitudes based solely on ignorance. Unfortunately, one's attitudes affect one's interpretation of such data. Even highly factual research data may be perverted to reinforce established prejudices. This does not indicate an abandonment of the rational approach; it means simply that informational programs should be used not in isolation but as supplements to other approaches. "Although facts can always be forgotten or distorted, in the long run, accurate information is a most important ally in the effort to improve human relations."[100]

Effective techniques in intergroup relations, including even the manner of presentation of factual material, address themselves to an emotional response. The exchange of information must be emotionally conditioned for the modification of attitudes. The psychology of learning that structured the formation of attitudes is equally sound in their modification. Briefly stated, effective techniques in changing of attitudes include the following: (1) rewarding for desired behavior, which reflects the expression of desired attitudes; (2) punishing for deviant behavior; (3) associating the new idea with positively charged symbols;[101] (4) associating the old attitude (prejudice) with negatively charged symbols; (5) entertaining (people are more receptive when in a pleasant mood); and (6) securing emotional involvement. Sociodrama is illustrative of the effective techniques of developing empathy as a preface to the presentation of information. Deliberate modification of attitudes involves action by persons or groups desiring the attitude modification. Some of these groups will be discussed subsequently.

Formal Workshops in Intergroup Education. The National Conference of Christians and Jews, the Anti-Defamation League, and the American Jewish Committee have fostered the development of workshops in intergroup education both as summer sessions at leading universities and as in-service programs in public school systems. Both educators and laymen are attending these workshops, studying the dynamics of intergroup problems and developing skills in techniques of combating them. The National Urban League goes beyond the informational techniques employed by these organizations. Workshops are held, it is true, but the emphasis of this organization is on persuading the federal government and/or the philanthropic foundations to translate their conclusions into action programs. The late

---

[100]Selma G. Hirsh, *The Fears Men Live By* (New York: Harper, 1955), p. 124.
[101]Note the authors' continuous equating of positive intergroup attitudes with values found both in democracy and in the Judaeo-Christian tradition.

1960's saw a mushrooming of the various interpretations of the sensitivity training pioneered in 1947 by the NEA in its National Training Laboratory at Bethel, Maine, and later extended to other centers. T-grouping, confrontation, rap sessions, and so on, increasingly are being used by industry, government, and education as devices for helping the individual better to know himself as a prime prerequisite for understanding others.[102] These strategies are discussed in Chapter 14.

Informal Study Groups.   Many parent–teacher associations have informal study groups discussing intergroup problems. Women's clubs, both professional and social, are taking an increased interest in this area. Unfortunately, some social women's clubs have been the traditional bulwarks of the forces perpetuating discrimination, representing the women whose husbands' income frees them for club work and whose consciousness of ancestry reinforces their feelings of superiority. If the upper-class woman recently has come from a lower class, she has a vested interest to protect; if she was born to the upper class, she is heir to all the prejudices illustrated in *Yankee City.* One encouraging facet of social women's club work is the overt action that often follows their study. They may adopt some civic project for the underprivileged. This firsthand contact with children and adults of minority groups can be of value in building understanding of these minorities; it is hoped that such contact will develop empathy rather than sympathy. The situation is not so structured, for it starts with an emphasis on difference in economic status rather than with an emphasis on building bridges of understanding through sharing likenesses.

Civic clubs such as Kiwanis, Rotary, Lions, and others long have been noted both for their programs of education of their members and for civic projects for the underprivileged. The American Legion, Veterans of Foreign Wars, and American Veterans Committee sometimes undertake projects. The men's civic clubs are prey to the same weaknesses as the women's social clubs. Too often a condescending sympathy blocks real understanding. The veterans' organizations are especially subject to chauvinism. Despite these weaknesses, both men's and women's clubs are making some progress in education in intergroup relations.

Literature in Intergroup Education.   If the proper literature finds its way into the hands of the previously listed groups, progress is accelerated. Fortunately, there is a wealth of excellent material available. The National Conference of Christians and Jews has a number of sound pamphlets on a variety of topics in intergroup education. These are concise, clearly written, authoritative capsules designed for lay consumption. The Public Affairs Committee, the Anti-Defamation League, and the American Jewish Committee (sometimes publishing as Community Relations Service) have similar series. The United States Chamber of Commerce has some pamphlets bearing on the same topics that will bear critical reading. The National Association for the Advancement of Colored People publishes a limited amount of materials. All these organizations furnish materials at nominal cost. The National Education Association has publications in this area by a number of its commissions, such as the Educational Policies Commission and the Defense

[102]Samuel A. Culbert, *The Interpersonal Process of Self Disclosure: It Takes Two to See One* (New York: N.T.L. Institute, 1968).

Commission. The American Council on Education has a scholarly research project in this field in progress. A number of its reports are available in bound form. These should provide expert professional assistance to educators and serve as stimulating reading for the informed layman. The National Training Laboratory has broadened its scope of operation (and changed its name to reflect that extension) and the range of its publication; "since 1960, the NTL Institute has conducted training programs designed especially for those who are engaged in community work." [103]

For the readers' convenience, these sources are listed:

American Association of School Administrators, N.E.A.; 1201 Sixteenth Street, N.W.; Washington, D.C. 20036. (Ask for *ERIC/CEA Abstracts* of the areas in which you are interested.)

American Civil Liberties Union, New York and local chapters.

American Council on Education; 744 Jackson Place; Washington, D.C.

American Jewish Committee; 386 Fourth Ave.; New York, N.Y. 10016.

Anti-Defamation League of B'nai B'rith; 515 Madison Ave.; New York, N.Y. 10022.

Catholic Interracial Council; 1307 South Wabash Avenue; Chicago, Illinois 60605.

Chamber of Commerce of the United States; 1616 H. St., N.W.; Washington, D.C. 20006.

The Council on Human Relations; 281 The Arcade; Cleveland, Ohio 44114.

Defense Commission of the N.E.A.; 1201 16th St., N.W.; Washington, D.C. 20036.

Educational Policies Commission of the N.E.A.; 1201 16th St., N.W.; Washington, D.C. 20036.

ERIC Clearing on Educational Administration; University of Oregon; Eugene, Oregon 97403. (Ask for *Implementing School Desegregation*; cites literature from 1966 through 1969.)

Ferkauf Graduate School of Education; Yeshiva University; 55 Fifth Avenue; New York, N.Y. 10003.

League of United Latin American Citizens; 2218 South Birch Street; Santa Ana, California.

N.T.L. Institute for Applied Behavioral Science; 1201 Sixteenth Street, N.W.; Washington, D.C. 20036.

National Association for the Advancement of Colored People; 20 West 40th St.; New York, N.Y. 10018.

National Association of Intergroup Relations Officials; 2027 Massachusetts Avenue, N.W.; Washington, D.C. 20036.

National Conference of Christians and Jews; 43 West 57th St.; New York, N.Y. 10019.

Negro Book Club; 160 West 85th Street; New York, N.Y. 10024.

Phi Delta Kappa's Commission on Education and Human Rights and Responsibilities; Eighth Street and Union Avenue; Bloomington, Indiana 47401. (Ask for *School Integration: A Comprehensive Classified Bibliography*.)

Public Affairs Committee; 22 East 38th St.; New York, N.Y. 10016.

Southern Regional Council; 5 Forsyth Street; Atlanta, Georgia.

Urban League; 55 East 52nd Street; New York, N.Y. 10022.

Other Agencies of Communication. Motion pictures, radio, and television have accelerated greatly the homogenization of America. Any factor that reduces differences among people retards discrimination by reducing the visibility of the minority group. In addition to this, documentary motion pictures such as *Gentleman's Agreement* provide sound education in inter-

[103]*Annual Laboratories in Community Leadership Training* (Washington, D.C.: N.T.L. Institute, 1970), p. iv.

group relations. Fortunately, production policy in most film, radio, television, and periodical and other publishing companies currently seems to be favorable to the promotion of better intergroup relations, in terms of the treatment of the stories they present. Members of minority groups are presented as human beings with problems, and in such a way as to merit respect. Respect is what is needed, not sympathy. Sympathy implies condescension. The agencies of public communication are to be commended on their traditional voluntary production policies. Governmental pressures of the Kennedy administration, the fear of Negro boycotts of their products, and eventually the Civil Rights Act of 1964 led to a far greater breakthrough in the early 1960's than any before. Negro performers began appearing in major roles on nearly every major radio and television show. Constant exposure to presentation of Negroes in serious dramatic roles, rather than the exclusively song/dance/comedy routines of previous years, must have had some influence on the attitudes of the audience.

Cultural Pluralism Versus the Melting Pot

Cultural monism was the traditional ideal of the American "melting pot." Immigrants were supposed to fuse the best of their diverse cultures into a common pattern. This cultural assimilation has not taken the ideal pattern that was intended. Vices have been assimilated as readily as virtues.

Cole has proposed "cultural democracy" as an ideal.[104] This would follow the pattern of American political democracy, preserving the good things in all cultures but building common strands of behavior to unify the nation. This would give prestige to all cultures, religions, and other groups, recognizing their variances and efficiencies as part of democracy. The basic weakness here is the same as in cultural monism: Who shall decide what the common strands will be?

Cultural pluralism is advanced by some authorities as the most feasible approach. This means, in effect, admitting that the practical working of the melting pot is superior to the ideal that was posited for it. We recognize that there is not one "American" but many "Americans," that there are many regional and subregional ways of life in America, rather than a common pattern, but with common strands of beliefs and behaviors unifying all groups into a national entity. These authorities would say that this cultural pluralism is good, that continued differences per se are not the problem, but that the discriminatory practices of the majority group are the problem. They cite as proof that impartial foreign social analysts such as Gunnar Myrdal identify a common "American character" among the various groups that make up America. They maintain that this proves that common strands of behavior will develop in time in a pluralistic culture.

The cultural pluralists have the weight of history in their favor. Any culture that failed to develop and maintain strong common strands of behavior in all its peoples has disintegrated. Until the 1970's America had been growing stronger. We have cited earlier the effect of public agencies of communication in building these common strands. Probably the effect of the

[104]Stewart G. Cole, I. James Quillen, and Mildred J. Wiese, *Charting Intercultural Education* (Stanford, Calif.: Stanford University Press, 1946), p. 58.

editorial policies of our newspapers in shaping political opinion was insufficiently developed at that time. Here is cultural pluralism at work. Some papers are Democratic, some are Republican, but most are alert to the threat of foreign wars and see the need for foreign commitments for hemispheric protection. Midwestern papers are complacent in their isolationism, but all support the government in time of war, no matter how many foreign commitments become necessary.

Itzkoff takes a more negative view of the pluralistic effects of American democracy, at least in the contemporary scene. He holds that cultural pluralism is not obsolete, but that, "The social conditions that have fostered pluralistic forms of behavior until recently have now been largely displaced by a new set of dynamics."[105] He cites the influence of modern technology, the standardization process, in making the world "more neutral qualitatively."[106] He notes the influence of such events as two world wars and of such institutions as the public schools and the mass media in causing Americans to seek common identity until the "character of life, the values, thought, and art of the nation are the same, whether one lives in Oregon or Maine."[107] He stresses man's basic need to be innovative and creative, and he claims that the stifling of this need in our modern era may destroy America:

> The man who has some creative control over the work he does, the environment in which he lives, and the rules he has to follow, who participates in building his culture, is likely to be an enthusiastic, happy and altruistic human being. If he learns that he is being manipulated for another's profit or exploited for the larger system, can we expect anything other than sullen hostility? Multiply this condition of each person millions of times and it is reasonable to expect conditions leading eventually to the dissolution of society.[108]

Itzkoff recognizes that restraints must exist on the actions of all groups, but he argues vehemently for the right—indeed, the need—for diverse communities to maintain unique values, patterns of life, and sense of identity. He sees as the greatest bulwark of cultural pluralism the right to dissent.[109] He sees in modern America not healthy dissent, but decadent universality of thought.

Others see contemporary dissent, the intergroup conflicts in modern American society in the early 1970's, as the forces which may destroy us: hawk vs. dove, black vs. white, labor vs. management, Establishment vs. youth, credibility gap between government and public, the need for public services vs. the resistance to taxes, and so on. *Time* presents the pessimistic question, "Is the U.S. Going Broke?"[110]

It is difficult to accept any prediction of the shape of the future, no

[105]Seymour W. Itzkoff, *Cultural Pluralism and American Education* (Scranton, Pa.: International Textbook Company, 1969), p. 93. Used by permission.

[106]Ibid., p. 106.

[107]Ibid., p. 107.

[108]Ibid., p. 110.

[109]Ibid., p. 122.

[110]"Is the U.S. Going Broke?" *Time*, March 13, 1972, pp. 52–69.

matter how scholarly the analysis of trends may be, as an inexorable consequence of those trends. We have noted earlier the glowing prediction that America will be one of only four postindustrial societies in the foreseeable future. We have cited differing views by cultural pluralists that America may be destroyed (1) by universality of thought or (2) by violent dissent. Economists question whether the cost of public services may exceed our abilities to pay taxes. The continued stress throughout this text, however, has been upon American democracy as a way of life, and upon faith in the future as one tenet of that cultural democracy. The authors have faith that America will solve her current problems and will fulfill the prediction of continued world leadership in the postindustrial era.

The problem facing the American schools, of course, is not so much whether cultural pluralism, cultural democracy, or cultural monism is the better ideal. Cultural pluralism currently exists. The educator's problem is to develop citizens who optimistically utilize respect, reason, and cooperation in dealing with differences.

THE ROLE OF THE SCHOOL

Formal education must be concerned with more than intellectual perception if the school is to make any contribution to improved Intergroup relations. We have indicated earlier the ineffectiveness of programs of information alone in the development and modification of the attitudes that guide our behavior. The schools must be concerned with understandings, and with tools for gaining understanding (the three R's) and high ideals and problem-solving abilities, but the crux of intergroup problems is human *emotions*.

This calls for a basic reorientation in the preservice preparation and the in-service training of the teacher. We shall summarize briefly the broad areas in which current practice needs to be re-examined: teacher purposes, teacher competencies, the scope and sequence of the public school curriculum in intergroup education, and the methodology of intergroup education.

Teacher Purposes

The task facing the teacher who is concerned with intergroup relations is that of developing in his students the understandings, ideals, and competencies necessary for effective, harmonious living as democratic citizens of a community, state, and nation in an interdependent world. This is no simple task of the presentation of the three R's. It demands of the graduates of our schools high levels of proficiency in the three R's, in understandings of our world and of the people in it, in techniques of working with people, in skills and attitudes of critical thinking, and in the development of high ideals. It means, further, that these competencies are to be expected of *all* children and youth, not just of the upper 10 per cent or 25 per cent or 50 per cent of the students, and certainly not just the white middle-class student about whom the public schools traditionally have been oriented. Some students will become more proficient than others, but the goal of the human-relations-minded teacher is effective citizenship for all his graduates.

One of the major purposes of teachers, particularly of those teaching in inner-city schools, must be to re-examine themselves. Gottlieb emphasizes that each teacher brings to the classroom his own cultural education, which colors his perceptions, which structures his actions. A study of teacher attitudes in a predominantly Negro inner-city school showed that the black teachers felt their students to be ambitious and cooperative, whereas the white teachers perceived them as lazy and talkative.[111] Miel and Kiester point out that the middle-class children of suburban parents will earn their adult livelihood in an integrated world, so that suburban teachers with a lack of either concern for or skills in human relations education are "teaching their children to be stupid."[112] Fantini and Weinstein make a case not only for all teachers to be skilled in human relations education, but for such content, indeed, to be the backbone of every school curriculum.[113] Educators seem to agree on the need for change. In a recent publication of the ASCD Council on Secondary Education, for example, Schneider speaks of "A Box —The School Ethos"[114] and of the consensus of the participants about the unimportance of much of the school curriculum and about the lack of meaningful involvement of teachers, students, and parents in the school program. However, Fantini and Weinstein are among the few modern educationists who offer concrete suggestions on "what to do about it." It seems clear, then, that prime purposes for all teachers should be (1) to examine their own prejudices, (2) to develop skills in intergroup education, and (3) to take positive steps toward incorporating human relations education into the curriculum.

The effective teacher guides his pupils throughout their years of common education through an ever-expanding orbit of social understandings and skills, roughly from competencies in living as a member of one's own family to competencies in living as a member of the human race. The stress needs to be on constructive human relations, plus all other understandings, skills, and values contributing to the improvement of human relations. This means that the successive teachers who work with the child should set up a series of progressive goals with the child working on successive developmental tasks as he gains the mental maturity and social skills requisite to their successful completion. These goals, in succession, are (1) clarification of concepts of self; (2) development of feelings of empathy (understanding of people cannot be accomplished unless the child can identify himself emotionally with them); (3) growth in skills in interpersonal relations; (4) growth in skills in group relations; and (5) growth in skills in intergroup relations. These tasks will need to be paralleled with continuous growth in (1) skills in forming value judgments and (2) skills in critical thinking. Students will work concurrently on several developmental tasks, but success

---

[111]David Gottlieb, "Teaching and Students: The Views of Negroes and White Teachers," *Sociology of Education*, Vol. XXXVII (Summer 1964), pp. 345–353.

[112]Alice Miel and Edwin Kiester, *The Short-Changed Children of Suburbia* (New York: Institute of Human Relations Press, The American Jewish Committee, 1967).

[113]Mario D. Fantini and Gerald Weinstein, *Toward a Contact Curriculum* (from manuscript in process for Harper & Row, Fantini and Weinstein. *The Disadvantaged: Challenge to Education*) New York: Anti-Defamation League.

[114]Frank Schnieder, "Teacher-Pupil Relationships in the Human School," from J. Galen Saylor and Joshua A. Smith (eds.), *Removing Barriers to Humaneness in the High School* (Washington, D.C.: A.S.C.D., N.E.A., 1971), pp. 74–75.

in the tasks further in social distance from the child must be built upon at least partial mastery of preceding tasks. For a discussion of the importance of building first skills first, with stress upon clarification of concepts of self and development of empathy, see *Elementary Curriculum in Intergroup Relations*.[115] This remains the classic in the field, for as Grambs notes, "The reports we have either are dated, mainly those of the *Intergroup Education Project* (Taba et al.) of the American Council on Education . . . or are scattered and fragmentary."[116]

Teacher Competencies

No teacher can hope to accomplish the preceding goals fully. Any capable teacher, however, can make substantial progress toward them. Certain personality characteristics, certain fields of knowledge, and certain abilities will contribute toward increased teacher efficiency. Basic to teacher success is a real concern for people, demonstrable so that children readily will recognize it. This is often referred to as a warm, outgoing personality. The teacher needs to include in his training a broad general education, with stress on the social heritage and on the social problems of his age. He needs specialized training in psychology and anthropology—the study of man, groups, and institutions. He needs, of course, specialized training in the basic theory and practice of teaching. Special abilities need to be developed in the human-relations-minded teacher. He needs to see the school as a society. He needs to recognize the significant evidence of children's needs as revealed in their work and play. He must free himself of his personal background for an objective evaluation of children's needs; this is particularly true in reference to his own middle-class values. He must at all times recognize the interdependence of physical, mental, social, and emotional learnings.

Scope and Sequence of Intergroup Education

The scope of an elementary school curriculum in intergroup education is the sum of the skills, knowledge, and attitudes necessary for accomplishment of the developmental tasks mentioned previously. Skills are necessary for working with people. Understanding of self is prerequisite to all other tasks. Knowledges about others are important mostly for their part in guiding the development of constructive attitudes; rather than just learning *about* people, intergroup education must foster emotional identification *with* and sensitivity *to* a variety of people, their feelings, and attitudes.[117] Attitudes are the most important end product, for they structure our behavior in these prejudicial areas.

The sequence has been indicated in an earlier section as successive goals of the teacher. The traditional content of the school subjects can serve as a base for the emphasis indicated here, for the stress is not on content but

[115]Hilda Taba (ed.), *Elementary Curriculum in Intergroup Relations* (Washington, D.C.: American Council on Education, 1950).

[116]Jean Dresden Grambs, *Intergroup Education* (Englewood Cliffs, N.J.: Prentice-Hall, 1968), p. 21.

[117]Taba, op. cit., p. 25.

on the provision of cooperative action in a problem-solving attack on all content. A school organized on a basic life-functions curriculum, rather than on the traditional subjects, may be more amenable to the human-relations emphasis, but again content is not the important part of the program. The end result is not acquiring a body of knowledge, but learning and habituating a way of approaching problems: with mutual respect, reason, cooperation, and high morale. In discussing a standard elementary school unit on transportation, Taba indicates the ways in which traditional content can be adapted to fit the purposes of intergroup education: "The study of communication (in the adapted unit) emphasized blocks instead of means of communication, because the aim of the unit was to develop insights into why people misunderstood each other; and a study of child's needs indicated their main difficulty was in not being understood." [118]

The secondary curriculum in intergroup education should continue the emphasis of the elementary school. Methodologically, the major block to an integrated curriculum in intergroup relations in the secondary school is the compartmentalization of course work, with the attendant impersonality in relations between teacher and student and the limitations in focusing the content of several traditional areas upon a central problem in human relations. Compounding the problem is the stress placed by many secondary teachers on the acquisition of knowledge in the separate disciplines, almost to the exclusion of attention to the development of skills and attitudes in human relations.

The leadership in constructive human-relations education shifts from the classroom teacher of the self-contained elementary school to the guidance department of the departmentalized secondary school. Conferences on individual and group problems, and the election of course patterns, are in the province of the guidance counselors. These counselors can do only part of the job. They can assist students in exploring their own potential, through testing, conferences, and patterns of exploratory courses. They can see that course patterns selected by students not only explore the potential of the student but also sample broadly the opportunities offered by the world. They can develop in individual and in group conferences, and through supervision of student cocurricular activities, the inseparability of individual and group welfare. They can urge the curriculum development department to offer to senior high school students those organized bodies of specialized knowledge in personal mental hygiene, family relations, and problems of democracy. But these tasks are administrative in nature. The real learning still occurs under the guidance of the classroom teachers who conduct the courses and who sponsor the cocurricular activities. Secondary classroom teachers must become human-relations minded if high school students are to receive guidance in the application of classroom concepts to the problems of life. The cocurricular program offers an excellent laboratory for the application of social understandings developed in the classroom. Values will become implanted and skills will be developed when these understandings are applied to areas of life *that are important to students.*

[118] Ibid., p. 207.

Methodoloy of Intergroup Education

An application of mental hygiene to classroom discipline is fundamental to the human-relations approach. A dictator can maintain order and can instill intellectual concepts more rapidly than can a democratic leader. A dictator can indoctrinate with an authoritarian philosophy through the use of highly emotional propaganda techniques. These authoritarian values are the antithesis of those valued in a democracy. Only in a permissive atmosphere, based on a sound knowledge of personality development, can attitudes and skills of democratic action be developed. Careful attention must be paid to the social climate of the group and to the personality adjustments of individuals.

Provisions for an extensive and varied base of three types of learning experiences are essential. First, situations involving strong emotional reactions must be structured. Second, discussion and analysis of those situations must explore those reactions, their causes, and ways of constructive adjustment to them. Finally, tasks requiring the ability to use inductive and deductive reasoning should include both these emotional situations and scientific ones, such as the gathering of research data to document discussion. We understand imperfectly how to develop the skills of problem solving.[119] The best solution seems to be the provision of much practice in the use of the technique, in order to develop a "mind set" for its use when one is faced with a problem.

Fostering understandings of people means more than the presentation of facts about them; it means an emotional identification with them. Producers of films for the elementary school studies program recognize this fact in focusing the content of the film on the children of other lands rather than on the adults. Primary teachers are adept in finding common strands that permit children to make a connection between what they know and understand and the strange and unfamiliar. John H. Elliott refers to this as "building bridges."[120] It means starting the study of other groups with an emphasis on likenesses, postponing the study of differences until the bridges of understanding are built. Finally, teaching should be organized in such a way as to support the relationship between ideas, facts, and insights that are most difficult to see and to understand. Logical organization provides many clues to children in their attempts to solve problems related to understanding other groups of people.

Building adequate concepts of self, developing empathy, and building skills in interpersonal relations are integral to the discussion in the preceding three paragraphs. Specifically, they mean freedom to practice interpersonal relations in the classroom and on the playground without the domination of the teacher. They mean class discussion of the successful and unsuccessful techniques evolving from the group, with stress upon understanding that all behavior is caused and that our behavior affects the other fellow. Sociological techniques such as panels, forums, sociodrama, and sociograms may serve to assist the teacher in better understanding her group and

[119]See Chapter 12 for a brief *schema*.
[120]John H. Elliott, *Building Bridges* (New York: Astoria Press, 1950).

in helping its members to understand themselves better.[121] The games theory probed by educational administrators in the 1950's by the Ohio State studies on leadership, funded by the U.S. Navy, and made more sophisticated by colleges of commerce in workshops for management personnel, is pervading much of the intergroup education strategy of the early 1970's. Many new materials may be expected from commercial sources. The personal involvement of games situations equates to the earlier sociodrama; the advantage of the game (the instrumented laboratory) is that the teacher has more materials and more precise instructions for their use and hence needs less training in order to achieve equivalent results.

Building skills in intergroup activities can be accomplished at the secondary school level, if the school is so oriented. These skills build on all that has preceded; further, the cocurricular program of the high school provides an excellent laboratory. The Stanford Workshop on Intercultural Education makes a number of suggestions applicable to intercultural education that are equally applicable to intergroup situations.[122] They stress capitalization upon traumatic incidents precipitating group conflicts to assist youth in probing for the *causes* of those conflicts—not the episode that precipitated the conflict, but the underlying causes. They stress the values of the unit approach to teaching. They emphasize discussions of parent–child conflicts, housing deficiencies, athletic contests, and other cocurricular topics. Student participation is stressed, through the preparation of panels, programs, newspapers, plays, fiestas, and the like. This active participation by students not only fosters the understanding necessary for effective intergroup action but also provides practice in the skills necessary for the solution of intergroup problems. Certainly Cole, Quillen, and Wiess were prophets far in advance of their times; they stress *involvement* and *relevance*. The new generation of writers in intergroup education—Anderson, Beck, Combs, Dillenbeck, Dunfee, Fantini, Foley, Fromm, Grambs, MacDonald, Trubowitz, Warden, Weinstein, Whiting, Wilhelms, and so on—lean heavily on the theoretical framework developed by the pioneers. They tend to develop strategies rather than new theory. Taba is a good example; she pioneered in theory and currently is developing strategies.[123] A host of new strategies may be expected to develop, judging by the belated but unanimous awakening of educators to the problem; for example, the Association for Supervision and Curriculum Development, a major force in American education, issued successive major publications at the start of the 1970's devoted to problems of intergroup education.[124, 125] School administrators also are getting into the action, with college classes devoted to human relations.[126]

[121]For a discussion of these techniques, see Hilda Taba et al., *Diagnosing Human Relations Needs* (Washington, D.C.: American Council on Education, 1951).

[122]Stewart G. Cole, I James Quillen, and Mildred J. Wiess, *Charting Intercultural Education* (Stanford, Calif.: Stanford University Press, 1946), pp. 36–41.

[123]Hilda Taba and Deborah Elkins, *Teaching Strategies for the Culturally Disadvantaged* (Chicago: Rand McNally, 1966).

[124]Maxine Dunfee, *Ethnic Modification of the Curriculum* (Washington, D.C.: A.S.C.D., N.E.A., 1971).

[125]*Dare to Care/Dare to Act: Racism and Education.* Addresses and Statements at the 1971 A.S.C.D. Annual Conference (Washington, D.C.: A.S.C.D., N.E.A., 1971).

[126]William W. Savage, *Interpersonal and Group Relations in Educational Administration* (Glenview, Ill.: Scott, Foresman, 1968).

THE CONTINUING SCHOOL INTEGRATION CRISES

The public school teacher of the great cities of the 1970's has no choice as to whether or not there shall be a curriculum in intergroup education in his classroom. The curriculum, after all, is the sum of the experiences shared by the teacher and his pupils. A significant portion of that total, for most of the 1960's and continuing into the 1970's, was that of dealing with the hostilities of his Negro pupils and of their parents (and, in specific cities, the hostilities of pupils and parents of Puerto Rican and Mexican extraction, whose fortunes tend to be tied to those of the Negro). Silberman analyzed the cultural matrix of the immediate future as it affected the business community in the early 1960's. Your authors see no reason to believe that the implications for the school community differ from those for the business community, and they see no significant change in the cultural matrix in the early 1970's. Partial quotation of the Silberman analysis follows:

> It would be fatuous to pretend that any set of policies adopted by business and government can bring racial peace within the next few years. For one thing, Negroes' impatience, bitterness, and anger are likely to increase the closer they come to full equality. This is not a quirk of Negro character but a characteristic of all disadvantaged groups; the closer they are to their goals, the harder it is to understand or justify the disparities that remain. Indeed, it is a commonplace of history that revolutions (and the Negro protest movement resembles a revolution in many ways) stem from hope, not despair; from progress, not stalemate. And the nearer to triumph the revolutionaries get, the tougher they usually become.[127]

To justify the faith that teachers are professional people rather than mere craftsmen, it seems essential that the teaching complex—teachers, supervisors, administrators, lay board members, state departments of education, college professors of teacher education, college administrators, and the U.S. Office of Education—face up to the challenge. If the welfare of the child is the concern of the professional educator, then the teacher must "deal with hostilities" in the ways suggested in the preceding section on methodology of intergroup education. As the classroom teacher applies the best of current knowledge to developing vital experiences in intergroup education within his classroom, it is the responsibility of the rest of the teaching complex to develop new and better ways of fostering constructive intergroup living and to disseminate this new knowledge and methodology to the teacher. One good example of a highly successful project in intergroup research is the program developed in the Banner District of St. Louis. Dr. Sam Shepard, Banner District Superintendent, is in constant demand to speak to professional and lay groups in other cities to explain the working of his plan and to suggest ways it might be applied to other cities. We have too few Sam Shepards. The teaching profession must invest much time and energy (and money) in action research in intergroup education if it is to meet the challenge of the times.

The public and private schools of America traditionally have been as notoriously niggardly in the allocation of funds for research as American industry has been successful in the generous investment of significant portions

[127]Charles E. Silberman, "The Businessman and the Negro," *Fortune*, September 1963, p. 193. Used by permission.

of its budget in research activities. The massive involvement of industry in the War on Poverty promised to yield significant dividends to American education. The education and training programs financed by the federal government under the Economic Opportunity Act of 1964 and other legislation appeared to be developing new approaches to old educational problems.[128] Unfortunately, the governmental bureaucracy stifled the research effort of industry by disallowing as legitimate contract expense most research endeavors. Washington said to industry, "Innovate; but don't waste any money on researching the new ideas, just implement them." It remains to be seen what role industry, and industrial research techniques, will play in the new manpower retraining program emerging from the Comprehensive Manpower Training Act of 1969. There were, of course, many action research projects involved in these government-sponsored programs of education and training. Men's urban Job Corps Centers will be used as an illustrative program. Many high Job Corps officials were disclaiming the research function as it applies to the operation of Job Corps Centers. This is understandable. Any new organization undergoes an early period of ferment in the development of policies and procedures. Job Corps was created in late 1964. "Policy Guide" was not developed until mid-1966. The newer governmental programs encompass the fifty states and other U.S. possessions and protectorates. They involve state and local governmental agencies, as well as private contractors drawn from industry, foundations, universities, local school boards, and other organizations such as Community Centers, Young Women's Christian Association, and so on. During the early days of Job Corps, the organizations operating the centers were under the loose and often contradictory controls of personnel from Job Corps headquarters in Washington. There appeared to be little coordination of the efforts of the various departments in headquarters; in fact, there appeared to be little continuity of individuals assigned to responsible positions in the various departments. The research function of the education and training programs in Job Corps centers was a major source of many divergent opinions.

The action research activities of the urban Job Corps centers both illustrate the divergence of opinion as to whether research is a function of a government-sponsored program of education and training and indicate the potential fruitfulness of this source of materials and methods for future application to the educational establishment. Within the diversity of opinions concerning research, the most commonly stated positions seemed to be the following: (1) Governmental funds for the operation of Job Corps centers shall not be utilized for research, but for the operation of the programs.[129] (2) The uniqueness of the student population of Job Corps demands innovative approaches to the education and training functions. Both positions concurrently were stated by many individuals, both in Job Corps headquarters and within the various training centers, with little or no apparent recognition

[128]For a comprehensive listing of the programs under the Office of Economic Opportunity and the other governmental agencies, see William A. Haddad, "Mr. Shriver and the Savage Politics of Poverty," *Harper's Magazine*, December 1965, pp. 46–47.

[129]While Job Corps center contractors were prohibited from spending contract funds for research activities, special grants were available for research projects designed by headquarters personnel. Contractors sometimes received these special grants for in-center research activities as approved by headquarters.

of the incongruity of these positions. Washington supervisors constantly stressed "trying new ideas." As new ideas are developed, implemented, and evaluated, action research results. The scope of this research is indicated by the fact that each of the large urban centers developed its own unique program.

The potential for development of materials and methods for application within the educational establishment, with particular reference to underprivileged children and youth, may be gleaned from a brief examination of the philosophic foundations on which one Job Corps program was based. In January 1966, Director James R. Bryner presented the program of the Atterbury Job Corps center, a synopsis of which follows. For a detailed description of the program, see Chapter 10, "Problems of the Depressed Areas."

The Job Corps program at Atterbury has three goals, two of which are traditional: teaching job skills and providing general education courses leading to a high school diploma. Not so obvious, but the tremendously exciting and more important goal, is the enculturation of educationally and culturally impoverished youth into the commonly accepted mores of American society.

If Dr. Bryner's goals were achieved at Atterbury, and if similar goals in other Job Corps centers were achieved, then one of the greatest contributions of Job Corps well may have been to present to the public and private schools of this country new ways of educating culturally and educationally disadvantaged youth, contributions based on action research!

De Facto Segregation. The major school issue of the 1960's was what the Negro organizations have chosen to call *de facto* segregation, as differentiated from the *de jure* segregation declared unconstitutional by the Supreme Court in 1954. Court battles, demonstrations, freedom marches, sit-ins, and so on, continued in the South, where only 18 per cent of the black students were integrated fifteen years after the Supreme Court decision mandating desegregation. The major Negro organizations fought valiantly to secure complete integration in the North, but the Supreme Court continued to consider de facto segregation constitutional, so Northern schools experienced minimal integration in the 1960's. The Stennis plea for "equality of treatment," in fact, threatened Southern integration in the early 1970's. As Southern whites fled to the suburbs, resegregation set in; the courts stepped in, declaring that "busing may be used as a means of desegregating public schools."[130] Significantly, "The ruling does not apply to Northern districts where segregation results from housing patterns."[131] Even so, many Northern legislatures appeared willing to integrate, until President Nixon publicly proclaimed (repeatedly) his opposition to busing as a means of eliminating de facto segregation. In 1970 and 1971, early legislation authorizing busing for elimination of de facto segregation in the North rapidly was being repealed. De facto segregation appeared to be a permanent part of the Northern scene and threatened to become increasingly significant in the South as the South became increasingly urbanized. The situation changed dramatically in the 1971–1972 school year, as the courts ignored the presidential opposi-

[130] "Court Okays Busing for Desegregation," *N.E.A. Reporter*, May 21, 1971, p. 1.
[131] Ibid.

tion to busing as a means of desegregation. For full discussion, see "busing" on pp. 351–352.

De facto segregation has been defined as racial segregation in the public schools brought about by residential patterns. The core areas of the great cities have tended to become almost exclusively Negro in composition. By contrast, the suburban areas (both within and outside the city limits of the parent city) have tended to become almost exclusively white. The only truly integrated schools in the great cities in recent years have been those schools whose sites fell approximately on the dividing line between the Negro residential areas and the white residential areas. Many schools became predominantly Negro through redrawing of district lines to exclude the white areas. (In all justice to school administration, this was a natural result of the heavier Negro inhabitation of what were formerly white residences; former white single-family residences usually became Negro multiple-family dwellings, with proportionately larger enrollments. Either the school buliding had to be enlarged or district lines had to be withdrawn.) James Farmer, executive director of the Congress of Racial Equality, said, "What we're getting in city after city in the North now is a black core at the center of the city and a white noose around it."[132] The schools in the black core are the subject of the de facto segregation battles.

In 1963 the Supreme Court refused to review the case in Gary, Indiana, in which the plaintiffs had contended that inferior education was provided in the predominantly Negro schools. Fresh attack by the NAACP attorneys unsuccessfully was instituted against the Cincinnati Public Schools, on completely different grounds from those on which the Gary case was lost by the NAACP in the lower courts. The legal briefs for the Cincinnati case paralleled as closely as possible the reasoning used by the Supreme Court in the 1954 decision, as follows: "To separate them [Negro children] . . . from others of a similar age and qualifications solely because of their race generates a feeling of inferiority as to their status in the community . . . which may affect their hearts and minds in a way unlikely ever to be undone."[133] The Supreme Court consistently failed to respond to such briefs in the 1960's, finding nothing unconstitutional in de facto segregation, in the North, but it came strangely close to that reasoning in attacking de jure segregation in the South, to the extent of not only removing the legal and administrative support of segregation but even of ordering busing for integration. As we have noted earlier, the South felt encouraged to resist such court orders in the light of President Nixon's repeated opposition to them. In the late 1960's, the fate of de facto segregation still was in doubt in the South, but it remained firmly entrenched in the North. In the early 1970's, de facto segregation rapidly was being eroded in the North, as a result of court orders for busing, despite congressional discussion of a constitutional amendment to outlaw busing for integration.[134]

Two factors lent credibility to Senator Stennis' plea for "equal treat-

[132]United Press International, "Negroes Will Dominate Cities if Trend Continues . . . Farmer," *Cincinnati Enquirer*, November 16, 1964.

[133]From a report, *Background Paper on the Integration Problem*, made by The Cincinnati School Foundation, March 1964. Used by permission.

[134]"The Fall Madness Over School Busings," *Business Week*, October 2, 1971, pp. 70–71.

ment" of de facto areas in Southern cities. The first was the Coleman Report. The second was the growing sentiment among black leaders that locally (black) controlled segregated schools in the core city may be preferable to centrally (white) controlled integrated schools.

Christopher Jencks reviewed the Coleman Report, saying, among other things:

> In the summer of 1964 Congress had decided to pass a civil-rights law which was expected to end *de jure* school segregation in the South by cutting off Federal funds from segregated systems. The question inevitably arose: what about *de facto* segregation in the North? The expedient answer was that the Commissioner of Education should investigate the problem and report back in two years.[135]

Under the leadership of Dr. James Coleman, a distinguished sociologist from Johns Hopkins University, nearly a million students in 6,000 schools were surveyed in the fall of 1965; then came the task of analyzing the data and reporting the findings so that Congress could draw conclusions from it. Long before the report possibly could be ready, Congress proceeded with the Elementary and Secondary Education Act of 1965, allotting huge sums of money for the improvement of the education of culturally disadvantaged children. At the very least, the Coleman Report questions the wisdom of such investment of federal funds; broadly interpreted, the report states that neither integration nor increased expenditures of money make any difference in the education of the disadvantaged child. Among the survey findings, as reported by Jencks, were (1) "black and white pupils are seldom in the same schools, even in the North"; (2) "black pupils do learn much less than the white pupils, at least judging by standardized tests of verbal and non-verbal skill, reading comprehension, arithmetic skill and general information . . . a 16-year-old is more than two years behind"; (3) the only major difference between black and white schools is that the black schools have more black teachers; (4) "neither black nor white children of a given family background did significantly better in schools with high expenditures, large libraries, accelerated curriculums and so forth"; (5) "there is reason to believe that children learn more from one another than from their teachers"; (6) a child is "influenced by his classmates' social class background rather than by their race"; (7) "by far the most important factor measured in the survey was the ethnic and socio-economic background of the individual child"; and (8) "even when family background and attitudes were taken into account, more than half the variations in individual achievement remain completely unexplained."[136]

Jencks reports some tentative conclusions of the Coleman Report as "black children were more sensitive to peer influences than white children"; there is "a strong association between teacher verbal ability and student achievement in secondary schools"; "parental expectations probably had an important influence on children's achievement"; "integration was a better

[135]Christopher Jencks, "A Reappraisal of the Most Controversial Educational Document of Our Time," *New York Times Magazine*, August 10, 1969, p. 12. © 1969 by The New York Times Company. Reprinted by permission.

[136]Ibid., pp. 12–13.

bet than what had come to be called compensatory education," but "*neither* strategy would help achievement much"; and "the major reasons for unequal academic achievement must be outside the school."[137] Jencks sees implications of the study as "black children's teachers also come from poorer homes and do worse on tests of academic ability"; school systems may be "assigning able teachers to schools with able pupils"; if black children attend schools where this informal curriculum is based on a vocabulary half as large and on concepts far less abstract than in a white school, their chance of developing academic skills is reduced"; and "a poor black child would *not* benefit from attending school with poor white children, but that he *would* benefit from attending school with middle class children, black or white . . . while a white child would suffer very little" (from integration).[138] Jencks noted that there is no consensus, even among the experts, about the policy implications of the Coleman Report. Antagonists of integration and opponents of using tax funds for compensatory education, however, certainly can find ammunition in the report.

The report was submitted at a time when American society was coming to the reluctant conclusion that it was sick, that much of the problem lay in the present educational programs for the disadvantaged. There was debate over whether the appropriate remedy was the integration of schools or the provision of compensatory education for the child in whatever school he might be found. The Coleman Report questioned whether either strategy would do any good; it questioned, in fact, if schools do any good. A major conclusion of the report seemed to be that only social reforms *outside* of the school would help the child in the school. If this is so, then why battle de facto segregation? Why not invest the resources of the nation in a more basic attack upon the roots of poverty? This continued to be President Nixon's position, as stressed in his nationally televised attack upon busing in March 1972. The courts continued to disagree with him.

The second factor ameliorating the attacks upon de facto segregation in the late 1960's was a shift in the attitudes of black leaders in the late 1960's and early 1970's; such a shift was not yet found among the masses of blacks, who still were clamoring for integration. Among other unanticipated consequences of integration in the South was the loss of jobs by thousands of black teachers and the virtual elimination of the black principal.[139] As early as November 1970, a twenty-one-member N.E.A. task force investigating school desegregation in Louisiana and Mississippi concluded that the "bad news about desegregation in the two states studied tragically outweighs the good."[140] Black leaders were relating this Southern phenomenon to its Northern counterpart and projecting current demographic trends in urban areas. They saw the loss of black leadership, both in the schools and in the community, as full control of the schools became vested in white boards of education and white school administrators under the various integration

[137]Ibid., pp. 13–42.

[138]Ibid., pp. 12–38.

[139]J. C. James, "The Black Principal," *The National Elementary Principal*, Vol. 1, No. 4 (February 1971), pp. 20–25.

[140]"Black Authority Disintegrates as the Schools Desegregate," *N.E.A. Reporter*, Vol. 9, November 27, 1970, p. 1.

schemes. In the early 1970's, they seemed to be concluding reluctantly that possibly the lesser evil was black schools with black teachers and black curriculum for black children of black areas *under black control.* As early as June 1970, Bickel was saying, "Negro leaders in the North are asking for black principals and black teachers for black schools." [141] As *black studies* became the "in term among educators" [142] in the early 1970's the Negro leaders saw yet another area dominated by whites; and their ardor for integration cooled still further. De facto segregation seemed to be here to stay; black control of black schools seemed destined to become the new battle. The courts did not see it this way. Court orders for massive busing to achieve integration accelerated in the early 1970's. Both de jure and de facto segregation in schools seemed to be outlawed by the courts.

School Adjustments to the Climate of the Times. Cities great and small, faced with charges of de jure and/or de facto segregation, developed a variety of ways to resolve their problems. Integration was painfully slow; in the eighteen years following the Supreme Court decision of 1954, only about one black child in four actually attended school with white children, and nearly all of this integration was accomplished in the final eight years. In the first ten years school systems were making their plans "with all deliberate speed"; in 1964, the Cincinnati School Foundation summarized the major plans to be implemented as follows:

A. *Appointment of Study or Advisory Commissions.*
   Public school systems have established commissions to study the problem and prepare recommendations for solution. In most cases the commissions have been composed of lay citizens, usually with professional staff participation. School systems which have reported the establishment of such commissions include Berkeley, Champaign, Chicago, Denver, Detroit, Englewood, Los Angeles, Minneapolis, New Rochelle, New York, Norwalk, Pasadena, Philadelphia, Plainfield, San Francisco, Stamford, Wichita, Boston.

B. *Statement of Policy by the School Board.*
   A number of school systems have adopted policy statements on de facto school segregation and/or equal educational opportunities for minority groups. Most cities have not issued such policy statements. On the state level, California, New Jersey, and New York have recognized that residential segregation results in segregated schools and that solutions to the educational aspects of this problem should be sought by the cities in those states. Cities which have issued policy statements include Detroit, Morristown (N.J.), New York, Norwalk, Pasadena, Wichita.

C. *Specific Plans to Promote Integration.*
   1. *"Princeton Plan"*
      Two formerly separate neighborhood schools with populations of different races are reorganized so that all children in grades 1–3 attend one school and all children in grades 4–6 attend the other school. This plan was initiated in Princeton, N.J., 15 years ago.
   2. *"Open Enrollment"*
      "Sending" and "receiving" schools are established to alter the racial proportions that exist in both schools. Free bus transportation is generally

---

[141]Alexander M. Bickel, "Desegregation: Where Do We Go From Here?" *Phi Delta Kappan,* Vol. LI, No. 10 (June 1970), p. 521.
[142]Rose Marie Walker Levy, *Education U.S.A. Special Report: Black Studies in Schools* (Washington, D.C.: N.S.P.R.A., N.E.A., 1970), p. 1.

needed to operate this plan. The term is also applied to "free-transfer" systems where parents may request the transfer of children to another school if there is space available.

3. *Pupil Dispersal*

In small communities a school with predominantly Negro pupils is closed and the students distributed among the other schools that are predominantly white.

4. *Rezoning*

School attendance zones are changed to promote a deliberate mixing of children from different ethnic backgrounds. This method is most applicable for contiguous areas having different racial compositions.

5. *Feeder Patterns*

The combinations of elementary schools which feed pupils to secondary schools are altered to minimize the concentration of one racial group in a particular junior high school.

6. *Selection of Sites for New Schools*

Criteria are established for planning of new schools that take into account the racial makeup of the areas, and school sites are selected to promote an attendance district that has a balance of races.

D. *Concomitant Steps Proposed to Improve Educational Opportunities.*

1. *Compensatory Education*

A greatly increased instructional program is instituted for children who come from "culturally disadvantaged" homes. Provisions include smaller class size, double periods in English, tutoring of individuals or small groups, assistance of psychologists and social workers. Major emphasis is placed on improving the achievement levels of students.

2. *Pre-school Programs for Children*

Efforts are concentrated on children from low socio-economic backgrounds, starting at the ages of 3 and 4 years in order to raise the level of communication and understanding before the children enter kindergarten.

3. *Use of Appropriate Textbooks*

Pictures and text of books, for lower grades particularly, show Negro children as well as white children; subject material includes situations that are familiar to the life of minority groups. Histories of the Negroes and their role in American history have been introduced in two school systems.

4. *Training for Human Relations*

The institution of training programs for teachers, counselors, and administrators to work with children in integrated classrooms, and to work with parents and groups in one community. [143]

By and large, these were the plans implemented. Only two major changes and two minor ones need comment. (1) The Educational Park was developed. (2) Open enrollment fell victim to the busing controversy; it was replaced with court-ordered plans for integration, with compulsory free busing to establish the same black–white ratio in both "sending" and "receiving" schools as prevailed in the entire school district, and all schools in the district became "sending" or "receiving" schools unless their neighborhood just happened to furnish the required black–white mix of students. Senator Stennis was bitter; these court-ordered plans for compulsory busing

[143]*Background Paper on the Integration Problem* (Cincinnati: Cincinnati School Foundation, March 1964), pp. 9–10. Used by permission.

affected only Southern schools. (3) Certainly the "academy" advocates support his "equal treatment" theory with vigor. The small but growing number of academies may be a minor problem nationally, but it is a severe financial burden on its adherents. (4) Tracking may offer them new hope.

The preceding four changes will be discussed, followed by brief comments on two related problems: urban schools and due process. The two latter problems are not necessarily related to integration, but they certainly are part of the crisis facing American schools in the 1970's.

Educational Parks. The educational park is the boldest and most imaginative proposal yet offered for coping with the segregated urban community and its school problems. The park is, in essence, a scheme for concentrating all the schools of a section of the city, or in some cases of the whole city, upon a single large campus.

> The plan applies to urban districts the principle, long accepted in rural areas, that when good schools cannot be provided close to a child's home, he should be transported to a site where an adequate program is possible. . . . Some advocates of the park plan would concentrate a whole school system in one large campus; some favor separate elementary and secondary centers; and others prefer several comprehensive parks strategically located about the periphery of the city.[144]

Despite the busing costs, adherents of the plan claim significant economies in over-all operation; for example, Syracuse, New York, estimates that "25 per cent more pupils can be served at a slightly higher cost" in its development of a campus plan to replace eight outmoded elementary schools.[145]

Busing. " 'Freedom of choice is dead!' This was the statement of Jerris Leonard of the Department of Justice when he came to Columbia, South Carolina, last Spring. He went on to say that extensive busing would take place and that Columbia had no choice but to comply." [146] "Nixon emphatically restated his position: 'I have consistently opposed the busing of our nation's school children to achieve a racial balance.' " [147] How dramatic can a school crisis become?

The tenor of Congressional legislation, of implementation by liberal civil right's administrators, and of court decisions made quite clear to the South that the latter half of the 1960's was a "get tough" time on school integration. State legislatures fell into line and codified this approach. In 1968, 68 per cent of Southern black children were in all-black schools; by 1970, only 18.4 per cent of Southern black children were in all-black schools! [148]

A turning point seemed to be apparent in 1970 as a result of the issuing of court-ordered plans for compulsory busing to achieve racial balance in

---

[144]John H. Fischer, "Desegregating City Schools," *The PTA Magazine*, Vol. 59, No. 4 (December 1964), pp. 12–13.

[145]Franklin S. Barry, *The Syracuse Campus School Plan.* (Paper presented at the *National Conference on Equal Educational Opportunity in American Cities*, sponsored by the U.S. Commission on Civil Rights in Washington, D.C., November 16–18, 1967.)

[146]Richard Gregel, "School Desegregation: A Student View," *New South*, Vol. 26, No. 1 (Winter 1971), p. 34.

[147]"Bus Stop," *Time*, August 16, 1971, pp. 14–15.

[148]David E. Wagoner, "The North, Not the South, Is Where School Desegregation Isn't Happening," *American School Board Journal*, Vol. 159, No. 3 (September 1971), p. 31.

the South. Prior to this time, some liberal civil rights administrators had been replaced by the Nixon administration, so some softening commenced in 1969, but the real shift in executive policy came in 1970, with the furor over busing. "State legislatures and Departments of Education, without prior notice, repealed state regulations aimed at integrating racially unbalanced schools . . . . Rochester, New York, with 33 per cent black enrollment, first adopted and then repealed a plan for total integration. . . . Many Southern districts . . . were stopped dead in their tracks on sniffing the new winds from Washington. Desegration plans well along the way were hastily withdrawn." [149] This seemed to solidify further the position of de facto segregation in the North and to threaten meaningful integration in the South. Court-ordered plans for busing remained in effect; but without vigorous action by the executive branch to enforce them, their fulfillment seemed doubtful.

The fall of 1971 saw extensive school compliance with court orders, despite executive (and popular) opposition. As the federal executive and the state legislatures apparently were turning their backs on busing as a way of securing racial balance, the courts apparently were expanding their view of its paramount importance. When the Denver School Board rescinded an integration plan (after an election resulting in a change in membership on the board), the court ordered the board to carry out the originally adopted plan. As Wagoner put it, "once board action has been taken to desegregate, there is no backing up—when the buses start to roll, there's no stopping." [150] Other court decisions of mid-1971 seemed to be even more significant. Briefly stated, they seemed to be saying that there can be no such thing as a walk-in school which maintains de facto segregation in a larger school district, that the very existence of racial imbalance in any school within the district makes the district guilty of de jure segregation. Further, they stressed achievement of racial balance in all schools of the district in the same ratio as pertained to the entire school population, and they stressed busing as the means to achieve it! The 1971–72 academic year saw courts ordering metropolitan consolidation of school systems, to integrate white suburban school children with the black residents of the core city.[151]

This very position taken by Southern courts precipitated the busing furor in early 1970 which led to presidential protests. By late 1971 the Northern courts were taking the same position as their Southern counterparts. This appeared to herald the end of de facto segregation in all larger school units, an end by busing. The same applied to the all-white suburban school system. By 1971 courts were ordering metropolitan school consolidation to further integration. A related issue, school finance, may be very significant in this regard. Court decisions in California, Minnesota, New Jersey, and Texas, in the early 1970's, challenged the traditional property tax as the basis for school support, on the grounds that wealthy districts with low tax rates provided plush educational systems whereas poor districts with high

[149]Ivor Kraft, "1970—The Year of the Big Sellout on Integration," Phi Delta Kappan, Vol. LI, No. 10 (June 1970), p. 524.

[150]Wagoner, op. cit., p. 32.

[151]"The Agony of Busing Moves North," Time, November 15, 1971, pp. 61–66.

tax rates still provided very few dollars for education.[152] If financial support becomes totally a state responsibility, why not state-wide ratios for racial balance, to be achieved by massive busing? This would be the logical extension of metropolitan consolidation of school systems comprised of black cities and white suburbs.

Academies. A minor movement by Southern parents to escape school integration has been the founding of private academies. It has been estimated that about 500 of these new academies sprang up in the South between 1954 and 1970.[153] Private education has never been a big factor in Southern education, for the economy could not support both public and private schools. (Less than 10 per cent of all Southern children traditionally have attended parochial schools.) As federal pressure for integration eases, with growing de facto segregation in Southern suburbs, the academy may cease to expand.

Tracking. Ability grouping (really a misnomer; reading scores are heavily weighted, so it really is achievement grouping) has been tried many times on the American scene, for many purposes. Now it appears to be another element of the Southern strategy to minimize integration. The Coleman Report clearly defined inequality of educational achievement between black and white children. On June 25, 1969, the U.S. District Court approved a plan for integration by tracking for the Sunflower County Schools:

> children in the first three grades will be given the California Test of Basic Skills or a comparable aptitude test by a disinterested outside agency. . . . children who rank in the top quarter on test scores will be sent to the nearest of the three schools in which all the (1,000) white children in the district are enrolled with 38 Negro children. Children in the lower three quarters will be sent to the nearest of five schools in which the remaining 4,100 Negro children and no white children are now enrolled.[154]

Score one for the academy! White professional parents will not send their children to predominantly black schools, and the range of human abilities makes inevitable that some of their children will score in the lower three quarters of test results.

Urban Schools. "A few years ago, this nation's best high schools were in the big cities; today, according to a secondary education survey prepared by three education professors, these same cities now have the worst schools." [155] "Between 1940 and 1960 the black population of metropolitan areas more than doubled, and by 1985, if present trends continue, it will double once more." [156] This is only one dimension of the crisis facing urban schools today: the cultural composition of the student body, as inner-city schools are flooded with poor whites and blacks. A second critical dimension

---

[152]"New Jersey School Aid Ruled Unconstitutional," *Education, U.S.A.*, January 31, 1972.

[153]John W. Yeates, "Private Schools and Public Confusion," *New South*, Vol. 25, No. 4 (Fall 1970), p. 83.

[154]"Integration by Tracking to Be Tried in Mississippi," *Inequality in Education*, Vol. 1, No. 1 (October 10, 1969), p. 9.

[155]"Inner City Hard Facts," *Concern*, Vol. 1, No. 3 (November 1970), p. 4.

[156]Whitney M. Young, "The Racial Whirlwind—Will It Finally Destroy U.S. Society?" *Cincinnatti Enquirer*, October 19, 1969, p. 14–A.

is the dwindling tax base, as the middle classes flee to the suburbs and industry moves to industrial parks beyond the city limits. HEW recognizes the problems, as noted in its *Final Report of the Task Force on Urban Education,* but school boards seemed less than enthusiastic about the HEW recommendations. A new Urban Education Act might coordinate existing funds effectively and provide new ones, but local boards fear increased federal control. The *Curriculum* proposal of the HEW draft of a new Act commences, "Curriculum is defined here as a clearly articulated master plan for the educative processes which includes student-oriented performance objectives; sequenced sets of experiences organized from task analyses; basic strategies for acquiring the knowledge, skills, and attitudes in these sequences; and evaluation based on these objectives." [157] True, under *Community Determination* HEW notes, "In order for that education to be effective, and truly relevant to the child's own frame of reference and environment, all components of the community need to be meaningfully involved in the educational process." [158] But they go on, under *Authority Structure,* to speak of the "need for restructuring of authority on all levels, Federal, State, municipal and community." [159] In case there remained any doubt in the minds of school board members as to the intentions of HEW with regard to federal control, a special section is devoted to "The Problems with Present Local Agents of Authority," saying, in part, "the authority figures, the policymakers and administrators, are often either too remote from or too indifferent to all of the constituencies that they are supposed to serve." [160] The junior author of this text has had bitter experience with twenty-two-year-old social workers on the Washington staff who claimed to know more about his problems as director of an Urban Job Corps Center than he did, and they had never visited the site, whereas he invested sixteen-hour days there, seven days a week. He sympathizes with the board position: we have enough problems, without Washington bureaucracy adding to them. The fact remains, of course, that urban schools are in a crisis situation, not just in the United States, but in Canada as well.[161] Urban problems will be discussed more fully in the next chapter, "Problems of Depressed Areas."

A new dimension may be imminent in the attack upon problems of the urban school. Whitney Young commented, in speaking of the changing composition of the population of the inner city, "This population shift places black people in potential political control of the very heart of our national power." [162] The 1970's may see a fresh attack, this time from black leaders, on the problems of the urban school, both through local (black) boards of education and through federal (civil rights) legislation. The most stimulating aspect of this prospect is the very real emergence of black pride. May the spirit of Reverend King prevail, as it did from Montgomery to Memphis.[163]

[157]*Urban School Crisis: The Problems and Solutions Proposed by the HEW Urban Education Task Force* (Washington, D.C.: N.S.P.R.A., N.E.A., 1970), p. 48.

[158]Ibid., p. 49.

[159]Ibid., p. 50.

[160]Ibid., p. 51.

[161]*The Poor at School in Canada* (Ottawa: Canadian Teachers Federation, 1970).

[162]Young, op. cit., p. 14–A.

[163]"A Powerful New Movie: King—from Montgomery to Memphis," *Ebony,* Vol. XXV, No. 6, April 1970, pp. 173–182.

Due Process. As though the school systems did not have enough problems of racial balance, the civil rights legislation of the late 1960's resulted in a number of court cases relating to the rights of students, one which "threatens to make public school operation a potential nightmare for many Boards of Education and administrators." [164] The essence of the problem is that constitutional safeguards of personal freedom, and legislative elaboration of these rights, is not limited to adults. This position may be endorsed by all in theory, but it makes a shambles of traditional "rules of conduct" for students in most schools. In addition it leaves boards, superintendents, principals, and teachers in severe doubt as to what real authority they possess. Both "integration" and "crisis" dimensions appear here, as dramatized in the *American School Board Journal:*

READ BUT DO NOT CRINGE
These are headlines quoted from recent newspapers:
Judge Orders School Board to Readmit Pregnant Girl
School Officials Must Readmit Boy Who Mutilates Flag
High Court Says Students May Wear Black Armbands in School
Due Process Not for Adults Alone, Courts Declare
Slacks OK Despite Board Rule Against Them
Long Hair No Bar to Public School Student, Courts Rule
Right to Ignore Flag Salute Upheld in Courts
Hair Style Falls Within the Right of Privacy
Court Bars Student Suspension Where No Disruption Occurs
Students Sue to Permit Wearing of Black Berets
Expulsion Without Due Process Is Forbidden, Court Holds
Dress Codes Unconstitutional, Court Declares
Underground School Newspaper Permitted
Board Must Prove Disruption to Control Dissent, Court Says
Grooming Code Exceeds Power of School Board
Students' Rights to Free Speech Not Controllable by Board
    And here is the U.S. Supreme Court speaking:
    "In our system, state operated schools may not be enclaves of totalitarianism. School officials do not possess absolute authority over their students. Students in school as well as out of school are 'persons' under our Constitution. They are possessed of fundamental rights which the state must respect, just as they themselves must respect their obligations to the state. . . . In the absence of a specific showing of constitutionally valid reasons to regulate their speech, students are entitled to freedom of expression of their views. . . ."
    Tinker v. *Des Moines*, 393 U.S. 503 (Iowa 1969)[165]

SUMMARY

Intergroup problems are emotional in nature. The major areas of conflict are race, class, religion, and national and regional origins. Prejudice is the common denominator of intergroup problems. It has its roots in ignorance and insecurity. Because of the nonrational origins of prejudice, it is resistant to change based solely on reason. Prejudice is most efficiently supplanted by constructive attitudes through the use of propaganda techniques. These

---

[164]M. Chester Nolte, "Due Process: And What It's Doing to Schools," *American School Board Journal*, Vol. 159, No. 1 (July 1971), p. 20.
[165]Ibid.

techniques supply the emotional involvement necessary to assimilation of reasoned understanding.

The short-term solution to intergroup problems is legal action. The long-range goals are twofold: social reform and education. Social reform is the responsibility of the larger society. The schools should focus on intergroup (human-relations) education. Most teachers have had little training in human relations. Success of the school in combating prejudice depends on the degree to which teachers can infuse human relations material and techniques into the total curriculum. This does not mean the addition of new bodies of knowledge for rote memorization but an application of democratic Judaeo-Christian values and problem-solving skills to problems of human relations as they arise in the regular curriculum.

The forces of history have thrown the spotlight on the public schools of the great cities as they attempt to resolve their integration problems. These problems were accentuated in the early 1970's by court-ordered metropolitan consolidation of school systems, with massive busing. Solutions do not seem to be readily apparent. The 1970's promise to be times of great turmoil as the schools search for practical application of democratic values to the schools' treatment of minority groups.

The thesis of this chapter, then, is that intergroup education is the capstone of a progressive curriculum in human relations. This curriculum is progressive in nature, with skills at each level based on those that preceded; but it is also concurrent in nature, in that basic attitudes of mutual respect, reason, cooperation, and optimism are essential at all levels. The progressive nature of a human-relations curriculum demands the application of these attitudes to an ever-expanding number of people at increasingly greater social and geographic distances from the individual. It is the application of the attitudes, then, that is progressive. The same democratic Judaeo-Christian attitudes that are essential for happy family living are equally essential for effective citizenship in an interdependent world.

Selected Bibliography

Altschuler, Alan. *Community Control: The Black Demand for Participation in Large American Cities.* New York: Pegasus, 1970.

Baltzell, E. Digby. *The Protestant Establishment.* New York: Random House, Inc., 1964. 430 pp. Traces the white Anglo-Saxon Protestant power structure from a ruling class dominating our institutional life and setting our cultural norms to its deterioration into a stubborn caste more concerned with protection of its privileges than with encouragement of the widest possible participation by talented citizens in the management of our country. Witty and informed.

Bloom, Benjamin, Allison Davis, and Robert Hess. *Compensatory Education for Cultural Deprivation.* New York: Holt, Rinehart and Winston, Inc., 1965. 179 pp.

Brophy, William A., and Sophie D. Aberle. *The Indian: America's Unfinished Business.* Norman: University of Oklahoma Press, 1966. 236 pp.

Carter, Thomas P. *Mexican Americans in Schools: A History of Educational Neglect.* College Entrance Examination Board, 1970. 235 pp.

Child, Irvin L. *Italian or American? The Second Generation in Conflict.* New York: Russell and Russell, 1970. 206 pp.

Clark, Kenneth B. *Dark Ghetto: Dilemma of Social Power.* New York: Anti-Defamation League, 1965. A sociological and psychological study of the Negro ghetto; an attempt to understand the combined problems of the confined Negro and the problems of the slum. 251 pp.

Coleman, James S. *Resources for Social Change: Race in the United States.* New York: John Wiley & Sons, Inc., 1971. 128 pp.

Coles, Robert. *Children of Crisis: A Study of Courage and Fear.* Boston: Little, Brown and Company, 1967. 401 pp. Dr. Coles sums up in this volume his many studies of the process on integration of the South, both Negro and white. A very useful and important study. Beautifully and humanely written.

Cordasco, Francesco, and Eugene Bucchioni (eds.). *Puerto Rican Children in Mainland Schools: A Source Book for Teachers.* New York: Scarecrow Press, Inc., 1968. 465 pp.

Cudlipp, Edythe. *Understanding Women's Liberation: A Complete Guide to the Most Controversial Movement Sweeping America Today.* New York: Paperback Library, Inc., 1971. 220 pp.

Ebony Magazine Editors, *The Negro Handbook.* Chicago: Johnson Publishing Co., Inc., 1967. Concise and accurate reference work documents the history and contemporary status of the American Negro.

Eddy, Elizabeth. *Walk the White Line: A Profile of Urban Education.* (Paperback.) Garden City, N.Y.: Doubleday Anchor, 1967. 187 pp. A publication growing out of *Project True*, Hunter College. An excellent discussion of what urban education is like.

Education U.S.A. Special Report: Black Studies in Schools. Washington, D.C.: National School Public Relations Association, N.E.A., 1970. 49 pp.

Education U.S.A. Special Report: High School Student Unrest. Washington, D.C.: National School Public Relations Association, N.E.A., 1969. 49 pp.

Education U.S.A. Special Report: Religion and the Schools. Washington, D.C.: National School Public Relations Association, N.E.A., 1970. 56 pp.

Elliott, John H. *Building Bridges.* New York: Astoria Press, 1950. 64 pp. (Pamphlet.) Stresses need for building mutual respect among all men as a means toward achieving international peace. Presents in capsule form the basic facts about religious and racial groups. Synthesizes personal guide lines toward elimination of prejudices through bridges of understanding.

Fantini, Mario, D.. and Gerald Weinstein. *Toward a Contact Curriculum.* New York: Anti-Defamation League of B'nai B'rith. 55 pp.

Fellman, David. *The Supreme Court and Education.* New York: Teachers College Press, Columbia University, 1969. 229 pp.

Flannery, Edward H. *The Anguish of the Jews: Twenty-three Centuries of Anti-Semitism.* New York: The Macmillan Company, 1965. 332 pp.

Glock, Charles Y., and Ellen Siegelman (eds.). *Prejudice U.S.A.* New York: Frederick A. Praeger, Inc., 1969. 196 pp.

Goldthorpe, John H., David Lockwood, Frank Bechhofer, and Jennifer Platt. *The Affluent Worker in the Class Structure.* New York: Cambridge University Press, 1969. 239 pp.

Grambs, Jean Dresden. *Intergroup Education.* Englewood Cliffs, N.J.: Prentice-Hall, Inc., 1968. 199 pp. Basic theory in basic English; summary of promising practices; appendixes of illustrative materials; and 110 pages of categorized, annotated bibliographies of books, pictures, films, recordings, journals, and organizations. *Must* reading for the *intergroup* human-relations educator!

Habens, Murray C. *The Challenges to Democracy.* New York: Anti-Defamation League of B'nai B'rith, 1965. Shows how our political unity has been threatened throughout our history—the Civil War, racial and religious bigotry, the Ku Klux Klan, Huey Long, Father Coughlin, McCarthyism—and discusses present-day dangers to American unity such as those connected with the acceptance government. The broad conclusions of this study are that our national unity is continuously in jeopardy, but that our democracy and nationalism are deeply rooted and possessed of considerable potential for survival. This book promises to become a classic on extremism in American life.

Hart, Richard L., and J. Galen Saylor (eds.). *Student Unrest: Threat or Promise?* Washington, D.C.: Association for Supervision and Curriculum Development, N.E.A., 1970. 124 pp.

Hirsh, Selma G. *The Fears Men Live By.* New York: Harper & Row, Inc., 1955. 164 pp. Lay interpretation of the monumental series in the dynamics of prejudice prepared by Max Herkheimer and Samuel H. Flowerman (eds.) for the American Jewish Committee, published by Harper & Row. Based largely on *The Authoritarian Personality.* Effectively presents the thesis that the origin of prejudice is fear.

Howe, Louise Kapp (ed.). *The White Majority: Between Poverty and Affluence.* New York: Random House, Inc., 1970. 303 pp.

Jeffers, Camille. *Living Poor.* Ann Arbor, Mich.: Ann Arbor Publishers, 1967. 123 pp. The insightful report of a woman who, with her children, lived as a participant-observer in an urban renewal project. Many myths and preconceptions about persons living in poverty are dispelled.

Lewis, Oscar. *La Vida: A Puerto Rican Family in the Culture of Poverty—San Juan and New York City.* New York: Random House, Inc., 1966. 669 pp. Relates the similarities and differences in the reaction to poverty in two settings.

Mack, Raymond W., and Troy S. Duster. *Patterns of Minority Relations.* New York: Anti-Defamation League, 1964. 61 pp. Based on Mack, *Race, Class, and Power.* Deals with minority status, especially the Jew and Negro in America.

Miel, Alice, and Edwin Kiester. *The Short-Changed Children of Suburbia.* New York: Institute of Human Relations Press, The American Jewish Committee, 1967. 68 pp. Report of a research study on the attitudes of children in suburbia regarding racial and economic differences and school programs. A "must" item for suburban educators.

Morgan, Robin (ed.). *Sisterhood Is Powerful: An Anthology of Writings from the Women's Liberation Movement.* New York: Random House, Inc., 1970. 602 pp. One of the best summaries of current status.

National Commission on Professional Rights and Responsibilities, N.E.A. *Detroit, Michigan: A Study of Barriers to Equal Educational Opportunity in a Large City.* Washington, D.C.: The Commission, March, 1967. A revealing and significant objective report of urban educational opportunity for all.

Riessman, Frank. *The Culturally Deprived Child.* New York: Harper & Row, Publishers, 1962. 140 pp. Particularly valuable for discussion of the values and uses of role-playing with children considered nonverbal. One of the most often cited books in the field.

Sebald, Hans. *Adolescence: A Sociological Analysis.* New York: Appleton-Century-Crofts, Inc., 1968. 537 pp.

Selznick, Gertrude S., and Stephen Steinber. *The Tenacity of Prejudice.* New York: Harper & Row, 1971. 248 pp. Volume Four in a series based on the University of California five-year study of anti-Semitism in the United States.

Silberman, Charles E. *Crisis in Black and White.* New York: Random House, Inc., 1964. 370 pp. The boldest and most profound attempt to understand the Negro crisis in America, not only in relation to its history, but with respect to its possible solution. Stresses the need for America to restore to the Negro the dignity, initiative, and the ambition of which his countrymen traditionally have deprived him. Covers all aspects of American life. Chapter IX, "The Negro and the School," should be required reading for all teachers.

———. *Crisis in the Classroom.* New York: Random House, Inc., 1970. 553 pp. Not of the caliber of *Crisis in Black and White,* but provocative reading.

Taba, Hilda, and Deborah Elkins. *Teaching Strategies for the Culturally Disadvantaged.* Chicago: Rand McNally & Co., 1966. 295 pp. Based on the authors' earlier work, with new insights gained from current experience. Highly recommended.

Urban School Crisis: The Problems and Solutions Proposed by the HEW Urban Educa-tion Task Force. Washington, D.C.: National School Public Relations Association, N.E.A., 1970. 63 pp.

Webster, Staten W. (ed.). *Knowing the Disadvantaged* (paperback); *Understanding the Educational Problems of the Disadvantaged Learner* (paperback); *Teaching the Disadvantaged Learner.* San Francisco: Chandler Publishing Company, 1966. All three titles by Webster available in one book or as three. Excellent material of practical help to the classroom teacher.

Selected Films

All the Way Home (Anti-Defamation League), 30 min. A house in an all-white neigh-borhood is for sale. When a Negro family stops to inquire about it, neighborhood fear and anxiety mount to a dangerous point while responsible community leader-ship asserts itself. An open-ended film.

Can We Immunize Against Prejudice? (Anti-Defamation League), 6½ min. Narrated by Eddie Albert. Three sets of parents use different methods to prevent prejudice in their children. When racial and religious bias develops nevertheless, the film asks where the parents have failed. A good audience participation film, since it pro-vides an open-end or stop-the-projector technique, at which point audience dis-cussion can take place.

The Captive (National Council of Churches), 28 min. Appalachia and the story of a man's struggle to escape from the crushing bonds of poverty. Should shock the complacent into reorganizing the responsibility that faces them for bringing new hope and freedom to the captive poor.

The Civil Rights Movement: Film Series. (Encyclopaedia Britannica)
The Civil Rights Movement: Historic Roots. 16 min.
The Civil Rights Movement: The Mississippi Project. 17 min.
The Civil Rights Movement: The North. 23 min.
The Civil Rights Movement: A Personal Review. 25 min.
The Civil Rights Movement: The South. 19 min.

Confronted (Indiana University Films), 1 hr. How or what does the Northern white feel when he is confronted by the demanding Negro?

Crisis in Levittown, Pa. (Brandon Films), 30 min. When the first Negro family moved into this community, on-the-spot reactions were captured by the film crew of the complex forces and reactions that were released. Insight into a community in turmoil over an integration crisis.

Dallas at the Crossroads (Anti-Defamation League), 8 min. Describes desegregation in the city of Dallas; is an appeal for law and order during the process of desegrega-tion in the public schools.

Democracy (EBF), 11 min. Presents the nature and meaning of democracy by analyzing four major concepts on which there is substantial agreement; points out how true democracy depends equally upon shared respect and shared power.

Epitaph for Jim Crow (Anti-Defamation League), 30 min. Series of illustrated film lectures focuses on the history and current situation of the American Negro. The historical, political, sociological, and psychological forces that shape patterns of prejudice and discrimination.

The Exiles (Kent Mackenzie, Contemporary Films), 1 hr., 17 min. Social problems of urbanized American Indians.

Face of the South (Anti-Defamation League), 30 min. Historical analysis of economic and social factors which influenced Southern life styles, attitudes, and behavior. An illustrated lecture by George Mitchell, former director of the Southern Regional Council.

Felicia (Anti-Defamation League), 12½ min. Shows the corrosive effects of prejudice. Felicia, a junior in high school, lives with her mother, an older brother, and younger sister in Watts. Felicia is black. Many adults in her community are jobless.

Most of her classmates see no future for themselves because of their color. But Felicia has a goal, education, and she wants to help make Watts a good place in which to live. The film is simple and honest, perfect for junior and senior high school students.

Free at Last (N.E.T.), 30 min. History of the American Negro from emancipation to the end of World War II, this film examines the Depression, the end of the so-called Negro renaissance of the 1920's, and past Negro leaders.

A Friendly Game (Cokesbury and Mass Media), 10 min. Depicts a "friendly" game of chess between a black man and a white man, and all the chances that attend the larger game in human relations that play with each other.

The Hard Way (N.E.T. Film Service, Indiana U.), 60 min. The problem of poverty in America, the richest country in the world, is discussed, emphasizing the ways in which the poor of today are different from those of past generations.

The High Wall (Anti-Defamation League), 30 min. This prize-winning film shows how the hostility of a teen-ager toward those of other national, religious, and racial groups is a product of the prejudices and frustrations of his parents, along with their emphasis on discipline instead of love. Shows some of the basic origins and meanings of prejudice. Develops ways of building confident, healthy personalities. This film represents an excellent, new approach to the re-education of the prejudiced.

Incident on Wilson Street (Anti-Defamation League), 15 min. Film dramatically reveals how skilled and sympathetic teachers bring enrichment into the lives of educationally disadvantaged children.

The Invisible Empire: Ku Klux Klan (Anti-Defamation League), 45 min. Traces the history of the Klan. Filmed sequences of an actual Klan meeting, footage of a Klan rally and cross-burning held in Ohio, and interviews with Klansmen reveal the bigoted savagery of this organization.

Joshua (Cokesbury), 15 min. The story of a Negro boy in Harlem who is about to enter college. His confrontation with whites in a park results in the realization of the possibilities of black-white partnership on terms of equality.

Just Like Me (Karl B. Lohmann, Jr.; Thorne Films), 9 min. Human relations; elementary grades.

Major Religions of the World (Encyclopaedia Britannica), 20 min. Beliefs and important rituals of Hinduism, Buddhism, Judaism, Christianity, and Islam. Animated diagrams illustrate rise of newer religions from older ones.

Marked for Failure (N.E.T. Film Service, Indiana U.), 60 min. This film report focuses on the problems facing both educators and children in America's slum schools and illuminates the reasons why these children, mostly Negro, are kept out of the cultural and, ultimately, the economic mainstream of society.

A Morning for Jimmy (National Urban League), 28 min. A young Negro boy, seeking a part-time job, encounters discrimination for the first time head on and is discouraged until his teacher takes him to visit Negroes successfully employed in many fields. Presents a strong case to finish school and to take a stand for your rights.

The Newest New Negro (Anti-Defamation League), 30 min. The meaning and value of the newest forms of direct-action protest against segregation are discussed with Whitney Young, late director of the National Urban League.

No Hiding Place (Mass Media and Cokesbury), 51 min. One of the most powerful and dramatic programs to be presented on the *East Side/West Side* television series. It is a daring drama about a Negro family who has moved into an all-white Northern suburban community. Ironically, it is a Southern white housewife and not her Northern husband who displays courage and understanding when some of their neighbors are panicked into selling their homes.

Now Is the Time (Anti-Defamation League), 32 min. Ruby Dee and Ossie Davis star in this film which re-creates, through the words of black poets and writers, the long, slow struggle from slavery toward equal rights. Included are works by James Baldwin, Countee Cullen, Langston Hughes; statements of black civil rights leaders; and music—spirituals, blues, jazz—set against photographs and film sequences.

Other Face of Dixie (Anti-Defamation League), 53 min. Progress report on Negro–white relations, as a vivid demonstration of integration achievement contrasting the old distrust with the new cooperative spirit among students in Clinton, Little Rock, Norfolk, and Atlanta.

Picture in Your Mind (International Film Foundation), 16 min. Through the use of symbols presents the earliest roots of prejudice and the reasons why any group, tribe, or nation thinks its way of life is superior to the other man's way of living. A forceful plea is made to every individual to re-examine his own mind to see whether his mental picture of the other man is distorted.

Portrait of a Disadvantaged Child: Tommy Knight (McGraw-Hill), 16 min. This film brings the viewer face to face with the reality of a day in the life of a slum child.

Portrait of the Inner City School: A Place to Learn (McGraw-Hill), 18 min. This film illustrates how, even unconsciously, a teacher can discriminate against pupils from disadvantaged homes and neighborhoods.

Social Class in America (McGraw-Hill), 15 min. Follows the lives of three young men representing the lower, middle, and upper classes. Points out that an individual may change his social status under certain conditions. Introduces such terms as vertical mobility and horizontal mobility.

That's Me (Contemporary), 15 min. A social worker tries to help a young Puerto Rican who finds it very difficult to adjust to life in New York City. This serio-comic dramatic sketch conveys the true situation with economy and wit.

To Live Together (Anti-Defamation League), 34 min. The difficulties encountered and experiences shared by children at an interracial summer camp. The film shows that to learn democracy, children must have a chance to live it.

The Troubled Cities (N.E.T.), 60 min. An inquiry into the crises of American cities and a report on the attempts of four metropolitan areas (New York, Detroit, Boston, and Newark) to solve their growing social and financial problems, including inadequate housing, low standards of living, racial tension, and crime.

Twelve Angry Men (United Artists), 1 hr., 35 min. Feature-length film, demonstrating how people can influence a group; also the role of prejudice and prejudgment in forming opinions and distorting reality. A powerful drama for high school students and adults.

The Victims (Anti-Defamation League), 50 min. Dr. Benjamin Spock, author, teacher, and pediatrician, diagnoses the cause of prejudice in children. He finds it a crippling disease, harmful to those who are the recipients of its insidious effects and to those who inflict it. A dramatically moving film showing youngsters and young adults—at play, in school, and in the frat house—as the victims. Poignant interviews with parents. Narrated by Pat Hingle. Produced by the Anti-Defamation League of B'nai B'rith in cooperation with Westinghouse Broadcasting Company.

Walk in My Shoes (Anti-Defamation League), 42 min. A documentary explores the innermost feelings of the Negro as he reacts to prejudice and discrimination in America.

We'll Never Turn Back (Brandon Films), 30 min. An extraordinary documentation of one of the most vital parts of the civil rights revolution: the attempt of Negro citizens in Mississippi to register and vote, as part of the Voter Registration Project in which all the major civil rights organizations cooperated.

The Young Americans (N.E.T.), 60 min. A study of the youth of America—who they are, what they want, where they fit in, how they affect society, what they believe in, and why.

Chapter 10

■■■■■■■■■■■■□□□□□□

Problems of the Depressed Areas

In considering "depressed areas" it may be asked what conditions constitute such a defined area? Why do these areas come into existence? What are the factors relating to economic deterioration? And what of the human suffering that is endured in these areas?

DEPRESSED AREAS

A depressed area is one that has failed to keep economic pace with the growth of the nation. It actually has moved backward while the rest of the nation has moved forward. Although no single remedy or short-term program offers itself as a solution, the United States government has moved ahead in the concern for these areas with far-reaching programs that provide varying measures and degrees of intensive aid.

This chapter will consider the far-reaching implications of the distressed areas and the human disability they engender. The constellation of factors are multiple in the human orientation: geographical, social, cultural, economic, and educational.

In an era of economic prosperity with vast scientific and technological innovations, there are geographical areas of substantial and persistent unemployment and underemployment in the United States. In the Public Works and Economic Development Act of 1965, Public Law 89–136, the following criteria, among others, determined whether a particular region has lagged behind the whole nation in economic development:

1. The rate of unemployment is substantially above the national rate.
2. The median level of family income is significantly below the national median.
3. The level of housing, health, and education facilities is substantially below the national level.
4. The economy of the area traditionally has been dominated by only one or two industries, which are in a state of long-term decline.
5. The rate of outmigration of labor or capital or both is substantial.

6. The area is adversely affected by changing industrial technology.
7. The area is adversely affected by changes in national defense facilities or production.
8. Indexes of regional production indicate a growth rate substantially below the national average.

The economic structure of depressed areas is typified by the following: (1) Large numbers of people are jobless who are ill equipped to find gainful employment. (2) Employment opportunities within the area are minimal because of lack of diversification in most of these areas.

Urban Depressed Areas

Lack of diversification is more severe in urban areas that are too small to be able to support the kind of diversification that would allow a self-adjusting process by means of shifting a variable labor force from one firm to another as economic opportunities change. Employment has often been dependent on a major industry. When it has declined, other local industries, if existent, have not been able to take up the slack. New industry has not moved in. The unemployed then cease to play a productive role in their community. The attitude of residents of the larger communities in which depressed areas are found tends to be, "They don't *want* to work!" These attitudes only perpetuate the ghettos of the unemployed.

This condition has been illustrated very clearly in areas dependent on coal mining in West Virginia, eastern Kentucky, Pennsylvania, and Illinois. Where anthracite and bituminous coal have lost out to gas or oil, or where technological improvements in the mines have increased productivity and thereby reduced the employment needs, the backbone of the economy is greatly altered and widespread unemployment results. In industries other than coal mining, causative factors have been at work to produce negative economic changes. Textile industries, through their manufacture of synthetic products, have cut into the market for wool, cotton, and silk. Manufacturing of railway equipment and railway repair has succumbed to the decline of rail passenger traffic and the rise of truck transportation. The decline in defense-oriented jobs, competitive forces within the automobile industry, competition from abroad, automation, and change because of locational advantages all have contributed to depression in urban areas. The human hardships involved in unemployment and the economic waste of human potential cause problems that are complex and numerous. The demography of depressed areas accentuates their depression. The more able, the more highly skilled leave the community. Property values deteriorate. New dwellers tend to be jobless or minimally employed, attracted by the lower rents and by the psychological salve of association with similarly deprived persons.

It can be asked, why do distressed areas persist and get worse? The social and physical deterioration that take place are by-products of economic distress, usually not the primary fault of the workers involved. A spirit of individual and community defeatism grows when lack of productivity renders people dependent, directly or indirectly, on public assistance. This, in turn, leads to disunity, disorganization, and even apathy.

Internal migration has always been a part of American life. However, to move from a known to an unknown area in the face of adversity does require money, experience, and spirit, all difficult in the face of defeat and failure. Although many have left, those who have not moved out of the depressed areas may be lacking in these requirements. They may lack knowledge of opportunities, or they may not possess skills for different jobs. Their familiarity with the home community, deep emotional ties with families and friends, or property investment may prevent their search for new opportunities. The factor that contributes most to continued depression is, however, the failure of new industry to move into the surplus labor area. Unfortunately, too often a single distressed region is lacking in appropriate occupational skills and in such locational advantages as utilities, school systems, and adequate local government; it often has poor local leadership, an eroded tax base, and heavy welfare burdens.

In Chapter 9 we have explored the problems of social class and minority groups. The problems of minority groups are intensified in the inner city; for example, the population of black minorities in the United States increased from 10 per cent to 11 per cent from 1960 to 1970, but in the inner city it has increased from 16 per cent to over 21 per cent. Other minorities multiply the problem.[1]

Large urban areas, containing diversification of industry, massive public utilities, schools, government, and many kinds of facilities and expert services are far more able to adjust to economic changes. Detroit, however, has been an example of a large metropolitan center with a concentration of employment in one or two major industries serving national markets. Until recently the decline in unemployment in these industries was not counterbalanced by other industries benefiting from the preceding factors. Recently, Detroit and other areas have attacked their problems through far-reaching economic development and urban renewal projects.

In 1970, 23 per cent of the total United States population lived in the ten largest metropolitan areas and about 35 per cent lived in the twenty-five largest metropolitan areas. Although the central cities were declining in their relative per cent, all cities still account for about 30 per cent of this total. (See Figure 19.) Data from the 1970 census reveal that all but one (Pittsburgh) of the twenty-five largest Standard Metropolitan Statistical Areas (SMSA's) gained in population during the last decade. SMSA's encompass central cities with a population of 50,000 or more, the county or counties in which they are located, and closely related counties. Only thirteen of the twenty-five largest cities had population gains. The inability of large cities to cope with the problems of crime, pollution, transportation, housing, and racial strife has speeded migration to the suburban rings and inhibited immigration.[2] The major depressed areas, in terms of people affected, continue to be inner-city locations, although suburbia is also becoming a problem.

Rural Depressed Areas

As the dynamic growth of technology has continued into a permanent industrial revolution, radical changes have taken place in agriculture, business,

[1] *Road Maps of Industry*, No. 1653 (November 1, 1970).
[2] Ibid.

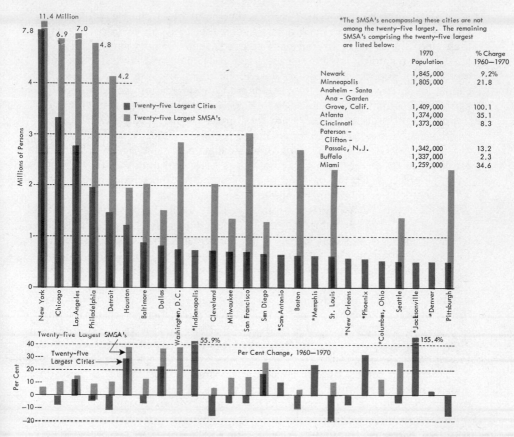

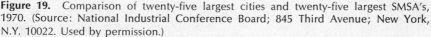

Figure 19. Comparison of twenty-five largest cities and twenty-five largest SMSA's, 1970. (Source: National Industrial Conference Board; 845 Third Avenue; New York, N.Y. 10022. Used by permission.)

industry, government, and labor throughout the United States and the world. The trend has been toward larger and larger enterprises. With mechanized farming methods, the agrarian system has changed from small units to big agricultural units. This has meant larger farms and less people needed to run them. In the decade 1960 to 1970 alone the farm population declined to slightly over 10 million from over 16 million in 1960.[3]

Before the days of industry and mechanized farming, the small rural community was largely isolated from other communities. Difficulties in transportation and communication led not only to geographical, social, and intellectual isolation, but also to well-established and provincial patterns of behaviors and attitudes. Strict adherence to those established ways was learned at an early age, and divergence was frowned upon. The mode of life was simple and continuing. The small farm unit allowed at least a marginal subsistence level and offered a life complete. However, this mode of life is for the most part becoming impossible.

[3]*The 1971 World Almanac and Book of Facts* (New York: Newspaper Enterprise Association, 1970), p. 408.

In the long run, the small farmers have not been able to profit from technology and have not been able to keep their way of living or to retain their land; the same end result has occurred where farmers have tilled marginal land, regardless of the size of the farm. Small land units or unfertile areas cannot support the cost of labor to till them, nor can they supply the capital necessary to invest in machinery. With increasing competition for agricultural commodities, governmental policies on acreage restriction for more efficient production, there are rural areas which, lacking diversification in other enterprises, also lack an adequate economic base. These factors have led to the social deterioration of rural society, depopulation, and a growing inadequacy of the old ways. Knowledge of opportunities and new ways have led either to leasing the land and becoming part-time labor in a nearby urban center or to migrating completely out of the rural area.

Those who have migrated from the rural to the urban centers have found all too often that this has not only failed to relieve their plight, but has led them to a situation in which they are unable to establish a satisfactory new life. These migrants are composed largely of Appalachian Mountain farmers, sharecroppers, tenant farmers (both black and white), landless Puerto Ricans, Mexicans, and reservation Indians who are generally poor and uneducated, with little chance for advancement. In this movement away from the land to the city, these people have found themselves the victims of a system they do not understand and over which they have no control. Their predicament is further compounded by racial and class prejudice and few or no marketable skills.

The urban center, large or small, has become the focal point of industry and organized community living. It has become the place for concentration of large numbers of wage earners. Discrepancies develop when technology outruns the wage earners' skills and when changed circumstances require social adjustments. The city is the place in which problems are met and institutional practices must be refashioned toward ultimate better human social adjustments and more widely available economic opportunity. The migration of rural people to the city has a historical background with old patterns and problems that are being seen today in new perspectives. The following section is a brief view of the city as it has grown and developed in human history.

THE CITY IN HUMAN CULTURE
The Polis

Predating even the most primitive village, nonliterate man's social and religious impulses, his need for protection, together with his practical needs, drew him to family and tribal groupings. Though nomadic and concerned with physical survival, the human need for expression and the search for meaning and understanding of life and death led to communal rites and meeting places.

Cooperative life grew with burial practices and communal rites, hunting activities, and feasts. Evidence exists of division of labor displayed in tools and weapon making and in highly developed art techniques.

The later domestication of animals and the practice of food production gave rise to the eventual establishment of more permanent settlements. With this humble beginning came the first expression of human institutions: the family and tribe, the religious shrine, and the protective fortress, all giving form to the primordial city.

The villages grew in number and size. As the invention of writing, engineering, and improved agricultural methods developed, old and new ways of living were brought into interaction, leading to the expansion of human energies and to the differentiation of occupational activities. The beginnings of organized law concerning justice, morality, and government gave rise to further structure in the lives of those whose village life was becoming more that of the city. For, as the village took root, trade came by way of merchant caravans that settled at the edges of the walled fortress. Here business was conducted; in case of danger, refuge could be sought inside the village. The influence of trade brought new life, growth, and complexity to the now emerging city. As ancient kingships were established, the city grew into the ultimate fusion of fortress, temple, and marketplace; it was the center of intellectual, artistic, economic, and political progress.

The cities, through the process just described, arose first in the areas of early Oriental civilizations: the Nile, Tigris, Euphrates, Yellow, and Indus Rivers. The development of a high level of civilization at this period of history is simultaneous with the rise of the city. In the Greek *polis* is found one of the most successful harmonizations of the city with its surrounding territory—the city-state. In Rome the city-state expanded into an empire and the city-states as such passed out of history until the rise of the great trading cities of the late medieval period.

The Medieval City

In medieval Europe the oldest cities were those that survived from Roman times. New cities grew out of population growths around castle strongholds, monasteries, or cathedrals. In the early Middle Ages the growth of the cities was relatively slow. Open spaces were plentiful for recreation and for such rural occupations as gardening and keeping animals. In this respect the use of land can be likened to the small country town of the United States, where such practices still exist in a limited sense today. In the later Middle Ages, population within these walls increased and became crowded. Land values rose, houses with upper overhanging stories were built to conserve land space, and the streets were dark, narrow, crooked, and unpaved. Life was crude and offered few refinements. Filth abounded as all refuse and garbage were thrown into the streets, to be removed only by rain or by the dogs and pigs which roamed at large. The frequently contaminated spring and well water supply served as fertile breeding grounds for disease. Certainly it can be said that the medieval city was beset by sanitation inadequacies. This problem continued to exist in the universal evolution of cities, with some making better provisions than others. Although today's modern cities often do create alleys of filth, make running sewers of the rivers, and contaminate the air into a disease-breeding element, Western civilization has made of the city a relatively sanitary environment, even within the depressed areas.

During the crusades in the late Middle Ages, profitable trade and commerce with the Near East grew rapidly. As this expansion took place, the cities grew in size, number, and importance. New markets developed and many people turned to manufacturing products like those of the Eastern cities. This resulted in the movement of much of the rural population to the cities to engage in commercial and industrial enterprises. A basic institution took the form of merchant and craft guilds, which were, in some respects—though superficially—the forerunners of present-day labor unions. These functioned to preserve the local market for their own members, to create a noncompetitive and stable economic system, and to maintain standards of goods, in addition to furnishing social services. The guilds served to raise the status of work and that of the wage earner, enabling him to become a free citizen; thus began the decline of a master–servant culture.

Although cities have emerged in different times and places and in different ways, it is significant that their growth has resulted primarily from a concentration of population, human energy, and social interaction, and the production of goods and services. The growth of industry, with its differentiated occupations drawing a labor force from the land to the city, is not a new phenomenon in human history.

The Modern Metropolis

The modern concept of the city is no longer one based on a fortress or religious shrine as in ancient and medieval times, but rather one based on the value of goods and services it facilitates. Changes in the internal patterns of cities have been occurring for centuries. With the extension of agriculture providing a varied food supply and with advance in medical science and sanitation, the world has experienced a vast increase in population. The commercial and industrial revolutions have accommodated this population by furnishing increased trade and more work opportunities in factories, all of which has made it possible for resourceful areas to support many people. The geographical concept of the metropolis includes the central city and its surrounding area, boroughs, villages, towns, and townships. These are the suburbs, and the whole is referred to as the greater metropolitan area.

Sociologically, cities are large and permanent population aggregates composed of heterogenous individuals involved in diversified and specialized occupational roles. Cities are self-maintaining and are in the constant process of creating order in the face of disturbing life forces. Heterogeneity and mass, although tending to break down class lines and to cause increasing integration of persons, paradoxically also lead to a complicated and segregated class structure, which at times undermines social solidarity through class, ethnic, and racial conflicts. Race relations with an urban culture are today presenting a challenge no longer limited to just the local metropolitan scene, but extending to the state and national scenes as well, even affecting the foreign image and policy commitments. Glaring contrasts of close physical contact and distant social relations; mobility, security, and instability; slums, gray areas, and affluent areas are also marks of the enlarged city. The individual, who is largely anonymous, finds his effectiveness in organized groups or institutions and in group actions that tend to serve the mass. It is from the metropolis that massive communication media emanate, such as newspapers, magazines and book publishing, radio, and television, and it is within this large city that dynamic financial and managerial moves are made.

Megalopolis

From the metropolis it is but a short step to Megalopolis. Wolf von Eckardt and other population and planning experts have identified several actual or potential Megalopolises in the United States. One such has been labeled Boswash and is the huge string of central cities, suburbs, and satellite areas that stretch along the eastern seaboard of the United States from north of Boston to south of Washington. It currently is the largest, wealthiest, and most productive region on earth.

This conglomeration includes arable land in spite of the spread of suburbs and growth of cities. It does, however, make less sharp the line of division between city and country and alters the balance between city and country. The quantity, expansion, and overgrowth of the megalopolis create one vast complex of industry, commerce, financial power, and high population density.

It draws hope through its concentration of skills, learning, talents, job opportunities, schools, affluence, and institutions. It draws despair in its unemployed and low-income people, its blighted areas, its need for more schools, its lack of adequate housing, its increasing tax burden, and its maladjusted—those who have not become "urbanized."

Urbanization involves the adjustment of a whole range of behaviors, attitudes, and relationships to the conditions imposed by urban life. Successful adjustment is a high degree of organization allowing personal freedom of social activity, economic self-sufficiency, and a productive role in the urban milieu. Lack of urbanization, or lack of adjustment, results in a condition characterized by personal disorganization, poor mental health, crime, corruption, and allied forms of social disorder.

Significantly, the suburban areas have experienced great growth in recent years. In 1970 they represented over 35 per cent of the population, a larger percentage than that of either the central cities or the nonmetropolitan areas. The farm areas have declined to 10 million population, less than 5 per cent of the total population. The suburbs represent the affluent society. Population will undoubtedly decline within the core cities, with their blighted areas. In the urban matrix the population of the depressed areas may live within sight of the industries from which the suburban commuters draw their livelihood, although many industries are also moving out. It is lack of job skills and discriminatory employment that keep the inner-city urban residents in depressed areas.

EFFECTS OF URBANIZATION
Specialization

Whereas in Europe the growth of cities has dominated, preceding the growth of national states, in America until recently, rural life and growth has been dominant, with the growth of national power preceding that of cities.

An urbanized society is rapidly emerging in the United States. The effects of this urbanization, although identified with abundance, security, and democratic freedoms, are also identified with negative social consequences, particularly in the core of the cities.

Specialization has developed as the nature of industry, and society has become more complex. Those knowledgeable within the limits of a particular occupation or service offer their limited roles to the whole of business or community enterprise.

Effective knowledge is professionalized and expert. In the complex metropolitan community, functions are performed better by those who possess knowledge and skills in specialized areas of influence. Persons find their roles occupationally and in social groups, and tend to function especially within these confines, thereby achieving their own special areas of living. The positive values of specialization notwithstanding, inherent dangers lie in overspecialization. It can foster passivity and even resistance to change and a lack of interpersonal and intergroup communication. The possibility of oversimplification resulting from specialization negates a comprehensive view of the vast and complex nature of the total society. The loss of interaction between specialized parts and the problem of recognizing the worth of the individual in relation to the whole of society have created human-relations problems requiring more and more attention and research from the behavioral sciences. Specialization demands skilled labor. The unskilled, whether from lack of ability or from lack of training, drift toward the depressed areas of the core city. Deprivation breeds violence. The large cities *must* retrain the workers of the depressed areas or face continuous riots of the magnitude of those of the 1960's.

Fragmentation

When society began to demand specialization, fragmentation began. Life at one time could be viewed more as a whole, with a view of a certain product of labor from its inception to its completion. The labor and its product were enmeshed in the whole tone of the family and the community. More and more persons play different roles that become compartmentalized. People go to work, to church, to social, recreational, and cultural events that are all more or less unrelated. Participation in the life of the city does not take place as a total activity, but more as one fragmented into certain selected parts. With the relentless increase in specialization, a different framework has been created that disrupts the continuity of the "whole." The fruits of a worker's labor can now represent only a small part of a whole complex operation. This change has brought about a subsequent fragmentation of relationships and created echelons of authority that are impersonal in human interaction. Today the importance of understanding human behavior, the realization that work is being done by people, has increased the need to understand the psychological needs in the large rank and file of wage earners.

Anonymity

Anonymity is the lack of adequate personal identification with the society in which one lives. With the impersonality fostered by *fragmentation,* associations are altered. On the urban scene the more intimate person-to-group relationship is replaced largely by a group-to-group relationship. Humans cannot tolerate a loss of individual identity, a sense of not belonging. According to some authorities, this in part explains the strength of labor unions. The union tends to give the worker a sense of belonging and it cares for his welfare. Men tend more to express themselves and gain identity through groups rather than individually.

Man measures himself in the structure of his values, beliefs, and work. He forms a sense of who and what he is. This is his ego identity, which involves self-concept, self-attitude, motivation, and aspiration. Simple personal relationships of a more rural past were a relatively easy adjustment for people. In the complex, mechanized urban society, these simple relationships are much more difficult to achieve at much more than a superficial and transitory level. People need a personal identity in the role they play in society, and this role is difficult to select. It is getting to be more difficult to function adequately and to achieve self-expression and to create a sense of belonging. If the individual sees society moving on regardless of his existence, he feels his impotence and his feeling of anonymity is intolerable. He may rationalize his victimization, his shortcomings, his lack of striving, his humiliation, and his predicament becomes his crutch. Apathy or aggressive and hostile behavior may be turned into weapons of sabotage against the anonymity he suffers.

Anomie

Anomie implies a social state of degradation in which the individual is so dissociated from any productive role in society that the common rules of conduct fail to influence his behavior. There is no longer any sense of values or goal direction. The symptomatology of anomie incorporates a state of alienation, progressing further to antisocial forms of behavior, and leading finally to a loss of sensitivity to reality. The sequela is a drifting and senseless existence devoid of cultural impact and lacking even rebellion in the form of hostile aggression. The finality of this anomic state is, upon reflection, identifiable only in the context of severe mental illness in which behavior no longer relates to reality, rationally or irrationally—a complete state of dehumanization or total withdrawal.

Anomie is decreasing in the depressed areas. Rebellions are based on hope of success as a result of the rebellious activities. The residents of the depressed areas are correctly concluding that the civil rights legislation of the mid-1960's was a direct result of the civil rights violence of the early 1960's. Success builds hope.

THE PROBLEMS OF THE CITY

Violence will accelerate until concrete improvement is visible in the lives of those who live in the depressed areas.

Urban problems have been articulated to some extent in the foregoing development of the city. The city has a rapid, intense pace, complicated by the forces of technology. Its culture has seen great physical and social changes. Crowding people into limited space results in increased demands, such as those for public utilities, traffic regulation and movement, police protection, parks and other recreation centers, civic centers, schools, libraries, public transportation, fire protection, health and welfare measures, and housing. Communities in their organization to meet these needs find both opportunities in physical improvements and growing social problems.

Urban Renewal

Urban renewal remains a controversial issue; many such projects have met with something less than long-range success. It is, however, generally agreed that the welfare of people is contingent on the prevention of slums and blight, that the preservation of natural beauty and the provision of decent homes and living environment are among the factors relevant to a healthy democratic society.

The problems of urban environment are enmeshed in critical issues of human welfare. Renewal projects precipitate the need to study housing, building codes, zoning and land use laws, traffic problems, and the disruption of private business and public enterprise. Such projects have been in effect, to one degree or another, since the Federal Housing Act of 1949. Very simply, the term *urban renewal* implies the rebuilding of a city through government subsidy and private enterprise. The procedure includes studies of the conditions mentioned previously and of the needs of the local community, with a proposed clearance of specific areas and plans for reuse. Development standards must be clarified in these plans and the whole submitted to the federal government. The cost of land, raising buildings, and resale of this land to private enterprise represent a large loss which, upon the condition of federal approval, is made up by federal and city subsidy.

With the more economically sufficient class of people leaving the city for the suburbs, thereby reducing taxable income, and with the basis of urban taxation in its property and improvements, many cities have found their dwindling basis of taxation in need of reconstruction. One remedy to aid in obtaining higher revenue is to impose income taxes on residents of suburban areas who still earn their living in the city. Detroit was successful in levying this tax, and even managed to cut its city property tax while in the midst of extensive renewal projects.

Diversity of values, class, and social groups—a pluralistic society—has always been thought to characterize the urban environment. However, the population trend is for the discriminated-against lower-class minority groups and elderly people to remain in the central city, with the middle and upper classes moving out to the fringes and suburbs. Thus the social distance between classes and ethnic groups becomes greater.

Housing

As urban renewal projects disrupt the small business merchants, so too do they involve the clearance of slums and subsequent removal of slum dwellers. Inadequate housing is a quantitative and qualitative problem of the city. Many residential areas located in the inner core are characterized by substandard dwellings. They are in a state of physical deterioration, housing too many people who are socially and economically impoverished. These areas, whose high population density demands greater facilities, are often lacking in parks, playgrounds, and appropriate educational opportunities.

In providing better public housing that will rent to low-income people, the Public Housing Authority pays a figure in lieu of taxes to the city and county, thus making it possible to provide good housing at reasonable cost for those who qualify. Rehabilitation of old housing has been pursued to some extent by nonprofit groups. Housing codes are effective in forcing the owners of property to improve it if there is adequate inspection service and if the courts enforce housing regulations. Effective zoning is another aspect of residential planning, be it new housing developments or the rehabilitation of older areas and the prevention of the encroachment of undesirable kinds of business and industry. It offers restrictions on the use of property and can prevent the deterioration of previously stable neighborhoods.[4]

It is recognized more and more that, in addition to a physical plan for renewal, a social plan is vital not only to serve people, but also to involve and educate people to the responsibilities of their care of property and their use of services. For neighborhood rejuvenation to succeed, the residents must, with intelligent leadership, participate in improvement of the neighborhood and must be instilled with civic pride. Civic organizations work in close alliance with the federal government. They try to achieve this citizen participation and to prove that the city is trying to improve itself, which is now a requirement in order to be granted government subsidy. The Community Action programs, developed in the 1960's, are logical outgrowths of the urban-redevelopment program. The emphasis in CAP is not upon housing alone, but upon job training and employment service and other community needs issues.

Traffic

Mass production has resulted in the use of the automobile, truck, and bus for the mass transportation of goods and people. These means of transportation have, in turn, resulted not only in urban congestion of traffic in the core of the city, but also in congestion on the routes into the city. Efforts thus far to render movement of traffic more efficient have resulted in the development of complex expressways leading into the city. Because of rapid growth, particularly of American cities, and the lack of planning, city streets are too narrow to be able to handle the heavy influx of traffic. Efforts to widen them and enforce complicated traffic regulations have alleviated the problem in a minimal and temporary way.

The problem of traffic is further compounded by the need for parking space, with areas above and below ground being utilized for this purpose. Expressways and garages and other parking areas consume land space, thereby reducing the space available for other purposes, such as parks, recreation areas, cultural centers, and residences

A number of procedures to remedy traffic ills have been proposed, and

[4]Further discussion of the problems of environmental conditions and man (human ecology) will be found in Chapter 11.

some have been incorporated into renewal projects. Perimeter parking facilities at strategic points enroute to the central city, with fast electrically driven public transportation to complete the journey, have been projected. Special underground routes have been suggested for inner-city traffic, especially facilitating the delivery of goods. Another device for commuters would be an underground tube through which passenger vehicles would travel at speeds in excess of 100 miles an hour. Within the core area, moving sidewalks and small electrically driven vehicles would be for pedestrian movement. The ideal is to enhance the core area for use by people and to offer flexibility of design in city planning.[5]

Crime and Delinquency

The preceding chapter dealt with crime and delinquency in its several forms. It will suffice here to remind the reader that they represent some of the most serious city problems. As the population migrates to the cities, there is more poverty, and when there is more poverty, there is more anti-social behavior. Crime is the manifestation of the social ills of a community. The circumstances of city life, such as poverty in the midst of material abundance, anonymity, the crowds of people, the need to conform to prevailing urban social mores, the lack of adjustment to these mores, and the fact that family activities frequently do not involve the family as a unit and take place away from the home—all evoke the problem of crime and delinquency.

THE CULTURALLY DISADVANTAGED

There is a growing concern stemming from the contrast of economic well-being for so many in the American society, and of the condition of economic poverty and social alienation for others. The technology that has created great material advantages, better working conditions, and high levels of aspiration both educationally and vocationally, has passed by growing numbers of this society. These are not only failing to advance, but seem to be insulated against advancements, forming a culture of the poor. The term *culturally disadvantaged* is relative and is one of several that have been used to identify a segment of society that is being recognized today as nonproductive economically. In addition, this part of society creates welfare burdens and social hazards, with a set of values, habits, attitudes, and behaviors that are different from those of the large middle class of America. Whereas these "different" elements of a more provincial culture may have been acceptable at another time and in another place, when moved to the urban scene, they no longer serve their bearers well. Nor do they serve the larger society in the urban milieu. Recognizing that these people do have a culture, that they are not "without" or "deprived" of a culture, it seems that they are a truly disadvantaged culture.

The middle-class influences demand some measure of conformity in matters of education, belief in the desirability of success, moral behavior,

[5]See William R. Ewald, Jr. (ed.), *Environment for Man: The Next Fifty Years* (Bloomington: Indiana University Press, 1967).

social adjustment, economic self-sufficiency, and belief and participation in the democratic way of living. It is possible that the very existence of a democratic form of government and way of life is contingent on a productive and educated citizenry.

Two cultures, though they may actually have a fundamental sharing of a basic democratic faith, cannot exist side by side without one assuming prominence over the other. To a degree the minor culture will have to be assimilated into the larger culture if a healthy society is to be maintained. This does not negate the right of subcultures to exist. That they do is healthy and good—offering, as they do, diversity of habits, talents, ideas, incomes, and institutions. However, when a subculture becomes insulated against the standards and norms that perpetuate the healthy survival of its offspring, and when it becomes enslaved in a downward spiraling cycle of poverty, then the whole of society is jeopardized. The culturally disadvantaged are those in American society who lack the resources—economically, educationally, and socially—to maintain norms acceptable in the middle-class culture and who cannot contribute to their own well-being or to that of society at large. These people are mostly of Southern origin, both black and white, and have been forced by economic necessity to leave their small farms or their positions as farm workers to seek employment in the cities. Millions of farm laborers and small farm owners either became migratory or crowded into the cities, looking for work. Many of the migrants are from depressed areas in which high unemployment has resulted from automation. These people move to the only area open to them in a large and confusing city, the slum. They bring with them few, if any, employable skills, their children, and their problems. The other minority groups, the Puerto Ricans, Mexicans, and Indians also comprise a part of the population of the slum. They too have the disadvantage of the lack of skills, and they face, because of language barriers and skin color, even more prejudice than the white population.

Although the case of the black is unique, it is unnecessary to go further into his plight, his history, and his enslavement to prejudice and discrimination. (See Chapter 9.) All that is said of the other disadvantaged groups may also be said of the black, but with considerably more emphasis.

Although the culturally disadvantaged cannot be stereotyped according to race, social class, nationality, or occupation, certain characteristics are held in common often enough to provide a clear picture.[6]

1. A position in the lower-income and class level.
2. A low aspirational and educational level and little upward mobility.
3. Victims of economic, class, and racial discrimination.
4. In a rural location in a depressed condition, or in a city location with a predominantly rural background and subsequent lack of adjustment to the urban environment.
5. Few, if any, marketable skills, with marginal or no employment.
6. Frequent regression to antisocial behavior.

[6]Martin Deutsch, "The Disadvantaged Child and the Learning Process," in A. Harry Passow (ed.), *Education in Depressed Areas* (New York: Bureau of Publications, Teachers College, Columbia University, 1963). See also Robert D. Havighurst, "Who Are the Socially Disadvantaged?" *The Education Digest*, Vol. 30, No. 3 (November 1964) and A. Harry Passow et al. (eds.). *Education of the Disadvantaged* (New York: Holt, 1967).

THE CULTURALLY DISADVANTAGED CHILD AND THE SCHOOL

From the family enmeshed in the defeating circumstances of poverty the child emerges. The disadvantaged child's environment and social relationships have not prepared him to grow and mature adequately.

What are the children like? What are their circumstances of poverty which so ill prepare them for healthy growth. To provide answers to these questions it is best to look at the different aspects of these children's environments: the home, attitudes, and social activity.

The home:

1. Is disorganized.
2. Provides inadequate space for play and study.
3. Is often characterized by maternal domination, with a poor male model.
4. Has inequality in eating and sleeping habits.

Attitudes:

1. Are fatalistic toward health.
2. Are accepting of illness.
3. Involve low aspiration.
4. Indicate a poor self-concept, a feeling of worthlessness and rejection.
5. Are distrustful of those in the larger society.

Social activity in which:

1. The child is confined to narrow sidewalks.
2. The child is kept close by parents.
3. The child is not exposed to a variety of middle-class cultural experiences.

The child in these circumstances is lacking on almost all fronts stressed by the middle-class school.[7]

The school represents a foreign culture. It has values of cleanliness and health. It offers a great variety of objects to be handled and identified— things to be seen and heard. It requires verbal expression and response. Long-range goals predominate over short-range goals. Emotional stability is a prerequisite. School learning requires regular attendance. Aggressive behavior is frowned upon. The educational process needs the parents' vital interest and involvement to motivate the child and help him to develop. For the middle-class child these are normal enough requirements. Why can the disadvantaged child not achieve in this orientation? This is discussed under the following headings:[8]

• *Cleanliness and health* are not the order in the home of poverty. Cleanliness holds a very secondary rating. The mechanical devices for cleaning taken for granted in a better home frequently do not exist. The rather fundamental knowledge of how to keep clean is also often missing.

Of considerably more importance is the factor of health, which affects the will to work and learn. The child has not only not learned good health habits, he has learned carelessness regarding health. His has been a poor diet resulting in low energy, upset stomach, poor teeth, and respiratory

[7]See Passow, op. cit., and Passow et al., op. cit.
[8]See also Deutsch, op. cit., pp. 163ff. for similar list.

problems. The family, usually large and living in small, inadequate, or dilapidated quarters, is disorganized and irregular concerning eating and sleeping habits, to say nothing of the lack of adequate beds, tables, and chairs. The attitude toward poor health is fatalistic—acceptance of poor health; the result is apathy and fatigue.

Sensory development is inadequate. The disadvantaged child's ingenuity with hands and mind has not been challenged. He does not have a variety of toys to play with and handle and with which to identify. He does not have picture books to look at or stories read to him. His home is sparsely furnished, bereft of decor and stimulating objects. Noise surrounds him, but much of it is meaningless. Intellectual stimulation does not exist; consequently, readiness to learn does not grow. Rather, it seems that he learns not to learn, not to see, not to hear, and not to be attentive. His is a restricted range of experiences and his concept formations are limited. This ill equips the child for the structure and demands of school activity.

• *Language development* in the impoverished home is usually of a restricted nature. It is used to convey essential, concrete, and immediate information for immediate consequences. The use of short, grammatically simple, and often unfinished sentences with little variety suffices. This meager language use is compounded usually by colloquialized expression. Concurrent with the minimal use of language is the inability to interpret and express impressions and reactions. With these restrictions the child is preset for poor language and cognitive development unless the school can offer compensatory measures.

• *Long-range vs. short-term goals* lie at the heart of middle-class values. The disadvantaged simply do not think this way. Life's basic needs are acute, and the effort expended to meet them is all-consuming. In addition, the attainability of future rewards is not realistic; the hurdles are too great. The feelings of insecurity and failure repudiate the promise of some distant security and success and make continued effort senseless. Only when basic needs are met and successful experiences in the early school years are achieved will long-range goals be meaningful to the child.

• *Emotional stability* is a part of being acceptable and secure. The impoverished child has his parents' feelings of worthlessness passed on to him, and school may offer more feelings of rejection and failure.

At home the child is subject to harsh and quick punishment for behavior that displeases, but he is seldom rewarded for behavior that is pleasing. The parents are more adept at communicating *what they feel about themselves*—disgust, disapproval, and rejection. It is hard to show love when bitterness, discouragement, ill health, and anxieties dominate. Frequently the home structure lacks a father, or the father, if present, is unemployed and presents a poor model to the child. There is no doubt that the need here is to help the child achieve and gain a good self-concept, and to provide parental education and guidance.

• *Good behavior* in the school means nonaggression. Compliance with rules, good sportsmanship, and rewards for success are indelibly inscribed in the middle-class concepts of good school behavior. As the deprived child progresses through school, he is often more and more of a behavior problem.

The rules of behavior are from another culture, and he has learned no respect for them. In his environment, fighting amounts to a way of life. Differences and arguments are not settled through logical reasoning. More often the child has not only witnessed the most gross physical exchanges between his peers, parents, and neighbors, but he has been a recipient of harsh punishment, many times undeserved. He has not been taught self-control. He has been taught quite the opposite and can be very volatile, with the result that subsequent school punishment for his aggression is ineffective. His is a life of survival, and he is ready to defend what seems to him to be the slightest infraction of his tenuous position. His weapons are few, and he uses what he has. What may be a good adjustment in his home environment, however, is a poor adjustment in the school.

• *Parental attitudes* are basically in favor of education. However, the attitude is ambivalent. The parent confusedly sees the need for education, but is opposed to the authority of the school. He himself has had only limited exposure to or success in school and has no knowledge of what is required for readiness to learn and for good study habits. The importance of regular attendance is not understood. The parent is embarrassed by his lack of education and is aware of his poor showing in the company of middle-class school personnel, and is actually fearful. The school is an outsider who takes the child away from the home to better him in ways not fully comprehended by the parent. The school appears to point an accusing finger at the culturally limited parent, and this bears the threat of humiliation and raises barriers.

EFFECTS OF THE CHARACTERISTICS COMMON TO DISADVANTAGED CHILDREN ON THEIR SCHOOL LIFE
Children

As the child enters school he may not give evidence of many or all of these disadvantages. However, the bridge between the slum culture and middle-class school culture is a large one, and problems increase with time. Frustrations and failures begin and accumulate until by the sixth grade the student is alienated and negative to the degree that success is doubtful.

Older Youth

Adolescence is a period when there is a search for a new identity, a quest for new experience, when peer group relations and conformity are increasingly important and future goals become more defined. All societies must have a set of universals—a set of values to which all persons must either adhere or face some ostracism. The child comes into conflict in the transition period between childhood and adulthood in his search for new self-identity. This is largely a case of maturing.

In contemporary American society, teenagers have developed a real culture that is considerably isolated from the adult culture. They have trouble relating to authority and seeing the adult as helpful. The young are also searching for identity in the world of skills and occupations. If there is a lack of proper identity development and adult relations, antisocial, delinquent, or outright psychotic behavior may result. The problem of youth then is threefold: (1) the search for new self-identity, (2) the adjustment to the adult world, and (3) the search for occupational identity.

For approximately one third of the youth who begin secondary education this critical period is one in which the student has little motivation and little aspiration for further education. He fails to see the relevance of his education to his living habits, and he has no clear vocational goals. The disadvantaged youth is rebellious and resentful of authority and school domination, which for him represents punishments and no rewards.

By ages fourteen to sixteen, the way to be "in" is to be hostile to the dominant society, with conformity to the peer culture in which the youth is growing up. Still, this presents an enigma. The youth knows that the completion of secondary education is essential to acquire work that will enable him to survive economically. But this awareness often does not generate the necessary will to overcome what are now internalized features of the poverty environment. He tends to push aside the grim reality of his future for immediate gratification. To the middle-class person this is an irrational response. To the psychologist it is the only rational response to his situation. From school truancy and dropping out, of course, come juvenile delinquency, adult crime, and the spontaneous riots of depressed areas.

One of every four unemployed today are under twenty years of age. The youth has been ill equipped since his early schools to take advantage of the educational opportunities available. Passow states that the unemployment rate of youth between the ages of fourteen and twenty-one is twice that of the labor force as a whole and is even greater among youth from minority groups.[9]

What is being said here is a natural conclusion to the preceding evaluation of the early school years of the disadvantaged child. The efforts of social and educational impoverishment are cumulative and culminate in the wasteful situation of school dropouts and unemployed youth. This concern is today being recognized as a problem of national dimensions in the United States. The school is recognizing that the deprivation endured by a child of the disadvantaged culture not only impinges on his academic achievement, but renders him incapable of ultimate social and economic adjustment, *within the framework of existing school programs,* both public and private. A new kind of education is needed.

PROGRAMS FOR THE ALLEVIATION OF THE EFFECTS OF POVERTY AND CULTURAL IMPOVERISHMENT

The culturally disadvantaged student does not make normal progress in school learning. This realization has affected all aspects of education, spurring educators and the public to view the immediacy of the problem and to define the task of reshaping curriculum and methods to attain full development for each individual. The need is for helping those who are impoverished to achieve personal dignity and freedom, thereby enabling them to identify with the larger society and to respond profitably to social and economic change. This calls for a system of education that can overcome deficiencies

[9]See Passow, op. cit.

in the learning development of the child. However, before we look at some of these, we should give a word of caution.

> Evidence from the Coleman Report and a number of other sources supports the conclusion that home conditions, general conditions of life, are more important predictors of school achievement than any of the variables that were studied. Although it is probably true that for an individual child, good schooling can possibly overcome many of the limitations of his background, for the population at large this relationship does not seem to exist. . . . With rare exceptions the available research relating to the disadvantaged treats the target population as if it were a homogeneous group despite the mounting evidence that heterogeneity within the several subgroups so designated may be a more crucial problem in educational planning. Similarly there appears to be a search for generic treatments or the one solution to the neglect of multiple solutions, individualization or the matching of treatment to specific characteristics. Studies in this area tend to depend excessively on quantitative measures and static variables to the neglect of the process variables and the qualitative analysis of the behaviors, circumstances and conditions studied.[10]

Enrichment and Compensatory Education

Special projects for schools with "problem" children evolve around a number of factors, and begin with the child at a preschool age. Considerations of adequate food, medical care, and clothing are fundamental. Programs to aid the perceptual and cognitive ability of the child by helping him to experience the world around him involve the structured nursery and kindergarten experience. In some areas these have existed as preschool academies, and in current federal programs are called Head Start. Through these, which may involve the child as young as three years, language is extended, and new insights and discoveries are made. The child learns to see the adult as a source of help and information. He becomes motivated and ready to learn. Communication and involvement with parents are essential at this early stage. They are informed of these early programs and are encouraged to observe the classes and, when possible, even to assist in their operation.

For those whose deprivation has culminated in a lack of learning, the progress may be early retardation, frustration, and failure within the first three grades of school. Compensations must be created to halt further failure that can only become more pronounced as the child proceeds through the upper grades. In these critical early years, careful evaluation of the social and intellectual characteristics of each child should be made, with adjustive teaching methods and the freedom to try new approaches geared to help each child. Enrichment and compensatory programs may include a longer school day with special instruction for small groups, summer programs, and tutorial programs. Exposure to the performing arts through concerts and plays, field trips to parks, museums, recreation areas, and places of business and industry are more and more being incorporated into programs to alleviate the effects of poverty.

The importance of a positive relationship between the school and

---

[10]Edmund W. Gordon, "Introduction" to issue on "Education for Disadvantaged Children," *Review of Education Research* (February 1970). Used by permission.

parents, thereby forming a conjunctive home–school effort, cannot be over-emphasized. The school reflects the community in terms of boys and girls, who in turn reflect their home environment and structure. As a community agent, the school can use neighborhood resources as a "community school." This concept involves a wide range of academic, vocational, recreational, and social pursuits that involve not only children, but also adults. Special classes operate on Saturdays and evenings through the week for children to acquire skills beyond those given during regular school hours. Adult education, recreation, health services, remedial education, social activities, and civic participation add special strengths to the school and community, and strengthen minority groups.

Study and work must have transfer value out of school. As the child progresses through secondary education, this statement claims more and more significance. Deprived students need special help in tutoring or small-group instruction, with emphasis on basic skills and vocational education. In a work–study plan, learning takes place through a relationship that holds concrete value, providing some income and motivation to complete what is so essential—the secondary school. The work–study program requires school leadership and counseling, and the cooperation of community agencies, business, and industry. From this can evolve an organized peer society in which adolescent youth may find positive identity and support from others in the group, as well as helpful adult leadership.

Not of least importance in school programs for the disadvantaged is the need to recognize the changes necessary in the school staff and their qualifications—more counselors for both students and parents at all levels, social workers, and leadership that can intelligently reach out into the community from the school. Teachers who are equipped to grasp the problems of the disadvantaged children and who are resourceful in coping with these problems need to possess certain characteristics both in personality and in training. The following are basic essentials:[11]

1. Knowledge and understanding of the disadvantaged culture, including specific ethnic differences.
2. Knowledge of the various forms of prejudice and discrimination and ways of counteracting them.
3. Exposure to an orientation program and specific training with regard to the problems and relevant issues of depressed areas.
4. An understanding of learning problems, with an emphasis on the students' fear of failure in the classroom.
5. The ability to evaluate students' strengths and weaknesses objectively.
6. Consistency in firmness and fairness of treatment, be it in disciplinary matters or structure of work.
7. An authoritative, straightforward, and direct approach, with the emphasis on physical presentation as opposed to a highly verbal presentation.
8. The ability to accept and respect children as they are.
9. The ability to establish good rapport and to motivate through interest, enthusiasm, and patience.
10. Conviction that these children can and will learn.

[11]See similar list in Passow, op. cit. See also Frank Riessman, *The Culturally Deprived Child* (New York: Harper, 1962) and Passow et al., op. cit.

School programs such as those just described are geared toward a better tomorrow for children—by raising their aspirational, educational, and vocational levels, by providing better cultural and recreational horizons, and by intensive guidance to help students want to achieve in the midst of opportunity.

ANTIPOVERTY PROGRAMS

The 88th and 89th Congresses of the United States enacted laws for the mid-1960's to strengthen the social and economic potential of people through education, training, work opportunity, and designs for a better living environment. This antipoverty legislation was overwhelming in its many aspects and perspectives, with extraordinary attempts to upgrade services in such broad fields as education, health and welfare, transportation facilities, employment, voting rights, farming, aid to distressed areas, and conservation. The legislation symbolized the growing outlook that the United States is a national community with problems that have grown to national dimensions.

Why is the country so concerned about its depressed areas and disadvantaged population? The economy is one of plenty and keeps moving upward. This is a society of affluence, and the relative downward mobility of a growing segment of society stands out in contrast to this affluence and upward mobility. Moreover, a careful look at the present and a further look into the future foretells even greater problems if we cannot develop human potential more fully.

In historical perspective, education has been the function of the state and local community, with controversy over the issue of federal aid. The state assumed this task, with the result that America became the first stronghold of universal education and that this concept became an integral part of democracy. As the cost of education has increased, the federal government has responded with caution. Thus, in the past, aid has come through the Morrill Act of 1862, a device for setting up land grant colleges to promote agricultural and mechanical arts education. During each succeeding war, further aid was enacted, designed largely to support vocational high school training, and after World War II, the famous G.I. Bill of Rights enabled veterans to gain higher education. With the advance into space by the Russians in 1957, Congress enacted the National Defense Education Act, which supported science, mathematics, and long-range instruction in the public schools by making further provision for loans to college students.

With the declaration that poverty must be eliminated, the legislation of 1964–1968 is of a vast nature and has long-range implications for fighting poverty on many fronts. It has provided federal initiative, but with allowance for local autonomy and latitude. Although most local communities had entered a war on poverty before 1964 and had supported their efforts by local foundations, the federal legislation made further funds available to existing or new agencies upon request, and subject to approval on the basis of utilization of the requested funds. These agencies have been organized as component parts of a whole antipoverty program, coordinated by a local community action commission. It is through this coordinating body that plans are made, funds are requested, and federal approval is obtained, to implement the program.

The Economic Opportunity Act of 1964 provided a work-training program giving part-time work to boys and girls in their local communities on projects picked by local government or organizations, thereby enabling them to stay in or return to school. Large training centers, the Job Corps, provided vocational training and educational skills, with an allowance and certain expenses paid for those sixteen to twenty-one years of age who are out of school and out of work. Work–study programs to help needy college students, community action projects such as tutoring, training, recreation centers, grants for adult education, work experience programs for needy unemployed, loans for poor farm families, projects involving mental health, migrant workers, and neighborhood improvement groups are areas of local effort. Organizations such as better housing leagues and American Committee to Improve Our Neighborhood (ACTION) are well-known examples of local organizations created to foster projects. Volunteers in Service to America (VISTA) is a federally operated domestic peace corps that serves in local areas with no pay.

The CCC corps of the 1930's and the NYA camps of the same period, together with the Job Corps of the 1960's and the Neighborhood Youth Corps of the same period, represent challenging opportunities for dealing with problems of youth. Political pressures, the Vietnam War, and other forces have set these programs back or eliminated them.

The Elementary and Secondary Education Act of 1965 offered aid to public, private, and parochial schools in low-income areas. Funds were allocated to school districts according to the number of pupils five to seventeen years old within their boundaries whose families have an annual income of less than $2,000. Educational centers were supplemented to provide for remedial instruction, to finance instructional materials, and to expand federally supported educational research. One illustration of a locally inspired, supported, and planned program conceived before this federal legislation is that opeated by the Mott Foundation in Flint, Michigan, since 1935. Based on the concept that the problems of society are the problems of the public schools, their program has involved families and homes in the schools' attendance areas and has attracted national and international attention. Briefly, this plan involves extra learning time after school hours and on Saturdays; adult educational, social, civic, and recreational activities; special classes for children with learning problems; and cooperative efforts and involvement of local businesses and clubs.[12]

The Public Works and Economic Development Act of 1965 provided assistance in improvements for public works and services, better employment opportunities, construction and rehabilitation within a redevelopment area, and aid to Appalachia. It actually extended and revised the Area Redevelopment Act of 1961.

[12]Peter L. Clancy, "The Urban Process," *The Community School and Its Administration*, Vol. 3, No. 6 (February 1965), pp. 1–6.

The Housing and Urban Development Act of 1965 offered financial assistance to make private housing available to lower-income families who are elderly, handicapped, displaced, victims of natural disaster, or otherwise qualifying occupants of substandard housing.

The Higher Education Act of 1965 in essence established funds to up-grade the quality of teaching by grants to colleges and universities. These grants extend services and resources within an institution; finance cost of cooperative exchanges of faculty, students, and facilities between institutions; provide student scholarships and loans; and finance advanced teacher preparation programs. The Vocational Act of 1963, revised in 1968, greatly expanded vocational education, making it available for occupations requiring skills of a simpler or less technical nature. Details and latest information about any or all of this legislation may be obtained by a request to the congressman of your district, or to one of your two senators.

After 1968, with a change in administration, the anti-inflation effort and the cost of the Vietnam War and the ABM (antiballistic missile) system caused appropriations to be curtailed.[13]

Family Allowance Proposals (Negative Income Tax)

Probably the most basic domestic decision President Nixon made on taking office was to opt for an income strategy against the problems of poverty and inequality. It was an option early in evidence. In April, 1969, the President proposed that the government stop taxing persons whose income was below the poverty level. A simple enough idea *in the context* of a mode of analysis that makes it simple; $650-million per year was involved in the administration proposal. . . .

Then came the Family Assistance Plan, the single most important piece of Then something important happened. Congress agreed. . . . social legislation to be sent to the Congress in a generation (or really two generations as we count them today) and the social initiative that will almost surely define the beginning of a new era in American social policy. The legislation established a floor under the income of every American family with children. It provides incentives for work and opportunities for work training, job placement, and child care. . . .

The principles of the program are simple. First, income assistance is not to be conditioned on dependency. Unlike the welfare system of what soon, we hope, will be the past, it is not a system that creates a class of dependent persons and then sustains them in their dependency. . . . Second, it provides incentives to work and to maintain fundamental family ties, in contrast to a system that had evolved with just the opposite incentives.[14]

An example of how the proposed Family Assistance Plan might work, using $3,920 as the level of earning for a family of four, follows:

[13]The legislative picture and administrative policy is subject to shifts and change. The National School Public Relation Associations frequently publishes reviews and assessments of trends. Latest at this writing: *Federal Aid: New Directions for Education 1970–71* (Washington, D.C.: National School Public Relations Association, 1970).

[14]Daniel P. Moynihan, "One Step We Must Take," *Saturday Review*, May 23, 1970, pp. 21–22. Copyright 1970 Saturday Review, Inc. Used by permission.

EARNED INCOME	BENEFIT	TOTAL INCOME
0	1,600	1,600
720	1,600	2,320
1,000	1,460	2,460
1,500	1,210	2,710
2,000	960	2,960
2,500	710	3,210
3,000	460	3,460
3,500	210	3,710
3,920	—	3,920

If the wage earner earns no money the federal government would allow $1,600, or $125 per month. These payments would be made until earnings reach $720, about what the extra expense of working would cost (bus fare, clothing, and so on). This would give the family of four $2,320. From this point on, the table shows the decrease in benefits until the $3,920 level is reached. At this point the benefits would cease. Of course the figures would vary with the size of the family and the cost of living. Food stamps would be available (up to $800 a year at this writing) and the states might supplement the federal program.

LONG-RANGE IMPLICATIONS FOR PROGRAMS

A healthy society provides effective roles for its members. It has physical, economic, education, governmental, and social aspects from which its members cannot be divorced. Civic pride and community conscience must be energized into involvement in setting goals for programs, and in determining values that prescribe the direction toward these goals.

Family planning services, which have existed in the past, must be made more effective for the future. Education in the material, physical, and psychological aspects of child rearing—so important to the development of physically and mentally healthy youngsters who later make up the adult social fabric—must be made more available to parents. Premarital education and marriage counseling must be made more available. (The difficulty here is that it is often hard to find, educate, and counsel those who need it most.) Communication is difficult on matters relating to family planning and other matters basic to the establishment of sound marriages.

The programs and the legislation just discussed have for the most part been constructed as a marshaling of resources to deal with complex and emergency situations. However, the immediate challenges must evolve into long-range measures that will effectively continue to prevent society from allowing inadequate roles for its members. Those concerned with human welfare cannot be indifferent to questions of poverty and its ills, education, social class and race, urban planning, rural environment, and physical and mental health. Basically, people must be educated to the problems that confront them and their society. The basis of this education must be laid early and proceed through the maturing of the individual as he develops into a functioning member of the family (see also Chapter 6), social, civic, and governmental groups. This education must be a positive approach and must develop a sensitivity to just and preventive treatment measures. Consideration should be given to the different kinds of impoverishment: intellectual, biological, cultural, educational, and emotional. A whole complex of factors is associated with poverty.

Community services of whatever nature must be a collaboration of lay people, professional educators, social scientists, and social planners. Underlying all endeavors, there must be a human orientation, the planning for people.

SUMMARY

In this chapter the problems of the depressed areas—those areas that have not kept pace with the economic growth of the rest of the country— and the problems of the culturally disadvantaged child have been considered. The urbanization of our society, with its attendant problems, has been fully discussed. The nature of the rural depressed areas has also been described.

The effects of urbanization and the attendant specialization of the society, its fragmentation into groups in which it is difficult to "live life as a whole," and the increase in the amount of anonymity (lack of identification), with the consequent increase in the number of persons who are in a complete state of degradation—i.e., "anomie"—were clarified. Also were discussed the problems of urban renewal, the problem of urban housing, and the city traffic and highway problems as these affect the life of the people.

The problems of the culturally disadvantaged and the characteristics of culturally disadvantaged children and youth in terms of their difficulties in adjusting to American social institutions, largely based on a middle-class set of values, were presented. Suggestions were made as to actions that might be taken to assist personnel working with disadvantaged children as these come into the schools or as they are helped by other social agencies.

Some of the programs developed as a part of the antipoverty movement, both by private and governmental groups, were discussed as these have come into play in recent years.

Selected Bibliography

Ablestrom, Winton M., and Robert J. Havighurst. 400 Losers. San Francisco: Jossey-Bass, 1971. 246 pp.

Alloway, David N., and Francesco Cordasco. Minorities and the American City. New York: David McKay Co., Inc., 1970. 124 pp.

Alsop, Joseph, et al. Ghetto Schools: Problems and Panaceas. Washington, D.C.: The New Republic, 1967. 56 pp.

Anastasiow, Nicholas. "Educational Relevance and Jensen's Conclusions," The Education Digest, Vol. XXXV, No. 4 (December 1969).

Arnold, David O. The Sociology of Subcultures. Berkeley, Calif.: The Glendessary Press, 1970. 170 pp.

Asbell, Bernard. The New Improved American. New York: McGraw-Hill Book Company, 1965. 272 pp.

Ashton-Warner, Sylvia. *Teacher.* New York: Simon & Schuster, Inc., 1963. 191 pp. (Paperback.)

Bagdikian, Ben H. *The Media and the Cities.* Chicago: University of Chicago Center for Policy Study, 1968. 90 pp.

Banfield, Edward C. *The Unheavenly City: The Nature and Future of Our Urban Crisis.* Boston: Little, Brown and Company, 1970. 308 pp.

Berland, Theodore. *Noise—The Third Pollution.* Public Affairs Pamphlet No. 449. New York: Public Affairs Committee, 1970. 20 pp.

Bernstein, Abraham. *The Education of Urban Populations.* New York: Random House, Inc., 1967. 416 pp.

Binzen, Peter. *Whitetown USA.* New York: Random House, Inc., 1970. 305 pp.

Blaustein, Arthur I., and Roger R. Woock (eds.). *Man Against Poverty: World War III, A Reader on the World's Most Crucial Issue.* New York: Random House, Inc., 1968. 456 pp.

Bottom, Raymond. *The Education of Disadvantaged Children.* West Nyack, N.Y.: Parker Publishing Co., 1970. 225 pp.

Bowers, C. A., Ian Housego, and Doris Dyke (eds.). *Education and Social Policy: Local Control of Education.* New York: Random House, Inc., 1970. 209 pp.

Brim, Orville G., Jr., David C. Glass, and others. *American Beliefs and Attitudes About Intelligence.* New York: Russell Sage Foundation, 1969. 291 pp.

Campbell, Alan K. (ed.). *The States and the Urban Crisis.* Englewood Cliffs, N.J.: Prentice-Hall, Inc., 1970. 224 pp.

Campbell, Ronald F., Lucy A. Marx, and Raphael O. Nystrand (eds.). *Education and Urban Renaissance.* New York: John Wiley & Sons, Inc., 1969. 148 pp.

Caplovitz, David. *The Poor Pay More.* New York: The Free Press, 1963. 220 pp.

Carson, Clarence B. *The War on the Poor.* New Rochelle, N.Y.: Arlington House, 1969. 283 pp.

Clark, Donald, Arlene Goldsmith, and Clementine Pugh. *Those Children: Case Studies from the Inner-City School.* Belmont, Calif.: Wadsworth Publishing Co., Inc., 1970. 334 pp.

Cohen, S. Alan. *Teach Them All to Read: Theory, Methods, and Materials for Teaching the Disadvantaged.* New York: Random House, Inc., 1969. 329 pp.

Coleman, James S. *Equality of Educational Opportunity.* Washington, D.C.: Government Printing Office, 1966. 325 pp.

Coles, Robert. *Uprooted Children.* Pittsburgh: University of Pittsburgh Press, 1970. 142 pp.

Committee for Economic Development, Research and Policy Committee. *Education for the Urban Disadvantaged: From Preschool to Employment.* New York: Committee for Economic Development, March 1971. 86 pp.

Community and the Schools. Reprint Series No. 3, *Harvard Educational Review.* Cambridge, Mass.: Harvard Educational Review, 1969. 176 pp.

Conant, James B. *Slums and Suburbs: A Commentary on Schools in Metropolitan Areas.* New York: McGraw-Hill Book Company, 1961. 128 pp.

Costikyan, Edward N. "Cities Can Work," *Saturday Review,* April 4, 1970.

Cowles, Milly (ed.). *Perspectives in the Education of Disadvantaged Children: A Multidisciplinary Approach.* Cleveland: The World Publishing Company, 1967. 314 pp.

Crain, Robert L. "School Integration and the Academic Achievements of Negroes," *Sociology of Education,* Vol. 44, No. 1 (Winter 1971).

Cranston, Maurice. *What Are Human Rights?* New York: Basic Books, Inc., Publishers, 1962. 105 pp.

Cronbach, L. J. "Heredity, Environment and Educational Policy," *Harvard Educational Review,* No. 39 (1969).

Cuban, Larry. *To Make a Difference: Teaching in the Inner City.* New York: The Free Press, 1970. 320 pp.

Daly, Charles U. (ed.). *The Quality of Inequality: Urban and Suburban Public Schools.* Chicago: Center for Policy Study, University of Chicago, 1969. 160 pp.

Damerell, Reginald G. *Triumph in a White Suburb.* New York: William Morrow & Co., Inc., 1968. 351 pp.

Dansereau, Pierre (ed.). *Challenge for Survival: Land, Air, and Water for Man in Megalopolis.* New York: Columbia University Press, 1970. 235 pp.

Dawson, Helaine. *On the Outskirts of Hope.* New York: McGraw-Hill Book Company, 1968. 329 pp.

Decker, Sunny. *An Empty Spoon.* New York: Harper & Row, Publishers, 1969. 125 pp.

Dennison, George. *The Lives of Children.* New York: Random House, Inc., 1969. 309 pp.

Dentler, Robert A., and Mary E. Warshauer. *Big City Dropouts and Illiterates.* New York: Frederick A. Praeger, Inc., 1968. 140 pp.

Deutsch, Martin, Irwin Katz, and Arthur R. Jensen. *Social Class, Race and Psychological Development.* New York: Holt, Rinehart and Winston, Inc., 1969. 423 pp.

Doll, Russell C. "Alternative Models of Institutional Change in the Slum School," *Phi Delta Kappan,* Vol. LII, No. 6 (February 1971).

Downs, Anthony. *Urban Problems and Prospects.* Chicago: Markham, 1970. 293 pp.

Durham, Joseph T. "Compensatory Education: Who Needs It?" *The Education Digest,* Vol. XXXV, No. 4 (December 1969).

Eckardt, Wolf von. *The Challenge of Megalopolis: Based on the Original Study of Jean Gottman.* Twentieth Century Fund Report. New York: The Macmillan Company, 1964. 126 pp.

Eddy, Elizabeth M. *Walk the White Line.* Garden City, N.Y.: Doubleday & Company, Inc., 1967. 188 pp.

Edelson, Edward. *The Battle for Clean Air.* Public Affairs Pamphlet No. 403 A. New York: Public Affairs Committee, 1967. 28 pp.

"Education in the News: Parkway's John Bremer," *Phi Delta Kappan,* Vol. LII, No. 6 (February 1971).

"Education for Socially Disadvantaged Children," *Review of Educational Research,* Vol. 25 (December 1965). Entire issue contains a review of research on the topic.

"Education of the Underprivileged," *School and Society,* February 18, 1967. Complete issue.

Education U.S.A. Special Report. *Federal Aid: New Directions for Education in 1970–71.* Washington, D.C.: National School Public Relations Association, N.E.A., 1970. 48 pp.

Eldredge, H. Wentworth. *Taming Megalopolis.* Two volumes. Garden City, N.Y.: Anchor Books, 1967. 1,166 pp.

Elias, C. E., Jr., James Gillies, and Svend Riemer (eds.). *Metropolis: Values in Conflict.* Belmont, Calif.: Wadsworth Publishing Co., Inc., 1964. 326 pp.

Ellul, Jacques. *The Meaning of the City.* Grand Rapids, Mich.: Wm. B. Eerdmans Publishing Co., 1970. 209 pp.

Endleman, Shalom (ed.). *Violence in the Streets.* Chicago: Quadrangle Books, Inc., 1968. 471 pp.

Etzkowitz, Henry, and Gerald M. Schaflander. *Ghetto Crisis.* Boston: Little, Brown and Company, 1969. 212 pp.

Fantini, Mario D. *The Reform of Urban Schools.* Washington, D.C.: National Education Association Center for the Study of Instruction, 1970. 100 pp.

_____, Marilyn Gittell, and Richard Magat. *Community Control and the Urban School.* New York: Frederick A. Praeger, Inc., 1970. 268 pp.

Fedder, Ruth, and Jacqueline Gabaldon. *No Longer Deprived.* New York: Teachers College Press, Columbia University, 1970. 211 pp.

Fellman, David (ed.). *The Supreme Court and Education.* New York: Teachers College Press, Columbia University, 1969. 231 pp.

Fitch, Lyle C., and Annmarie Hauck Walsh (eds.). *Agenda for a City: Issues Confronting New York.* Beverly Hills, Calif.: Russell Sage Foundation, 1970, 718 pp.

Friedman, Burton D. "Emphasizing the 'Urban' in 'Urban Education'," *Phi Delta Kappan*, Vol. LII, No. 7 (March 1971).

Friendly, Fred W. "Asleep at the Switch of the Wired City," *Saturday Review*, October 10, 1970.

Fuller, R. Buckminster, Eric A. Walker, and James R. Killian, Jr. *Approaching the Benign Environment.* University, Ala.: University of Alabama Press, 1970. 121 pp.

Gans, Herbert J. *The Levittowners: Ways of Life and Politics in a New Suburban Community.* New York: Pantheon Books, Inc., 1967. 474 pp.

_____. *The Urban Villagers: Group and Class in the Life of Italian Americans.* New York: The Free Press, 1962. 367 pp.

Gerson, Wolfgang. *Patterns of Urban Living.* Buffalo, N.Y.: University of Toronto Press, 1970. 113 pp.

Gittell, Marilyn (ed.). *Educating an Urban Population.* Beverly Hills, Calif.: Russell Sage Foundation, 1970. 320 pp.

Glaser, Daniel (ed.). *Crime in the City.* New York: Harper & Row, Publishers, 1970. 308 pp.

Goggin, Terrance P., and John M. Seidl. *Politics American Style: Race, Environment and Central Cities.* Englewood Cliffs, N.J.: Prentice-Hall, Inc., 1972. 384 pp.

Goldman, Marshall I. *Controlling Evolution: The Economics of a Cleaner Environment.* Englewood Cliffs, N.J.: Prentice-Hall, Inc., 1967. 175 pp.

Goldwin, Robert A. (ed.). *A Nation of Cities: Essays on America's Urban Problems.* Chicago: Rand McNally & Co., 1968. 128 pp.

Goodman, Paul. *Growing Up Absurd.* New York: Random House, Inc., 1960. 296 pp.

Gordon, Edmund W. Introduction to issue on "Education for Disadvantaged Children," *Review of Education Research* (February 1970).

Gordon, Ira J. *Parent Involvement in Compensatory Education.* Urbana, Ill.: University of Illinois Press, 1970. 88 pp.

Gordon, Sol. "The Bankruptcy of Compensatory Education," *The Education Digest,* Vol. XXXVI, No. 4 (December 1970).

Gottlieb, David, and Anne Lienhard Heinsohn. *America's Other Youth: Growing Up Poor.* Englewood Cliffs, N.J.: Prentice-Hall, Inc., 1971. 192 pp.

Gottman, Jean. *Megalopolis: The Urbanized North-Eastern Seaboard of the United States.* Cambridge, Mass.: The M.I.T. Press, 1964. 310 pp.

Graham, Grace. *The Public School in the New Society*, Third Edition. New York: Harper & Row, Publishers, 1969. 404 pp.

Graham, James J. *The Enemies of the Poor.* New York: Random House, Inc., 1970. 308 pp.

Grambs, Jean D. "The Culturally Deprived Child," *The Education Digest*, Vol. 30, No. 5 (January 1965).

Green, Constance McLaughlin. *American Cities in the Growth of the Nation.* New York: Harper & Row, Publishers, 1965. 258 pp.

Guthrie, James W., George B. Kleindorfer, Henry W. Levin, and Robert T. Stout. *Schools and Inequality.* Cambridge, Mass.: The M.I.T. Press, 1971. 253 pp.

Gutman, Robert, and David Popenoe (eds.). *Neighborhood, City and Metropolis: An Integrated Reader in Urban Sociology.* New York: Random House, Inc., 1970. 942 pp.

Hamilton, David. *A Primer on the Economics of Poverty.* New York: Random House, Inc., 1968. 133 pp.

Handler, Philip (ed.). *Biology and the Future of Man.* New York: Oxford University Press, 1970. 936 pp.

Hannerz, Ulf. *Soulside: Inquiries into Ghetto Culture and Community.* New York: Columbia University Press, 1969. 236 pp.

Harrington, Michael. *The Dynamics of Misery.* New York: Sidney Hillman Foundation, 1968. 24 pp. (Pamphlet.)

———. *The Other America: Poverty in the United States.* New York: The Macmillan Company, 1962. 191 pp.

Haskins, Jim. *Diary of a Harlem School Teacher.* New York: Grove Press, Inc., 1970. 150 pp.

Havighurst, Robert J. "The Reorganization of Education in Metropolitan Areas," *The Education Digest,* Vol. 36, No. 9 (May 1971).

———. "Who Are the Socially Disadvantaged?" *The Education Digest,* Vol. 30, No. 3 (November 1964).

———, and Daniel U. Levine. *Education in Metropolitan Areas,* Second Edition. Boston: Allyn & Bacon, Inc., 1971. 350 pp.

———, Frank L. Smith, and David E. Wilder. *A Profile of the Large City High School.* Washington, D.C.: National Association of Secondary School Principals, 1970. 182 pp.

Hazlitt, Henry. *Man vs. the Welfare State.* New Rochelle, N.Y.: Arlington House, 1969. 225 pp.

Heer, David M. (ed.). *Social Statistics and the City.* Report of a Conference held in Washington, D.C., June 22–23, 1967. Cambridge, Mass.: Joint Center for Urban Studies of the Massachusetts Institute of Technology and Harvard University, 1968. 186 pp.

Helfrich, Harold, Jr. (ed.). *The Environmental Crisis.* New Haven: Yale University Press, 1970. 187 pp.

Hellmuth, Jerome (ed.). *Disadvantaged Child,* Volume Two: *Compensatory Education: A National Debate.* New York: Brunner/Mazel, Inc., 1970. 466 pp.

———, *Disadvantaged Child,* Volume Two: *Head Start and Early Intervention.* New York: Brunner/Mazel, Inc., 1970. 466 pp.

Herndon, James. *The Way It Spozed to Be.* New York: Simon & Schuster, Inc., 1968. 188 pp.

Higbee, Edward. *A Question of Priorities: New Strategies for Our Urbanized World.* New York: William Morrow & Co., Inc., 1970. 214 pp.

Hilson, M., Francesco Cordasco, and F. P. Purcell. *Education and the Urban Community Schools and the Crisis of the Cities.* New York: American Book Company, 1969. 506 pp.

Hope, Frank L., Jr. "Building Entirely New Cities," *Current,* No. 125 (January 1971).

Horowitz, David. *The Abolition of Poverty.* New York: Frederick A. Praeger, Inc., 1969. 178 pp.

Hunt, J. McV. "Has Compensatory Education Failed? Has It Been Attempted?" *Harvard Educational Review,* Vol. 39 (1969).

Hurley, Rodger. *Poverty and Mental Retardation: A Causal Relationship.* New York: Random House, Inc., 1969. 301 pp.

Itzkoff, Seymour W. *Cultural Pluralism and American Education.* Scranton, Pa.: International Textbook Co., 1969. 202 pp.

Jacobs, Jane. *The Economy of Cities.* New York: Random House, Inc., 1969. 268 pp.

James, Dorothy Buckton. *Poverty, Politics and Change.* Englewood Cliffs, N.J.: Prentice-Hall, Inc., 1972. 224 pp.

Janowitz, Morris. *Institution Building in Urban Education.* New York: Russell Sage Foundation, 1969. 126 pp.

Jekel, James F. "Poverty and the Adolescent Parent," *Journal of the American Scientific Affiliation,* Vol. 22, No. 2 (June 1970).

Jensen, A. R. "How Much Can We Boost I.Q. and Scholastic Achievement?" *Harvard Education Review,* Vol. 39 (1968–69).

Johnson, Kenneth R. *Teaching the Culturally Disadvantaged.* Palo Alto, Calif.: Science Research Associates, 1970. 202 pp.

Jones, Loyal. "Appalachia," *Today's Education,* Vol. 60, No. 4 (April 1971).

Joseph, Stephen M. (ed.). *The Me Nobody Knows: Children's Voices from the Ghetto.* New York: Avon Books, 1969. 143 pp.

Josephson, Eric, and Mary Josephson (eds.). *Man Alone: Alienation in Modern Society.* New York: Dell Publishing Co., Inc., 1962. 592 pp.

de Jouvenel, Bertrand, René Dubos, et al. *The Fitness of Man's Environment.* New York: Harper & Row, Publishers, 1968. 250 pp.

Justice, Blari. *Violence in the City.* Fort Worth: Texas Christian University Press, 1969. 289 pp.

Kaplan, Bernard A. "Issues in Educating the Culturally Disadvantaged." *Phi Delta Kappan,* Vol. 40, No. 2 (November 1963).

Keach, Everret T., Robert Fulton, and William Gardner (eds.). *Education and Social Crisis: Perspectives on Teaching Disadvantaged Youth.* New York: John Wiley & Sons, Inc., 1967. 413 pp.

Klinzing, John. "The Invisible Man and Today's Education," *The Educational Forum,* Vol. XXXV, No. 4 (May 1971).

Kruszynski, Eugene. "The Nature of Urban Education," *School and Society,* Vol. 98, No. 2324 (March 1970).

Kvaraceus, William C., John Gibson, and Thomas Curtin. *Poverty, Education and Race Relations: Studies and Proposals.* Boston: Allyn & Bacon, Inc., 1967. 226 pp.

———, and others. *Negro Self-Concept: Implications for Schools and Citizenship.* New York: McGraw-Hill Book Company, 1965. 144 pp.

Lachman, Seymour P., and David Bresnick. "An Educational Ombudsman for New York City?" *School and Society,* Vol. 99, No. 2332 (March 1971).

Larned, Jeremy, and Irving Ilowe (eds.). *Poverty: Views from the Left.* New York: William Morrow & Co., Inc., 1969. 319 pp.

Lawson, Simpson. "Towns for the Urban and Rural Poor," *Current,* No. 125 (January 1971).

Leacock, Eleanor Burke. *Teaching and Learning in City Schools: A Comparative Study.* New York: Basic Books, Inc., Publishers, 1969. 263 pp.

Leinwand, Gerald. *Poverty and the Poor.* New York: Washington Square Press, Inc., 1968. 158 pp.

Levin, Henry M. (ed.). *Community Control of Schools.* Washington, D.C.: Brookings Institution, 1970. 318 pp.

Levin, Melvin R., and Alan Shank (eds.). *Educational Investment in an Urban Society: Costs, Benefits, and Public Policy.* New York: Teachers College Press, Columbia University, 1970. 425 pp.

Levine, Daniel U. (Guest Editor). "The Reform of Urban Education," *Phi Delta Kappan,* Vol. LII, No. 6 (February 1971). Entire Issue.

Levine, Murray, and Adeline Levine. *A Social History of Helping Services: Clinic, Court, School and Community.* New York: Appleton-Century-Crofts, Inc., 1970. 315 pp.

Levy, Gerald E. *Ghetto School: Class Warfare in an Elementary School.* New York: Pegasus, 1970. 178 pp.

Lindsay, John V. *The City.* New York: W. W. Norton & Company, Inc., 1970. 240 pp.

Lutz, Frank W. (ed.). *Toward Improved Urban Education.* Worthington, Ohio: Charles A. Jones, 1970. 343 pp.

McCall, Thomas D. "Urban Neighborhood Influences on High School Administration," *School and Society,* Vol. 99, No. 2332 (March 1971).

McDill, Edward L., Mary S. McDill, and J. Timothy Sprehe. *Strategies for Success in Compensatory Education: An Appraisal of Evaluation Research.* Baltimore: The Johns Hopkins Press, 1969. 83 pp.

McHarg, Ian. *Design with Nature.* Garden City, N.Y.: Natural History Press, 1969. 197 pp.

McKeown, James E., and Frederick I. Tietze (eds.). *The Changing Metropolis*, Second Edition. Boston: Houghton Mifflin Company, 1971. 200 pp.

McMurrin, Sterling M. (ed.). *Functional Education for Disadvantaged Youth*. New York: Committee for Economic Development, 1971. 128 pp.

Mangin, William P. *Peasants in Cities: Readings in the Anthropology of Urbanization*. Boston: Houghton Mifflin Company, 1970. 200 pp.

Marmer, Theodore (ed.). *Poverty Policy: A Compendium of Cash Transfer Proposals*. Chicago: Aldine Publishing Co.-Atherton Press, 1971. 256 pp.

Marris, Peter, and Martin Rein. *Dilemmas of Social Reform: Poverty and Community Action in the United States*. New York: Atherton Press, 1967. 248 pp.

Marris, Ronald W. *Social Forces in Urban Suicide*. Homewood, Ill.: The Dorsey Press, Inc., 1969. 214 pp.

Mayer, Martin. *The Schools*. New York: Harper & Row, Publishers, 1961. 446 pp. (Paperback.)

Meranto, Philip. *School Politics in the Metropolis*. Columbus, Ohio: Charles E. Merrill Books, Inc., 1970. 176 pp.

Miel, Alice, with Edwin Kiester, Jr. *The Shortchanged Children of Suburbia*. New York: Institute of Human Relations Press, 1967. 68 pp.

Miller, Harry L. *Education for the Disadvantaged*. New York: The Free Press, 1967. 288 pp.

——, and Marjorie B. Smiley (ed.). *Education in the Metropolis*. New York: The Macmillan Company, 1967. 303 pp.

——, and Roger B. Woock. *Social Foundations of Urban Education*. Hinsdale, Ill.: The Dryden Press, Inc., 1970. 544 pp.

Mink, Oscar G., and Bernard A. Kaplan (eds.). *America's Problem Youth: Educating the Disadvantaged*. Scranton, Pa.: International Textbook Co., 1970. 189 pp.

Morse, Dean. *The Peripheral Worker*. New York: Columbia University Press, 1969. 202 pp.

Morton, Malvin (ed.). *Can Public Welfare Keep Pace?* Published for the American Public Welfare Association. New York: Columbia University Press, 1969. 175 pp.

Moynihan, Daniel P. *Maximum Feasible Misunderstanding: Community Action in the War on Poverty*. New York: The Free Press, 1969. 218 pp.

Mozine, Harold, and Greta Mozine. *A Primer for the Inner-City School*. New York: McGraw-Hill Book Company, 1970. 1,969 pp.

Mumford, Lewis. *The City in History: Its Origins, Its Transformations and Its Prospects*. New York: Harcourt Brace Jovanovich, Inc., 1961. 657 pp.

Murphy, Gardner. *Freeing Intelligence Through Teaching*. New York: Harper & Row, Publishers, 1961. 64 pp.

Myrdal, Gunnar. *The Challenge of World Poverty*. New York: Pantheon Books, Inc., 1970. 518 pp.

Nagle, John M. *Urban Public Education: Problems and Prospects*. New York: Oxford University Press, 1970. 250 pp.

Nash, Roderick (ed.). *The American Environment: Readings in the History of Conservation*. Reading, Mass.: Addison-Wesley Publishing Co., Inc., 1968. 236 pp.

National Commission on Urban Problems. *Building the American City*. New York: Frederick A. Praeger, Inc., 1969. 502 pp.

"New Communities: Business on the Urban Frontier," Special Issue. *Saturday Review*, May 15, 1971. Articles by:
   Myron Lieberman. "Introduction."
   Wolf von Eckardt. "A Fresh Scene in the Clean Dream."
   Anthony Dow. "Private Investment and the Public Weal."
   Edward J. Logue. "Piecing the Political Pie."
   Leo A. Molinaro. "Truths and Consequences for Older Cities."

Nicholson, Max. *Environmental Revolution.* New York: McGraw-Hill Book Company, 1970. 366 pp.

Niederhoffer, Arthur. *Behind the Shield: The Police in Urban Society.* Garden City, N.Y.: Doubleday & Company, Inc., 1967. 360 pp.

O'Gorman, Ned. *The Storefront: A Community of Children on 129th Street and Madison Avenue.* New York: Harper & Row, Publishers, 1970. 75 pp.

O'Neil, Robert M. *The Price of Dependency: Civil Liberties in the Welfare State.* New York: E. P. Dutton & Co., Inc., 1970. 351 pp.

Ornstein, Allan C., and Phillip D. Vairo. *How to Teach Disadvantaged Youth.* New York: David McKay Co., Inc., 1969. 436 pp.

Orr, John B., and Patrick Nicholson. *The Radical Suburb: Soundings in Changing American Character.* Philadelphia: The Westminster Press, 1970. 201 pp.

Paradise, Scott. "Man's Relation to Nature, Our Vandal Ideology," *Current,* No. 115 (February 1970).

Passow, A. Harry, Mirian Goldberg, and Abraham Tannenbaum (eds.). *Education of the Disadvantaged: A Book of Readings.* New York: Holt, Rinehart & Winston, Inc., 1967. 503 pp.

Perel, William W., and Phillip D. Vairo. *Urban Education: Problems and Prospects.* New York: David McKay Co., Inc., 1969. 145 pp.

Pickard, Jerome P. "Is Megalopolis Inevitable?" *The Futurist,* Vol. 4, No. 5 (October 1970).

Pilisuk, Marc, and Phyllis (eds.). *Poor Americans: How the White Poor Live.* Chicago: Aldine Publishing Co., 1970. 160 pp.

Platt, John R. *Perception and Change: Projects for Survival.* Ann Arbor, Mich.: University of Michigan Press, 1970. 178 pp.

"Problems of Urban Education," *Phi Delta Kappan,* Vol. XLVIII, No. 7 (March 1967). Entire Issue.

Riesman, David. *Abundance for What?: And Other Essays.* Garden City, N.Y.: Doubleday & Company, Inc., 1964. 610 pp.

Riessman, Frank. *The Culturally Deprived Child.* New York: Harper & Row, Publishers, 1962. 140 pp.

———, Jerome Cohen, and Arthur Pearl (eds.). *Mental Health of the Poor.* New York: The Free Press, 1964. 648 pp.

Roberts, Joan I. *Scene of the Battle: Group Behavior in Urban Classrooms.* New York: Doubleday & Company, Inc., 1970. 441 pp.

Rogers, David. *Livingston Street: Politics and Bureaucracy in the New York City School System.* New York: Random House, Inc., 1968. 584 pp.

Rogers, Edward. *Poverty on a Small Planet.* New York: The Macmillan Company, 1964. 125 pp.

Rosenkranz, Richard. *Across the Barricades.* Philadelphia: J. B. Lippincott Co., 1971. 250 pp.

Rubinstein, Annette T. (ed.). *Schools Against Children: The Case for Community Control.* New York: Monthly Review Press, 1970. 299 pp.

Rudman, H. C., and R. L. Featherstone (eds.). *Urban Schooling.* New York: Harcourt Brace Jovanovich, Inc., 1969. 128 pp.

Ryan, William. *Blaming the Victim.* New York: Random House, Inc., 1971. 299 pp.

Sanders, Irwin T. *The Community.* New York: The Ronald Press Company, 1958. 431 pp.

Schaeffer, Francis A. *Death in the City.* Chicago: Varsity Press, 1969. 127 pp.

Seligman, Ben B. *Permanent Poverty: An American Syndrome.* Chicago: Quadrangle Books, Inc., 1970. 238 pp.

Sennett, Richard. *The Uses of Disorder: Personal Identity and City Life.* New York: Alfred A. Knopf, Inc., 1970. 198 pp.

Shepard, Paul, and Daniel McKinley. *The Subversive Science: Essays Toward an Ecology of Man*. Boston: Houghton Mifflin Company, 1969. 453 pp.

Shostak, Arthur B. *Blue-Collar Life*. New York: Random House, Inc., 1969. 299 pp.

Smith, Louis M., and Geoffrey William. *The Complexities of an Urban Classroom: An Analysis Toward a General Theory of Teaching*. New York: Holt, Rinehart & Winston, Inc., 1968. 277 pp.

Sommer, Robert. *Personal Space: The Behavioral Basis of Design*. Englewood Cliffs, N.J.: Prentice-Hall, Inc., 1969. 192 pp.

Stans, Maurice. "The U.S. Plan for Curbing Megalopolis," *The Futurist*, Vol. 4, No. 5 (October 1970).

Stein, Maurice R., and Arthur J. Vidich (eds.). *Identity and Anxiety: Survival of the Person in Mass Society*. New York: The Free Press, 1960. 658 pp.

Stone, James C., and Frederick W. Schneider. *Teaching in the Inner City: A Book of Readings*. New York: Thomas Y. Crowell Company, 1970. 512 pp.

Street, Paul. "Compensatory Education by Community Action," *Phi Delta Kappan*, Vol. LI, No. 6 (February 1970).

Strom, Robert D. *The Urban Teacher: Selection, Training and Supervision*. Columbus, Ohio: Charles E. Merrill Books, Inc., 1971. 160 pp.

Sturdivant, Frederick D. *The Ghetto Marketplace*. New York: The Free Press, 1969. 316 pp.

Swanson, Gordon I. "The Myth of Urbanism," *The Education Digest*, Vol. XXXVI, No. 1 (September 1970).

Taba, Hilda, and Deborah Elkins. *Teaching Strategies for the Culturally Disadvantaged*. Chicago: Rand McNally & Co., 1966. 295 pp.

Tabb, William K. *The Political Economy of the Black Ghetto*. New York: W. W. Norton & Company, Inc., 1970. 152 pp.

Task Force on Urban Education (Wilson C. Riles, Chairman). *The Urban Education Task Force Report*. New York: Frederick A. Praeger, Inc., 1970. 369 pp.

Theobald, Robert. *The Guaranteed Income: Next Step in Economic Evolution?* Garden City, N.Y.: Doubleday & Company, Inc., 1965. 233 pp.

Thurow, Lester C. *Poverty and Discrimination*. Washington, D.C.: Brookings Institution, 1969. 214 pp.

Toffler, Alvin (ed.). *The Schoolhouse in the City*. New York: Frederick A. Praeger, Inc., 1968. 255 pp.

Totten, W. Fred. "Community Education—Best Hope for Society," *School and Society*, Vol. 98, No. 2328 (November 1970).

Toynbee, Arnold. *Cities on the Move*. New York: Oxford University Press, 1971. 257 pp.

Tuckman, Bruce W., and John L. O'Brian (eds.). *Preparing to Teach the Disadvantaged*. New York: The Free Press, 1969. 311 pp.

Twente, Esther E. *Never Too Old: The Aged in Community Life*. San Francisco: Jossey-Bass, 1970. 246 pp.

Usdan, Michael, and Frederick Bertolaet (eds.). *Teachers for the Disadvantaged: The Report of the School–University Teacher-Education Project*. Chicago: Follett Publishing Company, 1966. 240 pp.

Vairo, Phillip D., and William M. Perel. *Urban Education: Problems and Prospects*. New York: David McKay Co., Inc., 1969. 160 pp.

Van Clef, Eugene. *Cities in Action*. New York: Pergamon Press, Inc., 1970. 325 pp.

von Eckardt, Wolf. "Rebuilding Cities We Have," *Current*, No. 125 (January 1971).

Warden, Sandra A. *The Leftouts: Disadvantaged Children in Heterogeneous Schools*. New York: Holt, Rinehart & Winston, Inc., 1968. 208 pp.

Warner, Sam Bass, Jr. (ed.). *Planning for a Nation of Cities*. Cambridge, Mass.: The M.I.T. Press, 1966. 310 pp.

Warner, W. Lloyd. *American Life: Dream and Reality*, Revised Edition. Chicago: University of Chicago Press, 1962. 291 pp.

Warren, Roland L. (ed.). *Politics and the Ghettos.* New York: Atherton Press, 1969. 214 pp.

Weaver, Thomas, Maurice Falk, and Alvin Magid (eds.). *Poverty: New Interdisciplinary Perspectives.* Chicago: Science Research Associates, Inc., 1969. 232 pp.

Weinstein, Gerald, and Mario D. Fantini (eds.). *Toward Humanistic Education: A Curriculum of Affect.* New York: Frederick A. Praeger, Inc., 1970. 228 pp.

White, William F. *Tactics for Teaching the Disadvantaged.* New York: McGraw-Hill Book Company, 1971. 274 pp.

Wilcox, Clair. *Toward Social Welfare: An Analysis of Programs and Proposals Attacking Poverty, Insecurity, and Inequality of Opportunity.* Homewood, Ill.: Richard D. Irwin, Inc., 1969. 402 pp.

Wilkerson, Doxey A., and others. *The Atlanta Area Workshop on Preparing Teachers to Work with Disadvantaged Youth,* Report Two, The NDEA National Institute for Advanced Study in Teaching Disadvantaged Youth. Washington, D.C.: American Association of Colleges for Teacher Education, 1968. 24 pp.

Will, Robert E., and Harold G. Vatter (eds.). *Poverty in Affluence: Social, Political and Economic Dimensions of Poverty in the U.S.* New York: Harcourt Brace Jovanovich, Inc., 1967. 274 pp.

Williams, Frederick (ed.). *Language and Poverty: Perspectives on a Theme.* Chicago: Markham Publishing Company, 1970. 459 pp.

Williams, Percy V. "Education of Disadvantaged Youth: Teachers vs. Administrators," *The Educational Forum,* Vol. XXXIV, No. 2 (January 1970).

Wilson, James Q. *The Metropolitan Enigma.* Garden City, N.Y.: Doubleday & Company, Inc., 1970. 320 pp. (Paperback.)

Wise, Arthur E. *Rich Schools, Poor Schools: The Promise of Equal Educational Opportunity.* Chicago: University of Chicago Press, 1968. 228 pp.

Wisniewski, Richard. *New Teachers in Urban Schools: An Insider's View.* New York: Random House, Inc., 1968. 24 pp.

Wogaman, Philip. *Guaranteed Annual Income: The Moral Issues.* Nashville, Tenn.: Abingdon Press, 1968. 158 pp.

Wolozin, Harold. *The Economics of Air Pollution.* New York: W. W. Norton & Company, Inc., 1966. 318 pp.

Woock, Roger R. (ed.). *Education and the Urban Crisis.* Scranton, Pa.: International Textbook Co., 1970. 264 pp.

Zimmer, Basil G., and Ames H. Hawley. *Metropolitan Area Schools: Resistance to District Reorganization.* Beverly Hills, Calif.: Russell Sage Foundation, 1968. 317 pp.

Selected Films

A Chance at the Beginning (Anti-Defamation League), 29 min. From the New York University Institute for Developmental studies. All aspects of the institute's preschool program are seen in operation. With a senior staff member as guide, the film demonstrates how these techniques may be adapted into traditional preschool curricula.

A Chance to Learn (N.E.A.), 30 min. Shows how the Elementary and Secondary Education Act of 1965 will open up educational opportunities to underprivileged children.

Air Pollution: Take a Deep Deadly Breath (McGraw-Hill), 54 min.

Approaches to Early Childhood Curriculum (Anti-Defamation League), 25 min.

Children Without (Anti-Defamation League), 30 min. Film shows a Detroit public school where teachers and counselors establish the warm relationships such children need, and provide positive learning experiences for them.

Children Without (American Association of School Administrators), 55 min.

The City—Cars or People? (Sterling Educational Films), 28 min.

The Cities and the Poor: Part I (N.E.T.), 60 min. Sections of Chicago and Los Angeles are examined to try to understand the nature of social welfare work.

The Cities and the Poor: Part II (N.E.T.), 60 min. Examination of continuing unrest in nation's slums.

The Cities: The Rise of New Towns (N.E.T.), 60 min. Comparison in planning and construction of new communities in the U.S. with past American developments.

Communication Makes a City Live (ICF), 15 min. This film will focus on the fact that communication is vital to any human society and especially important as the huge metropolitan agglomerates take form. The need for ways to end individual isolation, to have reliable information available, will continue to grow more pressing. Can the County Agent system of the Department of Agriculture be applied to the inner-city situation?

The Community (N.E.T.), 60 min. Two dissimilar communities are evaluated to reveal the cultural, educational, religious, and physical characteristics of two communities undergoing social and economic change.

Don't Crowd Me! (ICF), 15 min. Crowding, stress and anxiety situations and aggressive behavior are all under study by scientists and some believe that the results of their studies are of value to architects and social planners. This leads into an open-ended look at the problem of how to achieve civil order, and conversely, avoid civil disorder.

Drop Out (Atlantis Productions), 27 min. Studies the case of a school dropout. Explores the reasons for his action and the results.

The Dropout (N.E.A.), 29 min.

Elementary School Teacher Education Series (McGraw-Hill): *Elementary School Children, Part I, Each Child Is Different,* 16 min. *Part II, Discovering Individual Differences,* 25 min.

The Empty Lot (Instructional Media Center), 27.5 min. Portrays in three dramatic episodes some of the economic and social problems facing students, parents, educators, and other citizens and the role played by modern vocational education in meeting them.

Expanding City (University of Wisconsin), 14 min. Describes the problems of crowded schools, inadequate fire and police protection and the isolation of the individual in the growing city. Indicates that proper planning can help to solve or prevent these problems.

Green City (Stuart Finley Productions), 23 min. Civic action to preserve green space and open space as cities grow.

The Hard Way (N.E.T.), 60 min. The problem of poverty in America, the richest country in the world, is discussed, emphasizing the ways in which the poor of today are different from those of past generations.

Heart of the City (Sterling Educational Films), 28 min. Dramatizes the growing sterility, dullness, and congestion that is destroying vitality, breadth, and variety in cities.

How to Live in a City (N.E.T.), 30 min. Space problems involved in city housing.

How Things Get Done (N.E.T.), 30 min. Urban renewal in New York City area—pressures, politics, finances, and so on, involved.

Incident on Wilson Street (Anti-Defamation League), 15 min. Space problems involved in city housing. Film dramatically reveals how skilled and sympathetic teachers bring enrichment into the lives of educationally disadvantaged children.

An Intellectual Caste System (N.E.T.), 30 min. Intellectual placement system in elementary schools in the Dekalb County Schools in Georgia is discussed.

Living City (Encyclopaedia Britannica and the Twentieth Century Fund), 26 min. Historical review of the growth of cities resulting in slums and congestion. Discusses the need for a change in suburb–city relations and views the slum renewal programs now in progress in several cities.

Marked for Failure (N.E.T.), 60 min. Focuses on the problems facing both education and children in America's slum schools and illuminates the reasons why these children, mostly Negro, are kept out of the cultural and, ultimately, the economic mainstream of society.

Megalopolis: Cradle of the Future (Encyclopaedia Britannica), 22 min. Dynamics of urbanization and emphasis on the need for careful planning.

The Newcomers (Board of Missions, Methodist Church), 25 min.

Our Changing Environment (Encyclopaedia Britannica), 17 min. Man's increasing power to control his environment has created new pressures and problems for the modern city.

Overload in the Cities (ICF), 15 min. Our urban centers are deteriorating faster than we can keep up with even the minimum standards. Air and water are both heavily polluted and now need to be treated as something other than inexhaustible resources.

Pandora's Easy Open Pop-Top Box (Environmental Control Admin.), 15 min. Dramatic presentation of effects of uncontrolled urbanization.

A Place to Live (Brandon), 18 min. A film on housing problems. Relates the story of a school boy in squalid housing.

Portrait of a Disadvantaged Child: Tommy Knight (McGraw-Hill), 16 min. Documentary film highlighting a day in the life of a slum child—introducing special problems, needs, and strengths of the inner-city child.

Portrait of the Inner City (McGraw-Hill), 17 min. Viewing the streets, the schools, and the living quarters in the inner city of a large urban community in the United States, giving the viewer some idea of what life is like in the inner city, reflecting its uplifting as well as degrading aspects. You see the inhabitants who serve as models for young Tommy Knight: the shoeshine man, junkman, porter, car-wash man. You also see the more positive model of Tommy's older brother who works as a salesman in a store after school.

Portrait of the Inner City School: A Place to Learn (McGraw-Hill), 19 min. Focusing on Tommy Knight, shows many teaching techniques—some good, some ineffective, some harmful—and illustrates how a teacher can unconsciously discriminate against the culturally disadvantaged pupil. Shows teachers discussing methods which have proved successful or harmful.

Remedy for Riot (Mass Media), 37 min. The film speaks to the cause of race riots and what we can do about them.

Role Playing in Guidance (University of California), 14 min.

Step by Step (International Film Bureau), 20 min.

The Squeeze (Hank Newenhouse), 10 min. Throngs of people, jammed highways, rushing commuters, starving children graphically portray the population problems.

The Tenement (Anti-Defamation League), 40 min. Based on a *CBS Reports* documentary, filmed over a period of many months, in which members of nine families living in a slum on Chicago's South Side tell their own stories. *The Tenement* does not conceal the brutal facts of ghetto existence—indeed, it is a searing testimony to the contagion of hopelessness and despair. It will stimulate thought and discussion about the social and economic system that has stamped the mark of poverty on millions of people for generations.

Three Cures for a Sick City (N.E.T.), 40 min. Urban renewal efforts in Washington, D.C.

Urban Sprawl (Arthur Barr), 15 min. Shows the move of merchants and industries to the suburbs and points out the need for planning urban developments.

The Vicious Circle (McGraw-Hill), 28.5 min. Shows the search for ways to break the vicious cycle of poverty and ignorance in which those who are poor cannot get an education and those who are uneducated remain poor.

Worlds Apart (Anti-Defamation League), 16 min. From the New York University Institute for the Developmental Studies. Techniques for developing a sense of self-esteem, teaching concept formation and language efficiency are demonstrated in a prekindergarten class supervised by the institute. Contrasting scenes in a traditional classroom illustrate how middle-class teaching methods can doom the disadvantaged child to failure.

Chapter 11

■■■■■■■■■■■■■□□□□□□

Population Problems
and Trends

Population trends, both in America and the rest of the world, have experienced extreme shifts in recent years and have had significant effects on our social life and hence on education. During the period prior to World War II, a decreasing birthrate had a profound effect upon our economy and on our schools. During World War II, and immediately after, the increased birth rate in America and throughout the world has had enormous implications for population problems. The effect of this trend on education during the latter period has been particularly acute in America, where an effort is made to provide the opportunity for education for almost everyone in our society from age six to age eighteen. We provide higher education for a much larger percentage of our population than do many well-developed countries. In the sections that follow, the changing trends in population and some of the problems they entail are discussed in more detail, with the implications for education set forth in the latter part of this chapter.

WORLD POPULATION TRENDS AND FOOD SUPPLY
Recent Changes in World Population

Man, being an adaptive animal, is found over the entire land mass of the globe, but his numbers are concentrated in those places most favorable for his existence. There is no exact count of his numbers, for census-taking is accurate only in the more progressive regions. A total of 3.362 billion in 1970 appears to be a justified figure.[1] It is expected to double by the year 2010, and triple to around 11 billion by the year 2050. See Figure 20. Julian Huxley has estimated roughly that at about 8000 B.C., the beginning of agriculture, the world held about 10 million people (probably not more than 20 million and not less than 5 million). When the civilized era began—say, about 5000 B.C.—world population had increased to 20 million. There were perhaps 40 million when Egypt had its first dynasty, 100 million at the time of the Trojan War, and 175 million at the beginning of the Christian

[1]Estimate of UN Secretariat in an A.P. dispatch, June 21, 1970.

398

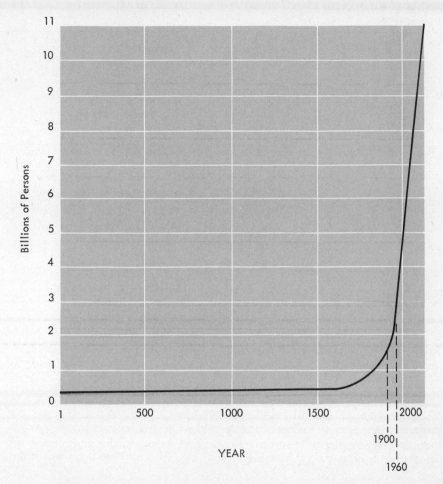

Figure 20. Twenty centuries of world population growth (to 2050).

Era. By 1650 there were about 500 million, and since then the climb has been rapid. Another way of illustrating the tremendous upsurge is the statement that probably 2 to 3 per cent of all human beings *(Homo sapiens)* who ever lived are still alive.[2] Figure 21 illustrates vividly the recent increase and projection—a real population bomb.

Estimates of human population by continents are helpful in interpreting these changes. In Table 14 will be found estimates of human population by continents from 1650 through 1970.

[2]Authorities vary on this, some going as high as one person out of seven; others, more conservatively, one out of twenty (5 per cent). The writers are conservative, but even their figure is startling, because only two or three generations are alive at once (now) out of perhaps 30,000 generations since 8000 B.C. Cf. Annabelle Desmond, "How Many People Have Ever Lived on Earth?" in Stuart Mudd (ed.), *The Population Crises and the Use of World Resources* (Bloomington: Indiana University Press, 1964), pp. 27–616.

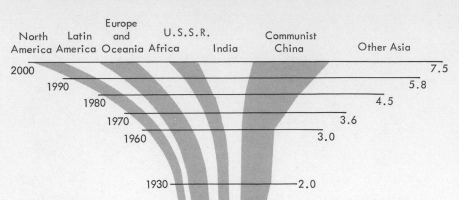

Figure 21. Growth of world population to the year 2000.
From "First Annual Report of the Council on Environmental Quality" (Washington, D.C.: Government Printing Office, 1970), p. 150.

The large increase in population has been a direct result of many important changes in the ways of man's living. The two checks in the past on population growth have been the shortage of food and the widespread toll of disease, both of which have been intensified by war. One need only think

TABLE 14
Population by Continents at Selected Years (in Millions)

CONTINENT	1650	1700	1800	1850	1900	1940	1950	1960	1970
North America	1	1	6	26	81	143	166	197	
Middle America	6	6	10	13	25	42	51	66	
South America	6	6	9	20	38	89	111	140	
Europe	100	110	187	266	401	543	559	639	
Asia	330	400	602	749	937	1,186	1,302	1,636	
Africa	100	98	90	95	120	157	198	235	
World Total	545	623	906	1,171	1,608	2,170	2,400	2,913	3,362

of the Black Death, the Thirty Years' War, and the modern famines of India and China to realize how millions of mankind have died in the past and are dying today. Better seeds and farming methods have resulted in more food; canning, freezing, and other means of preservation, together with better transportation, have made the food available. Better knowledge of health conditions and disease have allowed more to live—babies, mothers, and grandparents. Better means of production in factories have made men producers living in cities. With the possible exception of the Romans, it was not until about the middle of the eighteenth century that men had worked out satisfactory ways in which to supply any city, even a small one, with clean food and water, a minimal sanitary sewage disposal, moderately decent housing, and a small modern medical service. Wherever the benefits of the industrial revolution have spread, the people have been freed from a subsistence existence and their numbers have increased.

World Population and Food Supply

As soon as population and food supply are mentioned together, the name of Thomas Robert Malthus comes to mind. In 1791 Malthus presented the argument that population increases in a geometric ratio (1, 2, 4, 8, 16, 32, and so on), whereas food supply increases in an arithmetic ratio (1, 2, 3, 4, 5). Thus mankind must destroy himself through famine, pestilence, or war to maintain equality with his food! A review of history would, on the surface, apparently force one to agree with this. Even today, people frequently argue against aid to overpopulated countries by saying such aid will merely cause an increase in the birth rate and thus the problem will become worse instead of better.

An examination of the food supply of the more than 3 billion people in the world shows that most are underfed and undernourished. Two thirds of the people in the world have protein, vitamin, or mineral deficiencies in their diet (or deficiencies in all of these) that lead to slow starvation. This may be the result of poor soil, poor technology, poor land use, poor transportation, low standard of living, lack of incentive, religious and social taboos, or a combination of these factors.

For conditions at almost their worst, one can examine south China, where it was estimated in 1965 that over 3,500 agricultural people live on each square mile of farm land. Twenty-three per cent of the farms were under one-half acre in size, and each farm must support an average of 4.4 people. Each person got about 1,000 calories a day. In the United States, the average is about 3,400 calories. China at that time had a death rate of 30 per 1,000 per year, an infant mortality rate of 160 per 1,000, and a life expectancy of thirty-four years. (Life expectancy in the United States is now over seventy years.)

Again, those who believe Malthus point to India, where population increased 18 per cent from 1932 to 1942, whereas cereal production increased only 6 per cent. The rate of increase of population and food is roughly the same today. Accordingly, each person gets less cereal to eat—and cereal forms about 90 per cent of the diet. If reforms planned by the government are put into effect, India hopes merely to maintain the present level of food.

Further pessimism could come from an examination of probable populations in the future.

As Huxley says:

Let me spell out quantitatively what this (population increase) means. Today, the annual net increase in the total of people of the world's surface is over fifty million. That means that the world's population grows by about 150,000 people every 24 hours, the equivalent of a medium-sized town every day, 365 of them every year. To bring the facts home to American audiences may I point out that this is the equivalent of ten baseball teams, complete with coach, every minute of every hour of every day. And yet there are people who seriously talk of exporting our surplus population to Mars or some other planet!

The single country, China, contains well over six hundred million people. A few months ago its net annual increase was stated to be over thirteen million— much larger than the *total* population of Australia and New Zealand combined —but the latest information indicates that it is really over fourteen million. This means that by the mid-1970's the *increase* in China's population will be greater than the present *total* population of the United States. . . . Clearly this business of doubling cannot go on indefinitely, or indeed for more than a few decades, without leading to disaster. This is especially clear when we consider the *differential* rate of increase in different countries. The very high rates of increase are found mostly in the countries of Asia and in the tropical regions of Latin America and parts of Africa. The population explosion in these areas is undoubtedly due primarily to the great advances in medical science and its application in better health services.

To sum up, the world's demographic situation is becoming impossible. Man, in the person of the present generation of human beings, is laying a burden on his own future. He is condemning his children's children to increased misery; he is making it harder to improve the general lot of mankind; he is making it more difficult to build a united world free of frustration and greed. More and more human beings will be competing for less and less, or at any rate each will have to be content with a lesser cut of the world's cake. If nothing is done about this problem by us who are now alive, the whole of mankind's future will suffer, including the future of our own children and grandchildren. . . .

We must take a new look at the problem. We must stop thinking in terms of a race between production and reproduction, a race that never can be won. We must realize that our aim is not mere quantity, whether of people or goods or anything else, but quality—quality of human beings and of the lives they lead. Once we have grasped this, things begin to fall into place. . . . Meanwhile, of course, we must do everything in our power to increase all types of production—production of food, production of machines, production of what I may call the infrastructure of modern life; but equally of course we must pay the maximum possible attention to the conservation of resources. . . . Another thing that the advanced and privileged nations should do is to set their economists and social scientists to thinking out ways and methods of providing economic and social incentives for promoting a lower rate of population increase. Whether by means of family allowances, differential taxation, or other measures, it would undoubtedly be possible to devise economic and social methods that would exert pressure in favor of population decrease. As complement to this, we should set our psychologists and sociologists to studying ways of providing psychological motivation for small families and a sane population policy. In India the authorities are already beginning to try to persuade people that the whole future of the country depends on reducing the birth rate, and consequently that it is unpatriotic to have too many children. This has already been achieved in Japan, with the result that the Japanese have been able to cut their birth rate in half within a generation.

We should support all legislation—state, national, and international—that makes birth control easier and more socially approved. We must start discus-

sion groups and civic action groups and bring pressure to bear on our legislators and our governments.[3]

Did Malthus figure correctly? He lived just as the industrial revolution
was starting, and so he could not foresee the tremendous changes it wrought.
People's mental attitudes changed also. One of the results was a different
attitude toward family size, possibly because of the development of more
rational approaches to human problems. In the countries most affected by
the revolution, a planned limitation on family size has been the result.

More positive hope for man's future comes from a revolution in his food
supply. Through seed selection, better fertilizers, and more efficient use of
land, the amount of food that can be grown on the present farms of the
world could be greatly increased. But new developments are even more
startling, for mankind is changing nature to suit his needs. Soil conditioners
are changing soil texture; algae, containing trace elements, are being used
for fertilizer; work is going on to purify seawater for desert irrigation;
hormones are changing plant growth; crops grown in solutions (hydro-
ponics) eliminate the need for soil; algae, yeast, and seaweeds rich in food
value are now just beginning to be used. Each new idea produces a crop of
further ideas; by a change in education and food habits man can grow
enough to feed many billions more than there are now.

Some of the preceding developments are now economically feasible and
are being used; others need more experimentation. However, they all show
that starvation can be eliminated only if population growth can be slowed
or stopped. Most experts point out that the increase in production of food
is currently not matching the increase in population. As population further
expands, more land will be used for housing and highways, and the ultimate
productivity of new land not now being used is limited.

Borgstrom has canvassed and assessed the world's possibility carefully
and comes to these conclusions:

> In theory it is possible to produce, by means of rational exploitation of
> natural resources, enough food to nourish five billion human beings. But this
> can be accomplished only at the price of forced labor, a new kind of slavery,
> and tremendous investment—presumably pricing still more food than presently
> out of the markets of the poor.
>
> Although industrialization unquestionably would help to solve part of the
> economic woes of some poor countries, it is highly unlikely that it could come
> fast enough to overtake an unregulated population explosion. . . .
>
> The most serious fallacy of all is to believe that the world's resources are
> abundant and are limited only by man's ingenuity. It is commonly thought that
> man is capable of substituting technology for resources. This is feasible only to
> a very limited degree. Furthermore, the basic distinctions between renewable
> and nonrenewable resources are woefully neglected. The world's nonrenewable
> resources have lasted as long as they have principally because so few of the
> world's people have been using them. The United States, with 6 per cent of the
> world's population, is consuming more than one-third of the world's production
> of raw materials. Quite aside from the moral aspect of our right to this kind and

[3]Julian Huxley, *The Human Crisis* (Seattle: University of Washington Press, 1963), pp. 50, 51,
52, 79, 80, 81, 83, 85, 86. Reprinted by permission of the publishers.

degree of voracity, there is a much more far-reaching question. Will not the 2.5 billion poor people, multiplying within thirty years to more than 4 billion, demand their share?

It is sobering to keep in mind that in this very century, when the United States population doubled from 1900 to 1950, the "rising expectations" of the American people resulted in an eightfold increase in the use of minerals and a thirteenfold increase in the use of fuels. The total remaining resources of the globe are grossly inadequate to allow a similar extravagance among the have-nots; the meeting of even legitimate and reasonable demands will mean an unprecedented and devastating drain. In this light we have to examine our own blueprints for this other world. The average investment in machinery and equipment required on the farm in present-day United States agriculture exceeds 30,000 dollars per farm worker. This is in effect two to three times above that required for an average industrial worker. Even when recognizing chances for somewhat lower costs (in absolute figures) in poverty-ridden countries, it is still this disproportion that raises doubts whether this kind of capital-devouring agricultural operation is on the whole feasible in this hungry, poor world.[4]

John E. Mock,[5] director of the Georgia Science and Technology Commission (Atlanta), has declared that automation is the "hope of management, the despair of labor, the creator of employment, the destroyer of jobs, the harbinger of a better world, and the death knell of a familiar way of life." Mock indicates the following problems manifested in three ways:

1. Population explosion. The current American population of more than 200 million will increase to 300 million by the year 2000.
2. Population implosion. There will be a continuing rush from rural to urban communities, putting increasing pressure on urban facilities and institutions.
3. Population displosion. Changes within the metropolitan areas will continue, with the affluent moving to the suburbs, leaving behind the lower-income groups and thereby depleting the tax base.

AMERICAN POPULATION TRENDS AND EFFECTS
Effect of Recent Birth Rate on American Population

As noted in previous sections, the world is in the midst of a long-range trend of decreasing birth rate. This trend was temporarily reversed during the 1950's and 1960's. However, in spite of the enormous increase in the number of births, the rate did not reach that of 1925. The increased birth rate, together with longer life expectancy and the post-World War II immigration, did result in a major spurt in American population trends.

The increase in birth rate in America was due to several causes. More persons were married than ever before. (During the late 1960's there was the highest percentage of married persons in our population in the history of America.) More persons who married had at least one child. More families consisted of more than one child. However, there are fewer families that

---

[4]Reprinted with permission of The Macmillan Company from *Too Many: A Study of Earth's Biological Limitations*, by Georg Borgstrom (New York: Macmillan, 1969), pp. 332–34. Copyright © by Georg Borgstrom, 1969. See also Bates, Ehrlich, and Edward Rogers.

[5]Quoted in John Waring, "Automation, Society and Creative Capitalism," *Futurist* (February 1971), 16–17.

have gone beyond three children. The differential in birth rate between the various classes has tended to decrease. This is accounted for by increase in the number of persons born among middle-class families. All this served to accentuate the rapid increase in population in the United States. In the early 1970's it appears the U.S. birth rate has fallen to replacement-only rates.

A study of the predictions that have been made by population experts in the past does not give us any great confidence concerning any prediction of future population trends. In the past, the experts have been unable to predict such trends as the amount of decline in birth rate or such spurts as that coming after a war. Practically all population experts predicted that, although there would be a short spurt following World War II, it would not be as high as it turned out to be, nor would it last as long.

The following appraisal of the population trends in the United States by the Population Reference Bureau may serve to set the problems:

> The final published figures for the April 1 headcount show a total U.S. population of 204,765,770 (including Americans overseas). While the reported decennial increase of 25.4 million was the second largest in U.S. history, it reflected the second lowest growth rate—only 13.3 per cent. Only the depression decade of the '30s recorded a slower rate of increase.
>
> . . . the new range of possibilities for the U.S. population in the year 2000 is from 266 million to 321 million, compared with an earlier range of 281 million to 361 million. This official Census Bureau downward revision produced much talk about the imminent non-growth of the U.S. population and fueled a flareup of arguments that population was a problem for the poor nations, not for the United States. . . .
>
> On matters of distribution, however, the report found a very real and important challenge.
>
> "Plainly the country faces a problem in the distribution of its population regardless of policies to control its overall size. . . . Assuming that the trends continue unabated, most of the U.S. population growth over the next few decades will be concentrated in the 12 largest regions. . . . These trends have led to a prevalent sense of gloom for the future of both urban and rural America. . . . Hence, the choice of no change in public policy would run the high risk of bringing about the kind of future in which the communities of both urban and rural America would further deteriorate. It means that hundreds of American towns will continue to lose young people and economic opportunity and that the large metropolitan areas, already burdened with social and fiscal problems and characterized by fragmentation of governmental responsibility, may reach a size at which they will be socially intolerable, politically unmanageable and economically inefficient."
>
> The Goals report [National Goals Research Staff, *Toward Balanced Growth*, 1969], noting that the federal government can "provide leadership" for national strategy of balanced population growth, defined what it construed to be the current debate over tactics. It identified three choices: (1) generating growth in underpopulated rural areas; (2) generating growth in existing small towns and cities in non-metropolitan areas; and (3) creating new cities outside the big metropolitan regions. . . .
>
> Assume for a moment that . . . in the year 2000 the population of the United States is "only" some 280 million people. What might that mean to us and to the world?
>
> Each American has roughly 50 times the negative impact on the earth's life-support systems as the average citizen of India. Therefore, in terms of ecosystem destruction, adding 75 million more Americans will be the equivalent of

adding 3.7 billion Indians to the world population. . . . Clearly population
growth among Americans is much more serious than population growth in
underdeveloped countries.

. . . Even with luck we are doomed to continued population growth until
at least 2045, and the projected population size then will be over 300 million.
Hardly a pleasant prospect for a nation now failing to provide properly for 205
million people.

In May, the Population Reference Bureau pointed out that a wave of U.S.
women had begun to flood the prime reproductive ages of 20–29, and that this
trend might offset the drop in age-specific fertility (the number of children per
1,000 women in each age cohort). "In 1960," it said, "there were only 11 million
women aged 20–29; by 1980 there will be nearly twice as many about (20
million)." This population bulge is made up of the children of the post-World
War II "baby boom.". . .

The goal of the two-child family is closely linked to that of zero population
growth, since under current conditions of mortality in the United States, an
average of about 2.1 children per woman would, over a few generations, lead to
a stationary population. In February, addressing an environmental conference
jointly sponsored by the Public Affairs Council and the international Biological
Program, HEW Secretary Robert Finch momentarily endorsed this goal. When
asked what environmentally sound actions he would recommend to young
people, Finch replied: "I'd begin by saying, have only two children when they
get married."

This trial balloon, if it was one, was quickly deflated by other HEW spokesmen, who insisted the administration had no plans to encourage a policy on
family size. The ideal of a two-child family was popularized, however, by a new
citizen's group that grew spectacularly during 1970. Starting the year with a
membership goal of 10,000 members by the end of the year, Zero Population
Growth, Inc., now has over 25,000 members in about 425 chapters.[6]

Differential Birth Rate by Socioeconomic Status and Geographic Area

One of the characteristics of birth-rate trends throughout the United
States or, for that matter, the world) has been the differential of birth rate
among various socioeconomic classes and geographic areas. In general, in
the United States the over-all decline in birth rate during the last twenty
to twenty-five years has been more rapid in the cities than in rural areas and
has tended to be at a relatively lower absolute rate. Also, the decline that
occurred during the 1930's took place more rapidly among middle-class
families than among lower- or higher-class families. This differential in birth
rate coupled with a shift in the number of persons needed for agricultural
purposes has caused a tremendous movement of population from rural to
urban areas. This trend has continued since World War II.

There is some evidence that the differential birth rate has decreased
somewhat since World War II. In general, studies indicate that although
there is a decreasing size of the differential, there is still a differential among
the various socioeconomic classes. The highest birth rate occurs among the
low-income group, the second highest among the high-income group, with
the middle class coming third. There is still a higher birth rate among rural

[6]*Population Bulletin*, December 1970, "Population Developments in 1970," pp. 7–12,
passim. Reprinted with the permission of the Population Reference Bureau, Inc.

groups than among those in the cities. The main trend has been a decrease in the amount of differential.

Part of the difference in birth rates in geographic areas is due to the differing socioeconomic status of those areas. For example, there is a heavy birth rate in the southeastern part of the United States as compared with other parts. This is due largely to the agricultural nature of this area, together with the fact of its relatively lower socioeconomic status. This differential in birth rate, which will probably continue and may even be accentuated if the birth rate tends to resume its long-term decline following the post-World War II period, does pose rather serious problems. Even if we ignore the genetic implications of possibilities of inheritance of poor mental and physical characteristics, the fact that a large part of our population must grow up under environmental conditions that are less conducive to all-round development certainly does lead to discouragement, as far as the improvement of our society is concerned. However, the fact that the general prosperity of the postwar period has caused a rise in the level of living—so that even the poorer groups live at a level higher than did the middle class, for example, in 1900—has led to some optimism in regard to the possibly improved cultural background of those persons born into poor socioeconomic groups. Students of genetics do not seem to be completely agreed on the eventual effect upon the race of differential birth rates, as far as the type of physical and mental characteristics passed on to each new generation is concerned. At least at the moment, the increased cultural advantages apparently seem to cancel out or perhaps more than compensate for the disadvantages of the relatively lower environmental and, perhaps, inherited characteristics.

Mobility of American Population

The United States has always had a mobile population. It has been characterized for more than a century by a general westward movement and by a movement from the farms to the cities. Present major currents of population flow are (1) from the center of the country to the seacoasts, and (2) from the rural South to the industrial North. During the war periods and continuing during the postwar periods, there was a heavy mobility of our population resulting from the displacement caused by industrial expansion. See Figure 22.

The 1960's witnessed the continuation of the long-term trend of migration from rural to urban areas. The percentage of Americans living in metropolitan areas (cities of 50,000 or more, the county or counties in which they are located, and closely related counties) rose from 63 per cent in 1960 to 65 per cent in 1969. Simultaneously, they have been moving from the central cities to the suburban rings; in 1960 more people lived in the central cities than in the suburbs, while in 1969 the reverse was true. These population movements emphasize the high degree of mobility in the United States, made possible in part by well-developed transportation and communication networks. In the one-year period from March 1969 to March 1970 almost 36 million people—about 18 per cent of the population—changed their places of residence. These movements, together with other factors, contribute to the changing socioeconomic profile of the population.

In metropolitan areas, white-collar workers—professionals and managers

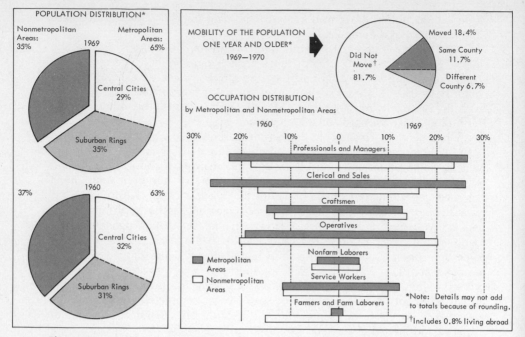

Figure 22. Profile of the U.S. population by area and occupation, 1960 and 1969. (Source: National Industrial Conference Board; 845 Third Avenue; New York, N.Y. 10022. Used by permission.)

and clerical and sales workers—were 52.5 per cent of the total work force in 1969, compared with 48.4 per cent in 1960. Blue-collar workers—craftsmen, operative, service workers, farmers, and farm and nonfarm laborers—were 47.5 per cent of the total in 1969, down from 51.6 per cent in 1960. The nonmetropolitan areas experienced the same trend, with white-collar workers accounting for 40.1 per cent of the total in 1969 versus 34.4 per cent in 1960. This trend reflects the increasing importance of the service of the economy where white-collar jobs predominate.[7]

   In recent years there has been a tendency toward moving from the centers of the cities to the suburbs and beyond. In many cases, this movement has been accentuated by urban renewal programs and by in-migration of minorities or southern mountaineers into the central city itself. This has led to the formation of middle-class suburbs and middle- and upper-class "exurbs." This tendency for the population to move from the major city outward to suburbs, coupled with the inability of cities to expand their legal limits to include the suburbs because of tradition and legal restrictions, has helped to accentuate the urban problems. In the first place, it tends to cause people living in the suburbs—a different political subdivision in most cases—to feel a lack of responsibility for the problems of the inner city. This attitude occurs even though they may work in the central city, or at least are economically tied to it. Secondly, it leads to an accentuation of the tendency

[7]*Road Maps of Industry*, No. 1654 (November 1970). The Conference Board. Used by permission.

for persons of different social statuses to live in different sections of the metropolitan area and, therefore, to an increased lack of understanding and less opportunity for acquaintance with persons from different social statuses. These problems have been discussed more fully in Chapter 12 and also in Chapter 10 (Depressed Areas).

Changing Life Span and Effect on American Population

One of the factors that has led to the population increase has been the increased years of life expectancy. This is due to a decreasing death rate, particularly in the early years. For example, in 1900 the number of deaths per thousand for persons under one year was 162.4 as compared to 33 in 1950 (a decrease of about 80 per cent); whereas the number of deaths in the range from sixty-five years of age to eighty-four changed from 123 per thousand to 93 per thousand, a decrease of just 22 per cent.[8] This changing death rate has increased the proportion of persons of sixty-five years of age or over in our population from 2.6 per cent in 1850 to over 10 per cent in 1970.[9]

The recent increase in birth rate has caused a temporary increase in the number of persons under fourteen years of age. This factor, together with the declining death rate, has caused a sizable increase in the number of of persons who are dependent on those who are working. In 1953 there was a ratio of 1.7 persons of working age to each dependant (below fifteen and above sixty-five). This ratio had decreased so that by 1970 it was less than 1.5.[10] What will happen when the persons born in the past ten years flood the labor market?

One of the interesting concepts for conjecture in the realm of changing life span is that of "life expectancy." In 1968 it was 70.2 years for all persons in the United States, 66.6 years for males and 74.0 years for females.[11] The concept of life expectancy is, of course, a fictitious one. It represents the average age that a person of each sex would reach if born in a given year (for example, 1965) and living his entire life according to the survival rates of that particular year. Quite likely the persons born that year will live on an average much longer than that, because the life expectancy rate will be continually raised if present trends continue.

Problems Related to Increase in Percentage of Aged

Not all the problems related to the increased numbers of aged have to do with dependency. The increase in Social Security programs, to be discussed in the next section, has helped to solve partially the problem of the support of the aged, although it in turn has led to some new problems. However, there are other problems that grow out of the increasing percentage of our population living to an older age than before. (See Figure 23.)

[8]Frederick Dewhurst and Associates, *America's Needs and Resources: A New Survey* (Washington, D.C.: Twentieth Century Fund, 1955), p. 61.

[9]*World Almanac, 1971* (New York: Newspaper Enterprise Associates, 1971), p. 172.

[10]*World Almanac, 1971.* pp. 92, 172.

[11]This represents a flattening out of the rise for total during the 1960's, a slight rise for women, and a rise then a slight fall for men.

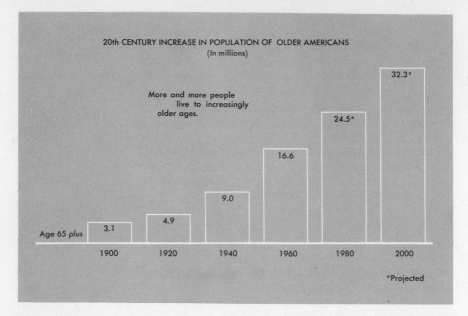

20th CENTURY INCREASE IN POPULATION OF OLDER AMERICANS
(In millions)

More and more people
live to increasingly
older ages.

32.3*

24.5*

16.6

9.0

4.9

Age 65 plus   3.1

1900   1920   1940   1960   1980   2000

*Projected

Figure 23. President's Council on Aging, *The Older American* (Washington D.C.: The Council, 1963), p. 4.

Part of the reason for the increasing longevity, of course, lies in the development of new medical techniques, including the use of antibiotics. This means that now death is seldom due to infectious diseases. Cancer, heart trouble, and other organic diseases of various kinds assume an increasing importance.

A whole new science of *geriatrics*, the medical treatment of the aged, has developed. Another new term is *gerontology*. The difference between gerontology and geriatrics is that the former deals with methods of preventing the ailments that affect the aged, whereas the latter deals with the treatment of such ailments.

Perhaps even more important is the problem of the place of the aged in our population. No longer able to hold a useful position for pay, the aged find themselves in a "useless" place in society. Sometimes deteriorating in mental and physical strength and increasingly living in the past, they find it difficult to find something in life that can maintain and hold their interest. An increasing interest is being shown in this problem by the organizing of leisure-time activities for the aged, such as clubs for aged persons and special recreational facilities. The trend in America toward the family unit increasingly being the immediate family makes it difficult for another generation to live satisfactorily with the husband, wife, and children of the immediate family. Increasingly there is need for housing, recreation facilities, and so on, for the aged among their kind. Some of these problems are receiving the attention of social workers and others in our society.

Effect on Social Security and Welfare Programs of the Increased Life Span in America

The increased longevity has, of course, been beneficial to the life insurance companies, because the expectancy has been always higher than predicted. However, when we take into account the various social security annuity plans, the increasing longevity raises serious financial problems. With an increasing percentage of our population sixty-five and over, the problem of providing adequate pension plans and other social security welfare plans becomes an increasing drain on the working population. Money collected from a population with one type of life expectancy is needed for payments to a much higher percentage of people than anticipated. This problem has been accentuated by the inflation of the dollar, which has left many pension plans utterly inadequate to provide even a minimal existence for persons in retirement. Other kinds of social security programs, such as workmen's compensation and mothers' pensions, have also helped to mitigate some of the social ills of our society. With an increased portion of our population below the age of eighteen, there will be an increase in money needed for aid to dependent children as well. Because there are more homes, there are more homes broken by death. The mothers then will need to be given aid through mothers'-aid laws.

The fact that these welfare programs are a heavy drain upon the money of the persons who are in active work does not necessarily detract from their value. Both as a protection for those persons who are unfortunate or who are aged and as a stabilizing economic influence in our society, social security programs are here to stay. The rapid increase in the extension of social securtiy to new elements of our population by both Democratic and Republican administrations emphatically indicates this trend. The development of unemployment insurance and encouragement of voluntary hospitalization plans are additional steps toward helping to stabilize our society and to protect the various individuals in it.

The development of systems of medical care, particularly for the aged, has been a recent concern. The Medicare program which began in July, 1966, represented a step toward an attempt to improve the quality of medical care for the aged. Under Medicare any person under Social Security can be covered for hospital insurance and, voluntarily, for an additional charge shared by the federal government and the individual, may be covered for supplementary medical insurance. The supplementary insurance is voluntary even for those persons under Social Security. The hospital insurance is automatic for those under Social Security.

The problem of medical care is a difficult enough problem for persons of normal age, because of increasing cost of the services and the scarcity of doctors and nurses in our rapidly expanding society. But the population increase in the percentage of our groups in the aged and the necessity for a great deal more care for persons in that age span makes special consideration necessary. It is possible for a person to have his life savings wiped out through one illness. For this reason Medicare has come into existence. It is really a federally financed payment of the premium for private hospital insurance, in many cases using the already available private insurance groups now used voluntarily by other persons in the various regions of the United States.

Some of the states experimented with extending Medicare on a volunteer basis to other medical services. Unwise administration of these laws led to skyrocketing medical costs and some obvious profiteering by some doctors. Early in the 1970's the U.A.W., through a committee appointed by the late Walter Reuther, issued a report calling on a greatly expanded medical care program to be financed by taxation something like Social Security. This would provide medical care, still operated on a private basis (like Medicare), with small annual charge to the users, the remainder to be funded by the tax.

Many authorities have documented deficiencies in the services provided by American medicine, ranging from poor efforts at prevention, to a lack of manpower, equipment, and facilities. The following paragraphs in this section, paraphrased largely from articles appearing in the August 22, 1970, issue of *Saturday Review*—called "Health Care: Rx for Change!" [12]—indicates some of these problems.

The shortage of doctors is due to the "professional birth control" (restriction of admission to medical school) the American Medical Association practiced in the 1930's, to the increased number of specialists, and to the tendency for doctors to go into teaching, research, industry, and public health instead of patient care.

Doctors are distributed unevenly throughout the country. A 1965 survey of 1,500 cities and towns in the upper Midwest showed that 1,000 had no doctor at all and 200 had only one. Highly populated areas also suffer from the doctor shortage.[13]

Medical schools face severe financial difficulties. Forty-three of 107 medical schools receive financial distress grants from the government. Lack of money has limited construction of new medical schools.

Specialized hospital expertise is unevenly distributed. A 1967 report of the President's Commission on Heart Disease, Cancer, and Stroke surveyed 777 United States hospitals equipped to perform open-heart surgery. One third of the hospitals had no open-heart surgery cases that year, better than 60 per cent had fewer than one a week, and 30 per cent had fewer than one a month.[14]

Hospital medical practice standards are not what they should be. Medical care is expensive, hard to get, and uneven in quality for the poor. The middle class is beginning to understand that this situation can result in death or disability, not only for the poor, but also for them.

We spend $63 billion a year, 6.7 per cent of our gross national product, $294 per person on medical care. No other nation spends as much.

A dozen countries do a better job in preventing infant deaths, twelve nations have lower maternal mortality rates, and the men of seventeen other countries live longer than our men. Women survive longer in ten other countries and the percentage of men who will die between the age of forty and fifty is less in seventeen countries.

Rough estimates indicate that the cost of medical care will reach $100

[12]Authored by Abraham Ribicoff, John H. Knowles, Carl M. Cobb, Rashi Fein, and Norman Cousins.

[13]Abraham Ribicoff, "The 'Healthiest Nation' Myth," *Saturday Review*, August 22, 1970, p. 18.

[14]Ibid.

billion by 1975 and that it may double by the 1980's. If the trend continues, 47 per cent of the increase will be due to rising prices caused by inflation, technology, wage increases, and higher charges. Thirty-five per cent will come from more services provided per person, and 18 per cent from population increases.[15]

The patient wants personal, comprehensive, high-quality care at a reasonable cost. Doctors also want this for their patients. The expansion of science and technology has resulted in specialization and a disappearance of the one-patient, one-doctor relationship; increasing costs have also resulted.

Resolution of the problems facing the health field demand changes in public and private financing methods, public education, manpower supply and use, regional planning, and medical education. This system must be changed to one that stresses preventive and rehabilitative services, early detection of diseases, and treatment outside of hospitals.

Well-organized group practice can produce more care for more patients than the same number of doctors in solo practice. This is especially true if the group uses nonphysician manpower as part of its practice.

Increased productivity requires delegating selected tasks to persons with less expensive training. Military corpsmen are trained to cope with medical situations ranging from minor lacerations to appendectomies. Programs attempting to utilize these skills are underway, such as the program called Medex at the University of Washington. Fifteen military corpsmen were enrolled in a three-month training program, then placed in one-year apprenticeships with rural physicians. Each rural doctor will hire his Medex student at the end of the apprenticeship.

In 1965 Dr. Eugene Stead at the Duke University Medical Center started a program to prepare civilians with some college training to assume many routine duties of the practicing physician. The physician assistants will aid the physician but will not be engaged with the physician in primary ambulatory care.[16]

Many services currently performed by gynecologists and obstetricians, including routine prenatal care, supervision during labor, postpartum care, and family and premarital counseling, could be performed by a nurse midwife.

A midwife training program was launched at Johns Hopkins in 1961. Designed for R.N.'s holding baccalaureate degrees, the course lasted nine months. In 1969 the course was changed to a two-year course leading to a master's degree in public health. The graduate will not be involved in direct patient care. Programs designed to produce nurse midwives directly involved in patient care are underway at Kings County Hospital in Brooklyn, at the University of Mississippi, and in Hyden, Kentucky, as part of the Frontier Nursing Service.[17]

The pediatric nurse practitioner could be involved in well-baby care, innoculations, camp physicals, screening tests for hearing and vision, and routine home visits.

There are other ways to increase physician productivity. Computers are being used to interpret electrocardiograms, take patient histories, and aid

[15]Ibid., p. 19.
[16]Carl M. Cobb, "Solving the Doctor Shortage," *Saturday Review*, August 22, 1970, p. 25.
[17]Ibid.

doctors in making diagnoses. Closed-circuit television cameras are being used to bring consultations to rural physicians and their patients. Massachusetts General Hospital is using closed-circuit television to link a first aid station at Logan International Airport with the hospital, where specialists are available for consultation.

Many individuals who need financial protection are thought of as uninsurable because their medical conditions make high expenditures predictable. Inclusion of high-risk individuals with other subscribers means higher insurance premiums; excluding them leaves those who are most vulnerable to fend for themselves.

One of the problems with voluntary private insurance is that it offers little incentive toward economy and efficiency in provisions of health services, or toward substitution of less expensive services for more expensive ones.

A system of national health insurance could be financed through general revenues derived in large part from the progressive income tax. Persons with more income would pay more than those with less income. Unless tax rates are increased, health insurance funds could be obtained only by cutting funds from other governmental programs.

Another approach is to finance the program through Social Security. Social Security taxes would be increased to pay for all or part of the services. The Social Security system involves employee and employer contributions based on wages of the employee up to a maximum wage level, without taking into account family size or other obligations. The tax does not reflect ability to pay.

Finally there is the tax credit approach. Assistance would be given to purchase private insurance by an offset against taxes. The amount of credit against taxes due would decline as the tax due increases, and persons who would not benefit fully because their tax is too low would receive the difference between the credit and the tax due. Whether such a program is progressive enough and offers enough assistance depends on the rates selected. Aside from how to finance national health insurance, there is the problem of breadth of coverage and comprehensiveness of benefits. It is important that the scope of coverage not distort the choice between medical services.

The total costs of the program must be considered. We must not exclude certain coverages or have high deductibles or coinsurance provisions to reduce the impact on the governmental budget. If these reduce costs to government, they would increase them to the individual, because these provisions entail high administrative and bookkeeping costs.

Provisions for health insurance coverage for all the population would bring benefits; however, without restructuring the delivery system and the method by which providers are paid costs would escalate. Government cannot announce it will pay for all services and permit the providers of the service to fill in a blank check.

HUMAN ECOLOGY: ENVIRONMENTAL PROBLEMS RELATED TO POPULATION

At the close of the 1960's and with increasing vigor in the 1970's, the youth and many others began to raise questions about environmental pollution. Evidence began to mount that the air was increasingly being filled with pollutants, the waters of the lakes, rivers, and oceans were being polluted by human and industrial wastes, including such chemicals as pesticides and detergents. These were largely the result of increasing population and the lack of effective means of rendering the wastes harmless before discharge. Even the future use of relatively "clean" atomic energy raises questions of disposal of radioactive materials and the increase in the water temperature of lakes and streams resulting from warm water discharged from the plant, which has a deleterious effect on water life.

Some concerned scholars have referred to man as a planetary disease capable of destroying the earth. Man is the largest killer and destroyer of other species. He tends to destroy and pollute the area where he lives. Further, the more advanced man is technologically, the more resources he exploits and destroys and the more he pollutes with automobiles, industrial wastes, throw-away bottles, elaborate packaging, and so on. Population growth itself is the greatest threat to environmental pollution, but a run-away GNP, with its exploitation of unreplaceable natural resources, is the bane of the advanced countries. It may be that the emphasis of the future will have to be on holding down growth in GNP and on working to improve the quality of the product so that it lasts and is not thrown away. Education would help people to be more careful and saving; instead of discarding freely, they would be taught to use things up and thereby cut down on waste.

The following paragraphs, paraphrased from an article appearing in the *Scholastic Teacher*,[18] indicate what must be done to save the environment.

Air

To clean the air, we need to establish Federal standards, set stricter standards, and enforce existing laws. Automobile manufacturers need to develop cleaner engines, and de-leaded gasolines need to be developed. Power companies (both fossil fuels and nuclear plants) must clean up their pollutants.

Water

To clean the water supplies, all pollution control laws must be enforced. Government must clean up water pollution, helping industry to find the way. Crash programs must be instigated to check organic and chemical pollution from farms, factories, chemical transports, etc.

Timber

To conserve our timber supply we must develop adequate substitutes for timber, recycle and reuse paper, more efficiently utilize sawdust and other by-products, and encourage better timber management.

Wildlife

In order to preserve wildlife, we need to consider animals in any plans for land redevelopment, encourage the establishment of wildlife habitats, and stop the use of long-lasting pesticides.

[18] "America Is in Trouble," *The Scholastic Teacher*, October 5, 1970, Advertising Section, p. A13. Prepared by the Sierra Club.

Soil

In order to conserve our soil, we must set up a national land use plan, encourage better soil conservation practices, and the Federal government must be sure that soil conservation practices are built into farm programs.

Minerals

All metals must be reclaimed and recycled, rigid conservation policies must be established, and strip miners must restore the surface of the land.

Living Space

Population growth must be slowed down, green areas near population centers must be set aside for recreation, zoning laws must be comprehensive, programs for natural beauty must be developed, and programs for solid waste disposal and noise pollution must be established.

Starting in 1965 with President Johnson, attention has been called on an official United States government level to the population problem. The topic of conservation of natural resources goes back at least to Theodore Roosevelt. On March 16, 1970, President Nixon signed a bill creating a Commission on Population Growth and the American Future. This commission is to collect data on population and population movement and distribution and determine their impact on the quality of life.

The Ash Council on Governmental Reorganization has found that there are eighty-four overlapping agencies and bureaus of the federal government dealing with environmental problems. This council has suggested an Environmental Protection Authority to deal with problems of water, air, and solid wastes, including radiation problems. Other bodies proposed are a National Ocean and Atmosphere Agency to collect facts on pollutants of entire oceans and the atmosphere of the earth, a National Energy Council, and a National Land Use Board. These four agencies would coordinate the work of the eighty-four agencies. It may well be that pollution problems are to the world as great a threat as the atomic bomb, and perhaps even more difficult to bring under control.

POPULATION TRENDS AND EDUCATION
Effect of Increased Birth Rate on American Schools

Changes in population will naturally change or influence the schools. The babies of yesterday become the pupils of today and tomorrow. Although the previous discussion was concerned with long-range changes in population, present-day schools are affected by current fluctuations. The lower birth rate during the 1930's produced smaller classes, just as the booming birth rate following World War II brought about a flood that engulfed the schools. The tidal wave hit the high schools in the early 1960's; by 1965 it had pressed on the colleges. Merely to maintain the style of education of the immediate past more classrooms and more teachers had to be provided. The current oversupply of teachers is due in part to limited finances, which prevent expansion. We must consider greater possibilities in adult education and an expansion of educational services in quantity and diversity even if our population were stabilized.

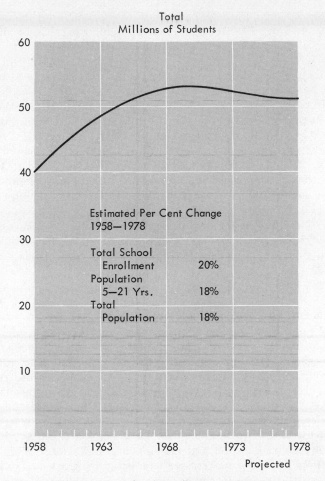

Figure 24.   School enrollment, 1958–1978.

Of great importance to educators and to all citizens is the number of children who are of school age. Figure 24 shows persons in the school population projected to 1978. (The children in school for this decade have already been born.) Nonpublic institutions are quite sensitive to economic conditions, and so the continuing rise in their enrollments depends upon continuing prosperity and their ability to meet rising education unit costs.

By 1978 the high school enrollment will increase to 87 per cent more than that of 1958. Today over 90 per cent of the adolescents of high school age are actually in school; about 88 per cent will graduate. It is estimated that college enrollment will be 232 per cent more in 1978 than in 1958, with 68 per cent of all high school graduates going on to college! Over half of these will complete their college degrees.

All of these facts show clearly that the schools must provide more classroom space and more teachers, and this takes more tax money. The problem has been heightened by past troubles. From 1930 to 1940 the schools did not keep up their building pace because of economies needed during the Depression; from 1940 to 1946 they fell behind because of World War II; and now they have fallen still farther behind because of the increased birth rate.

The problem is complex. With more people over sixty-five years of age, there may be competition for public support. As indicated earlier in this chapter, the population is highly mobile. The population of the West Coast increased 49 per cent in one decade, from 1940 to 1950; many rural areas have gone down 12 per cent in the same length of time. This, of course, affects the school population directly. One fourth of all school children moved from at least one county to another. Besides the trend to the West, there is a strong one from the South to the North. Suburban industrial areas have grown greatly, with the result that schools in some sections are more hard pressed than those in others.

In 1970 teacher supply caught up with demand for elementary and secondary school teachers in most fields. This was due to a slackening of demand as well as an increased supply because of expanded university enrollment.[19]

Implication of Population Problems for Education

The first and most obvious implication of the population problems for education grows out of the effect of the birth rate on the elementary and secondary schools. The problem of providing an adequate number of teachers from the young adult population, at low ebb because of the reduced birth rate of the 1930's, was extremely difficult during the late 1950's and early 1960's. By 1955 the increase in number of persons in college made it much more easy to solve this problem, but there were other factors that contributed to the lack of teachers in a great number of areas of teaching, such as elementary education and mathematics and science. One of these was the competition for the college graduates in areas that were more remunerative than that of teaching.

By far the most difficult implications for the period of the late 1960's and on into the era of 1970's related to the problem of the expanding college. The amount of money necessary to build the buildings, to enlarge the campuses, to provide the additional equipment, and so forth, for the large number of students entering college is enormous. The colleges and universities had expanded greatly between 1950 and 1965 because an increased percentage of the population had become interested in going to college. Then the "population bulge" hit the colleges, thereby necessitating even more expansion.

The problem of getting adequate and competent staff at all levels remains great. However, in 1970 the teacher supply and demand situation had reversed at the elementary and secondary levels (see Figure 25) and, at least at the Ph.D level, was much less critical for colleges and universities (see Figure 26). In interpreting Figure 26 it should be noted that the percentage

[19]See *Newsweek*, July 29, 1970, p. 58

TEACHER SUPPLY AND DEMAND

(000)   1965—1970

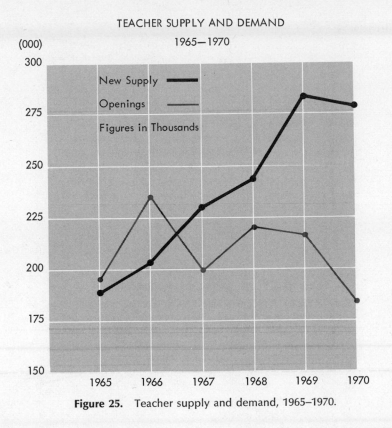

Figure 25. Teacher supply and demand, 1965–1970.

of Ph.D's completing their work who go into teaching may be declining, so the gap does not necessarily represent "unemployed Ph.D's."

Another implication arises from the kind of education to be given in the world of the future. One of the things that makes the educational problem much more acute is the extent to which people desire more schooling. From less than 10 per cent of persons going to college before 1930, the figure had risen to more than 40 per cent in 1965 and will eventually go higher than the over 50 per cent of the population in 1970. Similarly, the percentage going to high school has risen to more than 90. This demand for education is proper in the light of the greater complexity of our world and the necessity of training to live in it and cope with its problems. The unbelievable expansion of human knowledge in the past few years and the inability of people to secure this knowledge merely from casual contacts with their culture present an unanswerable argument for the necessity for more education.

Still another implication arises from the necessity of providing schooling for a much longer period of time. The population trends point toward a need for additional educational or quasieducational facilities for persons aged sixty-five or over. In many cases there may be a necessity for re-educating these people to live a different kind of life after their work period

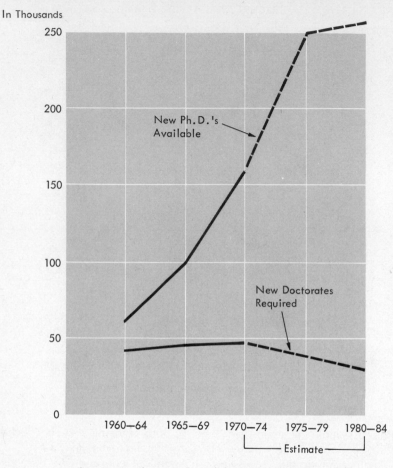

Figure 26.   Ph.D supply and demand, 1960–1984.

has passed, to help them face the many additional years of life in which, under our present family structure, they must depend largely upon their own resources. The challenge for this kind of education for the aged is very great.

The challenges faced by the schools seem unsurmountable: rapidly swelling enrollments, limited teacher supply, inadequate numbers of classrooms, inadequate facilities in classrooms, the need for the extension of education, a challenge to improve education better to fit the conditions of the changing world, and an immediate need to improve the high school to meet the needs of the great heterogeneous mass of individuals now presenting themselves for education. The situation seems to be an almost impossible one to meet, even for a country as wealthy as the United States. It certainly means that we must put an increasing amount of our energies, money, and time into the enterprise of education.

SUMMARY

In this chapter the details of the tremendous expansion of the world's population, frequently called the population explosion, have been set forth.

The possibilities of solution of this problem through the increase of the supplies of food and other necessities have been fully considered. The impact of the population changes both within America and throughout the world has been discussed in terms of the effect of these population changes upon such things as the care of the aged, social security and welfare programs, and the problems of getting schools ready to take care of the increased number of persons who desire more education because of a longer life span. There is both a longer period for formal education and a prolonged education in the form of adult education. Closely related to this is the increased demand for education at the college level, together with demands for additional schooling to upgrade skills made necessary by technological changes.

Implications in terms of the possibilities in population control and of the kind of life on this planet to expect if the population remains unchecked have been considered in this chapter.

Selected Bibliography

The American Assembly, Columbia University. *Overcoming World Hunger*. Englewood Cliffs, N.J.: Prentice-Hall, Inc., 1969. 177 pp.

_____. *Uses of the Sea*. Englewood Cliffs, N.J.: Prentice-Hall, Inc., 1968. 202 pp.

"America Is in Trouble." *Scholastic Teacher* (October 5, 1970), A1-A16. Advertising section, prepared by the National Wildlife Federation.

"Atomic Power: Paradise Lost or Found," *Cincinnati Enquirer*, February 7, 1971, n.p. Excellent presentation of the possibilities and problems in the use of atomic energy.

Baker, Paul T., and J. S. Weiner (eds.). *The Biology of Human Adaptability*. Oxford: Clarendon Press, 1966. 541 pp.

Bardach, John. *Harvest of the Sea*. New York: Harper & Row, Publishers, 1968. 301 pp.

Bates, Marston. *Expanding Population in a Shrinking World: Readings for an Age of Change No. 4*. New York: American Library Association in cooperation with the Public Affairs Committee, 1963. 32 pp.

Bell, E. Moberly. *Storming the Citadel: The Rise of the Woman Doctor*. London: Constable & Co., Ltd., 1953. 200 pp.

Berland, Theodore. *Noise—The Third Pollution*. Public Affairs Pamphlet No. 449. New York: Public Affairs Committee, 1970. 20 pp.

Berrie, W. D. *The Growth and Control of World Population*. London: Weidenfeld and Nicolson, 1970. 340 pp.

Blaug, Mark (ed.). *The Economics of Education*, Vol. I. Baltimore: Penguin Books, Inc., 1968. 442 pp.

Blaustein, Arthur I., and Roger R. Woock (eds.). *Man Against Poverty: World War III, A Reader on the World's Most Crucial Issue*. New York: Random House, Inc., 1968. 465 pp.

Borgstrom, Georg. *Too Many: A Study of Earth's Biological Limitations*. New York: The Macmillan Company, 1969. 368 pp.

Boyer, William H. "Education for Survival," *Phi Delta Kappan*, Vol. LII, No. 4 (January 1971).

Braden, William. *The Age of Aquarius: Technology and the Cultural Revolution*. Chicago: Quadrangle Books, Inc., 1970. 307 pp.

Brennan, Michael, Philip Taft, and Mark Schupack. *The Economics of Age*. New York: W. W. Norton & Company, Inc., 1967. 246 pp.

Brooks, Robert R. R. "People Versus Food," *Saturday Review*, September 5, 1970.

Brown, Harrison. "After the Population Explosion," *Saturday Review*, June 26, 1971.

Brown, Lester R. *Seeds of Change: The Green Revolution and Development in the 1970's.* New York: Frederick A. Praeger, Inc., 1970. 204 pp.

Browning, Harley L. "Life Expectancy and Life Cycles," *Current,* No. 114 (January 1970).

Butler, Robert N. "Recycling Rigid Life Patterns," *Current,* No. 114 (January 1970).

Calder, Nigel. *Technopolis: Social Control of the Uses of Science.* New York: Simon & Schuster, Inc., 1970. 376 pp.

Cancro, Robert. "Preserving the Species," *Saturday Review,* March 6, 1971.

Carnow, Bertram W. "Pollution Invites Disease," *Saturday Review,* July 4, 1970.

Carson, Rachel. *Silent Spring.* Boston: Houghton Mifflin Company, 1962. 368 pp.

Chasteen, Edgar R. *The Case for Compulsory Birth Control.* Englewood Cliffs, N.J.: Prentice-Hall, Inc., 1971. 240 pp.

Claiborne, Robert. *Climate, Man and History.* New York: W. W. Norton & Company, Inc., 1970. 444 pp.

Clark, Colin, and Margaret Haswell. *The Economics of Subsistence Agriculture,* Third Edition. New York: The Macmillan Company, 1967. 245 pp.

Cobb, Carl M. "Solving the Doctor Shortage," *Saturday Review,* August 22, 1970.

Cochrane, Willard W. *The World Food Problem: A Guardedly Optimistic View.* New York: Thomas Y. Crowell Company, 1969. 331 pp.

Cohen, Yehudi A. (ed.). *Man in Adaptation: The Cultural Present.* Chicago: Aldine Publishing Co., 1968. 433 pp.

Commager, Henry Steele. "America's Heritage of Bigness," *Saturday Review,* July 4, 1970.

Commoner, Barry. *Science and Survival.* New York: The Viking Press, Inc., 1966. 150 pp.

Cook, Robert C. "The Population Prospect: The Years Just Ahead," *Social Education,* Vol. 29 (February 1965).

Cooley, Richard A., and Geoffrey Wandestorde-Smith (eds.). *Congress and the Environment.* Seattle: University of Washington Press, 1970. 277 pp.

Council on Environmental Quality, First Annual Report. *Environmental Quality.* Washington, D.C.: Government Printing Office, 1970. 326 pp.

Cousins, Norman. "Can Doctors Cause Disease?" *Saturday Review,* August 22, 1970.

Curtis, Richard, and Elizabeth Hogan. *Perils of the Peaceful Atom: The Myth of Safe Nuclear Power Plants.* Garden City, N.Y.: Doubleday & Company, Inc., 1969. 274 pp.

Dansereau, Pierre (ed.). *Challenge for Survival: Land, Air and Water for Man in Megalopolis.* New York: Columbia University Press, 1970. 235 pp.

Dasmann, Raymond. *A Different Kind of Country.* New York: The Macmillan Company, 1968. 276 pp.

Davies, J. Clarence, II. *The Politics of Pollution.* New York: Pegasus, 1970. 321 pp.

Dickinson, Robert E. *Regional Ecology: The Study of Man's Environment.* New York: John Wiley & Sons, Inc., 1970. 199 pp.

Disch, Robert (ed.). *The Ecological Conscience: Values for Survival.* Englewood Cliffs, N.J.: Prentice-Hall, Inc., 1970. 206 pp.

Domhoff, G. William. *Who Rules America?* Englewood Cliffs, N.J.: Prentice-Hall, Inc., 1967. 184 pp.

Dubos, René. *Reason Awake: Science for Man.* New York: Columbia University Press, 1970. 280 pp.

Editors of Ramparts. *Eco-Catastrophe.* San Francisco: Canfield Press, 1970. 158 pp.

Ehrlich, Paul R. *The Population Bomb.* New York: Ballantine Books, Inc., 1968. 223 pp.

_____, and Anne H. Ehrlich. *Population Resource Environment: Issues in Human Ecology.* San Francisco: W. H. Freeman & Co., Publishers, 1970. 385 pp.

_____, and John P. Holdren. "Deceptive Birth Rates," *Saturday Review,* October 3, 1970.

_____. "The Heat Barrier," *Saturday Review,* April 3, 1971.

———. "The Hidden Effects of Overpopulation," *Saturday Review*, August 1, 1970.

———. "The People Problem," *Saturday Review*, July 4, 1970.

Elling, Ray H. (ed.). *National Health Care: Issues and Problems in Socialized Medicine.* Chicago: Aldine-Atherton, 1971. 304 pp.

Esposito, John C. (ed.). *Vanishing Air: Ralph Nader's Study Group Report on Air Pollution.* New York: Grossman Publishers, Inc., 1970. 328 pp.

Ettinger, Robert C. W. *The Prospect of Immortality.* Garden City, N.Y.: Doubleday & Company, Inc., 1964. 190 pp. Deals with the arrestment of aging.

Ewald, William B., Jr. (ed.). *Environment and Change.* Bloomington: Indiana University Press, 1968. 397 pp.

———. *Environment and Policy: The Next Fifty Years.* American Institute of Planners' Fiftieth Year Consultation. Bloomington: Indiana University Press, 1968. 459 pp.

Fagley, Richard Martin. *The Population Explosion and Christian Responsibility.* New York: Oxford University Press, 1960. 260 pp.

Fair, Charles M. *The Dying Self.* Middletown, Conn.: Wesleyan, 1969. 288 pp.

Fanning, Odom. "The Environment Boom," *Saturday Review*, May 1, 1971.

Fawcett, James T. *Psychology and Population: Behavioral Research Issues in Fertility and Family Planning.* New York: The Population Council, 1970. 149 pp.

Fein, Rashi. "The Case for National Health Insurance," *Saturday Review*, August 22, 1970.

Fischer, John. "Why and How to Build Another U.S.A.," *Current*, No. 114 (January 1971).

Fisher, Tadd. *Our Overcrowded World.* New York: Parent's Magazine Press, 1969. 256 pp.

Foreman, Harry (ed.). *Nuclear Power and the Public.* Minneapolis: University of Minnesota Press, 973 pp.

Fraser, Dean. *The People Problem: What You Should Know About Growing Population and Vanishing Resources.* New York: American University Press, 1971. 248 pp.

Friedmann, Wolfgang. *The Future of the Oceans.* New York: George Braziller, Inc., 1971. 128 pp.

Fry, John. *Medicine in Three Societies: A Comparison of Medical Care in the USSR, USA and UK.* New York: American Elsevier Publishing Co., Inc. 1969. 249 pp.

Fuller, R. Buckminster. *Operating Manual for Space-Ship Earth.* Carbondale: Southern Illinois University Press, 1969. 143 pp.

———, Eric A. Walker, and James R. Killian, Jr. *Approaching the Benign Environment.* University, Ala.: University of Alabama Press, 1970. 121 pp.

Gans, Herbert J. *The Levittowners: Ways of Life and Politics in a New Suburban Community.* New York: Pantheon Books, Inc., 1967. 474 pp.

Gerber, Alex. *The Gerber Report.* New York: David McKay Co., Inc., 1971. 242 pp.

Geyelin, Philip L., and Payler Cates. *American Medicine: Adequate or Not?* Washington, D.C.: American Institute for Public Policy Research, 1970. 104 pp.

Ginzberg, Eli, with Mirian Ostow. *Men, Money and Medicine.* New York: Columbia University Press, 1969. 291 pp.

Goldman, Marshall I. (ed.). *Controlling Pollution: The Economics of a Cleaner Environment.* Englewood Cliffs, N.J.: Prentice-Hall, Inc., 1967. 175 pp.

Graham, Frank. *Since Silent Spring.* Boston: Houghton Mifflin Company, 1970. 288 pp. (Also Fawcett paperback.) Excellent source on the effect of pesticides.

Greenberg, Daniel S. *The Politics of Pure Science.* New York: The New American Library, Inc., 1967. 303 pp.

Greenberg, Selig. *The Quality of Mercy: A Report on the Critical Condition of Hospital and Medical Care in America.* New York: Atheneum Publishers, 1971. 385 pp.

Gross, Martin L. *The Doctors: A Penetrating Analysis of the American Physician and His Practice of Medicine.* New York: Random House, Inc., 1966. 605 pp.

Gullion, Edmund A. (ed.). *Uses of the Seas.* Englewood Cliffs, N.J.: Prentice-Hall, Inc., 1968. 202 pp.

Handler, Philip (ed.). *Biology and the Future of Man.* New York: Oxford University Press, 1970. 936 pp.

Hardin, Clifford M. (ed.). *Overcoming World Hunger.* Englewood Cliffs, N.J.: Prentice-Hall, Inc., 1969. 177 pp.

Hardin, Garrett J. "Ecology Versus Economics," *Current,* No. 116 (March 1970).

———. *Population, Evolution and Birth Control.* San Francisco: W. H. Freeman & Co., Publishers, 1969. 386 pp.

———. *Science and Controversy: Population, A Case Study.* San Francisco: W. H. Freeman & Co., Publishers, 1971. 30 pp.

Harrington, Alan. *The Immortalist.* New York: Random House, Inc., 1970. 324 pp.

Heer, David M. (ed.). *Readings on Population.* Englewood Cliffs, N.J.: Prentice-Hall, Inc., 1968. 234 pp.

Heilbroner, Robert L. *Between Capitalism and Socialism.* New York: Random House, Inc., 1970. 294 pp.

———. "Our Simple but Compelling Needs," *Current,* No. 116 (March 1970).

Helfrich, Harold W., Jr. (ed.). *Agenda for Survival.* New Haven: Yale University Press, 1970. 175 pp.

——— (ed.). *The Environmental Crisis.* New Haven: Yale University Press, 1970. 187 pp.

Herfindahl, Orris C., and Allen V. Kneese. *Quality of the Environment: An Economic Approach to Some Problems in Using Land, Water and Air.* Baltimore, Md.: The Johns Hopkins Press, 1965. 96 pp.

Herndon, James. *How to Survive in Your Native Land.* New York: Simon & Schuster, Inc., 1971. 192 pp.

Hersey, Jean, and Robert Hersey. *These Rich Years: A Journal of Retirement.* New York: Charles Scribner's Sons, 1969. 270 pp.

Holloway, Mark. *Heavens on Earth.* New York: Dover Publications, Inc., 1966. 246 pp.

Hudson, Liam (ed.). *Ecology of Human Intelligence.* Baltimore: Penguin Books, Inc., 1971. 368 pp.

Hughes, Donald J. *Science and Starvation.* New York: Pergamon Press, Inc., 1968. 161 pp.

Huxley, Julian. *The Human Crisis.* Seattle: University of Washington Press, 1963. Contains an essay on the world population problem.

Johnson, Huey D. (ed.). *No Deposit—No Return: Man and His Environment, A View Toward Survival.* Reading, Mass.: Addison-Wesley Publishing Co., Inc., 1970. 351 pp.

Jorstad, Erling. *The Politics of Doomsday: Fundamentalists of the Far Right.* Nashville, Tenn.: Abingdon Press, 1970. 190 pp.

de Jouvenel, Bertrand, René Dubos, et al. *The Fitness of Man's Environment.* New York: Harper & Row, Publishers, 1968. 250 pp.

Kennedy, Edward M. *In Critical Condition: The Crisis in America's Health Care.* New York: Simon and Schuster, 1972. 252 pp.

Kiser, Clyde V., Wilson H. Grabill, and Arthur A. Campbell. *Trends and Variations in Fertility in the United States.* Cambridge, Mass.: Harvard University Press, 1968. 338 pp.

Knowles, John H. "Where Doctors Fail," *Saturday Review,* August 22, 1970.

Kormonday, Edward J. *Concepts of Ecology.* Englewood Cliffs, N.J.: Prentice-Hall, Inc., 1968. 209 pp.

Lapp, Ralph E. "Nuclear Power for Electricity," *Current,* No. 127 (March 1971).

Laycock, George. *The Diligent Destroyers.* Garden City, N.Y.: Doubleday & Company, Inc., 1970. 225 pp.

Lear, John. "The Enemy Is Us," *Saturday Review,* March 1970.

———. "Peace, Health, and the Doctor," *Saturday Review,* April 17, 1971.

Linton, Ron M. *Terracide: America's Destruction of Her Living Environment.* Boston: Little, Brown and Company, 1970. 376 pp.

Loraine, John A. *Sex and the Population Crisis.* St. Louis, Mo.: C. V. Mosby Co., 1970. 200 pp.

MacDonald, Gordon, J. F. "How Man Endangers the Climate," *Current*, No. 114 (January 1970).

Mannix, Daniel P. *Troubled Waters*. New York: E. P. Dutton & Co., Inc., 1969. 247 pp.

Marine, Gene. *America the Raped: The Engineering Mentality and the Devastation of a Continent*. New York: Simon & Schuster, Inc., 1969. 312 pp.

Marx, Wesley. *The Frail Ocean*. New York: Coward-McCann, Inc., 1967. 248 pp.

May, Sigmund H. *Crowning Years*. Philadelphia: J. B. Lippincott Co., 1969. 191 pp.

McCormack, Arthur. *The Population Problem*. New York: Thomas Y. Crowell Company, 1970. 264 pp.

McHale, John. *The Ecological Context*. New York: George Braziller, Inc., 1970. 188 pp.

McHarg, Ian. *Design with Nature*. Garden City, N.Y.: Natural History Press, 1969. 197 pp.

Michener, James A. *The Drifters*. New York: Random House, Inc., 1971. 751 pp.

Miller, Harry L., and Roger R. Woock. *Social Foundations of Urban Education*. Hinsdale, Ill.: The Dryden Press, Inc., 1970. 433 pp.

Millett, Kate. *Sexual Politics*. Garden City, N.Y.: Doubleday & Company, Inc., 1970. 393 pp.

Morris, Desmond (ed). *Primate Ethology*. Chicago: Aldine Publishing Co., 1967. 374 pp.

Myrdal, Gunnar. *The Challenge of World Poverty: A World-Anti-Poverty Program in Outline*. New York: Pantheon Books, Inc., 1970. 518 pp.

Nam, C. B. (ed.). *Population and Society: A Textbook of Readings*. Boston: Houghton Mifflin Company, 1968. 708 pp.

Nash, Roderick (ed.). *The American Environment: Readings in the History of Conservation*. Reading, Mass.: Addison-Wesley Publishing Co., Inc., 1968. 236 pp.

———. *Wilderness and the American Mind*. New Haven: Yale University Press, 1967. 256 pp.

National Academy of Science, National Research Council. *Resources and Man*. San Francisco: W. H. Freeman & Co., Publishers, 1969. 259 pp.

Nelkin, Dorothy. *Nuclear Power and Its Critics: The Cayuga Lake Controversy*. Ithaca, N.Y.: Cornell University Press, 1971. 160 pp.

Nicholson, Max. *Environmental Revolution*. New York: McGraw-Hill Book Company, 1970. 366 pp.

Paddock, William, and Paul Paddock. *Famine 1975!: America's Decision. Who Will Survive?* Boston: Little, Brown and Company, 1967. 276 pp.

Paradise, Scott I. "Old Now Is Earth," *Presbyterian Life*, September 15, 1970.

Parker, Garland G. *The Enrollment Explosion: A Half-Century of Attendance in U.S. Colleges and Universities*. New York: School and Society, 1971. 163 pp.

Peel, John, and Malcolm Potts. *Textbook of Contraceptive Practice*. New York: Cambridge University Press, 1969. 297 pp.

Pendleton, Don. *1989: Population Doomsday*. New York: Bee-Line Books, Inc., 1970. 129 pp. A novel of the future.

Perin, Constance. *With Man in Mind: An Interdisciplinary Prospectus for Environmental Design*. Cambridge, Mass.: The M.I.T. Press, 1970. 135 pp.

Perloff, Harvey S. (ed.). *The Quality of the Urban Environment: Essays on "New Resources" in an Urban Age*. Washington, D.C.: Resources for the Future (distributed by Johns Hopkins Press, Baltimore, Md.), 1969. 332 pp.

Petersen, William. *Population*, Second Edition. New York: The Macmillan Company, 1969. 735 pp.

Phelan, William D., Jr. "Is Constitutional Democracy Doomed?" *Current*, No. 116 (March 1970).

Pickard, Jerome P. "Is Megalopolis Inevitable?" *The Futurist*, Vol. 4, No. 5 (October 1970).

Platt, John R. *Perception and Change: Projects for Survival*. Ann Arbor, Mich.: University of Michigan Press, 1970. 178 pp.

———. *The Step to Man*. New York: John Wiley & Sons, Inc., 1966. 216 pp.

Pohlman, Edward. *The Psychology of Birth Planning*. Cambridge, Mass.: Schenkman, 1969. 496 pp.

Population Bulletin. Washington, D.C.: Population Reference Bureau. All issues.

"Population Developments in 1970," *Population Bulletin*, Vol. 16, No. 6 (December 1970). (Pamphlet.)

Prehoda, Robert W. *Extended Youth: The Promise of Gerontology*. New York: G. P. Putnam's Sons, 1968. 256 pp.

Price, Daniel O. (ed.). *The 99th Hour: The Population Crisis in the U.S.* Chapel Hill: University of North Carolina Press, 1967. 130 pp.

Quinn, Francis X. (ed.). *Population Ethics*. Washington, D.C.: Corpus, 1968. 144 pp.

Ramsey, Paul. *Fabricated Man: The Ethics of Genetic Control*. New Haven: Yale University Press, 1970. 174 pp.

Reich, Charles A. *The Greening of America*. New York: Random House, Inc., 1970. 399 pp.

Report of the Special Commission on the Social Sciences of the National Science Board. *Knowledge Into Action: Improving the Nation's Use of the Social Sciences*. Washington, D.C.: Government Printing Office, National Science Foundation, 1969. 95 pp.

Revelle, Roger, and Hans H. Landsberg. *America's Changing Environment*. Boston: Houghton Mifflin Company, 1970. 314 pp.

Ribicoff, Abraham. "The 'Healthiest Nation' Myth," *Saturday Review*, August 22, 1970.

Rienow, Robert, with Leona Train Rienow. *Man Against His Environment*. San Francisco: Sierra Club; New York: Ballantine Books, Inc., 1970. 307 pp.

_____. *Moment in the Sun: A Report on the Deteriorating Quality of the American Environment*. New York: The Dial Press, Inc., 1967. 286 pp.

Riley, Matilda White, Anne Foner, and associates. *Aging and Society*. Volume I: *An Inventory of Research Findings*. New York: Russell Sage Foundation, 1968. 636 pp.

_____, John W. Riley, Jr., Marilyn E. Johnson, and associates (eds.). *Aging and Society: Aging and the Professions*, Vol. II. New York: Russell Sage Foundation, 1969. 410 pp.

Rockefeller, Nelson A. *Our Environment Can Be Saved*. Garden City, N.Y.: Doubleday & Company, Inc., 1970. 176 pp.

Rosenfeld, Albert. *The Second Genesis: The Coming Control of Life*. Englewood Cliffs, N.J.: Prentice-Hall, Inc., 1969. 327 pp.

Rubin, Isadore. *Sexual Life After Sixty*. New York: The New American Library, Inc., 1965. 224 pp.

Sauvy, Alfred. *General Theory of Population*. New York: Basic Books, Inc., Publishers, 1970. 550 pp.

Schaeffer, Francis A. *Pollution and the Death of Man: The Christian View of Ecology*. Wheaton, Ill.: Tyndale, 1970. 125 pp.

Schrag, Peter. "Who Owns the Environment?" *Saturday Review*, July 4, 1970.

Seaborg, Glenn T. "Those Good New Days," *Saturday Review*, March 6, 1971.

Segal, Judith A. *Food for the Hungry: The Reluctant Society*. Baltimore: Johns Hopkins Press, 1970. 83 pp.

Shanas, Ethel. *Old People in Three Industrial Societies*. New York: Atherton Press, 1968. 478 pp.

Sheldon, Alan, Frank Baker, and Curtis P. McLaughlin (eds.). *Systems and Medical Care*. Cambridge, Mass.: The M.I.T. Press, 1970. 360 pp.

Shelesnyak, Moses C. (ed.). *Growth of Population*. New York: Gordon and Breach Science Publishers, Inc., 1969. 480 pp.

Shepard, Paul. *Man in the Landscape: A Historic View of the Esthetics of Nature*. New York: Alfred A. Knopf, Inc., 1967. 290 pp.

_____, and Daniel McKinley (eds.). *The Subversive Science: Essays Toward an Ecology of Man*. Boston: Houghton Mifflin Company, 1969. 453 pp.

Simon, Herbert A. *The Sciences of the Artificial.* Cambridge, Mass.: The M.I.T. Press, 1969. 118 pp.

Simpson, George Gaylord. *Biology and Man.* New York: Harcourt Brace Jovanovich, Inc., 1969. 175 pp.

Simpson, Ida Harper, and John C. McKinney (eds.). *Social Aspects of Aging.* Durham, N.C.: Duke University Press, 1966. 341 pp.

Singer, S. Fred (ed.). *Global Effects of Environmental Pollution.* New York: Springer-Verlag, Inc., 1970. 220 pp.

Smith, Harmon L. *Ethics and the New Medicine.* Nashville, Tenn.: Abingdon Press, 1970. 174 pp.

Smith, Robert, Richard Axen, and Devere Pentony. *By Any Means Necessary.* San Francisco: Jossey-Bass, 1970. 370 pp.

Smithsonian Annual II. *The Fitness of Man's Environment.* Washington, D.C.: Smithsonian Institution Press, 1968. 250 pp.

Spock, Benjamin. *Decent and Indecent: Our Personal and Political Behavior.* New York: McCall, 1970. 210 pp.

Stamp, L. Dudley. *Land for Tomorrow.* Bloomington: Indiana University Press, 1952. 230 pp.

Stans, Maurice. "The U.S. Plan for Curbing Megalopolis," *The Futurist,* Vol. 4, No. 5 (October 1970).

Stoler, Donald. "Environmental Education as Liberation," *The Education Digest,* Vol. 36, No. 9 (May 1971).

Strickland, Stephen P., and Margot Davis (ed.). *Population Crisis.* Washington, D.C.: Socio-Dynamics Industries, 1970. 481 pp.

Talland, George A. (ed.). *Human Aging and Behavior: Recent Advances in Research and Theory.* New York: Academic Press, Inc., 1968. 322 pp.

Taylor, Gordon Rattray. *The Biological Time Bomb.* New York: The New American Library, Inc., 1968. 239 pp.

——. *The Doomsday Book.* New York: World Book Company, 1971. 335 pp.

——. "People Pollution . . . How the Stress of City Life Scars Our Minds and Bodies," *The Ladies Home Journal,* October 1970.

——. "The Threat to Life in the Sea," *Saturday Review,* August 1, 1970.

Toffler, Alvin. *Future Shock.* New York: Random House, Inc., 1970. 505 pp.

Train, Russell. *America the Beautiful.* An address before the 90th Annual Meeting of the American Forestry Association held jointly with the National Council of State Garden Clubs, Jackson Lake Lodge, Grand Teton National Park, Wyoming. Washington, D.C.: The Conservation Foundation, September 6, 1965. (n.p.) (Pamphlet.)

——. *Challenge to Youth.* An address given at the National Youth Conference on Natural Beauty and Conservation, Washington, D.C., June 29, 1966. Washington, D.C.: The Conservation Foundation, 1966. 14 pp. (Pamphlet.)

Turner, James S. *The Chemical Feast: Ralph Nader's Study Group Report on the Food and Drug Administration.* New York: Grossman Publishers, Inc., 1970. 273 pp.

Twente, Esther. *Never Too Old: The Aged in Community Life.* San Francisco: Jossey-Bass, 1970. 246 pp.

United Nations, Economic and Social Council, Report of the Population Commission. "World Population Situation." New York: United Nations, 1970. 28 pp.

Ward, Barbara. *Spaceship Earth.* New York: Columbia University Press, 1966. 152 pp.

Warner, Aaron W., Dean Morse, and Thomas E. Cooney (eds.). *The Environment of Change.* New York: Columbia University Press, 1969. 186 pp.

Watson, Richard A., and Patty Jo Watson. *Man and Nature: An Anthropological Essay on Human Ecology.* New York: Harcourt Brace Jovanovich, Inc., 1969. 172 pp.

Watts, D. G. *Environmental Studies.* New York: Humanities Press, 1969. 117 pp.

Weiser, Eric. *Years in Hand: New Ways to a Longer and More Fruitful Life.* New York: Abelard-Schuman Limited, 1969. 159 pp.

Wheeler, Harvey. "The Politics of Ecology," *Saturday Review*, March 7, 1970.

White, Theodore H. "How Do We Get from Here to There?" *Life*, June 26, 1970. An appraisal of the environmental crisis and the complicatedness of federal action, where, at this date, some eighty-four bureaus have some parts of the responsibility, and where coordination is essential. Purposes and methods need to be formulated and clarified.

Whittaker, Robert H. *Communities and Ecosystems*. New York: The Macmillan Company, 1970. 162 pp.

Wilson, Mitchell A., and the Editors of *Life*. *Energy*. New York: Time, Inc., 1963. 200 pp.

Wilson, Thomas W., Jr. "The Environment: Do the Polluted Clouds Have a Silver Lining?" *The Futurist*, Vol. 5, No. 1 (February 1971).

Wolff, Kurt. *The Emotional Rehabilitation of the Geriatric Patient*. Springfield, Ill.: Charles C Thomas, 1970. 232 pp.

"World Population." *The Annals of the American Academy of Political and Social Science*, Vol. 369 (January 1967).

Wrigley, Edward A. *Population and History*. New York: McGraw-Hill Book Company, 1969. 256 pp.

Your Right to Clear Air: A Manual for Citizen Action. Washington, D.C.: The Conservation Foundation, August 1970. 108 pp.

Selected Films

Aging (N.E.T.), 30 min. Suggests that by re-establishing the natural roles of grandparents as useful participants in family situations, the child, parent, and grandparents may benefit.

Aging—A Modern Achievement (University of Michigan), 30 min.

Air Pollution (Encyclopaedia Britannica), 15 min.

America's Crises: Old Age—The Wasted Years (N.E.T.), 60 min. Interviews with senior citizens, government officials, and social workers attempting to answer the challenge posed by this ever-increasing segment of society.

Banquet of Life (Audio-Visual Center), 54 min. Documents the view that increasing food production alone will not solve the population problem. Voluntary family planning is indispensable. Excellent content; beautiful photography from all over the world.

Before the Day (Social Security Administration), 15 min. Gives an account of the founding of the several programs that make up social security and the story of what happened before social security started. Above all, it is the story of people who can face the future with greater confidence because they know the system they have built is working for them long before the day of need occurs.

Brazil: The Gathering Millions (Audio-Visual Center), 30 min.

Bulldozed America (Carousel), 25 min. Explores the problem of vanishing natural beauty in the U.S. as a result of construction by commercial interests. Interviews with William O. Douglas, and Stewart Udall are included.

Can the Earth Provide? (Contemporary/McGraw-Hill), 28 min.

Can the World Be Fed? (ICF), 15 min. Today the prospect of mass starvation is very real for countries such as India and China. What is the outlook for preventing famine, and what should we do? What should the endangered countries do?

Challenge to Mankind (McGraw-Hill), 28 min. Five world experts speak of threat of overpopulation.

Crisis on Our Rivers (Health Educational Service), 14 min. Discusses stream pollution, emphasizing that pollution is the responsibility of every citizen.

The European Experience (Audio-Visual Center), 30 min.

Fair Chance (Parthenon), 14 min. An expectant father, unhappy about the impending birth of his fourth unplanned child, learns in the waiting room how Planned

Parenthood helps couples have only as many children as they want. In flashback, a Planned Parenthood Center's activity is shown.

First Mile Up (McGraw-Hill), 28 min. Problems of air pollution and its effect on human health.

Five Million (PPWP), 10 min. Dramatic profile of the 5 million impoverished U.S. women dependent on subsidized services for birth control, presented through a real-life picture of a day in the life of one family. Dynamic, factual, and surprising —a refutation of long-held stereotypes about the poor. Derived from a special U.S. Census Bureau tabulation.

For All to Enjoy (Conservation Foundation), 20 min. Satirical approach to uncontrolled development in national parks.

Glen Canyon (Sierra Club), 29 min. That uniquely beautiful stretch of the Colorado River, before and after the construction of the dam; a poignant film experience.

The Global Struggle for Food (Contemporary Films/McGraw-Hill), 28 min.

Happy Family Planning (PPWP), 6 min. This charming, witty animated cartoon explains in pictures and musical accompaniment the benefits of family planning and methods. Wordless, except for the names of the contraceptives shown, in seven languages. *Happy* is the word for this film designed especially for hospital family-planning clinics and useful in many different national settings.

India: Writings in the Sand (Audio-Visual Center), 30 min.

Japan: Answer in the Orient (Audio-Visual Center), 30 min.

Learning for Life (O.E.A., N.E.A.), 29 min. New developments in adult education.

Life with Grandpa (March of Time Forum Films), 17 min. Portrays problems confronting older people in our society: disease, economic insecurity, emotional difficulties. Suggests several solutions.

Man and His Resources (Contemporary/McGraw-Hill), 28 min.

Multiply and Subdue the Earth (Indiana University Audio-Visual Center), 60 min.

No Room for Wilderness (Association Films), 25 min. Examines the fundamental nature of ecology and indicates the relationship of primitive man to his environment through the use of African examples. Demonstrates the disruptive impact of civilization and the need to preserve the wilderness, and pleads for world population control.

No Room for Wilderness (Sierra Club), 30 min. A beautiful film, photographed in the African wilderness, which describes how civilization and overpopulation have destroyed the delicate balance of nature. Contains a strong plea for population control to preserve wilderness.

Noise—The New Pollutant (Audio-Visual Center), 30 min. Dr. Vern O. Knudsen's demonstration of the nature of sound and the sensation of hearing is supplemented by several research projects into the harmful effect of noise.

Old Age—Out of Sight Out of Mind (N.E.T.), 60 min. Hospitals, nursing homes, etc., are observed in terms of treatment and rehabilitation facilities available to the aged and the concerns of medical experts and government officials.

Old Age—The Wasted Years (N.E.T.), 60 min. The individual who has retired and the worker who loses his job because of advancing years are seen in terms of the limited social opportunities and living situations available to them.

Our Crowded Environment (Encyclopaedia Britannica), 11 min.

People by the Billions (McGraw-Hill), 28 min.

A Plague on Your Children (BBC), 72 min. Very graphic.

Poisoned Air (Carousel), 50 min. Secretary of Health, Education, and Welfare John W. Gardner discusses methods of dealing with pollution with representatives of the automobile and petroleum industries.

Poisons, Pests and People (Contemporary), 30 min. each. Two parts.

Population Ecology (Encyclopaedia Britannica), 19 min. Examines factors limiting the growth of plant and animal populations in their natural environments in contrast to man's success in shaping his environment to meet his needs. Reviews the explosive growth rate of human populations and considers its cause and related problems. Designed for high school biology classes, but suitable for college and adult levels.

Population Ecology (McGraw-Hill), 28 min. Ecological consequence if population is not brought under control.

The Population Explosion (CBS Reports), 43 min. A close and sobering look at the grave consequences of the abnormally high current rate of growth in the world's population, which may double in the next thirty years. India, the largest democracy in the world, is the locale of this film and is the most prominent example of a growing crisis that soon may become the world's number one problem—an excess of population over available food supplies.

Population Explosion (McGraw-Hill), 15 min. Thomas Malthus, in his *Essay on the Principle of Population*, pointed out that population tends to increase geometrically while the wealth-producing sector increases only arithmetically. For a time his theory's postulates were not seriously tested; at present, however, the problem is an acute one. *Population Explosion* shows how advances in medical technology are reducing mortality, thereby giving rise to a great shortage of food for the people of the world. Efforts to increase food production output in underdeveloped nations are explained. A National Film Board of Canada Production.

The Problem Is Life (Contemporary/McGraw-Hill), 28.5 min. This film focuses on the population explosion in India and various aspects of the vast birth control program underway there; the Indian clinics, the village visits by family-planning workers, the intensive publicity campaign. Includes interviews with program leaders. Beautiful photography. Compelling presentation.

Problem with Water Is People (McGraw-Hill), 30 min. Narrated by Chet Huntley.

Proud Years (Columbia University), 20 min. Film on the aged.

Questions and Answers About Birth Control (PPWP), 30 min. A group of young adults ask Dr. Alan F. Guttmacher the questions they have about birth control. The answers are frank, direct, and factual and are supplemented by line drawings and actual contraceptive devices. Cleared for television.

Redwoods—Saved? (Sierra Club), 3.5 min. A brief but powerful statement of the continuing threat to the coast redwoods.

Silent Spring of Rachel Carson (McGraw-Hill), 54 min. Black and white/CBS Reports.

The Steps of Age (International Film Bureau), 25 min. Portrays the confusion, fears, and far from easy struggle to understand that Mrs. Potter, sixty-two, faced as she embarks on the last quarter of her life. The picture suggests that people need to begin early in life to handle well the situations that come with increasing age.

Third Pollution (Stuart Finley, Inc.), 23 min. Describes America's solid waste problem and its relation to air and water pollution. Outlines alternatives for community action, including procedures for obtaining federal or state assistance.

The Time of Man (Ealing Co.), 50 min. Mankind is viewed in context of the earth's natural environment from his prehistoric ecological and cultural context and today's environmentally entrapped situation. The rich imagery and pertinent examples create a large audience for this film.

To Each a Rightful Share (Contemporary/McGraw-Hill), 28 min.

To Live Till You Die (N.E.T.), 60 min. Two contemporary and contrasting Western points of view concerning the aged (in Sweden and Italy) reveal old age as a social problem in one case and as a traditional family problem in the other.

U.S.A. Seeds for Change (N.E.T.), 30 min. Population trends in the United States.

Wasted Woods (Sierra Club), 15 min. A biting commentary on the destructive logging carried on in the nortnwestern part of the United States.

Water Famine (Carousel), 54 min. Problems of water shortage and pollution.

What Is Ecology? (Encyclopaedia Britannica). Consideration of man and his environmental interrelationships.

The Yosemites (Sierra Club), 10 min. A needed scenic-recreations resource was lost with the damming of the Yosemite's twin valley, Hetch Hetchy. The tragedy of the lost Yosemite.

Chapter 12

▓▓▓▓▓▓▓▓▓▓▓▓▓□□□□

Problems Related to Representative Government and Communications Media

Many of the problems we face are those peculiarly related to the fact that we live under a representative type of government—one in which the people must ultimately make the decisions. This fact has certain implications for the structure of the government and also for the type of communication facilities. Especially pertinent are problems of the limitations of communication facilities and the lack of public sensitivity to propaganda. The rapid increase in the accessibility and pervasiveness of the communications media pouring out words and pictures in tremendous quantity raises questions concerning the extent to which reality itself is being replaced by the media.

COMMUNICATIONS FACILITIES

This availability and quality of the communications in a democracy, particularly a very large, complex, and intricately interrelated one, becomes of crucial importance to that society. Furthermore, it has enormous implications for the school in terms both of the availability of mass communication facilities for educational purposes and of the possibility of the schools' assistance in improving the communication facilities.

Modern Communication Facilities

Certainly there is no lack of opportunity for the citizens in America (as in many others of the highly industrialized nations) to gain access to any information that they may need, not only for understanding their roles in citizenship but also for their own cultural enlightenment and vocational improvement. The quantity of books, newspapers, and magazines is increasing at a rate faster than that of our population. In spite of television, the circulation of books in libraries is increasing at least as fast as the population, if not faster. Radio and television, each with a very large mass audience, constitute two other important media of communication.

Technological improvements in the sending of reports from one point to another facilitate the almost immediate availability of news to all parts of the world. The greater ease of transportation and communication enables every corner of the world to be readily accessible to news-gathering agents and to persons trying to obtain information for educational purposes. The extent of communication facilities in the United States is truly amazing:

Newspapers. In 1969 there were 1,652 English-language newspapers in the United States with a combined circulation of 61,966,623. There were 582 Sunday papers with 49,840,827 circulation.[1] Because it is estimated that there were over 50 million families (households) in the United States in 1969, the extent of the circulation of the newspaper is readily apparent. (In a later section we shall discuss the extent of increasing concentration of newspaper control and ownership.)

Radio and Television. It was estimated that in 1971 there were about 237 million radio and television sets in use in the United States out of about 482 million in the entire world. Of this number there were approximately 57 million homes with radios in the United States; 18 million radios in business places, institutions, and other such locations; 47 million radios in automobiles; and 61.5 million television sets.[2] For comparison, it was estimated that in 1948 there were just 75 million radios in use in the United States, and only 900,000 television sets. Over 98 per cent of the population in the United States was within sufficient distance of transmitting stations to view television broadcasts.

Magazines and Books. In 1971 there were more than 100 magazines in the United States that had over 430,000 circulation.[3] There were two magazines with over 10 million circulation, ten others with over 5 million circulation, and eleven others with over 2 million circulation. In 1969 there was a total 21,787 new books published, as compared to 11,901 in 1954.[4] Bernstein states,[5] "During the 1960's, while United States population increased about 10 per cent, sales in the book industry doubled."

This increase has occurred in the face of enormous increase in TV coverage and in other recreational and leisure-time opportunities.

Advertising

One of the characteristics of America and of all other countries that have competitive economic systems is advertising. Advertising certainly is increasing in the United States. The public is bombarded with advertising from billboards, radio programs, newspapers, and countless other sources.

Undoubtedly advertising has contributed greatly to the vaunted American standard of living. Through continual enticing of the buyer to spend his money as rapidly as possible for products, particularly for new types of products—the latest model—the economic system is stimulated to operate

[1]*World Almanac, 1971* (New York: Newspaper Enterprise Association, 1970), p. 175.

[2]This includes "homes" (or rooms) with single persons, not "households."

[3]*World Almanac, 1971*, p. 174. See also John Tebbel, *The American Magazine: A Compact History* (New York: Hawthorne, 1969).

[4]Ibid., p. 818.

[5]Robert L. Bernstein, "A Publisher Looks at Publishing," *Education Digest*, Vol. XXXVI, No. 4 (December 1970), pp. 40–43.

at a rapid rate. Money does not stay long in the pockets of the consumer. Some advertising, of course, does not contribute much to economic improvement, because it is competitive advertising for different brand-name products that are equivalent in quality. The tendency of such mass advertising is eventually to drive one or more of such competitive products out of business in favor of the ones that have better advertising campaigns, thus contributing to monopolistic or oligopolistic practices.

Although the opinion of liberal economists and others is, in general, not so much opposed to excessive advertising as it was during the 1930's, there is a question as to whether or not all advertising can be justified as making a contribution toward the economic system. Certainly advertising responsibilities consume the energies of persons who might be better engaged in improving the product (or increasing the number of producers in our economic system—producers of actual products that can be consumed). One can well ask whether or not all advertising does contribute to the total economic betterment of our society. It does actually add to the cost of the article, unless the increased volume of sales contributes to lower unit costs in production. It is true that advertising does subsidize some of our communications, such as newspapers, magazines, radio, and television. It is also true that it partially controls what it subsidizes.

It is likely that advertising is with us to stay. Efforts should probably be made toward increasing the responsibility of advertisers for truthfulness. Legal action should probably be taken against advertisers who actually use false claims for their products, particularly in the field of food and drugs.

Readability

What about the problem of communicating ideas accurately and adequately? Many studies have been made concerning the readability of mass communications media. Such studies indicate that much of the material in the newspapers is not readable. This may be entirely due to the type of vocabulary used, but it also may be due to the wording of the material. The material needs to be supplemented with pictures, graphs, and other concrete illustrations. Although it is beyond the scope of this book to indicate the suggestions for readability, certainly responsible publishers should be constantly alert to this problem. This does not necessarily mean bringing the contents "down to the audience's level." What it does mean is presenting the ideas and facts in a context and in a manner that will be understood.

PROPAGANDA AND PUBLIC OPINION

The problem of communication is not solved when mass media presents ideas effectively. The problems of the control of the opinion and of possible biases may exist. These will be explored in the next sections.

Growth of Newspaper Monopoly

For a considerable period in American history (since 1909), the number of separate English-language daily newspapers in the United States decreased at a fairly constant rate up to about 1949. Since that point there has been a very slight increase. During this same period there has been a large increase in the population. The peak in the number of separate dailies was reached with about 2,600 in 1909.[6] In 1970 the number was 1,652.[7] Furthermore, the study from which the former figures were taken reports that only about 8 per cent of the cities in which daily newspapers are published had competing dailies even in 1947. At that time there were ten states in which there were no cities with competing dailies and twenty-two states in which there were no cities with competing Sunday newspapers. In this same study 40 per cent of the estimated total daily newspaper circulation at that time was judged to be noncompetitive. It is true that nationally syndicated columnists and cartoons may be more influential than local editors in molding opinion on national and international issues. However, in cities with no competing papers, all these may be chosen so that they present similar views.[8]

There has also been a heavy concentration of mass circulation among a few very popular magazines. Of course, any study of the growth of monopoly among newspapers and magazines should always include the figures in the total increased circulation and the increased number of small magazines. However, the great mass of readers do read magazines published by a relatively few companies, and therefore the control that these companies potentially could exercise over the mass mind represents a possible threat. Advertisers (or the people who control the advertising budget) also can wield tremendous power over newspapers and magazines.

Possibilities of Bias in Communication

Rapidity of communication and massiveness of communication facilities may be utilized to disseminate accurate and unbiased information, or they may be used to propagandize a people. (Witness the silencing of *La Prensa* by Perón and the control of mass media for their own purposes by the Nazis, fascists, and Communists.) Even freedom of communication may result in mass dissemination of false concepts. In the first place, in both magazines and newspapers there is a bias in favor of that which is interesting. Sometimes a diet of the sensational aspects of the news or of developments in our country does not adequately portray what is really happening. There is also a bias in the mind of the reader toward the sensational as opposed to the humdrum. For example, stories about juvenile delinquency that may involve only 4 to 5 per cent of our juvenile population may be given publicity that causes the public to feel that most young people are delinquent. Comparatively overlooked are the approximately 95 per cent who may be more ambitious, sober, and industrious than were young people of the same age fifty to seventy-five years ago. Reading the daily press and magazines would not give this impression to the reader. Yet this may not be deliberately done on the part of the magazine and newspaper editors or writers.

Other kinds of bias that may or may not be intentional arise out of the fact that newspaper publishing is "big business." As we have shown in the

[6]Commission of Freedom of the Press, *A Free and Responsible Press: A General Report on Mass Communication; Newspapers, Radio, Motion Pictures, Magazines, and Books* (Chicago: University of Chicago Press, 1947), p. 37.

[7]*The World Almanac*, 1971, p. 175.

[8]Commission of Freedom of the Press, op. cit., p. 38.

last section, the concentration of the newspaper and the publishing industry in ever larger companies is increasing. Because the persons who control newspaper policy are in big business, they themselves tend sometimes to favor attitudes of big business toward news. An unconscious, or sometimes conscious, bias appears in the selection of news items, in the writing of headlines, and in other aspects of the publication. This is especially evident on the editorial page, where the viewpoints, political philosophy, and so on, of the publisher of course are, and *should be*, expressed. Editorial viewpoints, however, may not adequately represent popular opinion.

Propaganda Analysis

In the preceding sections we have talked about possible biases of the press and other means of communication resulting from matters that were more or less unconscious. In America and elsewhere throughout the world there is also much deliberate attempt to influence public opinion. Where the attempt is deliberate through the manipulation of the means of communication and is for the purpose of influencing action on the part of the recipient, the term *propaganda* is applied to it. Although there may be an element of propaganda in education itself at times, ordinarily propaganda differs from education in that every attempt should be made in the case of education to give the learner many points of view other than that which the teacher or writer considers to be appropriate. In education none of the pertinent facts should be omitted.

The following are the seven types of propaganda that are commonly recognized.

1. The name-calling device.
2. The glittering-generalities device.
3. The transferral device.
4. The testimonial device.
5. The plain-folks device.
6. The card-stacking device.
7. The band-wagon device.

Name calling is used to prejudice the person against an idea by attributing it to a group that, for a variety or reasons, is considered to be bad. Once a name is applied to an idea, such as the adjectives *fascist* or *communistic,* it is condemned. Such use of names in a stereotyped manner is a short circuit to appropriate thinking and must be considered to be a propaganda technique. Yet it is used frequently, both in the totalitarian countries and in the democratic countries, to persuade persons to a point of view without having them consider at all the facts of the situation.

Glittering generalities is applied to the use of broad terms, sometimes called virtue words, such as *love, brotherhood, Christianity, religion, democracy,* or the *American way.* Through the use of these terms a person can be persuaded to accept other ideas because they are part of a "total acceptance" pattern. Name calling gets one to reject an idea; glittering generalities make one accept or approve it without completely examining the evidence one way or the other.

Transfer is the third device. In this case, a symbol such as the cross representing the Christian church or the flag representing America, is used to stir up our emotions so that we will accept or reject an idea. Cartoonists use such symbols as Uncle Sam to cause people to accept an idea they are trying to portray.

The *testimonial device* is a technique of getting an outstanding person in some field to indicate that he is for an idea, thereby indicating that, because outstanding people are for it, the rest of us should be for it also. We quite often overlook the fact that sometimes the person to whom the testimonial is attributed may not be in a position to judge with respect to this matter, even though he may be well qualified in certain other areas.

The *plain-folks device* is quite often used by a politician to indicate he is a "man of the people." By using nicknames and folk terms, sometimes a person tries to appeal to other people by giving the impression that he is one of them and therefore would understand their problems. Advertising or political articles may be written in such a way as to appeal to the common man, who may sometimes have a feeling that he has been left out of representation when decisions are made.

The *card-stacking device* refers to a situation where evidence, which quite often is true, is quoted. However, what is quoted is not all the evidence but only that part of it that supports the desired point of view. Evidence that does not support the point of view is suppressed or wrongly interpreted.

The *band wagon* is quite often used in politics. "Everybody is doing it"; therefore, it must be good. "Let's get on the band wagon."

The preceding is only one of the many analyses of propaganda that could be made, but it should help teachers to get students interested in an analysis of propaganda. There is, of course, one danger in this proceeding—both the propaganda of our opponents *and that of our friends* may be recognized. There is no way of teaching the intelligent person to think critically without having him apply critical thinking to what the teacher may say as well as what the other person says. This is good, because the student who can recognize propaganda on whatever side should be able better to evaluate material pertinent to his needs.

THE MEDIA IMPACT: McLUHAN'S HYPOTHESIS

In considering the media impact, one should examine first the changes in the media.

We come then to a . . . problem which . . . may appropriately be called the "Change Revolution." In order to illustrate what this means, we will use the media again and the metaphor of a clock face. Imagine a clock face with 60 minutes on it. Let the clock stand for the time men have had access to writing systems. Our clock would thus represent something like 3,000 years, and each minute on our clock 50 years. On this scale, there were no significant media changes until about nine minutes ago. At that time, the printing press came into use in Western culture. About three minutes ago, the telegraph, photograph, and locomotive arrived. Two minutes ago; the telephone, rotary press, motion pictures, automobile, airplane, and radio. One minute ago, the talking pictures. Television has appeared in the last ten seconds, the computer in the last five, and communications satellites in the last second. The laser beam—perhaps the most potent medium of communications of all—appeared only a fraction of a second ago.[9]

Marshall McLuhan is famous for his books on the revolutionary nature of the change wrought by the media on man. His hypothesis has been paraphrased in the following paragraphs:

Man's method of thinking is formed by the environment, which he in turn has created. Environment is not a protective wrapping, or container, into which man is thrust, but rather a continuously shifting process of which man is both integral part and creator.

Every medium, all technology, is an extension of man. Print is an extension of speech and speech an extension of thought. T.V. and electric circuitry is an extension of the central nervous system. Each bit of technology is significant because it ultimately creates a totally new environment through the influence it exerts on the pattern, pace, or scale of human affairs.

Media and methods of communication change the environment and alter our sense perceptions. When the ratio among the sense perceptions is changed, man's manner of thinking and acting is changed. The advent of print moved man from the interdependence of tribal life, enabling him to gain information without having to rely on the elders for the information necessary for the maintenance of life. Print liberated man and gave rise to the cult of the individual. Print is responsible for the process of linear, sequential thought which has come to be recognized as the "rational" or "logical" method of thought. Sequential thought, or block-by-block thought, created the public which consists of separate individuals all with separate fixed points of view. Linear thinking separates thought from action.

Electric circuitry has profoundly affected the way men think. The change was brought about not by the content of the media (the "content" of any media is always another media), but through the way the media affect our perceptual senses. Printing isolates or classifies data for man to absorb at his leisure. The new technology bombards man with information instantaneously and continuously. When this information is acquired, he is bombarded with newer information. Man is no longer able to sort or classify isolates. His senses are being trained by the media to view the entirety, the whole process of his environment and experience in a state of constant interplay.

This constant interplay of environment and experience has created a "global village," making man an integral part of the environmental process of the entire globe, not just his city, state or country. It has awakened in man a new social awareness and brought thought and action into closer proximity. Man creates media, which alters his environment, and becomes the mode of defining his role within it. Circuitry has altered our methods of perception, thereby changing our environment, and the way we think of ourselves and others.[10]

Suggestions Toward the Improvement of Public Information Channels

By far the best study of the whole problem of communication in America, with particular emphasis upon the press, was made by the Com-

[9]Neil Postman and Charles Weingartner, Teaching as a Subversive Activity (New York: Delacorte, 1969), p. 10. Used by permission.

[10]Marshall McLuhan, The Medium Is the Massage (New York: Bantam, 1967).; The Gutenberg Galaxy (New York: New American Library, 1969); Understanding Media: The Extensions of Man (New York: McGraw-Hill, 1965). The summary was prepared by Irene Thorman.

mission of Freedom of the Press, which issued its general report in 1947.[11] The members of this body made certain recommendations after having studied carefully the status of communication facilities, including newspapers, radio, motion pictures, magazines, and books. They did not recommend a whole set of new laws controlling these facilities. They did recommend: (1) That the constitutional guarantees of the freedom of the press be extended and protected. (2) That governmental agencies continue to use their own communication facilities to supply the people with information concerning their activities both in this country and abroad. (3) That responsibility for maintaining standards of integrity and for the avoidance of either propaganda or bias with respect to its news items be placed on the communications industry as a quasipublic institution (perhaps the most important recommendation). This was not meant in any way to restrict the freedom of the newspaper to maintain positions in editorial columns or to restrict the freedom of other commentators within the paper. (4) That competence, independence, and effectiveness of the staffs of the newspapers be improved. (5) That the various nonprofit educational agencies accelerate the publishing of readable materials on a completely unbiased basis. This would include institutions such as libraries, educational radio, and FM and TV stations. (6) That an annual survey be conducted on the performance of the press with respect to the problem of bias. With such a survey cases might be spotted where newspapers had been notoriously biased with respect to important issues.

It should be remembered through all the discussions of this and the preceding sections that in spite of the shortcomings of communications facilities in America, the American people, relatively speaking, are very privileged in this respect. By and large, the American press is free. By and large, the American people have access to more facts and information untrammeled by censorship than any other people of the world. The suggestions that have been made are meant to improve and enlarge upon the free flow of information to the American people. However, the problem of adequate communication is not solved with getting the information to the people. There must also be consideration of the responsibility of education through other sources in preparing the people to utilize the information properly.

Public Forums, Community Discussion Groups, and Other Means of Stimulating Adult Thinking

Access to adequate information is of little avail if adults do not make sense out of the immense amount of information that is necessary to understand this rapidly changing world. This section is focused on the part-time education of adults, mostly postschool-age persons. In later sections we will discuss the role of the schools with children and youth.

It is probable that if a person would read *and study carefully* all the material that is found in a good newspaper during a year's time, he would have the basis for a very good college education. It would require, however, that the person have learned how to read properly and how to evaluate information. It would also require that he be willing to look up and give

[11]Commission of Freedom of the Press, op. cit.

further study to matters that were raised in newspaper articles and commentaries. Newspapers and magazines are trying to appeal to a wide variety of people; consequently, they have all types of information. No one person ever reads carefully all the articles found in an ordinary newpaper.

Through adult education classes and classes in the public schools, people can be taught to evaluate information and to use the library and other resources for further study of the problems that are raised. In addition to formal and informal adult classes, communities should arrange for various kinds of community discussion groups in public forums. Some of these public forums can be on a national level and promulgated by means of radio and TV. Some of the group discussions, which are for the purposes of getting together all the facts on a given current problem, are excellent. Others have speakers, sometimes bitterly partisan, discuss differing viewpoints with respect to a problem. Sometimes such a debate or discussion becomes so heated as not to throw much light on the situation. Such discussions should use persons who are well informed and who can see the viewpoint of others readily, without emotion. There are, of course, times when the presentation of a point of view by a partisan is also educational in its nature.

DEVELOPMENT AND PRESENT NATURE OF REPRESENTATIVE GOVERNMENT

The exact nature of government is important as an aspect of the total culture of a society. Most Americans feel that they understand the general nature of our American governmental structure. However, it seems wise that a more careful analysis now be made in order to see ways in which the schools may play a part in preparing better citizens and in helping toward the solution of many of the political problems we face in the United States.

America, a Representative Form of Government with Checks and Balances

There is still some controversy within the American democratic culture concerning whether or not our form of government is a republic or a democracy. As we shall show in the next section, there was some inclination among the founding fathers toward the setting up of a form of government that would not be completely amenable to the will of the popular majority. This means the trend was toward a republic form of government in which the powers of the people were somewhat limited. However, evolution made it clear that we were establishing one in which the ultimate power lay in the hands of the people.

Our government today is a representative democracy with numerous types of checks and balances. In the first place, our national government is a federal-type government with limitations of sovereignty. Some of the sovereign powers have been allocated among the various states. Within the federal government itself, as well as in the various state governments, there has been division of power, with checks and balances. The division of power between the upper and the lower houses of the legislature is one of these. The independence of the executive, judicial, and legislative branches is another. The complex procedure through which the Constitution can be amended is a third. These checks and balances were obviously intended to give stability to the government and to prevent a wave of mass hysteria from causing steps to be taken foolishly without full realization of the consequences.

Although it is obvious that the founding fathers had fundamental respect for the intelligence of man and felt that ultimately the citizen should make his own decisions in regard to problems, they feared that some wave of emotion or mass reaction might destroy important institutions or even democracy itself. Certainly some of the events in republics elsewhere in the world have indicated that this easily can occur.

Although ultimately the stability of any form of government depends on the character of the people making up the nation, it is probable that the form of government must be adapted to the particular state of the people at a given time. The evolution of the American government toward more democratic forms was in line with the increasing enlightenment of the American people and their ability to make political decisions.

We may summarize this section by saying that we do have a representative democracy, or a republic, in which certain powers have been allocated to the national or federal government, certain powers reserved to the states, and, in most cases, many powers in turn allocated to local governments within the states. The American people as a whole have thought the allocation of more powers to the central government to be dangerous, and sometimes they have held to that belief well beyond the period when it had become obvious that power had to be centralized to meet urgent social and economic needs. As such services as transportation and communication became more complete and rapid, as industry became more intricately tied in with all parts of the country, it became necessary to give the central government more powers in order to meet the problems with which the country was confronted.

Some of the problems that are faced in a period of adjustment to the new and intricate world in which we find ourselves are discussed in a later section.

Evolution of Governmental Form and Theory in America

Many of the men who were influential in writing such documents as the Declaration of Independence were strongly influenced by political theorists like Hobbes and Locke. Because of their experiences with an autocratic, oligarchic form of government, they feared a strong central government and a strong executive. They had great faith in the intelligence of the middle class but feared the concentration of power in the hands of a ruling group. Because of fear of the masses, the franchise was considerably limited during pre-Revolutionary days and in the immediate post-Revolutionary days. Various restrictions of property and rank made the suffrage available to only a minority of the community. Men of property and of standing were considered, however, to be capable of making decisions that were wise for their own self-government.

The influence of the frontier was very strong toward emphasis upon the individual and upon the extension of suffrage to a more complete democracy. Although the form still remains, the theory of selecting the president not directly by the voters but by a group of electors chosen by the voters was for all practical purposes done away with in the early years of the republic. This device was originally set up to guarantee the careful selection of an executive in terms of his qualifications rather than on the basis of his popularity with the masses. It was one example of a lack of complete faith in the ability of the masses to choose their leader. Another example was the selection of senators by members of the state legislatures; this was not completely changed until the passing of the Seventeenth Amendment to the Constitution in 1913, which provided for universal popular election of senators.

The elimination of laws in regard to the restricted inheritance of property (e.g., primogenitive) and other such matters was also a move toward the democratization of American society. Along with these social developments, there were numerous others that led to the extension of democracy from a political concept to social concepts as well. The elimination of the class structure of early American society, discussed more fully in Chapters 4 and 9, was partly indicative of this change in ideas.

We have shown how the supposedly laissez-faire theory of government with respect to economic matters was gradually changed over a period of years, so that by 1930 the governments at both state and national levels were involved considerably in economic matters. As society became more complex and as new problems developed that needed solving, increasingly, men turned to government for action. All of this meant an increased amount of government and a strengthening of the government. Many of the decisions of the Supreme Court over a period of years strengthened the power of the central government by reinterpreting the Constitution. Quite early in the history of America a "loose" interpretation of the Constitution enabled the federal government to buy the Louisiana territory, to help in the development of canals, later to help in the development of railroads, and still later to participate in numerous projects leading more directly to the welfare of the individual.

The early theory held by most Americans, including the founding fathers, was that the "least" government governs best and that as much as possible should be left to the local government. As the problems became more intricate and complex, however, it was found that some matters that had been left with the local government must of necessity be turned over to higher levels. A lag in this respect constitutes one of the problems of American government that we shall discuss in a later section. By and large, the theory openly expressed by the American people is very similar to that of the earlier period. The type of problems we face already has required us in practice to change our institutions greatly. The "least" government at the present time is a great deal more government than in earlier times because of the complexity and intricacy of the problems we face.

Some of the trends toward further democratization are seen in the use of the *initiative*, the *referendum*, and the *recall*[12] in some of our state governments. We do not have any of these operating at the federal level.

---

[12]*Initiative:* the placing of a proposed law or constitutional amendment on the ballot by petition.

Referendum: the placing of an existing or proposed law on the ballot by petition or by action of the legislature.

Recall: a reconsideration by a special election through petition of the right of a person to hold his office. If he were turned down (or recalled), the position would be filled in accordance with regular procedures when a vacancy exists.

On the whole, the American people believe in the democratic form of government and the democratic way of life. There are many differences of opinion as to what this actually means. In Chapter 14 we shall indicate some of the values that can be considered to be fairly well accepted by all people in the American democratic society. There are, of course, a few persons on the extremes, both right and left, who do not really believe in democracy, however broadly it can be defined. Some, on the reactionary right, do not trust the people to make the correct decision, and quite often they argue that we have a republic rather than a democracy. By this they mean that through various kinds of control the people should be prevented from making decisions. They go on to point out that the check-and-balance ideas contained in our Constitution were in response to a realization that the upper classes should rule. On the other extreme we have "left-wing" persons who would like to do away with the freedom of our institutions in certain other respects through doctrinaire approaches to our economic problems, such as complete socialization or even communistic methods and a dictatorship of the proletariat, albeit a supposedly temporary one. Both of these extremes certainly lie beyond the sphere of democratic thinking as ordinarily understood.

GOVERNMENTAL AND POLITICAL PROBLEMS IN AMERICA

It is important to go into some detail in regard to the political problems that we face in America, in order to get a better understanding of how we might go about strengthening our government through the schools.

Problems Inherent in the American Form of Government

There are problems inherent in the particular structure of any government. Other problems are inherent in the weaknesses of the people that make up the government. The problem of government is primarily that of getting a structure that will work best for the particular people, country, and culture that are involved. There are, of course, certain difficulties inherent in the American governmental structure.

A first problem lies in the bicameral type of legislature. One state, Nebraska, early recognized this and created a unicameral legislature. In many cases in the past, legislation has been prevented from going through because the measure had to pass two houses. This means duplication of effort on every bill. Furthermore, it increases the number of lawmakers, so that it is more difficult for the public to know a given lawmaker and to hold him responsible. A relatively small unicameral legislature fixes the responsibility more directly upon the members for their voting. The bicameral legislature does have some advantages, for it sometimes prevents bad laws from slipping through and also provides for the correction of defects in laws that do not pass one house. Of course, if there is only one house, the bill might be checked more carefully before being permitted to pass.

A second inherent problem relates to the complete separation of the executive and legislative branches. Because the president is elected independently of the legislature and is not responsible to it, situations arise frequently in which the president and Congress are at odds with one another. This may be because they are of different political parties, or it may be that the president does not truly have the leadership as far as his fellow party members in the legislature are concerned. Many of the other democratic countries of the world have a responsible prime minister who serves at the pleasure of the majority of the legislature. This insures that he represents the will of the legislature; any time that he fails to do so his governments falls and a new government is set up or there is a new election. In England and in several of the members of the British Commonwealth with what amounts to a two-party system this has worked out fairly well. In France, which has a multiple-party system, it has led to a great deal of instability in government. France, of course, also has a president, corresponding to the monarch of England, to give some stability to the government. There is in the United States, England, and France a permanent government secretariat (or civil service) which gives stability to the ordinary running of government when there is a change of the administration.

A third basic problem arises from the division of powers between the federal and state governments. Many problems are broader than state lines, yet the Constitution is not always clear with regard to the jurisdiction of the federal government. An example in recent years was the control of the pollution of rivers. Although the Constitution clearly gives the federal government the right to control commerce on rivers, it apparently does not give the right to control the dumping of sewage and other waste into them. Numerous makeshift devices, such as interstate or regional commissions, have to be set up to control the purity of rivers or to take care of the diversion of river water for irrigation, city water supply, and other purposes. Such a problem of jurisdiction would not arise in a country that had a unitary-type government as opposed to a federal-type government.

Another type of problem arises out of the practice of leaving a great deal of jurisdiction to the local governments and permitting the incorporation of villages. As cities grow and expand from their boundaries, quite often they are hemmed in by small cities and villages on their outskirts. Apparently there is no way under American jurisprudence for a village that has once been set up as a corporation to be merged later with a larger governmental unit except by the wishes and permission of that village. The problem of placing a contiguous industrial, metropolitan area under a single government for more efficient operation and for a unified attack on its problems exists not only in America but throughout the world. It has been an especially difficult matter in the United States, where there are constitutional precedents to prevent action on the annexation or consolidation of existing communities even when they border on each other and have common problems that they ought to face together. Toronto, Canada, is often cited as the only major city in the world that has been able to solve this problem. London, England, is a notorious example of a city that has not been able to do so satisfactorily.

Another set of problems in this general area of conflicting jurisdictions is the extreme chaos that exists in the marriage and divorce laws among the separate states. It is imperative that each state recognize the marriage and divorce laws of the other states, but so wide are the differences among the states that the problem becomes very complex; the validity of some divorces is even questionable.

A set of problems has also arisen out of police and judicial procedures in the United States. Because of recent judicial decisions relating to the treatment of prisoners or persons apprehended for investigation for criminal acts. there have been very strong restrictions placed upon police procedures. These procedures relate to such matters as informing the apprehended individual of his right to counsel before he gives a confession, and using force in the investigation or the obtaining of a confession. There is a fine line of distinction here between protecting the rights of the individual and making investigation by the police and other law officials so difficult as to make the apprehension of criminals almost impossible. Although generally agreed that this protection may at times be needed, the police must be much more sophisticated on legal procedures and rights if they are to avoid mistakes.

Another problem of current significance that arose during the mid-1960's concerns the matter of equal representation in the lower house of the state legislatures. Many of these houses have indicated their representation on the basis of units or counties, which because of the rapid urbanization of certain counties has caused the rural areas to be more highly represented than the urban areas. The variation in ratio sometimes is quite high. The Supreme Court has ruled that there must be equal representation in the various states. Many states were forced to pass legislation to conform to this Supreme Court rule. Similar questions are being raised with regard to local elections.

Problems Resulting from Social and Economic Changes

In addition to problems of the type listed in the preceding section, there are others that could not possibly have been foreseen by the founding fathers. The development of the complex, interrelated, industrial world based upon mass production technology, let alone automation, could not have been envisioned by even the most prophetic. The development of large corporations involving the lives of many people with resources exceeding those of many of our states could not have been foretold. Problems arose quite early in regard to interstate commerce, such as the regulation of railroad rates in the latter part of the nineteenth century, where it became obvious that the federal government would have to establish its power. By a series of interpretations of the Constitution and by certain amendments, such as the income tax amendment, the power of the federal government has been extended to meet many of these problems. There is, however, still considerable disagreement regarding the extent to which the federal government should increase its power beyond the point that is really necessary in order to meet the most urgent situations. There are still areas of debate, such as federal aid to education in the field of general instruction.

One of the problems that needed to be faced as a result of social and economic change was that of providing protection for the welfare of workers in our industrial society. Another problem was the prevention of certain companies from monopolizing a given industry and thereby hampering the economy by charging exorbitant prices or by holding back progress. The tromondous complexity of government needed to meet these problems as well as to provide information and services of a wide variety, such as weather bureau reports, aid to business and to farmers, and many others, necessitated passing laws that give wide discretion to elected officials in making decisions. Even in the case of laws and regulations themselves, there has been an increasing tendency at both federal and state levels to pass legislation that permits administrative regulations to be set up. Under appropriate safeguards these often have the force of law. This means, in effect, that the legislature delegates the details of many governmental policies to appointed or civil service officials. This is the field of the so-called administrative law. Many problems, however, develop in regard to providing necessary safeguards in this field, such as public hearings and provisions for repeal, changes, or revisions.

Because of the necessity for increasing regulations of various kinds related to the complexity of our social order, various kinds of safeguards are necessary; one of these is a safeguard against the bureaucracy itself. We have seen how democracy was protected by the advent of the initiative, the referendum, and the recall. We have seen that protection is given by legal aid societies, and in some states by the public defender, against the power and majesty of the law itself.

There has arisen in recent years in the Scandinavian countries a new government official called the *ombudsman*, which has now become an international word and can be translated best perhaps as "commissioner of complaints and grievances." This office has been in operation in Sweden, Finland, Denmark, Norway, New Zealand and West Germany for some time. Great Britain instituted a similar plan in 1967. The ombudsman in Finland is established by the legislature as a protection of the ordinary individual against bureaucracy. Quite often the persons who handle the application of administrative rules and regulations are insensitive to the problems of the person involved. The individual is unaware of the rules and regulations and how they can be applied, so he has no way of defending himself against a bureaucratic ruling. He knows that there is something wrong with the ruling, but he has no way to defend himself. This can be called to the attention of an ombudsman, who then investigates the complaint to see whether or not it is justified. In many cases it has been found that there was a misunderstanding on the part of the complainant. The reason for this misunderstanding, in a few cases, is that the complainant is not able to state his case properly in order to secure the justice due him. In still other cases, perhaps not more than 10 per cent, it has been necessary for the ombudsman to take some action in order to bring about justice. In some cases this has involved a legal mandamus suit through the courts in order to protect the individual. The desirability of an ombudsman is being investigated in this country as well as those with one.

With the increasing use of the computer and with the almost universal use of Social Security numbers as a key to the location of data for individuals, the possibility arises that all data on an individual from birth to death may be available on demand from an interlocking national computer system. All these data, whether accurate or appropriate at a later time, can be printed out without being evaluated. This constitutes a very serious threat to the personal rights of all individuals.[13]

Problems Related to Political Indifference

One of the most important problems facing a democracy is the indifference or ignorance of the voting public. That such a small percentage of

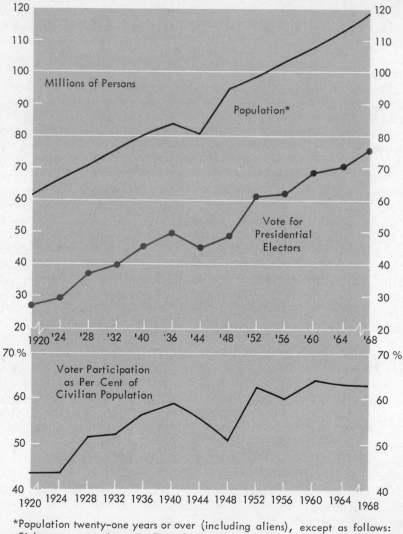

*Population twenty-one years or over (including aliens), except as follows: Eighteen years and over in Georgia since 1944, eighteen years and over in Kentucky since 1956, nineteen years and over in Alaska since 1958; and twenty years and over in Hawaii since 1958.

Figure 27. Voting population for president, 1920–1968. (Source: National Industrial Conference Board; 845 Third Avenue; New York, N.Y. 10022. Used by permission.)

[13]See Jerry M. Rosenberg, *The Death of Privacy* (New York: Random House, 1969). The April 17, 1971, issue of *The Saturday Review* also deals with this topic.

the citizens in America exercise their voting rights and privileges is appalling. At best, only slightly over 50 per cent of the eligible population vote at any given election, including presidential elections. (See Figure 27.) This means that most issues are decided by a plurality rather than by a majority of those persons eligible to vote. Of course, the effect that a higher percentage of voting would have on the ultimate issue is not known. Many other or more enlightened countries of the world have a much higher percentage of voting. Some of the free countries, such as those in Scandinavia, may have as high as 80 or 85 per cent. Totalitarian countries sometimes have claimed percentages as high as 98 or 99. However, in those cases voters usually have no real choice, and penalties are often placed upon those who do not vote.

It has been suggested by some that there be compulsory voting, with fines or other penalties assessed against those people who do not exercise their rights. Some of the democratic countries of the world, such as Australia and Belgium, have compulsory voting statutes and do attempt to enforce them. Most of the penalties are monetary fines rather than imprisonment. Some penalties merely consist of publishing the names of the offenders. There are some persons in the United States who have advocated compulsory voting. Abraham, after a very careful study of the problem and the difficulties of enforcement even in smaller countries, decides that such a law would be unwise, unconstitutional, and probably unenforceable under the conditions of American democracy.[14]

This means that the problems of increasing the number of voters and the enlightenment of those who do vote demand the attention of educators. Several suggestions that have been made in other sections of this chapter and throughout the book should be helpful.

Suggestions for the Alleviation of Governmental Problems

Numerous suggestions have been made from time to time as to how our government might be modified to meet better the problems we face. However, it should be pointed out that, with some exceptions where the rigid and fixed structure of our government built for one period handicaps us in the present age, the basic task is to get the people to understand our problems and then to be willing to work with their officials toward their solution.

Attempts to solve such problems as river pollution, garbage collection systems in metropolitan areas, traffic, and so forth, face almost insurmountable difficulties because of the many conflicting local subdivisions. Such barriers just do not make sense in the present age. Provisions should be made that areas that are joined together by economic institutions (banks, industries, and stores), sewage, garbage collection, and other facilities should also be joined politically. This may cause a loss of some of the feeling of local autonomy that people have enjoyed heretofore. Consequently, some new scheme probably should be worked out where problems involving the entire community would be solved on a higher level, but where the city would be divided into smaller communities to solve local, neighborhood, and community problems on a basis entirely different from the township or

[14]Henry J. Abraham, *Compulsory Voting* (Washington, D.C.: Annals of American Government, Public Affairs Press, 1955), pp. 16–20, 30–33.

small-town governments of an earlier era. The writers can point to no place where this has been done at present.

For the solution of problems that are too big for the state but that do not require the attention of the national government, the use of regional-type bodies has been suggested. The Ohio River compact for the control of pollution by the states bordering on the river is one example of a voluntary association to solve a problem that had been unsolvable on the basis of the present division of powers between state and federal government. In an entirely different type of venture the Tennessee Valley Authority attempts to solve the problems of conservation, flood control, and power production in a valley covering parts of seven states. Recent attempts to do the same thing in certain other areas have not met with approval as far as public opinion is concerned. It is difficult to see where the Tennessee Valley Authority approach to the problem has in any way been detrimental, even to the welfare of established private businesses. The number of private industries and businesses coming into the Tennessee valley since the development of public power has been enormous.

The federal government's power to levy taxes where the money is and to distribute it where it is needed already has been put to use in numerous areas, such as unemployment compensation, aid to mothers and handicapped children, vocational education, and so on. In such cases money is granted to the states on a matching basis or on a basis of a formula, leaving the states to distribute the money and to administer its expenditure under their constitutional prerogative.

This combination of federal and state action seems to be a good compromise in a situation of divided sovereignty, such as our federal–state type of government. This same approach has been used with respect to federal aid to general education in the Elementary–Secondary Education Act of 1965 and its successors. The reason for the development of federal financing is that quite often the areas that have the greatest needs have also the least resources with which to meet them. The head offices of corporations tend to be concentrated largely in New York and its metropolitan area; consequently, income and other tax sources are heavily concentrated in those areas, even though the money may originally come from all parts of the United States. Such states as Alabama, Mississippi, and Georgia have few sources to be taxed, yet the welfare of the people of Georgia, Mississippi, and Alabama is important to the welfare of the entire country. It is as much to the interest of New York State that the people of Georgia, Mississippi, and Alabama be well educated as it is that the people of New York should be. This is due not only to the very great mobility of our population, but also to the fact that our country is an economic unit and the prosperity of one part contributes to the prosperity of the whole.

EDUCATIONAL IMPLICATIONS

The implications of this chapter for educational curriculum should be fairly obvious. The student must be made aware of the historic concept of our American democratic representative government as well as the ways in which it has changed in recent times through gradual evolution. He should also be aware of the many problems that are faced. Being made aware of the problems does not necessarily mean that the student is taught any one method of solving them. Perhaps, in some cases, it is better not to change the structure but to work on the problems on an intelligent basis within the present structure (which it may be important to safeguard for other reasons). The fact that there are serious problems needing solution should be made clear. Important suggestions that have been made by various groups for the alleviation of problems through changes of structure or other means should be discussed fully so that the student will have these ideas clearly in mind when problems arise and he must make some type of a decision as a citizen. Many solutions that forty or fifty years ago were not considered possible in a democracy are now not only accepted but considered to be an integral part of American democratic society.

Throughout all of the school curriculum should be found materials related to problems covered in this chapter. The student should be made clearly aware of what the problems are and also of alternatives in their solution. He should also be helped to develop a sense of dedication, to attempt to improve his country by thinking through the problems, proposing solutions, and bringing about whatever change may be necessary to build a political structure that can face its problems adequately.

Use of Current History in the Schools

One of the problems of the schools is that of providing a background for understandings of current history. One of the improvements in recent years is the increased availability of materials in current trends written especially for use in our schools. Carefully edited and unbiased materials of this kind are now available at different maturity levels.[15] Writers of such materials usually expend greater effort to secure proper balance of material on both sides than do those of our ordinary newspapers and magazines. These materials should be used, particularly at the beginning of consideration of these problems. Emphases upon such current materials in the schools will certainly not eliminate the history, literature, and other courses already offered. In most cases these publications tie in with much of the current curricular materials and serve to enrich their study.

Current materials should not be limited to those specially prepared for the schools themselves. Otherwise the students would not get experience in evaluating the kind of materials they will read as adults. Examples in current magazines and newspapers of bias and propaganda techniques, such as are indicated earlier in this chapter, should be pointed out by the teacher and identified by the students.

Education or Discrimination and Critical Thinking

Very little has been said so far in this chapter concerning the educational values of those media that are primarily concerned with entertainment—

[15]Three of the most widely used sets of materials of this kind are published by the following companies: American Education Press, Civic Education Service, and Scholastic Magazines.

plays, movies, and so on. However, these do have an educational value. It is important that the school prepare people to appraise such media adequately. One of the jobs of a school is to broaden the student's taste and interests so that he will appreciate some of the things he has not previously met in his environment. Interest in such cultural matters as the legitimate stage, symphony, and ballet can be fostered by the school. The improvement of taste will insure that the students will choose more carefully the materials they read and the entertainments they enjoy. This is an important part of the problem of communication. A student or adult who reads little but comic books and "cheap" novels is losing a lot of the pleasure and satisfaction he should get out of life.

Another important thing, of course, is education for critical thinking. An aspect of this has already been covered in the discussion of propaganda analysis. The school should stress continuously the use of the scientific method of arriving at conclusions.

It is this problem of critical thinking that is the key to America's future. It has been referred to in Chapter 8 as a problem-solving approach to life. The difficulty lies in that professional educators do not know how to endow the youth of the nation with critical thinking. Problem solving as a learning technique has been advocated for some years. The theory is beautiful. If all graduates of our schools possessed a high degree of problem-solving ability and the attitude of using this rational approach to attack our social problems, the cultural lag between our technological inventions and our social inventions would be reduced rapidly. Unfortunately, we do not as yet understand the mental processes involved in the construction of relevant hypotheses— what some psychologists refer to as the "ah-hah" phenomenon. This step is the heart of the technique.

The basic schemeta of the technique of the scientific process have been developed by Thorndike, Francis Bacon, Dewey, and many others. The best statement has perhaps been made by Dewey.[16] A workable sequence of steps consolidated from several sources is as follows:

1. An awareness of the problem.
2. Clarification of the problem.
3. Definition of needed data—construction of a "search model."
4. Collection and organization of data.
5. Formulation of tentative hypotheses.
6. Logical testing of hypotheses.
7. Drawing of conclusions.
8. Testing of conclusions.
   a. Logically.
   b. Empirically.

The major difficulties involved in teaching critical thinking as a method of attack are the psychological (and emotional) nature of many of life's problems, the need for extensive experimental bases, and the lack of understanding of how to develop generalizing ability in students. Each difficulty will be briefly summarized.

[16]John Dewey, *How We Think* (Boston: Heath, 1937).

Critical thinking is a logical procedure, not a psychological one. We are creatures of reason only to a degree. Logical reasoning breaks down in pre-judicial areas, and those are the areas in which our major social problems lie. The propaganda techniques described in an earlier section of this chapter capitalize on that fact.

A broad base of experiences is necessary before one can become aware of a problem, clarify it, construct a search model, know where to seach for data, or scientifically test the conclusion. This does not mean that teaching for critical thinking should be deferred. It means, rather, that problems posed to students at all ages should be appropriate to their mental maturity and experiential background.

The ability to generalize is necessary for the construction of hypotheses (the "ah-hah" phenomenon) and their logical testing ("if-then" thinking). We do not fully understand how to teach for generalizing ability. We do know that it is limited by native intelligence. This psychological fact has been capitalized upon by those who attempt to discredit democracy and who plead for a government by the elite. We know from experience, however, that the average person has enough native ability to generalize on most of life's problems. Our dilemma, as professional educators, is that we know too little about how to capitalize on this native ability in teaching for generalization.

Some things we do know. We know that mere possession of all the data does not ensure intelligent decisions. We know, further, that the emotional attitude of consistently applying critical thinking to life's problems significantly increases the ratio of intelligent decisions. Pending further research into generalizing ability per se, the best available procedures for all teachers to follow are these:

1. Help the pupil become aware of the process (schema) he is using.
2. Provide the class with many problems appropriate to their mental maturity and experiential base.
3. Assist the class in applying the schema to the solution of their problems.
4. At the all-important step of formulating hypotheses, give many hints toward possible solutions. This has been proved to be our most effective technique in developing generalizing abilities.
5. Insist upon scientific testing of conclusions. It is at this point that most classroom teachers fail in the social subjects. Mathematics teachers insist that solutions be proved; social studies teachers tend to accept results of class discussions as final.

SUMMARY

We have indicated that our complex, industrialized modern life poses many problems that could not have been foreseen by our founding fathers. It pays tribute to their wisdom that our form of government, with minor revisions, has proved so nearly adequate to the solution of our modern problems.

The crux to the solution of these problems lies not in the basic structure of our government but in the wisdom of man. We have indicated the importance of our modern communications system in providing basic data.

We have delineated the destructive forces of bias, propaganda, and false interpretations. The tremendous increase in the impact of the media quantitatively has raised the possibility that man will lose contact with reality. The danger of this development to democracy and to individual freedom has been set forth. The final solution to these problems, however, rests upon the ability of the common man to utilize the basic data effectively and to recognize and combat the force of bias and propaganda. Educators bear a major responsibility to increase these abilities in the common man. We have referred to this complex of abilities as critical thinking.

In Chapter 14 we will set forth a possible list of basic values on which such thinking might be based. The degree of success with which educators can implant high ideals and skills of critical thinking in our youth will determine to what degree the social and governmental problems of America will be solved.

Selected Bibliography

Adler, Norman (ed.). *The Learning of Political Behavior.* Glenview, Ill.: Scott, Foresman and Company, 1970. 224 pp.

Agee, Warren K. (ed.). *Mass Media in a Free Society.* Kansas City: University Press of Kansas, 1969. 96 pp.

Ake, Claude. *A Theory of Political Integration.* Homewood, Ill.: Dorsey Press, 1967. 173 pp.

Ashley, Paul Pritchard. *Say It Safely: Legal Limits in Publishing, Radio and Television*, Fourth Edition. Seattle: University of Washington Press, 1969. 181 pp.

Bagdikian, Ben H. *The Information Machines.* New York: Harper & Row, Publishers, 1971. 359 pp.

Barkun, Michael (ed.). *Law and the Social System.* Chicago: Aldine-Atherton, 1972. 128 pp.

Bazelon, David T. *Power in America: The Politics of the New Class.* New York: New American Library, 1967. 407 pp.

Bendiner, Robert. *The Politics of Schools: A Crisis in Self-government.* New York: Harper & Row, Publishers, 1969. 240 pp.

Bennis, Warren G. (ed.). *American Bureaucracy.* Chicago: Aldine Publishing Company, 1970. 187 pp.

Boorstin, Daniel J. *The Decline of Radicalism: Reflections on America Today.* New York: Random House, Inc., 1969. 142 pp.

Bowers, C. A., Ian Housego, and Doris Dyke (eds.). *Education and Social Policy: Local Control of Education.* New York: Random House, Inc., 1970. 224 pp.

Braden, William. *The Age of Aquarius: Technology and the Cultural Revolution.* Chicago: Quadrangle Books, Inc., 1970. 306 pp.

Brickman, William W. "The Mass Media as Educators," *School and Society*, Vol. 98, No. 2323 (February 1969).

Brooks, Harvey. *The Government of Science.* Cambridge, Mass.: The M.I.T. Press, 1968. 343 pp.

Brucker, Herbert. "Can Printed News Save a Free Society?" *Saturday Review*, October 10, 1970.

Buckley, William F., Jr. (ed.). *Did You Ever See a Dream Walking?: American Conservative Thought in the Twentieth Century.* Indianapolis: The Bobbs-Merrill Company, Inc., 1970. 554 pp.

Burns, Haywood. "Race and Fair Trial," *Current*, No. 121 (September 1970).

Camien, Laiten Lester. *Education: The Process and Social Institution.* New York: Vantage, 1964. 165 pp.

Center for the Study of Democratic Institutions. *The Elite and the Electorate: Is Government by the People Possible?* Santa Barbara, Calif.: The Center and the Fund for the Republic, 1964. 22 pp.

_____. *The Mazes of Modern Government: The States, the Legislature, the Bureaucracy, the Courts.* Santa Barbara, Calif.: The Center and the Fund for the Republic, 1964. 38 pp.

Cleary, Robert E. *Political Education in the American Democracy.* Scranton, Pa.: Intext Educational Publishers, 1971. 185 pp.

Cohen, Carl. *Civil Disobedience: Conscience, Tactics, and the Law.* New York: Columbia University Press, 1971. 222 pp.

_____. "How Far Electronics Surveillance?" *Current,* No. 129 (May 1971).

Cone, Fairfax. "When Advertising Talks to Everyone," *Saturday Review,* October 10, 1970.

Coons, John E., et al. *Private Wealth and Public Education.* Cambridge, Mass.: Harvard University Press, 1970. 520 pp. Three lawyers expose the discrimination by wealth inherent in existing state systems of school finance. They propose a solution based on manipulation of state and local taxes and demonstrate that judicial intervention is the primary hope for change.

Cowen, Zelman, et al. *Fair Trial vs. a Free Press.* Santa Barbara, Calif.: The Center for the Study of Democratic Institutions, 1965. 37 pp.

de Crespigny, Anthony (ed.). *Contemporary Political Theory.* Chicago: Aldine Publishing Company, 1971. 320 pp.

Cumming, Elaine. *Systems of Social Regulation.* New York: Atherton Press, 1968. 324 pp.

Dewey, John. *How We Think.* Boston: D. C. Heath, 1933. 301 pp.

Domhoff, G. William. *Who Rules America?* Englewood Cliffs, N.J.: Prentice-Hall, Inc., 1967. 184 pp.

Douglas, Jack D. (ed.). *Freedom and Tyranny: Social Problems in a Technological Society.* New York: Alfred A. Knopf, Inc., 1970. 384 pp.

Dye, Thomas R. *Understanding Public Policy.* Englewood Cliffs, N.J.: Prentice-Hall, Inc., 1972. 400 pp.

Easton, David, and Jack Dennis. *Children in the Political System.* New York: McGraw-Hill Book Company, 1969. 440 pp.

The Economist (London). "Will There Be Less Violence?" *Current,* No. 115 (February 1970).

Ellul, Jacques. *The Political Illusion.* New York: Alfred A. Knopf, Inc., 1967. 258 pp.

Engel, A. S. "A Case Against Censorship," *Current* (November 1970).

Ernst, Morris L., and Alan U. Schwartz. *Censorship: The Search for the Obscene.* New York: The Macmillan Company, 1964. 288 pp.

Estrin, Herman A., and Arthur M. Sanderson (eds.). *Freedom and Censorship of the College Press.* Dubuqe: William C. Brown Company, 1966. 310 pp.

Etzioni, Amitai. *The Active Society.* New York: The Free Press, 1968. 698 pp.

Fellman, David (ed.). *The Supreme Court and Education.* New York: Teachers College Press, 1969. 229 pp.

Final Report of the National Commission on the Causes and Prevention of Violence. *To Establish Justice, to Insure Domestic Tranquility.* New York: Bantam Books, Inc., 1970. 277 pp.

Ford Foundation and the Danforth Foundation (eds.). *The School and the Democratic Environment.* New York: Columbia University Press, 1970. 115 pp.

Forester, Arnold, and Benjamin R. Epstein. *Danger on the Right.* New York: Random House, Inc., 1964. 204 pp. The attitudes, personnel, and influence of the radical right.

Fried, Morton H. *The Evolution of Political Society*. New York: Random House, Inc., 1967. 242 pp.

Friendly, Fred W. "Asleep at the Switch of the Wired City," *Saturday Review*, October 10, 1970.

_____. "Today's Short Supply of Air Time," *Current*, No. 124 (December 1970).

Gans, Herbert J. *The Levittowners: Ways of Life and Politics in a New Suburban Community*. New York: Pantheon Books, Inc., 1967. 474 pp.

Gardner, John W. *The Recovery of Confidence*. New York: W. W. Norton & Company, Inc., 1970. 189 pp.

Gattegno, Caleb. *Towards a Visual Culture: Educating Through Television*. New York: Outerbridge and Dienstfrey, 1969. 117 pp.

Gerlack, Vernon S., and Donald P. Ely. *Teaching and Media: A Systematic Approach*. Englewood Cliffs, N.J.: Prentice-Hall, Inc., 1971. 480 pp.

Geyelin, Philip L., and Douglas Cater. *American Media: Adequate or Not?* Washington, D.C.: American Enterprise Institute, 1970. 104 pp.

Golan, Tamar. *Educating the Bureaucracy in a New Polity*. New York: Teachers College Press, 1968. 78 pp.

Gore, Albert. *The Eye of the Storm: A People's Politics for the Seventies*. New York: Herder and Herder, 1970. 212 pp.

Greene, Theodore P. *America's Heroes: The Changing Models of Success in American Magazines*. New York: Oxford University Press, 1970. 387 pp.

Greenstein, Fred I. *Personality and Politics: Problems of Evidence, Inference and Conceptualization*. Chicago: Markham, 1969. 200 pp.

Grier, William H., and Price M. Cobbs. *The Politics of Protest*. New York: Ballantine Books, Inc., 1969. 419 pp.

Hardin, Oscar, and Mary Handlin. *The Dimension of Liberty*. Cambridge, Mass.: Harvard University Press, 1961. 264 pp.

Harris, Richard. *Justice: The Crisis of Law, Order and Freedom in America*. New York: E. P. Dutton & Co., Inc., 1970. 268 pp.

Hayes, Dennis. "Can We Bust the Highway Trust?" *Saturday Review*, June 5, 1971.

Hazlitt, Henry. *Man vs. the Welfare State*. New Rochelle, N.Y.: Arlington House, 1969. 225 pp.

Hersch, Jeanne. *Birthright of Man: A Selection of Texts Prepared Under the Direction of Jeanne Hersch*. New York: UNESCO, 1969. 591 pp.

Hodgkinson, Harold L., and L. Richard Meeth (eds.). *Power and Authority*. San Francisco: Jossey-Bass, 1970. 215 pp.

Hohenberg, John. *Free Press/Free People: The Best Cause*. New York: Columbia University Press, 1971. 325 pp.

Holloran, Richard. "What Curbs on Government Surveillance?" *Current*, No. 129 (May 1971).

"The Invasion of Privacy," *The Saturday Review* (April 17, 1971), Special section. Articles by Ralph Nader, "The Dossier Invades the Home," pp. 18–21, 58–59; Peter Schrag, "Dossier Dictatorship," pp. 24–25; Ramsey Clark, "Demeaning Human Dignity," pp. 29–32.

Johnson, Nicholas. "What Can We Do About Television," *Saturday Review*, July 11, 1970.

Katope, Christopher, and Paul Zelbrod. *The Rhetoric of Revolution*. New York: The Macmillan Company, 1970. 553 pp.

Kennedy, Thomas. "Should We Abolish All Strikes?" *Current*, No. 121 (September 1970).

Kirst, Michael W. (ed.). *The Politics of Education at the Local, State and Federal Levels*. Berkeley, Calif.: McCutchan, 1970. 406 pp.

Klein, Alexander. "Toward Participatory Citizenship," *Current*, No. 121 (September 1970).

Knopf, T. A. "Race and the Press," *Current*, No. 121 (September 1970).

Knowles, Laurence W. "Student Rights Find a Friend in Court(s)," *The Education Digest,* Vol. XXXVI, No. 9 (May 1971).

Kuh, Richard H. *Foolish Figleaves? Pornography In and Out of Court.* New York: The Macmillan Company, 1967. 368 pp.

Lachman, Seymour P., and David Bresnick. "An Educational Ombudsman for New York City?" *School and Society,* Vol. 99, No. 2332 (March 1971).

Laing, R. D. *The Politics of Experience.* New York: Pantheon Books, Inc., 1967. 138 pp.

Lamont, Corliss. *Freedom of Choice Affirmed.* New York: Horizon Press, 1967. 214 pp.

Lane, Robert E. *Political Thinking and Consciousness.* Chicago: Markham, 1969. 375 pp.

Lang, Kurt, and Gladys Engel Lang. *Voting and Non-Voting: Implications of Broadcasting Returns Before Polls Are Closed.* Waltham, Mass.: Blaisdell Publishing Co., 1968. 172 pp.

Lindenfeld, Frank (ed.). *Reader in Political Sociology.* New York: Funk & Wagnalls Company, Inc., 1968. 622 pp.

Linton, Thomas E., and Jack L. Nelson. *Patterns of Power: Some Foundations of Education.* New York: Pitman Publishing Corp., 1967. 602 pp.

Lipset, Seymour Martin. *Politics and the Social Sciences.* New York: Oxford University Press, 1969. 328 pp.

＿＿＿, and Earl Raab. *The Politics of Unreason: Right Wing Extremism in America, 1790–1970.* New York: Harper & Row, Publishers, 1970. 547 pp.

MacIver, Robert M. *Politics and Society.* New York: Atherton Press, 1969. 571 pp.

MacNeil, Neil. *Forge of Democracy: The House of Representatives.* New York: David McKay Company, 1963. 496 pp.

Malik, Rex. "The Databank Society: Can We Cope?" *Current,* No. 129 (May 1971).

Markman, Sherwin. *The Election.* New York: Random House, Inc., 1970. 208 pp.

Martin, Warren Bryan. *Conformity: Standards and Change in Higher Education.* San Francisco: Jossey-Bass, 1969. 264 pp.

Martindale, Don, and R. Galen Hanson. *Small Town and the Nation: The Conflict of Local and Translocal Forces.* Westport, Conn.: Greenwood, 1969. 211 pp.

Massialas, Byron G. *Education and the Political System.* Reading, Mass.: Addison-Wesley, 1969. 219 pp.

Mayntz, Renate (ed.). *Theodore Geiger on Social Order and Mass Society: Selected Papers.* Chicago: University of Chicago Press, 1969. 242 pp.

McClellan, Grant S. (ed.). *Censorship in the United States.* New York: H. H. Wilson Company, 1967. 222 pp.

McDonald, Donald, with William H. Parker, Chief of Police of Los Angeles. *The Police.* Santa Barbara, Calif.: The Center and the Fund for the Republic, 1962. 30 pp. One of a series of interviews on the American character.

McGinniss, Joe. *The Selling of the President, 1968.* New York: Trident Press, 1969. 253 pp.

McIntosh, Donald. *The Foundations of Human Society.* Chicago: University of Chicago Press, 1969. 341 pp.

McKinnon, Frank. *The Politics of Education: A Study of the Political Administration of the Public Schools.* Toronto: University of Toronto Press, 1960. 187 pp.

McLuhan, Marshall. *Counterblast.* New York: Harcourt Brace Jovanovich, Inc., 1969. 143 pp.

＿＿＿. *The Gutenberg Galaxy.* New York: The New American Library, 1969. 350 pp.

＿＿＿, and Quentin Fiore. *The Medium Is the Massage.* New York: Bantam Books, Inc., 1967. 157 pp.

＿＿＿. *War and Peace in the Global Village.* New York: McGraw-Hill Book Company, 1968. 190 pp.

McLuhan, Marshall, and Wilfred Watson. *From Cliche to Archetype.* New York: The Viking Press, Inc., 1970. 213 pp.

Meehan, Eugene J. *The Foundations of Political Analysis: Empirical and Normative.* Homewood, Ill.: Dorsey Press, 1971. 275 pp.

Melman, Seymour. *The Political Economy of War*. New York: McGraw-Hill Book Company, 1970. 290 pp.

Meranto, Philip. *School Politics in the Metropolis*. Columbus, Ohio: Charles E. Merrill Publishing Company, 1970. 176 pp.

Mickelson, Sig. "The First Eight Years," *Saturday Review*, October 24, 1970. Deals with mass communication since Telstar.

Miller, Arthur R. *The Assault on Privacy: Computers, Data Banks and Dossiers*. Ann Arbor: University of Michigan Press, 1971. 333 pp.

Miller, Clyde R. *How to Detect and Analyze Propaganda*. New York: The Town Hall, 1939. 36 pp.

Millett, Kate. *Sexual Politics*. New York: Doubleday & Company, Inc., 1970. 395 pp.

Mills, C. Wright. *Power, Politics, and People*. New York: Oxford University Press, 1967. 657 pp.

Minor, Dale. *The Information War*. New York: Hawthorn Books, Inc., 1970. 212 pp.

Montagu, Ashley. *The Anatomy of Swearing*. New York: The Macmillan Company, 1967. 370 pp.

Morse, Dean, and Aaron W. Warner (eds.). *Technological Innovation and Society*. New York: Columbia University Press, 1966. 214 pp.

Mumford, Lewis. *The Myth of the Machine, Vol. II: The Pentagon of Power*. New York: Harcourt Brace Jovanovich, Inc., 1970. 496 pp.

Nelson, Jack, and Gene Roberts, Jr. *The Censors and the Schools*. Boston: Little, Brown and Company, 1963. 208 pp.

Nieburg, H. L. *Political Violence: The Behavioral Process*. New York: St. Martin's Press, 1969. 184 pp.

Nisbet, Robert A. *The Social Bond: An Introduction to the Study of Society*. New York: Alfred A. Knopf, Inc., 1970. 448 pp.

Ozmon, Howard (ed.). *Contemporary Critics of Education*. Danville, Ill.: Interstate Printers and Publishers, Inc., 1970. 223 pp.

Packard, Vance. *The Hidden Persuaders*. New York: David McKay Co., Inc., 1957. 275 pp.

Parsons, Talcott. *Politics and Social Structure*. New York: The Free Press, 1969. 557 pp.

Pearson, Drew, and Jack Anderson. *The Case Against Congress*. New York: Pocket Books, 1969. 464 pp.

Perrin, Noel. *Dr. Bowdler's Legacy: A History of Expurgated Books in England and America*. New York: Atheneum Publishers, 1969. 296 pp.

Postman, Neil, and Charles Weingartner. *Teaching as a Subversive Activity*. New York: The Delacorte Press, 1969. 219 pp.

Quade, Quentin L., and Thomas J. Bennett. "Coping with Bureaucracy," *Current*, No. 57 (March 1967).

Rae, Douglas W., and Michael J. Taylor. *The Analysis of Political Cleavages*. New Haven: Yale University Press, 1970. 152 pp.

Randall, Richard. *Censorship of the Movies: The Social and Political Control of a Mass Medium*. Madison: University of Wisconsin Press, 1968. 280 pp.

Rembar, Charles. *The End of Obscenity: The Trials of Lady Chatterley, Tropic of Cancer and Fanny Hill*. New York: Random House, Inc., 1968. 528 pp.

The Report of the Commission on Obscenity and Pornography. New York: Bantam Books, 1970. 700 pp.

Report of a Conference sponsored by the Danforth and Ford Foundations. *The School and the Democratic Environment*. New York: Columbia University Press, 1970. 115 pp.

Rogers, David. *110 Livingston Street: Politics and Bureaucracy in the New York City Schools*. New York: Random House, Inc., 1968. 584 pp.

Rose, Arnold M. *Libel and Academic Freedom: A Lawsuit Against Political Extremists*. Minneapolis: University of Minnesota Press, 1968. 287 pp.

Rosenberg, Jerry. *The Death of Privacy.* New York: Random House, Inc., 1969. 236 pp. Deals with the threat of data banks to individual rights.

Rossi, Peter H., and Bruce J. Riddle. *The New Media and Education: Their Impact on Society.* Garden City, N.Y.: Doubleday & Company, Inc., 1966. 460 pp.

Rubenstein, Richard E. *Mass Political Violence in the United States.* Boston: Little, Brown and Company, 1970. 201 pp.

_____. *Rebels in Eden: Mass Political Violence in the United States.* Boston: Little, Brown and Company, 1970. 201 pp.

Sagarin, Edward. *The Anatomy of Dirty Words.* New York: Lyle Stuart, 1968. 220 pp.

Salisbury, Harrison E. *The Many Americas Shall Be One.* New York: W. W. Norton & Company, Inc., 1971. 204 pp.

Schaller, Lyle E. *The Impact of the Future.* Nashville, Tenn.: Abingdon Press, 1969. 246 pp.

Schiller, Herbert I. *Mass Communications and American Empire.* New York: August M. Kelley, 1969. 170 pp.

Schramm, Wilbur (ed.). *Mass Communications.* Urbana: University of Illinois Press, 1969. 695 pp.

Schur, Edwin M. *Law and Society: A Sociological View.* New York: Random House, Inc., 1968. 239 pp.

Segal, Ronald. *The Americans: A Conflict of Creed and Reality.* New York: The Viking Press, 1969. 340 pp.

Shell, Kurt L. (ed.). *The Democratic Political Process: A Cross-National Reader.* Waltham, Mass.: Blaisdell Publishing Company, 1969. 509 pp.

Sierra Club. *Ecostactics: The Sierra Club Handbook for Environmental Activities.* New York: Pocket Books, 1970. 288 pp.

Spinard, William. *Civil Liberties.* Chicago: Quadrangle Books, 1970. 355 pp.

Stambler, Sookie (ed.). *Women's Liberation: Blueprint for the Future.* New York: Ace Books, 1970. 283 pp.

Stearn, Gerald Emanuel (ed.). *McLuhan Hot and Cool: A Primer for the Understanding and a Critical Symposium with a Rebuttal by McLuhan.* New York: New American Library, 1967. 304 pp.

Stretton, Hugh. *The Political Sciences: General Principles of Selection in Social Science and History.* New York: Basic Books, Inc., Publishers, 1969. 453 pp.

Talese, Gay. *The Kingdom and the Power: Story of the New York Times.* New York: The World Publishing Company, 1969. 555 pp. The story of the men who influence the institution that influences the world.

Tebbel, John. *The American Magazine: A Compact History.* New York: Hawthorn Books, Inc., 1969. 279 pp.

_____. "The Miniaturization of the Book," *Current,* No. 126 (February 1971). Indicates possibilities of storage and retrieval of books (printed information) easily and reasonably.

Tobin, Richard L. "The Coming Age of News Monopoly," *Saturday Review,* October 10, 1970.

_____. "Publishing by Cathode Ray Tube," *Saturday Review,* October 10, 1970.

_____. "When Officials Shackle the News," *Saturday Review,* December 12, 1970.

Tocqueville, Alexis de. *Democracy in America.* New York: Alfred A. Knopf, Inc., 1945. Vol. 1, 434 pp. Vol. 2, 401 pp. A well-printed, intelligently edited new edition of the "greatest study of one country by a citizen of another," one of the earliest works to sense the critical implications of the American experiment in self-government.

Triezenberg, George. "How to Live with Due Process," *The Education Digest,* Vol. XXXVI, No. 9 (May 1971).

Turnstall, Jeremy (ed.). *Media Sociology: A Reader.* Urbana: University of Illinois Press, 1970. 574 pp.

Usdan, Michael D., David W. Minar, and Emanuel Hurwitz, Jr. *Education and State Politics: The Developing Relationship Between Elementary-Secondary and Higher Education*. New York: Teachers College Press, Columbia University, 1969. 190 pp.

Watts, Alan. *The Book: On the Taboo Against Knowing Who You Are*. New York: Pantheon Books, Inc., 1966. 146 pp.

Wheeler, Harvey. "The Politics of Ecology," *Saturday Review*, March 7, 1970.

Wilhelmsen, Frederick D., and Jane Bret. *The War in Man: Media and Machines*. Athens: University of Georgia Press, 1970. 122 pp.

Yu, Frederick T. C. (ed.). *Behavioral Sciences and the Mass Media: A Report of an Arden House Conference Jointly Sponsored by Russell Sage Foundation and the Graduate School of Journalism, Columbia University*. New York: Russell Sage Foundation, 1968. 270 pp.

Zinn, Howard. *The Politics of History*. Boston: Beacon Press, 1970. 390 pp.

Zunderveld, Anton C. *The Abstract Society: A Cultural Analysis of Our Time*. Garden City, N.Y.: Doubleday & Company, Inc., 1970. 216 pp.

Selected Films

Allo! Hallo! Alo! (McGraw-Hill), 9 min. An animated film that shows the history of communications from tom-toms to satellites.

Community Governments: How They Function (Coronet), 14 min. This film looks into the advantages and disadvantages of the mayor–council and other forms of government. It focuses on the participation of the people and the general interest in local problems on their part.

Crisis in the Classroom (ICF), 15 min. How can today's students be motivated to take an active and positive role in the process of education? How much authority should a teacher have in the classroom? What part should students play?

Decision at Laurel Falls (Pennsylvania Department of Internal Affairs), 28 min. Demonstrates that good government is the result of a vital and continuing partnership between the elected and the elector.

Due Process of Law Denied (Teaching Film Custodians), 20 min. Excerpted from the feature-length motion picture, *Ox-Bow Incident*.

Freedom to Read (Columbia University), 15 min. How a library can best serve freedom. Stresses the place of competing philosophies in a democratic society.

Great Lessons in American Politics: The State and the Nation (McGraw-Hill and Omnibus), 25 min.

How to Judge Facts (Coronet), 10 min. How to separate facts from assumptions and faulty reasoning. Using a case study of a false story, the film points out the common errors of reasoning. Helps to be on guard against assumptions, false analogies, irrelevant facts, and words with double meanings.

More Than Words, 14 min. Animated outline of basic principles and methods of communication. The film can be applied to any activity where dealing with people plays a key role.

Polling the Public (EBF), 30 min. This film is an analysis of the uses and methods used in polling public opinion. It conveys the message that it is the duty of every American to keep an interest in and to express an opinion about national issues.

Pressure Groups (EBF), 20 min. Explains what pressure groups are and reveals that, when democratically used, they are a necessary instrument for decision making in a democracy. Illustrates methods used by a representative democratic pressure group to bring about legislation for a desirable civic project. Contrasts these methods with the underhanded and behind-the-scenes manipulation employed by a group attempting to prevent the passage of a bill.

Propaganda Techniques (Coronet), 10 min.

Public Opinion (EBF), 10 min. Sets up criteria by which public opinion may be judged and measured, illustrating through an example of the development of public opinion that produced a waterworks project in a small community. An enlightened public opinion must have access to the facts; press and radio must be balanced in their presentation of the facts; competent witnesses or experts are needed; and the public must overcome prejudice and think objectively. In short, an analysis of public opinion—what is is, how it is formed, and what it can accomplish.

Public Opinion in Our Democracy (Coronet), 11 min. This motion picture explains clearly the importance of public opinion and shows how it is formed and determined on a significant community issue. Students will learn from it the importance of their opinions and the obligations they have to express their opinions in terms of responsible action.

The Social Animal (Encyclopaedia Britannica), 29 min. Investigates some of the ways in which man is influenced and changed by society. Studies group pressures to conform and shows the consequences of publicly stating ideas contrary to one's private belief. From the Focus on Behavior series.

United States Elections: How We Vote (Film Associates), 14 min. Shows process by which citizens vote—registration, voting machines, ballots, and so on.

Chapter 13

■■■■■■■■■■■■■■■□□□

Problems of the United States in an Interdependent World

Sufficient documentation is found in the previous chapters to establish thoroughly that we do live in an interdependent world. The typical "100 per cent American" each day utilizes ideas and material products that have been incorporated into the American culture from sources all over the world; in some cases, the products are imported in the final manufactured or refined form. This interdependent nature of the world, however, does not automatically lead to increasing understanding and cooperation. The realities of the present world center around the nation-states that evolved in the late medieval period. Man's loyalties, once centered within the tribe and later in his religion, are now focused rather definitely upon the nation-state. By and large, now it is only treason to one's nation, not to one's religion, that is punishable by death. Those who wish to help work toward an improvement in the solution of problems in the world must take into account this all-important fact of *nationalism* as a force in the present-day world.

Theoretically, nation-states are sovereign; that is, there is no power that can dictate to them what they should do. This means that, theoretically, we live in a state of international anarchy. Actually, it is only a state of relative anarchy, ameliorated by voluntary international agreements regulating such major matters as communications, transportation, commerce, tourist and commercial travel, and the rules of war. Departments of foreign affairs of each nation facilitate and regulate these international agreements through elaborate diplomatic protocol, including foreign embassy and consular posts. As individuals, we have long since realized that one's freedom and rights must end at the point where they conflict with the common concerns of the group. This principle is generally recognized among the free nations, but it can operate only on the basis of an agreed-upon cooperation. There is little disposition at present to solve international problems through an all-encompassing group, such as a world government, that would define the areas of freedom and responsibilities for each of the nations. It is within a framework of a group of nation-states, still free and independent, and not in the area of a possible immediate world government, that we apparently must explore the problems of the interdependent world.

The dominant fact in the field of international relations in the immediate post-World War II period was the bipolarization of world power. One section of the world, under the hegemony or domination of the Soviet Union (Russia) has been opposed by another, under the somewhat reluctant leadership of America. By and large, this bipolarization of power represented a totalitarian group of countries with almost completely socialized economics and little internal freedom opposed by a group of free nations with a variety of economies and a variety of conditions of internal freedom. The second group has been composed mainly of democratic nations. This interpretation is now far too simple.

Mainland China has asserted her independence, defiance, and hostility toward both the United States and the U.S.S.R. Japan and the two Germanies are emerging as large industrial powers and thus potential political and military powers.

In the sections to follow, we shall first analyze some of the potential and actual problem areas and summarize important developments on the world scene. Then we shall look at the major conflicts for example, the "Communist" world versus the United States for leadership of the world and a developing "third world" attempting to avoid dependence on either. Finally, we shall point out some educational implications.

SOURCES OF STRESS BETWEEN NATIONS

An analysis of the problems that cause difficulty among nations is necessary to determine ways in which these groups can work together and set up machinery for resolving their conflicts in some positive way.

Wide Range of Ideologies in the World

There is a wide range of cultural patterns within the American scene, and a much wider range of cultural patterns throughout the world. Many examples may be cited—the attitudes toward the sacred cow in India, toward polygamous marriage in Africa, toward "Western-style" progress in many countries. This wide range of ideologies poses a challenge as to how to enable the differing groups to get along together. Just as it is necessary for those of us in the United States to study and understand persons within the American democratic framework who are different from ourselves, so it is necessary for world understanding to study the cultural backgrounds of other persons in the world.

Population Variability

There are extreme differences in the number of people living upon the land in various areas because of the differences in the ability of the soil and its accompanying resources to support a population. There are also differences in the number of persons on the different lands that have the

same potential for supporting a population. This is due to the technological stage at which the people find themselves or to the slowness of
population growth in some lands that have been newly discovered.

The average population per square mile of the world at present is
approximately 50 persons. It ranges from about 3 per square mile in semi-
arid areas or in tropical forest areas, through over 40 in the central part of
the United States and in Russia, to 180 in the northeastern part of the
United States, 310 in western Central Europe, 410 in India and Ceylon,
and up to 500 in Korea and Japan.

Variability of Resources, Utilized and Unutilized

There is also tremendous variability in the amounts of the natural
resources existing in different places on the earth's surface. The fertility
of the land, the extent of forest, the amounts and kinds of minerals and
oil, and the coal and water-power resources vary greatly. The most important economic differential among nations, however, seems to be the
state of technology. For example, Great Britain has a high level of prosperity but has low potential in forest and water power and in petroleum
and natural gas. At the same time, such places as the highlands of eastern
Africa, where a low level of living exists, have great potential in terms of
water power, minerals, and soil.

It can help to visualize the present world situation if we can consider,
as an illustration, the present population, consisting of around 3.4 billion,
to be compressed into a single town of 1,000 people.[1] In this imaginary
town, sixty persons would represent the Americans in the town, whereas 940
would represent all the other countries. These sixty Americans would receive
one half of the total income of the town, whereas the remaining 940
persons would share the other half.

Just 300 of the total population would be Christians, leaving the remaining 700 for all the other beliefs. The next largest would be Moslems,
numbering approximately 150. Approximately eighty of the town's population would actually be card-carrying Communists. Three-hundred seventy of
the town's population would be in countries which are Communist dominated. Less than 300 of the town's population would be white or Caucasian,
whereas more than 700 would be nonwhite.

The sixty Americans would have a life expectancy of slightly over
seventy years. The life expectancy of all others would average below forty
years. The Americans would produce about one sixth (16⅔ per cent) of the
town's food. Most of the 940 others would be hungry most of the time. The
Americans would use 15 per cent of the food supply and would store the
remainder.

Each of the sixty Americans would have twelve times as much electricity,
twenty-two times as much coal, twenty-one times as much oil, fifty times as
much steel, and fifty times as much general manufactured equipment as each
of the 940 remaining in the town.

---

[1]These comparisons have been developed from recent figures that can be found widely
scattered throughout the literature. They have been quoted many times in the public press
and in magazine articles.

The *lowest* income group of Americans would be better off than the *average* of the other 940.

EARLIER EFFORTS TOWARD WORLD ASSOCIATION AND COOPERATION

Ever since early times there have been conflict and warfare when men of different groups have come in contact, but there has also been cooperation on the basis of mutual advantage, usually through trade, which has helped bring about the diffusion of culture. In the recent years, with the development of the nation-states, mankind has attempted to set up a system of diplomacy to enable the peoples of the world to get along with each other. However, the world has been subjected to a series of wars, which have been growing in their intensity. There has apparently been no direct relationship between the enlightenment of the nations in respect to education, religion, or other such cultural advancement and their ability to get along without resort to war. Consequently, man from time to time has sought to develop better methods of world association and cooperation through direct diplomacy. After the devastating World War I, an attempt was made to work out such an association in the League of Nations. There were several reasons why the League of Nations did not prove to be successful. One was that several of the powerful nations, including the United States, did not join it. Another was weakness of the structure of the League of Nations, arising as a result of the power conflict following World War I and from its consequent close tie-in with the Versailles Treaty, which was an outgrowth of the animosities of World War I. In the midst of World War II the United States, with its allies, attempted to work out a system of world cooperation in the United Nations. This is not a world government but is an attempt to set up a systematic method of world consultation and joint action based upon a rational way of solving the problems that the nations face.

THE UNITED NATIONS

The present United Nations organization started as a development among those nations that were associated in the fight against the Axis powers. In San Francisco on July 26, 1945, these nations adopted the United Nations Charter. This was later ratified by the respective governments of the countries concerned. Nearly 130 nations are members of the United Nations at this writing.

Structure

Basically, the United Nations consists of the Security Council composed of eleven representatives of which five are permanent—namely China,[2] France, the U.S.S.R., the United Kingdom (Great Britain), and the United

[2]This seat had been filled by so-called Nationalist China, the exiled government of Chiang Kai-shek on the island of Taiwan, until 1971 when the People's Republic of China (mainland China) was admitted to the U.N. and took the seat on the Security Council.

States—and the General Assembly, composed of the delegations from each member nation, each with one vote. Closely associated with the United Nations is the International Court of Justice, which was in existence prior to the United Nations but has now become an integral part of it. (See Figure 28.)

The idea behind the Security Council was that the major nations would agree on cooperative efforts to prevent war. The five permanent members have a veto power over any actions of the Security Council. This was deemed necessary, because the actions of the Security Council amounted to a commitment of the nations concerned to take military action if necessary. Neither the United States nor the U.S.S.R. would have joined without it. However, this power has been one of the stumbling blocks in the way of decisive action in the Security Council. The U.S.S.R. has used its veto in a number of issues, thus blocking some of the important actions of the Council. This problem was partially alleviated after the Korean episode by a provision whereby the General Assembly can be called into action very quickly in case of a crisis to take action on any matter on which the Security Council may be deadlocked. This has tended to reduce somewhat the importance of the Security Council.

Under the General Assembly there are three main groups: the Trusteeship Council, the Economic and Social Council, and the Secretariat (the permanent staff).

Under the Economic and Social Council there are many other commissions as well as certain specialized agencies that have a link with the United Nations but that actually are separate groups. Nations belonging to the United Nations may or may not belong to a specialized agency, and nations not belonging to the United Nations may affiliate with the specialized agencies. Some of these agencies will be discussed in a later section.

Successes and Failures

Since the United Nations was formed it has undertaken numerous problems. Many of these have been handled quite successfully. However, these have not made the headlines as often as the basic conflict largely outside the United Nations between the U.S.S.R. and the People's Republic of China on the one hand and the United States on the other. Numerous clashes that might have led to war in Syria, Lebanon, Iran, Indonesia, Greece, Palestine, Kashmir, and elsewhere, all were given careful attention by United Nations staff members, and in many cases satisfactory solutions were worked out.

The crucial conflict in Korea, of course, developed into a small-size war and entailed considerable loss of life. This issue has not yet been decided, and it constitutes one of the failures of the United Nations to discover a peaceable method for the solution of international conflicts. Moreover, the Arab–Israeli situation has not yet been ameliorated. The United Nations failed again on the matter of the control of atomic energy and weapons, because of the basic opposition of Russia to an inspection system.

In areas other than military, the United Nations has done a good job

THE UNITED NATIONS

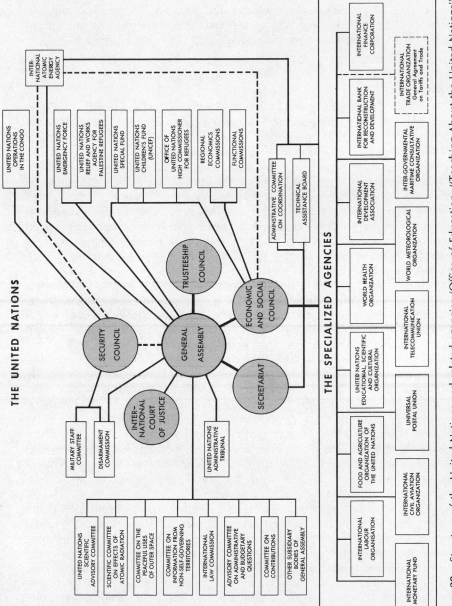

Figure 28. Structure of the United Nations and related agencies (Office of Education, "Teaching About the United Nations").

465

in sponsoring technical aid (including medical aid) to various "have-not" countries. The Commission on Human Rights has drafted the Universal Declaration of Human Rights, which was adopted in the Assembly on December 10, 1948. Many of the specialized agencies of the United Nations to be discussed later have also been quite successful in their programs.

Weaknesses

The weaknesses of the United Nations can be appraised from two viewpoints. One of these is held by those who desire a much stronger international structure bordering on, or going over completely to, a form of world government. The United Nations is not at present a world government. It has very little power unless its actions are backed by the moral and military forces of the nations that make it up. On the other hand, criticism also comes from those persons who think that participation in the United Nations constitutes an unwarranted weakening of the freedom of action of the individual nations concerned. These people are prone to "point with alarm" at such things as the Declaration of Human Rights, claiming that they abridge some of the rights of each nation to determine such matters internally.

Careful study of the United Nations does uncover certain basic weaknesses, which stem from inherent weaknesses of structure, on the one hand, and from public opinions and attitudes, on the other. Both types of weaknesses are difficult to remedy. The veto power of the five major nations constitutes a definite weakness that can stymie action. The inability of the United Nations to enforce its decisions because it lacks a sufficient permanent military force also causes it to be weak. Another basic weakness lies in the fact that the United Nations is not wholeheartedly supported by the peoples of the world. Its successes and failures in the future will certainly be measured in terms of the support that it has from the peoples of the earth in demanding that their governmental representatives act in accordance with the welfare of the globe as a whole. The world is apparently not yet ready for world government. We still live in a real world of independent nation-states. People still feel their security is dependent on their own nation-states and not on a world organization.

The crucial problem, of course, is not whether world government is imminent but whether world destruction impends. A nuclear war could destroy modern civilization. The after-effects of such a war, including "fallout" of atomic dust on the areas of human habitation, could destroy the human race. Human energies must be directed in massive proportions toward peaceful coexistence between the non-Communist and the Communist world. A legitimate part of this effort is the tremendous expenditure for nuclear and other devices for military preparedness, and for the exploration of the military potential of space. Much greater efforts must be expended, however, toward economic and diplomatic means of maintaining and stabilizing the present uneasy peace. The present structure of the UN provides only a limited avenue for the accomplishment of permanent peace. Upon the efforts of the independent nation-states, such as the United States, depends the question of peace or war, and possible extermination.

UNESCO

A section is devoted to a discussion of UNESCO because it is the organization affiliated with the UN that is most closely related to education. The letters stand for the United Nations Educational, Scientific, and Cultural Organization. The purpose of UNESCO "is to contribute to peace and security by promoting collaboration among the nations through education, science, and culture in order to further universal respect for justice, for the rule of law, and for human rights and fundamental freedoms which are affirmed for the people of the world, without distinction of race, sex, language, or religion, by the charter of the United Nations."

Thirty-one nations made up the original list of members (now over 100) in this organization. It has a regular secretariat, which has been located in Paris. Most of its work is related to such things as the improvement of educational facilities, the promotion of international educational understanding, and the fight against illiteracy. It also promotes international scientific cooperation and the exchange of cultural activities in the various arts. It tries to assist in the free flow of information between the various member countries, particularly information that will be of help to the less advanced countries. UNESCO provides experts for technical assistance in various areas.

The United States became an original member of UNESCO by an overwhelming majority of the House of Representatives and by unanimous action of the Senate. The United States (as have other of the nations represented) has developed a national commission, which prepares policies that its representatives carry out in the general conferences of UNESCO. Important elements in our society, such as the Federal Council of Churches, Catholic and Jewish organizations, labor organizations, all have representatives appointed to the commission of UNESCO.

In the United States, UNESCO has proved to be the most controversial of all the agencies of the United Nations. Some school systems have prohibited the use of UNESCO materials. Prominent organizations in the United States have been vigorous in their condemnation of this agency. They have accused it of being Communist and atheist and of promoting the ideals of world government as opposed to nationalism. In the 1950's a committee of the American Legion, including two former Legion presidents, made a careful study and declared that UNESCO was neither Communist and atheist nor in favor of world government; the committee recommended that the American Legion support UNESCO wholeheartedly. The American Legion in convention refused to accept the recommendation of its committee and went on record again as condemning it. It did, however, approve the United Nations.

Many important groups in the United States, including both political parties, have repeatedly endorsed the aims of UNESCO. Many school systems are utilizing its materials in the same fashion that other materials are utilized in the school curriculum.

Other UN Agencies

In addition to UNESCO, there are other specialized agencies that have done important work in developing international relations:

1. International Labor Organization (ILO). This is an organization with a delegation from each of the countries, composed of two members representing the government and one each representing management and labor. This agency works on such problems as labor conditions in the various countries of the world.
2. Food and Agricultural Organization of the United Nations (FAO). This agency deals with basic food problems of the countries. It collects information and distributes it in relation to developing better facilities for the production of food.
3. International Civil Aviation Organization (ICAO). This takes care of all matters related to nonmilitary aviation arrangements between the various countries.
4. International Bank for Reconstruction and Development (BANK). This agency helps to facilitate the interchange of credit facilities among the various countries.
5. International Monetary Fund (FUND). This is a fund to facilitate the exchange of currencies between the various countries.
6. World Health Organization (WHO). This is an organization concerned with distributing information and technical assistance in regard to health matters in the various countries of the world.
7. Universal Postal Union (UPUN). The early machinery of this organization existed long before the United Nations. The Universal Postal Convention, which has been in effect for a great many years, is now organized through the Universal Postal Union. Practically all the countries of the world are members of this organization.
8. International Telecommunication Union (ITU). This is an organization that correlates problems related to telegraph and radiotelegraph.
9. World Meteorological Organization (WMO). This organization correlates weather information.

There are other organizations that were in existence but that have now ceased to operate, as well as some that are not yet in existence but that are planned.

THE WORLD IN BLOCS

Political life within a free country is usually organized into various political parties. This is to be expected in a country where there is freedom for opinion. People do not agree, and, not agreeing, they tend to organize in groups. In the case of the nations making up the United Nations and of those outside that body, the world has tended to organize around certain major power blocs. Nations within these blocs tend to vote together in the U.N. and to pursue policies somewhat in common.

The Communist Blocs

The Communist bloc, which developed rapidly after World War II, was composed mainly of the Union of Socialist Soviet Republic (Russia) and the so-called People's Republic of China. However, these two countries are quite independent and in the 1960's drew apart.[3] The two separate Communist blocs and the United States seemed to be seeking the support of the uncommitted of what used to be called the third world.

Closely associated with them are the so-called satellite countries, such as Poland, Hungary, Rumania, North Korea, and North Vietnam. One of the countries that is avowedly Communist, Yugoslavia, apparently is independent of Russia and sometimes appears to go along with the democratic bloc. Rumania and Hungary appear to pursue a fairly independent foreign policy. The Communist bloc is thus far from united.

Arab and Moslem Blocs

There is some tendency toward the development of a so-called Moslem bloc. This could include all the nations that are officially or nominally of the Moslem faith: Iran, Iraq, Lebanon, Egypt, Syria, Pakistan, Indonesia, Yemen, Turkey, and others. These nations, however, all pursue a partially independent policy. Some are pro-West but most tend to be anti-West and anti-Soviet, part of the third force. There was some evidence after the mid-1950's and into the 1960's of the attempted formation of an Afro-Asian bloc in the U.N., including the Arab and Asian countries, but this has not completely materialized.

The Arab–Israeli conflict, involving Israel against Syria, Jordan, Egypt, and to a lesser extent Iraq, poses serious obstacles to world peace. The Soviets have interests and commitments in Egypt and other Middle Eastern countries which makes possible a confrontation between the United States and the Soviet Union there.

South American Problems

To the South of the United States lie a group of countries, which, because of geographical position and other reasons, should have interests aligned closely with those of the United States and Canada. Because of a relatively retarded economic development, a large lower class, and poor development of some resources, these countries tend to be somewhat erratic in their governments and thus run a danger of swinging over to the Communist orbit. The predominant religion of South America (Roman Catholic), however, tends to be a stabilizing influence against Communist leanings. Very few South American countries have stable governments. They are subject to quite frequent revolutions. Although most are generally considered to be democratic nations, they are certainly not democratic in the way the United States or the members of the British Commonwealth of Nations are.

Chile in 1970 legally elected the first Marxist-Socialist government in the New World.

India and Other "Neutrals"

There are other countries of the world that tend to consider themselves as neutrals. The most prominent of these, of course, is India. India, antago-

---

[3]See Harrison Salisbury, *War Between Russia and China* (New York: Norton, 1969).

nistic to the West because of her colonial experience with Great Britain, tends at times to be closely sympathetic with the Communist bloc. The Indians claim, however, that they do not have any predilection toward either side. This frees them to accept economic assistance from all sources. The Russians currently are financing the building of huge steel mills in India. The United States recently sent vast quantities of surplus grain to India. The Indians claim that they are in favor of peace. They *have* dealt strenuously with any Communist terrorists who have attempted to destroy the internal well-being of India. "Peaceful" India is very belligerent when her own border security is immediately threatened, which is attested to by her disputes with Pakistan and China. It remains to be seen what this vast country and the other neutral countries like her would do if a general conflict should arise.

The "Democratic" Nations

At the opposite pole from the Communist bloc there is the so-called bloc of the democratic nations. This includes the United States, the Philippines, and most of the British Commonwealth of Nations (the United Kingdom, Canada, Australia, New Zealand) and the other countries of Western Europe, except Spain, Portugal, and Greece. Almost all these nations can certainly be called democratic in the Western meaning of the term. The Union of South Africa is developing rapidly into an oligarchic state where a minority group, the European whites, is pursuing a policy of domination. The South American countries tend to go along with the democratic bloc of nations on most issues. Spain also seems to pursue a foreign policy that is closely related to that of the democratic bloc. Spain, in its internal policies, is probably the nearest example of a fascist state at present among those being discussed.

WORLD CONFLICTS

There are many conflicts between the two major powers, the United States and Russia, that emerged from World War II; some of these are important issues but minor in nature as causes of a possible future world war, others are major in nature. There are also conflicts between nations that have similar cultures and governmental structures.

Conflicts Among Democratic Nations

Not all the conflicts that afflict the world are between countries that differ in regard to their political ideology. There are numerous conflicts among the so-called democratic nations. They are in trade competition with each other. In some cases this is a matter of being in competition to sell to a third country. In other cases the competition exists between companies in the various countries to sell to customers within one or both of the countries concerned. For example, England and the United States, both being industrial countries, are in conflict in regard to the sale of manufactured goods of various kinds.

Sometimes there are conflicts between "democratic" countries over territories. Some of the boundary lines in South America, for example, are still not fully settled. There are also differences in regard to the ways to solve economic problems. The difference in the approaches of England and America to the solution of some of their economic problems is a source of friction; England tends more toward a socialist and welfare state, whereas America tends to be somewhat more conservative in this matter. Some of the democratic nations are "have" nations and some are "have-not." This leads to conflicts of interest and attitude. Some of the democratic countries of the world were formerly colonies of other democratic countries. They may tend to be antagonistic toward the former "imperialistic" overlords and toward countries friendly to the latter. An example of this is India and its relationship to England and her friends. Other areas of the world, not yet nations, are striving for autonomy in government. This leads to friction and serves as a possible source of war. The differences in the way in which the Union of South Africa is handling its race problems and the ways in which some other countries in Africa and Europe, and even the United States, are handling theirs, are also sources of possible conflict.

Major Conflicts Between the Soviet Union and the United States

There are some issues between the United States and the Soviet Union that are sources of conflict but that, in the view of many thinking persons (including the authors of this book), should not be considered to be causes for war. These can be summarized under forms of government, economic systems, and religious policies.

The American people, believing as thoroughly as they do in democracy as a political form and as a way of life (see Chapter 14), are very much upset when a country fails to practice even the semblance of democracy as they see it. On paper even the Soviet Union constitution has democratic forms, in some respects more so than the United States; however, in practice the form of government is a *de facto* dictatorship by an oligarchy. All elections are controlled by the Communist Party, which in turn is controlled by a relatively few persons who hold high positions. The voters have no real choice in their elections. However, the local Party members may exercise some choice in those selected to "run." In the state of terrorism maintained by the secret police, very little opportunity is given for the criticism of the basic premises of political ideals or economic practices in Russia. Although the American people would prefer to see a different governmental policy in the Soviet Union, we certainly are committed to the self-determination of peoples in regard to their government and could not go to war to change the methods that are now being used in the Soviet Union for the political operation of their government.

The second minor conflict relates to the type of economic system in the Soviet Union. Our American Constitution does not commit us to any single way of solving our economic problems. We have, in fact, solved different economic problems within our country in diverse ways. In some cases this has involved private ownership with governmental control; in other cases it has involved public ownership.[4] Certainly we would not

---

[4]See Chapter 5.

deny the right of another country to solve its internal economic problems as it pleases; however, most Americans would think that the Soviet Union has been unwise in the way in which it has done so, even though they would not wish to go to war on that particular issue.

The religious issue is the one of the three discussed here about which many persons would feel most strongly. Most Americans consider themselves to be religious and most Americans believe in religious freedom. Although, theoretically, the Soviet state is supposed to practice religious freedom, there is very little freedom of religion in the Western sense. For many years the Soviet state has propagated an atheist point of view and substituted a philosophy of Marxist materialism for religion. Although in recent years there has been some freedom of worship, there is certainly not any encouragement of, nor is there even a neutral position with respect to, religion. It is quite likely that no prominent position in government or in other aspects of life in the U.S.S.R. can be held by a person too closely identified with any religious point of view. Certainly, however, the experience that the Western world has had with religious wars should discourage us from ever making war over a problem of religion. The question of religious freedom is one that all people will have to work out internally within their own country.

Minor Conflicts Between the Soviet Union and the United States

This brings us to the problem of the basic conflicts between the two countries that have involved us in the cold war. It appears to the writers that these are two in number and that they do constitute not only a serious threat to America but also to the other democratic nations of the world. The first of these conflicts has been the tendency of the U.S.S.R. to follow an expansionist policy, a continuation of trends under the old Czarist regime. This expansion has recently come about through taking over countries lying at its border under one pretext or another, dominating them either actually or behind the scenes, and making them a part of the so-called Communist bloc of nations. This tendency, in the range of history, is not unique to the Russians; however, the present Communists have added to the age-old Russian expansionist policy the drive to spread the Marxist–Leninist economic philosophy. This goes far outside the nature of being an internal problem of Russia; it involves all of us. There can be no freedom for any nation as long as one nation, however small or insignificant, is threatened by another that violates international law and order. Soviet (or Communist Chinese) expansionism presents a threat to freedom-loving countries and consequently a threat to the entire world. The preservation of world peace and order depends upon the security of any nation against being forced to join other nations against its desire. The Soviet system of supposedly independent but affiliated Communist states (satellites) is a thinly disguised use of force. The revolts of the mid-1950's in Poland, Hungary, and East Germany; the independent policies in Rumania; and the suppression of a Czechoslovakian liberal movement by force in the late 1960's all indicate considerable nationalist feeling even among Communists in these countries.

The other major conflict between the two nations is the policy of propagandizing for communism by means of activities within the various nations of the world. It has been definitely a policy of the Communists to set up organizations within all the countries of the world to propagandize and to work by devious means to spread their philosophy in those countries. These political groups have also been used as part of the overseas apparatus of Russia and have engaged in espionage and other related activities. The official policy of these political parties or groups in the other countries has borne little relationship to the problems within these countries but has followed very closely striking shifts in the foreign policy of the U.S.S.R. This was particularly noticed as the Soviet Union changed her attitude toward Hitler at least twice during the period from 1939 to the end of World War II. The policy of trying to put over a philosophy within another country by subversive means through agents in the pay of the first country is one that freedom-loving nations cannot tolerate. So long as such tactics are used, whether by the Soviet Union or by an overly aggressive policy of our American Central Intelligence Agency (C.I.A.), they will be a source of antagonism between the U.S.S.R. and the United States and could lead to war.

During the decades of the 1950's and 1960's, there was considerable emphasis by Soviet and American leaders on competition between the two nations with respect to their economic and military systems *without resort to war.* An apparently sizable improvement in productivity in the U.S.S.R., the success of the Russians in sending up the first satellites, and information reaching this country concerning the enormous expansion of the Russian educational system all serve to point up the fact that Russian society has been making some progress in many fields. It would seem that peaceful competition of this kind, as long as it involves real progress, is helpful. In the late 1960's there was some sharing of technological advances as in the space program. This policy of friendly competition and limited sharing, seemingly pursued by both countries in the late 1960's and into the 1970's, should be stimulating and rewarding to both nations.

The rapprochement between the United States and the People's Republic of China, which came to light in 1971 and was vividly dramatized by the 1972 visit by President Nixon, holds much promise and of course also involves new possibilities of danger in the Far East relations of the Western world.

MILITARY PREPAREDNESS

The state of tension and the condition of cold war with which the world is confronted have led to frantic efforts to maintain the United States and other countries in a state of military preparedness. It is necessary to assess some of the problems that the terrific costs of military preparedness, in both money and effort, lay upon the country.

Economic Costs

One approach to the problem of maintaining world peace through military preparedness is a consideration of its tremendous cost to the world. It has been estimated that the total cost for the world currently is approximately $185 billion annually. The United States alone spends over $75 billion annually for defense. The total cost figures are not readily available, nor are they easily ascertainable. Moreover, numerous problems arise in connection with the classification and interpretation of such figures. For example, an expenditure may be classified by the Bureau of the Budget as military in one annual report, but it may not be so listed in a later annual report. Also, most sources do not include the cost of interest on the portion of the national debt resulting from costs of previous armament and wars. In addition, veterans payments are not included. Other complications arise when some appropriations are carried over from one fiscal period to another, so that spending in any one year may be far greater than the appropriation for that particular year.

Few people are aware of the large percentage of our national budget that is set aside for military preparedness. The Federal Internal Revenue Service has estimated that at least 60 cents of every tax dollar are spent for military purposes, but this figure does not include benefits to veterans nor interest on the indebtedness. Another aspect of military preparedness is its increasingly higher cost. It has been estimated that in Caesar's time it cost 75 cents to kill a man, as compared to $50,000 in World War II.

Hemisphere and regional defense pacts created and sponsored by the United States during the past eight or ten years are adding millions of dollars annually to the foregoing figures. These pacts definitely commit us to a program of global proportions. Thus we see that any future war will involve more people, more resources, and far greater costs.

Economic and Other Effects of Military Preparedness

Budgetary expenditures, defense pacts, and such do not nearly approach the "real" or total cost of military preparedness. Other economic factors of startling proportions must be included, factors on which it is almost impossible to place a price tag. In reviewing the total situation, some economists have been concerned about the many dangers of prolonged military spending and its impact upon the long-range economy of our country. They are well aware of the displacement of industries and personnel. They realize the implications of the great diversion of human effort and strategic materials from consumer channels. They see personnel being trained for highly specialized military jobs for which there is little or no counterpart in normal consumer production. They see the civilian market being stripped of doctors, dentists, nurses, technicians, and other professional people who are sorely needed by their own communities. They see the shifts of population toward industrial centers, with the resultant overcrowding of those communities. The enormous expenditures for the highly technical materials of the modern electronic warfare have created an industrial–military complex that threatens to be destructive to the economic and political freedom of the United States. Finally the economists see the great readjustment that is needed when cutbacks in the military spending program are made. The economic costs of military preparedness thus cannot be clearly estimated or shown on graphs.

The Social–Psychological Costs of Military Preparedness

We cannot deal with the cost of military preparedness only in terms of money, because the "real" cost includes the human cost that a military atmosphere levies upon the social–psychological health of our nation. Social scientists are aware of the dangers of a prolonged state of military domination and emphasis in any culture or society. Continued military programs can cause strong government controls and bring about centralization to a dangerous degree, as has been demonstrated in Germany and Russia.

One of the costs of military preparedness is its possible effect upon attitudes of our civilian population. There is a danger that even a democratic people could become militaristic in its outlook on life in a world in which militarism becomes increasingly dominant. There is a genuine conflict between democratic ways and military ways of operating. A completely militarized state would, of necessity, become a fascist state.

The effect of military preparedness on the democratic countries would include uneasiness and tensions toward each other as well as toward those who are opposed to democracy. It is difficult to relieve tensions in a world of nations armed to the teeth. The real solution to our international problems must come when there is some way of putting down disturbers of the peace by means of an international police force. This course lies well in the future.

Other social–psychological disturbances caused by continued mobilization might be

1. Migration of great numbers of people to areas ill equipped for such influx of population. (Included in this would be housing shortages, water shortages, traffic problems, and the like.)
2. Hasty marriages, broken homes, numerous divorces, juvenile delinquency.
3. General unrest, mentally disturbed men and women.
4. Increase in crime, breakdown in morals, and increase in alcoholism and drug addiction.

There is little doubt that "brink of war" conditions have far-reaching effects on the nation's leaders as well as on the population as a whole. These social–psychological disturbances are extremely dangerous in our society, and we as educators must be concerned about them. What, then, is the total cost? It is far too great, yet it is a problem that requires long-range planning and some intense soul searching. There is evidence of course in the recent antiwar and anti-Establishment protests that many persons are concerned about the military establishment and its effect.

Necessity for Military Preparedness

The realities of the present world indicate that free nations must prepare themselves for any kind of eventuality. We do not now have guaranteed or enforced international law and order. We do not have a world government that can enforce the decisions of a world council on the member nations or upon the member citizens. The situation is something similar to that of vigilante days in the western parts of the United States, where raw force tended to prevail. Persons sought protection by allying themselves with neighbors of like mind. Finally order came about through the establishment of strong local governmental units. Similarly, for the moment, military preparedness of the most technologically efficient kind possibly is a necessity for survival on the part of the larger nations of the world. Strangely enough, on the whole the smaller nations—being pawns among the great powers—do not have the same necessity for military preparedness that the larger nations do.

With such vast sums of money being allocated for the military and aerospace programs, other much-needed federal aid programs are being sacrificed in attempts to keep down governmental spending. Education, health, and welfare must compete with the military for public funds. If only a fraction of the nearly $2 trillion spent on World War II had been allocated to education, many of the critical school building and classroom shortages could have been prevented and the substandard teacher salaries could have been raised to attract better people to the teaching profession. Yet the military draws heavily upon the products of our educational system for personnel for their further specialized training and service. It would seem that increasing the support of the schools through larger federal appropriations would be of benefit to the national defense effort.

Positive and Negative Effects of Military Preparedness on Education

Military policy since World War II has permitted many thousands of servicemen the opportunity to continue their education or to learn new skills upon discharge through the now famous G.I. Bill of Rights. While serving in the armed forces, men were subjected to almost continuous training programs in military schools throughout the nation and operational areas. Thus the Army became a giant education system in itself. Nearly all armed forces personnel were permitted to take college extension courses through the United States Armed Forces Institute (USAFI).

In many instances, colleges and universities throughout the nation were encouraged to set up courses for military personnel as well as to participate in laboratory experimentation and projects. It was at the University of Chicago that Fermi, Compton, and others built the first atom smasher.

Military preparedness has resulted in some hardships on education through the drafting of young teachers, and, as stated previously, through competition with education for public funds. In addition, large defense industries have located in sparsely settled unincorporated areas near cities and towns where tax assessments are quite low. These industrial plants draw upon the labor market for miles around, an area that may encompass many school districts. Eventually these plants attract additional families into the general region, thereby causing the overcrowding of the surrounding school districts, which receive no increase in their local or state tax allotment. Thus a large industry that could support adequate schools avoids its share of responsibility.

ALLEVIATION OF CAUSES OF CONFLICT

We discussed earlier in this chapter some of the reasons that lead to conflict among nations. One of the potential dangers is that involved in the underdeveloped nations becoming restive and seeking short cuts in order to arrive at the same economic level of the more developed nations. It is on this basis and as a bulwark against the possibility of communism that the United States has engaged in a program of economic and technical aid to other countries. This may, of course, also involve at times military aid to certain countries threatened by neighboring countries. However, in this chapter we wish to discuss aid to countries that is not on a military basis.

Aid to Foreign Countries

Economic aid itself may mean loaning money or sending food or other raw or manufactured materials to the country in order to help out when there is a lack. This, in effect, is emergency short-term aid. It is obvious that countries cannot live forever upon some kind of aid from countries from the outside. Thus it becomes more and more important to consider the next form of aid, namely, technical aid.

In the latter part of the Truman administration, President Truman proposed to develop a program of technical aid to countries—"Point Four" in his address to Congress at that time. In other words, he proposed to teach them to help themselves. On this basis an enormous program of aid was developed. In some cases this has meant some giving of technical equipment to countries and teaching them how to use it; in other cases it has been merely a matter of helping them to develop better methods for working with their country's resources. Technical aid has far-reaching, long-range effects and does not cost nearly as much as short-range economic aid. In the end, the country should be enabled to become self-sufficient because of the improved level of technology brought about by the technical aid. In the long run this program is much less costly than direct economic or monetary aid.

A more recent version of technical aid that has perhaps been more successful and promising is the Peace Corps. This program was proposed by the United States first as a nation-state venture, although similar programs had long existed in church and in private philanthropic bases before this governmental venture. Since that time, other countries have also developed some kind of an aid program similar to our Peace Corps. Under the Peace Corps program, well-trained individuals are given special instruction, including a knowledge of the language and culture of the country, and are then sent to work side by side with the persons in that country on some enterprise, such as teaching, farming, engineering, health, and so on. The Peace Corps aid has advantages over the technical aid under the "Point Four" Program in general because members of the Peace Corps actually demonstrate how things should be done. In many cases under the earlier technical aid programs, the cooperative effort was entirely at the upper levels; Americans worked with and trained the people who supervise, not those who actually do the work. The Peace Corps was quite successful in the 1960's. More recently there has been some disenchantment and the numbers of persons seeking to join has declined. An international peace corps devoid of any possible taint of nationalism probably would be more desirable.[5] The ideal would be training of citizens from "have-not" nations, and then these citizens returning as the trainers of their own people. Canada has tried this with disappointing results—the trainees remain in Canada rather than returning to help their own people. This creates a "brain drain" on the countries who can least afford it.

EDUCATION FOR WORLD UNDERSTANDING

It seems that the biggest contribution that education might take to world understanding would be the education of the generation now in school to the realities of the world situation. This means assessing realistically the nature of the world in which we live. It also means a positive effort toward international understanding. This is not necessarily in conflict with the ideal of loyalty to or pride in our own country. In the present world the best interests of our country demand not only that we understand and faithfully adhere to our values, but also that we learn to work with others in developing, if possible, a world in which we all can cooperate. The following are some of the elements that could be involved in decisions related to the teaching of international or world understanding as related by Frankel, then Under Secretary at the Department of State.[6]

[There are] certain ineluctable imperatives that have changed the meaning of the phrase "education for world responsibility." These imperatives define the problem with which we have to deal and set the limits within which a good solution must fall.

The first of these imperatives is that American education has an international responsibility whether it makes any conscious decision to fulfill that responsibility or not.

. . . There was a time . . . when we Americans had a choice: to educate for world responsibility or not to do so. This freedom of choice is no longer ours.

Today we have options with regard to the way in which we ought to define our responsibilities in the rest of the world. But we do not have any option with regard to the question whether we have world responsibilities. If we choose to use our power as a nation, we make a choice that deeply affects our fellows on this planet. If we choose not to use our powers, this choice also affects our fellows.

The same applies to the choices we make in education. We can ignore the international scene . . . we can recognize how little we really know or really feel about the facts of life in other parts of the world and take steps to repair this state of affairs. Whatever we do, however, we make a decision that has not only national but international impact. We shall educate or miseducate for world responsibility. . . .

. . . we must not exaggerate. As Secretary (of Defense) Robert McNamara said in Montreal in May 1966: "The United States has no mandate from on high

---

[5]See Marshall Windmiller, *The Peace Corps and Pax Americana* (Washington, D.C.: Public Affairs Press, 1970).

[6]Charles Frankel, "Some Thoughts on Education for World Responsibility," *School and Society*, April 1967, pp. 219–220. Used by permission.

to police the world and no inclination to do so." . . . we have no mandate to educate the world, and this government has no desire to do so. Indeed, we do not have the power or resources to do so, even if we so desired. We Americans have a large task on our hands merely educating ourselves.

But the task of educating ourselves requires us . . . to be in close and steady touch with others. Educational cooperation abroad is an indispensable tool of international education at home. And international education at home Is essential if American education is to succeed in equipping Americans with the knowledge and guiding ideas they require to make sense of the world in which we live.

When we think of education today we must think in international terms for a number of reasons.

First, the very materials of education today are international. Science is international. Technology is international. To an increasing extent, literature and the arts are produced for an international audience and are responses to problems whose major elements are common to many nations.

Second, American education has the task . . . of meeting the demands of a new generation. The most serious and dedicated members of this generation want an education that is serious and dedicated. If we are to give them what they want . . . we cannot cut the schoolroom and the campus off from the great drama which the human race is now enacting. . . .

Third, education is emerging progressively as the indispensable ingredient in the complex and painful process to which we have given the bland name of "economic and social development." The development of the poorer countries . . . is not . . . a material process, even though it has material conditions and material rewards. Development is a psychological process, a moral transformation. If this transformation is to take place in a reasonably peaceful way, education must be our main hope.

Accordingly, if we have knowledge or educational techniques and resources that can be of assistance to other nations in their educational efforts, and if they want this assistance from us, it is in our own interest to give such assistance. Indeed, it is in our educational interest. For we, too, are a changing and developing country. And one of the respects in which we are changing most rapidly is that the international environment has penetrated our domestic scene so deeply. We will cope with this environment more effectively in our own classrooms if more of our students and teachers have the opportunity to work in classrooms elsewhere.

SUMMARY

In this chapter a description has been given of the problems of the United States in the contemporary, complex, interdependent world. First, the necessity for solving these problems in the near future within the context of a group of sovereign nations—i.e., within a concept of nationalism—is set forth. The efforts of the United Nations and associated groups to work with some kind of cooperative relationship among the nations of the world and the problems involved thereby are described. The conflicts between the Soviet Union and the United States are discussed, and the possibility of a competitive economic race between the two countries without resort to war is presented. The effects of military preparedness on education and on attitudes in general are discussed. Some suggestions are made for better education for world understanding, which, if carried out by all countries, might eventually eliminate war.

Selected Bibliography

Alt, Herschel, and Edith. *The New Soviet Man.* New York: Bookman, 1964. 304 pp.

Amalrik, Andrei. *Will the Soviet Union Survive Until 1984?* New York: Harper & Row, Publishers, 1970. 93 pp.

Arensberg, Conrad M., and Arthur H. Niehoff. *Introducing Social Change: A Manual for Americans Overseas,* Second Edition. Chicago: Aldine Publishing Company, 1971. 288 pp.

Barnet, Richard J. *The Economy of Death.* New York: Atheneum Publishers, 1969. 201 pp.

Bauer, Peter T., and Basil S. Yamey, *The Economics of Under-developed Countries.* Chicago: University of Chicago Press, 1957. 271 pp.

Baumgartner, John Stanley. *The Lonely Warrior: Case for the Military Industrial Complex.* Los Angeles, Calif.: Nash, 1970. 237 pp.

Beck, Robert H., et al. *The Changing Structure of Europe: Economic, Social, and Political Trends.* Minneapolis: University of Minnesota Press, 1970. 286 pp.

Becker, Benjamin M. *Is the United Nations Dead?* Philadelphia: Whitmore, 1969. 163 pp.

Blatchford, Joseph H. "The Peace Corps: Making It in the Seventies," *Foreign Affairs, An American Quarterly Review,* Vol. 49, No. 1 (October 1970).

Blaustein, Arthur I., and Roger R. Woock (eds.). *Man Against Poverty: World War III, A Reader on the World's Most Crucial Issue.* New York: Random House, Inc., 1968. 456 pp.

Borgese, Elizabeth Mann. *A Constitution for the World.* Santa Barbara, Calif.: Center for the Study of Democratic Institutions, 1965. 110 pp.

Braden, Thomas W. "I'm Glad the CIA is 'Immoral,'" *Saturday Evening Post,* May 20, 1967. On Braden see the *New York Times,* May 8, 1967.

Brinton, Crane. *From Many, One: The Process of Political Integration: The Problem of World Government.* Cambridge, Mass.: Harvard University Press, 1948. 126 pp.

On Co-existence. New York: The Center and the Fund for the Republic, 1965. 44 pp.

Crabb, Cecil V., Jr. *Nations in a Multipolar World.* New York: Harper & Row, Publishers, 1968. 702 pp.

On the Developed and the Developing. New York: The Center and the Fund for the Republic, 1965. 22 pp.

Douglas, William O. *International Dissent: Six Steps Toward World Peace.* New York: Vintage Books, 1971. 155 pp.

Dragnich, Alex N. *Major European Governments,* Third Edition. Homewood, Ill.: Dorsey Press, 1970. 510 pp.

Dux, Dieter. *Ideology in Conflict: Communist Political Theory.* Princeton, N.J.: Van Nostrand Co., Inc., 1963. 198 pp.

Escalona, Sibylle. *Children and the Threat of Nuclear War.* New York: Child Study Association of America, 1962. 20 pp.

Farnsworth, Lee W., and Richard B. Gray (eds.). *Security in a World of Change: Readings and Notes on International Relations.* Belmont, Calif.: Wadsworth Publishing Co., Inc., 1969. 432 pp.

Foreign Policy Association (eds.). *Toward the Year 2018.* New York: Cowles, 1968. 177 pp.

Galbraith, John Kenneth. *A Contemporary Guide to Economics, Peace and Laughter.* Boston: Houghton Mifflin Company, 1971. 382 pp.

Gardner, Richard N. "Ten Steps for UN Reform" *Current,* No. 120 (August 1970).

_____. "United Nations Procedures and Power Realities: The International Apportionment Problem.—Reprinted from the *Department of State Bulletin,* May 10, 1965. 25 pp.

Gaylin, Willard. *In the Service of Their Country: War Resisters in Prison.* New York: The Viking Press, Inc., 1970. 344 pp.

Goldman, Marshall I. *The Soviet Economy: Myth and Reality*. Englewood Cliffs, N.J.: Prentice-Hall, Inc., 1968. 176 pp.

Goldston, Robert. *The Rise of Red China*. Indianapolis: The Bobbs-Merrill Company, Inc., 1967. 256 pp.

Gollin, Albert E. *Education for National Development: Effects of U.S. Technical Training Program*. New York: Frederick A. Praeger, Inc., 1969. 280 pp.

Goulden, Joseph C. *Truth Is the First Casualty: The Gulf of Tonkin—Illusion and Reality*. Chicago: Rand McNally & Co., 285 pp.

Greenstein, Fred I. *Personality and Politics*. Chicago: Markham, 1969. 200 pp.

Griffin, Willis H., and Ralph B. Spence. *Cooperative International Education: Background Paper 1*. Washington, D.C.: N.E.A., 1971. 80 pp.

Gullion, Edmund A. (ed.). *Uses of the Seas*. Englewood Cliffs, N.J.: Prentice-Hall, Inc., 1968. 202 pp.

Gyorgy, Andrew, and George Blackwood. *Ideologies in World Affairs*. Waltham, Mass.: Blaisdell Publishing Co., 1967. 262 pp.

Haas, Ernst B. *Tangle of Hopes: American Commitments and World Order*. Englewood Cliffs, N.J.: Prentice-Hall, Inc., 1969. 306 pp.

Hacker, Andrew. *The End of the American Era*. New York: Atheneum Publishers, 1970. 239 pp.

Hayden, Tom. *Rebellion and Repression*. Cleveland: The World Publishing Company, 1970. 186 pp.

Henderson, James L. *Education for World Understanding*. New York: Pergamon Press, Inc., 1968. 160 pp.

Jacob, Philip E., Alexine L. Atherton, and Arthur Wallenstein. *The Dynamics of International Organization*, Revised Edition. Homewood, Ill.: Dorsey Press, 1971. 400 pp.

Kalb, Marvin, and Elie Abel. *Roots of Involvement: The U.S. in Asia, 1784-1791*. New York: W.W. Norton & Company, Inc., 1971. 336 pp.

Keenleyside, Hugh L. "What's Wrong at the United Nations?" *Saturday Review*, June 19, 1971.

Kenworth, Leonard S. *The International Dimension of Education: Background Paper II*. Washington, D.C.: Association for Supervision and Curriculum Development, 1971. 120 pp.

Knoll, Erwin, and Judith Nies McFadden. *American Militarism, 1970*. New York: The Viking Press, Inc., 1969. 150 pp.

Lie, Trygve. *In the Cause of Peace: Seven Years with the United Nations*. New York: The Macmillan Company, 1954. 473 pp.

Littell, Robert (ed.). *The Czech Black Book*. New York: Frederick A. Praeger, Inc., 1969. 303 pp.

Lodge, George C. *Engines of Change: United States Interests and Revolution in Latin America*. New York: Alfred A. Knopf, Inc., 1970. 411 pp.

Lowenthal, Richard. *World Communism*. New York: Oxford University Press, 1966. 296 pp.

Luce, Don, and John Sommer. *Viet Nam: The Unheard Years*. Ithaca, N.Y.: Cornell University Press, 1969. 336 pp.

Magdoff, Harry. "The Logic of Imperialism," *Current*, No. 125 (January 1971).

McLuhan, Marshall, and Quentin Fiore. *War and Peace in the Global Village*. New York: McGraw-Hill Book Company, 1968. 190 pp.

Melman, Seymour. *Pentagon Capitalism: The Political Economy of War*. New York: McGraw-Hill Book Company, 1970. 290 pp.

Melvin, Kenneth. *Education in World Affairs*. Lexington, Mass.: D. C. Heath & Company, 1970. 198 pp.

Miel, Alice, and Louise Berman (eds.). *Report of the World Conference on Education in Asilomar, California. in 1970, sponsored by the ASCD Commission on International Cooperation in Education. Educating the Young People of the World*.

Washington, D.C.: Association for Supervision and Curriculum Development, N.E.A., 1971. 144 pp.

Miller, S. M., Roy Bennett, and Cyrill Alapatt. "A New American Imperialism? Does the U.S. Economy Require It?" *Current,* No. 125 (January 1971).

Moos, Elizabeth. *Soviet Education 1970.* New York: National Council of American-Soviet Friendship, 1970. 63 pp.

Morris, Bernard S. *International Communism and American Policy.* New York: Atherton Press, 1966. 179 pp.

Morris, Richard B. *The Emerging Nations and the American Revolution.* New York: Harper & Row, Publishers, 1970. 238 pp.

Myrdal, Gunnar. *The Challenge of World Poverty: A World-Anti-Poverty Program in Outline.* New York: Pantheon Books, Inc., 1970. 518 pp.

N.E.A. Committee on International Relations. "Introduction to UNESCO," *NEA Journal* (October 1970).

Office of Education Committee. *Teaching About the United Nations.* Washington, D.C.: U.S. Department of Health, Education and Welfare, 1964. 110 pp.

Ojha, Isher C., and Daniel Tretiak. "Toward a New Beginning," *Current,* No. 130 (June 1971), U.S.A.–China relations.

Orata, Pedro T. *Education for a World Community.* Columbus, Ohio: College of Education, Ohio State University, 1965. 24 pp.

Pauling, Linus (ed.). *On the Developed and the Developing.* Santa Barbara, Calif.: The Center for the Study of Democratic Institutions, 1965. 24 pp.

Pentagon Papers, The, as Published by *The New York Times.* New York: Bantam Books, 1971. 677 pp. (Paperback.)

Pincus, John A. (ed.). *Reshaping the World Economy: Rich Countries and Poor.* Englewood Cliffs, N.J.: Prentice-Hall, Inc., 1968. 176 pp.

Preston, Ralph C. (ed.). *Teaching World Understanding.* Englewood Cliffs, N.J.: Prentice-Hall, Inc., 1955. 207 pp.

Proxmire, William. *Report from Wasteland: America's Military-Industrial Complex.* New York: Frederick A. Praeger, Inc., 1970. 248 pp.

Rogers, Edward. *Poverty on a Small Planet.* New York: The Macmillan Company, 1964. 125 pp.

Salisbury, Harrison E. *War Between Russia and China.* New York: W. W. Norton & Company, Inc., 1969. 224 pp.

Sargent, Lyman Tower. *Contemporary Political Ideologies: A Comparative Analysis.* Homewood, Ill.: Dorsey Press, 1969. 203 pp.

Schram, Stuart R. *The Political Thought of Mao Tse Tung,* Revised and Enlarged Edition. New York: Frederick A. Praeger, Inc., 1969. 479 pp.

Spock, Benjamin. *Decent and Indecent: Our Personal and Political Behavior.* New York: McCall, 1970. 210 pp.

Staar, Richard E. (ed.). *Aspects of Modern Communism.* Columbia: University of South Carolina Press, 1968. 416 pp.

Textor, Robert B. (ed.). *Cultural Frontiers of the Peace Corps.* Cambridge, Mass.: M.I.T. Press, 1966. 363 pp.

Toynbee, Arnold J. *America and the World Revolution and other Essays.* New York: Oxford University Press, 1962. 231 pp. Excellent presentation of the thesis that America did represent a truly revolutionary development and that her present challenge is to continue her revolution.

Trials of the Resistance. Introduction by Murray Kempton. New York: Random House, Inc., 1970. 246 pp.

"The U N at 25," *Saturday Review,* June 27, 1970. Contains three articles, one each by Lester B. Pearson, Richard Walton, and Clark M. Eichelberger.

The United Nations: Who Needs It? Dobbs Ferry, N.Y.: Oceana Publications, 1964. 60 pp.

"Universal Declaration of Human Rights." United Nations, Office of Public Information.

Ward, Barbara. *The Rich Nations and the Poor Nations.* New York: W. W. Norton & Company, Inc., 1962. 159 pp.

Windmiller, Marshall. *The Peace Corps and Pax Americana.* Washington, D.C.: Public Affairs Press, 1970. 178 pp.

On the World Community. New York: The Center and the Fund for the Republic, 1965. 33 pp.

Selected Films

America and the European Common Market (Indiana University), 31 min. This film reveals the role of America in world trade and its relation to the national economy.

Americans All (U.S. Govt.), 25 min. Film on South America. Published during the war by the U.S. government.

Atomic Power (McGraw-Hill), 19 min. A basic film on atomic power and the bomb.

The Awakening (McGraw-Hill), 28½ min. Explores the enormous difficulties involved in providing teachers for the children of the developing world, where education is an absolute necessity.

Born Equal (Library Films), 10 min. Interprets the United Nations Declaration of Human Rights, with special emphasis on rights for children.

The Children (UN), 10 min. This film describes UNICEF's attack on the problems of the world. We see the food production, the health programs, and the educational activities that are carried out in many areas to make a happier, healthier, and more hopeful world for tomorrow's citizens.

Communism (UWF), 32 min. Documentary film on communism and its history, contrast between communism and the American system, and a warning to avoid labeling as Communists all who disagree with the majority.

Crossroads of Life (UN), 35 min. This film highlights several cases of children with serious problems who are helped to understand their needs and become healthier people. There are scenes showing therapeutic work with children, which helps them to relieve their aggressive feelings.

Defense of the Peace (UN), 12 min. Animated charts and maps, together with live-action scenes, show how the UN machinery provides a realistic way to deal with political and economic problems. The functions and structure of the General Assembly, Security Council, International Court of Justice, Economic and Social Council, and Trusteeship Council are described. The film ends with an appeal for citizen cooperation in action for peace.

Earth and Its Peoples Series (Louis de Rochemont Assoc.), 20 min. each. Includes the titles Malaya—*Nomads of the Jungle;* Norway—*Farmer-Fisherman;* Java—*Tropical Mountain Land;* Guatemala—*Cross Section of Central America;* South Africa—*Riches of the Veldt;* and Argentina—*Horseman of the Pampas.* The Malaya film is particularly recommended.

Expanding World Relationships (U.S. State Department), 11 min. Contrasts the slow transportation and communication of Thomas Jefferson's day with the machine age, in which technological advances have lightened men's work and brought all the countries of the world into close contact and interdependence on raw materials and manufactured goods; emphasizes the necessity for worldwide cooperation.

Fable for Friendship (McGraw-Hill), 10 min. An animated humorous short that illustrates aims and ideas of UNESCO.

The Global Struggle for Food (Contemporary Films/McGraw-Hill), 28 min.

I.L.O. (NFB), 30 min. International Labor Organization, an agency that survived the League of Nations and as part of the United Nations is active today in meeting worker's needs throughout the world.

India: Asia's New Voice (McGraw-Hill), 17 min.

India: Writings on the Sand (N.E.T.), 30 min. An exploding population in a country where there is barely enough food to feed the people.

Introduction to Foreign Trade (Coronet), 10 min. First establishes the importance of foreign trade to our economy and then presents a general picture of the mechanics of international commerce. The role of monetary standards and control, national policies in reference to those controls, distribution of raw materials and markets are shown. Then, in an actual exchange of goods, the detailed domestic and foreign operations involved in the sale, shipment, and payment are portrayed.

The Land and Its People (UN), 23 min. This film sets the stage for the sequel *New Horizons* (listed below). It is a description of the Patzcuaro district, the home of the Trascan Indians. It tells something of the history, geography, and culture of these Mexican people and of their modern daily life before the UNESCO Fundamental Education Centre was established. The history and source of current problems are outlined and the need for the UNESCO project is defined. This film is most significant when shown as a prelude to New Horizons.

Mission of Discovery (Peace Corps), 15 min.

New Horizons (UN), 26 min. This film brings you an actual account of the work of the United Nations Educational, Scientific and Cultural Organizations in Patzcuaro, Mexico, where teachers from twenty Latin-American countries are being trained for an organized attack on illiteracy. Dominant throughout the film is the emphasis UNESCO places on creating a desire for knowledge and a realization that through their own efforts the people can create a better life for their entire community.

Of Human Rights (UN), 20 min. An incident involving economic and racial prejudice among children is used to dramatize the importance of bringing to the attention of the people of the world their rights as human beings, as set forth in the Universal Declaration of Human Rights, proclaimed by the UN General Assembly in December, 1948.

One World—Or None (Film Publishers), 9 min. Federation of American (Atomic) Scientists assisted technically with this film. Chiefly through animation, the international aspect of atomic research is emphasized; control of mass-destruction weapons by the UN and measures to outlaw wars are advocated.

The Revolution in Human Expectations (N.E.T.), 30 min. The needs of underdeveloped areas of the world.

The Task Ahead (UN), 20 min. Getting the needs of all the people of the world for food, for literacy, for technical and scientific skills, and above all for peace is the mission of UNESCO. Among these are educational reconstruction; international exchange of literature, art, and science; the UNESCO coupon system for books, films, and technical equipment for soft-currency countries; studies of technical needs in press, film, and radio; fundamental education; draft agreements for free flow of educational material.

This Is the Challenge (UN), 10 min. This film has been designated not only to remind us of some of the peace-making achievements of these first years but to throw into dramatic perspective the determined attack launched by the United Nations and its member states upon the basic causes underlying dispute and war, causes that have remained obdurate and unchanging throughout man's troubled history. Overshadowed by wars and rumors of wars, the work of the United Nations experts goes too often unnoticed.

This Is the United Nations (UN), 30 min. Series starting with Screen Magazine #1 and continually being added to, giving current developments.

UNESCO (McGraw-Hill), 10 min. A basic film on UNESCO that gives a comprehensive picture of the organization's major activities in the fields of education, science, and culture.

The U.N. in a Revolutionary World (N.E.T.), 30 min. The role of the United Nations in maintaining peace.

United Nations (UN), 30 min. Check additional films by writing for latest list to Department of Public Information, United Nations, New York, N.Y.

United Nations in Korea (UN), 30 min. This authentic, accurate, and objective film is a unique record of how the United Nations Unified Command with troops from sixteen member states repulsed aggression and gained a truce through international cooperation, thus reaffirming in practice the concept of collective security.

The U.S. in a Revolutionary World (N.E.T.), 30 min. The issue of isolation versus involvement in world affairs.

Who Owns the Bottom of the Ocean? (ICF), 15 min. The exploration of the continental shelf leads us not only to look at the resources in minerals and food which are opening up to man's use, but also to a new field in international law. What are the steps for the nations of the world to take to assure freedom to harvest the resources of the oceans?

Who Owns the Moon? (ICF), 15 min. Legal and social problems never before encountered are created by man's thrust Into the planetary system. Solutions will require new concepts of law and closer cooperation among the nations of the world. If there are vast mineral resources on the moon, who will own them?

Part IV

▓▓▓▓▓▓▓▓▓▓▓▓▓▓▓▓▓▓▓▓

The Role of the School in Modern America

Part IV organizes the implications of the materials presented earlier in this book. First comes a clarification of democratic values, based on some of the concepts set forth earlier but also on some new materials, particularly the results of recent research in the fields of group dynamics and group relations. The challenges to those values and the challenge to man to live up to them in an age of protest and confrontation are delineated in Chapter 11. Second, a careful philosophical analysis is made of the contemporary conflicting viewpoints as to the role of the school, including the new radical left (and what is sometimes called the third world). In Chapter 15 the writers do not themselves indicate that one of those views is clearly preferable to another. The final chapter, Chapter 16, presents a summary of the main findings from the entire book. This consists of the ideas concerning man and society that have been developing from research in the social sciences within years and the clarification of democratic values from man's experience over his history. It includes the kind of problems which our culture faces as a result of social changes and some of the implications of these problems for schools. Then a view of the "foreseeable future" is presented. Finally, the authors set forth some of their recommendations for the school in American society.

Chapter 14

■■■■■■■■■■■■■■■■□□

Democratic Values
and Processes in an
Age of Protest

In this chapter we shall explore the nature of democratic values. We shall try to indicate the sources of such values, the relationship between democracy and freedom, the problems of authority in democracy, and some of the conflicts concerning democratic values. We also shall attempt to indicate some consensus concerning them. In the latter part of the chapter we shall discuss processes that are related to democracy, including the whole area of developments in group dynamics and the new area of concern with sensitivity through the development of "human potential" groups. The protest movement and the politics of confrontation are surveyed and their potential for violence is assessed.

DEMOCRATIC IDEAS: PRODUCT OF LONG PERIODS OF HUMAN EXPERIENCE

Students of history no longer think of democracy as being of ancient origin. Although there were cases among primitive men (including the Germanic tribes of Europe) in which there was some voting to select chieftains, this was a very crude form of democracy, if it was democracy at all. Such a chieftain had enormous powers after his election. There were, however, cases in which decisions were made by consultations among the leading persons, elders, of the tribe. Democratic values have emerged quite recently, even though they are a result of the application of ethical principles that developed over a long period of years.

Democratic ideas, insofar as they are actually practiced, are by and large a product of the Western world after the medieval period. Their roots do, of course, go back into the medieval period and into the time of the Greeks. Among the Greeks, for example, there was a great deal of freedom of thinking and action. There was a strong emphasis upon individual rights. There was an almost pure democracy at times with respect to the formation of laws. The citizenry met as a group to propose and to adopt laws. However,

Greek democracy was extended to only a very small group. It included neither the "noncitizens" nor the slaves; hence it excluded the great mass of the Greek people.

There was also a kind of democracy among the primitive Christians. This far exceeded that of the Greeks. In some cases they completely shared all their property, thus forming a type of communal democracy. This was of limited duration and did not constitute a political government.

There were at least two important factors that brought about a new emphasis upon the common man. One was the technological development resulting in such changes as the invention of gunpowder, which made one man with a gun the equal of several knights without firearms. Another was the commercial revolution, which gave prosperity to the middle class and made it reasonably free of the feudalistic rule of the barons. In this struggle the bourgeoisie (or middle class) appealed to the kings, as opposed to the barons, and was able to wrest certain freedoms for their commercial city-states. This struggle for freedom gave rise to the development of thoughts about the fundamental nature of such freedom. Such philosophers as Rousseau, Locke, and others began to write about the natural rights of men. These writings strongly influenced American thinking before, during, and after the Revolutionary period.

From the long struggle for freedom emerged certain important documents. The Magna Carta is generally considered to be one of the first of these. It concerned mainly the freedom of the barons in their struggle against the king. Town charters secured from the king by commercial groups constitute another type of written affirmation of freedom. Many of these rights were won first in England and then in other parts of the world. After the Glorious Revolution of 1688, the English Bill of Rights of 1689 was passed. This was a forerunner to the American Constitution.

It should be noticed, however, that the early bills of rights were for the bourgeoisie or wealthy middle and upper merchant classes, rather than for all the people. Over a period of years, in America as well as in England, the rights of suffrage and certain other freedoms were extended to all people. As these freedoms were won, various theories of freedom for all commenced to appear in written documents and gradually began to win widespread support. Such documents as our Constitution and Declaration of Independence are good examples. The development of workmen's compensation and other kinds of social insurance, from 1900 on, was a further extension of democracy and freedom. These are only a few of the major steps toward the development of democratic ideas. At each stage our democratic ideas and the application of them were quite incomplete. Democracy itself is continually growing. It may mean quite different things in different periods—or in different countries during the same historical period.

The recent concern with protection of the rights of the individual against the pressures of conformity, the civil rights movement, and other protests have culminated in a general increase in the use of confrontation techniques. The increased use of such techniques to secure one's desired ends poses new challenges but also gives a potential for the further development of democracy.

DEMOCRACY MORE A SET OF VALUES THAN A POLITICAL STRUCTURE

Some students of society have noted that democracy may exist under many forms of political structure. These are as different as the constitutional monarchies of Great Britain and The Netherlands, which have ministries responsible to the people, and the American system, with its president and bicameral legislature. To the scholar this indicates that, after all, democracy is basically a set of values held by the people rather than any particular form of political structure. This is borne out by the experiences of the South American countries, which indicate that political form and structure do not necessarily guarantee freedom or democratic procedures. Basically, then, a free people has a set of verbalized values concerning freedom. They continually talk about and strive for these values. The accomplishment of these values is facilitated but not guaranteed by an appropriate type of political structure. Furthermore, because these sets of values change from time to time as new problems arise, the specific values in any of the democratic countries vary from time to time. Later in this chapter we shall indicate a set of values that are fairly well agreed upon by various groups in our American democratic culture at the present time.

DEMOCRACY AND FREEDOM

Ask anyone in the Western culture to define democracy and he will invariably use the word *freedom* or *liberty*. Yet the extreme of freedom or liberty is not democracy, but anarchy. Democracy is a social order in which we have freedom, on the one hand, but responsibilities—duty, group action —on the other.

The concept of freedom in a democratic culture has to be defined more explicitly than the freedom to "do as you please as long as you do not interfere with anyone else's freedom." That would be a negative approach that would hinder *group* action. In this modern, interdependent world, where people must act conjointly, it is necessary at times to restrict freedoms in certain areas in order to increase the total amount of freedom. A simple concrete example of this is the ordinary traffic light. By restricting the freedom of a person to enter an intersection at any time that he pleases, we increase total freedom, because we prevent traffic jams and allow for the better flow of the total traffic. Another example is the compulsory-education law. By withholding from the child or his parents the right to decide whether or not he shall go to school, in the long run we increase the child's freedom of choice because we assure him an opportunity for a better background of education. Restriction for the sake of freedom may also be characteristic of many of the other regulations and rules that are found in a democratic society. We restrict the immediate freedom of an individual in order to insure the larger freedom.

There are several reasons why freedom must be given such a prominent place in democratic culture. First, there is no final authority to which we can turn in a democracy to find the answer to a problem. Consequently the minority must be free at any time to speak and to agitate for changes in the ideas and procedures of a democratic culture. Democracy itself, and the framework in which democratic principles may operate at any given time, must be subject to continual scrutiny. There can be no closed areas. The minority of one generation may well become the majority of the next. If there were not freedom of the minority (actually of any of the *many* minorities) to agitate for change, change would be prevented. Second, society grows only through the possible change that comes about as someone becomes dissatisfied with conditions the way they are. This means not only that a democracy *should permit* freedom of speech and of criticism but that this freedom *must be encouraged.* Third, although the fundamental unity of the people must be encouraged, we must also encourage diversity and a maximum of local and individual freedom. This diversity gives richness to the culture and permits things to be tried out in small areas that may be later adopted in the larger unit.

It was out of experiences where the minority, denied their rights, eventually became the "majority" by force that the Bill of Rights and other freedoms were eventually hammered out in the Anglo-Saxon tradition of liberty and in Western culture as a whole. Certainly, in the extremely complex, interdependent society that is now emerging and that in the future probably will become more complex, there must always be a place for freedom of inquiry and agitation and for freedom of choice among diverse ways of life.

THE NATURE OF AUTHORITY IN A DEMOCRACY

Although democracy is centered upon the theme of freedom, it does represent a kind of social order. Consequently there must be inherent in it some kind of authority to give it structure. It is important for those helping children and youth develop into effective citizens in a democracy, as well as for all citizens as they exercise their freedom, to understand the nature of authority in society.

In societies other than democracy or anarchy, final authority always is vested in some kind of fixed system—an absolute, hereditary, or constitutionally limited monarchy; an oligarchy of a small ruling class; a party (as in Russia); or, in the case of a theocratic state, religious leaders. In a complete democracy there is no such authority. In most democracies there is a written constitution that theoretically has transferred certain rights and responsibilities of government from the people to the political structure. These constitutions serve to define the limits of authority for a period of time. However, all constitutions are subject to continual scrutiny and possible change and thus do not constitute a sacrosanct document.

The analysis in this section is not based primarily on government but on the authority that is inherent in any situation where free people associate together to take action. This may be a democratic government, or it may be just a group of people who meet to accomplish certain things on an informal basis. The writers are indebted, in this analysis, to a very important early study by Benne.[1] In this analysis of authority, Benne identifies the natural

[1]Kenneth D. Benne, *A Conception of Authority: An Introductory Study* (New York: Bureau of Publications, Teachers College, Columbia University, 1943).

kinds of authority inherent in any situation where people associate together in some form of common action. He identifies these as of three kinds: the authority of the "expert"; the authority of the "rules of the game"; and the authority of the community. The following analysis, while developed around Benne's three types of authority, does not follow completely his discussion of them.

The Authority of the "Rules of the Game"

Whenever people are associated together, whether in playing a game or in any other kind of enterprise, they are unable to work together at all unless there is some agreement as to the "rules of the game." This can be readily observed if one watches young children attempting to play a game before they understand the importance of rules. The young children quite often wish to change the rules according to their own individual interpretation. The game is able to progress only after they learn that there must be a common agreement upon the rules before the game is any fun. This represents a stage of maturity in the young child. Rules of the game primarily concern matters in which the decisions in and of themselves are not important. No group of people can work together—whether in an informal game, a committee meeting, a legislature, or a prisoners' enterprise—unless there is some agreement as to how they will work together and on the importance of having rules. Actually, just what rules are finally established does not matter much as long as rules exist. In football or basketball the rules could be quite different and the game could still go on. However, there *must be* rules; otherwise there can be no game. Similar is the authority of the "rules of the game" found throughout all of our society. One example of such rules of the game in America would be that of driving on the right side of the road rather than on the left. It is not particularly important which side is decided upon, but there must be agreement. In informal groups such rules often do not assume legal status, although the rules of parliamentary order frequently do. In governments such agreements are usually enforced by law. Unless the people by and large agree upon the rules of the game, society lacks any kind of coherence.

The Authority of the "Expert"

A second type of authority in any group is that of the "expert." An accident occurs, a crowd gathers, there is uncertainty as to what to do. Finally a man steps up and says, "I am a doctor." Automatically the crowd adjusts itself to the authority of the expert in this situation. He is the natural leader, and, because of a peculiar background of training and experience, he *is* best able to cope with this problem. In other kinds of emergencies other persons would be the expert, for example, a plumber, a minister, a lawyer, or a sailor. There are some areas in which we do not as yet recognize the authority of the expert as readily as we do that of the medical doctor in case of illness or accident. In problems involving economics, education, or other social issues, for example, every one considers himself to be an expert.

There are, of course, problems arising even within a field of expertness where the decision cannot be made wholly by the expert alone. Faced with such problems, society as a whole must make the decision after full utilization of the experience of the expert. Thus, in certain matters related to the social aspects of medicine, the final decision must be made by the public as a whole rather than by the medical profession. In problems involving such fields as economics, the same is true. However, the expertness of the economists and others ought to be recognized as contributing in a special way to such problems and to proposed decisions for the public welfare. This has been increasingly the case in recent years, when such events have occurred as the appointment of special economic advisors to the president of the United States or the employment of economic advisors on the staffs of most business corporations and other large groups, including labor unions.

In the school situation the teacher is the expert because of his special knowledge. He also has the "authority of the community," which is to be discussed in the next section. There is also, in the classroom situation, the authority of the rules of the game. Certain understood rules there must be in order that a group of people may be able to carry on successfully in the school situation or in any situation.

The Authority of the Community

The third kind of authority is the authority of the community. Whatever the use of expertness and the means of establishing the rules of the game, there must also be some procedures worked out to enable the community (whether local, regional, state, national, or international) to come to some conclusions with respect to the certain important problems that it faces. These are problems that *really* make a difference. Decisions *must* be made. After full discussion and full representative action, usually the community does make a decision. Whatever the decision may be, the minority must conform to that decision whether or not it agrees. The minority may wish to agitate for a change, but it must conform temporarily in order that societal operations may go on. In a democratic society it is assured that only when the action of the community is such as to cause excessive violation of the individual's rights would he ever rebel against the authority of the community. A democratic society ought not, of course, to take action that unnecessarily restricts the rights of individuals. However, there are cases in which such action might rightly be taken. A person following some type of religious cult in which harm was being done to his children or to others might expect the authority of the community to be visited upon him, at least with respect to this aspect of his behavior. Such procedures are illustrated in the cases of the "snake" religious cults of the Appalachian Mountains and the practice of polygamy among the Mormons in the latter part of the nineteenth century. In most cases the authority of the community is expressed in some kind of law or regulation. However, in some instances it is enforced only by general agreement. These informal (extralegal) regulations may not be necessarily merely rules of the game. They may be basic rules that have not been given the force of law but that are still of crucial importance in the community.

CONFLICTING VALUES WITHIN AMERICAN DEMOCRATIC SOCIETY

Persons who live in a society where the right of the minority to agitate for change is recognized and where diversity is encouraged can expect numerous conflicts concerning any ideas that may be expressed. This is certainly true of the concept of democracy. Democracy is a growing concept. At any time there is considerable difference of opinion as to what it means in action. Although there is a wide area of agreement within the American culture, there are also areas of conflict. In some cases where there is agreement as to wording, there are major disagreements as to what it means in action.

In the famous study of Middletown the Lynds discovered conflicting ideas about the American value system, and Robert S. Lynd expressed them succinctly in a later publication:

> Individualism, "the survival of the fittest," is the law of nature and the secret of America's greatness; and restrictions on individual freedom are un-American and kill initiative.
>
> BUT: No man should live for himself alone; for people ought to be loyal and stand together and work for common purposes.
>
> Democracy, as discovered and perfected by the American people, is the ultimate form of living together. All men are created free and equal, and the United States has made this fact a living reality.
>
> BUT: You would never get anywhere, of course, if you constantly left things to popular vote. No business could be run that way, and no business-man would tolerate it.
>
> The family is our basic institution and the sacred core of our national life.
>
> BUT: Business is our most important institution and, since national welfare depends upon it, other institutions must conform to its needs.
>
> Religion and "the finer things of life" are our ultimate values and the things all of us are really working for.
>
> BUT: A man owes it to himself and his family to make as much money as he can.
>
> Honesty is the best policy.
>
> BUT: Business is business, and a businessman would be a fool if he didn't cover his hand.
>
> Education is a fine thing.
>
> BUT: It is the practical men who get things done.
>
> Children are a blessing.
>
> BUT: You should not have more children than you can afford.
>
> Patriotism and public service are fine things.
>
> BUT: Of course, a man has to look out for himself.
>
> The American judicial system insures justice to every man, rich or poor.
>
> BUT: A man is a fool not to hire the best lawyer he can afford.

While these conflicts are real and do serve to cause uncertainty about human action, they do not represent fundamental weaknesses in our society. While it is important for people to clarify their values and for our society to eliminate conflicts, it is true that the growing edge of a culture may reveal conflicts at a given time. If an entire culture agrees upon a value, the result is monolithic, like the oriental type of society described in Chapter 2, with very little chance of growth.[2]

As we shall indicate in the next section, there are wide areas in which the American people do, by and large, agree on a basic set of values in the American democracy.

THE BASIC PREMISES OF AMERICAN LIBERTY

There have been many efforts to set forth the basic values inherent in American culture. Some of these have been made in connection with education. In the presentation of the Seven Cardinal Principles in 1918 there was an excellent discussion of the nature of democracy. In 1932 a committee on socioeconomic goals in America proposed a list of ten goals as a basis for educational and social development in our country.

There have also been statements of goals consistent with democracy from persons not in the field of education. President Roosevelt, during wartime, defined the goals of democracy in terms of the four freedoms: freedom from fear, freedom from want, freedom of speech, and freedom of religion. Attention should also be drawn to the Universal Declaration of Human Rights proclaimed by the United Nations on December 10, 1948.[3] This set of principles, developed by a joint group of the United Nations, not all from countries called democratic, actually contains many of the values inherent in democracy. Although this list is not extensive, it is an example of a wide range of agreement among the nations of the world. Certainly there is disagreement among the various countries as to what these values mean. In addition, there is considerable difference within any country, including the United States, concerning the extent to which the basic values are realized.

At the close of World War II a venture called the Citizenship Education Project was set up by Teachers College, Columbia University. This was to some extent encouraged by Dwight D. Eisenhower, who was at that time president of Columbia University. Among other things, this project developed a statement of the "Premises of American Liberty" to which the reader is referred.[4]

There certainly will be much disagreement as to what should be considered the basic "premises" of our American liberty. There are, however, some well-established values to be strived for in our culture and values toward which we have already made some progress by law and through practice. On the other hand, in almost every case instances can be cited where they have been violated. There are even some cases in our country where people are in violent opposition to some of the values stated here and are making no effort to carry them out. This is notable, of course, in the area of minority rights.

[2]Adapted from Robert S. Lynd, Knowledge for What?: The Place of Social Science in American Culture, pp. 60–62. Copyright, 1939, Princeton University Press. Used by permission.

[3]"Your Human Rights": The Universal Declaration of Human Rights Proclaimed by the United Nations, December 10, 1948 (New York: Ellner, 1950), p. 71.

[4]When Men Are Free: Premises of American Liberty, Citizenship Education Project. Copyright 1955, Teachers College, Columbia University, and Houghton Mifflin Co.

DEMOCRACY AS A WAY OF LIFE

Democracy has been defined in this chapter as a set of values, not merely as a set of procedures or a kind of structure. An increasing number of students have indicated that democracy *really* involves a complete way of life. That is, it permeates all aspects of American culture. There are, of course, groups in our society that would object to this concept, even some who deny that our government is a democracy. For instance, they insist that it is a republic, not a democracy in a strict sense. By and large, events in our culture indicate that democracy is far more than a purely political or governmental concept. It is a way of life, and as such it defines relationships between persons in many areas. We have mentioned in Chapter 7 that family life is becoming democratized. This is not a matter of government but the result of a change in the climate of social opinion. The patriarchal or matriarchal family is no longer consistent with American culture.

The fact that democracy has become a way of life that permeates our culture does not mean that there is no place for individual sets of values. Most persons in American culture adhere to a set of values that have been derived in part from a religious authority or tradition. Because of our policy of diversity within unity, these values do not, in most cases, conflict with our democratic values. In many cases, such persons can adhere to the entire set of basic premises of American liberty just quoted and also to their religious ideas. As a matter of fact, many of these persons would insist that their religious ideas give a solid foundation to the democratic values. This is not to deny that at times there are serious conflicts between a point of view that is primarily authoritarian and unchanging in nature (such as is typical of some religions) and the nonauthoritarian concepts of American democracy. These conflicts, of course, will have to be worked out in the same way that other conflicts are. In some cases, the minority religious group may have to forego in practice the achievement of what they consider the implications of their belief because of the lack of acceptance by the majority group. Wherever possible, however, in American culture these minorities are permitted to pursue their own ways of life within the general framework of the democratic society.

There needs to be an effort on the part of all persons in our society, including educators, to try to develop the distinctive nature of the values of our democratic culture. This is important if these values, contrasted with those of the nondemocratic areas of our world, are to be fully understood and if their practice is to be most fully realized. The later sections of this chapter indicate ways in which groups can operate on the more democratic basis—the whole science of group dynamics and group action.

"TEACHING" MORAL VALUES

Earlier we traced the changing relationships between the church and the state and the relation of both to education (Chapters 3 and 4). Although the school has always placed some emphasis on moral values, attention was directed more closely to them in the late 1950's and 1960's. Some have felt the problem was so acute that it might be necessary to change the policy of the separation of church and state sufficiently to enable public schools to teach religious ideas as a base for moral and spiritual values. The increase in crime and juvenile delinquency and the general world conditions resulting from the cold war between American capitalistic democracy and Russian communism have caused a new interest in the basic values of our culture.

The school had always taught and was continuing to teach moral values. However, it was believed that a bettter job could be done. Discussion of this topic continued during the postwar period. The Educational Policies Commission, after careful consideration of a policy, issued a pioneer statement in 1951.[5] They presented a careful study of the place of moral and spiritual values in the public schools. They reaffirmed a central place for such values in the school program. They reviewed the problem of the separation of church and state and reaffirmed the necessity for the public school to refrain from teaching sectarian doctrines.[6] The commission further explored some of the common values of American culture, irrespective of any theological background upon which they might have been based. They listed a total of ten values (actually cores of values). These are as follows:[7]

1. Human Personality—The Basic Value
Among the values here proposed, the *first* is fundamental to all that follow. The basic moral and spiritual value in American life is *the supreme importance of the individual personality.*
2. Moral Responsibility
If the individual personality is supreme, *each person should feel responsible for the consequences of his own conduct.*
3. Institutions as the Servants of Men
If individual personality is supreme, *institutional arrangements are the. servants of mankind.*
4. Common Consent
If the individual personality is supreme, *mutual consent is better than violence.*
5. Devotion to Truth
If the individual personality is supreme, *the human mind should be liberated by access to information and opinion.*
6. Respect for Excellence
If the individual personality is supreme, *excellence in mind, character, and creative ability should be fostered.*
7. Moral Equality
If the individual personality is supreme, *all persons should be judged by the same moral standards.*
8. Brotherhood
If the individual personality is supreme, *the concept of brotherhood should take precedence over selfish interests.*
9. The Pursuit of Happiness.
If the individual personality is supreme, *each person should have the*

[5]N.E.A., Educational Policies Commission, *Moral and Spiritual Values in the Public Schools* (Washington, D.C.: N.E.A., 1951).

[6]Ibid., p. 6.

[7]From N.E.A., Educational Policies Commission, *Moral and Spiritual Values in the Public Schools,* pp. 18–30. Copyright, 1951, National Education Association. Used by permission. (Italics added.)

greatest possible opportunity for the pursuit of happiness, provided only that such activities do not substantially interfere with the similar opportunities of others.

10. Spiritual Enrichment.

If the individual personality is supreme, each person should be offered the emotional and spiritual experiences which transcend the materialistic aspects of life.

The commission goes on to say that because life is a continuing series of moral decisions, the schools should help the students by teaching them how to make choices. There are two kinds of moral decisions that we face in life. One involves the decision as to whether or not to act in accordance with a value that we acknowledge and have agreed to follow. The second is one where certain of one's values are in conflict. Examples of such conflict of values might be (1) loyalty to our family as opposed to loyalty to our country; (2) a conflict between the values of equality and of respect for excellence; (3) a conflict between the value of brotherhood and the value of common consent. The book also illustrates the problem of moral choices with samples of different kinds of sanctions, such as justice, the law, property rights, and so on. Throughout this volume the whole intent is toward making the *study of values* the central core of the school. There is no suggestion that a set of values be imposed on the pupils. The commission saw the job of the teacher as being one of helping each boy and girl to clarify his values and to apply them to life decisions.

The ideas expressed in this volume have gained wide acceptance. However, there is a group of persons of many differing points of view who feel that spiritual values cannot be taught apart from theology. These persons have advocated teaching theology by various kinds of proposals. One would be the increase of released time, which is still legal under Supreme Court decisions if conducted off the school premises. Others advocate a change, if necessary, through amendments of our constitutions, to permit sectarian doctrines to be taught as electives in public schools. Recently there has been a proposal to solve the problem of teaching religious ideas through *shared time* and still possibly avoid constitutional questions. According to this proposal a student would be permitted to attend two accredited and recognized high schools at the same time. He might be a regular student at a public high school and go to a private, sectarian high school for some instruction. Or he might be a regular student at a sectarian high school and attend the public school for certain classes. It is argued that at the present time a student may freely move from one high school to another at the end of each year and transfer his credits. It is argued that all shared time would be the transfer of credits simultaneously to one of two high schools the pupil attends. It can be seen that the administrative complexities involved in simultaneous attendance and scheduling would be quite great. Moreover, there have been questions raised concerning the constitutionality of shared time in some states.

Other points of view emphasize the teaching *about* religion as an adjunct of the curriculum, rather than the direct teaching of sectarian doctrines. This point of view holds that because religion is a part of our culture, the school's curriculum should be as much concerned with it as with other aspects of the culture. This seems to be constitutionally satisfactory. It contemplates an objective study of the different religions just as we study other aspects of the culture. Problems are found in the availability of skilled teachers and objective materials.

Without a doubt an increased emphasis upon moral and ethical values is good for education, and it is certain that the efforts of the schools will be improved as we know and understand more about helping boys and girls to clarify their values and to act in accordance with them.

UNDERLYING ALL SOCIAL PROBLEMS ARE PROBLEMS OF HUMAN RELATIONS

It has become increasingly evident to students of our culture that the problems we face are now largely problems of our own making. Furthermore, they are now more predominantly problems of persons lacking the desire and knowledge of how to act together on common needs than they are of those lacking the knowhow to tackle the source of the problems. Increasingly, then, students and others have come to the position that most of our problems are basically problems of human relations.

When man knew little about the world in which he lived, he was ill equipped to solve his problems even with the best of cooperative effort. As we have developed technical competence in one physical area after another, it has become increasingly important that we develop appropriate value standards and the disposition to apply them to the solution of our problem. The ability of the individual to forget his own selfish interest in terms of a cooperative effort toward the common good, and in the long run for his own individual good as well, becomes of increasingly urgent importance.

We still have not been able to control the path of the hurricane; we still have not been able to conquer the scourge of cancer completely; we still have some technological problems to solve with respect to the automated factory; and we still have not solved the problem of photosynthesis. But at least partial control of the environment may be effected even in the case of some of the problems that may be insoluble, such as the hurricane, through the cooperative effort of all persons. Warning systems, preparation for the storm, damage-control installations, fire-and-rescue parties, and salvage squads may mitigate the severity of damage.

As to most of our problems, including practically all those discussed in this book, it becomes increasingly apparent that because man has created the conditions that have caused them to exist—at least in their present form —it is up to man to solve them through some sort of cooperative action. To summarize: It is the belief of the present authors that man must be made aware that he is in charge of his own destiny; that he must use all his powers and all his increasing knowledge of the world; and that he must bring this knowledge to bear upon his problems without prejudice with respect to past solutions and existing institutions.

In the area of human relations, one of the historic difficulties has been a lack of knowledge of the ways in which groups function and of appropriate means to increase their efficiency. Quite often one has heard persons say, "I suppose we ought to do it the democratic way, but if we do, we will get nothing but a lot of talk. Nothing will get done." This, of course, means that the person does not understand the "democratic way" or that techniques have not been developed to do it the "democratic way." In recent years there has been considerable research into the ways in which groups work, in which leaders can work with groups, and in which individuals within groups should work within the democratic framework. This growing area is the field of group dynamics.

THE DEVELOPMENT OF GROUP DYNAMICS

We have seen (in Chapter 2) that mankind apparently always has lived in groups. We have seen the important part that culture plays in the lives of humans, with the very quality of "humanness" arising from the transmission of culture within the group. Moreover, as we have indicated in Trend IV, Chapter 4, group activity and cooperation have become more important with increased specialization and the complexity of the various social and technological processes. At one time most achievements and advances were made by individuals, although certainly they were influenced by what the individual had learned from others. At the present time many of our most important advances are the result of the work of teams of individuals in research laboratories, in social organizations, and so on. It becomes of increasing importance, then, to understand more about group activity and about how members of groups function. The name that has been applied to the field of study concerned with how groups work and function and ways in which they can do so more effectively is *group dynamics*. Research workers in the field of group dynamics have been interested in helping the members of groups better to understand the forces operating in situations that tend to help or to hinder group action. They have also attempted to develop instruments and skills to facilitate the diagnosis of cases in which groups do not function properly. They have attempted to clarify the various aspects of group leadership and the role of the members necessary to the successful action of the group. They also have attempted to devise techniques of training individuals for better group membership and for the various leadership roles. Furthermore, they have tried to help members of the group bring about improvements in the group situation and to develop techniques and procedures for evaluating group relationships. An example of one of the bodies in this field is the National Training Laboratory in Group Development, which has done considerable research in group dynamics in the postwar period at summer workshops at Bethel, Maine.

A new field that has been closely related to group dynamics and actually draws its materials partially from the same areas of study is the field of *action research*. This is defined as research where the individuals are as much interested in putting the research into action and feeding back the results in further research as they are in the "pure" results of the research itself. It includes the involvement in the research of many persons who will be in a position to put the results into operation.

The Function of the Leadership in Groups

Even though the emphasis in group dynamics turns the attention from the leader to the group, it is essential that a group have a good leader if it is to function effectively. One common weakness of group action in America is the lack of leaders skilled in techniques for keeping groups working in democratic fashion. Good leadership has been commonly thought to be the ability of a person to get other persons to "go along" in accomplishing the purposes of the leader. This, of course, is an authoritarian concept and arises out of the fact that democracy is relatively a latecomer on the scene. There have been, in general, two types of leaders prior to democracy. One was the leader who had prestige because of the respect and affection in which he was held by the group. He was able to exercise leadership because the group felt that he had the answers to all the problems it faced. The other type of leader achieved results because he was feared, the group not daring to go contrary to his will. Neither of these types produces effective democratic processes.

The democratic leader succeeds by helping the group solve its problems through cooperative action. The assumptions for this kind of leadership are the same as the assumptions of democracy and are based on faith that human beings are capable of making their own decisions and of controlling the processes necessary to make changes in their own activities. This type of leadership is not the laissez-faire type, where the leader merely tells the group to go ahead and do as it wishes and that he as a leader will help them to accomplish whatever they desire. It is apparent from the research done at Bethel and elsewhere that the leader must take a much more active role in helping the group to define what it wishes to accomplish. In laissez-faire leadership, usually someone else in the group becomes the aggressive leader if the leader himself does not effectively help the group accomplish its purposes.[8]

The following are some of the positive things that leaders should do in order to help the group operate effectively:

1. The leader must help the group to clarify completely its purposes and to determine the scope and limits of the particular problem at hand.
2. The leader must see to it that all members of the group clearly understand the group's purposes and are involved in the process.
3. The leader must see to it that the group members are sensitized to the need for getting facts and evidence and for going far beyond the "talk stage" in attacking the problem.
4. He must help the group organize itself for specialized work in seeking information that will be helpful in making group decisions, and in having this information brought back to the group and used in deliberation.
5. From time to time he must help the group from straying from its purposes, either through one individual attempting to dominate or sway the group by monopolizing its time or other means, or by the group straying from its purposes by taking up extraneous matters.
6. He must help the group from time to time to realize that the final goal is action and decision rather than the process of deliberation.

Individuals in groups play roles that are as important as that of the leader. One of the leader's roles is to help each person identify and play his

[8]For further information on this, the reader is referred to Darwin Cartwright and Alvin Zander (eds.). *Group Dynamics: Research and Theory* (New York: Harper & Row, 1968).

role. In the following analysis we have followed materials common to the literature on group dynamics. Group roles are constantly changing as the needs of the group progress. It is not intended that this analysis be more than suggestive or that it be used as any kind of stereotype.

1. Group task roles
   a. The Initiator–Contributor. Suggests new ideas and new ways of working.
   b. The Information Seeker. Asks for clarification, for more authoritative information, for additional research to get more facts.
   c. The Opinion Seeker. Searches for facts and tries to get an interpretation of the shared attitudes and values of the group.
   d. The Information or Opinion Giver. Gives facts and opinions relative to the problem.
   e. The Elaborator. Suggests, in terms of examples, and tries to predict the results of other suggestions.
   f. The Coordinator. Shows relationships between ideas and tries to find common points in order to clarify the matter under discussion.
   g. The Orienter. Reviews what the group has done, defines the position of the group with respect to the purpose agreed upon, and raises the question of whether the group is moving in the direction planned.
   h. The Evaluator–Critic. Subjects the accomplishments of the group to some set of standards, raises questions about the practicality, usefulness, or logic of the course of discussion.
   i. The Energizer. Prods the group for decisions.
2. Group building and maintenance roles. These are some of the roles taken in order to extend group-centered attitudes and to prevent the group from falling apart.
   a. The Encourager. Accepts the contributions of others, praises, and commends.
   b. The Harmonizer. Reconciles conflicting views in order to relieve tensions, either through jest or a congenial approach.
   c. The Compromiser. Differs from the harmonizer and operates from within the conflict in which his own ideas or position are involved. He may offer a compromise to someone with a different position.
   d. Communication Facilitator. Keeps the lines of communication open and tries to assure that each person has an opportunity to speak.
   e. The Standard Setter or the Ego Ideal. Proposes the standards the group ought to achieve with respect to both group action and the quality of the group process.
   f. The Group Observer. Keeps records of the group process and reports findings and interpretations during the periods of group evaluation.
3. Destructive roles within the group. Many groups contain people who are oriented to the group process or who are handicaps to group action.
   a. The Aggressor. Tries to inflate his own ego by deflating the status of others.
   b. The Blocker. Tends to be very resistant, disagreeing and opposing beyond reason.
   c. The Recognition Seeker. Tries to call attention to himself by acting unusual or by using physical or facial antics.

    d. The Self-confessor. Tries to use the group situation to express personal feelings irrelevant to the situation.

    e. The Playboy. Exhibits cynicism, nonchalance, or frivolity.

    f. The Dominator. Tries to assert his authority or superiority by manipulation of the group.

    g. The Help Seeker. Tries to gain sympathy by expressing confusion or self-deprecation.

    h. The Special-Interest Pleader. Plans to promote the welfare of a group to which he belongs, other than the one in which he is now operating.

4. Techniques to be used to help groups in action. Much experience in group work has suggested techniques that will help the groups to produce changes:

    a. Reality Practice or Role Playing. Role playing is a technique where the group arranges to have parts of the group dramatize a situation, problem, procedure, or type of group structure. By use of this technique it is possible to sensitize members of the group to operational problems, emotional factors, and other blocks. An important part of role playing is the analysis by the spectators of what has been taking place.

    b. The "Buzz" Session. This turns the larger group into smaller groups for talking freely, each taking up some aspect of the problem or all the subgroups attacking the same problem. After discussion, the groups then report back to the main group.

    c. Brainstorming. This is a method that has been developed in industrial and other research groups in order to get hypotheses or ideas for investigation. In this procedure the persons concerned are brought together, and, after the problem has been stated, suggestions are secured as rapidly as they can be given, and without criticism. This is to avoid any inhibition to the thinking process. After the group has exhausted the possibilities of suggestions, and only then, does it begin to analyze and pick out the more promising ones for further investigation.[9]

    d. The Sociodrama. In this case a situation is set up deliberately, in order to have persons express their feelings with regard to something. This is a method of catharsis—the release of pent-up feelings and tensions. In the sociodrama and other methods of catharsis (which include, in addition to sociodrama, letting each person "speak their piece," insuring full individual participation), members of the group are enabled to rid themselves of some of the feelings that may block group action.

    e. Group Discussion. The group-discussion technique is a very common one. Here the group as a whole tries to work out proposed actions appropriate to a democratic society.

Other techniques, such as demonstration, decision-making practice with respect to some smaller problem that can be demonstrated, or group recreational experiences so that the group can meet each other in matters not related to their work, are also helpful. Bringing in experts for panel discussions, reports, field trips, utilization of special member talents are all familiar procedures sometimes used in the group process.

[9]See Alex F. Osborn, *Applied Imagination* (New York: Scribner, 1957).

SENSITIVITY TRAINING: HUMAN POTENTIAL GROUPS

Groups dealing with the promotion of candor, trust, and intimacy have become increasingly popular. These groups have an assortment of names—sensitivity training, T-groups, or encounter groups. The message of each of these groups is, as Rasa Gustaitis said in her book *Turning On*:

> to be fully present at whatever one is in at a particular moment and ready to accept the next moment, whatever it might bring. It is not a matter of performing well but of fully being; not a question of developing a mature attitude toward adult responsibilities but of experiencing anger, love, grief and joy, perceiving subtler inner and outer events and relationships and responding to them clearly and directly.[10]

Esalen, at Big Sur, California, is perhaps the largest and best-known "growth center." The emphasis at Esalen is psychological and sensual, never on the exploration of neurosis and the possible cure, but on individual growth and self-actualization. The people at Esalen feel that the way to change systems is to change people. Groups are planned to help people behave less dishonestly with others, to express the way they feel without fear of the displeasure those expressions might arouse.

The National Training Laboratories Institute for Behavioral Science (mentioned earlier) in Bethel, Maine, has been conducting T-Groups (*T* for training), which are related in format and spirit to the encounter groups. An encounter group is a gathering for a few hours, or a few days, of twelve to eighteen normal people. The purpose is to help each individual, by being candid, to try to gain insight into the way he behaves in groups.

Esalen and NTL are perhaps the largest of the human potential, or human growth, centers. Throughout the country centers are growing. These groups enjoy a wide spectrum of methods of attaining the goal of "self-actualization," from the mysticism at the Zen Mountain Center at Tassajara Springs, California, to the drug culture at Morningstar Ranch, the games played at Synanon, and the sensory awareness techniques practiced by Charlotte Selve in New York.

All these groups have become the object of skepticism on the part of more conservative elements in American society, primarily because sensitivity groups have become equated with nudity, drugs, and sexual promiscuity. Nude groups can be found, as can drug-oriented groups and groups which encourage sexual contact. Each has its own rationale for the particular methods employed. Most groups, however, do not employ these tactics, feeling that sexual contact is not necessary for intimacy, that inhibitions can be released without nudity, and that drugs are really a "cop-out," a refusal to accept the responsibility for achieving congruity.

Groups can cause psychological damage if the leader of the group is not experienced. Jane Howard, in her book *Please Touch*, quotes Dr. William Schultz, "We go in deeper, quicker, faster, . . . but people are safer with us than they might be elsewhere. We don't just leave them after we've opened up. . . . We work them through."[11]

---

[10]Reprinted with permission of The Macmillan Company from *Turning On*, by Rasa Gustaitis (New York: Macmillan, 1969), p. x. Copyright © by Rasa Gustaitis, 1969. The summary of the human sensitivity movement which follows was prepared by Irene Thorman.

[11]Jane Howard, *Please Touch* (New York: McGraw-Hill, 1970), p. 233.

Whether the groups are effective is a question of much debate. Monographs and dissertations say that sensitivity training has been shown to make people better managers, abler than they were to listen accurately, perceive the complexities of relationships, and tolerate pressures and differences.

Carl Rogers has found that groups lead people toward becoming "more spontaneous, flexible, closely related to their feelings, open to their experience, and closer and more expressively intimate in their interpersonal relationships. . . . If we value this type of behavior, then clearly the group process is a valuable process." [12]

As for the educational use of the T-group, the statement by Harrison summarizes the possibilities very fully, although perhaps very ideally:

> Develop the ability to listen, to express and articulate feelings to others; give up the notion of control and manipulation and learn to interact with sensitivity in the the context of other people's needs and abilities; grow beyond the fears of exposure and rejection; develop the ability to express naturally tenderness and love to others; become able to put other people at ease at initial contact; learn how to preserve sense of self within a group. [13]

There of course has been criticism of the sensitivity movement. Bruce Maliver, in a well-balanced article, points out some dangers.

> Many observers feel that there is in the encounter movement the essence of a profound emotional fascism. Not necessarily a political fascism, but one that elicits emotional conformity, demands the correct behavior and the correct emotion at the designated time, and suppresses criticism.
>
> It has often been pointed out that American culture has a profoundly right-wing component, and it strikes me as interesting that among the population groups that have most readily taken encounter to their bosoms have been churches from the least emotionally expressive Protestant denominations, suburban school systems and business organizations. . . .
>
> Let me make it clear that I don't think the encounter movement is all bad. It already has had an effect on many conventional therapists, giving them second thoughts about some of their long-cherished beliefs, particularly with respect to how the body expresses, and interacts with, personality. Therapists have long been concerned that their treatment techniques may be too heavily rooted in the verbal interchanges known as intellectualizing (". . . so he said he felt this, and then I said I feel that," etc.). Perhaps the most important result of the encounter cult is that many conventionally trained psychotherapists, myself included, are selectively incorporating encounter techniques into our group work and even into our individual practices.
>
> Competent, carefully planned group process can work wonders, both in clinical practice and organizational settings. But the risks of such experiments are too great unless the leaders are professionally trained and strive for an atmosphere of confidentiality, nonpressure and above all, respect for the individual's right to maintain his own life-style or social adaptation if he so chooses. [14]

[12]Quoted by Rasa Gustaitis, *Turning On* (New York: Macmillan, 1969), p. 236–237. Used by permission.

[13]Charles H. Harrison, "The Teacher and the T-Group," *Scholastic Teacher*, February 1, 1971, p. 6. Reprinted by permission. © 1971 by *Scholastic Magazines, Inc.*

[14]Bruce Maliver, "Encounter Groupers Up Against the Wall," *The New York Times Magazine*, January 3, 1971, p. 43. © 1971 by The New York Times Company. Reprinted by permission.

PROTEST AND CONFRONTATION POLITICS

Perhaps one of the most significant and far-reaching social changes, and potentially the greatest threat of all, in the United States and the world, is the growing use of protest and confrontation politics and the violence that frequently flows from it. The worldwide trend in this mode of political expression within countries with a democratic tradition arises out of the sense of frustration by social reformers, largely youth, at the response of society to wrongs that seemed to them so obvious.

The civil rights sit-ins and marches at Selma, Alabama, and elsewhere seemed to be successful, just as the similar movement of Ghandi was in India. However, there was a growing resistance to further proposed reforms. particularly those protesting the Vietnam War. Violence flared, as shown by the assassinations of Robert Kennedy and Martin Luther King and by the violent and fatal riots in Watts, Detroit, and Chicago and at Kent State and Jackson State.

Violence is not new in American life, although Americans like to minimize its prevalence. Skolnick in his report to the National Commission on the Causes and Prevention of Violence[15] has sketched some of the previous instances as including:

1. American Indians.
2. Farmers (1740 and 1790).
3. Pre-Revolutionary American colonists.
4. White Southerners.
5. Northern abolitionists.
6. White Anglo-Saxon Protestants (WASPs).
7. Immigrant groups.
8. Working men.
9. Women.

Thus violence has been a fact of life in American society. Of great concern to the educator is the prevalence of overt, violent student rebellions. The causes for these rebellions are as diverse as human nature, but perhaps understanding the causes should begin with an understanding of students. Paul H. Cashman has attempted to categorize the types of students in the university today.

1. Moderate student activists—prefer to work within the system. Their interests are in major changes in the educational system and in society. They become disruptive only when they sense intolerable behavior.
2. Cause-oriented students—interested in a specific cause—war, poverty, race, academic reform, democratic freedoms. They work within the system as long as the university and community appear to be working on the problem. They will use radical methods to obtain change.
3. Revolutionary students—are in rebellion against the university and the community and see no value in retaining the "establishment."
4. Hip students are alienated by society and have as little contact with it as possible. They are usually not a factor in disruption.

[15]Jerome H. Skolnick, The Politics of Protest (New York: Ballantine, 1969), pp. 10–17.

5. Noninvolved students are career oriented and resent disequilibrium caused by activists.[16]

Cashman[17] feels that the general public does not understand the life style of the students. They have different interests, goals, and tactics from those of the World War II generation. The concept of authority based upon relationships and special knowledge, which so many young people embrace, is hard for the older generation to understand. It is equally hard for the students to understand the concept of authority based upon status and title, which has been a part of the older generation's life.

The young people want solutions to the problems of international conflict, racism, and poverty. They want an educational system flexible enough to meet their needs, permit innovation, and take advantage of new knowledge about society. They want a means by which the democratic freedoms of speech and the press can be guaranteed fully. Cashman feels that in order to satisfy these needs, we must establish relationships between the youth and nonyouth based upon the authority that comes from a helping relationship.

Frederick C. Neff, in an article in *Insights*, advances the idea of meaningful dialogue as a method of coping with student unrest and sets up the following criteria to obtain this end: For dialogue to be successful, it cannot resort to harangue, badgering, or harassment. It progresses better if it begins with broad areas of agreement. The language employed must consist of concepts and terms that have a shared meaning. Each side must concede that it could be wrong, that it can learn something from the other side, that its stand is modifiable. It is advisable to formulate a position which represents the contributions of opposing factors and is forged out of the process of exchanging and interchanging ideas.[18]

Official recommendations for riot control have offered a two-pronged approach, combining a program for the reduction of social tensions and a policy of containment of disruptive factions through the use of force. Skolnick attacks this policy and offers other suggestions. He says that implicit in the two-pronged theory is the assumption that reform measures and firepower measures have the same prospect of gaining executive and legislative support, but that this seems not to be the case. Commissions from the Chicago Commission of 1919 to the Kerner Commission have adopted this approach only to see control recommendations being implemented and social recommendations more or less neglected. Order has been given priority over justice.

An approach that gives equal emphasis to force and reform fails to measure the consequences of employing force; and it fails to appreciate the political significance of protest. A democratic society cannot use force as its answer to long-standing, legitimate grievances. We must, he says, either carry through a firm commitment to massive political and social reform or develop into a society of garrison cities.[19]

[16]Paraphrased from Paul H. Cashman, "Working with the Modern Student," *Journal of Higher Education,* Vol. XLI (April 1970), pp. 266–267.

[17]Ibid., pp. 270-273.

[18]Frederick C. Neff, "Campus Climates," *Insights,* April 1970, pp. 1–2.

[19]Skolnick, op. cit., pp. 342–346.

A common response to student protest is to portray it as a monolithic movement and ascribe to its participants a common motivation. The greatest shortcoming to such simplistic theories is that they oversimplify the diverse themes of student unrest, as Stuart Langton points out, namely, the "survival of mankind," "response to misery and suffering," "repudiation of the present style of life by the advantaged children of the affluent." [20]

Although Langton feels that there is no clear comprehensive ideological system among students, there are some clear ideological convictions that are widely accepted, here summarized:

1. *The Liberal Spirit.* A large proportion of students assume the basic liberal assumptions of "natural rights," personal liberty, meaningful consent in their government, right of property and equality of opportunity. The crucial issue in student protest is the applicability of liberal values. The real antagonist of student rebels is not so much "liberalism" as the liberals who fail to make it work.

2. *The Sense of Alienation.* Alienation has many meanings to students in protest. It may refer to their sense of powerlessness, depersonalization, normalness, or lack of opportunity for meaningful fulfillment. The students assume that the structure of the existing social order separates them from meaningful relationships to it. There is a conviction among the young that the normal and preferable state of man's social existence is to live in a community that is both tolerant and responsive to human needs.

3. *A Commitment to "Praxis."* Many young people are gaining an awareness that they can manipulate social and political institutions, rather than be manipulated by them. There is an emerging ideological conviction to be involved in the determination of social and political Issues.[21]

Students are seeking to cope with the complexities of our society with commitment and passion that is alien to the methods of a generation ago. However, perhaps this intense commitment is reason for hope for a better world. Further, opinion polls made after 1970 and other appraisals indicate that the advocacy of the use of violence is limited to a very few, even of the so-called radical left.

THE AMELIORATION OF CONFLICTS BETWEEN GROUPS

One of the trends in our society (compare Trend X, Chapter 4) has been the increasing division of our society into groups that are antagonistic toward one another. Therefore one of our central problems in attempting to solve the situations in which we find ourselves is to develop some way for these groups to learn to get along better with each other. In other words, we must apply what we know about human relations and group dynamics in helping groups better to know and to understand each other as well as in helping group members to work well *within their own groups.*

[20]Stuart Langton, "Demythologizing the Student Revolt," *Phi Delta Kappan,* June 1970, pp. 540–541.
[21]Ibid., p. 543.

Richard Rubenstein states the problem well in *Rebels in Eden*:

First stage: Relative isolation. The group exists outside the area of economic and political interest of those in positions of great power. While its members are aware of their collective identity (the awareness is often based on shared ethnic characteristics), this group consciousness is not "nationalistic"; that is, it has no political content. Leadership rests with a small elite whose interests are similar to upper-class elites in power. The group's isolation, of course, is not absolute; it may be systematically exploited in certain respects (for example, as a labor force). But on its own territory, where it is generally left alone, it enjoys a high degree of local autonomy and social organization along traditional lines. Examples are Indians of the early seventeenth century. Appalachian farmers and American colonists before 1740, southern whites before 1820, western farmers before 1860, most European immigrant groups during and immediately after their peak years of immigration, urban Negroes before 1920 and Appalachian whites at present.

Second stage: Confrontation. The group is drawn into closer contact with governmental authority and more powerful groups as well as with other outgroups in neighboring territories with whom it engages in conflicts or makes alliances. It begins to pursue political activity along nonviolent lines, under middle-class leadership which wished to integrate its members into the larger society. Group consciousness moves toward the level of "nationalism"; both expectations and dependence vis-à-vis those in power rise. Toward the end of this period the group often makes significant political gains. If, on the local level, its members have achieved sufficient organization to enable them to feel that they can control their own territory and group destiny, it may enter the stage of coalition politics. If, on the other hand, dependence deepens significantly, it begins a revolt. Examples of groups in the confrontation stage are Appalachian farmers between 1730 and 1765, southern whites 1830 and 1865–67, settled first-generation immigrants, urban blacks 1920–60, western farmers 1865–95, Spanish Americans at present.

Third stage: Coalition politics. If the group has secured a local power base either before or after a revolt, it can then enter coalition politics on a national level. If successful, it gains entry into one of the major party coalitions and becomes entitled to share the special privileges of power. If not, it retreats to the local base and awaits its day. Similarly, if the economic needs of the larger society require services which group members are capable of performing, the group will advance to a position of economic power nationally; if not, its members will perform services for each other at the local level. Participation of such "successful" groups in American life involves either a political transformation permitting implementation of group demands or very rapid integration of the group's members individually into the middle class. Examples: German Americans after 1850, Irish Americans after 1880, Jewish Americans after 1930, western farmers after 1935, skilled union members after 1938.

Fourth stage: Revolt. If, in spite of initial political gains the group's dependence deepens to the extent that members see themselves losing control over the local power base and slipping into permanent servitude, a resort to violence is predictable. The violence itself often follows a detectable pattern, with individual civil disobedience followed, in order, by mass civil disobedience, marches and demonstrations, spontaneous rioting, and more selective organized violence. As the group moves through these phases its leadership becomes progressively more militant and the group itself more politically conscious. If the basic problem of group dependence is not resolved, a war of group liberation—which may take the form of mass military mobilization of insurgents or mass acquiescence in guerilla activity—begins. It does not end until the problem of dependence is solved, either by destruction of the insurgents, victory of the rebellion, or implementation of radical political changes. Examples have been given in Chapter 2 but others could be suggested—Hudson Valley farmers during the anti-rent wars of the 1840's, Rhode Islanders during the Dorr Rebellion of the same period, etc. . . .

The process is closely analogous to that which, on the international stage, we call colonialism. In fact, it involves the *internal colonization* of less-developed groups, for whom (as for their foreign analogues) it is an exceedingly painful experience. Contact with the modernizers creates hope, ambition and rising expectations and ends the fatalism characteristic of traditional societies. Simultaneously, it creates a new consciousness of group identity and destroys the old group life, generates a desire for power and weakens the group's traditional power base. Not surprisingly, if dependence deepens, the group begins to behave like a colonized nation. After all, the internal development of the United States involved the same motivations and pressures, and generated many of the same reactions, as the developments of colonial territory by the Great Powers. The perceptions of various out-groups to this effect, although at times overpersonalized and oversimplified, have a basis in fact.

There are fewer differences than one may think between the British or French colonial office and the United States Bureau of Indian Affairs, Freedmen's Bureau or Department of Housing and Urban Development. Like imperial civil servants our internal colonial administrators have traditionally offered their benighted clients the hope of radical self-improvement while, with the best intentions, they disrupted traditional institutions, siphoned off locally produced wealth to the outside, and bought off the indigenous leadership by trading local power for guarantees of the status quo. The same middle-class church groups which dispatched missionaries to the Africans and Chinese attempted, often simultaneously, to save and "civilize" American Indians, waterfront Irish, eastern European factory workers and ghetto blacks. The same business interests which saw Asia and Latin America as a source of raw materials, cheap labor and potential markets moved to exploit the land, labor and purchasing power of domestic "natives"—Indians, southerners, immigrants or Negroes. The same politicians who set out to democratize the world, American style, extended the benefits of the United States Constitution even to domestic outcasts, while troops used to suppress disorder in the Phillipines or Lebanon might also be used to put down revolt in the Coeur d'Alene or Detroit.

Always, the colonizers have had the same dream: unity and prosperity under one law. Always, the colonized come to the same dream: independence. Thus the predominance in so many domestic revolts of the theme of secession, from the Burr conspiracy and Kentucky and Tennessee secession schemes to the current demand of some black nationalists for a separate territory in the South or West. In the context of internal colonization it is hardly surprising that some domestic revolts have been miniature wars of national liberation.[22]

Whenever two groups have a problem concerning the solution of which they do not agree, it usually means that they have that problem in common because they have common, overlapping interests. Quite often when they meet to take up a particular problem, they immediately begin to emphasize their differences. In almost all cases where the groups live in the same culture or similar cultures, they have more points in common with respect to the

[22]From *Rebels in Eden*, by Richard E. Rubenstein (Boston: Little, Brown, 1970), pp. 43–48, by permission of Little, Brown and Co. Copyright © 1970 by Richard E. Rubenstein.

problem than they have differences. Consequently, the first step should be to clarify the problem to see whether or not the nature of the problem itself and at least part of the facts can be agreed upon. Second, they should set forth the areas of agreement with respect to the solution of the problem. There will then be left an area or areas within which are found their differences. Before any attempt is made to resolve or compromise these differences, every effort should be made to get at the facts to see whether or not there can be a decision based solely upon the agreed-upon facts and the common values. They should look at the problem from the point of view of the welfare of both groups and particularly of the long-range welfare of their society. If a common decision that embraces the welfare of both groups and of society cannot be reached, then compromises must be made. Each group must sacrifice something to the common welfare.

Even in a democracy, where the individual is supreme, some decisions must of necessity impair the immediate welfare of some groups. The adoption of labor-saving devices is a case in point. In such cases, the contribution to the welfare of the total society is such that common decency demands that the total society assume the responsibility for assisting the displaced persons in orienting themselves to new ways of living. Thus the dignity of the individual is maintained, even though his old ways of living have become obsolete.

SUMMARY

In this chapter the nature of our American democracy is described. It is indicated that American democracy is more a set of values than it is a political structure. The nature of the authority in our democratic social order is elaborated, and some of the main values that have been formulated as the basis for American democracy are clarified. The problem of people in groups, the field of "group dynamics" is discussed. The new use of groups in sensitivity training and human potential development is described.

Finally the possibility of the elimination of the difficulties between conflict groups within our culture by some kind of effective, peaceful method of obtaining intergroup agreement is suggested. The protest movement, leading to confrontation politics and its accompanying potential (and actual) violence, is considered in a critical vein.

Selected Bibliography

Aaron, Daniel. *Writers on the Left.* New York: Avon Books, 1969. 480 pp.

Aaron, Raymond. *The Elusive Revolution: Anatomy of a Student Revolt.* New York: Frederick A. Praeger, Inc.. 1969. 200 pp.

Academic Freedom and Civil Liberties of Students in Colleges and Universities. New York: American Civil Liberties Union, 1970. 47 pp.

Aldridge, John W. *In the Country of the Young.* New York: Harper & Row, Publishers, 1970. 128 pp.

Alinsky, Saul D. *Reveille for Radicals.* New York: Random House, Inc., 1971. 235 pp.

American Civil Liberties Union. "A Conspiracy Against the Black Panthers?" *Current,* No. 115 (February 1970).

American Council on Education, Special Committee on Campus Tensions, Sol M. Linowitz, Chairman. *Campus Tensions: Analysis and Recommendations.* Washington, D.C.: American Council on Education, 1970. 61 pp.

Ashby, Lloyd W., and John A. Stoops (eds.). *Student Activism in the Secondary Schools: A Practical Outlook*. Danville, Ill.: The Interstate Printers & Publishers, Inc., 1970. 250 pp.

Axelrod, Joseph, Marvin B. Freedman, and others. *Search for Relevance: The Campus in Crisis*. San Francisco: Jossey-Bass, 1969. 244 pp.

Barzun, Jacques. *The American University: How It Runs, Where It Is Going*. New York: Harper & Row, Publishers, 1968. 319 pp.

Bassiouni, M. Cherif (ed.). *The Law of Dissent and Riots*. Springfield, Ill.: Charles C Thomas, Publisher, 1971. 498 pp.

Bazelon, David. "Notes on the New Youth," *Change* (May–June 1971).

Bell, Daniel, and Irving Kristol (eds.). *Confrontation: The Student Rebellion and the Universities*. New York: Basic Books, Inc., Publishers, 1969. 191 pp.

Benne, Kenneth D. *A Conception of Authority*. New York: Teachers College Press, Columbia University, 1943. 227 pp.

Bennis, Warren G., Edgar Schein, Fred Steele, and David Berlew (eds.). *Interpersonal Dynamics*. Homewood, Ill.: Dorsey Press, 1968. 766 pp.

———, and others (eds.). *The Planning of Change: Readings in the Behavioral Sciences*. New York: Holt, Rinehart & Winston, Inc., 1961. 781 pp.

———, and Philip E. Slater. *The Temporary Society*. New York: Harper & Row, Inc., 1968. 147 pp.

Berger, Peter L., and Richard J. Neuhaus. *Movement and Revolution*. Garden City, N.Y.: Doubleday & Company, Inc., 1970. 168 pp.

Bermann, Marshall. *The Politics of Authenticity: Radical Individualism and the Emergence of Modern Society*. New York: Atheneum Publishers, 1970. 325 pp.

Bernstein, Saul (ed.). *Further Explorations in Group Work*. Boston: Boston University School of Social Work, 1970. 148 pp.

Berrigan, Philip. *Prison Journals of a Priest Revolutionary*. New York: Holt, Rinehart & Winston, Inc., 1970. 198 pp.

Bingham, Jonathan B., and Alfred M. Bingham. *Violence and Democracy*. New York: World Book Company, 1971. 188 pp.

Birenbaum, William M. *Overlive: Power, Poverty and the University*. New York: Dell Publishing Co., Inc., 1969. 208 pp.

Birmingham, John (ed.). *Our Time Is Now: Notes from the High School Underground*. New York: Frederick A. Praeger, Inc., 1970. 262 pp.

Blackstone, Tessa, and others. *Students in Conflict: London School of Economics in 1967*. London: London School of Economics, 1970. 352 pp.

Bloomberg, Edward. *Student Violence*. Washington, D.C.: Public Affairs Press, 1970. 91 pp.

Bode, B. H. *Democracy as a Way of Life*. New York: The Macmillan Company, 1937. 114 pp.

Bondurant, Joan V., and Margaret W. Fisher (eds.). *Conflict: Violence and Nonviolence*. Chicago: Aldine Publishing Co., 1971. 200 pp.

Boorstin, Daniel J. *The Decline of Radicalism: Reflections on America Today*. New York: Random House, Inc., 1969. 141 pp.

———. (ed.). *The Sociology of the Absurd, or the Application of Professor X*. New York: Simon and Schuster, Inc., 1970. 94 pp.

Borton, Terry. *Reach, Touch and Teach*. New York: McGraw-Hill Book Company, 1970. 213 pp. Very good in the application of the "human potential" techniques in the classroom.

Braden, William. *The Age of Aquarius: Technology and the Cultural Revolution*. Chicago: Quadrangle Books, Inc., 1970. 306 pp.

Brown, George. *Now: The Human Dimension*. New York: McGraw-Hill Book Company, 1970. 194 pp. A report on a training program for teachers which combined cognitive and effective learning to create a "humanistic education."

Brown, George Isaac. *Human Teaching for Human Learning: An Introduction to Confluent Education.* New York: The Viking Press, Inc., 1971. 298 pp.

Brown, Richard Maxwell (ed.). *American Violence.* Englewood Cliffs, N.J.: Prentice-Hall, Inc., 1970. 170 pp.

Brubacher, John S. (ed.). *The Public Schools and Spiritual Values: A Seventh Yearbook of the John Dewey Society.* New York: Harper & Row, Publishers, 1944. 22 pp.

Buchanan, James M., and Nicos E. Devletoglou. *Academia in Anarchy: An Economic Diagnosis.* New York: Basic Books, Inc., Publishers, 1970. 187 pp.

Buckley, William F., Jr. (ed.). *Did You Ever See a Dream Walking?: American Conservative Thought in the Twentieth Century.* Indianapolis: The Bobbs-Merrill Co., Inc., 1970. 554 pp.

Burton, Arthur (ed.). *Encounter: Theory and Practice of Encounter Groups.* San Francisco: Jossey-Bass, 1969. 207 pp.

Butts, Robert Freeman. *The American Tradition in Religion and Education.* Boston: Beacon Press, 1950. 230 pp. The most authoritative source on the history of the separation of church and state in American history, particularly as it relates to education.

Butz, Otto (ed.). *To Make a Difference: A Student Looks at America, Its Values, Its Society and Its Systems of Education.* New York: Harper & Row, Publishers, 1967. 174 pp.

Callahan, Daniel (ed.). *The Secular City Debate.* New York: The Macmillan Company, 1966. 218 pp.

Cantor, Norman F. *The Age of Protest: Dissent and Rebellion in the Twentieth Century.* New York: Hawthorn Books, Inc., 1969. 368 pp.

Carling, Francis. *Move Over: Students, Politics, Religion.* New York: Sheed & Ward, 1969. 154 pp.

Cartwright, Dorwin, and Alvin Zander (eds.). *Group Dynamics: Research and Theory.* Third Edition. New York: Harper & Row, Publishers, 1968. 580 pp.

Cashman, Paul H. "Working with the Modern Student," *Journal of Higher Education,* Vol. XLI, No. 4 (April 1970).

Chomsky, Noam. "The Student Movement," *The Humanist* (September–October 1970).

Citizenship Education Project. *When Men Are Free: Premises of American Liberty.* Boston: Houghton Mifflin Company, 1955. 167 pp. Developed by this project set up by Teachers College, Columbia University, for use with junior and senior high schools. Contains a listing of the "basic premises" of American liberty together with a description of their meaning.

Clark, Ramsey. *Turbulent Times.* New York: Sidney Hillman Foundation, 1970. 9 pp.

Cohen, Carl. *Civil Disobedience: Conscience, Tactics and the Law.* New York: Columbia University Press, 1971. 222 pp.

Collins, Gary R. "The Manipulation of Human Behavior: A Psychologist's Perspective," *Journal of the American Scientific Affiliation,* Vol. 22, No. 1 (March 1970).

Combs, Arthur W., Stephen M. Corey, and Elinor K. Corey. "Sensitivity Education: Problems and Promise," *Educational Leadership* (December 1970). Washington, D.C.: Association for Supervision and Curriculum Development, N.E.A., 1970.

Commager, Henry Steele. "Is Freedom Dying in America?" *Look,* July 14, 1970.

Cooke, Alistair. *Talk About America.* New York: Alfred A. Knopf, Inc., 1968. 310 pp.

Corey, Stephen M., and Elinor K. Corey. "Sensitivity Education," *The Education Digest,* Vol. XXVI, No. 7 (March 1971).

Cowan, Paul. *The Making of an Un-American: A Dialogue with Experience.* New York: The Viking Press, Inc., 1970. 370 pp.

Crabtree, Walden B. "An Age of Irrelevancy," *Educational Theory,* Vol. 21, No. 1 (Winter 1971).

Dahl, Robert A. *After the Revolution?: Authority in a Good Society.* New Haven: Yale University Press, 1971.

Daly, Charles U. (ed.). *Urban Violence.* Chicago: Center for Policy Study, University of Chicago, 1969. 81 pp.

Danforth Foundation and the Ford Foundation. *The School and the Democratic Environment:* Papers and other materials drawn from a conference sponsored by the Danforth Foundation and the Ford Foundation. New York: Columbia University Press, 1970. 115 pp.

Demaris, Ovid. *America the Violent.* New York: Cowles, 1970. 404 pp.

Deutsch, Steven E., and John Howard (eds.). *Where It's At: Radical Perspectives in Sociology.* New York: Harper & Row, Publishers, 1970. 610 pp.

Dietze, Gotfried. *Youth, University and Democracy.* Baltimore: Johns Hopkins Press, 1970. 117 pp.

Divoky, Diane (ed.). *How Old Will You Be in 1984?: Expressions of Student Outrage from the High School Free Press.* New York: Avon Books, 1969. 350 pp.

Domhoff, G. William. *Who Rules America?* Englewood Cliffs, N.J.: Prentice-Hall, Inc., 1967. 184 pp.

Dorsen, Norman (ed.). *The Rights of Americans: What They Are—What They Should Be.* New York: Pantheon Books, Inc., 1971.

Douglas, Jack D. (ed.). *Freedom and Tyranny: Social Problems in a Technological Society.* New York: Alfred A. Knopf. Inc., 1970. 289 pp.

Douglas, William O. *Points of Rebellion.* New York: Vintage Books, 1970. 97 pp.

Dow, Robert Arthur. *Learning Through Encounter.* Valley Forge, Pa.: Judson Press, 1971. 174 pp.

Draper, Hal. *Berkeley: The New Student Revolt.* New York: Grove Press, 1965. 246 pp.

Dressel, F., Craig Johnson, and Philip M. Marcus. *The Confidence Crisis.* San Francisco: Jossey-Bass, 1970. 268 pp.

The Economist (London). "Terrorism Rampant," *Current,* No. 124 (December 1970).
———. "Will There Be Less Violence?" *Current,* No. 115 (February 1970).

Ehrenreich, Barbara, and John Ehrenreich. *Long March, Short Spring: The Student Uprising at Home and Abroad.* New York: Monthly Review Press, 1969. 189 pp.

Eichel, Lawrence E., Kenneth W. Jost, and others. *The Harvard Strike.* Boston: Houghton Mifflin Company, 1970. 381 pp.

Endleman, Shalom (ed.). *Violence in the Streets.* Chicago: Quadrangle Books, Inc., 1968. 471 pp.

Erlich, John, and Susan Erlich (eds.). *Student Power, Participation and Revolution.* New York: Association Press, 1971. 254 pp.

Eurich, Alvin C. (ed.). *Campus 1980.* New York: The Delacorte Press, 1968. 327 pp.

Fact-Finding Commission on Columbia Disturbances. *Columbia: Report of the Fact Finding Commission Appointed to Investigate the Disturbances at Columbia University in April and May, 1968.* New York: Vintage Books, 1968. 222 pp.

Fairlie, Henry. "A Minority Report on U.S. Violence," *Current,* No. 114 (January 1970).

Fanon, Frantz. *The Wretched of the Earth.* New York: Grove Press, Inc., 1963. 316 pp.

Farber, Jerry. *Student as Nigger.* New York: Pocket Books, Inc., 1969. 147 pp.

Faust, Clarence H., and Jessica Feingold (eds.). *Approaches to Education for Character: Conference on Science, Philosophy and Religion.* New York: Columbia University Press, 1970. 395 pp.

Feldman, Saul, and Gerald Thielbar. *Life Styles: Diversity in American Society.* Boston: Little, Brown and Company, 1971. 480 pp.

Ferry, W. H. "Is a Police State Emerging?" *Current,* No. 115 (February 1970).

Feuer, Lewis S. *The Conflict of Generations: The Character and Significance of Student Movements.* New York: Basic Books, Inc., Publishers, 1969. 543 pp.

Final Report of the National Commission on the Causes and Prevention of Violence. *To Establish Justice, to Insure Domestic Tranquility.* New York: Bantam Books, Inc., 1970. 277 pp.

Fitts, W. H. *Interpersonal Competence: The Wheel Model.* Nashville, Tenn.: Rich Printing Co., 1970. 99 pp.

Frankel, Charles. *Education and the Barricades.* New York: W. W. Norton & Company, Inc., 1968. 90 pp.

Freire, Paulo. *Pedagogy of the Oppressed.* New York: Herder and Herder, Inc., 1970. 186 pp.

Friedenberg, Edgar Z. (ed.). *Anti-American Generation.* Chicago: Aldine Publishing Co., 1970. 160 pp.

Fromm, Erich (ed.). *Socialist Humanism.* New York: Anchor Books, 1966. 461 pp.

Gardner, John W. *The Recovery of Confidence.* New York: W. W. Norton & Company, Inc., 1970. 189 pp.

Geiger, Louis, and Helen Geiger. "The Revolt Against Excellence," *American Association of University Professors Bulletin,* Vol. 56, No. 3 (November 1970).

Gert, Bernard. *The Moral Rules.* New York: Harper & Row, Publishers, 1970. 239 pp.

Gerzon, Mark. *The Whole World Is Watching: A Young Man Looks at Youth's Dissent.* New York: The Viking Press, Inc., 1969. 274 pp. Excellent—has a broad religious conclusion.

Glasser, Ira. "Protecting Student Rights," *Current,* No. 115 (February 1970).

Glazer, Nathan. *Remembering the Answers: Essays on the American Student Revolt.* New York: Basic Books, Inc., Publishers, 1970. 320 pp.

Golembiewski, Robert T., and Arthur Blumberg (eds.). *Sensitivity Training and the Laboratory Approach: Readings About Concepts and Application.* Itasca, Ill.: Peacock, 1970. 515 pp.

Goodman, Mitchell (Assembler). *The Movement Toward a New America: The Beginnings of a Long Revolution.* New York: Alfred A. Knopf, Inc., 1971. 752 pp.

Gotesky, Rubin, and Ervin Laszle (eds.). *Human Dignity: This Century and the Next.* New York: Gordon and Breach Science Publishers, Inc., 1970.

Governors Commission on the Los Angeles Riots. *Violence in the City: An End or a Beginning.* Los Angeles: College Book Store, 1965. 101 pp. The "McCone Report" on the Watts Riot of 1965.

Graham, Hugh Davis, and Ted Robert Gurr. *The History of Violence in America.* New York: Bantam Books, Inc., 1970. 822 pp.

Greeley, Andrew M. "Intellectuals as an 'Ethnic Group,' " *The New York Times Magazine,* July 12, 1970.

Greer, Colin, *Cobweb Attitudes: Essays in American Education and Culture.* New York: Teachers College Press, Columbia University, 1969. 70 pp.

Greer, Mary, and Bonnie Rubinstein. *Will the Real Teacher Please Stand Up?: A Primer in Humanistic Education.* Pacific Palisades, California: Goodyear Publishing Company, Inc., 1972. 236 pp.

Gregg, Richard B. *Power of Nonviolence,* Revised Edition. Nyack, N.Y.: Fellowship Publications, 1959. 192 pp.

Grey, Alan L. (ed.). *Man, Woman and Marriage: Small Group Process in the Family.* New York: Atherton Press, 1970. 225 pp.

Grier, William H., and Price M. Cobbs. *The Politics of Protests.* New York: Ballantine Books, Inc., 1969. 419 pp.

Gurr, Ted Robert. *Why Men Rebel.* Princeton, N.J.: Princeton University Press, 1970. 421 pp.

Gustafson, James M., et al. *Moral Education: Five Lectures.* Cambridge, Mass.: Harvard University Press, 1970. 136 pp.

Gustaitis, Rasa. *Turning On.* New York: The Macmillan Company, 1969. 326 pp.

Haberman, Jurgen. *Toward a Rational Society: Student Protest, Science and Politics.* Boston: Beacon Press, 1970. 132 pp.

Hacker, Andrew. *The End of the American Era.* New York: Atheneum Publishers, 1970. 239 pp.

Hamachek, Con E. *Encounters with the Self.* New York: Holt, Rinehart & Winston, Inc., 1971. 288 pp.

Harman, Willis W. "The New Copernical Revolution," *Journal of the American Scientific Affiliation*, Vol. 23, No. 2 (June 1971). Human sensitivity.

Harrington, Michael. "Toward Legalizing Revolution," *Current*, No. 122 (October 1970).

Harris, Janet (ed.). *Students in Revolt.* New York: McGraw-Hill Book Company, 1970.

Harrison, Charles H. "The Teacher and the T-Group," *Scholastic Teacher*, February 1, 1971.

Hart, Richard L., and J. Galen Saylor (eds.). *Student Unrest: Threat or Promise.* Washington, D.C.: Association for Supervision and Curriculum Development, N.E.A., 1970. 124 pp.

Hartman, Robert S. *The Structure of Value: Foundations of Scientific Axiology.* Carbondale, Ill.: Southern Illinois University Press, 1967. 384 pp.

Hayden, Tom. *Trial.* New York: Holt, Rinehart & Winston, Inc., 1970. 168 pp. On the Chicago conspiracy trial.

Heilbroner, Robert L. *Between Capitalism and Socialism.* New York: Random House, Inc., 1970. 294 pp.

Hensman, C. R. *From Ghandi to Guevara: The Polemics of Revolt.* London: Allen Lane (Penguin Press), 1969. 490 pp.

Hentoff, Nat. *Our Children Are Dying.* New York: The Viking Press, Inc., 1966. 141 pp.

_____. "Why Students Want Their Constitutional Rights," *Saturday Review*, May 22, 1971.

Hersch, Jeanne. *Birthright of Man: A Selection of Texts,* prepared under the direction of Jeanne Hersch. New York: UNESCO, UNIPUB, 1969. 591 pp.

Hills, Christopher, and Robert B. Stone. *Conduct Your Own Awareness Session.* New York: New American Library, Inc., 1970. 238 pp.

Hines, Paul D., and Leslie Wood. *A Guide to Human Rights Education.* Washington, D.C.: National Council for Social Studies, 1969. 139 pp.

Hofstadter, Richard, and Michael Wallace. *American Violence: A Documentary History.* New York: Alfred A. Knopf, Inc., 1971. 478 pp.

Holmes, Robert Merrill. *The Academic Mysteryhouse: The Man, the Campus, and Their New Search for Meaning.* Nashville: Abingdon Press, 1970. 208 pp.

Hook, Sidney. *Academic Freedom and Academic Anarchy.* New York: Cowles, 1970. 269 pp.

Hoopes, Ned. E. (ed.). *Who Am I? Essays on the Alienated.* New York: Dell Publishing Co., Inc., 1969. 386 pp.

Horowitz, Irving Louis. *The Struggle Is the Message.* Berkeley, Calif.: Glendessary, 1971. 175 pp.

Howard, Jane. *Please Touch: A Guided Tour of the Human Potential Movement.* New York: McGraw-Hill Book Company, 1970. 271 pp.

Howe, Irving (ed.). *The Radical Papers.* New York: Doubleday & Company, Inc., 1966. 391 pp.

"Human Potential: The Revolution in Feeling," *Time*, November 9, 1970. Excellent summary of the T-Group, sensitivity training movement, popularly written.

Illich, Ivan D. "The Alternative to Schooling," *Saturday Review*, June 19, 1971.

Jacobs, Paul, and Samuel Landau. *The New Radicals: A Report with Documents.* New York: Random House, Inc., 1966. 333 pp.

Jerome, Judson. *Culture Out of Anarchy: The Reconstruction of American Higher Learning.* New York: Herder and Herder, Inc., 1970. 330 pp.

Jorstad, Erling. *The Politics of Doomsday: Fundamentalists of the Far Right.* Nashville: Abingdon Press, 1970. 190 pp.

Kaplan, Abraham (ed.). *Individuality and the New Society.* Copublished with Reed College, Second Sanctity of Life Symposium. Seattle: Washington University Press, 1970. 168 pp. Six distinguished thinkers from the field of biology, economics, philosophy, psychology, government and political sociology probe basic issues concerned with the future of the individual in contemporary society.

Kaplan, Morton A. *Dissent and the State in Peace and War: An Essay on the Grounds of Public Morality.* New York: Dunnelon, 1970. 172 pp.

Karier, Clarence J. *The Quest for Orderly Change.* Paper presented at Midwest Regional Meeting, History of Education Society, Chicago, Illinois, October 30, 1970. 22 pp. (Mimeographed.)

Katope, Christopher, and Paul Zolbrod. *The Rhetoric of Revolution.* New York: The Macmillan Company, 1970. 553 pp.

Katz, Joseph, and associates. *No Time for Youth: Growth and Constraint in College Students.* San Francisco: Jossey-Bass, 1968. 463 pp.

Kavanaugh, Robert. *The Grim Generation.* New York: Trident Press, Inc., 1970. 219 pp.

Kelley, Earl. *In Defense of Youth.* Englewood Cliffs, N.J.: Prentice-Hall, Inc., 1962. 145 pp.

Kelman, Steven. *Push Comes to Shove: The Education of Student Protest.* Boston: Houghton Mifflin Company, 1970. 287 pp. (Paperback.)

Keniston, Kenneth. *Young Radicals: Notes on Committed Youth.* New York: Harcourt Brace Jovanovich, Inc., 1968. 368 pp.

Klein, Alexander (ed.). *Natural Enemies?: Youth and the Clash of Generations.* Philadelphia: J. B. Lippincott Company, 1969. 553 pp.

Knowles, Asa S. "A President's View of Campus Unrest," *School and Society,* Vol. 99, No. 2331 (February 1971).

Kopkind, Andrew, and Frances Lang. "How Far Repression?" *Current,* No. 115 (February 1970).

Kotschnig, Walter M., and Elined Prys (eds.). *The University in a Changing World.* New York: Books for Libraries Press, 1969, 224 pp.

Kunen, James Simon. *The Strawberry Statement: Notes of a College Revolutionary.* New York: McGraw-Hill Book Company, 1972. 292 pp.

Laing, R. D. *The Politics of Experience.* New York: Pantheon Books, Inc., 1967. 138 pp.

Lakin, Martin. *Interpersonal Encounter: Theory and Practice in Sensitivity Training.* New York: McGraw-Hill Book Company, 1972. 292 pp.

Larner, Jeremy, and Irvin Howe. *Poverty: Views from the Left.* New York: William Morrow & Co., Inc., 1969. 319 pp.

Lasch, Christopher. *The Agony of the American Left.* New York: Alfred A. Knopf, Inc., 1969. 212 pp.

Lawlor, John (ed.). *The New University.* New York: Columbia University Press, 1968. 200 pp.

Lehr, Stan, and Louis Rossetto, Jr. "Libertarianism: A New Right Credo?" *Current,* No. 127 (March 1971).

LeMelle, Tilden J., and Wilbert J. LeMelle. *The Black College: A Strategy for Relevancy.* New York: Frederick A. Praeger, Inc., 1969. 133 pp.

Lemon, Richard. *The Troubled American.* New York: Simon & Schuster, Inc., 1970. 256 pp.

Levine, Maryl, and John Naisbitt. *Right On! A Documentary on Student Protest.* New York: Bantam Books, Inc., 1970. 249 pp.

Lewis, Howard R., and Harold S. Streitfeld. *Growth Games: How to Tune in Yourself, Your Family, Your Friends.* New York: Harcourt Brace Jovanovich, Inc., 1970. 292 pp.

Libarle, Marc, and Tom Seligson (eds.). *The High School Revolutionaries.* New York: Random House, Inc., 1970. 276 pp.

Lifton, Robert Jay. *Boundaries: Psychological Man in Revolution.* New York: Random House, Inc., 1969. 113 pp.

Lipset, Seymour Martin, and Earl Raab. *The Politics of Unreason: Right Wing Extremism in America, 1790–1970.* New York: Harper & Row, Publishers, 1970. 547 pp.

Lipset, Seymour Martin, and Philip G. Altbach (eds.. *Students in Revolt.* Boston: Houghton Mifflin Company, 1970. 561 pp.

Lipton, Lawrence. *The Erotic Revolution: An Affirmative View of the New Morality.* Los Angeles: Sherburne, 1965. 322 pp.

Littell, Franklin H. *Wild Tongues: A Handbook of Social Pathology.* New York: The Macmillan Company, 1969. 173 pp.

Lockwood, Lee. *Conversation with Eldridge Cleaver (Algiers).* New York: McGraw-Hill Book Company, 1970. 131 pp.

Lothstein, Arthur (ed.). *"All We Are Saying . . . ": The Philosophy of the New Left.* New York: G. P. Putnam's Sons, 1970. 381 pp.

Lucas, Christopher J. "The Invisible Dissenters," *Educational Studies,* Vol. 2, No. 1–2 (Spring–Summer 1971).

Lynd, Robert S. *Knowledge for What?: The Place of Social Science in American Culture.* Princeton, N.J.: Princeton University Press, 1939. 268 pp.

———, and Helen M. Lynd. *Middletown: A Study in Contemporary American Culture.* New York: Harcourt Brace Jovanovich, Inc., 1937. 604 pp.

Maliver, Bruce L. "Encounter Groups: A Dangerous Game?" *Current,* No. 126 (February 1971), 3–12.

———. "Encounter Groupers Up Against the Wall," *The New York Times Magazine,* January 3, 1971.

Mann, John. *Encounter: A Weekend with Intimate Strangers.* New York: Grossman Publishers, Inc., 1970. 235 pp.

Mann, Richard D. *Interpersonal Styles and Group Development: An Analysis of the Member-Leader Relationship.* New York: John Wiley & Sons, Inc., 1967. 305 pp.

Marcson, Simon (ed.). *Automation, Alienation and Anomie.* New York: Harper & Row, Publishers, 1970. 479 pp.

Martin, David (ed.). *Anarchy and Culture: The Problem of the Contemporary University.* New York: Columbia University Press, 1969. 212 pp.

Martin, Malachi. *The Encounter: Why the Major Religions—Christianity, Judaism, and Islam—Are in Crisis, and How They Have Failed Modern Man.* New York: Farrar, Strauss & Giroux, Inc., 1969. 488 pp.

Maslow, Abraham. *Religions, Values, and Peak Experiences.* Columbus: Ohio State University Press, 1964. 123 pp.

Mays, John B. *The Young Pretenders: Teenage Culture in the Contemporary Society.* New York: Schocken Books, Inc., 1966. 206 pp.

McCord, James H. (ed.). *With All Deliberate Speed: Civil Rights Theory and Reality.* Urbana: University of Illinois Press, 1969. 205 pp.

McGrath, Earl J. *Should Students Share the Power?* Philadelphia: Temple University Press, 1970. 124 pp.

Mead, Margaret. *Culture and Commitment: A Study of the Generation Gap.* New York: Natural History Press, 1970. 113 pp.

Means, Richard L. *The Ethical Imperative: The Crisis in American Values.* Garden City, N.Y.: Doubleday & Company, Inc., 1969. 360 pp.

Metefsky, George, et al. *Six Essays on Hip Culture: Yippie, Third World, Feminist, Marxists. High School Student, Anarchist.* New York: Times Change Press, 1970. 62 pp.

Metzger, Walter P., and others. *Dimensions of Academic Freedom.* Urbana: University of Illinois Press, 1969. 121 pp.

Michaelsen, Robert. *Piety in the Public School.* New York: The Macmillan Company, 1970. 274 pp.

Michener, James A. *The Drifters.* New York: Random House, Inc., 1971. 751 pp.

Miller, Michael V., and Susan Gilmore (eds.). *Revolution at Berkeley.* New York: The Dial Press, Inc., 1965. 348 pp.

Mintz, Morton, and Jerry S. Cohen. *America, Inc.: Who Owns and Operates the United States.* New York: The Dial Press, Inc., 1971. 424 pp.

Moberg, David O. "The Manipulation of Human Behavior: A Sociologist's Perspective." *Journal of the American Scientific Affiliation,* Vol. 22, No. 1 (March 1970).

Morison, Robert S. *Students and Decision Making.* New York: Public Affairs Press, 1970. 136 pp.

Muessig, Raymond H. "The Greening of America: An Imaginary Conversation Between Charles A. Reich and William Socrates, Jr.," *Phi Delta Kappan,* Vol. LII, No. 10 (June 1971).

Muir, William K. *Prayer in the Public Schools.* Chicago: University of Chicago Press, 1967. 170 pp.

Muller, Herbert J. *The Children of Frankenstein: A Primer on Modern Technology and Human Values.* Bloomington: Indiana University Press, 1970. 431 pp.

Neff, Frederick C. "The College and Social Upheaval—some Reflections." Insights of the Members of the John Dewey Society for the Study of Education and Culture, Vol. 7, No. 2 (April 1970). (Excerpts from an address of the Conference of California State Colleges.)

Nichols, David C. (ed.). *Perspectives on Campus Tensions.* Washington, D.C.: American Council on Education. 1970. 232 pp.

——, and Olive Mills (eds.). *The Campus and the Radical Crisis.* Washington, D.C.: American Council on Education, 1970. 309 pp.

Nisbet, Robert. *The Degradation of the Academic Dogma: The University in America, 1945–1970.* New York: Basic Books, Inc., 1971. 252 pp.

——. *The Social Bond: An Introduction to the Study of Society.* New York: Alfred A. Knopf, Inc., 1970. 448 pp.

Nobile, Philip (ed.). *The Con III Controversy: The Critics Look at the Greening of America.* New York: Pocket Books, 1971. 273 pp.

Nyberg, David. *Tough and Tender Learning.* Palo Alto, California: National Press Books, 1971. 186 pp.

O'Banion, Terry, and April O'Connell. *The Shared Journey: An Introduction to Encounter.* Englewood Cliffs, N.J.: Prentice-Hall, Inc., 1970. 203 pp.

Oglesby, Carl (ed.). *The New Left Reader.* New York: Grove Press, 1969. 312 pp.

Olson, Mancur, Jr. *The Logic of Collective Action: Public Goods and the Theory of Groups.* Cambridge, Mass.: Harvard University Press, 1965. 176 pp.

O'Neil, Robert M. *The Price of Dependency: Civil Liberties in the Welfare State.* New York: E. P. Dutton & Co., Inc., 351 pp.

Osborn, Alex F. *Applied Imagination: Principles and Procedures of Creative Thinking,* Revised Edition. New York: Charles Scribner's Sons, 1957. 379 pp. A book describing the process used by industry to develop new ideas, sometimes called brainstorming.

Paradise, Scott. "Man's Relation to Nature, Our Vandal Ideology," *Current,* No. 115 (February 1970).

Peck, Richard. "Can Students Evaluate Their Education?" *The Education Digest,* Vol. XXXVI, No. 9 (May 1971).

Pei, Mario. *The America We Lost.* New York: The New American Library, Inc., 1969. 191 pp.

Pettitt, George A. *Prisoners of Cultures.* New York: Charles Scribner's Sons, 1970. 291 pp.

Platt, John R. (ed.). *New Views of the Nature of Man.* Chicago: University of Chicago Press, 1965. 152 pp.

Pratte, Richard. "The New Sensorium: The New Student," *School and Society,* Vol. 99, No. 2332 (March 1971).

President's Commission on National Goals. *Goals for Americans.* New York: Columbia University Press, 1960. 372 pp.

Putman, Howard. "Campus Unrest: Its Cause and Cure," *School and Society,* Vol. 98, No. 2327 (October 1970).

Rae, Douglas W., and Michael J. Taylor. *The Analysis of Political Cleavages.* New Haven: Yale University Press, 1970. 152 pp.

Ramsey, Paul. *Fabricated Man: The Ethics of Genetic Control.* New Haven: Yale University Press, 1970. 174 pp.

Rejai, M. (ed.). *Decline of Ideology: Empirical and Comparative Perspectives.* Chicago: Aldine Publishing Company, 1970. 200 pp.

Report of the Conference sponsored by the Danforth and Ford Foundations. *The School and the Democratic Environment.* New York: Columbia University Press, 1970. 115 pp.

The Report of the President's Commission on Campus Unrest. *Campus Unrest.* Washington, D.C.: Government Printing Office, 1970. 537 pp.

Report of the Select Committee on Education. *Education at Berkeley.* Berkeley: University of California Press, 1968. 252 pp.

Resnik, Henry S. *Turning on the System.* New York: Pantheon Books, Inc., 1970. 299 pp.

Revel, Jean-François. *Without Marx or Jesus: The New American Revolution Has Begun.* Garden City, N.Y.: Doubleday & Company, Inc., 1970. 269 pp.

Rexroth, Kenneth. *The Alternative Society: Essays from the Other World.* New York: Herder and Herder, 1970. 196 pp.

Riesman, David, and others. *Academic Values and Mass Education: The Early Years of Oakland and Montieth.* Garden City, N.Y.: Doubleday & Company, Inc., 1970. 286 pp.

Robinson, Paul A. *The Freudian Left: Wilhelm Reich, Geza Roheim, Herbert Marcuse.* New York: Harper & Row, Publishers, 1969. 253 pp.

Rockefeller, John D., III. "Reconciling Youth and the Establishment," *Saturday Review,* January 23, 1971.

Rogers, Carl H. *Freedom to Learn.* Columbus, Ohio: Charles E. Merrill Books, Inc., 1969. 344 pp.

––––. *Carl Rogers on Encounter Groups.* New York: Harper & Row, Publishers, 1971. 172 pp.

Rosenbaum, Robert A. (ed.). *Growing Up in America.* Garden City, N.Y.: Doubleday & Company, Inc., 1970. 380 pp.

Roszak, Theodore. *The Making of a Counter Culture.* Garden City, N.Y.: Doubleday & Company, Inc., 1969. 303 pp.

Rubenstein, Richard E. *Rebels in Eden: Mass Political Violence in the United States.* Boston: Little, Brown and Company, 1970. 201 pp.

Rubin, Jerry. *Do It!* New York: Simon & Schuster, Inc., 1970. 256 pp.

Rubinstein, Annette T. (ed.). *Schools Against Children: The Case for Community Control.* New York: Monthly Review Press, 1970. 299 pp.

Ruitenbeek, Hendrik M. *The New Group Therapies.* New York: Avon Books, 1970. 240 pp.

Sampson, Edward E., and Harold A. Korn. *Student Activism and Protest.* San Francisco: Jossey-Bass, 1970. 265 pp.

Sanford, Nevitt. *Where Colleges Fail.* San Francisco: Jossey-Bass, 1967. 229 pp.

Sax, Joseph L. "Civil Disobedience—The Law and the Injustice," *Saturday Review,* September 28, 1968.

Schick, Edgar B. "The Student Conservative Revolution and Faculty/Student Conflict," *Educational Theory,* Vol. 21, No. 1 (Winter 1971).

Schmuck, Robert A., and Patricia A. Schmuck. *Group Processes in the Classroom.* Dubuque, Iowa: Wm. C. Brown, 1971. 156 pp.

The School and the Democratic Environment. Edited for the Danforth and Ford Foundations. New York: Columbia University Press, 1970. 115 pp.

Schrag, Peter. *Out of Place in America: Essays for the End of an Age.* New York: Random House, Inc., 1970. 247 pp.

Schutz, William C. *Here Comes Everybody.* New York: Harper & Row, Publishers, 1971. 295 pp.

———. *Joy: Expanding Human Awareness.* New York: Grove Press, Inc., 1967. 223 pp.

Seale, Bobby. *Seize the Time.* New York: Random House, Inc., 1970. 429 pp.

Select Committee on Education of the Academic Senate, University of California, Berkeley. *Education at Berkeley.* Berkeley: University of California Press, 1968. 252 pp.

Servan-Schreiber, Jean-Jacques. *The Radical Alternative.* New York: W. W. Norton & Company, Inc., 1971. 207 pp.

Sharp, Gene. *Exploring Nonviolent Alternatives.* Boston: Porter Sargent, 1970. 160 pp.

Shepard, Martin, and Marjorie Lee. *Marathon 16.* New York: G. P. Putnam's Sons, Inc., 1970. 253 pp. An account of a human sensitivity group weekend.

Sherif, Muzafer. *In Common Predicament: Social Psychology of Intergroup Conflict and Cooperation.* Boston: Houghton Mifflin Company, 1966. 192 pp.

Short, James F., Jr., and Marvin E. Wolfgang (eds.). *Collective Violence.* Chicago: Aldine-Atherton, 1972. 416 pp.

Shostrom, Everett L. *Man, the Manipulator: The Inner Journey from Manipulator to Actualization.* Nashville: Abingdon Press, 1967. 256 pp.

Silberman, Charles E. *Crisis in the Classroom.* New York: Random House, Inc., 1970. 495 pp.

Simpson, Elizabeth Leonie. *Democracy's Stepchildren.* San Francisco: Jossey-Bass, 1971. 240 pp.

Skelnick, Jerome H. *The Politics of Protest.* New York: Ballantine Books, Inc., 1969. 419 pp.

Slater, Philip. *The Pursuit of Loneliness.* Boston: Beacon Press, 1970. 154 pp.

Smith, M. Brewster. *Social Psychology and Human Values.* Chicago: Aldine Publishing Company, 1969. 438 pp.

Stein, Maurice, and Larry Miller. *Blueprint for Counter Education: Curriculum, Handbook, Wall Decoration, Shooting Script.* Garden City, N.Y.: Doubleday & Company, Inc., 1970. No pagination. Included in the "box" are three charts and a book, the tools for creating a "new educational environment."

Stoff, Sheldon, and Herbert Schwartzberg (eds.). *The Human Encounter: Readings in Education.* New York: Harper & Row, Publishers, 1969. 433 pp.

Stumpf, Samuel Enoch. "Freedom and Order on the Campus," *School and Society,* Vol. 98, No. 2328 (November 1970).

Sutton, Horace. "Fanon," *Saturday Review,* July 17, 1971.

Task Force on Youth. "Youth and Establishment Collaboration?" *Current,* No. 127 (March 1971).

Taylor, Harold. *Students Without Teachers: The Crisis in the University.* New York: McGraw-Hill Book Company, 1969. 333 pp.

Theobald, Robert. *An Alternative Future for America II: Essays and Speeches.* Chicago: Swallow, 1970. 199 pp.

Thompson, Sheila, and J. H. Kahn. *The Group Process as a Helping Technique.* New York: Pergamon Press, Inc., 1970. 158 pp.

Touraine, Alain. *The May Movement: Revolt and Reform.* New York: Random House, Inc., 1971. 373 pp.

Train, Russell. *Challenge to Youth:* Washington, D.C.: The Conservation Foundation, 1966. 14 pp. An address given at the National Youth Conference on Natural Beauty and Conservation, Washington, D.C., June 29, 1966.

Turney, Billy L. *Catcher in the Wrong: Iconoclasts in Education.* Itasca, Ill.: Peacock, 1968. 270 pp.

Tussman, Joseph. *Experiment at Berkeley.* New York: Oxford University Press, 1969. 139 pp.

Uman, Shelley. *The Management of Education: A Systematic Design for Educational Revolution.* Garden City, N.Y.: Doubleday & Company, Inc., 1970. 226 pp.

University of California, Berkeley Academic Senate. *Education at Berkeley: Report of the Select Committee on Education.* Berkeley: University of California Press, 1966. 236 pp.

Urofsky, Melvin (ed.). *Why Teachers Strike.* Garden City, N.Y.: Doubleday & Company, Inc., 1970. 349 pp.

Velvel, Lawrence R. *Undeclared War and Civil Disobedience: The American System in Crisis.* New York: Dunnellen, 1970. 405 pp.

Vizinczey, Stephen. *The Rules of Chaos.* New York: McCall, 1970. 239 pp.

Voss, John, and Paul L. Ward (eds.). *Confrontation and Learned Societies.* New York: New York University Press, 1970. 126 pp.

Walcott, Fred G. *The Origins of Culture and Anarchy.* Toronto: University of Toronto Press, 1970. 161 pp.

Walker, Daniel. *Rights in Conflict: Chicago's Seven Brutal Days.* New York: Grossett & Dunlap, Inc., 1968.

Wallerstein, Immanuel. *University in Turmoil.* New York: Atheneum Publishers, 1969. 160 pp.

———, and Paul Starr (ed.). *The University Crisis Reader.* New York: Vintage Books, 1971. 300 pp.

Warner, Aaron W., and others. *The Environment of Change.* Chicago: Rand-McNally & Co., 1971. 309 pp.

Waskow, Arthur I. *Running Riot: A Journey Through Official Disaster and Creative Disorder in American Society.* New York: Herder and Herder, 1970. 174 pp.

Waxman, Chaim I. (ed.). *End of Ideology Debate.* New York: Funk & Wagnalls, 1969. 397 pp.

Weaver, Gary R., and James H. Weaver. *The University and Revolution.* Englewood Cliffs, N.J.: Prentice-Hall, Inc., 1970. 180 pp.

Weinstein, Michael A. (ed.). *Identity, Power and Change.* Glenview, Ill.: Scott, Foresman & Company, 1970. 288 pp.

Weisse, Edward B. "A Proposal for Combating Campus Revolution," *School and Society,* Vol. 98, No. 2328 (November 1970).

Weldon, Lynn L. *Conflicts in Our Schools.* Columbus, Ohio: Charles E. Merrill Books, Inc.. 1971. 288 pp.

Westley, William A. *Violence and the Police. A Sociological Study of Law, Custom and Morality.* Cambridge, Mass.: M.I.T. Press, 1971. 222 pp.

Wheeler, Harvey. *The Politics of Revolution.* Berkeley, Calif.: Glendessary, 1971. 308 pp.

Wiener, Norbert. *The Human Use of Human Beings: Cybernetics and Society.* New York: Avon Books, 1967. 288 pp.

Williams, Daniel Day. *What Present-Day Theologians Are Thinking.* New York: Harper & Row, Publishers, 1952. 400 pp.
Williams, J. Paul. *What Americans Believe and How They Worship.* New York: Harper & Row, Publishers, 1952. 400 pp.
Winter, Gibson. *Being Free: Reflections on America's Cultural Revolution.* New York: The Macmillan Company, 1970. 158 pp.
Wolin, Sheldon S., and John H. Schaar. *The Berkeley Rebellion and Beyond.* New York: New York Review of Books, 1970. 158 pp.
Yablonsky, Lewis. *The Tunnel Back: Synanon.* New York: The Macmillan Company, 1965. 403 pp.
Yankelovich, Daniel. *Youth and the Establishment:* A Report on Research for John D. Rockefeller, III, and the Task Force on Youth. New York: JDR, 3rd. Fund, Inc., 1971. 89 pp.
Young, Michael. *The Rise of the Meritocracy, 1870–2033.* Baltimore: Penguin Books, Inc., 1958. 190 pp.
Young, Richard P. (ed.). *Roots of Rebellion: The Evolution of Black Politics and Protest Since World War II.* New York: Harper & Row, Publishers, 1970. 482 pp.
Your Human Rights: The Universal Declaration of Human Rights Proclaimed by the United Nations, December 10. 1948. New York: Ellner, 1950. 71 pp.
Zinn, Howard. *The Politics of History.* Boston: Beacon Press, 1970. 390 pp.
Zorsa, Richard. *The Right to Say We.* New York: Frederick A. Praeger, Inc., 1970. 214 pp.

Selected Films

Almanac of Liberty (Anti-Defamation League), 48 min. A film on Supreme Court Justice Douglas's book by the same name is a drama highlighting Bill of Rights Day. Justice Douglas's book, published in late 1954 by Doubleday, is a group of 366 short essays dealing with landmarks in America's struggle for freedom.
Belonging to the Group (EBF), 16 min. Examines the meaning of the idea of respect and explains its essential relation to living in a democracy. Illustrates the origin and the development of some of the barriers to respect, and suggests ways for eliminating them. Indicates how respect must be exchanged among all members of society.
Born Equal (MP, UN Film Board), 11 min. Uses specific examples to interpret the Declaration of Human Rights as it emerges out of the United Nations Charter. Stresses the acceptance of individual responsibilities as well as rights and emphasizes the necessity for nations to support the provisions of the Declaration.
Crisis in the Classroom (ICF), 15 min. How can today's students be motivated to take an active and positive role in the process of education? How much authority should a teacher have in the classroom? What part should students play?
Defining Democracy (EBF), 18 min. A combined version of the films *Democracy* and *Despotism*. Illustrates the conditions that lead toward democracy or despotism.
Discussion Techniques (United World Films), 28 min. Various methods used in conducting a discussion hour: Forum, symposium, debate, panel, conference, committee, and informal techniques. Stresses importance of trained discussion leaders.
Due Process of Law Denied (Teaching Film Custodians), 30 min. Excerpted from the feature-length motion picture *The Ox-Bow Incident.*
Education for Democracy (Missouri State Teachers Association), 22 min. Depicts with actual classroom scenes the manner in which Missouri schools achieve the purposes of education in our American democracy as outlined by the Educational Policies Commission of the N.E.A.

Four Religions (Ind.), 60 min. This film examines four of the higher religions of mankind: Hinduism, Buddhism, Islam, and Christianity.

The Great Rights (Brandon), 14 min. This film attempts to alert the public to violations of rights in the first ten amendments: violations made possible by ignorance of the Bill of Rights. It tells how the public can defend itself against infringements on freedom of press, speech, worship, assembly, and trial by jury.

Heritage (McGraw-Hill), 10 min. A short film of clever cartoon animation that defines the natural rights of man and indicates how these rights can be maintained by any individual. Produced by the Anti-Defamation League, Catholic Youth Organization, and Christian Youth Movement.

Learning Democracy (Ed. Film Service), 20 min. How young people can gain experience in the democratic process through participation in school–community projects. Filmed in sixteen Michigan communities. The cast is made up of the actual participants in the projects shown.

Of Human Rights (UN), 21 min. On December 10, 1948, the Universal Declaration of Human Rights was proclaimed by the General Assembly of the United Nations. The importance of the fundamental human rights set forth in this declaration and the necessity of bringing these articles again to the attention of the peoples of the world are portrayed through a discussion between the editor of a small-town newspaper and his two employees.

Practicing Democracy in the Classroom (EBF), 25 min. A high school social studies class explores techniques of planning, sharing, gaining and giving information, evaluating, and deciding. Shows group dynamics in action. Emphasizes democratic methods as adaptable to any subject and age level. Provides interpretation of schools' purposes and methods related directly to community needs. Helpful to adult groups.

Production 5118 (MOT), 30 min. A dramatic story of understanding one another— communication.

Role Playing in Human Relations Training (N.E.A.), 25 min. Demonstrates the role playing of human-relations situations as an educational method. A training film on use of role playing and how to do it, gaining insight into human relations problems by demonstrating and analyzing effects of different behavior, uncovering interperson relationships that are hindering group progress, practicing new behavior before trying it out in real-life situations, communicating human relations skills. Also develops skills required to use role playing—how to take an inventory of problems, how to select one problem upon which the group agrees to work, how to find a real-life example of the problems, and how to set up. get under way, and stop role playing scene demonstrating the problem, how to lead the discussion after the role playing. Note: Role playing is a discussion technique and a complicated and interesting one, not a gimmick.

Secure the Blessings (N.E.A.), 27 min. In school the children of America learn the ways of liberty that they must practice tomorrow to keep America free. Typical adults are faced with decisions that involve the democratic way of living.

Understanding the Law (EBF), 12 min. Explains the rights of individuals to be protected from the law and by the law. Illustrates step-by-step functions in due process of law with a series of dramatic sequences in actual courtrooms. Duties of the state and federal courts in the American judicial system are sketched and dramatized.

Why We Respect the Law (Coronet), 14 min. Respect for the law is developed by a realization that law represents accumulated wisdom, that it is in harmony with laws of nature, and that it is necessary to prevent trouble. A young boy learns through case histories how respect is necessary to enable the law to operate properly.

Chapter 15

■■■■■■■■■■■■■■■■□

Contrasting Viewpoints
as to the School's Role

In spite of some fundamental agreements there are in our democratic society numerous and conflicting points of views as to how the school should operate in a period of social change. In the next section we shall present an overview of the more important of these, and in the following sections we shall describe each one in more detail.

There is a sense in which *all* these alternative points of view tend partially to reflect the fundamentally democratic nature of our culture. As a matter of fact, the authors present in this chapter only those ideas that are in general harmony with the democratic point of view as it is found in our American society, including those of the so-called New Left. However, we do not present the point of view of the American Communists, which represents a kind of extreme totalitarianism of the left; neither do we present the point of view of the extreme Rightists in American society, who believe that there is only the "American way." According to the latter, there should be no unsettled issues. They define the "American way" strictly in terms of their own narrowly conservative point of view; there is no respect for persons who hold conflicting opinions. The American principles, handed down to us by tradition, are to be passed on unchanged and unquestioned to the next generation. Only the principles selected and defined by the extreme rightists are accepted by them as being "American"—all other positions are "Communist." In the opinion of the authors, these extreme rightists violate a basic principle of the American way of life in thus ignoring respect for the individual.

The immediate post-World War II period found Americans divided on the question of education. More recently, we have seen the rise of existentialism; a new philosophical approach, "philosophical analysis"; and, very recently, a nonaligned "New Left." We shall first analyze the situation in the decades between the end of World War II and 1965.

CONTEMPORARY CONFLICTING VIEWS ON THE NATURE OF THE SCHOOL AS RELATED TO SOCIAL CHANGE

The accompanying table (Table 15) is a schematic attempt to set forth the prevailing, conflicting viewpoints present in American democratic society, with respect particularly to the role of the school in a period of social change. These were pre-eminent in the period between 1945 and 1965 and still exist but have become obscured by the rise of newer viewpoints.

Any attempt to delineate the various points of view on any issue in any period in American society will have numerous weaknesses, two of which are particularly significant for this discussion. In the first place, the very way in which the various opinions are classified will be affected somewhat by the position of the person making the classification. Secondly, because any creative thinker will diverge somewhat from all other persons, even those who are close to him in their points of view, any attempt to group persons under a small number of classifications will tend to do some injustice to the unique positions of individuals.

Every philosopher tends to be somewhat individualistic. He has specific points at which he is not in agreement with other persons who, in general, *do* agree with him. In spite of weaknesses and shortcomings, a classification system has merits. It serves to give the student an overview, simplified to be sure, of the range of possibilities. It also gives points of reference when more detailed discussions as to specific points may cause him to lose sight of the larger issues.

The classification system used in the charts and presented first in this chapter will be helpful in setting the patterns against which the present emerging situation can be seen.

The first point of view in the chart is what the authors have labeled *humanism.*[1] This point of view is also called *neohumanism* by some of its proponents. One of several views under this general heading has been called *neo-Thomism*, perhaps better termed *perennialism.* There are many different positions, based on somewhat differing philosophical assumptions, that have been lumped together under the term *neohumanism* as used here; for example, it includes both those persons who are religious humanists and those whose views are not primarily based upon any sectarian religious points of view. In general, the various schools of thought included by the authors under *perennialism* tend to have the following views in common. They believe that there are certain unchanging truths that exist in what is fundamentally an unchanging universe; that the main job of education is to pass on these truths; and that the prime function of education is the cultivation of the intellect.

Robert M. Hutchins, formerly Chancellor of the University of Chicago, was probably the leading proponent of neohumanism, even though he may not have been quite as explicit in the underlying philosophical assumptions as some of the less well-known progenitors. Mortimer Adler, professor of philosophy at the University of Chicago, has stated this point of view very clearly in numerous sources.[2]

The next point of view (Table 15), which is called by Justman *social evolutionism*, roughly corresponds to what has been called by some *essentialism.* (See Essentialist Manifesto discussed later in this chapter.) This point

---

[1]*Humanism* is currently used in so many senses that it is confusing. The use here was in the historic sense as related to the humanism of the Renaissance—interest in man's works.

[2]For example, Mortimer Adler, "In Defense of the Philosophy of Education," Chapter V in John Brubacher (Chairman), *Philosophies of Education*, Forty-first Yearbook, N.S.S.E. (Chicago: The Society, 1942), pp. 197–249.

TABLE 15

Conflicting Philosophies Compared
Prevailing 1945–65

POINTS OF COMPARISON	EXPERIMENTALISM (PRAGMATISM)	RECONSTRUCTION-ISM	EDUCATIONAL LAISSEZ FAIRE
Leading Proponents	Mortimer Adler Robert Hutchins Jacques Maritain	W. C. Bagley C. H. Judd H. C. Morrison	F. S. Breed T. H. Briggs J. B. Conant
Central Ideas Related to the Nature of Education	Prime purpose of education is the development of intellect. The best method of developing intellect is contact with the product of great minds, the classics (great books), or with subject disciplines.	Main function of education is the passing on of the time-tested elements of our social heritage—those essential to social advance: primarily, language (reading and writing), computation, and essential character traits.	Schools exist to help develop individuals for effective social living—to teach people to do better what they would do anyway.
Basic Philosophical Assumptions	Reality dualistic; composed of two essences, matter and ideas (or spirit and form). Knowledge secured by scientific method for matter; ideas and values by reason, intuition, revelation, or faith.	A real knowable universe which is in a state of evolving. Scientific method paramount in getting of knowledge.	
		Social progress result of man's social inventions.	Social progress result of utilization of scientific method by man to accomplish his goals.
Ideas on the School in Relation to Social Change; Other Suggestions as to Curriculum and Method	Social changes are surface phenomena; pose problems, do not change basic truths. Basic values, basic principles and assumptions unchange. Job of school to help student to find basic truths, which can then be applied to current problems.	The subject-matter curriculum of the past is satisfactory to the extent that it represents real aids to man's successful adaptation to his social and physical environment. Methods and adaptations of curriculum to individual differences need improvement.	Schools must quickly change; pupils must be taught to live in present society.

TABLE 15 (continued)

POINTS OF COMPARISON	EXPERIMENTALISM (PRAGMATISM)	RECONSTRUCTION-ISM	EDUCATIONAL LAISSEZ FAIRE
Leading Proponents	Boyde H. Bode John L. Childs W. H. Kilpatrick George Counts	T. Brameld Harold Rugg B. O. Smith Kenneth Benne	Probably does not exist in pure form; may be traced historically to Rousseau.
Central Ideas Related to the Nature of Education	Main purpose of education is to develop critically minded individuals capable of living creatively in their society and of improving society in line with their clarified values.	Main purpose of education is to develop individuals with the ability and desire to create a better social order along the lines dictated by social knowledge.	Main purpose of education is to encourage the fullest development of the individual. Stress on individuality in the handling of students.
Basic Philosophical Assumptions	Reality is that of human experience. The world is dynamic, changing, parts in interaction. Knowledge is tested human experience. Values arise out of experiences and are tested in experience. Both knowledge and values must be continually retested.	Similar to experimentalism—greater emphasis on hypothesis as predeterminant to the solution of the problem.	Similar to experimentalism—greater emphasis on physical environment and on the individual's creative expression.
Ideas on the School in Relation to Social Change; Other Suggestions as to Curriculum and Method	School's job is to help individuals develop, to become creative in problem solving in line with scientific ideas. Curriculum is selected experiences under guidance of the teacher.	Schools should find out the kind of society needed as a result of social change, prepare individuals to create.	Very little emphasis on society.

of view represents, by and large, the positions of Henry C. Morrison, Charles H. Judd, and William C. Bagley. It differs markedly from humanism in its basic assumptions in that it does include the belief in a fundamentally changing, evolving world—one that, however, changes gradually. It holds that the main job of education is the transmission of only those elements from the culture that have become thoroughly established in the onward evolution of man's society. This means that man looks back in his history to discover those essential things that have been helpful in promoting his onward and upward development. The job of the school is, then, to help insure the continuance of these things by passing them on to the young. These elements constitute the essentials of our civilization. Although there may be certain more or less permanent changes coming about at present, one will never know the exact nature or degree of permanence of these current problems, which may represent merely ebbs and flow in our culture. The main job of the school is, then, to pass on those essentials that can be recognized as thoroughly established by man's previous history.

The next point of view (Table 15) is that of which Justman speaks as *social realism*. There are many kinds of realism, including, of course, the realism of Judd and Morrison found under the previous point of view. Philosophically, realism takes many forms. This particular form of realism, social realism, is more of a social philosophy than it is a metaphysical one. Persons of this school of thought, who constitute a sizable majority among the school administrators and others who make up such organizations as the American Association of School Adiminstrators and the National Association of Secondary School Principals, believe that it is the job of the school to keep up with social change and to see to it that the currently prevailing values and ideas of our society are made clear to each generation. It is primarily the job of the school to fit each individual to meet the demands that his society places upon him. We look, therefore, to contemporary society for our values and for the subject matter for the curriculum for our schools. As society changes, so should the school. It should take on the general tenor of the society at any given time.

Another point of view (Table 15), which has been called *pragmatism* by the general philosophers and *experimentalism* in its educational version, tends to place the emphasis upon the development of critically minded, intelligent individuals to live and operate in a changing society. This group believes that one of the most significant features of our culture, or any culture. is the possibility (yes, the certainty) of change. Therefore it emphasizes provisions for experiences in problem-solving situations, and thus in making decisions that are in accordance with scientific methods and with conditions present in a given period of change. Its main goal is to develop critically minded indviduals who seek to operate in accordance with the main values that have emerged and have been found important in our democratic culture.

The next point of view (Table 12) is called *reconstructionism* and is an offshoot of experimentalism. The reconstructionists agree with the experimentalists with respect to most of the latter's interpretations of the nature of social change and also with respect to most of their metaphysical assumptions. They differ largely in their conception of the place of the school with respect to social change. They believe it is the main job of the school to help society make the necessary changes in its institutions in order to meet the demands created by the rapid changes in society. Indeed, it is held that such a reconstruction of our society is so urgent that the school *must* play this part if civilization is to be preserved. Therefore, according to the reconstructionist, the teachers and leaders of our schools must clearly think through what should be the nature of the future society, using the knowledge made available through the progress that has been made in the social sciences. We should then prepare the individuals in our schools to live and operate in such a way as to bring about the new society as quickly as possible.

There is one other point of view (Table 15), which does not have any well-identified proponents at present in our culture but which does represent a point of view sometimes erroneously identified with "modern education." This is the view Wynne calls *educational laissez faire*. Its proponents hold that the main job of the school is to study the child and to develop an educational program or curriculum based upon the *felt* needs and desires of each child (as opposed to adult-recognized present and future needs of the child) and in accord with his particular stage of development. There is no social philosophy[3] inherent in this view except that of an extreme laissez faire (in a broader sense than the economic one). It is doubtful that there are very many individuals who hold strictly to this philosophy or practice it completely, but it does represent a point of view that many people incorrectly ascribe to the so-called progressive educators. It has also been ascribed wrongly to John Dewey. The members of the Progressive Education Association (from which the term *progressive education* originated) represented many points of view having only one common central idea, namely to try to bring about an improvement of education away from what is termed the "traditional" school. A more complete explanation of the laissez-faire view, as related to so-called progressive education, will be found later in this chapter.

In addition to the systematic points of view that we have already indicated, two others gained prominence in the United States in the later years of the 1945–1965 period and are today quite prominent. One of these is existentialism. This will be discussed more fully later, but at this time suffice it to say that existentialism is a philosophical approach that places great emphasis on individual choice and on individual responsibility for that choice. The other point of view is called philosophical analysis or, sometimes in a narrower version, logical positivism. This is rapidly gaining adherents in the general philosophy departments of the United States. This view holds that the primary role of philosophy is to explore the meaning of statements people make. It is closely related to linguistics. It is concerned with the analysis of what is meant when a statement is made. Most of the statements of traditional philosophy are meaningless to this group, because they hold that there is no way of verifying whether or not the statements are true and hence the statements have no real meaning for human existence. These points of view will also be discussed more fully in the next six sections; then the newer movements will be discussed.

[3]It extends through the so-called Romantic philosophers at least as far back as Jean-Jacques Rousseau. See his *Emile*.

SCHOOLS FOR THE DEVELOPMENT OF THE INTELLECT—
PERENNIALISM (HUMANISM, RELIGIOUS AND CLASSICAL)

The way in which the school can serve present society best, according to the humanist position, is in concentrating its efforts on the mental development of outstanding individuals who can become the leaders of our present society. It is the job of the schools carefully to select the best thoughts of the past, representative of the best minds, and transmit them to the present—at least to those persons who are capable of understanding and utilizing these thoughts in the solution of our pressing problems.

Certain main metaphysical assumptions are for the most part held in common by persons having this point of view, whether they are classical or religious humanists.

By and large this group adheres to the concept of a dualistic world composed of two substances or essences, the one of matter and the other of ideas (or spirit or form). The student of philosophy will recognize this concept as going back historically as far as the ancient Greek controversies on the nature of matter. It includes both the Platonic and the Aristotelian concepts. The student of philosophy will also recognize that there is a wide variety of viewpoints that may be taken with respect to the nature of these two types of essences and also with respect to the relationships between them. Also, it will be recognized that some individuals holding the other points of view may be dualists to a greater or lesser extent.

In general, the theory of knowledge that is adhered to by those in the perennialist tradition places less emphasis upon the scientific development of knowledge, in the modern connotation of the word *science* as necessarily involving careful experimentation, and more upon the securing of knowledge through the use of reason or the rational process. In some cases, of course, faith, intuition, or revelation are added to other methods for arriving at ideas of values. The scientific method in general *is* accepted by this group only as a method of securing knowledge concerning the material world. For more basic knowledge, including that of the metaphysical principles and certainly for the realm of values, we must go to other processes. These are held to lie in the realm of ideas where the scientific method is not applicable.

Man himself is considered to differ from animals because he possesses mind. Mind is the "quality of rationality" that makes man different from animals. In general, the chief values for this group are those that are in harmony with the unchanging values that have accredited by the great figures and writers of the past.

Although the American adherents to the perennialist view are for the most part enthusiastic supporters of our democratic society, there certainly is a difference between their point of view toward democracy and some of the points of view to be described later. In general, those in the humanist position accept only the political definition of democracy: namely, that it is a form of government in which the main officers or representatives are chosen by the people. Political equality is not held to mean social or intellectual equality. This group emphasizes quite strongly that everyone should recognize that there is a difference in the kind of contribution different individuals can make to our society. The humanists advocate improvement of the ability of the masses to select as their leaders members of the intellectual elite who can make the proper decisions for the rest of us. The perennialists, for the most part, believe very strongly in the individual's civil liberties and think that we should protect them because individuals must be free to make decisions they wish to make.

In general, those matters that we have usually termed social change, such as those described earlier in this book, are held by those in the perennialist position not to be changes in the basic ideas underlying the universe. Consequently, although these changes pose problems, it becomes all the more important that we should not lose sight of the unchanging principles. The main job of the school, therefore, in times of slow change as well as in times of rapid change, is to see to it that methods of rational thinking are used in facing our problems. Thinking through to the basic principles that underlie solution of the problems we face is held central and paramount in the educational process.

One of the implications of this, of course, is that the school should not be concerned basically with current events. By being too much taken up with current problems, we lose perspective and sometimes do not get at the basic principles in the crosscurrents of our poltical and other problems. Once our minds have been trained to think rationally by coming in contact with the great minds through study of the great books or of the subject disciplines, we shall then be able to use our trained intellects in the solution of the present problems with which we are faced.

This apparent lack of interest by formal education in our present social problems does not mean that persons adhering to this philosophy are not concerned about them. Many of them are. Robert Hutchins, for example, tends to be a social liberal, even though, in his educational philosophy, he harks back to an earlier form of education, which he thinks will enable us to develop leaders to help us solve the social problems we face.

In the perennialist point of view, the best form of education, at least the education of the intellectual elite, is that which was used in our schools in an earlier period: namely contact with the great classics and the lecture method, perhaps supplemented by discussion in seminars with professors familiar with the classics. The student will thereby be stimulated to think, through contact with the ideas that are being promulgated in the great books curriculum or in the subject disciplines. Contact with a great mind that uses rational thinking is more important than practice in the utilization of proper procedures in the actual solving of concrete problems. After it has been ascertained in elementary school or early in high school that certain individuals cannot attain any very great intellectual accomplishment, they should be given vocational training and training for citizenship so that they will be able to make wise decisions in choosing their political leaders. Such training should not be called education, because real education is the development of the intellect.

SCHOOLS TO PASS ON THE TESTED HERITAGE FROM MAN'S HISTORICAL DEVELOPMENT—ESSENTIALISM (SOCIAL EVOLUTIONISM)

Again as in the case of the perennialist, those we have called the essentialists (social evolutionists) represent a number of related points of view. In this case the points of view probably are more similar in their basic philosophical assumptions. This general point of view differs markedly from that of the perennialists with respect to its naturalistic approach to the universe and to man: This point of view, and the others of the series to follow, date (in their more mature forms) from the period after man had discovered the scientific method. What is here called social evolutionism probably can be traced at least as far back as Spencer, the scientist who first applied the Darwinian point of view to the field of social evolution. It is most definitely found within the scientific–evolutionary view of the nature of man and the universe.

In contrast to this emphasis on change, the conclusions for education tend to be of a conservative nature. Whereas the perennialists tend to go back to an earlier period for both the subject matter of the schools and the methods, the essentialists, for the most part, are satisfied with the present curriculum of the school, although some of them may have suggestions for the improvement of methods of teaching. In this group there are wide differences of opinion with respect to certain matters. For example, there is a difference of opinion as to the validity of intelligence tests. William C. Bagley was very critical of the use that was being made of their results in his time. There are also differences as to emphasis. Bagley emphasized adaptability of methods to the individual; Morrison carefully worked out detailed units of study for the various subjects, and Judd emphasized the cultivation of the higher mental processes.

As indicated earlier, the name most aptly applied to this group is *essentialists*. This word is derived from the so-called Essentialist Manifesto which was issued by the Essentialist Committee for the Advancement of American Education and which included among its sponsors William C. Bagley and Henry C. Morrison, who are both listed among the social evolutionists in our classification. This committee also included some persons who might be classified better as humanists or social realists. This Essentialist Manifesto called for more emphasis upon the essential knowledge and skills to be passed on by the school and less emphasis upon "interest, freedom, immediate needs, personal experience, psychological organization and pupil initiative." [4] The contemporary Council for Basic Education would also, in general, be in agreement with this position.

In the discussion of essentialism to follow, we shall limit ourselves to those positions that for the most part are held in common by the persons to be indicated later as the proponents of this general point of view.

The essentialists look to man's evolutionary development in order to get a basis for their ideas about the specific purposes of the school. They note that a study of man's social development indicates that man has been enabled to make progress because of specific adaptations or inventions he has made. Man learned to associate with his fellows for improved ability to secure food and to protect himself from danger. Later, speech developed and still later, the art of writing. Various forms of organization that enabled man

[4]William C. Bagley, "An Essentialist Platform for the Advancement of American Education," *Educational Administration and Supervision*, Vol. 24 (April 1938), pp. 241–256; quoted in John P. Wahlquist, *The Philosophy of American Education* (New York: Ronald Press, 1942). See also the related article, Gurney Chambers, "Educational Essentialism Thirty Years Later," *School and Society*, Vol. 97 (January 1969), pp. 14–15.

to carry on his organization more effectively were developed. Many kinds of adaptation of technology and food getting were discovered and then passed on culturally.

The net result of all this is that man owes his very quality of "humanness" to the social environment in which he is found. Society is pre-eminent. Man gets his individuality from his contact with the society in which he is found.

Education, according to the essentialist view, develops as a separate institution when its functions become so important or so complex that they must be performed by specialists. Then main function of education is to see to it that those great inventions of the past that have enabled man to make such progress are passed on to the young. The school acts as a preserver of the cultural heritage. The school as an institution must carefully study the past, determine those aspects of the past that are worthy of being passed on, and see to it that the new generation is then given the necessary skills, attitudes, and character traits that have been validated by societies of the past. By and large, the traditional curriculum, consisting of the subjects that incorporated the past successful discoveries of mankind, did contain those elements that needed to be passed on to the new generation. The school must do the most effective job possible in seeing to it that these essentials of our time-tested cultural heritage are passed on.

There is implicit in this point of view the assumption that the direction of social evolution is inevitably upward and onward and that the direction is good. Holders of other points of view are not so sanguine in their opinion that the evolution of mankind will necessarily continue in a direction that can be called good. The social evolutionists do recognize that the course of evolution has not always been upward. There have been dips downward. In general, however, they believe mankind will continue in the onward and upward evolutionary progress. In contrast, we will find that the experimentalists, and reconstructionists in particular, believe that man must consciously seek and work for good social progress rather than leave matters to "blind" social evolution.

There are three persons who have done most of the writing that would adhere fairly closely to this point of view as we have described it. Those men are William C. Bagley, Charles H. Judd, and Henry C. Morrison. Certainly there are many others who have similar viewpoints but who are not such prolific writers. Many persons who believe in the same general point of view with respect to the curriculum have not worked out its underlying assumptions so carefully.

In examining the basic philosophical assumptions of this point of view, we run into some fundamental problems, because some of these persons cannot be clearly classified in any of the "standard" general philosophical fields. Judd and Morrison are definitely realists in their basic metaphysical assumptions and could be classified on this aspect very similarly to the persons with the next point of view, social realism. Bagley tends to be more of an idealist, although his writings are not entirely clear in this respect.[5] Many of the

[5]W. C. Bagley, *Education and Emergent Man* (New York: Nelson, 1934); C. H. Judd, *Education and Social Progress* (New York: Harcourt, 1934); H. C. Morrison, *Basic Principles of Education* (Boston: Houghton, 1934).

lesser-known persons holding this view could certainly be classified as having a dualistic interpretation of the nature of the universe and of man (similar to that of the humanists, involving matter and ideas).

To those of this group who base their concept of man on biological evolution, mind is a function of the organism that arose as a part of man's physical evolution. The mind, to this group, is that function of the organism that enables it to solve its problems and to adapt itself in other ways to the various environmental conditions it faces.

For most of the persons in this school of thought, the approach to the problem of knowledge, of course, comes largely through the scientific method. (The historical method is one aspect of the scientific.) Certainly the scientific method should be used to verify facts concerning the nature of the world and of man. The scientific method can also be used in establishing the facts of history. It is from history that, according to this point of view, the values for the use of the school are obtained. The values lie in the preservation of those things that have been validated through their success in man's previous history. The purpose of life, therefore, seems to be to build a society that would operate in terms of those values that have been fully established in man's previous social history.

Because the school is to validate its curriculum and its values by a study of the history of the race, educators need not be concerned about the events that are happening contemporaneously in the society. Indeed, at this very point, when society is in a state of crisis, the school is needed most to act as a conservator or "balance wheel" to support basic social values. This does not mean that there is no change (over a long period of time) in certain basic values as man goes onward in his societal evolution and has new insights. For example, the development of democracy was a new insight that arose out of man's experience and was gradually proved to be helpful for his onward and upward evolution. The school plays no part, however, in these advances of society. It is enough that the school's program assures that the time-tested values and essentials of our culture are passed on, once they are established. By so doing, it will prevent the various societies from moving rather hastily in unknown directions. Any lack of attention to essential values and to man's past heritage may cause a society to deteriorate. As a matter of fact, they note, a study of history indicates this. In many cases a more gradual, and therefore a better, evolution of society would have occurred had the school done a more effective job of passing on the time-tested values of a culture.

For the essentialist, the curriculum of the school should consist of those essentials of subject matter, skills, attitudes, and character traits that have been time-tested and therefore have proved to be good in terms of man's past history. These essentials, for the most part, have traditionally (at least in the recent past) been held to be of most importance in the curriculum of the school. The present school subjects are satisfactory as far as they contain the essentials (knowledge and skills).

The central idea of this point of view can be summarized in the statement, "It is the school's job to pass on the essentials as effectively as possible to the greatest number of persons in our culture in order to insure the optimum conditions necessary for the further onward development of our society." To this group the main function of the school is to facilitate the onward development of our civilization by seeing to it that the essentials of our cultural heritage are passed on as unimpaired as possible to the next generation. Emphasis was upon mastery of essentials by all; no provision was made for leadership training for the gifted few.

SCHOOLS TO ADJUST INDIVIDUALS TO PRESENT SOCIETY— SOCIAL REALISM

The point of view here called *social realism* tends to represent more of a social philosophy than a general metaphysical point of view. For the most part, however, its proponents do adhere to a general philosophical point of view—that of realism. There are many kinds of realism, so we have attempted to differentiate them by calling this one *social realism*. The precise nature of the metaphysical assumptions will be set forth in a later section. As has already been noted, this point of view is a currently prevailing one among school administrators.

In general, this point of view arose (as did social evolutionism) in response to the scientific movement, which came about in the Western world in the latter part of the seventeenth century. The scientific movement did not affect seriously the study of psychology until late in the nineteenth century, with the work of Wundt and others in Europe and the group in America under the stimulation of William James. The point of view underlying almost all of science of that time was a strongly realistic one, philosophically speaking. It was felt that by a careful use of the scientific method we could amass a whole set of facts, each one established in an isolated investigation. These individual facts could then be added together until man could establish all knowledge, and on the basis of this knowledge he could develop the kind of world he wanted. In the field of science and in the scientific study of man, there was little place for values. As a matter of fact, in the early part of this period it was felt that, in order to be scientific, it was necessary to lay aside for the moment all questions of values. Consequently this group was very little interested in the problem of values as such. Indeed some of this group were, and are, quite antagonistic toward philosophy. In the period of the 1920's, when certain extreme aspects of this point of view were quite evident, in the movement of education called *scientism*, there was very little interest in a philosophical approach to the problems of education.

The social realists felt that the job of education is to insure that individuals are prepared to adjust to the present society. The emphasis was upon preparing individuals to *live in our present society*. Consequently one of the main procedures to be used in the selection of a curriculum was to conduct a careful study of the present society, in order to determine just what would be demanded of the students when they got out of school.

The basic philosophical assumptions of the social realists are similar in some respects to those of the social evolutionists. The social realists believe very definitely in a real, knowable world that can be known apart from the particular knower. In other words, this is not a subjective world. It can be known objectively. The means of knowing the world is through the scientific method, whereby knowledge can be validated. Most of the realists formerly

thought that knowledge could be obtained by careful isolation of a phenomenon and by examining it in piecemeal fashion in accordance with the Newtonian scientific tradition. The newer point of view of Einsteinian science
indicates that phenomena must always be studied in the total field of interrelationships. The realists hold that, when man has determined the facts concerning the world in which he lives, the problem remaining is to use them
in accordance with the prevailing purposes and values of his culture. For the
most part the implication is that as teachers and educators we may arrive at
these values by a careful study of our culture. For example, as school administrators, we must study our culture objectively to determine its prevailing
values and then we must proceed to develop the practices of the institution
called the school so that it operates in such a way as to achieve those prevailing values.

The realists recognize that we live in a changing world. Consequently
the school as an institution must change, both to keep up with the world
and to be in touch with whatever values may become predominant at different times in our culture. The realists would agree with those points of view
that hold that the values predominant in a democratic culture are different
from those in, let us say, a feudalistic culture, and that the school at present
must reflect in its practices the democratic nature of our culture.

We have seen that the proponents of the social-realist point of view by
and large desire that the school keep up with the changes in our society. A
special problem arises when we recall that, if in an era of social change we
are preparing people for the now-present society, the society to which they
will have to adjust will be a different one within the next few years. Some of
the social realists have recognized this problem and have arrived at answers
similar to those of the experimentalists. They have become more concerned
about the development of adaptable individuals because of the changing
nature of our society. Another point that many of this group apparently have
neglected is the existence of many conflicts in our society. It is difficult to
find out what values are predominant. At any given time a whole series of
values is in conflict. Sometimes sudden changes are made, perhaps rever-
sions to previous ideas or values. Do we get our values merely by "counting
noses" at a particular time? Does the school follow every change in the
political and social weather vane? This issue appears to be faced in two
different ways by different groups of realists. One approach is to ignore
for the most part those values that are in serious conflict. Instead we may
look at the fundamental activities in which man engages and attempt to dup-
licate them in the school, so that a man can learn as a child or youth to
make proper adjustments in his social activities. Another approach among
the realists is to handle this problem in a fashion similar to that of the experimentalists. The school would teach the student to handle problems of a
controversial nature in a scientific manner and attempt to help him to arrive
at satisfactory answers to the problems with which individuals and groups in
our society are faced. In this latter process, an attempt is made to help the
student to clarify his own values among the varieties of multiconflicting
values found in our society. This latter approach would differ very little in
operation from the methods usually used by the experimentalists. Only the
underlying philosophical assumptions would be somewhat different.

To return now to the discussion of social realism in general, the curriculum of the school should be made up of those activities and selected subject matter that would be of direct, functional, practical value to the persons who are going to live and operate in our culture. The learning situation should be such as to secure maximum learning of facts and skills.

The emphasis on the part of some realists on the wide differences among individuals in regard to capabilities and the activities they will pursue later in life leads them to set up a number of differentiated curricula, particularly in the secondary school, according to the kind of life the individual plans to pursue later. Of course there will be a core of common studies, but there will also be curricula of many kinds, differentiated for persons of differing abilities and with respect to the quite different vocations into which they will enter. Some of the realists advocate plans that use homogeneous grouping of the students with respect to their abilities, so that both curriculum and methods can be more readily adapted to students of similar ability. This point of view has been manifest, of course, in some contemporary secondary schools. Although there is still emphasis on special classes for those people requiring special help, such as the slow learner and the gifted, the general trend today is away from such a heavy emphasis on homogeneous grouping, even among some of the realists.

The realists in general advocate that the methods of teaching should be discovered through scientific research to determine the most effective way of accomplishing whatever purposes or values can be arrived at by the methods described.

SCHOOLS TO DEVELOP INDIVIDUALS WITH ABILITY TO REFINE CRITICALLY THE SOCIAL HERITAGE AND TO IMPROVE SOCIETY—EXPERIMENTALISM

Experimentalism is the point of view that has been ascribed to John Dewey and others of his school of philosophy. In the field of general philosophy, it is based on what is called the pragmatic viewpoint. It is more commonly known as experimentalism as far as the implications for education are concerned. The word *instrumentalism* has sometimes been applied to it because of the stress upon the instrumental nature of the hypothesis or idea in assisting the human organism in solving its problems. This point of view has developed primarily within the American democratic culture, and it stems from democratic values coupled with the scientific method of getting at knowledge and with the general "practical" realistic point of view found in American society. John Dewey assimilated these elements into an integrated point of view to form his pragmatic philosophy.

Most of the persons adhering to the experimentalist position place emphasis on the process of getting at knowledge through the method of tested human experience. Education as the construction and progressive "reconstruction of experience" is John Dewey's way of stating the relation of the educational process to ongoing activity.

The main purpose of education, then, is to develop critically minded individuals who are capable of seeking and finding (at least tentatively) creative answers to the problems they face in their society. Not only should they be able to find answers to their own personal problems, but they should be able to work well with others in a group solution to common problems. There is emphasis among the experimentalists on the clarification of the values of the students as a part of the educational process.

The preceding concepts mean that the curriculum is primarily to be thought of in terms of carefully selected experiences under the guidance of the teacher, in order to develop the kind of individuals who will be capable of the solution of their own problems and of common problems in conjunction with fellow students and later with fellow men.

John Dewey[6] is considered by almost all experimentalists as being their outstanding progenitor. Although his ideas go back to those of William James and thence to Charles S. Peirce, as far as general pragmatic philosophy is concerned, there are important differences in fundamental assumptions and emphasis between the philosophy of John Dewey and that of these other two.

Dewey has had several rather outstanding followers who have served to carry his philosophy much further and to sharpen and clarify it: William H. Kilpatrick and John L. Childs,[7] both of Teachers College, Columbia University, and the late Boyd H. Bode[8] of the Ohio State University. This point of view, by and large, also has been accepted, at least verbally, by a sizable number of the persons who are now teaching courses in various teacher-education institutions in the United States. It is interesting to contemplate the amount of influence that John Dewey has had on educational philosophy and teaching method as taught in teacher-education institutions. John Dewey was not a very dynamic teacher himself, rather soft-spoken and fairly easygoing. He was actually in the Department of Philosophy at Columbia University and was not on the staff of a teachers college. His writings are not particularly easy to read, nor are they particularly clear. Once a person is able to read through the difficult style, the ideas are found to be quite revolutionary in terms of the deep philosophical assumptions involved. It has remained primarily for his followers to spell out in more concrete terms the implications of his philosophy for the schools.

John Dewey held that there are some metaphysical problems the solution of which we can never hope to find. Consequently we should begin to work on our practical problems without trying to settle in advance the answers to all those that are metaphysical. There is, however, a necessary set of assumptions under which the experimentalist operates. The earlier idealistic philosophy held that there are two basic essences of the universe, matter and spirit. The experimentalist tries to resolve this dualism, and along with it many other types of dualisms, by holding that reality is one, the reality of human experience. It is within this reality of human experience that mankind must seek the answers to its problems. This world of human experience in which we find ourselves and in which we attempt to solve our problems is a dynamic, changing world, the parts of which are in constant interaction

[6]John Dewey, *Democracy and Education* (New York: Macmillan, 1931). John Dewey, *Reconstruction in Philosophy* (New York: New American Library, 1953).

[7]John L. Childs, *Education and the Philosophy of Experimentalism* (New York: Appleton-Century-Crofts, 1931).

[8]Boyd H. Bode, *Democracy as a Way of Life* (New York: Macmillan, 1937).

with each other. All knowledge in that universe is tentative and is based upon tested human experience. Each new hypothesis for human action must be tested in terms of consequences for further human action. Hypotheses dealing with values arise out of human experiences in the same way that hypotheses dealing with facts do, and they are tested in that human experience. Both knowledge and values are tentative and must be retested continually.

Almost all experimentalists find three values emerging out of their experience that seem to be fairly universal. These values, also central to our democracy (see Chapter 14), can be summarized as follows: (1) respect for individual personality; (2) use of the reflective–scientific method as a basis for the solution of human problems; and (3) widening of the area of common concern through the increasing participation of all in the solution of problems.

These basic principles, which are much simpler than those of most of the other philosophies, are held by the experimentalists to be sufficient to define a point of view, but they are broad enough to be susceptible to a variety of meanings related to human experience as such experiences change through enrichment and through contact with a changing world. These assumptions are not held to be absolute but are subject to scrutiny and possible change from time to time.

In general, the experimentalists hold it to be the school's job to help individuals to develop so as to become creative in problem solving in line with the scientific method. The curriculum is to be selected experiences under the guidance of the teacher. The following principles of procedure in teaching, generally characteristic of experimentalists, can be listed: (1) experiential learning; (2) student participation in the selection and development of learning experiences; (3) integrated learnings; (4) individualization of the study of the child; (5) emphasis on intrinsic motivation; (6) continuous evaluation by group and self; (7) emphasis on social adjustment; (8) teaching as guidance; (9) emphasis on cultivation of problem-solving abilities; and (10) emphasis on refinement of the cultural heritage.

Some of these principles are accepted also by persons holding other points of view, and, of course, individual experimentalists may well interpret them quite differently in light of their own individual experiential background. In general, these points of view do serve to define a pragmatic approach to the problems of the curriculum and methods of the school.

SCHOOLS TO DEVELOP INDIVIDUALS FOR A NEW SOCIETY BASED ON BEST SOLUTIONS TO PRESENT CONDITIONS AND TRENDS—RECONSTRUCTIONISM

The point of view called *reconstructionism* has become clearly defined only in quite recent years. Theodore Brameld, emeritus professor at Boston University, has played a prominent part in its inception. Reconstructionism has stemmed from the experimentalist point of view and agrees with it in many of the basic philosophical assumptions. The reconstructionists, however, have become quite impatient with the experimentalist teacher, who, they say, hesitates to take a position as a teacher with respect to a definite answer to the problems that the student faces, holding that the student must be "free" to make his own decisions.

Central Ideas Related to the Nature of Education

To the reconstructionists, the main purpose of education is to develop individuals with the ability and the desire to create the new social order now possible. The method to be used in discovering and developing the new social order is the scientific method. The school, however, must have examined available knowledge and must have arrived in advance at a possible solution as to the kind of society that we need in light of our present knowledge and of problems with which we are faced. The teacher then presents this solution to the student, with the evidence pro and con. The student, of course, is permitted to make his own decision with respect to whether or not he accepts or rejects the kind of society that the reconstructionist, in light of his interpretation of the evidence, has found that we need in order to deal effectively with the very crucial problems that we face.

Reconstructionism is a relatively new school of educational philosophy, and the persons who, in general, adhere to this point of view are not entirely agreed upon what should be the exact nature of the new society. Many of those listed below have not directly indicated in writing or otherwise (as far as is known) their particular adherence to it. The following people are here listed on the basis of an examination of their writings as being in general accord with this point of view: Theodore Brameld,[9] B. Othaniel Smith, Kenneth Benne, and William O. Stanley.[10] Although these persons would not entirely agree on all aspects of the kind of school needed, they do agree in general that the nature of the school is determined by the urgency and the kinds of problems that we face. We must, because of the critical times in which we live, rapidly produce a new generation that will have the disposition to create the better society that our scientific knowledge indicates is needed in order to solve the problems we face.

The assumptions of the reconstructionist as to the nature of the world and their answers to other metaphysical problems are similar to those of the experimentalists. At times, some of them do stress the greater emphasis upon the hypothesis as a necessary determinant of the way in which we approach the solution of a problem. There is also on the part of these theorists, such as Harold Rugg, a greater emphasis on the esthetic and on other aspects related to validating knowledge or values other than that of the tested experience emphasized by the experimentalists. For example, Rugg holds that an esthetic experience is intrinsically good in and of itself, rather than because it has been validated by testing its consequences for further human action.

In determining the curriculum of the school, the reconstructionists feel that teachers and others concerned with education must first examine the facts and principles of knowledge that have been discovered by the social sciences and from them determine the kind of society we need. Then they should set up the school's curriculum in such a way as to present these facts

[9]Theodore Brameld, *Education for the Emerging Age* (New York: Harper, 1965).

[10]William O. Stanley, *Education and Social Integration* (New York: Bureau of Publications, Teachers College, Columbia University, 1953).

and principles, including the "blueprint of the new society," so that the student may know what is needed to solve the social problems we face. Although the individual would be given arguments on other sides and would be permitted to choose whether or not he wanted to accept the new society, it is felt that in general he would accept the new society because it would be based upon scientific knowledge and principles. The nature of the new society is held to be readily apparent, given the facts of the situation and the facts and principles developed by the social sciences. It will be acceptable to the student if it is presented fairly to him along with the evidence. The main job of the school, then, is to prepare individuals to have the various skills needed and to know how to use the various procedures needed to bring about the new society.

SCHOOLS WITH EMPHASIS ON SELF-CREATIVITY AND INDIVIDUAL GROWTH—EDUCATIONAL LAISSEZ FAIRE

The point of view with emphasis on "self-creativity and individual growth" is the one labeled *educational laissez faire* in Table 15. On the contemporary scene, this point of view does not exist in any sharply defined form. Sometimes we find it approximated among some persons who lay extreme emphasis on the child-study approach, or sometimes among those who have an extremist approach stemming originally from psychiatry (or at least from a smattering of psychology). In this point of view, there is very little emphasis upon society itself as a basis for determining the nature of the curriculum of the school. The emphasis is upon the individual child and his development trends. The main purpose of education is to encourage the fullest development of the individual. The stress of educational method is on individuality in handling pupils. There is great emphasis upon the individual's physical environment (to be sure that we have an environment that is conducive to his good development), and there is an emphasis upon trying to bring out the individual's creative expression. There is particular opposition to efforts that might thwart the individual's creative expression and his wholesome development.

Some of the persons holding this point of view realize that the pupil does live in and grow with a dynamic, pervasive society, and they do help him to understand his society and to learn to live within it. In this case, the point of view does not differ too greatly from that of experimentalists. The extreme point of view that some popular writers erroneously associate with the term *progressive education*, that of "permitting a child to do as he pleases," stems philosophically from the laissez-faire point of view. This extreme point of view has been erroneously ascribed to John Dewey, even though Dewey in *Experience and Education*,[11] and Boyd Bode, in *Progressive Education at the Crossroads*,[12] have clearly set forth the differences between their point of view, experimentalism, and an extreme point of view among some "progressive" educators of the 1930's, similar to educational laissez faire.

Experimentalism does have a very definite social philosophy in order to

[11]John Dewey, *Experience and Education* (New York: Macmillan, 1938).
[12]Boyd H. Bode, *Progressive Education at the Crossroads* (New York: Newson and Co., 1938).

give it a definite direction, which Bode described as "democracy." The Progressive Education Association was organized originally by persons whose only common philosophy was a desire to move away from traditional practices. Some of them perhaps did go to extremes. In 1941, however, the society did officially adopt a philosophic point of view within the experimentalist position.[13]

NEWER MOVEMENTS (1945–1965)

Existentialism

Existentialism as a point of view and as a well-defined system of thinking goes back to at least the nineteenth century. Some persons have held that it goes back to some aspects of Thomas Aquinas' thinking or even to Socrates and the ancient Greeks. In its more modern version it has a great deal of acceptance among French intellectuals. It arose largely in the nineteenth century as a theological point of view in order to explain the nature of religion in a world in which scientific explanation seemed to do away with any logical basis. However, in the modern form it has two branches—theistic and nontheistic, or atheistic. Jean-Paul Sartre is the most prominent proponent of the nontheistic branch. There are many prominent representatives of the theistic point of view, including Martin Buber, Jacques Maritain, and Paul Tillich, who represent three different theological traditions—Jewish, Catholic, and Protestant, respectively.

Basically the existentialists hold that man lives in a world of despair that is bound to end up in an absurd, tragic finish. In this world in which there is no meaning to be found outside a man's own efforts to find or determine a meaning for himself, the most important thing is for man to recognize the necessity for choosing, and to accept his responsibility to live in accord with his particular choice. One cannot get the answer to the meaning of one's existence from science or any other discipline. Certainly the extent to which man has attempted to probe the meaning of existence in literature and the arts may help other persons to some extent, but basically the question comes back to one's own self, and each must finally make his own choice. What is the nature of my existence and what do I wish to become? "Existence precedes essence." We first recognize we exist; we then choose; and then we develop into the "essence" (or nature) of our choice. This point of view has implications for education in terms of getting youngsters ready to recognize the necessity for choice and to prevent them from being pushed into conformity and standardization without facing up to the necessity for their own choice. This whole point of view is an antisystem. Consequently, there is no well-defined program of action for education. It is more of an attitude or temper than a program.[14]

When we broaden our scope a little and take into account many other points of view related to existentialism, such as phenomenology and personalism, we add a great number of views that are very similar to existentialism. Table 16, taken from Cofer and Appley, illustrates the variety.

[13]See "Progressive Education: Its Philosophy and Challenge," *Progressive Education,* Vol. 8, No. 5 (May 1941), pp. 241–264. (Yearbook issue with special supplement.)

[14]See Van Cleve Morris, *Existentialism in Education* (New York: Harper, 1965).

TABLE 16

List of Recent Theorists Classified as Emphasizing Self-actualization and the Term Each Uses*

Kurt Goldstein (1939): Self-actualization

Erich Fromm (1941): The productive orientation

Prescott Lecky (1945): The unified personality; self-consistency

Donald Snygg and Arthur Combs (1949): The preservation and enhancement of the phenomenal self

Karen Horney (1950): The real self and its realization

David Riesman (1950): The autonomous person

Carl Rogers (1951): Actualization, maintenance, and enhancement of the experiencing organism

  Fully functioning person (1955b)

Rollo May (1953): Existential being

Abraham Maslow (1954): Self-actualization

Gordon W. Allport (1955): Creative becoming

Source: C. N. Cofer and M. H. Appley, *Motivation: Theory and Research* (New York: Wiley, 1964), p. 666. Used by permission.

*A number of theological writers, like Martin Buber and Paul Tillich, could be included. We here confine our consideration to psychoanalysts, psychologists, psychiatrists, and sociologists.

Philosophical Analysis

Philosophical analysts have some difficulty with the problem of values. For some of them, such as Ayer,[15] most value statements are nothing but expressions of the emotive feelings of the speaker. There are others, however, particularly the so-called ordinary-language philosophical analysts, who follow the "later" Wittgenstein.[16] Wittgenstein in late life tried to analyze what is the meaning of the speaker when he makes a "value statement." The former attitude toward value problems makes it difficult for these analysts to determine purposes for education and, therefore, the implications of their philosophy for education. However, it can be assumed that there should be great emphasis upon the study of language, particularly on linguistics, and upon the careful use of logical analysis in exploring the subject disciplines as far as the schools are concerned. The point of view is a very rigorous, highly intellectual one, and certainly it has important implications for the school in terms of the kind of subjects to be emphasized and the approach to be used in teaching them.

It can be recognized that neither existentialism nor philosophical analysis fit into a system. Consequently they can be considered as "mavericks" as far as a systematic analysis of points of view is concerned. We will continue now with the presentation of a point of view that crosses over the lines of points of view within classifications systems, viz., the eclectic position.

---

[15]For example, see A. J. Ayer, *Language, Truth, and Logic* (New York: Dover, 1936), Chapter VI, p. 160.

[16]George Pilcher, *The Philosophy of Wittgenstein* (Englewood Cliffs, N.J.: Prentice-Hall, 1964). Also, David Pole, *The Later Philosophy of Wittgenstein: A Short Introduction with an Epilogue by John Wisdom* (New York: Oxford University Press, 1963).

ECLECTIC POINT OF VIEW

There are many persons who work in the field of education, including indeed some who are definitely students of philosophy of education, who have points of view that do not fit into the classification structure used in this chapter. The word *eclectic* has been applied frequently to those whose point of view does not fit into a standard philosophical position. In the first place, it should be noted that many eclectics are so classified only because they do not happen to fit into a particular structure as it has been set up by someone else. Were the structure different, they might well fit. Second, there is a sense in which all persons who have thought clearly and creatively develop ideas somewhat different from others whose general points of view are similar. This, of course, means they quite often have ideas that are also found in some other point of view. This would automatically make them "eclectics" by definition. Their particular combination of ideas may be very consistent (according to their assumptions) and may fit together into a well-coordinated point of view though it does not fit into a "standard" classification.[17]

In a sense, each of the philosophical positions discussed in preceding sections may be "eclectic" according to one of the other points of view. If, for example, we were to ask an experimentalist how he would handle the problems of passing on the cultural heritage (in which we might be somewhat critical of his apparent lack of emphasis upon past tradition), the experimentalist would probably indicate that he had taken care of the matter because of his emphasis upon the "clarification or refinement of the cultural heritage." In other words, he would not ignore some of the things that are emphasized in other points of view; he would merely stress them in other ways. Similar questions directed at other groups, such as the place of scientific thinking for the humanist or of the importance of cultural change for the essentialist, would be answered in ways to indicate that they had taken into account that particular point but had answered it in a different way. All of them would deny that they were overlooking the emphasis of the other points of view.

All of this discussion on eclecticism indicates that each individual in a democratic society must work out his own point of view for himself in light of whatever criteria or assumptions he considers essential. In general, the point of view that the person may take will depend somewhat upon his own background of experiences. In continuously clarifying and examining his particular point of view, he will have to make his own decisions as to what *his* *assumptions* are. As a matter of fact, in our democratic society we stress the richness of our culture because we do have the diversity possible when each person is free to think for himself. It is not likely that in a democratic society we will ever have complete uniformity of point of view among thinking persons, unless someone enforces a single point of view from a single position of authority. The existence of such an authority is not consistent with the basic assumptions of a democratic society as seen by the authors.

[17]A third possibility, particularly for the less advanced students, is that their everyday operations are based upon conflicting philosophic assumptions not clearly revealed in the writings of the "authorities" nor clearly known to them.

THE NEW LEFT AND THE POLITICIZING OF EDUCATION

It was pointed out at the start of this chapter that since 1965 there has been a reorientation of political and social philosophies in the United States. Most of it was centered on campuses (discussed more fully in Chapter 14) and involved criticism of both education and governmental policies. The force behind this criticism has come mainly from the so-called New Left, which has opposed conservative political groups and the liberal center, all of which have been categorized as "the Establishment." On the other hand, the rightists, in their condemnation of the New Left, quite often included the liberals (who agree with many of the New Left's criticisms but deny their methods) with the New Left, and have called them the "radiclibs."

Carl Oglesby, in his introduction to *The New Left Reader*, writes thus:

> The New Left is properly so called because in order to exist it had to overcome the memories, the certitudes, and the promises of the Old Left. Russia-firstism had been made insupportable by Hungary and then unintelligible by the Sino-Soviet split, well before Czechoslovakia was to make it grotesque. The doctrine of coexistence had therefore lost such binding practical authority as it had formerly possessed. The internationalizing of the class war, momentous event, along with the directly connected triumph of international monopoly as the prime mode of Western economic organization, called implicity for a new conception of the participants in the ongoing conflict of classes. . . .
>
> SNCC and SDS (Students for a Democratic Society) were answering to the name New Left early in the Sixties, but this needs two cautions. Both groups shared a pathological distrust for what they sneeringly called ideology. . . . They wanted . . . to go south and get their hands and their heads—their lives—into [the] dangerous, the moral and therefore the authentic. The instinct from the beginning was to discover the streets, and there was nothing at all anti-intellectual about this. It embodies rather a refusal to tolerate the further separation of thought from its consequences: books argued with each other and lied and in any case did not make much of a difference; only direct experience was incontrovertible.
>
> There are four basic positions on the New Left.
>
> The first is held by a variety of left-wing liberals and Millsian radicals who believe either that the System can produce a worthwhile self-reform, or (the case with the Millsians) that the absence of radical alternatives forces one to hope that it can. The New Left is understood then as a generator of challenges, or critical energy and ideas which may bear some fruit within the evolving structure of enlightened capitalism.
>
> Second, the most familiarly radical position, is that the industrial workers remain the essential driving force of an inevitable socialist revolution. The student movement's main current purposes must be the building of a radical base among the intellectuals and the making of such ties with the factories and the black groups as may be possible.
>
> Third, an exclusively New Left position, is that the composition of the work force has been significantly altered by the massive assimilation of industry and technology. . . . The factory of the post-industrial state is the multiversity. Students are the new working class.
>
> Fourth is a position which has not yet been argued in a sustained way, although it is perhaps suggested in some of the writings by André Gorz, Louis Althusser, and Martin Nicolaus. Diverging from the conclusions but not the

methods of Marx, this view would share with the new-working-class theory the notion that students can no longer be understood as if the modern university retained all the key features of the medieval university. . . . Such a view implies several departures from classical Marxism. First, it denies that bourgeois society in anything like the original model still exists: bourgeois society was above all a scarcity society, a fact which determined its chief legal, political, and economic features. What we have now, inadequately termed post-scarcity and post-industrial, is, in fact, merely the fulfilled industrial society. Second, it denies that bourgeois society (or any other) is the last of the contradictory social systems. On the contrary, there is more reason to believe that each historically successful revolution will produce a new class with a new conception of need and possibility, new objectives which will motivate new historical practices. Third, it denies that the mission of the proletariat was to make the socialist revolution. The objective evidence indicates rather, that its mission was to industrialize society—a mission which brought it into sharp conflict with the bourgeoisie. Fourth, it denies that current world politics can be understood as a clash of rival socioethical systems. Capitalism and socialism, as defined by their practices, are different means, corresponding to different material and political situations, for pursuing the common and general aim of industrialization. Fifth, far from hero-worshipping the proletariat, the new class (unnamed and no doubt at this point unnameable) repudiates in part and in part carries forward the proletarian culture in much the same way that the proletariat both absorbed and transcended bourgeois culture. That an embryonic new class will seek alliances with the proletariat in its struggle with the bourgoisie—this has the same kind of meaning as the fact that the embryonic proletariat made alliances with the bourgeoisie in the latter's struggle against Versailles.[18]

One person who has been identified as a spokesman for the New Left is Herbert Marcuse. His writings are difficult to understand. Robert Marks, in his *The Meaning of Marcuse,* suggests a clarification as follows:

[there are] many paradoxes in the Marcuse story. Bereft of any support from Left, Right, or Center, he has nevertheless more general popularity than any other living philosopher. His books are held by almost everyone who has struggled with them to be uniformly unreadable, yet they are best-sellers in academic circles, and have been translated into some fifteen languages, including Catalan and Serbo-Croatian. His claim for support lies chiefly in his appeal to students and members of the disenfranchised minorities; yet most of the former have not read him, and the latter have not heard of him. He is pictured by his detractors as a political menace whose programs would plunge the world into an Orwellian, Big-Brother-is-watching nightmare; yet he is a soft, gentle scholar, devoted in heart to the spirit of the Enlightenment and the lyric sweetness of Papageno.

Now let us try to list in approximate order of priority the important issues of this day:

1. That all civilization, perhaps all human life, perhaps all life on earth, is in danger of extermination as a consequence of nuclear warfare.
2. That pollution of the environment may so alter the planet that the conditions for sustaining human life will deteriorate to a point of marginal subsistence.

[18]Carl Oglesby (ed.), *The New Left Reader* (New York: Grove, 1969), pp. 13–19. Reprinted by permission of Grove Press, Inc. Copyright © 1969 by Carl Oglesby.

3. That unchecked population growth will multiply the problems of survival beyond the limits of technological solution.
4. That a vastly improved society, based on the maximum use of automation and its associated technology, although now feasible, is not now in the process of development; rather, the reverse is the case—the existing technology is employed in augmented programs of destruction.
5. That "happiness" (or, at least, the minimization of unnecessary suffering) is a realizable goal, but is not admitted in present-day society as a valid goal—and is not approached by institutional means.

The devil in this case is the Establishment.

Marcuse's remedy is to oppose one-dimensionality with negativity. Exert the force of the great refusal. Extirpate the Establishment.

The promised land can be found, he feels, only after the one-dimensional society [i.e. dominated by industrial-technology–materialist goals] has been successfully confronted with its negation. The evils of existing society are a consequence of two factors: (1) the nature and ideals of the society, and (2) the nature of man as he exists in this society—one-dimensional man. But a society which has succeeded in the pacification of the struggle for existence, which has eliminated surplus domination and surplus repression, will witness the emergence of a new kind of man. And this kind of man will not repeat the mistakes of his predecessors because his needs will be different. He will be the Orphic-Narcissistic man whose goals are love, play, and contemplation. Such a man, armed with the ripening fruits of an ongoing technology, will operate under the aegis of Eros. And it is within his power to solve all the essential problems of the world. . . .

In spite of his expressed sympathies for the political aims of Castro and Che Guevara, Marcuse has no liking for the masses, or the values of the masses. These he regards as mutilated men, and the preference of mutilated men; they are consequences of a system which denies to society the development, the degree of perfectibility, which is society's potential in a technologically oriented world. His own tastes are aristocratic, academic, romantic. He foresees the possibility of men acclimated to beauty—however it is defined; men joined in friendship and affection, softened by the instinct for play and the charm of contemplation. What is significant in his purview is the transvaluation of values which can occur once men are freed from rigors of labor and the corruptions of getting-on. With such a change in the quality of society, the term "masses" loses its pejorative meaning, and the values now associated with popular tastes diminish to a vanishing point.[19]

Although the groups working with the New Left have many differences among themselves, they are strongly against the present status quo in the capitalistic countries and, in some cases, the Soviet Union. They are influenced by Mao Tse Tung, Che Guevara, and Herbert Marcuse. They want the universities to become committed to these viewpoints. The liberals in the center are opting for the traditional noncommitment "academic freedom." The New Left argues that control through money and influence has already produced a political, and a conservative, university, i.e. pro-military, pro-industry, and so on.

Many liberals fear that politicizing will mean the early end of academic

[19]Robert Marks, The Meaning of Marcuse (New York: Ballantine, 1970), pp. 8, 123–24, 129–30. Used by permission. Although Marcuse has been identified with the extreme left, early in 1971 he was reported as rejecting violence or even sit-ins. Dr. Spock also at this time took this same attitude against the use of violence.

freedom; consequently, they oppose the official commitment of the university. The conservatives' reaction to the New Left has hardened their views with respect to restrictive policies. The battle is being fought more on a political level than on a deeply philosophical or ideological one.

Specific examples of the changes the New Left would make either in the political sphere or in education after the destruction of the establishment are hard to find. There is a strong anarchist element present. However, we find them quoting freely from such new "authorities" as Paul Goodman,[20] John Holt,[21] and Jonathan Kozol.[22]

These persons do not offer many specific proposals. They seem to be opposed to set curricular requirements, grading, and "systems" in general. They seem to favor the "free school" (or voluntary school), to oppose compulsory attendance, and to place emphasis on the choice of the learner. They want education to be "relevant," that is, to be clearly and exclusively "practical" in terms of the urgent problems of society and the needs of the individual. The Philadelphia experiment (involving a situation where there are no school buildings as such and only designated persons and resources to whom individuals may go for help) generally seems to be the type favored.[23] It is unclear whether any one proposal, other than that of resisting the present system, is accepted by all the members of the extreme New Left. The movement at present seems to be controlled by individuals completely dissatisfied with the present. However, many who oppose much of the present system would rather work to change the system than to destroy it and opt for no system.

SUMMARY

In this chapter there is a discussion of some of the viewpoints on what the school's role in a rapidly changing society should be. Several different viewpoints historically held in recent time were described in some detail. Some would stay with the classical tradition; some would conserve those important elements established in the past by man's societal evolution; some would prepare students to live in current society; some would develop critically minded individuals capable of solving their own problems in a changing society; some would emphasize the schools' participation in the development of the new social order; some would limit themselves to helping individuals grow in ways in line with their own inner tendencies. Certain other groups would break completely with all the preceding approaches. The analytical philosophers, for example, hold that the whole problem of philosophy is one of language. The existentialists, on the other hand, place the emphasis upon the necessity for each individual making his own nonrational value choice. The approach of the proponents of the New Left is not definitely defined categorically, because there is no single point of

[20]Paul Goodman, *Compulsory Mis-education and the Community of Scholars* (New York: Vintage, 1962). *Growing Up Absurd* (New York: Random House, 1960).

[21]John Holt, *How Children Fail* (New York: Dell, 1970).

[22]Jonathan Kozol, *Death at an Early Age* (New York: Bantam, 1968).

[23]See Ivan Illich, "Education Without School: How It Can Be Done," *The New York Review of Books,* Vol. XV, No. 12 (January 7, 1971). pp. 25–31.

agreement among the various proponents. One point of view is that the society can produce worthwhile self-reform; another view is that the working class will inevitably produce a socialist revolution; another view is that the students have evolved into the working class and it is they who will produce the revolution. Some of the more radical seem to support the notion of the complete abolition of the school and compulsory education.

Many persons of our society have developed an eclectic point of view in regard to philosophy and to what they conceive to be the role of the school in a period of rapid social change.

Selected Bibliography

Aaron, Daniel. *Writers on the Left.* New York: Avon Books, 1969. 480 pp.

Ackerman, Nathan W., et al. *Summerhill: For and Against.* New York: Hart, 1970. 263 pp.

Adler, Mortimer J. *The Conditions of Philosophy: Its Checkered Past, Its Present Disorder, and Its Future Promise.* New York: Atheneum Publishers, 1965, 302 pp.

Alinsky, Saul D. *Reveille for Radicals.* New York: Vintage, 1969. 235 pp.

Allport, Gordow W. *Becoming! Basic Considerations for a Psychology of Personality.* New Haven: Yale University Press, 1955. 106 pp.

————. *The Individual and His Revolution.* New York: The Macmillan Company, 1950. 147 pp.

Archanbault, Reginald D. *Philosophical Analysis and Education.* New York: Humanities Press, 1965.

Ayer, Alfred J. *The Problem of Knowledge.* Baltimore: Penguin Books, Inc., 1956. 224 pp.

Axelrod, Joseph, et al. *Search for Relevance: The Campus in Crisis.* San Francisco: Jossey-Bass, 1969. 244 pp.

Bandman, Bertram, and Robert S. Guttchen (eds.). *Philosophical Essays on Teaching.* Philadelphia: J. B. Lippincott Company, 1969. 326 pp.

Barral, R. M. *Progressive Neutralism: A Philosophical Aspect of American Education.* Louvain: Nauwelaerts Publishing House, 1970. 140 pp.

Bayles, Ernest E. *Pragmatism in Education.* New York: Harper & Row, Publishers, 1965. 146 pp.

Beck, Carlton E., and others. *Education for Relevance.* Boston: Houghton Mifflin Company, 1968. 260 pp.

Becker, Ernest. *Beyond Alienation: A Philosophy of Education for the Crisis of Democracy.* New York: George Braziller, Inc., 1967. 305 pp.

Berkson, I. B. *Ethics, Politics, and Education.* Eugene: University of Oregon Press, 1968. 348 pp.

Berman, Marshall. *The Politics of Authenticity: Radical Individualism and the Emergence of Society.* New York: Atheneum Publishers, 1970. 325 pp.

Bigge, Morris L. *Positive Relativism: An Emergent Educational Philosophy.* New York: Harper & Row, Publishers, 1971. 182 pp.

Bloch, Ernest. *A Philosophy of the Future.* New York: Herder and Herder, 1970. 149 pp.

Bloomberg, Edward. *Student Violence.* Washington, D.C.: Public Affairs Press, 1970. 91 pp.

Bode, Boyd H. *Democracy as a Way of Life.* New York: The Macmillan Company, 1937. 114 pp. A short statement on a modern view of the nature of democracy.

Boorstin, Daniel J. *The Decline of Radicalism: Reflections on America Today.* New York: Random House, Inc., 1969. 142 pp.

_____ (ed.). *The Sociology of the Absurd or: The Application of Professor X*. New York: Simon & Schuster, Inc., 1970. 94 pp.

Borton, Terry. *Reach, Touch and Teach*. New York: McGraw-Hill Book Company, 1970. 213 pp.

Bowyer, Carlton H. (ed.). *Philosophical Perspectives for Education*. Glenview, Ill.: Scott, Foresman and Company, 1970. 402 pp.

Braden, William. *The Age of Aquarius*. Chicago: Quadrangle Books, Inc., 1970. 306 pp.

Brameld, Theodore. *The Climactic Decade: Mandate to Education*. New York: Frederick A. Praeger, Inc., 1970. 210 pp.

_____. *Education as Power*. New York: Holt, Rinehart & Winston, Inc., 1965. 160 pp.

_____. *Patterns of Educational Philosophy: Divergence and Convergence in Culturological Perspectives*. New York: Holt, Rinehart & Winston, Inc., 1971. 608 pp.

Breines, Paul (ed.). *Critical Interruption: New Left Perspectives on Herbert Marcuse*. New York: Herder and Herder, 1970. 188 pp.

Brenecke, John H., and Robert G. Amick. *The Struggle for Significance*. Beverly Hills, Calif.: Glencoe Press, 1971. 347 pp.

Broudy, Harry Samuel. "The Philosophical Foundations of Educational Objectives." *Educational Theory*, Vol. 20, No. 1 (Winter 1970).

Brubacher, John S. *Modern Philosophies of Education*, Fourth Edition. New York: McGraw-Hill Book Company, 1969. 393 pp.

Buber, Martin. *The Knowledge of Man*. London: George Allen and Unwin, 1965. 184 pp.

Buford, Thomas G. *Toward a Philosophy of Education*. New York: Holt, Rhinehart & Winston, Inc., 1969. 578 pp.

Burns, Robert W., and Charles J. Brauner (eds.). *Problems in Education and Philosophy*. Englewood Cliffs, N.J.: Prentice-Hall, Inc., 1965. 160 pp.

Butler, J. Donald. *Four Philosophies and Their Practice in Education and Religion*, Third Edition. New York: Harper & Row, Publishers, 1968. 528 pp.

Cahn, Steven M. *The Philosophical Foundations of Education*. New York: Harper & Row, Publishers, 1970. 433 pp.

Callahan, Daniel (ed.). *The Secular City Debate*. New York: The Macmillan Company, 1966. 218 pp.

Camus, Albert. *Resistance, Rebellion, and Death*. New York: Alfred A. Knopf, Inc., 1961. 272 pp.

Chamberlain, J. Gordon. *Toward a Phenomenology of Education*. Philadelphia: The Westminster Press, 1969. 201 pp.

Chickering, Arthur W. *Education and Identity*. San Francisco: Jossey-Bass, 1969. 367 pp.

Child, John L. *American Pragmatism and Education: An Interpretation and Criticism*. New York: Holt, Rinehart & Winston, Inc., 1956. 373 pp. A comprehensive survey of pragmatism and its implications for education.

Cohen, Carl. *Communism, Fascism and Democracy: The Theoretical Foundations*. New York: Random House, Inc., 1962. 704 pp.

Cox, Harvey (ed.). *The Situation Ethics Debate*. Philadelphia: Westminster Press, 1968. 285 pp.

D'Angelo, Edward. *The Problem of Freedom and Determinism*. Columbia: University of Missouri Press, 1968. 107 pp.

Danto, Arthur C. *Analytical Philosophy of Knowledge*. Cambridge, England: Cambridge University Press, 1968. 269 pp.

Denton, David E. *The Language of Ordinary Experience: A Study in the Philosophy of Education*. New York: The Philosophical Library, 1970. 160 pp.

Dewey, John. *Democracy and Education*. New York: The Macmillan Company, 1931. 434 pp. A reprint of Dewey's famous classic. Originally published in 1916.

_____. *Experience and Education*. New York: The Macmillan Company, 1938. 116 pp. A philosophic statement of the nature of experience as related to the means and goals of education. A criticism of certain extremes in progressivism.

_____. *Reconstruction in Philosophy*. New York: The New American Library, 1953. 168 pp. One of Dewey's clearest presentations of his philosophy.

Divoky, Diane (ed.). *How Old Will You Be in 1984?: Expressions of Student Outrage from the High School Free Press*. New York: Avon Books, 1970. 350 pp.

Ellul, Jacques. *To Will and to Do: An Ethical Research for Christians*. Philadelphia: Pilgrim Press, 1969. 320 pp.

Emmet, Dorothy, and Alasdair MacIntyre (eds.). *Sociological Theory and Philosophical Analysis*. New York: The Macmillan Company, 1970. 232 pp.

Fann, K. T. *Wittgenstein's Conception of Philosophy*. Berkeley: University of California Press, 1969. 178 pp.

Faust, Clarence H., and Jessica Feingold (eds.). *Approaches to Education for Character*. New York: Columbia University Press, 1970. 395 pp. Conference on science, philosophy, and religion.

Fischer, David H. *The Revolution of American Conservatism*. New York: Harper & Row, Publishers, 1965. 455 pp.

Fisher, William H. "Value Judgements and Neo-Behaviorism," *School and Society*, Vol. 98, No. 2323 (February 1969).

Fletcher, Joseph. *Situation Ethics: The New Morality*. Philadelphia: Philadelphia Press, 1966. 176 pp.

Fleming, Donald. "The Mood of the New Revolutionaries," *Current*, No. 105 (March 1969).

Frankena, William K. *Three Historical Philosophies of Education: Aristotle, Kant, Dewey*. Glenview, Ill.: Scott, Foresman and Company, 1965. 216 pp.

Fromm, Erich. *Man for Himself*. New York: Holt, Rinehart & Winston, Inc., 1964. 2,456 pp.

_____ (ed.). *Socialist Humanism: An International Symposium*. Garden City, N.Y.: Doubleday & Company, Inc., 1965.

Gallagher, Donald, and Idella Gallagher (eds.). *The Education of Man: The Educational Philosophy of Jacques Maritain*. Garden City, N.Y.: Doubleday & Company, Inc., 1962. 191 pp.

Garcia, John David. *The Moral Society: A Rational Alternative to Death*. New York: Julian Press, Inc., 1971. 353 pp.

Gert, Bernard. *The Moral Rules*. New York: Harper & Row, Publishers, 1970. 239 pp.

Glasser, William. *Schools Without Failure*. New York: Harper & Row, Publishers, 1969. 235 pp.

Goodman, Paul. *Compulsory Mis-education and the Community of Scholars*. New York: Vintage Books, 1962. 339 pp.

_____. "Freedom and Learning: The Need for Choice," *Saturday Review*, May 18, 1968.

_____. *Growing Up Absurd*. New York: Random House, Inc., 1960. 296 pp.

_____. *The New Reformation: Notes of a Neolithic Conservative*. New York: Random House, Inc., 1970. 208 pp.

Gorowitz, Samuel, and Ron G. Williams. *Philosophical Analysis*, Second Edition. New York: Random House, Inc., 1969. 170 pp.

Greeley, Andrew M. "Intellectuals as an 'Ethnic Group,'" *New York Times Magazine*, July 12, 1970.

Greenberg, Herbert M. *Teaching with Feeling*. New York: The Macmillan Company, 1969. 219 pp.

Greenberg, James D., and Robert E. Roush. "A Visit to the 'School Without Walls': Two Impressions," *Phi Delta Kappan*, Vol. LI, No. 9 (May 1970).

Greene, Maxine (ed.). *Existential Encounters for Teachers.* New York: Random House, Inc., 1967. 174 pp.

Greer, Colin. *Cobweb Attitudes: Essays in American Education and Culture.* New York: Teachers College Press, Columbia University, 1970. 70 pp.

Grene, Marjorie. *Introduction to Existentialism.* Chicago: University of Chicago Press, 1962. 149 pp.

Gribble, James. *Introduction to Philosophy of Education.* Boston: Allyn & Bacon, Inc., 1969. 198 pp.

Gross, Ronald, and Beatrice Gross (eds.). *Radical School Reform.* New York: Simon & Schuster, Inc., 1970. 350 pp.

Gutel, Gerald L. *The Educational Theory of George S. Counts.* Columbus: Ohio State University Press, 1970. 277 pp.

Hampden-Turner, Charles. *Radical Man.* Cambridge, Mass.: Schenkman Publishing Co., Inc., 1970. 512 pp.

Hart, Leslie A. *The Classroom Disaster.* New York: Teachers College Press, 1969. 354 pp.

Hendrick, Irving G., and Reginald L. Jones (eds.). *Student Dissent in the Schools.* Boston: Houghton Mifflin Company, 1970. 400 pp.

Hoffer, Eric. *The Temper of Our Time.* New York: Harper & Row, Publishers, 1967. 111 pp.

Holt, John. *How Children Fail.* New York: Dell Publishing Co., Inc., 1970. 223 pp.

Hook, Sidney. *Academic Freedom and Academic Anarchy.* New York: Cowles, 1970. 269 pp.

—— (ed.). *Dimensions of Mind: A Symposium.* New York: The Macmillan Company, 1969. 250 pp.

—— (ed.). *In Defense of Academic Freedom.* Indianapolis: Pegasus, 1971. 256 pp.

Howe, Irving (ed.). *The Radical Papers.* Garden City, N.Y.: Doubleday & Company, Inc., 1966. 391 pp.

Hurwitz, Emanuel, Jr., and Robert Maidment (eds.). *Criticism, Conflict, and Change: Readings in American Education.* New York: Dodd, Mead & Company, Inc., 1970. 484 pp.

Hutchins, Robert M. *The Learning Society: A Major New Statement on Educational Policy.* New York: Frederick A. Praeger, Inc., 1968. 154 pp.

Illich, Ivan. "Education Without School: How It Can Be Done," *The New York Review of Books,* Vol. XV, (January 7, 1971).

——. *Deschooling Society.* New York: Harper & Row, Publishers, 1971. 186 pp.

Jarrett, James L. *Philosophy for the Study of Education.* Boston: Houghton Mifflin Company, 1969. 473 pp.

Junell, Joseph S. "Is Rational Man Our First Priority?" *Phi Delta Kappan,* Vol. LII, No. 3 (November 1970).

Justman, Joseph. *Theories of Secondary Education in the United States.* New York: Teachers College, Columbia University Press, 1940. 481 pp. This is the original piece of research used as a primary basis for the classification system of this chapter.

Kaplan, Abraham. "The Travesty of the Philosophers," *Change,* Vol. 2, No. 2 (January–February 1970).

Katope, Christopher, and Paul Zolbrod. *The Rhetoric of Revolution.* New York: The Macmillan Company, 1970. 553 pp.

Katz, Aaron Hillel. *Mission of Man.* New York: Philosophical Library, Inc., 1970. 104 pp.

Kaufman, Arnold S. *The Radical Liberal: New Man in American Politics.* New York: Atherton Press, 1968. 175 pp.

Keniston, Kenneth. *Young Radicals: Notes on Committed Youth.* New York: Harcourt Brace Jovanovich, Inc., 1968. 368 pp.

Knoller, George F. *Existentialism and Education*. New York: Philosophical Library, Inc., 1958. 170 pp.

Kohl, Herbert R. *The Open Classroom*. New York: Vintage Books, 1970. 116 pp. (Paperback.)

Kozol, Jonathan. *Death at an Early Age*. New York: Bantam Books, 1968. 242 pp.

Kranzberg, Melvin, and C. W. Pursell, Jr. *Technology in Western Civilization*. New York: Oxford University Press, 1967. 772 pp.

LaBenne, Wallace D., and Bert I. Greene. *Educational Implications of Self-concept Theory*. Pacific Palisades, Calif.: Goodyear, 1969. 134 pp.

Laing, Ronald David. *The Divided Self*. London: Tavistock Publications, 1960. 240 pp.

Lamont, Corliss. *Freedom of Choice Affirmed*. New York: Horizon Press, 1967. 214 pp.

Lasch, Christopher. *The Agony of the American Left*. New York: Alfred A. Knopf, Inc., 1969. 224 pp.

Laszlo, Ervin. *System, Structure and Experience: Toward a Scientific Theory of Mind*. New York: Gordon and Breach, 1969. 120 pp.

Lee, Edward N., and M. Mandelbaum. *Phenomenology and Existentialism*. Baltimore: The Johns Hopkins Press, 1969. 268 pp.

Leonard, George B. *Education and Ecstasy*. New York: Dell Publishing Co., Inc., 1968. 239 pp.

Lerner, Max. *Education and a Radical Humanism*. Kappa Delta Pi Lecture Series, Vol. XXXIII. Columbus: Ohio State University Press, 1962. 63 pp. Notes toward a theory of the educational crisis.

Littell, Franklin H. *Wild Tongues: A Handbook of Social Pathology*. New York: The Macmillan Company, 1969. 173 pp.

Lothstein, Arthur (ed.). *All We Are Saying . . .: The Philosophy of the New Left*. New York: G. P. Putnam's Sons, 1970. 381 pp.

Lucas, Christopher J. *What Is Philosophy of Education?* New York: The Macmillan Company, 1969. 313 pp.

Maccia, Elizabeth S., and George S. Maccia. *Development of Educational Theory Derived from Three Educational Theory Models*. U.S. Department of Health, Education, and Welfare: Project 5-0638, Contract 0E4-10-186. Columbus: The Ohio State University Research Foundation, 1966. 188 pp.

MacIntyre, Alasdair. *Herbert Marcuse: An Exposition and a Polemic*. New York: The Viking Press, 1970. 114 pp.

Marcel, Gabriel. *The Existential Background of Human Dignity*. Cambridge, Mass.: Harvard University Press, 1963. 178 pp.

_____. *The Philosophy of Existentialism*, Second Edition. New York: Citadel Press, Inc., 1962. 128 pp.

Marcuse, Herbert. *Eros and Civilization: A Philosophical Inquiry into Freud*. New York: Vintage Books, 1955. 256 pp.

_____. *An Essay on Liberation*. Boston: Beacon Press, 1969. 91 pp.

_____. *Negations: Essays in Critical Theory*. Boston: Beacon Press, 1968. 290 pp.

_____. *One Dimensional Man: Studies in the Ideology of Advanced Industrial Society*. Boston: Beacon Press, 1968. 260 pp.

Marks, Robert W. *The Meaning of Marcuse*. New York: Ballantine Books, Inc., 1970. 136 pp.

Martin, Jane Roland. *Readings in the Philosophy of Education: A Study of Curriculum*. Boston: Allyn & Bacon, Inc., 1970. 432 pp.

Martin, Malachi. *The Encounter*. New York: Farrar, Straus & Giroux, Inc., 1970. 488 pp.

Maslow, Abraham H. (ed.). *New Knowledge in Human Values*. New York: Harper & Row, Publishers, 1959. 268 pp.

Masters, R. E. L. *Forbidden Sexual Behavior and Morality*. New York: Matrix House, 1966. 431 pp.

May, Rollo. *Existential Psychology*. New York: Random House, Inc., 1961. 126 pp.

———. *Love and Will*. New York: W. W. Norton & Company, Inc., 1969. 352 pp.

———, Ernest Angel, and Henri F. Ellenberger (eds.). *Existence: A New Dimension in Psychiatry and Psychology*. New York: Basic Books, Inc., 1961. 425 pp.

McClellan, David C. *The Achieving Society*. New York: The Free Press, 1961. 498 pp.

McClellan, James E. *Toward an Effective Critique of American Education*. Philadelphia: J. B. Lippincott Company, 1968. 324 pp.

McClellan, David. *Marx's Grundrisse*. London: Macmillan, 1971. 152 pp.

Mead, Margaret. *The School in American Culture*. Cambridge, Mass.: Harvard University Press, 1951. 48 pp.

Meehan, Eugene J. *Value Judgment and Social Science: Structures and Processes*. Homewood, Ill.: Dorsey Press, 1969. 171 pp.

Merleau-Ponty, Maurice. *The Visible and the Invisible*. Evanston, Ill.: Northwestern University Press, 1968. 275 pp.

Metzger, Walter P., Sanford H. Kadish, and others. *Dimensions of Academic Freedom*. Urbana: University of Illinois Press, 1969. 121 pp.

Mischel, Theodore (ed.). *Human Action: Conceptual and Empirical Issues*. New York: Academic Press, Inc., 1969. 277 pp.

Morris, Van Cleve. *Existentialism in Education: What It Means*. New York: Harper & Row, Publishers, 1966. 163 pp.

Nagel, Ernest. "Philosophy of Science and Educational Theory," *Studies in Philosophy and Education*, Vol. VIII, No. 2 (Fall 1969).

Nash, Paul. *Authority and Freedom in Education: An Introduction to the Philosophy of Education*. New York: John Wiley & Sons, Inc., 1966. 342 pp.

N.E.A. *Moral and Spiritual Values in the Public Schools*. Washington, D.C.: National Education Association, 1951. 100 pp. Defines commonly agreed-upon values of American democracy as a way of life. Stresses the role of the school in transmitting to youth an intelligent and fervent loyalty to those moral and ethical principles that have made America great.

Neff, Frederick C. *Philosophy and American Education*. New York: The Center for Applied Research in Education, 1966. 116 pp.

Nietzsche, Friedrich. *Beyond Good and Evil*. New York: The Macmillan Company, 1907. 268 pp.

Nordstrom, Carl, Edgar Z. Friedenberg, and Hilary A. Gold. *Society's Children: A Study of Ressentiment in the Secondary School*. New York: Random House, Inc., 1967. 209 pp.

Novak, Michael. *The Experience of Nothingness*. New York: Harper & Row, Publishers, 1970. 147 pp.

Oglesby, Carl (ed.). *The New Left Reader*. New York: Grove Press, Inc., 1969. 312 pp.

O'Neill, William. *Readin', Ritin', and Rafferty: A Study of Educational Fundamentalism*. Berkeley, Calif.: Glendessary Press, 1969. 147 pp.

Ortega y Gasset, Jose. *The Revolt of the Masses*. London: George Allen & Unwin, Ltd., 1932. 204 pp.

Ozmon, Howard (ed.). *The Contemporary Critics of Education*. Danville, Ill.: Interstate Printers & Publishers, Inc., 1970. 223 pp.

———. *Utopias and Education*. Minneapolis: Burgess Publishing Company, 1969. 157 pp.

Parker, Don H. *Schooling for What?" Sex/Money/War/Peace*. New York: McGraw-Hill Book Company, 1970. 270 pp.

Patka, Frederick. *Values and Existence: Studies in Philosophic Anthropology*. New York: Philosophical Library, Inc., 1964. 239 pp.

Peters, R. S. (ed.). *The Concept of Education*. London: Routledge and Kegan Paul, 1967. 223 pp.

Phenix, Philip H. (ed.). *Philosophies of Education*. New York: John Wiley & Sons, Inc., 1961. 137 pp.

Pitcher, George. *The Philosophy of Wittgenstein*. Englewood Cliffs, N.J.: Prentice-Hall, Inc., 1964. 340 pp.

Pole, David. *The Later Philosophy of Wittgenstein: A Short Introduction*. New York: Oxford University Press, 1963. 132 pp.

Postman, Neil, and Charles Weingartner. *Teaching as a Subversive Activity*. New York: The Delacorte Press, 1969. 219 pp.

Pratte, Richard. *Contemporary Theories of Education*. Scranton, Pa.: Intext Educational Publishers, 1971. 338 pp.

Pritzkau, Philo T. *On Education for the Authentic*. Scranton, Pa.: Intext Educational Publishers, 1970. 148 pp.

Rasmussen, Victor. "Towards a Freer School," *The Education Digest*, Vol. XXXVI, No. 9 (May 1971).

Raywid, May Anne. "Subjectivism—The Self-Destructing 'Philosophy of Education,'" *The Educational Forum*, Vol. XXXIV, No. 4 (May 1970).

Reid, Louis Arnaud. *Philosophy and Education: An Introduction*. New York: Random House, Inc., 1965. 203 pp.

Reiner, Everett. *School Is Dead: Alternatives In Education*. Garden City, N.Y.: Doubleday & Company, Inc., 1971. 215 pp.

Rexroth, Kenneth. *The Alternative Society: Essays from the Other World*. New York: Herder and Herder, 1970. 196 pp.

Rich, John Martin. *Education and Human Values*. Reading, Mass.: Addison-Wesley Publishing Co., Inc., 1968. 163 pp.

_____. *Humanistic Foundations of Education*. Worthington, Ohio: Charles A. Jones, 1971. 342 pp.

Roberts, J. Deotis. *Liberation and Reconciliation: A Black Theology*. Philadelphia: The Westminster Press, 1971. 205 pp.

Robinson, Paul A. *The Freudian Left: Wilhelm Reich, Geza Roheim, Herbert Marcuse*. New York: Harper & Row, Publishers, 1969. 253 pp.

Rogers, Carl R. *Freedom to Learn*. Columbus, Ohio: Charles E. Merrill Books, Inc., 1969. 358 pp.

Rokeach, Milton. *Beliefs, Attitudes and Values: A Theory of Organization and Change*. San Francisco: Jossey-Bass, 1968. 214 pp.

Roszak, Theodore. *The Making of a Counter Culture*. Garden City, N.Y.: Doubleday & Company, Inc., 400 pp.

Roubiczek, Paul. *Ethical Values in the Age of Science*. New York: Cambridge University Press, 1969. 318 pp.

Rucker, Darnell. *The Chicago Pragmatists*. Minneapolis: University of Minnesota Press, 1969. 188 pp.

Sartre, Jean Paul. *Existentialism*. New York: Philosophical Library, Inc., 1947. 92 pp.

_____. *Existentialism and Human Emotions*. New York: Philosophical Library, Inc., 1957. 96 pp.

Schaffer, Jerome A. *Reality, Knowledge and Value: A Basic Introduction to Philosophy*. New York: Random House, Inc., 1971.

Scheffler, Israel (ed.). *Conditions of Knowledge: Introduction to Epistemology and Education*. Glenview, Ill.: Scott, Foresman and Company, 1965. 117 pp.

_____. (ed.). *Philosophy and Education: Modern Readings*. Boston: Allyn & Bacon, Inc., 1958. 311 pp. Selection of readings tends toward analytical philosophy.

Schon, Donald A. *Technology and Change: The New Heraclitus*. New York: The Delacorte Press, 1967. 248 pp.

Sciama, D. W. *The Physical Foundations of General Relativity*. Garden City, N.Y.: Doubleday & Company, Inc., 1969. 104 pp.

Shaw, F. Alden. "The Essentialist Challenge to American Education," *School and Society*, Vol. 99, No. 2333 (April 1971).

Shermis, S. Samuel. *Philosophic Foundations of Education*. New York: American Book Company, 1967. 292 pp.

Shinn, Robert L. *Existentialist Posture*. New York: Association Press, 1970. 128 pp.

Skolnick, Jerome H. *The Politics of Protest*. New York: Ballantine Books, Inc., 1969. 419 pp.

Slater, Philip. *The Pursuit of Loneliness: American Culture at the Breaking Point*. Boston: Beacon Press, 1970. 154 pp.

Smith, B. Othaniel and Robert H. Ennis (eds.). *Language and Concepts in Education*. Chicago: Rand McNally & Company, Inc., 1961. 211 pp.

Smith, Huston. *Condemned to Meaning: Seventh John Dewey Society Lecture*. New York: Harper & Row, Publishers, 1965. 94 pp.

Smith, Philip G. *Theories of Values and Problems of Education*. Urbana: University of Illinois Press, 1970. 252 pp.

———. *Philosophy of Education: Introductory Studies*. New York: Harper & Row, Publishers, 1967. 276 pp.

Soderquist, Harold O. *The Person and Education: A New Approach to Philosophy of Education for Democracy*. Columbus, Ohio: Charles E. Merrill Books, Inc., 1964. 200 pp.

Spielgelberg, Herbert. *The Phenomenological Movement: A Historical Introduction*, Vols. 1 and 2. The Hague: Martinus Nijhoff, 1969. 391 pp., 735 pp.

Stein, Maurice, and Larry Miller. *Blueprint for Counter Education*. Garden City, N.Y.: Doubleday & Company, Inc., 1970.

Stenius, Erik. *Wittgenstein's Tractatus: A Critical Exposition of its Main Lines of Thought*. Oxford, England: Blackwell, 1960. 241 pp.

Strain, John Paul (ed.). *Modern Philosophies of Education*. New York: Random House, Inc., 1970. 554 pp.

Strawson, P. F. *Individuals: An Essay in Descriptive Metaphysics*. Garden City, N.Y.: Doubleday & Company, Inc., 1959. 263 pp.

Teilhard de Chardin, Pierre. *The Future of Man*. New York: Harper & Row, Publishers, 319 pp.

Teodori, Massimo. *The New Left*. Indianapolis: The Bobbs Merrill Co., Inc., 1970. 501 pp.

Thayer, H. S. *Meaning and Action: A Critical History of Pragmatism*. Indianapolis: The Bobbs Merrill Co., Inc., 1968. 572 pp.

Tillich, Paul. *The Courage to Be*. New Haven: Yale University Press, 1952. 197 pp.

Toffler, Alvin. *Future Shock*. New York: Random House, Inc., 1970. 505 pp.

Turney, Billy L. (ed.). *Catcher in the Wrong: Iconoclasts in Education*. Itasca, Ill.: F. E. Peacock Publishers, Inc., 1968. 269 pp.

Vandenberg, Donald. *Being and Education: Essays in Existential Phenomenology*. Englewood Cliffs, N.J.: Prentice-Hall, Inc., 1971. 228 pp.

Walcott, Fred G. *The Origins of Culture and Anarchy*. Toronto: University of Toronto Press, 1970. 161 pp.

Wheelis, Allen. *The Quest for Identity*. New York: W. W. Norton & Company, Inc., 1958. 146 pp.

White, Winston. *Beyond Conformity*. New York: The Free Press, 1961. 230 pp.

Wingo, G. Max. *The Philosophy of American Education*. Boston: D. C. Heath & Company, 1965. 438 pp.

Wittgenstein, Ludwig. *Philosophical Investigations*. Oxford: Blackwell, 1953. 232 pp.

———. *Preliminary Investigations*. Oxford: Blackwell, 1958. 185 pp.

Wynne, John P. *Philosophy of Education from the Standpoint of the Transaction Theory*. Farmville, Va.: Longwood College Foundation, 1971. 400 pp.

Wynne, John P. *Theories of Education: An Introduction to the Foundations of Education.* New York: Harper & Row, Publishers, 1963. 521 pp.

Young, Michael. *Rise of the Meritocracy: An Essay on Education and Equality.* Baltimore: Penguin Books, Inc., 1958. 190 pp.

Selected Films

Philosophies of Education Series (N.E.T.). 29 min. each.
  The Classical Realist Approach to Education.
  Education for Cultural Conservation.
  Education for Cultural Reconstruction.
  Education for a Free Society.
  Education as Intellectual Discipline.
  Education for Life Adjustment.
  Education for Moral Character.
  Education for Psychological Maturity
  Education for National Survival.
  An Experimentalist Approach to Education.
  A Jewish View of Education.
  Protestant Philosophy of Education.
  A Roman Catholic View of Education.

Chapter 16

■ ■ ■ ■ ■ ■ ■ ■ ■ ■ ■ ■ ■ ■ ■ ■ ■ ■

The School's
Role in Social Change

In this final chapter, the authors draw together the ideas that have been brought out throughout the book into an over-all conception of the role of the school in an era of social change. The authors realize that many times their conclusion with respect to an issue is only one of several possible conclusions. It is also their contention that the contrasting philosophical conceptions that have been set up in Chapter 15 constitute only one aspect of the problem of choice. This book has been written primarily in the field of educational sociology and social foundations of education. It has therefore stressed material drawn largely from the social sciences. Decision making with respect to the program of the school, as far as it is based upon sound scholarship, may be founded upon three bases:

1. Philosophy, the scholarly area, to assist in the clarification of the values that must be used by any institution in designing its program.
2. Sociology and the other social sciences, to give an understanding of our culture and of the nature of human civilization in order to help in the appropriate selection of pertinent subject matter.
3. Psychology, to provide better understanding of the learner and the learning process.

The suggestions that the authors make in this chapter are based on all three of these foundational fields.

SCHOOLS AS RELATED TO THEIR SOCIETIES

We have noted in Chapter 3 that the school tends to reflect the type of society in which it is found. There were times in the history of education when the school tended to reflect merely one of many prevalent points of view in its culture. As a matter of fact, it did so more frequently than not in the period prior to the development of the common school. In pre-Christian societies, when the school was largely in the hands of the priestly class, it tended to reflect the point of view of that class. This was also true during the Middle Ages, the period of the dominance of institutional Christianity. Later, the humanistic ideas of the Renaissance and of the periods immediately following tended to reflect the social points of view of the ruling class. This narrow representation of social views in the school was primarily due to the fact that the privilege of education was limited to a small segment of persons of the culture, rather than to any deliberate attempt to indoctrinate all persons of the culture with a particular restricted point of view.

It is important to note that the methodology of the school, in contrast to the restrictive nature of its curriculum and its population, tended to reflect the prevailing point of view in society toward children and toward learning. Examples of issues: whether or not the society in general encouraged creativity, and whether or not there was rigid discipline. For example, in the early period of the Renaissance, with its general concern for man and emphasis on this world, there tended to be a greater trend toward creativity and toward gentleness in discipline than there was in the period of the Protestant Reformation. In the latter period there was a very rigid attitude toward the child, which reflected the strict moral point of view of the Protestant culture in which the school functioned.

THE LAG OF THE SCHOOL BEHIND SOCIETY

We have already pointed out in Chapters 2 and 3 the nature of the lag of the school behind society. As soon as the school became institutionalized, it was inevitable that a lag would appear. There is, moreover, another reason for the school to lag behind other institutions: it has always had a "conservator" function—that of preserving the ideals of a culture, particularly in periods of stress. This means that, by and large, the school is fearful of experimentation and the public is afraid to have it experiment. Because the school is dealing with the youthful and the immature, society is very careful to have it teach only the tested and tried. There is a fear, culturally originating when society is prone to instability and new ideas tend to upset the stability, that the young might take up the new ideas too quickly or go off on some tangent that would be detrimental to society.

This fear has a very real basis in fact today. Our technological and economic progress has far outstripped our philosophic and governmental progress. Physical inventions have revolutionized modern life. Social inventions are few and are slow to be accepted. Many people justly feel that some educators, impatient with the rapidly growing lag between social and material progress, may indoctrinate the young with hastily formed panaceas for our social ills.

As a matter of fact, according to almost all points of view, the school *does have* a conservator function. Any society that develops an institution such as the school would require that it transmit the universals of the culture; that is, those elements that various groups within the culture agree upon at any given time. If the school did not have such a function, the society would disintegrate rapidly and a new and perhaps drastically different society would develop. Most points of view (except a most revolutionary one, such as anarchism) would certainly agree that the stability of a society is at least partially assured when the various agencies of the society assist it in passing on the important elements of its cultural heritage. Many of the items listed in Chapter 14 are matters of agreement in our culture, and one of the important jobs of the school should be to help our young understand clearly the nature of these ideas. There are many aspects of our culture that are not ideological in nature but that do represent the best of the past in terms of skilled ways of solving certain problems. An example of this might be the use of the Arabic number system in preference to the Roman number system. A negative example, in Western culture, is the preference not to use the abacus in actual computation. Other examples in all literate cultures would be grammatical usage and spelling. There are few or no questions about these particular points, and it is obvious that the school should play an important part in the transmission of these knowledges and skills.

On the other hand, there is certainly no well-developed point of view that would have the school teach patterns of behavior found in a society but generally recognized as deteriorative, even though such may be known to exist and even though they may be somewhat apologetically tolerated by the society. An example would be the institution of gambling. It is not likely that the adherents of any of the philosophic points of view would advocate that the school deliberately teach youngsters better ways of gambling. There are other aspects of our culture that, although tolerated by the society, are not usually recognized as falling within the scope of the school. The school has, in other words, a selective function in transmitting only the best elements of our culture to the young and immature.

Because of its institutional nature, then, and also because persons of many points of view explicitly hold the primary role of the school to be the preservation and passing on of the social heritage, the school has always tended to lag behind society in periods of change. This lag is not only in the facts, skills, values, and ideas taught, but also in the methods of working with boys and girls. It has already been pointed out that in the early period of American history, when ideas of democracy were prevalent on the frontier (such as, "one man is as good as another," in the Jacksonian epoch), the schools were still operating in a highly autocratic way. The schoolmaster was to be carefully checked before employment to see whether his ideas were in accord with the prevailing mores of the community. In the strict discipline of the schools of that day, the schoolmaster's word was law, and he was expected never to allow questioning, in any way, of what he said, not only with respect to discipline but also with respect to what he taught. As the predetermined spokesman for the community, then, his word was to be respected as authority by the child.

THE ROLE OF THE SCHOOL IN A DEMOCRATIC (NONAUTHORITARIAN) SOCIETY

Before we can discuss what the nature of the school ought to be in a democratic (nonauthoritarian) society, we have to be clear as to the nature of such a society. As shown in Chapter 14, there are many differences regarding what constitutes democracy. Perhaps this is rightly so. One of the characteristics of a democratic society is that there apparently is no authoritative source other than the universals of the culture itself that can set forth a single, unchallengeable point of view. There should be a wide range of ideas competing for attention at any time in the democratic society, even ideas about the fundamental nature of democracy itself, in order for the term to have real meaning. However, so that there can be communication among the different groups, those ideas should center around some agreed-upon key concepts. We have pointed out in Chapter 14 what some of those concepts might be. Central among them are (1) the respect for the personality of the individual, (2) the use of the scientific method in solving a problem, (3) the widening of the areas of common concern.[1]

At this time we shall discuss fully only the first of these points, because it is most pertinent to the topic at hand. The respect for the individual personality in the democratic society means that each person has a right to propose ideas in accordance with his own thinking. At any given time, however, the majority point of view does prevail as far as action is concerned. If the school is to be thought of as an institution to aid the society in perpetuating itself, and if one of the characteristics of a democratic society is its ability to change peacefully, then the school might have some part to play in enabling people to bring about necessary changes in an intelligent fashion. This would definitely mean that the role of the school in a democratic (or nonauthoritarian) society would be quite different from that in an authoritarian society, where only one official point of view could be promulgated by any of the existing institutions. Apparently many persons, especially among the young, feel the school is not functioning effectively in this area. (Witness the protest movements against schools and college policies.)

THE MEANING OF THE SCHOOL AS AN "AGENT OF SOCIETY"

Ever since the school has existed as a separate institution in any culture, it has been an agent to carry out that culture's values. In the days when the schools were either private enterprises charging tuition or philanthropic enterprises, they existed almost as much in the capacity of agents of their society as in the present day, when the public schools are legally authorized and established as a function of government. The various agencies of government have developed in society as devices for carrying out many activities beyond the scope of the individual or even of the large corporation or labor union. The decision as to whether to make the school a public institution offering education free to all persons was debated over a considerable period of time, and many points were not immediately clarified. Eventually it became clear that the decision for the free public school *definitely* made the school *an agent of society*. When education became compulsory, even more did the school become an agent for carrying out certain ideas and principles that that particular society had established.

Once having established the proposition that the school is an agent of society, we must then define its function as an agent of society. Certainly there are very few persons who would conceive that function to be doing the exact bidding of society. It would be difficult to justify the use of specialized professional people with skilled backgrounds, or even the necessity for a separate institution such as a school, if it were not to offer some kind of leadership as the agent of society in doing the job that society wants done. We might present here an analogy from the field of law. If it were the job

[1] Cf. Chapter 14, pp. 490–500.

of a lawyer employed by, let us say, a businessman merely to carry out the law as it is conceived by the businessman (in other words, to operate purely as a technician, a hireling employed by the businessman), it is difficult to see what his special function as an agent would be. Lawyers are to interpret the law as it is and to advise businessmen on the results of proposed future courses. We employ persons with professional abilities to help us so that we can take advantage of the special training, experiences, and other types of background they may have, in order to lead or guide us in the solution of our problems.

If we examine the various points of view described in Chapter 15, we can see that each interpretation of the role of the school is quite different. The perennialist (or neohumanist) conceives of the main job of education as the development of the intellect and the transmission of the great ideas (unchanging ideas) of the past, so that they will be thoroughly understood by at least the elite of the present generation; he could not conceive of the school being limited by the vision of the present state of knowledge of the society in which it is found. The school must stand as a beacon light guiding and leading the society toward new goals, even those that the society may not conceive. The basic principles that are envisioned by the neohumanists are not necessarily those that are customarily found among the prevailing ideas in our body politic.

The essentialists (or social evolutionists), with their emphasis upon the role of the school in passing on those things found essential in the past, do not think their job is limited to passing on those things that are prevailing in the culture at any given time. As a matter of fact, they emphasize the importance of the school as an agency for preserving the culture against some of its own defects—such as forgetfulness of the essentials of the past and the tendency to be carried away by the exigencies of the moment.

The social realists would perhaps come closest to considering the school as an agent of society in the simpler sense. Certainly to most social realists the values that the school should be teaching are those that are prevailing in the culture. However, scientific research, which is not always available to the culture itself, may be needed to determine the best methods to carry out these values. Sometimes the body politic does not know the best method of carrying out the values that it does express. However, it is difficult to find social realists who envision any kind of a concept of the school as the agent of society in the sense of helping to achieve new social values or to clarify present values at least in terms of the means of arriving at those values.

The experimentalists, of course, do conceive of the job of the school quite definitely as to develop critical-minded thinkers and thereby persons who will exercise creative leadership at all levels. The school in this sense is definitely an agency of society. It is an agent of society in its own development, for example, by improving the methods and procedures that are used by the individuals of that society in clarifying their values and in carrying out those values. Sometimes, when individuals are helped to clarify their values and are encouraged to carry them out, they may arrive at values that are not those commonly accepted by our population. Most new ideas originate as minority ideas, and often they are vigorously challenged by the majority point of view. Even though the experimentalist may thus be in the position of trying to lead society in a direction it does not wish to go, he would deny that that is his intention. In the first place, he conceives of the values he holds as subject constantly to further critical study, not as absolutes. Second, he thinks that the central values that he holds are those that have clearly emerged in our democratic culture. Furthermore, he thinks the school that will produce the intelligent, critically minded individual is the school that exemplifies best the values held dear in our democratic culture. Consequently, as long as the school is helping people to clarify their values and to develop scientific–reflective ways to achieve them, without furnishing any preconceived answers to the problems that we face as individuals, as small groups, or as a total society, it would not be in conflict with a democratic conception of the school as an agent of our society.

The reconstructionists are most concerned about a new interpretation of the proposition that the school is an agent of society. We are living, say the reconstructionists, in an age of crisis. As a matter of fact, the crisis is so acute that unless we quickly bring to bear upon the solution of our problems the knowledge and understanding we already possess, we are in danger of losing our civilization. One of the ways society organizes itself, in order to be able to utilize the new data arising from the social sciences and other sources and bring them to bear upon a solution of our problems, is through the school. In this institution the young can be exposed to facts from the social sciences. These facts, say the reconstructionists, indicate very definitely certain positive solutions to the problems we face. These solutions should be clarified and presented by the teachers, together with the supporting facts and arguments as the answers to the problems we face; and the students should be guided in their study of the proposed solutions to recognize them as the best-supported alternatives. This position does not call for blind indoctrination. We live in a democratic society, and the students should study the alternative points of view to the solutions proposed. However, it is the view of the reconstructionists that the teacher should take a position as to the answers that, they say, the facts quite definitely indicate. To summarize, the reconstructionist point of view is that the school as an agent of society should help society to accomplish that which it is not able to do by itself, namely, its own reconstruction. The school guides the growth of society in the light of the most advanced knowledge we have and helps the new generation to understand and interpret that knowledge in the light of certain rather definite answers to the solution of the problems that our society faces.

Persons holding the laissez-faire view are usually not too much concerned about the school as an agent of society, save perhaps in the sense in which the school is trying to help each individual to his own best self-realization. The existentialists are not so much concerned with social philosophy as they are with the individual and the necessity for his free choice, nor are the philosophical analysts greatly concerned with social philosophy.

THE SCHOOLS, CONTROVERSIAL ISSUES, AND "RELEVANCE"

One of the questions faced by the schools is the extent to which there should be discussion of controversial issues, such as those discussed earlier in this book. No major philosophical point of view would deny the place of controversial issues in the school upon the basis of any kind of restriction of the teacher's academic freedom. If there are differences of opinion among American philosophies of education, they follow from differences in their premises as to the function of the school and from differences in their relative emphases. All these philosophical points of view would accord to the teacher the same right as that of any citizen in stating his viewpoint, both in the classroom and out. But certainly several of them would think it educationally undesirable for the teacher to use his classroom for the promotion of a partisan point of view with respect to some of the major controversial issues in our society. Much of the controversy about relevance (discussed some in Chapter 14) really relates to a desire on the part of the protagonists to have the professor or teacher state a position, usually in agreement with his. However, the issue of relevance is deeper. It is philosophical in one dimension, but, more important, it usually involves a lack of sensitivity on the part of the teacher to the students' need to see possible relevance of material presented.

With the humanists, because their emphasis is upon either the great ideas that have come down to us from the past or the content and organization of the subject-matter disciplines, there is no immediate critical need to look at the problem of controversial issues, unless we begin to talk about some of the implications of these ideas for solving the problems we face. Robert Hutchins, the leading proponent of neo-humanism at the college level, has been outspoken in regard to many issues we have faced, in some cases taking what would be a minority and unpopular view. However, this is his right as a citizen, not merely his right as an educator. Hutchins' statements on academic freedom are among the strongest that have been made by anyone in the profession. However, the main emphasis in the school curriculum, as Hutchins and others of his point of view would maintain, should not be upon the clarification of controversial issues as such, but upon the development of the intellect and the training in rational methods of thought that would enable at least the leaders of our country to think through clearly the basic nature of issues involved in our controversies. Emphasis upon the controversial issues themselves might cause us to overlook the more basic ideas—the principles and values—that lie behind them

The emphasis of the social evolutionists on passing on the essentials of our social heritage causes them to have little concern with current events or with controversial issues in our society.

As we have seen, the realists differ among themselves with respect to the importance of controversial issues. Some tend to ignore them and to emphasize cultural agreements without too much attention to the problems within our society. Some emphasize particularly those things established by means of the scientific method, conceived in its more rigid sense. Others, however, feel that one of the things demanded of us in our present society is to handle the many controversies that rage at any given time; therefore, we must have instruction in our schools on how to handle controversial issues. This includes the development of skills in the collection and verification of data, in the utilization of data in the development of hypotheses, in the testing of hypotheses, and in the application of tentative conclusions. Those who hold this latter point of view would advocate practices and experiences in the schools that would not differ greatly from those advocated by the experimentalists.

The experimentalists feel that helping the student in the solution of his problems is the main purpose of the school. Consequently, the school must help him tackle all kinds of issues and problems, both those that he faces as an individual and those that society as a whole faces. The freedom to consider and to tackle controversial issues is essential to that type of school. The school itself does not take any particular side with respect to these controversial matters, but helps the child (as in the case of the second form of realism just discussed) to formulate his ideas, to test them, and to apply them.

The reconstructionists believe that controversial issues should be carefully discussed and that the answers determined by the facts and understandings given to us by the social sciences should be set before the child, so that he can see what the possibilities are.

If we are going to teach controversial issues in our schools, there are questions that may arise as to the ways in which the teaching should be handled. One of the questions is, "What constitutes a controversial issue?" Some things are controversial in some communities, but uncontroversial in others. Some things are controversial to some persons, but not to others. An example of the first is certain facets of the theory of biological evolution. An example of the second is the bacterial theory of disease, which is not accepted by, for example, Christian Scientists. What constitutes a controversial issue? A rough working definition might well be the following: A controversial issue is one on which sizable groups of a given community have taken different sides. There should be added to this, of course, cases where an entire community may take one side but where the issue is still controversial in our society. This may occur where a view toward which the evidence may strongly point is not even considered by anyone in a particular community as a conceivably correct answer to the problem. Such an issue would be controversial, even though not so recognized in a particular community.

Another question is, "What shall the teacher do in respect to revealing his own particular point of view on a controversial issue?" If we are going to teach controversial issues in a democratic society, we should present all sides of the problem fairly. The reconstructionists, who believe that the teacher must have and present a point of view of his own, agree to this. If the teacher must have a point of view, do the pupils have a right to know at some time during the discussion of an issue what his point of view is, or should he conceal it from them? If the teacher does give the student his point of view, at what point in the educational process should he do so? Quite often if the teacher gives his answer too early, it tends to stifle the thinking process. On the other hand, if he never reveals his viewpoint he has abdicated his position of leadership. Very few teachers fail to reveal their viewpoint; either consciously or otherwise, their own professional judgment as to the "correct" answers channel the thinking of the group into the "desired" directions.

It is perhaps best for the teacher, where appropriate, to give his view but to withold it during early discussion.

Questions such as these either have not been fully and clearly answered by the philosophies discussed in this chapter or are matters concerning which there is no agreement within any particular school of philosophy. Some of the points raised here call for research. The question for research might well be stated, "What are the best ways of teaching controversial issues for the most effective development of clear thinking and critical-minded individuals with a will to action based upon sound moral and ethical principles as well as a will to think and to talk about the problems they are facing?"

THE FREEDOM OF THE TEACHER— LIMITS AND RESPONSIBILITY

One of the implications that flows from the fact that we live in a free, democratic society is the right of the teacher, both as a citizen and as a professionally trained person to be as free as possible with respect to what he teaches and the method he uses in teaching. Of course, on the other hand, when an individual accepts responsibility as a teacher, he assumes certain obligations and responsibilities and certain limits must be placed upon his freedom. However, let us first discuss his right to freedom as a citizen and as a professional leader. The following quotation, taken from a statement prepared by a committee of the Philosophy of Education Society, is only one of many on this issue that are consistent with the nature of our democratic society and its best traditions.

> Consequently, the freedom to inquire is a public necessity. Our society will be renewed not by those who know no other way to live, but only by those who, knowing others, prefer the democratic way. Thus the rights to inquire, to hear, to speak, are not rights we hold privately, but rights we share in common through our citizenship. . . .
>
> A democratic people puts its trust in procedures that provide a hearing for contending beliefs and the weighing of different ideas. Anything which prevents or restricts the process of public inquiry and free communications of ideas interferes with the process by which the people decide what is good in every aspect of their life. In this manner, they seek to improve the institutions which serve them. . . .
>
> It is the obligation of a democratic community to provide the maximum opportunity for the full, free, and responsible exchange of ideas on matters of public concern.[2]

There are, of course, limitations even to the freedom of speech of the citizen. The citizen is not free to make slanderous statements with respect to other persons in our society, statements that would be damaging to his character or reputation, unless they are true. A person is not permitted to make obscene or degrading remarks in an excessive manner that would tend to endanger public morals. A person may not use his freedom of speech to make threats against the lives of public officials or others in our democracy. All these restrictions, which apply to citizens in general, apply to teachers.

When a teacher accepts a position in a school, he has become in effect an official for carrying out certain obligations that government has assumed.

[2]A. Stafford Clayton, Chairman, and others, "A Statement by the Philosophy of Education Society" (pamphlet). Printed for the Society by the Journal Press, Columbia, Mo., n.d.

Consequently, there are certain limitations on the freedom of the teacher in the classroom that do not apply to him outside the classroom. First and foremost, the teacher must not use his classroom for the promulgation of a partisan point of view. The school must belong to all the people and must be an open forum for ideas. Second, in the discussion of controversial issues, the teacher must take into account the maturity level of the pupils with whom he works. Although there are many matters of controversy that can be taken up as early as the preschool or kindergarten age (such as how we get along with each other, how we treat persons who serve us, such as the mailman, the policeman, and the fireman), some of the issues that we face are of such a complex nature that they have little meaning for young children or involve emotions that would be somewhat disturbing to them. The teacher must use his professional knowledge and wisdom in choosing the topics and the methods under which he discusses topics of a controversial nature within the particular community. It should be noted that at a time when important issues are current that seriously involve the welfare of all of us, the teacher must bring out the facts. One example is provided by the impending ecological crisis. It has controversial aspects, but the fact of possible, imminent destruction should not be considered to be one of them.

The question of the rights and responsibilities of the teacher in the classroom immediately gives rise to a further question as to the selection of the kind of person who can adequately teach in the public school in a changing social order. The immediate question might well be, "What shall we do about teachers who are not sympathetic to our democratic social order?" An immediate case in point in our society is that of the Communist teacher. One of the prerequisites for a teacher given academic freedom in the classroom is that he be free to examine all the evidence and draw his own conclusions, whatever they may be. If it can be ascertained that the teacher is sworn in advance to arrive at only certain predetermined conclusions, then one may seriously question his competence as a teacher leading a group in the consideration of all sides of controversial issues. Increasingly in our society it is becoming recognized that a person who is a member of the American Communist Party is not for the most part free, under his obligations to the Party, to pursue each problem wherever it may lead. As has been pointed out by many, including Sidney Hook, persons who are members of the Communist Party are members of a conspiracy that is committed to bringing about a change of government, not by persuasive democratic action but by overthrowing the existing government by whatever techniques or methods are necessary.

There are others in our society who are blinded by prejudice or some other type of preconceived notion toward certain definite conclusions on some controversial issues. Unless it can be proved that this is part of a conspiracy in order to change our way of life, the evidence of such prejudice per se should not disqualify the person from teaching. But it is obvious from our discussion that persons not able to examine all the data and to look at them without prejudice do not make the kind of teachers we need in a changing society. It should be equally obvious that the teacher, as an agent of society, is responsible for loyalty to those basic principles upon which the society is founded.

THE PROCESS OF DETERMINING EDUCATIONAL OBJECTIVES

Although the local boards of education throughout the United States have been given the legal responsibility for determining the policies of the school, in a democratic society this means that the policies should be broad enough to permit discretion on the part of the professional staff, in order to develop a school program consistent with its educational philosophy, with the particular problems in the community, and with the group of children in the particular school. The fact that we live in a democratic society means that we should give as much freedom as possible to the individual teacher to do what seems best to do for the boys and girls in his particular room.

Educational groups at all levels, including official and nonofficial groups, have set up statements of purposes, or goals, for education. The authors hold, however, that such statements are of little value unless the persons most concerned in the educative process, the teachers, accept these goals and carry them out. The only point where learning takes place in the school is the point where teacher and child meet. Any statements promulgated from a central source without being wholly accepted in all their implications are of very little value.

Statements concerning educational values usually are not accepted unless the persons who are going to use them—in this case, the teachers—have participated in developing them. This seems to imply that those teachers who work together in a face-to-face situation in a building should work together in setting up their educational objectives and policies, within limitations posed by the general policies of their particular school district. We have already noted that persons (teachers and laymen alike) differ widely with respect to their conceptions of the school's purposes and of the curriculum, and with respect to some of their basic philosophical assumptions; how then can teachers get together on a set of objectives?

Because all the teachers live and work in a democratic society, it is assumed that on the operational level there will be many more points on which they agree than on which they disagree. It is also assumed that, when the group members think through their problems together, there may be sizable areas of agreement at the operational level, even though the various group members may be drawing their implications from differing philosophical assumptions. Now if there are some areas of school policy within the building on which a decision has to be made but on which no unanimous opinion appears possible, it may be necessary to operate on administrative edict based on a consensus. The settling of matters by the faculty of a school, of course, is to be done only with respect to problems that have been left to its discretion by its board of education. Boards of education by and large should leave as much discretion as possible to the teachers working in a face-to-face situation in a local school building.

After common agreement on some problems has been reached and certain other matters settled by a majority vote, areas of disagreement or differing preferences may still remain. The authors envision a school where a teacher would be free to operate (within the limits indicated earlier in this section), to work with his children in accordance with his own values. Authority to define these areas of freedom is vested in the school administration, through policy statements of the board of education. In working with his children, the teacher should seek to get all information possible from all the sources available, including his administrators, fellow teachers, board of education, state department of education, and professional organizations. The important point to stress here is the final responsibility of the teacher for putting into action the values to which he has tentatively agreed on the basis of his understanding of the nature of our culture. A good teacher should continue the clarification and reclarification of those values in the light of any changes that may come about in our culture, and of new research in child growth and development and in the psychology of learning. This position is predicated upon the development of a teaching staff with training and abilities more nearly comparable with the training and abilities of the other professions. Among other things, this implies improvement in both the quantity and the quality of teacher training offered in our teachers' colleges and universities. It implies also an upgrading of selective teacher-recruitment policies and increased emphasis upon in-service training of our present teachers. Professional teachers will demonstrate by their abilities the right to ever-increasing freedom in working with children in accordance with values dynamically derived and modified by the teacher.

A SUMMARY OF SOCIAL FACTS, TRENDS, AND PROBLEMS

The authors now draw together some of the important information and data that have been collected in this book and indicate some of the possible future actions that seem to be indicated for the school by these data. First, let us summarize some of the important facts, trends, and problems found in Chapters 1 through 13.

Information that has been rapidly accumulating from the social sciences, particularly sociology, social anthropology, and psychology, has indicated the all-important place of culture in the formation of the characteristics of a human being. There have been no important changes in the biological nature of man for perhaps 40,000 to 50,000 years. The changes are primarily those of culture. Man, born with a plastic nervous system, is able to absorb the changing aspects of his culture and thus keep up with whatever advances have been made in previous years.

A study of man's social evolution from the first development of simple societies reveals several distinct stages: (1) the stage of the nonliterate man, where only such culture as could be passed on directly could be sustained; (2) the stage of the Oriental-type culture, where a relatively high degree of civilization had been reached, bulwarked by opposition to change or progress; (3) the stage of Western civilization, with its central theme of progress, the latter stages of which have been centered on concepts of democracy, the use of the scientific method, and the application of improved technology; and (4) the possibility of a new stage of modern man, which would be based completely upon man's use of his own intelligence through the scientific method toward the solution of the problems he faces.

The school, however, did not exist as an institution among many of the nonliterate peoples; the function of education was performed by the tribe as a whole. The school eventually developed as a separate institution to do certain things that the tribe could not do. As an institution, it has reflected the fundamental nature of the culture in which it is found. However, it has typically lagged behind the culture and has not often provided leadership toward the improvement of that culture. It has acted primarily as a conservative factor in the culture, preserving those things that might otherwise be lost and doing specialized jobs, such as teaching literary skills.

An analysis of the cultural characteristics of America in recent times has revealed twelve outstanding characteristics, which can be summarized concisely under twelve headings:

1. Development of atomic energy and automation.
2. Increased leisure time made possible by technological efficiency.
3. Continued social lag of institutions behind material changes.
4. Increased demand and necessity for specialization and the consequent need for a common general understanding of the universe as a whole.
5. Increased necessity for cooperative action and for a sense of responsible participation in all cooperative enterprises.
6. Increased necessity for long-range planning.
7. Increased social control and increasing remoteness of social control.
8. Increased potential for differentiation for individuals.
9. Vigorous assertion of the right of the individual and the denial of traditional authoritarian controls over human conduct.
10. Increased strains and tensions.
11. Developing biological technology, population pressure, and pollution.
12. America's increased involvement in a position of world power and responsibility in the space age.

In spite of these enormous changes taking place in American culture, there are certain persistent values that are characteristic of our culture and that serve to distinguish it from other cultures and also to give it a certain stability. One of the jobs of the school certainly ought to be to help boys and girls to understand the nature of these accepted values and to apply them to problems they face.

Among the serious social problems we are facing are those related to the economic factors of our society. Spurred on by the use of the scientific method, one of the over-all impelling factors in American social change is the rapid advance in technology. This technology, coupled with changes in the structure of American industry, is bringing about enormous changes in our economic life. We have undergone basic changes from a theoretically laissez-faire society to a complex mixture of corporation capitalism, state capitalism, socialism, and cooperatives. We still face many serious problems of an economic nature. We have not yet solved the problems of the business cycle. The rapid expansion of industrial technology and the exploitation of natural resources are destroying much of our store of such resources and polluting the remainder. The American people, as a whole, are not well informed on economic matters. The scientific study of economics in its modern form is quite young. Enormous implications for the school flow from the challenge of bringing the vast majority of the population up to a minimum level of economic understanding so that they can participate in policymaking in regard to economic problems.

The most important basic institution in all cultures, including the present, is the family. There are some factors in the present culture that make the family of crucial importance now. It is structuring the basic personalities of the future citizens of an uncertain world. Mutual respect and adaptability seem to be desirable personality characteristics in an America that is becoming increasingly dependent upon the rest of the world at a time when the very nature of that world is rapidly changing. The family, like other institutions, is also in a process of change; it is probable that there will emerge a type of family based on mutual respect and companionship, better suited to the uncertain future than the authoritarian family of pioneer America. Many trends in present society, including biological technology, threaten the family.

The age of anxiety in which we live now has given rise to an enormous increase of problems in the area of mental health. The extreme complexity of our culture and the rapidity of change have confronted many individuals with conditions that undermine their basic emotional security. Frustrations and anxieties beset many people. An increasing number of persons in our culture are being hospitalized for mental illness. The school bears a responsibility to prepare individuals to be better equipped to deal with the problems of modern life. Other social institutions must cooperate in alleviating these problems that are related to mental hygiene.

Emotional problems relate not only to the personality disorganization that results in damage to the affected individual, but also to those persons who become antisocial and seek their security and recognition through committing acts that are contrary to the law of the land. Among these is the special and rapidly growing group, the juvenile delinquents. Both juvenile and adult crime are increasing. The disorganization of the home, the emphasis upon materialism in our culture, and the uncertainty about values—all are factors contributing to juvenile delinquency. Increased personal and social guidance of youth is a necessity. Home, school, church, and other social agencies must cooperate in this task.

Population pressures are very heavy in some parts of the world, where the number of persons far exceeds the presently developed resources to house, clothe, and feed them. It is also a problem in America, where the development of adequate schools, housing, and so forth has become important, even in a country as wealthy and as technologically advanced as the United States. There is, in the United States, no immediate danger of a scarcity of food and other resources, considering the country as a whole. Eventually, the problem of what is the maximum population the world can support will have to be faced on the world level. Population growth is overtaking advances in food technology and even the present population is rapidly destroying our resources.

Among the other problems that the world faces are those related to differing groups and their ability to live and work together. We have primarily considered this problem within the American scene. The goal to be sought is found in the ideals of American democracy and of all the major religions. However, the immediate next steps and the processes by which we arrive at those goals are not so clear. Research in human dynamics, including human encounter groups, has developed new and promising techniques in recent years. It then becomes a matter of education and cooperative endeavour to enable these techniques to be put into operation for the gradual improvement of the relationship between differing groups in our culture. Recently the polarization of the population on some issues—the rise of the new left and campus and ghetto riots, for example—has challenged our ability to solve these problems peacefully.

We live in a democracy characterized by a responsible, representative government. Many problems have arisen in this democracy: (1) problems of communication in an extremely complex culture; (2) problems of keeping communication free and untrammeled (to avoid the "credibility gap"); (3) problems of the appropriate interpretation of the information received and the ability of the masses to arrive at appropriate decisions with respect to the information; (4) some problems of governmental structure, rising out of situations in which the governmental machinery set up for one age with one type of transportation (horse and buggy) cannot meet the problems of an age of jet propulsion. Among these problems are those of the conflicting political jurisdictions of metropolitan areas in which a growing percentage of our people live.

Another of the big problems that we now face is that of living together with many other sovereign, independent nation-states in the world. This problem is aggravated because of a bipolarization of power between two nations, the United States and Soviet Union, and their immediate friends and affiliates. The development of a "third world" unwilling to cooperate with either further complicates the situation. The ability of these nations to work together to resolve differences and to operate through the United Nations and other international organizations must be improved in order to assure even the continued existence of the world. We have the possibility now that a worldwide war might result in the destruction of civilization as we know it. The threat of war and arming as a deterrent to possible aggression have vital implications for the internal policies of all countries, including the United States, where a large proportion of our energies are devoted to paying for past wars and preparing for new ones.

We have now traced some of the outstanding facts, problems, and trends that have been set forth in Chapters 1 through 13. In the next section we shall draw together some of the trends of the foreseeable future as these have been recently outlined by numerous experts.

THE FORESEEABLE FUTURE

Numerous scientists and other writers in recent years have freely predicted the future on the basis of what we now know.[3] This is referred to as the "foreseeable future," in contrast to some of the wild guesses often found in science fiction. A whole new area of scholarship, that of the futurologist, has been born.

It appears to be agreed by scientists that the rate of technological change

[3]Among the better sources are Fritz Baade, *The Race to the Year 2000: Our Future a Paradise or the Suicide of Mankind* (New York: Doubleday, 1962); Burnham Beckwith, *The Next 500 Years* (New York: Exposition, 1967); Nigel Calder (ed.), *The World in 1984* (Baltimore: Penguin, 1965); Stuart Chase, *The Most Probable World* (New York: Harper, 1968). Additional sources are cited in the bibliography at the end of this chapter.

for the next twenty-five years, and most likely to the year 2000, will be at an ever-increasing pace. In the first place, the use of nuclear energy and the better use of other energy sources will enable us to increase our gross national product, so that by the year 2000 the 250 million or more people in the United States will have an average income of $7,500 per person, or $30,000 for a family of four persons (1970 dollars). This is approximately four times the average income at the present time.

Furthermore, the use of electronic and other automatic devices will enable the work of the factory and office to be more efficiently done so that the work week undoubtedly can be reduced to twenty-four hours.

Furthermore, the strides that have been made in medical science, increasing the span of life from fifty to seventy years in the past century, will certainly continue. A life span of at least eighty years will be attained within the next ten years. Thus, any child born today might be expected to live to the middle of the twenty-first century.

There will be a rapid increase in transportation and communication. With the use of commercial jets for long trips and the helicopter for short trips, the remote parts of the earth will be next door. We will soon have telephone service to *all* parts of the world. Worldwide TV programs have been made possible by satellites.

Advances in agriculture and in food preservation will probably enable man to feed the population of the world, which will be at least 6 billion by the year 2000 (present population over 3 billion). However, beyond that date or figure the remaining resources probably would be inadequate. Soon space would become a serious problem. If pollution is not stopped serious problems will arise in ten to fifteen years, not thirty.

There will be great advances in the science of understanding human behavior and in the ability to use chemicals to control behavior and to alter personality patterns in some cases (tranquilizer pills are a current example). It is not likely that we will have solved completely all the problems in the field of anxieties, neuroses, and psychoses by the end of the twentieth century, but it is likely that we will be much nearer to a solution than we are at the present time.

Herman Kahn and Anthony J. Wiener are members of a group of persons studying possible future trends. In their book *The Year 2000* they set forth many aspects of the problem. Tables 17, 18, and 19 set forth the very likely, the less likely, and a few selected "far-out" possibilities up to the year 2000. If these are not available by that year, they probably will be by 2030.

TABLE 17
One Hundred Technical Innovations Very Likely in the Last Third of the Twentieth Century

---

1. Multiple applications of lasers and masers for sensing, measuring, communication, cutting, heating, welding, power transmission, illumination, destructive (defensive), and other purposes
2. Extreme high-strength and/or high-temperature structural materials
3. New or improved superperformance fabrics (papers, fibers, and plastics)
4. New or improved materials for equipment and appliances (plastics, glasses, alloys, ceramics, intermetallics, and cermets)

TABLE 17 *(continued)*

5. New airborne vehicles (ground-effect machines, VTOL and STOL, superhelicopters, giant and/or supersonic jets)
6. Extensive commercial application of shaped-charge explosives
7. More reliable and longer-range weather forecasting
8. Intensive and/or extensive expansion of tropical agriculture and forestry
9. New sources of power for fixed installations (e.g., magnetohydrodynamic, thermionic and thermoelectric, and radioactivity)
10. New sources of power for ground transportation (storage battery, fuel cell, propulsion [or support] by electro-magnetic fields, jet engine, turbine, and the like)
11. Extensive and intensive worldwide use of high-altitude cameras for mapping, prospecting, census, land use, and geological investigations
12. New methods of water transportation (such as large submarines, flexible and special purpose "container ships," or more extensive use of large automated single-purpose bulk cargo ships)
13. Major reduction in hereditary and congenital defects
14. Extensive use of cyborg techniques (mechanical aids or substitutes for human organs, senses, limbs, or other components)
15. New techniques for preserving or improving the environment
16. Relatively effective appetite and weight control
17. New techniques and institutions for adult education
18. New and useful plant and animal species
19. Human "hibernation" for short periods (hours or days) for medical purposes
20. Inexpensive design and procurement of "one of a kind" items through use of computerized analysis and automated production
21. Controlled and/or supereffective relaxation and sleep
22. More sophisticated architectural engineering (e.g., geodesic domes, "fancy" stressed shells, pressurized skins, and esoteric materials)
23. New or improved uses of the oceans (mining, extraction of minerals, controlled "farming," source of energy, and the like)
24. Three-dimensional photography, illustrations, movies, and television
25. Automated or more mechanized housekeeping and home maintenance
26. Widespread use of nuclear reactors for power
27. Use of nuclear explosives for excavation and mining, generation of power, creation of high-temperature–high-pressure environments, and/or as a source of neutrons or other radiation
28. General use of automation and cybernation in management and production
29. Extensive and intensive centralization (or automatic interconnection) of current and past personal and business information in high-speed data processors
30. Other new and possibly pervasive techniques for surveillance, monitoring, and control of individuals and organizations
31. Some control of weather and/or climate
32. Other (permanent or temporary) changes—or experiments—with the overall environment (e.g., the "permanent" increase in C-14 and temporary creation of other radioactivity by nuclear explosions, the increasing generation of CO_2 in the atmosphere, projects Starfire, West Ford, and Storm Fury)
33. New and more reliable "educational" and propaganda techniques for affecting human behavior—public and private
34. Practical use of direct electronic communication with and stimulation of the brain
35. Human hibernation for relatively extensive periods (months to years)

TABLE 17 (continued)

36. Cheap and widely available central war weapons and weapon systems
37. New and relatively effective counterinsurgency techniques (and perhaps also insurgency techniques)
38. New techniques for very cheap, convenient, and reliable birth control
39. New, more varied, and more reliable drugs for control of fatigue, relaxation, alertness, mood, personality, perceptions, fantasies, and other psychobiological states
40. Capability to choose the sex of unborn children
41. Improved capability to "change" sex of children and/or adults
42. Other genetic control and/or influence over the "basic constitution" of an individual
43. New techniques and institutions for the education of children
44. General and substantial increase in life expectancy, postponement of aging, and limited rejuvenation
45. Generally acceptable and competitive synthetic foods and beverages (e.g., carbohydrates, fats, proteins, enzymes, vitamins, coffee, tea, cocoa, and alcoholic liquor)
46. "High quality" medical care for undeveloped areas (e.g., use of medical aides and technicians, referral hospitals, broad spectrum antibiotics, and artificial blood plasma)
47. Design and extensive use of responsive and supercontrolled environments for private and public use (for pleasurable, educational, and vocational purposes)
48. Physically nonharmful methods of overindulging
49. Simple techniques for extensive and "permanent" cosmetological changes (features, "figures," perhaps complexion and even skin color, and even physique)
50. More extensive use of transplantation of human organs
51. Permanent manned satellite and lunar installations—interplanetary travel
52. Application of space life systems or similar techniques to terrestrial installations
53. Permanent inhabited undersea installations and perhaps even colonies
54. Automated grocery and department stores
55. Extensive use of robots and machines "slaved" to humans
56. New uses of underground "tunnels" for private and public transportation and other purposes
57. Automated universal (real time) credit, audit and banking systems
58. Chemical methods for improving memory and learning
59. Greater use of underground buildings
60. New and improved materials and equipment for buildings and interiors (e.g., variable transmission glass, heating and cooling by thermoelectric effect, and electroluminescent and phosphorescent lighting)
61. Widespread use of cryogenics
62. Improved chemical control of some mental illnesses and some aspects of senility
63. Mechanical and chemical methods for improving human analytical ability more or less directly
64. Inexpensive and rapid techniques for making tunnels and underground cavities in earth and/or rock
65. Major improvements in earth moving and construction equipment generally
66. New techniques for keeping physically fit and/or acquiring physical skills
67. Commercial extraction of oil from shale
68. Recoverable boosters for economic space launching
69. Individual flying platforms

TABLE 17 *(continued)*

70. Simple inexpensive home video recording and playing
71. Inexpensive high-capacity, worldwide, regional, and local (home and business) communication (perhaps using satellites, lasers, and light pipes)
72. Practical home and business use of "wired" video communication for both tele-phone and TV (possibly including retrieval of taped material from libraries or other sources) and rapid transmission and reception of facsimiles (possibly including news, library material, commercial announcements, instantaneous mail delivery, other printouts, and so on)
73. Practical large-scale desalinization
74. Pervasive business use of computers for the storage, processing, and retrieval of information
75. Shared time (public and interconnected?) computers generally available to home and business on a metered basis
76. Other widespread use of computers for intellectual and professional assistance (translation, teaching, literature search, medical diagnosis, traffic control, crime detection, computation, design, analysis and to some degree as intellectual collaborator generally)
77. General availability of inexpensive transuranic an other esoteric elements
78. Space defense systems
79. Inexpensive and reasonably effective ground-based BMD
80. Very low-cost buildings for home and business use
81. Personal "pagers" (perhaps even two-way pocket phones) and other personal electronic equipment for communication, computing, and data processing program
82. Direct broadcasts from satellites to home receivers
83. Inexpensive (less than $20), long lasting, very small battery operated TV receivers
84. Home computers to "run" household and communicate with outside world
85. Maintenance-free, longlife electronic and other equipment
86. Home education via video and computerized and programmed learning
87. Stimulated and planned and perhaps programmed dreams
88. Inexpensive (less than one cent a page), rapid high-quality black and white reproduction; followed by color and high-detailed photography reproduction—perhaps for home as well as office use
89. Widespread use of improved fluid amplifiers
90. Conference TV (both closed circuit and public communication system)
91. Flexible penology without necessarily using prisons (by use of modern methods of surveillance, monitoring, and control)
92. Common use of (longlived?) individual power source for lights, appliances, and machines
93. Inexpensive worldwide transportation of humans and cargo
94. Inexpensive road-free (and facility-free) transportation
95. New methods for rapid language teaching
96. Extensive genetic control for plants and animals
97. New biological and chemical methods to identify, trace, incapacitate, or annoy people for police and military uses
98. New and possibly very simple methods for lethal biological and chemical warfare
99. Artificial moons and other methods for lighting large areas at night
100. Extensive use of "bilogical processes" in the extraction and processing of minerals

TABLE 18
Some Less Likely but Important Possibilities

1. "True" artificial intelligence
2. Practical use of sustained fusion to produce neutrons and/or energy
3. Artificial growth of new limbs and organs (either in situ or for later transplantation
4. Room temperature superconductors
5. Major use of rockets for commercial or private transportation (either terrestrial or extraterrestrial)
6. Effective chemical or biological treatment for most mental illnesses
7. Almost complete control of marginal changes in heredity
8. Suspended animation (for years or centuries)
9. Practical materials with nearly "theoretical limit" strength
10. Conversion of mammals (humans?) to fluid breathers
11. Direct input into human memory banks
12. Direct augmentation of human mental capacity by the mechanical or electrical interconnection of the brain with a computer
13. Major rejuvenation and/or significant extension of vigor and life span—say 100 to 150 years
14. Chemical or biological control of character or intelligence
15. Automated highways
16. Extensive use of moving sidewalks for local transportation
17. Substantial manned lunar or planetary installations
18. Electric power available for less than .3 mill per kilowatt hour
19. Verification of some extrasensory phenomena
20. Planetary engineering
21. Modification of the solar system
22. Practical laboratory conception and nurturing of animal (human?) foetuses
23. Production of a drug equivalent to Huxley's soma
24. A technological equivalent of telepathy
25. Some direct control of individual thought processes

Herman Kahn and Anthony J. Wiener, *The Year 2000: A Framework for Speculation Next Thirty-three Years* (New York: Macmillan, 1967), p. 57. Used by permission.

TABLE 19
Ten Far-Out Possibilities

1. Life expectancy extended to substantially more than 150 years (immortality?)
2. Almost complete genetic control (but still homo sapiens)
3. Major modification of human species (no longer homo sapiens)
4. Antigravity (or practical use of gravity waves)*
5. Interstellar travel
6. Electric power available for less than .03 mill per kw hour
7. Practical and routine use of extrasensory phenomena
8. Laboratory creation of artificial live plants and animals
9. Lifetime immunization against practically all diseases
10. Substantial lunar or planetary bases or colonies

*As usually envisaged this would make possible a perpetual motion machine and therefore the creation of energy out of nothing. We do not envisage this as even a far-out possibility, but include antigravity, even though it annoys some physicist friends, as an example of some totally new use of a basic phenomena or the seeming violation of a basic law.

Herman Kahn and Anthony J. Wiener, *The Year 2000: A Framework for Speculation the Next Thirty-three Years* (New York: Macmillan, 1967), p. 57. Used by permission.

Even Servan-Schreiber, a sober commentator on the contemporary scene, sees a tremendous change.

Thanks largely to the influx of American technology and organization, Europeans are now being swept along on a tide of progress. But we have been slow to react to this power unleashed in our midst. Our creative abilities have been strangely paralyzed, and within this general forward tide we are mired in second place—far behind the Americans.

Before analyzing exactly how economic dependence slows down and limits progress, we might take a look at the future with the Hudson Institute, which has recently made a preview of the world 30 years from now—the world of the next generation in the year 2000.

In 1968 Herman Kahn and the Hudson Institute published a 1,000 page report of life in the year 2000, based on projections of current information. Here are some of its major points.

In 1968 the nine leading powers in terms of per capita income were: The United States, Sweden, Canada, Germany, Britain, France, U.S.S.R., Italy, Japan.

Two other countries were also studied by the Hudson Institute—India and China. Although their per capita income is small, their future importance is very great. This makes 11 countries.

During the next 30 years our generation will see the advent of what Daniel Bell calls the "post-industrial society." We should remember this term, for it defines our future. It involves such fundamental changes that for certain industrialized countries life in the year 2000 may be as different from what it is today as our societies now are from Egypt or Nigeria.

In the new society, according to Bell and Kahn:

1. Industrial revenue may be 50 times higher than in the pre-industrial society;
2. most economic activity may have shifted from the primary (agriculture) and secondary (industrial production) area to the third and fourth areas (service industries, research institutes, non-profit organization);
3. private enterprise may no longer be the major source of scientific and technological development;
4. the free market may take second place to the public sector and to social services;
5. most industries will be run by cybernetics;
6. the major impetus for progress will come from education and the technological innovations it utilizes;
7. time and space will no longer be a problem in communications;
8. the gap between high and low salaries in the post-industrial society may be considerably smaller than today.

According to this study, a country starts reaching the post-industrial level when per capita income exceeds $4,000 a year.

Per capita income in the United States is already over $3,500 a year, $1,800 in Western Europe, and $1,000 in the Soviet Union.

The following chart by Herman Kahn classified societies according to per capita income.

TYPES OF SOCIETIES

Pre-Industrial	$50 to $200 per capita
Partially Industrialized or Transitional	$200 to $1,500 per capita
Industrial mass Consumption or adv. Ind.	$1,500 to $4,000 per capita
Post-Industrial	$4,000 to $20,000 per capita

The United States and Western Europe (with Russia catching up) are both advanced industrial societies, despite obvious differences in the level, distribution, and use of income.

The Hudson Institute study goes on to show how nations are likely to be ranked 30 years from now. This serves as a useful basis for thought. The post-industrial societies will be, in this order; the United States, Japan, Canada, Sweden. That is all.

The advanced industrial societies that have the potential to become post-industrial include: Western Europe, the Soviet Union, Israel, East Germany, Poland, Czechoslovakia, Australia, and New Zealand.

The following nations will become consumer societies: Mexico, Argentina, Venezuela, Chile, Colombia, South Korea, Malaysia, Formosa, and the other countries of Europe.

The rest of the world—China, India, most of South America, the Arab countries, and black Africa—will not have even reached the industrial stage.

Thus an extraordinary historical change is calmly presented to us. Within a single generation there may no longer be a difference of degree between our situation and that of the advanced countries—but a difference of kind. We would belong to a different world, a world somewhere between the advanced societies and the undeveloped ones.

A few rare countries, like Japan and Sweden, by carefully managing their resources, concentrating their talents, and adapting themselves to the demands of the new society, will manage to stay among the front runners—but not Western Europe.

The purpose of our analysis, and of this book, is not to point out how shameful it would be to resign ourselves to gradual decadence, but rather to find a way by which Western Europe can reverse this perilous situation and stay in the race among competing civilizations by regaining control over her own destiny.

In 30 years America should be a post-industrial society with a per capita income of $7,500. There will be only four days a week of seven hours per day. The year will be comprised of 39 work weeks and 13 weeks of vacation. With weekends and holidays this makes 147 work days a year and 218 free days. All this within a single generation.[4]

The following, paraphrased from Victor Ferkiss' Technological Man,[5] sets an ideological basis for the new man in the postindustrial society.

Technological man will be a new cultural type, not a new ruling class, personality type, or biological type. He will be in control of his development within the context of a philosophy of the role of technology in human evolution.

The new philosophy will embrace three basic elements:

1. New Naturalism—man is a part of nature rather than something apart from it. Nature is not a rigid, mindless, deterministic machine. The universe is a moving equilibrium of which man is a part.
   Man is the highest element of nature. His mind is the most complex thing in the universe. His mechanical creations are insignificant in complexity compared to man.
2. The New Holism—the realization of the interconnectedness of all things. The idea of becoming destroys traditional distinctions between being

[4]Servan-Schreiber, op. cit., pp. 31–36. Used by permission.
[5]Victor C. Ferkiss, Technological Man: The Myth and the Reality (New York: Braziller, 1969), pp. 245–272.

and non-being. No part is meaningful outside the whole, no part can be defined or understood except in relation to the whole. The totality consists of mind, body, society, nature. All men are linked to each other, and with their social and physical environment.

3. New Immanentism—the whole shapes itself. Nothing is isolated. Life exists within systems, and the system creates itself.

These three principles must dominate human society if man is to survive. Technological man must internalize these principles, so that they form his personal, political and cultural life. If man and nature are one, then society and environment are one. Therefore, social policies must be ecological in character. Any change affects everything in the total system.

Because man and nature are intermingled, nature and man have rights. The new holism insists there are no individual decisions, since decision making is part of a seamless process. Man is affected by the actions of others, and others are affected by the action and decisions of man.

The new immanentism means that the whole shapes itself. Order is a structure of interrelationships created by the activity of its elements. Each element is responsible for the result his acts have upon the totality.

Technological man through this basic world view will be able to evolve ethical norms which will make survival possible.

The norms that guide technological man rest upon his data about the nature of the universe. The first norm is that man is a part of nature and cannot conquer it but must live in harmony with it.

Man's economic and social life demand co-ordination and his exploitation of natural resources must be determined by what is optimum for the total system.

Man must retain the distinction between himself and the machine, and control his own evolution. He is capable of controlling evolution even to the extent of slowing down, or stopping it.

In this new civilization, man has the task of finding himself, and defining his role in the totality.

Technological man, as an intelligent, aware part of the universe, with full responsibility for himself and the totality, cannot come into being without a reorientation of human culture.

Since control of all aspects of human culture is not possible, the one essential for the development of a technological civilization is that each person realize that there is a totality which he does not totally represent, and that the one intolerable act is for one person or group to assume dominance.

This new culture demands tremendous changes in our economic and political systems. Our capitalistic system fails because the false assumption is made that an "invisible hand" will direct everything to the common good.

This assumption becomes less tenable as society becomes more complex, and population more dense. The increased number and kinds of patterns of interaction demands changes that will constantly take into account the interests of others.

The pace of technological change and the rate of population growth make it imperative that man assume control of his society. But the problem of considering the needs of the whole and distributing gains and losses equitably cannot be met through socialism. Special interest groups go their own ways in both socialistic and capitalistic societies.

A holistic view of the world in terms of government is necessary. Technology makes the idea of world government possible. Attitudinal changes and the breaking down of nationalistic boundaries must occur before a world government is possible.

Even the relatively conservative report of the National Goals Research staff sets forth the need for a major change in our response to these challenges.

Ours is a society which until recently, rarely questioned the virtue of continued economic growth per se. We were further proud of our ability to generate a flood of new technology and consumer products, and of our ability to expand our scientific knowledge and educational resources. But today there is an explicit challenge to the view that we can or should continue to encourage or permit the unfettered growth of our economy, population, technology, use of materials and energy, flow of new products, and even of our scientific knowledge. Some manifestations of this challenge are too sweeping to deserve policy consideration, but others are unquestionably reasonable, and the circumstances precipitating them sufficiently concrete and urgent as to warrant priority attention by public policymakers. Viewed in historical perspective, these challenges signify that a profound re-examination is taking place of man's view of his relationship to nature, to his institutions, and to his fellow man.

The growing challenge to established viewpoints by new concepts is the substance of certain emerging debates that come about not only because of some doubts about the effectiveness of our institutions and the anticipation of worsening future problems, but also because our wealth now provides the latitude and the ability to alter parts of the national life that are found wanting. For example, pollution has become a national problem not only because its symptoms are evident, but also because the promise exists that resources and programs to deal with it may become available; both a visible dissatisfaction and the ability to intervene in the causes of dissatisfaction encourage debate.

This call for a growth policy occurs in the midst of a period of rapid social change marked by problems that indicate that even more change is needed. A growth policy is only one element in the total process of social change. It is one set of principles that will influence that change. . . .

Population. The traditional view of population growth as a source of national pride and strength is being re-examined. Some authorities argue for zero population growth on the ground that population stability is imperative for survival, or will improve the quality of our society. (For example it might enable us to avoid the issue of limitation on the use of energy and materials.)

The merits of sheer size now appear more debatable than heretofore, particularly in the case of large metropolitan areas. Large concentrations of population generate serious pollution problems, traffic congestion, and higher per capita public expenditures. And they are unduly vulnerable to power failures, riots, and other disruptive social action. Thus, major questions are asked: should we limit our population size, and if so, how? And should we redistribute our population, and if so, how?

Environment. Historically, our concern over resources focused on whether there would be enough food, energy, and materials to meet our needs. Today, in the United States, the concern is about the ability of land, air, and water to absorb all the wastes we generate. We already have violated the aesthetic limits of pollution and, from time to time and place to place, we have violated health and survival limits of pollution. Some argue that the long-run issue may well be our survival. Questions often asked are: What can be done to repair the damage already done? To what extent and by what means will future pollution be contained within tolerable limits? Are there fixed limits of environmental tolerance that might make it imperative to limit the size of our population or set per capita quotas on the amount of energy and material we may use?

Education. Throughout its history, America's educational system has had to meet a variety of needs for a growing Nation. Today this system, after a long stretch of phenomenal growth, finds itself the target of deepening dissatisfaction. The nature and degree of the dissatisfaction implies the existence of unmet educational needs in our society. As the education system met earlier needs, a reciprocal relation was formed between our society and the schools. When society needed more skilled citizens it turned to the schools; in turn, the schools raised the knowledge and skill level of society, nurturing additional development in a continuing spiral of mutually supported growth. The question raised in the chapter on education is: What relation might be established between the educational system and a rapidly changing, complex society to achieve growth? A number of specific issues arise, such as whether or not our colleges and universities should assume service roles in society as opposed to the traditional role of discipline-oriented institutions searching for knowledge for its own sake. Also, there are questions relating to individual self-development, equality of opportunity, educational achievement standards, and the financial problems of schools. And, should we develop a wider diversity of post secondary opportunities?

Basic Natural Science. To the extent that it was discussed at all in the past, it was generally agreed that science should grow according to its own internal logic as dictated by the structure of evolving knowledge and the criteria and judgements of the scientific community. In America since World War II, basic science continued to develop in its traditional spontaneous fashion because the available funds were so large compared to the capacity of the scientific community that almost everything scientifically worthwhile was funded.

Today, the relationship of the scientific establishment to its funding is being reversed. In relation to the capacity of the research establishment to do research, funds are deficient. Furthermore, many persons, including members of the scientific community, are concerned over the possibility that the knowledge they develop will be used for ends they do not approve. Thus, knowledge no longer is seen as necessarily good. Furthermore, scientists and others have become acutely aware of social and environmental problems for which systematic knowledge may offer solutions, and basic science is asked to address these problems. Thus, the traditional "guidance" mechanism of science is being challenged at a time when funds have declined in relation to the capacity of the scientific community.

Among the questions asked are: To what extent should basic natural science be permitted to develop in a free unguided manner? How much support should the Nation give to development of basic science and scientists (whether or not in the capacity for which they were originally trained) be pressed to solve specific social problems?

Technology Assessment. The sophisticated products of our Nation's technologists have been a source of pride and, sometimes, wonder. Largely free of governmental constraint, technology has tended to develop according to the internal logic of its usual industrial, public, and business sponsors. What seemed feasible and profitable was tried. What proved possible and profitable tended to be used. Technology accounts, to a large extent, for the productivity of our economy, our standard of living, our ability to keep a high proportion of the potential work force in school, our achievements in space, and —granting the perils of a nuclear age—our military security. But we have become increasingly aware of technology's adverse effects. Some highly sophisticated drugs produce severe side effects. Airplanes and automobiles make intolerable noise and foul the air. Advanced technology of all sorts produces unexpected and often unwanted indirect consequences. A movement called "technology assessment" now advocates a more pervasive and systematic assessment of the social costs and benefits of both new and existing technology. The main issues are: To what extent should the use of new and old technology be restricted because of adverse side effects? What institutional mechanism might assess and regulate technology? What effect would such a policy have on economic growth and on the size and nature of our technological and scientific establishments?

Consumerism. While technology is a source of strength in our economy, the abundant flow of new consumer goods has been viewed as a clear indication that the economy brings vast direct benefits to the American people. Yet, in the past decade, this virtue has been questioned. A movement labeled "consumerism" contends that the rapid introduction of new products produces confusion, that the technical complexity of new products makes it impossible to evaluate their benefits or dangers and makes them difficult to repair, and that pressure on business firms to introduce new products and services breeds marketing practices of a dubious nature.

The traditional doctrine of "consumer sovereignty" holds that the consumer is capable of protecting his own interests. Today, the proponents of the consumer movement argue that the consumer does not have the information with which to make an informed choice. The internal guidance system of the marketplace is challenged. The issues include To what extent and in what ways is the consumer actually the victim of these circumstances? How should he be protected? In the course of this, how can a healthy business environment be maintained? . . .

Undoubtedly the call for a national growth policy evokes many different images of what the policy will deal primarily with, as well as what its composition might be. . . .

Therefore, pursuit of a national growth policy may be characterized as both a search for coherence among the many activities of our society, and a search for actions supportive of the human values and qualities which we would most hope to further.

It is not a policy for government alone to develop. Because it is national in scope and covers all areas of our life, the Federal Government must take the leadership initiative. But the effort can be successful only if all Americans engage themselves in the search—both in their capacity as private citizens and in their various institutional roles. The constellation of policies which will comprise the new national growth policy will not be just governmental, but will encompass every form of social institution.

We should embark on this search with the understanding that it will not be soon completed. It is both a long-term, continuing and a national process. Therefore, we can correctly say that the goal of a national growth policy is a long-term goal in these respects: it deals with the shaping of our quality of life both now and as it will be at the conclusion of the century and beyond; it will not be developed full-blown within a year or so, but rather will evolve in varying pieces throughout the 1970's; and it will probably never be completed, because by the virtue of the dynamic nature of events, it will be open-ended.

The successful pursuit of this new national growth policy will require many modifications to our present way of approaching decisions for action and some major institutional and social reforms. In fact, as is indicated in the chapters on environment and technology assessment, some of the changes are so deep as to affect our fundamental philosophical assumptions of "world views." . . .

POSSIBLE NEW TREND-SETTING DEVELOPMENTS OF THE 1970's

. . . One cannot plan for the future simply on the assumption that it will evolve just from trends now a part of our life. Many developments in the future—which may or may not be foreseeable—will act in unpredictable ways upon present trends. Some of these new developments will generate new trends not yet a part of human experience. Therefore, to obtain a realistic picture of what the future may be, we must go beyond today's realities. . . .

Of course any analysis of future developments must be regarded as speculative. Unpredictable breakthroughs from basic science will occur. Other presently familiar technologies such as computers are pregnant with possibilities for major social change as their use is extended and new applications are made.

However, the following are just a few illustrations of developments which many experts now believe will be emerging in the 1970's. These selected developments are not necessarily the most important of those now foreseen. . . .

Communications Developments

Communication techniques and tools are likely to change radically during the coming decade. Picture phones, already in limited use, may become widely disseminated. Three-dimensional TV, portable individual telephones, and tape libraries for individual programming of home TV may be in use by 1980. Such changes could have significant impacts on education, government, business, and family life.

Some experts believe that new tools of communication can reduce the need for business travel. Many types of workers may find it increasingly possible to do much of their work at home. This will be particularly true when it becomes economically feasible to connect home facilities with central computers and closed-circuit TV. For example, combining of picture phones, communication satellites, and equipment for reproducing facsimiles of documents and signatures already make it possible for individuals at many different points on the globe to converse face-to-face on a matter, draft final documents, and have signed copies simultaneously.

Significant education potentials could be opened through audio-visual tapes for home TV sets, much education might take place outside traditional educational institutions. The cost of "attending" college courses might be greatly reduced, while at the same time the quality of such courses may be raised, since lectures could combine the powerful educational tools of gifted lecturers with graphics and pictures. These changes, if they are employed, would require new institutional arrangements.

Weather Developments

Steps are being taken to build effective meteorological monitoring systems that will eventually encompass the globe. The combination of satellite technologies, ocean buoys, and computerized weather models may make longer range and more accurate weather forecasting a reality by the end of the decade.

An increasing number of experts feel that some capability for modifying weather could become feasible during the decade. For example, precipitation levels might be increased by modest percentages. Some techniques for fog and smog control could become a reality during the decade. In the longer range future there may be substantial capability for both predicting and modifying weather. Before this capability can be employed, much additional information will be necessary on the effects of weather modification. A risk is associated with the potential that capabilities for beginning weather control might emerge before we have complete information and knowledge about their consequences or have the means to handle these consequences. Should they emerge, such capabilities will raise a number of important policy issues for both domestic and international policies and relationships.

Possible Ocean Developments

Scientific exploration of the sea is getting seriously underway. Although the resources of the ocean have been used for centuries in various ways, a variety of technological advances of the 1970's may greatly expand the uses of the ocean. These developments in new knowledge may also begin to place constraints on some current uses: for instance, many waste-disposal procedures now use the ocean as the ultimate "sink" (the place where waste is finally deposited). The development of ocean ecology is already beginning to bring information about the effects of these practices upon the pollution of the ocean. The debates over these issues are just beginning to emerge and can be expected to increase during the decade as the consequences of our actions become clear and as new uses of the ocean are developed.

Some forecasters anticipate the development of "ocean farming." At present most food from the ocean comes largely from hunting and gathering rather than careful cultivation, or "aqua-culture," but cultivation of the oceans may become significant in future decades just as land cultivation has been in the past.

It is expected that in a decade it will be feasible to do offshore drilling farther from shore and perhaps begin to exploit the ocean floor and the geological resources beneath international waters.

These developments promise to have great impact upon man's source of nutrition, wealth, and recreation.

Possible Developments in Biological and Health Sciences

The health sciences have shown accelerating change during the past two decades. A number of additional changes appear to be on the horizon and could be coming into use by 1980. An increasing array of human organs could be transplanted as a normal treatment for malfunctioning body processes. Preparations are being made now to adapt legal codes to those new capabilities. A number of state legislatures now are making modifications to their laws that will make it possible to transplant human organs. The political and social implications of these prospective developments are little understood.

Some experts believe that during the 1970's a number of new capabilities for the influence of learning processes and improving memory through chemical stimulation of various aspects of the neurophysiological processes will be successfully demonstrated. If these developments occur, they will give a variety of new tools for which experience gives little adequate guidance.

Our information on genetics may have progressed by the end of the decade to a more complete understanding of the likely consequences of two partners bearing offspring. What will be society's responsibility to an unborn infant if it can be determined that there is a high chance that the infant, if conceived, will have deformities likely to affect the quality of his existence and greatly increase the cost to society which must provide for him.

Engineering developments promise to provide more and more mechanical organs either to assist in controlling the physiology of the body or perhaps even to replace certain of its vital organs. The forerunners of these new technologies are such things as electronic heart-pacers and the variety of prosthetic devices now in use.

As research on human reproduction processes continues, new forms of fertility control may be developed. Some of these may permit relatively longer term control which could substitute a "shot per year" for a "pill per day." [6]

Charles Reich, in *The Greening of America*, has traced the change in terms of what he calls Consciousness I, Consciousness II, and Consciousness III.[7]

Consciousness I developed in the nineteenth century and is defined by Reich as the traditional outlook of the "American farmer, small businessman, or worker trying to get ahead." The man who made good was a moral being, and his triumph would come from the ordinary virtues—plainness, character, honesty, and hard work.

Consciousness II, Reich holds, was formed in the first half of this century, and is the belief held by the New Deal, the Kennedy men, the Great Society, idealistic lawyers, young doctors, general reformers, and liberals. Consciousness II regards all individual liberty as subject to the overriding public interest of the corporate state.

Consciousness III is in the process of emerging, among youngsters, college students, and very few enlightened older people. Reich holds that Consciousness III's commitment lies in the concept of full personal responsibility. The Consciousness III person feels that he must respond to those issues which affect him, his society, his environment. He believes in the search for self, individual liberty, honesty, and full responsibility. He denies the importance of hierarchy, status, authority, position. There is a total rejection of competition.

In the confusion that comes to all of us out of the welter of possibilities open in the future, one should remember that there are possibilities, not necessarily all desirable. Man must make choices among the possibilities or face an armoral, chaotic world, the nightmare of so many utopias.

Reich's book created considerable controversy and was a best seller. It was almost uniformly panned by the critics, conservative, liberal, and radical. However, all seemed to feel he had done a good job in his delineation of Consciousness I and II. They disagreed with his optimism concerning the possibility of a nonviolent revolution, his underestimation of the seamier aspects of the youth movements, and his political naïveté in thinking that the establishment could wither away and that we could still have a technology adequate to maintain the affluence necessary to support Consciousness III.[8]

[6]Report of the National Goals Research Staff, *Toward Balanced Growth: Quantity with Quality* (Washington, D.C.: Government Printing Office, July 4, 1970), pp. 27–31, 162–163, 214–217.

[7]Charles A. Reich, *The Greening of America* (New York: Random House, 1970).

[8]Philip Nobile (ed.), *The Con III Controversy: The Critics Look at the Greening of America* (New York: Pocket Books, 1971).

Keyes and Fresco, in their recent utopia *Looking Forward*, indicate clearly what the choices are:

> If anyone wished to spell out in useful detail some of the forms of our future, we believe he must pick the right horse in three different races:
>
> 1. He must correctly assess what man will want to do—what he *really values most*.
> 2. He must accurately find out how he's going to try to do it—what *methods of thinking* he will rely upon most.
> 3. He must analyze the tools that man will have for accomplishing what he sets out to do—he must pinpoint the significant *technological developments* that will play major roles in the future.
>
> All three factors interact with each other. The value structure not only influences the method of thinking and the technology, but it is, in turn, influenced by them. The method of thinking that man employs is affected by his value structure and the technology of the age, but it also plays a part in modifying both of these. Similarly, the technology of any given civilization interacts in a mutual way with the value structure and the methods of thinking. These pregnant factors might be viewed as three gears that mesh with each other.[9]

EDUCATION FOR THE FORESEEABLE FUTURE

The authors believe that the information obtained from the social sciences, from the past history of man's social trends, and from these forecasts of the future has certain definite implications for education. They have drawn specific implications in each of the chapters as the data have been presented. On the basis of their understanding of the nature of our culture and its recent changes as developed from data from the social sciences and psychology and on the basis of a set of values they consider appropriate to education in a democratic society, they set forth the following as over-all suggestions for persons responsible for decision making for education. Many of these are related to the basic questions raised in Chapter 1 as part of their purposes in writing a book presenting this analysis of society.

There are numerous consequences of these enormous scientific and technical advances. One is that we will have to teach respect for new ideas. This must include both the acceptance of technological changes themselves and the acceptance of the new patterns of living and institutions these changes make necessary. One of the characteristics of life in the future will be an enormous increase in the amount of leisure time. That leisure might mean that we could have a new renaissance of culture in America. The part that the school can play in this is, of course, quite basic. One of the main educational jobs of society and of the school, society's institution for doing that job, would be to teach for "adjustability," not for "adjustment" only. "Adjustment" implies education for a static society, whereas "adjustability" implies that the student can adjust himself and his institutions to changes that come about after his education has been completed.

The authors believe that the schools have a very definite responsibility

[9]Kenneth Keyes and Jacques Fresco, *Looking Forward* (New York: Barnes, 1969), pp. 41–42. Used by permission.

for providing a curriculum that will keep boys and girls apprised of the changes occurring in our society, the nature of the emerging society, and the trends in that society. Because the amount of knowledge is so great and being added to so rapidly, it is impossible ever to teach boys and girls all of the information they will need. It therefore becomes important that we teach boys and girls the process of seeking knowledge when needed—the scientific method and how to use the resources from the social and other sciences. This means that to the fundamental processes—important as they may be—must be added the basic job of teaching boys and girls to locate, verify, interpret, and apply knowledge (in short, research skills).

The fact that we live in a changing world means further that we must help boys and girls to develop a quality of adjustability. To be educated for adjustability means that the child must develop the ability to change as conditions warrant, must be able to recognize his own limitations and adjust to them, and must learn not only to operate within those limitations but also to grow within them. The youngster must develop a frame of mind that will enable him to see that new conditions require new remedies. The idea of adjustability and more is found in all of these concepts. We are educating children now who will live a great part of their lives in the twenty-first century under conditions different in many ways from those we have at present.

The increased amount of leisure time means that we must educate the youngsters for creative use of leisure. This does not mean a purely passive use of leisure or a routine whiling away of time. It means teaching for the creative use of talents, perhaps in a new intellectual renaissance. Creativity can be encouraged in all fields. The amount of wealth we have and the amount of time now available should enable us, with an appropriate background from our educational system, to forge ahead in the field of the creative arts.

The fact that our boys and girls must have a readiness to use unknown ways to solve problems that are not known means that we must teach problem solving—the scientific method. About the only way to teach the problem-solving procedure is to give youngsters practice in solving problems while they are in school. An important part of problem solving is, of course, getting the facts and information necessary for such solutions. But facts and information are not enough. Boys and girls must have practice in the actual solving of problems that are important to them.

The recent developments of the social sciences that indicate the fact that we as human beings are a product of our culture have many implications for the quality of the experiences we have in school. We are a product of our experiences. To the extent to which we adopt democratic methods in our schools, are taught how to solve our problems, and are helped to clarify our values, to that extent we will be better able to operate as adults in this very complex democratic social order.

What the effect of automation will be upon the nature of the school's job in the area of vocational and general education is not fully known at this time. However, it probably means that we ought to have a good general-education program for all of our students and postpone specific vocational education to nearer the time when the person is certain about the occupation he will follow. Very likely this specific training for the highly technical jobs of the period of automation ought to be given in institutions that are post-high school as high schools are now understood—two more years for boys and girls of ages eighteen or nineteen. There is much evidence that the post-high school vocational institute or junior college is entering a period of rapid expansion. For the more highly complex jobs, the technical, professional, and engineering schools would be more appropriate institutions.

In the book *High School 1980*,[10] edited by Alvin C. Eurich, the contributors paint a challenging picture of what the high school *could* be by 1980, but they are not all certain that these changes actually will come about. Students are referred to this source for a detailed, considered presentation of possibilities.

The breakdown of values, caused by the rapidly changing society, and the urbanization of our culture, with the consequent juxtaposition of differing and conflicting value systems, have led to confusion in values on the part of many individuals. The school must place more emphasis upon helping each boy and girl to arrive at a set of values he can live by.

Educators need to become greatly concerned with education in the area of values.

> Any idea that the thinker's job is to teach only his subject matter, his discipline, and not values is a major crime.
>
> It is not enough to help children know their values. We must also assist children in their ability to collect evidence, compare, and select the priority value when they are confronted with conflicting values.
>
> Further, teachers can be a "significant other" if they are not hollow men.
>
> Teachers should stand for the basic American values that enable a person to live effectively in plural cultures.
>
> They should stand for the continuation of the human race. If human life is blotted from the face of the earth, there is no point in discussing other values.
>
> They should be for the development of the potential of each human being. Simply maintaining mankind is not enough.
>
> They should make the inclusive approach, which accepts all men as being important.
>
> They should not want all people to accept the American culture, but work to develop a single moral community where all possess the same fundamental rights and obligations.
>
> They should value an inclusive approach that will assign all men the same rights without insisting that they live by the same light.
>
> They should stand for freedom of thought, worship, press and speech.
>
> They should see differences and the exploration of it as the doorway to new insight, not as a threat to our cherished values.
>
> They should see the interaction of peoples as the mutual seeking of more insight.
>
> They should become more open rather than more protective.
>
> They should be optimistic. They should believe that the future can be better.
>
> They should see change as progress because they make intelligent choices and [use] each action as a move in the direction of our destiny. Un-

[10]Alvin C. Eurich (ed.), *High School 1980: The Shape of the Future in American Secondary Education* (New York: Pitman, 1970). This book was prepared by the staff of the Academy of Educational Development.

less a given step is final, each advance can increase our vision and make possible more intelligent planning of our future.[11]

In this emerging educational system—based upon the educational implications of the findings of the social sciences, particularly philosophy, sociology, and psychology—the authors envision the schools and the teachers as being leaders of our cultural life and playing an important part in the communities in which they are located. Their leadership would operate not only among the children and youth but also among the adults. The authors do not envision the school as determining the direction or the nature of society, but as stimulating thinking and helping all the people to use the problem-solving methods learned in school to develop appropriate institutions and appropriate behavior for the kind of world that is emerging. The center of study of this school of the future would be man himself and his relations with other men—the new "humanities."

In a recent book by Bennis and Slater, Bennis sets forth the "Human Problems Confronting Contemporary Organizations." [12] (See Table 20.) Concerning revitalization, he further states:

I introduce the term "revitalization" to embrace all the social mechanisms that stagnate and regenerate, as well as the process of this cycle. The elements of revitalization are:

An ability to learn from experience and to codify, store, and retrieve the relevant knowledge.
An ability to learn how to learn, that is, to develop methods for improving the learning process.
An ability to acquire and use feedback mechanisms on performance, in short, to be self-analytical.
An ability to direct one's own destiny.[13]

In the same book Bennis indicates the role of education and the challenge of the future as follows:

Our society and particularly our educational systems should be involved in helping to develop the necessary interpersonal competencies rather than, as tends to be true of most education, working against our full human development. Our educational system should (1) help us to identify with the adaptive process without fear of losing our identity, (2) increase our tolerance of ambiguity without fear of losing intellectual mastery, (3) increase our ability to collaborate without fear of losing our individuality, and (4) develop a willingness to participate in social evolution while recognizing implacable forces. In short, we need an educational system that can help us make a virtue out of contingency rather than one which induces hesitancy or its reckless companion, expedience.

Most education shies away from or shuns these adaptive capacities, wishfully hoping that the student will possess them or that, like sex, he can find out about them from his buddies. So for the most part we learn the significant things informally and badly, having to unlearn them later on in life

[11]Dr. Kimball Wiles in *ASCD News Exchange* (April 1964), p. 15. By permission.
[12]Warren G. Bennis and Philip R. Slater, *The Temporary Society* (New York: Harper, 1968).
[13]From p. 71, "Human Problems Confronting Contemporary Organizations" by Warren G. Bennis, from *The Temporary Society* by Warren G. Bennis and Philip E. Slater. Copyright 1968 by Warren G. Bennis and Philip E. Slater. Reprinted by permission of Harper & Row, Publishers, Inc.

TABLE 20
Human Problems Confronting Contemporary Organizations

PROBLEM	BUREAUCRATIC SOLUTIONS	NEW TWENTIETH-CENTURY CONDITIONS
Integration Integrating individual needs and organizational goals.	No solution because there is no problem. Individual vastly over-simplified, regarded as passive instrument. Tension between personality and role disregarded.	Emergence of human sciences and understanding of man's complexity. Rising aspirations. Humanistic-democratic ethos.
Social Influence Distributing power and sources of power and authority.	An explicit reliance on legal-rational power, but an implicit usage of coercive power. In any case, a confused, ambiguous, shifting complex of competence, coercion, and legal code.	Separation of management from ownership. Rise of trade unions and general education. Negative and unintended effects of authoritarian rule.
Collaboration Producing mechanisms for the control of conflict.	The "rule of hierarchy" to resolve conflicts between ranks and the "rule of co-ordination" to resolve conflict between horizontal groups. Loyalty.	Specialization and professionalization and increased need for interdependence. Leadership too complex for one-man rule or omniscience.
Adaptation Responding appropriately to changes induced by the environment.	Environment stable, simple, and predictable; tasks routine. Adapting to change occurs in haphazard and adventitious ways. Unanticipated consequences abound.	External environment of firm more turbulent, less predictable. Unprecedented rate of technological change.
Identity Achieving clarity, consensus, and commitment to organizational goals.	Primary goal of organization clear, simple, and stable.	Increased complexity due to diversity, multipurpose capability, intersector mobility. Creates role complexity, conflict, and ambiguity.
Revitalization Dealing with growth and decay.	Underlying assumption that the future will be certain and at least basically similar to the past.	Rapid changes in technologies, tasks, manpower, raw materials, norms and values of society, goals of enterprise and society all make constant attention to the process of revision imperative.

From pp. 68–69, "Human Problems Confronting Contemporary Organizations" by Warren G. Bennis, from *The Temporary Society* by Warren G. Bennis and Philip E. Slater. Reprinted by permission of Harper & Row, Publishers, Inc.

when the consequences are grave or frightfully expensive, like a five-day-a-week analysis.

I would like to see educational programs in the art and science of being more fully human, which would take very seriously the kind of world we are living in and help produce students who could not only cope with and understand this world but attempt to change it. We should help our students develop the necessary interpersonal competencies, which would include at least the following: (1) learning how to develop intense and deep human relationships quickly—and learn how to "let go." In other words, learning how to get love, to love, and to lose love; (2) learning how to enter groups and leave them; (3) learning what roles are satisfying and how to attain them; (4) learning how to widen the repertory of feelings and roles available; (5) learning how to cope more readily with ambiguity; (6) learning how to develop a strategic comprehensibility of a new "culture" and finally, (7) learning how to develop a sense of one's uniqueness.

One final consideration, which I suspect our educational system cannot provide, nor can we hope to acquire it easily. Somehow with all the mobility, chronic churning and unconnectedness we envisage, it will become more and more important to develop some permanent or abiding commitment. If our libidinal attachments, to return to a theme of Slater's, become more diffused, it will be essential that we focus commitment on a person or an institution or an idea. This means that as general commitments become diffuse or modified, a greater *fidelity* to something or someone will be necessary to make us more fully human.

I think that the future I describe is not necessarily a "happy" one. Coping with rapid change, living in temporary work systems, developing meaningful relations and then breaking them—all augur social strains and psychological tensions. Teaching how to live with ambiguity, to identify with the adaptive process, to make a virtue out of contingency, and to be self-directing—these will be the tasks of education, the goals of maturity, and the achievement of the successful individual.

In these new organizations of the future, participants will be called upon to use their minds more than at any other time in history. Fantasy, imagination, and creativity will be legitimate in ways that today seem strange. Social structures will no longer be instruments of psychic repression but will increasingly promote play and freedom on behalf of curiosity and thought.[14]

The challenge to education based on emerging problems and on the roles we need to assume to meet them is very great. The demands made on the teacher are heavy. By and large, teachers are at present inadequately equipped to discharge the duties necessitated by the problems posed by the changing society. There are many communities in our society that at present are not prepared to support the teacher adequately, either financially, socially, or with sympathetic approval as to the difficulty of his task. The status of the teacher of America must be greatly improved. He must be given compensation adequate for living a greatly enriched life. Efforts must be made to help him gain a comprehensive and profound understanding of the nature of the society in which we live and of the implications of that society for education. The net result of all this will be to develop a school system that

14From pp. 127–128, 75–76, "Human Problems Confronting Contemporary Organizations," by Warren G. Bennis, from *The Temporary Society* by Warren G. Bennis and Philip E. Slater. Reprinted by permission of Harper & Row, Publishers, Inc.

will help the American people to achieve more fully the greatness inherent in the American democratic society, and to achieve it while maintaining a *free* democratic society.

Selected Bibliography

Abt, Clark C. "Forecasting Future Social Needs," *The Futurist,* Vol. V, No. 1 (February 1971).

Aerospace Education Foundation. *Technology and Innovation in Education: Putting Education to Work in America's Schools.* New York: Frederick A. Praeger, Inc., 1968. 149 pp.

Alexander, William M. *The High School of the Future: A Memorial to Kimball Wiles.* Columbus, Ohio: Charles E. Merrill Books, Inc., 1969. 280 pp.

Allen, James E., Jr. "Education for Survival," *American Education,* Vol. 6, No. 2 (March 1970).

Asimov, Isaac. *Is Anyone There?* New York: Ace, 1969. 319 pp.

Axelrod, Joseph, Mervin B. Freedman, and others. *Search for Relevance.* San Francisco: Jossey-Bass, 1969. 244 pp.

Baade, Fritz. *The Race to the Year 2000, Our Future: A Paradise or the Suicide of Mankind.* Garden City, N.Y.: Doubleday & Company, Inc., 1962. 246 pp.

Bagdikian, Ben H. *The Information Machines.* New York: Harper & Row, Publishers, 1971. 359 pp.

Baier, Kurt, and Nicholas Rescher (eds.). *Values and the Future: The Impact of Technological Change on American Values.* New York: The Free Press, 1969. 527 pp.

Barnett, Lincoln. *The Universe and Dr. Einstein.* New York: The New American Library, 1957. 128 pp. Probably the most readable of the lay books on the implications of Einsteinian science.

Bates, Frederick L. "Social Trends in a Leisure Society," *The Futurist,* Vol. V, No. 2 (February 1971).

Beckwith, Burnham P. *The Next 500 Years.* New York: Exposition University, 1967. 341 pp.

Behrman, S. J., et al (eds.). *Fertility and Family Planning: A World View.* Ann Arbor: University of Michigan Press, 1969. 503 pp.

Bennis, Warren G., et al. (eds.). *The Planning of Change: Readings in the Behavioral Sciences.* New York: Holt, Rinehart & Winston, Inc., 1961. 781 pp.

———, and Philip E. Slater. *The Temporary Society.* New York: Harper & Row, Publishers, 1968. 147 pp.

Berger, Peter L., and Brigitte Berger. "The Bluing of America," *Current,* July–August, 1971.

Berg, Ivar. *Education and Jobs: The Great Training Robbery.* New York: Frederick A. Praeger, Inc., 1970. 194 pp.

Berrien, F. Kenneth. *General and Social Systems.* New Brunswick, N.J.: Rutgers University Press, 1968. 231 pp.

Blaustein, Arthur I., and Roger R. Woock (eds.). *Man Against Poverty: World War III, A Reader on the World's Most Crucial Issue.* New York: Random House, Inc., 1968. 456 pp.

Bloch, Ernst. *A Philosophy of the Future.* New York: Herder and Herder, 1970. 149 pp.

Boguslaw, Robert. *The New Utopians: A Study of Systems Designs and Sound Change.* Englewood Cliffs, N.J.: Prentice-Hall, Inc., 1965. 213 pp.

Boulding, Kenneth E. *The Meaning of the Twentieth Century.* New York: Harper & Row, Publishers, 1964. 199 pp.

Bowers, C. A., Ian Housego, and Doris Dyke (eds.). *Education and Social Policy: Local Control of Education.* New York: Random House, Inc., 1970. 209 pp.

Bowles, Samuel. *Planning Educational Systems for Economic Growth*. Cambridge, Mass.: Harvard University Press, 1969. 245 pp.

Braden, William. *The Age of Aquarius: Technology and the Cultural Revolution*. Chicago: Quadrangle Books, Inc., 1970. 306 pp.

Brameld, Theodore. *The Climactic Decade: Mandate to Education*. New York: Frederick A. Praeger, Inc., 1970. 210 pp.

———. *The Use of Explosive Ideas in Education: Culture, Class and Evolution*. Pittsburgh: University of Pittsburgh Press, 1965. 224 pp.

Brinkman, William W., and Stanley Lehrer (eds.). *Automation, Education and Human Values*. New York: School and Society Books, 1966. 419 pp.

Bronowski, Jacob. "What We Can't Know," *Saturday Review*, July 5, 1969, 44–45. A noted philosopher of science indicates some of the uncertainties of predictions of the possible future.

Bronwell, Arthur B. (ed.). *Science and Technology in the World of the Future*. New York: Interscience Publishers, Inc., 1970. 393 pp.

Brown, George Isaac. *Human Teaching for Human Learning: An Introduction to Confluent Education*. New York: The Viking Press, Inc., 1971. 298 pp.

Brown, Lester R. *Seeds of Change: The Green Revolution and Development in the 1970's*. New York: Frederick A. Praeger, Inc., 1970. 205 pp.

Browne, Ray B., et al. (eds.). *Frontiers of American Culture*. Layfayette, Ind.: Purdue Research Foundation, 1968. 201 pp.

Brzezinski, Zbigniew. *Between Two Ages: America's Role in the Technotronic Era*. New York: The Viking Press, Inc., 1970. 334 pp.

Caffrey, John (ed.). *The Future Academic Community: Continuity and Change*. Washington, D.C.: American Council on Education, 1969. 327 pp.

Calder, Nigel (ed.). *Technopolis: Social Control of the Uses of Science*. New York: Simon & Schuster, Inc., 1970. 376 pp.

"Can We Afford Tomorrow? A Report on America's Needs and Resources in Co-operation with Committee for Development," *Saturday Review*, January 23, 1971.

Carter, Anne P. *Structural Change in the American Economy*. Cambridge, Mass.: Harvard University Press, 1970. 292 pp.

Cetron, Marvin J. *Technological Forecasting: A Practical Approach*. New York: Gordon and Breach, 1969. 345 pp.

Chase, Stuart. *The Most Probable World*. New York: Harper & Row, Publishers, 1968 239 pp.

———. "Two Cheers for Technology," *Saturday Review*, February 20, 1971.

Chorfas, D. N. *The Knowledge Revolution*. New York: McGraw-Hill Book Company, 1968. 143 pp. (Paperback.)

Cohen, Yehudi A. (ed.). *Man in Adaptation: The Cultural Present*. Chicago: Aldine Publishing Co., 1968. 433 pp.

Coleman, James S. *Resources for Social Change: Race in the United States*. New York: John Wiley & Sons, Inc., 1971. 128 pp.

Counts, George S. *Education and American Civilization*. New York: Bureau of Publications, Teachers College, Columbia University, 1952. 491 pp. A careful examination of the implications of the American way of life for education.

———. *Education and the Foundations of Human Freedom*. Pittsburgh: University of Pittsburgh Press, 1962. 104 pp.

Cox, George W. (ed.). *Readings in Conservation Ecology*. New York: Appleton-Century-Crofts, 1969. 595 pp.

Davidson, R. Michael. "Man's Participatory Evolution," *Current*, No. 105 (March 1969).

Diebold, John. *Man and the Computer: Technology as an Agent of Social Change*. New York: Frederick A. Praeger, Inc., 1969. 157 pp.

Divoky, Diane (ed.). *How Old Will You Be in 1984?: Expressions of Student Outrage from the High School Free Press*. New York: Avon Books, 1969. 350 pp.

Douglas, J. W. B., J. M. Ross, and H. R. Simpson. *All Our Future*. London: Peter Davies, 1968. 241 pp.

Drucker, Peter F. *The Age of Discontinuity: Guidelines to Our Changing Society*. New York: Harper & Row, Publishers, 1969. 402 pp.

Dubos, René. *Man, Medicine and Environment*. New York: Frederick A. Praeger, Inc., 1968. 125 pp.

———. "On Controlling Technology," *Current*, No. 119 (June 1970).

———. *Reason Awake: Science for Man*. New York: Columbia University Press, 1970. 280 pp.

Dupuis, Adrian M. (ed.). *Nature, Aims and Policy*. Urbana: University of Illinois Press, 1970. 344 pp.

Ehrlich, Paul R. *The Population Bomb*. New York: Ballantine Books, Inc., 1968. 223 pp.

———, and Anne H. Ehrlich. *Population Resources Environment: Issues in Human Ecology*. San Francisco: W. H. Freeman & Co., Publishers, 1970. 383 pp.

———, and John P. Holdren. "The People Problem," *Saturday Review*, July 4, 1970.

Elam, Stanley, and William P. McLure (eds.). *Educational Requirements for the 1970's: An Interdisciplinary Approach*. New York: Frederick A. Praeger, Inc., 1967. 266 pp.

Ellul, Jacques. *The Technological Society*. New York: Vintage Books, 1964. 449 pp.

Epstein, Herman T. *A Strategy for Education*. New York: Oxford University Press, 1970. 122 pp.

Ernst, Leonard. "Can Chemicals Stimulate Learning Capacity?" *The Education Digest*, Vol. XXXV, No. 9 (May 1970).

Etzioni, Amitai. *The Active Society*. New York: The Free Press, 1968. 698 pp.

Eurich, Alvin C. (ed.). *Campus 1980*. New York: Delacorte, 1968. 327 pp.

——— (ed.). *High School 1980: The Shape of the Future in American Secondary Education*. New York: Pitman Publishing Corp., 1970. 304 pp.

———. *Reforming American Education: The Innovative Approach to Improving Our Schools*. New York: Harper & Row, Publishers, 1969. 269 pp.

Evans, Wayne O. "Mind Altering Drugs and the Future," *The Futurist*, Vol. V, No. 3 (June 1971).

Ewald, William R., Jr. (ed.). *Environment for Man: The Next Fifty Years*. Bloomington: Indiana University Press, 1967. 397 pp.

Ewing, David W. *The Human Side of Planning: Tool or Tyrant?* New York: The Macmillan Company, 1969. 216 pp.

Fabun, Don. *The Dynamics of Change*. Englewood Cliffs, N.J.: Prentice-Hall, Inc., 1967. 190 pp.

Ferkiss, Victor C. *Technological Man: The Myth and the Reality*. New York: George Braziller, Inc., 1969. 336 pp.

Field, Frank L. *Freedom and Control in Education and Society*. New York: Thomas Y. Crowell Company, 1970. 195 pp.

Fischer, John. "Why and How to Build Another U.S.A.," *Current*, No. 114 (January 1970).

Fischer, Robert B. *Science, Man and Society*. Philadelphia: W. B. Saunders Co., 1971. 124 pp.

Fisher, Robert J., and Wilfred R. Smith (eds.). *Schools in an Age of Crisis*. New York: Van Nostrand, Reinhold, 1972. 224 pp.

Foreign Policy Association. *Toward the Year 2018*. New York: Cowles, 1968. 177 pp.

Frankel, Charles. *The Case for Modern Man*. New York: Harper & Row, Publishers, 1956. 240 pp. An excellent survey and appraisal of man's cultural development, with a look to the future.

Frank, Lawrence K. *Nature and Human Nature*. New Brunswick, N.J.: Rutgers University Press, 1951. 175 pp. An excellent summary of modern knowledge about man.

Fromm, Erich. *The Revolution of Hope: Toward a Humanized Technology.* New York: Harper & Row, Publishers, 1969. 178 pp.

—— (ed.). *Socialist Humanism.* Garden City, N.Y.: Anchor, 1966. 461 pp.

Fuller, R. Buckminster. *Utopia or Oblivion: The Prospects for Humanity.* New York: Bantam Books, 1971. 366 pp.

——, Erich A. Walker, and James R. Killian, Jr. *Approaching the Benign Environment.* University, Ala.: University of Alabama Press, 1970. 121 pp.

Gardner, John W. *The Recovery of Confidence.* New York: W. W. Norton & Company, Inc., 1970. 189 pp.

Garth, Eleanore. "The A-Sexual Society." Santa Barbara, Calif.: Center for the Study of Democratic Institutions, 1971. Processed.

Gilkey, Langdon. *Religion and the Scientific Future.* New York: Harper & Row, Publishers, 1970. 193 pp.

Gore, Albert. *The Eye of the Storm: A People's Politics for the Seventies.* New York: Herder and Herder, 1970. 212 pp.

Gorman, Burton W. *Secondary Education: The High School Americans Need.* New York: Random House, Inc., 1971. 389 pp.

Gouldner, Alvin. *The Coming Crisis of Western Sociology.* New York: Basic Books, Inc., 1970. 528 pp.

Goulet, Richard R. (ed.). *Educational Change: The Reality and the Promise.* New York: Citation, 1968. 288 pp.

Grace, Alonzo G. "Education in the 21st Century," *The Educational Forum,* Vol. XXXV, No. 4 (May 1971).

Graham, Robert Klark. *The Future of Man.* North Quincy, Mass.: Christopher, 1970. 200 pp.

Greeley, Andrew M. *Religion in the Year 2000.* New York: Sheed and Ward, 1969. 175 pp.

Haberman, Jurgen. *Toward a Rational Society: Student Protest, Science, and Politics.* Boston: Beacon Press, 1970. 132 pp.

Hack, Walter G. et al. *Educational Futurism, 1985: Challenges for Schools and Their Administrators.* Berkeley, Calif.: McCutchan, 1971. 225 pp.

Hacker, Andrew. *The End of the American Era.* New York: Atheneum Publishers, 1970. 239 pp.

Handler, Philip (ed.). *Biology and the Future of Man.* New York: Oxford University Press, 1970. 936 pp.

Harcleroad, Fred F. (ed.). *Issues of the Seventies.* San Francisco: Jossey-Bass, 1970. 192 pp.

Harrington, Alan. *The Immortalist.* New York: Random House, Inc., 1970. 324 pp.

Harrington, Michael. *The Accidental Century.* Baltimore: Penguin Books, Inc., 1965. 322 pp.

——. *Toward a Democratic Left: A Radical Program for a New Majority.* New York: The Macmillan Company, 1968. 314 pp.

Harrison, John F. C. (ed.). *Utopianism and Education: Robert Owen and the Owenites.* New York: Teachers College Press, 1968. 257 pp.

Havelock, Ronald G., et al. *Planning for Innovation.* Ann Arbor: Publications Division Institute for Social Research, The University of Michigan, 1970. 538 pp

Heilbroner, Robert L. *The Future as History.* New York: Harper & Row, Publishers, 1968. 217 pp.

Helfrich, Harold W., Jr. (ed.). *The Environmental Crisis.* New Haven: Yale University Press, 1970. 187 pp.

Hellman, Hal. *Biology in the World of the Future.* New York: M. Evans & Co., Inc., 1971. 188 pp.

——. *Transportation in the World of the Future.* New York: M. Evans & Co., Inc., 1968. 187 pp.

Hillegas, Mark R. *The Future as Nightmare: H. G. Wells and the Anti-Utopians*. New York: Oxford University Press, 1967. 200 pp.

Hirsch, Werner Z., et al. *Inventing Education for the Future*. San Francisco: Chandler Publishing Co., 1967. 353 pp.

Hitchcock, James. "Comes the Cultural Revolution," *New York Times Magazine*, July 27, 1969.

Hope, Frank L., Jr. "Building Entirely New Cities," *Current*, No. 125 (January 1971).

Hoyle, Fred. *Encounter with the Future*. New York: Trident Press, Inc., 1965. 108 pp.

Hunnicutt, Clarence W. (ed.). *Education A.D. 2000*. Syracuse, N.Y.: Syracuse University Press, 1956. 321 pp.

Hurwitz, Emanuel, Jr., and Charles A. Tesconi, Jr. (eds.). *Challenges to Education: Readings for Analyses of Major Issues*. New York: Dodd, Mead, 1972. 560 pp.

Hutchins, Robert M. *The Learning Society*. New York: Frederick A. Praeger, Inc., 1968. 142 pp.

Huxley, Julian. *Man in the Modern World*. New York: New American Library, 1952. 191 pp.

Illich, Ivan. "The Alternative to Schooling," *The Saturday Review*, June 19, 1971.

_____. "Education Without School: How It Can Be Done," *The New York Review of Books*, Vol. XV, No. 12 (January 7, 1971).

_____. "Why We Must Abolish Schooling," *The New York Review of Books*, Vol. XV, No. 1 (July 2, 1970).

Jencks, C. A., and David Riesman. *The Academic Revolution*. Garden City, N.Y.: Doubleday & Company, Inc., 1968. 580 pp.

Jerome, Judson. *Culture Out of Anarchy: The Reconstruction of American Higher Learning*. New York: Herder and Herder, 1970. 330 pp.

Jonas, David, and Doris Klein. *A Study of the Infantilization of Man*. New York: McGraw-Hill Book Company, 1970. 362 pp.

de Jouvenel, Bertrand. *The Art of Conjecture*. New York: Basic Books, Inc., 1967. 307 pp.

_____, René Dubos, et al. *The Fitness of Man's Environment*. New York: Harper & Row, Publishers, 1968. 250 pp.

Kahl, Joseph A. *The Measurement of Modernism*. Austin: University of Texas Press, 1968. 210 pp.

Kahn, Herman, and Anthony J. Wiener. *The Year 2000*. New York: The Macmillan Company, 1967. 431 pp. A framework for speculation on the next thirty-three years.

Kaplan, Abraham (ed.). *Individuality and the New Society*. Co-published with Reed College, Second Sanctity of Life Symposium. Seattle: University of Washington Press, 1970. 168 pp.

Kateb, George (ed.). *Utopia*. Chicago: Aldine Publishing Company, 1971. 200 pp.

Keyes, Kenneth S., and Jacques Fierro. *Looking Forward*. New York: A. S. Barnes & Co., Inc., 1969. 204 pp.

Keyserling, Leon H. *Growth with Less Inflation or More Inflation Without Growth?* Washington, D.C.: Conference on Economic Progress, 1970. 79 pp. (Pamphlet.)

Kirkendall, Lester A., and Robert A. Whitehurst (eds.). *The New Sexual Revolution*. New York: Donald W. Brown, 1971. 236 pp.

Koch, Adrienne. *Philosophy for a Time of Crisis: Key Writings by 15 Great Modern Thinkers*. New York: E. P. Dutton & Co., Inc., 1959. 382 pp.

Korten, F. F., S. W. Cook, and J. I. Lacey (eds.). *Psychology and the Problems of Society*. Washington, D.C.: American Psychological Association, 1970. 450 pp.

Kosa, John (ed.). *The Home of the Learned Man*. New Haven, Conn.: College and University Press, 1968. 192 pp.

Kostelanetz, Richard (ed.). *Social Speculations: Visions for Our Time*. New York: William Morrow & Co., Inc., 1971. 307 pp.

Krech, David. "Don't Use the Kitchen Sink Approach to Enrichment," *Today's Education—The NEA Journal* (October 1970).

———. "Psychoneurobiochemeducation." Speech before the A.A.S.A. in *American Association of School Administrators Official Report*, 91–105. Washington, D.C.: American Association of School Administrators, 1969.

Kroll, Arthur M. (ed). *Issues in American Education: Commentary on the Current Scene.* London: Oxford University Press, 1970. 202 pp. These ten essays, presented originally at the Graduate School of Education at Harvard University, discuss a cross section of issues presently confronting American education, such as student attitudes and values, technological influences, integration within cities, vocational guidance, and labor relations.

Lachman, Seymour P., and David Bresnick, "An Educational Ombudsman for New York City?" *School and Society*, Vol. 99, No. 2332 (March 1971).

Landsberg, Hans H., et al. *Resources in America's Future: Patterns of Requirements and Availabilities, 1960–2000.* Baltimore: Johns Hopkins Press, 1963. 1,017 pp.

Lear, John. "Predicting the Consequences of Technology," *Saturday Review*, March 28, 1970.

Lederberg, Joshua. "What Controls for Genetic Engineering?" *Current*, No. 121 (September 1970).

Lerner, I. Michael. *Heredity, Evolution and Society.* San Francisco: W. H. Freeman & Co., Publishers, 1968. 307 pp.

LeShan, Eda J. *The Conspiracy Against Childhood.* New York: Atheneum Publishers, 1968. 368 pp.

Lessinger, Leon. *Every Kid a Winner: Accountability in Education.* New York: Simon & Schuster, Inc., 1970. 231 pp.

Lonsdale, Richard C. "Education in a Changing Society," *The Education Digest,* Vol. XXXVI, No. 2 (September 1970).

Lundberg, Ferdinand. *The Coming World Transformation.* Garden City, N.Y.: Doubleday & Company, Inc., 1963. 395 pp.

Lundsberg, Hans H., et al. *Resources in America's Future: Patterns of Requirements and Availabilities, 1960–2000.* Baltimore: Johns Hopkins Press, 1913. 1,017 pp.

Lyon, Harold C., Jr. *Learning to Feel and Feeling to Learn: Humanistic Education.* Columbus, Ohio: Charles E. Merrill Books, Inc., 1971. 288 pp.

"Man into Superman: The Promise and Peril of the New Genetics." *Time*, April 19, 1971. An excellent, up-to-date account of genetic, electrical, chemical possibilities for human improvement.

Martin, Reed. "Performance Contracting: Making It Legal," *The Education Digest*, Vol. XXXVI, No. 8 (April 1971).

McHale, John. *The Future of the Future.* New York: George Braziller, Inc., 1969. 322 pp.

McLain, John. "Developing Flexible All-Year Schools," *The Education Digest*, Vol. XXXVI, No. 9 (May 1971).

Mesthene, Emmanuel G. *Technological Change: Its Impact on Man and Society.* Cambridge, Mass.: Harvard University Press, 1970. 127 pp.

Metzger, Walter P., et al. *Dimensions of Academic Freedom.* Urbana: University of Illinois Press, 1970. 121 pp.

Meynaud, Jean. *Technocracy.* London: Faber and Faber, 1968. 315 pp.

Michael, Donald N. (ed.). *The Future Society.* Chicago: Aldine Publishing Co., 1970. 131 pp.

———. *The Next Generation: The Prospect Ahead for the Youth Today and Tomorrow.* New York: Random House, Inc., 1965. 218 pp.

———. *The Unprepared Society: Planning for a Precarious Future.* New York: Basic Books, Inc., 1968. 132 pp.

Miller, S. M., and Pamela Roby. *The Future of Inequality.* New York: Basic Books, Inc., 1970. 272 pp.

Millett, Kate. *Sexual Politics*. Garden City, N.Y.: Doubleday & Company, Inc., 1970. 393 pp.

Mitzel, Harold E. "The Impending Instruction Revolution," *Phi Delta Kappan*, Vol. LI, No. 8 (April 1970).

Montagu, Ashley. "A Scientist Looks at Love," *Phi Delta Kappan*, Vol. LI, No. 9 (May 1970).

_____. *The Directions of Human Development: Biological and Social Bases*. New York: Harper & Row, Publishers, 1955. 404 pp. An excellent summary of what is now known about man—a set of facts and understanding quite in contrast with nineteeth-century and earlier knowledge.

_____. *Education and Human Relations*. New York: Grove Press, Inc., 1958. 191 pp.

_____. *Modern Man*. Chicago: Science Research Associates, 1956. 48 pp. "The story of his present development and future possibilities."

Morphet, Edgar L., and Charles O. Ryand (eds.). *Designing Education for the Future: No. 2*. New York: Citation, 1967. 323 pp.

_____. *Implications for Education of Prospective Changes in Society*. New York: Citation, 1967. 337 pp.

_____. *Planning and Effecting Needed Changes in Education*. New York: Citation, 1967. 331 pp.

Moynihan, Daniel P. "What Role for Social Science Elites?" *Current*, No. 124 (December 1970).

Mumford, Lewis. *The Myth of the Machine: Vol. II, The Pentagon of Power*. New York: Harcourt Brace Jovanovich, Inc., 1970. 496 pp.

_____. *The Transformation of Man*. New York: Harper & Row, Publishers, 1956. 249 pp. A well-written essay on the development of modern man and an outlook for the future.

Nobile, Philip (ed.). *The New Eroticism: Theories, Vogues and Canons*. New York: Random House, Inc., 1970. 238 pp.

Oettinger, Anthony G. *Run, Computer, Run: The Mythology of Educational Innovation*. Cambridge, Mass.: Harvard University Press, 1969. 302 pp.

Ong, Walter J. (ed.). *Knowledge and the Future of Man: An International Symposium*. New York: Simon & Schuster, Inc., 1968. 276 pp.

Otto, Herbert A. "Communes: The Alternative Life-Style," *Saturday Review*, April 24, 1971.

Paddock, William, and Paul Paddock. *Famine 1975!: America's Decision: Who Will Survive?* Boston: Little, Brown and Company, 1967. 276 pp.

Parker, Don H. *Schooling for What?: Sex/Money/War/Peace*. New York: McGraw-Hill Book Company, 1970. 270 pp.

Perrucci, Robert, and Marc Pilisuk. *The Triple Revolution Emerging: Social Problems in Depth*, Second Edition. Boston: Little, Brown and Company, 1971. 800 pp.

Platt, John R. "The Crisis of Transformation," *Current*, No. 115 (February 1970).

_____ (ed.). *New Views of the Nature of Man*. Chicago: University of Chicago Press, 1965. 152 pp.

_____. *Perception and Change. Projections for the Future*. Ann Arbor: University of Michigan Press, 1970. 178 pp.

_____. *The Step to Man*. New York: John Wiley & Sons, Inc., 1966. 216 pp.

Poor, Riva (ed.). *4 Days, 40 Hours*. Cambridge, Mass.: Bursky and Poor, 1970. 175 pp.

Pratte, Richard. "The New Sensorium: The New Student," *School and Society*, Vol. 99, No. 2332 (March 1971).

Rainwater, Lee. *Family Design: Marital Sexuality, Family Size and Contraception*. Chicago: Aldine Publishing Co., 1965. 349 pp.

Ramsey, Paul. *Fabricated Man*. New Haven: Yale University Press, 1970. 171 pp.

Rasmussen, Victor. "Towards a Freer School," *The Education Digest*, Vol. XXXVI, No. 9 (May 1971).

Reich, Charles A. *The Greening of America*. New York: Random House, Inc., 1971. 395 pp.

Reiss, Albert J., Jr. (ed.). *Schools in a Changing Society*. New York: The Free Press, 1965. 224 pp.

Report of a Conference sponsored by the Danforth and Ford Foundations. *The School and the Democratic Environment*. New York: Columbia University Press, 1970. 115 pp.

Report of the National Goals Research Staff. *Toward Balanced Growth: Quantity with Quality*. Washington, D.C.: U.S. Government Printing Office, July 4, 1970. 227 pp.

Reynolds, Jerry D. "Performance Contracting . . . Adapted," *Education Digest*, Vol. XXXVI, No. 8 (April 1971).

Rimmer, Robert. *Proposition 31*. New York: The New American Library, 1969. 285 pp. Deals with a "way-out" concept of family.

Rockefeller, Nelson A. *Our Environment Can Be Saved*. Garden City, N.Y.: Doubleday & Company, Inc., 1970. 176 pp.

Rohrlich, George F. (ed.). *Social Economics for the 1970's*. New York: Dunellen, 1970. 189 pp.

Rokeach, Milton. *Beliefs, Attitudes and Values: A Theory of Organization and Change*. San Francisco: Jossey-Bass, 1968. 214 pp.

Roland, Jon D. "Alternative Paths to World Order," *The Futurist*, Vol. V, No. 4 (August 1971).

Rosenfeld, Albert. *The Second Genesis: The Coming Control of Life*. Englewood Cliffs, N.J.: Prentice-Hall, Inc, 1969. 327 pp.

Ruttenbert, Stanley H. *Manpower Challenge of the 1970's: Institutions and Social Change*. Baltimore: Johns Hopkins Press, 1970. 126 pp.

Sarason, Seymour B. *The Culture of the School and the Problem of Change*. Boston: Allyn and Bacon, 1971. 246 pp.

Schneider, Kenneth R. *Autokind vs. Mankind: An Analysis of Tyranny, a Proposal for Rebellion, a Plan for Reconstruction*. New York: W. W. Norton & Company, Inc., 1971. 267 pp.

Scobey, Mary M., and Grace Graham (eds.). *To Nurture Humaneness: Commitment for the 1970's*. Washington, D.C.: Association for Supervision and Curriculum Development, NEA, 1970. 257 pp.

Servan-Schreiber, J. J. *The American Challenge*. New York: Atheneum Publishers, 1969. 291 pp.

Sexton, Patricia Cayo. *School Policy and Issues in a Changing Society*. Boston: Allyn & Bacon, Inc., 1971. 426 pp.

Shane, Harold G., and Owen N. Nelson. "What Will the Schools Become?" *Phi Delta Kappan*, Vol. LII, No. 10 (June 1971).

Shofield, Andrew. "Futurology: A New Science?" *Current*, No. 105 (March 1969).

Shostrom, Everett L. *Man, the Manipulator*. Nashville: Abingdon Press, 1967. 256 pp.

Silber, Irwin. *The Cultural Revolution: A Marxist Analysis*. New York: Times Change Press, 1970. 62 pp.

Silberman, Charles E. *Crisis in the Classroom: The Remaking of American Education*. New York: Random House, Inc., 1970. 553 pp.

Staff of the Wall Street Journal. *Here Comes Tomorrow: Living and Working in the Year 2000*. New York: Dow Jones, 1970. 196 pp.

Steinberg, Ira S. *Educational Myths and Realities: Philosophical Essays on Education, Politics, and the Science of Behavior*. Reading, Mass.: Addison-Wesley Publishing Co., Inc., 1968. 240 pp.

Taylor, Gordon Rattray. *The Biological Time Bomb*. New York: The New American Library, 1968. 239 pp.

Teilhard de Chardin, Pierre. *The Future of Man*. New York: Harper & Row, Publishers, 1964. 319 pp.

Tesconi, Charles A., and Morris Van Cleve. *The Anti-Man Culture. Bureautechnocracy and the Schools*. Urbana, Ill.: University of Illinois Press, 1972. 248 pp.

Theobald, Robert. *An Alternative Future for America*. Chicago: Swallow, 1970. 199 pp.

————. *The Guaranteed Income; Next Step in Economic Evolution?* Garden City, N.Y.: Doubleday & Company, Inc., 1965. 233 pp.

Tishler, Max. "A New Goal for Science: Discovering What Can Be Done Is No Longer Enough; Research Must Focus on What Should Be Done," *Saturday Review*, June 5, 1971.

Toffler, Alvin. *Future Shock*. New York: Random House, Inc., 1970. 505 pp.

Touraine, Alain. *The Post Industrial Society: Tomorrow's Social History—Classes, Conflicts, and Culture in the Programmed Society*. New York: Random House, Inc., 1971. 244 pp.

Toynbee, Arnold J. *American and the World Revolution and Other Essays*. New York: Oxford University Press, 1962. 231 pp. Excellent presentation of the thesis that America did represent a truly revolutionary development and that her present challenge is to continue her revolution.

Umans, Shelley. *The Management of Education: A Systematic Design for Educational Revolution*. Garden City, N.Y.: Doubleday & Company, Inc., 1970. 226 pp.

The Unfinished Journey: Issues in American Education. New York: The John Day Company, Inc., 1968. 202 pp.

U.S. Department of Health, Education and Welfare. *Head Start—A Child Development Program*. Washington, D.C.: U.S. Government Printing Office, 1970. 16 pp. (Pamphlet.)

Van Til, William. *Curriculum: Quest for Relevance*. Boston: Houghton Mifflin Company, 1971. 390 pp.

————. "Curriculum for the 70's," *Phi Delta Kappan*, Vol. LI, No. 7 (March 1970).

Vaux, Kenneth. *Subduing the Cosmos: Cybernetics and Man's Future*. Richmond, Va.: Knox, 1970. 197 pp.

Venn, Grant. *Man, Education and Manpower*. Washington, D.C.: American Association of School Administrators, 1970. 281 pp.

Von Eckardt, Wolf. " 'Life-Style' Education," *Saturday Review*, April 3, 1971.

Waring, John. "Automation, Society and 'Creative Capitalism'," *The Futurist*, Vol. V, No. 1 (Febraury 1971).

Warner, Aaron W., Dean Morse, and Thomas E. Cooney (eds.). *The Environment of Change*. New York: Columbia University Press, 1969. 186 pp.

Warshofsky, Fred. *The 21st Century: The Control of Life*. New York: The Viking Press, 1969. 181 pp.

Watson, James D. "Moving Toward the Clonal Man: Is This What We Want?" *The Atlantic*, Vol. 227, No. 5 (May 1971).

Ways, Max. "What Hope for the Future?" *Current*, No. 124 (December 1970).

Weaver, W. Timothy. "The Delphi Forecasting Method," *Phi Delta Kappan*, Vol. LII, No. 5 (January 1971).

Weinstein, Gerald, and Mario D. Fantini (eds.). *Toward Humanistic Education: A Curriculum of Affect*. New York: Frederick A. Praeger, Inc., 1970. 228 pp.

Weinstein, Michael A. (ed.). *Identity, Power and Change: Selected Readings*. Glenview, Ill.: Scott Foresman & Company, 1917. 288 pp.

Wilcow, Clair. *Toward Social Welfare: An Analysis of Programs and Proposals Attacking Poverty, Insecurity and Inequality of Opportunity*. Homewood, Ill.: Richard D. Irwin, 1969. 402 pp.

Wilson, Thomas W., Jr. "The Environment: Do the Polluted Clouds Have a Silver Lining?" *The Futurist*, Vol. V, No. 1 (February 1971).

Winick, Charles. *The New People: Desexualization in American Life*. New York: Pegasus, 1968. 384 pp.

Wirth, Arthur G. *Education in the Technological Society.* San Francisco: Intext Educational Publisher, 1972. 237 pp.
Wise, John E. "Science and Human Values," *School and Society,* Vol. 99, No. 2331 (February 1971).

Selected Films

Assignment: Tomorrow (N.E.A.), 32 min. Deals with the vital role of the teacher in our culture; points out importance of the teacher as a teacher, as a community member, as a professional person, indicating roles played and contributions made in each. Also shows the activities in a modern schoolroom that help students to develop the ability to think for themselves, to be conscious of community needs, and to participate and cooperate with others. Contrasts this type of school with that in which adequate support is not supplied by the community.

Bertrand Russell Discusses Mankind's Future (Chantern), 13½ min. In speaking of his fears and hopes for the future, Lord Russell sees the possibility of a world so organized and static that "there will be no fun to be had anywhere." On the positive side, he feels that with education and the realization that many of the world's troubles lie in individual psychology, we could abolish war, poverty, and disease.

Better Tomorrow (Overseas Branch of OWI), 20 min. Shows progressive education systems in three New York schools, demonstrating how learning is connected with everyday experiences in children's lives on the preschool, junior high, and senior high school levels.

Broader Concept of Method (McGraw-Hill), 32 min. Two reels. First reel: "Developing Pupil Interest" (13 min.). Presents the conventional teacher-dominated, lesson-hearing type of school, followed by some alternative techniques designed to achieve broader educational objectives. Shows effects of methods on attitudes, response, and learning. Second reel: "Teacher and Pupil's Planning Together" (19 min.). Students learning to work together. They organize into functional groups, plan and carry out an investigation, prepare and present their findings, evaluate what they have learned.

The Child of the Future: How He Might Learn (McGraw-Hill), 59 min. How some of the products of modern technology are being used in the classroom.

Community Resources in Teaching (Iowa State University), 19 min. Explains how the schools can profitably use the community as a laboratory; follows a social studies class as it visits a newspaper plant during a study of communications. Also points out the value of having resource people from the community come into the classroom.

Crisis in the Classroom (ICF), 15 min. How can today's students be motivated to take an active and positive role in the process of education? How much authority should a teacher have in the classroom? What part should students play?

Design of American Public Education (McGraw-Hill), 16 min. Compares and contrasts the operation of the "assembly-line" kind of educational process with one that is tailored to meet the needs of today's young people and the needs of the community. Typical state, county, and local situations are presented.

Education for Democracy (Missouri State Teachers Assn.), 22 min. Depicts with actual classroom scenes the manner in which Missouri schools achieve the purposes of education in our American democracy as outlined by the Educational Policies Commission of the N.E.A.

Learning Democracy Through School-Community Projects (University of Michigan and D.A.R.), 21 min. Depicts experiences in democratic learning that are provided in Michigan schools; includes student councils, student elections, Junior Red Cross, youth centers, a community conference, a school safety patrol, an audiovisual service club, and a rural field day.

Learning for Life (N.E.A.), 28 min. Gives the view of adult education as a new force in public schools through which people can learn to live for themselves and their communities.

New Schools for Old (M.M.A.), 10 min. Contrasts little red school house, its methods and results with modern classrooms and up-to-date techniques.

Preparation of Teachers (U.S. State Department), 20 min. Uses the experiences of two prospective teachers during their training period to show that teaching is not just the business of getting information across, but also the sharing of children's experiences and excitement. Emphasizes the fact that a teacher must have a well-rounded background in order to help children to become useful and responsible citizens.

Satellites, Schools and Survival (N.E.A.), 30 min. A pictorial history of education in the United States during the last half century. Points up the challenge of present problems.

School (IND), 24 min. Shows a progressive education school in action. The dialogue is by fifth-grade children in the classroom. Indicates that intelligent citizenship in democracy is best achieved by permitting children at school to develop their own aptitudes and interests according to their individual abilities.

School in Centerville (N.E.A.), 20 min. Depicts a life-centered program in a rural community setting. Has the character of a documentary report.

School and Community (McGraw-Hill), 13 min. Animated film. Shows a school isolated from community neither benefiting its community nor being benefited by it; then describes the advantages to be derived from school and community cooperation.

Schoolhouse in the Red (Kellog), 42 min. Describes a typical rural community debating whether to change from a system of individual small rural schools to a larger school-district system; discusses the sociological and psychological factors involved and pictures the facial expressions, actions, and opinions of the local citizens; shows how the little school has become outmoded and emphasizes the considerations involved in the change of an educational system.

We Plan Together (Teachers College, Columbia University), 20 min. An eleventh-grade core class illustrates its ways of working, showing how needs and abilities are used in relation to problems, interest, and fields of knowledge.

Wilson Dam School (TVA and Alabama State Department of Education), 22 min. Depicts daily activities at the Wilson Dam School in Alabama. From the time the elementary pupils arrive in school buses until they leave, they are seen engaging in functional learning experiences, including such activities as taking care of pets and chickens, group singing, gardening, and games that require coordination and imagination. A medical examination given at the beginning of each year and parent cooperation and visitation are also shown.

Index

abortion, 202
Abraham, Henry J., 447
academic, as word, 51
academies, Southern, 353
academy, 59
ACTION, 383
action research, 501
activism, student: coping with, 308–310, 508; reasons for, 65, 306–308, 507–509, 547–550, 588
Adler, Mortimer, 527
administered economy, 151–152
administered prices, 142
administrative organization of schools, 42
adolescents: black, 296–297; disadvantaged, 378–379
adult education, 438–439
AFL–CIO, 327
aged, the, 210–213, 411
agriculture, changes in, 126
agriculture stage, 29
alienation: of working class, 313–314; of youth, 306–310, 509
American Association of School Administrators, 530
American economics, *see* economics, American
American population: and birth rate, 406–407; and education, 416–420; and life span, 409; mobility of, 407–409; and social security, 411–414; and welfare programs, 411-414; *see also* birth rate *and* population
American productivity, 116–117
animals: hominoid, 27; social cooperation among, 26–27
animatism, 26
animism, 25
anomie, 371
anonymity, 370–371
anti-Catholicism, 300–302
antipoverty programs, 142, 382–385

anti-Semitism, 299–300
Arab bloc, 469
Area of Redevelopment Act of 1961, 383
Aristotle, 35, 52
Aryan superiority, 311
atomic energy, 147–148
Atterbury Job Corps Center, 345
attitudes, learning of, 316
authority in democracy, 492–495
automation, 95–96, 143–144
automobiles and society, 85
Ayer, A. J., 545

Bacon, Francis, 35
Bagley, William C., 530, 534
Beard, Charles A., 41
behavior, 341, 377–378
Benne, Kenneth D., 492–493, 542
Bennis, Warren G., 592–594
bicameral legislature, 442
Biesanz, John, 14
Biesanz, Mavis, 14
Bill of Rights, 492
birth control, 208–209
birth rate: and birth control, 208–209; differential, 406–407; recent, 404–406; wartime, 191
Black Americans: and antipoverty programs, 292; and boycotting industry, 326; caste of, 286, 289; children, 296–297; in Cincinnati, 349–350; compensatory employment for, 325; and crime, 297; as culturally disadvantaged, 375; culture of, 297; and delinquency, 297; discrimination against, 291–297, 317–330; economic situation of, 293–294; as educators, 348–349; and extremist groups, 292–293; and first-class citizenship, 291–293; industrial recruitment of, 323; and integration, 318, 322–330, 343–354; King, Martin Luther, and, 291–293,

607